The New Music Record Guide

Omnibus Press

London/New York/Sydney/Cologne

Originally published 1983 in the USA
© Trans-Oceanic Trouser Press Inc.
Revised edition published 1985
© Ira A. Robbins by Charles
Scribner's Sons, New York.
This edition (second revision)
© Copyright 1987 Omnibus Press
(A Division of Book Sales Limited)

Book designed by Sands Straker
Cover designed by Pearce Marchbank

ISBN 0.7119.1115.0
Order No. OP 44320

Exclusive distributors:
Book Sales Limited
8/9 Frith Street, London W1V 5TZ, UK.
Music Sales Corporation
24 East 22nd Street, New York,
NY 10010, USA.
Omnibus Press
GPO Box 3304, Sydney,
NSW 2001, Australia.
To the Music Trade only:
Music Sales Limited
8/9 Frith Street, London W1V 5TZ, UK.

Typeset from disc by
Serious Software.
Printed in England by
Billings, Worcester.

The
New
Record Guide
Music

Edited by Ira Robbins

PREFACE

This book began in 1982 as an attempt to review all of the extant records that had emerged via the "new wave"—i.e., records that either led to or resulted from the 1976/77 upheaval spearheaded by the Sex Pistols, Ramones, Clash, Blondie, etc. The first edition was fairly parochial, essentially containing only British and American rock records. It was fine for what it was, but the ceaseless development and cross-fertilization of pop musics quickly made it seem narrow and limited. A second edition, published in 1985, broadened the concept and abandoned the defunct notion of new wave for a more general slice of the musical pie. The concept of the book became more valid and useful, but the ability to explain the overriding aesthetic concept largely evaporated.

This third edition—the first to be published in the United Kingdom—is even harder to explain, so I won't even try. Suffice it to say we've updated the original entries through the Spring of 1986 while also endeavoring to add a greater variety of artists than ever before, concentrating especially on Third World performers, whose influence on and appeal to the rock community continues to grow. So the final result may not make describable sense in terms of whose records are covered, but a general standard does continue to guide the selection process: bands that favor experimentation, adventure, innovation and making music not just for the potential financial rewards are included. Musicians who can't be said to have added anything original, fresh or exceptionally entertaining to the culture are generally not covered here. Some readers may disagree with the selection process, but that's both expected and desirable.

About the Editor

Ira Robbins co-founded *Trouser Press* magazine in 1974 while an electrical engineering student; he was Publisher and Editorial Director at the time of its demise 96 issues (and 10 years) later. He is presently Senior Editor at *Video* magazine. His writing has also appeared in numerous music magazines, including *Rolling Stone*, *New Musical Express*, *Musician*, *The Face* and *Creem*. He has edited and contributed to various books about popular music. A rock'n'roll fanatic ever since hearing Del Shannon's "Hats Off to Larry" in 1961, he lives in New York City.

THE CONTRIBUTORS

ag: Altricia Gethers
bk: Bud Kliment
cpl: Charles P. Lamey
df: David Fricke
ds: Dave Schulps
dgs: David Sheridan
ep: Elizabeth Phillip
gf: Graham Flashner
iar: Ira Robbins
jg: Jim Green
jl: John Leland
jw: John Walker
jy: Jon Young
kh: Kathy Haight
ks: Karen Schlosberg
mf: Mark Fleischmann
mp: Michael Pietsch
rg: Richard Gehr
rnp: Robert Payes
sg: Steven Grant
si: Scott Isler
tr: Terry Rompers
wk: Wayne King

ACKNOWLEDGMENTS

Without whom: David Sheridan, Linda Robbins, Lisa Hayes, Binky Philips, Chris Charlesworth, Andrew King, Madeleine Morell, Michael Pietsch, Kathy Haight, Bud Kliment, Richard Gehr, Trish Gethers, Jon Young, Jim Green, Dave Schulps, Bill Ashton, Michael Krumper, Nick Cucci, Melani Rogers, Toby Mamis, Joanne Brown, B. George/Archive of Contemporary Music, Cary Baker, Danny Beard, Rick Orienza, Barry Feldman, Don Ireland, Clint Forer, Tony Cece, Fran DiFeo, Peter Gordon, Fred Wasser, Pier Platters, Mike Carducci, Jim Khambatta, Gerard Cosloy, Arthur Levy, Jim Bessman, Falling James, Nick DeBenedetto, Toby Mamis, David Pierce, Louis and Estelle Robbins, Sara Schoenwetter.

This book is respectfully dedicated to the memories of my grandparents, Jenny and Harry Rubenoff.

Ira Robbins

INTRODUCTION

The format is straightforward: entries are arranged purely alphabetically by the last names of individuals or the first letter of group names, with no precedence given to acronyms, abbreviations, numerals, etc. Untraditional perhaps, but appropriate for the unpredictability encountered here. Pseudonyms notwithstanding, groups taking their name from a member are alphabetized as if they were individuals; fabrications are treated as band names. Articles (except for names not in English) have generally been dropped from names in headings. Those groups who get to keep an article as part of their name are alphabetized as such. Groups that have gone by more than one name are listed under all their recording monikers, but alphabetized under the most significant and/or recent. What it comes down to is this: there's a good reason why the entries are arranged as they are, and if something isn't where you think it should be, keep looking and it'll turn up.

Headings include complete album listings through the Spring of 1986, as many EPs as could be included, and the occasional critical single (indicated by quote marks around the title). All efforts have been expended to research, check and confirm discographical information; the inevitable errors are just that. Our apologies in advance.

The label information inside the parentheses is of several varieties:

One label name, no slash, no country abbreviation: the record was released in the UK and the US on the same label.

A slash and one or two labels indicated, separated by a slash: the record was released in the UK on the label to the left of the slash, and in the US on the label listed to the right. If an "nr" appears on either side, the record was never released in the corresponding country.

A country abbreviation, one label and no slash: the record has never been issued in either the US or UK but did appear originally in the country indicated.

Reissues are noted by a second set of parens and a second year; if only a plus sign and a year appears, the record was reissued by the same label(s). Reissues outside the US and UK are not noted. No attempt has been made to determine deletions—records are listed regardless of their potential unavailability. Furthermore, given small record companies' tendency to not remain in one place indefinitely, no label addresses are provided. The purpose of this book is to describe and critique records, not sell 'em.

The notation "tape" inside brackets signifies a cassette-only release. The "EP" designation covers everything from titled three-song maxi-singles to six-song mini-albums, regardless of how the records themselves are billed. With the exception of records with very long tracks that amount to albums, anything with six or fewer cuts is called an EP here; by the same token, a 12-inch record with seven or more songs, even a 15-minute hardcore quickie, is considered an album.

Two provisos about release dates: The year given is always that of earliest known release. The UK and US releases may have appeared in different years; the date given is the earlier of the two. For a record that was originally released outside the UK and US and later released in one or both of those countries, the date is that of the original release, although the labels shown aren't.

For a variety of reasons (mostly notification of forthcoming records that were not received until after our deadline), an occasional record listed in a heading is not actually discussed in the accompanying text. In the interests of full-fledged discographies, no titles have been deleted just because the records aren't reviewed.

Because of updating and cross-editing, some entries are bylined with more than one set of initials. (See the list of contributors for a key to who's who.) Generally, the first-named wrote the main piece, and the second updated and/or overhauled it.

Political note: music critics often refer to "white music" and "black music" as if skin color determined the sound of music one is obliged to make. In the hopes of avoiding the racism inherent in such simple-minded generalizing (especially in light of the movement against artistic segregation along color lines), when the phrases are used here, the quote marks are meant to stress that it's a musical style, not genetics, being invoked.

Reggae note: as this is the first edition to seriously incorporate reggae artists, it should be noted that those discographies are less complete and precise than the rest of the book's. It was not possible to adequately identify original Jamaican labels and release dates, so many of the references are only to English or American releases.

Nit-pickers, fact-checkers, friends and relatives are encouraged to write the editor with corrections, omissions, disagreements, praise, etc. c/o Music Sales Limited, 8/9 Frith Street, London W1V 5TZ.

EXPLANATORY NOTES

Abbreviations

Aus.	Australian
Bel.	Belgian
Can.	Canadian
EP	3—6 song record
Fr.	French
Ger.	German
Hol.	Dutch
Ice.	Icelandic
It.	Italian
Jam.	Jamaican
Jap.	Japanese
Nor.	Norwegian
nr	not released
NZ	New Zealand
Port.	Portuguese
Sp.	Spanish
Sw.	Swiss
[tape]	released only on cassette
UK	British
US	American

ABC

The Lexicon of Love (Neutron/Mercury) 1982
Beauty Stab (Neutron/Mercury) 1983
How to Be a ... Zillionaire! (Neutron/Mercury) 1985

ABC revolves around the talented but often misguided Martin Fry, whose detailed notions of style include, on the band's first album, setting his own Ferry/Bowiesque vocals in lustrous pop production (by Trevor Horn) laden with keyboards and strings, mostly to a supple techno-soul disco pulse. He succeeds admirably with "Poison Arrow" and "Look of Love," but an entire album on the same subject—Fry is stuck in the lexicon's "lack-of/loss-of love" section—can be a strain; taken in toto, his melodies seem like retreads, and his attempts at urbane metaphoric wit seem forced.

With **Beauty Stab**, ABC suddenly became a rock band, using guitar for the main instrumental fabric on most tracks. Fielding the same lineup as latter-day Roxy Music (vocals, guitar, sax) and, coincidentally, joined by the session bassist and drummer (Alan Spenner and Andy Newmark, respectively) Roxy used on **Flesh & Blood**, ABC offers a remarkable impression (discounting Fry's usual howler lyrics) of that band on "That Was Then and This Is Now." ABC makes additional overtures towards Roxyish guitar rock but with little aptitude in direction, identity or grace. Quotes from Bo Diddley, the Move and other rock staples abound, but ABC has utterly no clue what to do with them.

Fry and his guitar/keyboard-playing partner Mark White then took a long vacation, returning in '85 with **Zillionaire!**, a mixed bag of sarcasm ("So Hip It Hurts," "Vanity Kills," "How to Be a Millionaire") and sweetness ("Be Near Me") largely influenced by hip-hop sounds. (American techno-rhythm king Keith LeBlanc figures prominently on the album.)

Alternately (sometimes simultaneously) clever, charming, obnoxious and insufferable, ABC can't help but be misunderstood. [jg/iar]

A BLAZE COLOUR

A Blaze Colour EP (Hol. Plurex) 1982

Lots of sonic space on this Belgian duo's EP, just synths, "rhythms" and some vocals, in staccato phrases with a few drones thrown in for variation. Attractive in its own way, despite the pair's obvious attempt to maintain a pose of Suffering for Art—putting dire lyrics to a musically jolly little slice of dance rock for robots. [jg]

A CERTAIN RATIO

The Graveyard and the Ballroom [tape] (Factory/nr) 1979 & 1985
Do the Du EP (Factory) 1980
Blown Away EP (Factory/nr) 1980
To Each ... (Factory/nr) 1981
Sextet (Factory/nr) 1981
I'd Like to See You Again (Factory/nr) 1982
The Old and the New (Factory/nr) 1985

Hailing from Manchester and managed by Factory label head Tony Wilson, A Certain Ratio (ACR) used horns and other instruments to play a soulful brand of modern music that has proven significantly influential to many outfits.

Do the Du is an original, exciting post-punk dance record that does ACR proud. Although their funk trip later turned fatal, check out "Shack Up" for the decay of modern social values. With this first release, ACR seemed certain to join Public Image in the vanguard of the New Rock Left. The **Graveyard** cassette compiles '79 material—half studio work produced by Martin Hannett, the rest live from their hometown's famed Electric Ballroom. Musically, it anticipates the studied tedium of the band's first full-length album, **To Each ...** , which snuffed the band's early promise, burying itself in dreary rhythms and astonishing self-indulgence. Leader Simon Topping—he of the free-form trumpet that stamped songs like "The Fox" (here on a subdued remake from **Do the Du**)—evidently believed that ACR would fill the gap left by Joy Division. Unfortunately, while Joy Division was at least lyrical in its despair, A Certain Ratio is merely monotonous. **Blown Away** is a three-song 12-inch of non-LP blasts of horns and rhythms.

ACR relocated their energy on **Sextet**, but didn't apply it in the right places. There's no real focus to the discoish beats and wailing female vocals (Martha Tilson); ACR don't seem especially interested in what they're doing.

I'd Like to See You Again suffers from the absence of Tilson's singing, and stumbles about, evidencing self-consciousness and conservatism in place of a previously aggressive experimental attitude.

The Old and the New compilation was originally released with a bonus 45 of "Shack Up." [gf]

ACT

Too Late at 20 (Hannibal) 1981

Impeccable production gives singer/songwriter Nick Laird-Clowes' controlled passion and the band's tight, tasteful playing the clearly-deserved chance to be heard. Elvis Costello and Tom Petty appear to be major influences, and there are nods to the Byrds and Springsteen, but Clowes and company rise above derivation, giving such songs as "Touch and Go" and "The Long Island Sound" indelible emotional authenticity. [mf]

See also *Dream Academy*.

ACTIFED

Dawn of a Legion EP (Jungle/nr) 1984

Produced by ex-Gen X-er Tony James, this four-song 12-inch pounds out powerful semi-bleak rock with dense guitar noise. Neither awesome nor awful, Actifed (perhaps the only band ever named after a brand of antihistamine) are muscular but undistinguished. [iar]

!ACTION PACT!

Mercury Theatre—on the Air! (Fall Out/nr) 1983
Survival of the Fattest (Fall Out/nr) 1984

George Cheex—!Action Pact!'s female singer—sounds perenially outraged, terrified and amazed, all at once. She doesn't quite shriek, but comes damn close to it, which makes the London foursome rather tiresome, especially as the music manages nowhere near the same level of aggression, holding rather to relatively tame medium-speed punk. Lyrics on **Mercury Theatre** are pointedly political, addressing royalty ("Blue Blood"), yellow journalism ("Currant Bun"), racism, etc. Commendable but barely listenable although, aided by guest saxophone, "London Bouncers" does resemble X-Ray Spex a bit.

Survival of the Fattest (no one said this lot weren't clever) introduces a new member, Thistles (taking over bass from Dr. Phibes), joining George, Grimly Fiendish and Wild Planet in the lineup. The group's lyrics are slightly refined and subtler; likewise, the music offers more variety and better playing, but George's artless singing—despite flashes of adequacy—remains their undoing. [iar]

ADAM AND THE ANTS

See *Adam Ant*.

KING SUNNY ADÉ AND HIS AFRICAN BEATS

Juju Music (Island/Mango) 1982
Synchro System (Island/Mango) 1983
Aura (Island) 1984

Nigerian King Sunny Adé came to prominence in Europe and the US in 1982, following a decade spent establishing himself as one of Africa's most prolific and successful pop artists. Almost unanimously embraced by critics (if not consumers) everywhere, he plays a music known as juju, a flowing, sonorous style which has its origins in the Yoruba people of Nigeria. He has made about four dozen albums; only three have so far been released in the US and UK.

Adé's music is almost as formulaic as it is intoxicating. His songs are long (often filling an entire side on African releases) and contain some of the most irresistible grooves anywhere. As many as a half-dozen guitarists and an equal number of percussionists play simple figures to collectively weave an intricate web that serves as background for call-and-response vocals. Within this framework, Adé adds his own touches, borrowing from many other cultures. **Juju Music**, a compilation culled from several prior LPs, relies heavily on synthesizers, Hawaiian steel guitars and reggae dub techniques. It has the densest sound of the three: ghostlike guitars float through one another with near-vocal textures for perhaps as organic a sound as can be produced with electric instruments. **Synchro System** is more melodically stripped down; percussion dominates, especially the bubbling sound of the talking drum, an African instrument of variable pitch. On **Aura**, Adé sets his pancultural sights even further, and the rhythm tracks are almost pure beat-box in style. Also, vocal harmonies in all his work have a distinctive Latin feel.

Adé has been tagged by many as the heir apparent to Bob Marley as preeminent Third World musical/cultural ambassador to the world. But even with all of Marley's well-earned popularity, he lacked the musicological instincts which enable Adé to incorporate such a wide range of idioms into a truly global pop style. (He and his band are said to listen mostly to country-western while touring the US.) Quite simply, Adé is one of the most captivating and important musical talents anywhere in the world today. [dgs]

ADICTS

Songs of Praise (Dwed Wecords/nr) 1981
Sound of Music (Razor/nr) 1982
This Is Your Life (Fall Out/nr) 1985
Smart Alex (Razor/nr) 1985

Although neither startling nor overly original, this glam-punk quartet from Ipswich make highly enjoyable records that owe more to the Ramones than anyone else. The image is lifted directly from *A Clockwork Orange*, but the music—played hard'n'fast with vicious thick rhythm guitar—is memorable, definitely teenage and, best of all, fun.

Following the group's 1984 signing (as the AD-X) to Sire, an Adicts retrospective was compiled from 1978—1980 demos, singles and radio sessions. **This Is Your Life** may be poorly annotated but the fifteen tracks are musically entertaining. Many of the studio numbers sound like early Clash; the slightly rawer live-in-the-studio takes more resemble prototypical punkers like Chelsea or the Members. If you've never heard the Adicts, this odds-and-ends album is as good a place as any to introduce yourself. [cpl/iar]

A DROP IN THE GRAY

Certain Sculptures (Geffen) 1985

The good news about this California-based Scottish-American trio is that they're not as pretentious or as distant as their name. The bad news is they're close to it. Utterly without personality or purpose, the eleven slickly produced tracks (with titles like "Heartache Feeds Heartache" and "Past Your Frame") blur into one another, the smooth, modern sound of guitars and keyboards approximating an updated Moody Blues. Except for Dan Phillips' cloyingly over-emotional, gimmicky vocals, these sculptures are faultless to a fault. [iar]

ADVERTISING

Jingles (EMI/nr) 1978

Advertising was a clever young pop quartet with a penchant for quirky but catchy tunes, punny teenager lyrics and the color pink. They had a near brush with chart success via a 45 called "Lipstick" (included on **Jingles**); their failure to win a large following caused an early breakup. This album (produced separately by Andy Arthurs and Kenny Laguna) is chockablock full of engaging numbers, cheery vocals and snappy, clean playing; the songs (written by Tot Taylor and Simon Boswell, the band's guitarists) are literate and charming. Highly recommended to pop fans. In their post-Advertising lives, Tot Taylor records under his own name, while Boswell became a producer and formed Live Wire, who made three swell albums. [iar]

See also *Data, Tot Taylor*.

ADVERTS

Crossing the Red Sea with the Adverts (Bright/nr) 1978

(Butt/nr) 1982
Cast of Thousands (RCA/nr) 1979

When the four Adverts (including female bassist Gaye Advert) debuted on a 1977 Stiff 45 with "One Chord Wonders," the young Londoners could barely play their instruments, but that didn't keep Tim Smith's song from being a witty commentary on earnest yet incompetent bands. By the time they re-recorded it for their first LP, the Adverts had acquired just enough proficiency to make a positive difference. In its own way, **Red Sea** is the equal of the first Sex Pistols or Clash LP, a hasty statement that captures an exciting time. Smith's tunes almost always offer a new wrinkle on issues of the day, and when they fall into a rut, as in "Bored Teenagers," his breathy, urgent vocals compensate. It's too bad the album didn't include the ghoulishly funny "Gary Gilmore's Eyes," a wicked single about a blind person who receives a transplant from you-know- (but-may-not-remember)- who.

Oddly, **Cast of Thousands** is as feeble as **Red Sea** is vital. Fatigue and depression permeate the LP, suggesting that Smith's muse had made a hasty exit. One need only read the cover quote from 1 John 2:15 to get the picture: "Love not the world, neither the things that are in the world." Pretty punky, huh? [jy]

See also *T.V. Smith's Explorers*.

A FLOCK OF SEAGULLS

Telecommunication EP (Jive) 1981
A Flock of Seagulls (Jive) 1982
Listen (Jive) 1983
The Story of a Young Heart (Jive) 1984
Dream Come True (Jive) 1986

Amidst all the talented and adventurous bands from the second Liverpool explosion, A Flock of Seagulls was ironically the first to score a gold record in the US. Led by singer/keyboardist/guitarist Mike Score (he of the ludicrous hairdo) and including his brother Ali on drums, the quartet's first break came when Bill Nelson released a single for them on his own Cocteau label; the 12-inch EP (somewhat different in the UK) includes the Nelson-produced title track, also on their debut LP.

Although the EP has a catchy tune or two, it wasn't until AFOS entered the studio with producer Mike Howlett and cut **A Flock of Seagulls** that they developed any real style of their own. Relying on guitarist Paul Reynolds' U2-influenced textural wash, distended strains of synthesizer and some fancy studio maneuvers, the band's inadequacies (mainly dumb lyrics and limited concepts) fade into the background, and are replaced by listenable, danceable techno-rock that has proven to have broad appeal.

Faced with the challenge of following a hugely successful album, the Seagulls' second longplayer was recorded again with Howlett (except for one cut) and hits some real highs. They retreated from gimmicky sci-fi themes (despite the circuit-board cover photo) and found an affecting path in the lushly pretty, languid "Wishing (If I Had a Photograph of You)" and the understated "Nightmares," but fouled out on several boring tracks and "What Am I Supposed to Do," which starts off alright but winds up repeating

the title endlessly as the song fades out. Score does the same thing on "(It's Not Me) Talking," but a propulsive synth-dance-beat and some neat sonic maneuvers keep it exciting.

Dispensing with Howlett, **The Story of a Young Heart** is decidedly inferior. The bland romantic ballads on the first side lack character, have tedious vocals and point up the group's finite songwriting skill. "The More You Live, The More You Love" comes closest to succeeding but is nonetheless plodding and forgettable. The rockier songs on the flipside are marginally better, but can't carry the record on their own. The best effort is the formulaic "Suicide Day" which at least offers a catchy refrain and some emotional intensity. A vain attempt at artistic maturity and sophistication, the real story here is one of over-ambition at odds with realistic capabilities.

Reynolds left and AFOS made their next record as a trio (augmented by half a dozen different guitarists), with Mike Score producing. Although somewhat lacking in personality, the almost modestly appointed **Dream Come True** is reasonably listenable, a collection of simpleminded romantic numbers led by the single, "Heartbeat Like a Drum." [iar]

AFRAID OF MICE

Afraid of Mice (Charisma/nr) 1982

This Liverpool quartet's sole LP is humorless Bowiesque dance-rock, produced by former Bowie collaborator Tony Visconti. Leader Philip Franz Jones, who wrote all but one of the songs, performs on sax, flute and keyboards in addition to providing mannered lead vocals. For all his versatility, Jones' songs are not particularly memorable, and the dour, self-centered views of life and romance he expresses, while fashionable, seem petty and witless. Sophomoric boredom. [ds]

AFTER THE FIRE

Signs of Change (Rapid/nr) 1978
Laser Love (CBS/nr) 1979
80-F (Epic/nr) 1980
Batteries Not Included (CBS/nr) 1982
ATF (nr/Epic) 1982
Der Kommissar (CBS/nr) 1982

This smart foursome from East London and Essex update traditional Anglo-rock values. Think of the sonic characteristics of Queen, Supertramp, Yes, 10cc and then (before you puke) imagine a composite that's too young and irreverent and modest to get bogged down in excess soloing and flash for flash's sake, too full of beans to sit still for ponderous epics or pompous pronunciations. That's After the Fire.

Unfortunately, after perking up A&R ears with a do-it-yourself debut LP, the band was shunted from one producer to another, despite chart action on its first UK CBS 45, "One Rule for You"—like minimalist Genesis, with a lonesome synth hook. **Laser Love** and **80-F** display a moderately talented, promising band trying its hand at a number of approaches (even '80s Ventures-cum-guitar'n'synth) with results never less (but rarely more) than decent.

By **Batteries Not Included**,

though, the group's obvious melodic capabilities, effervescent playing and frequently tongue-in-cheek attitude were most profitably harnessed by Queen/Sparks producer Mack. Instruments mesh cleverly over a snappy drum line while the harmonies (even football shouts) nicely complete the picture on consistently strong songs.

The last two LPs are compilations, the US stressing more commercial programming and UK ranging further afield to better results (save the omission of "One Rule for You"). Both have the English language version of Falco's "Der Kommissar," which was a hit for the group in 1983. [jg]

AGENT ORANGE

Living in Darkness (nr/Posh Boy) 1981
Bitchin' Summer EP (nr/Posh Boy) 1982
When You Least Expect It . . . EP (nr/Enigma) 1984

Picture a band that combines the best elements of the Sex Pistols, the Ventures and early Blue Oyster Cult. Got that? Then you've got Agent Orange, a Fullerton, California punk trio whose style hybridizes surf-twang sounds, smart-metal chops and punky drive. The trio's debut album is a short (by LP standards), concise collection of originals like "Bloodstains" plus such appropriate memory-tweakers as the instrumental classic, "Miserlou." **Bitchin' Summer** furthers the band's connection with guitar instrumentalists while retaining full burn potential.

The four songs on the 1984 EP display relative restraint, sub-ordinating Mike Palm's guitar to a secondary role in favor of his echoed vocals on the pop "It's Up to Me and You." The two instrumentals are likewise less enflamed, although that doesn't stop "Out of Limits" from being great. A tepid, pointless cover of the Jefferson Airplane's "Somebody to Love," however, is a total mistake. [rnp/iar]

JANE AIRE AND THE BELVEDERES

Jane Aire and the Belvederes (Virgin/nr) 1979

Another talented singer from Akron, Ohio whose career really got started outside her homeland. Accompanied here by a sharp four-piece English band otherwise known as the Edge, Aire works confidently through a solid set of tunes that includes the oft-recorded "Breaking Down the Walls of Heartache," Pearl Harbor's "Driving," Holland/Dozier/Holland's "Come See About Me," plus some of producer Liam Sternberg's better original compositions. [iar]

ALARM

The Alarm EP (nr/IRS) 1983
Declaration (IRS) 1984
Strength (IRS) 1985

If these four young Welshmen weren't so studiedly intense, they might be able to drop their junior-Clash pretensions and use their evident talent to make more enjoyable records. Bassist Eddie MacDonald and singer Mike Peters write catchy, anthemic songs, but after a while the tireless exhortation becomes tiring and, worse, laughable.

Compiling UK singles, **The Alarm** contains "The Stand," which must be the only pop song based on a Stephen King novel, as well as "Marching On" and three more slices of the group's roughed-up folk-rock. **Declaration** further exploits the pose (and the haircuts), offering another batch of memorable tunes ("Sixty Eight Guns," "Blaze of Glory," "Where Were You Hiding When the Storm Broke?") all smeared with Peters' overly dramatic bawling. Although often compared to U2, the Alarm has none of the subtlety that keeps their Irish compatriots from sounding histrionic.

Strength was produced by Mike Howlett, who managed to rein in some of the Alarm's brassiness, slowing them down, focusing Peters' vocals, and opening up the sound with dynamics and silence. Keyboards add to the overall improvement; the songs are a bit stronger as well. But it's still an Alarm LP. Highlights: The title track, which rips off Billy Idol to amusing effect, and "Spirit of '76," a Springsteenish crypto-ballad. Other tracks sound like old Gen X and Mott the Hoople. Weird, but encouraging. [iar]

ALBANIA

Are You All Mine (Chiswick/nr) 1981

Albania's strength was prolix, interesting lyrics about winning and losing at romance, delivered over stylistically multi-national rock with guitars, keyboards and saxophone providing the basic sound and K-Y McKay's songs and vocals adding personality. The music stretches from polka to punk—like Deaf School and other quasi-theatrical outfits—but it's really the words that make the band. [iar]

WILLIE ALEXANDER AND THE BOOM BOOM BAND

Willie Alexander and the Boom Boom Band (MCA) 1978
Meanwhile . . . Back in the States (MCA) 1979

WILLIE "LOCO" ALEXANDER

Solo Loco (nr/Bomp) 1981
Taxi-Stand Diane EP (Fr. New Rose) 1984
Greatest Hits (New Rose/nr) 1985

WILLIE ALEXANDER AND THE CONFESSIONS

Autre Chose (Fr. New Rose) 1982
A Girl Like You (Fr. New Rose) 1982

Long-time Boston scene patriarch Alexander is an intriguing figure whose redoubtable career even includes a stint in a late incarnation of the Velvet Underground. With countless club gigs under his belt and abiding admiration for the beat poets, Alexander's credentials are impressive; unfortunately, his records haven't been very good.

His first album, **Willie Alexander and the Boom Boom Band** is dedicated to and includes the tribute "Kerouac," which was a cult hit when it appeared as an independent single in early 1977. The song's a real heartfelt standout; the rest of the record is routine bar-band rubbish, wanting for both songs and style. **Meanwhile . . .** follows the same path, but is noticeably better, thanks to Alexander's looser singing; for him, sloppiness is definitely an asset.

Willie left the Boom Boom Band behind for **Solo Loco**, relying instead on his own keyboards and percussion, with some outside guitar assistance. The record is a real departure, using occasional synthesizers to support extended, moody numbers that refer back to his earliest recorded work and a voice that seems at once weary and optimistic. The material is uneven; when it's good, the record shines brightly. (**Solo Loco** was originally released on French New Rose; the American version is slightly different.)

Autre Chose—two disques of live Willie—was recorded in France during a March/April 1982 tour with a new backing trio. The choice of material is eclectic, beginning with "Tennesse [sic] Waltz" performed a cappella and including all of his best(-known) songs, plus some new things.

The Confessions on **A Girl Like You** (recorded in an American studio but unreleased outside France) include a saxophonist, the same bassist and guitarist, but no drummer; Willie picks up the sticks for this effort. Like a low-key version of a '70s Rolling Stones album, there's a little rock'n'roll, a blues number, lots of sex (including the painfully tacky cover), and actually some good times. Probably as good as Alexander's going to get, **A Girl Like You** shows various sides of an eclectic and mature—if limited—performer. [iar]

ALIEN SEX FIEND

Who's Been Sleeping in My Brain (Anagram/Relativity) 1983
Acid Bath (Anagram/Relativity) 1984
Liquid Head in Tokyo (Anagram/nr) 1985
Maximum Security (Anagram/nr) 1985
I Walk the Line EP (Flicknife/nr) 1986

More ugly noise from the Batcave: Alien Sex Fiend flail away with all their might yet still produce nothing of merit on their first album. The quartet croons moronic slices of morbidity that read like Cramps discards, but the music never rises above sub-Dead Boys—a glum, muddy mix of identispeed drums, sporadic blurts of guitar and synth and wanky, over-stylized-shout-singing. The net result is a headache with a beat and some comic book images that lack humor, drama or impact of any kind. Utterly awful.

The second album doesn't deserve many kind words either, but smarter, sharper production turns the group's basic components into something almost sensual and then bakes on gimmicky effects to further help counteract the inherent miserableness. (The US version contains an extra track and two alternate versions.)

Recorded as a trio, **Maximum Security** employs tedious electronic percussion, murky guitar noise, and little else, making the lengthy tracks unbelievably boring. Thankfully not ear-splitting, it's still too loud to function effectively as a sleeping aid. Who likes this swill? **Liquid Head** is an unnecessary live album. [iar]

ALLEZ ALLEZ

African Queen (Kamera/nr) 1982
Promises (Virgin/nr) 1982

On **African Queen**, we have a Belgian sextet with Briton Sarah Osbourne's strong, sure alto voice out front producing lush discoid funk material of no great consequence. On **Promises**, aside from more contrast between Osbourne and low-pitched male vocal backing, Allez Allez and their producer (Martyn Ware of Heaven 17/B.E.F.) were unable to create anything more than pleasant dance music with unfortunately pretentious lyrics. The group may think this is subtle and elegant art, but the hard truth is that they offer little music to remember, and a few phrases best forgotten (e.g., the stuff about "My name is culture . . . her name is the devil"). [jg]

STEVE ALMAAS

See *Beat Rodeo*.

MARC ALMOND AND THE WILLING SINNERS

Vermin in Ermine (Some Bizzare-Phonogram/nr) 1984
Stories of Johnny (Some Bizzare-Virgin/nr) 1985

MARC AND THE MAMBAS

'Untitled' (Some Bizzare/nr) 1983
Torment and Toreros (Some Bizzare/nr) 1983

Leaving the evident confines of Soft Cell behind—while still a member and subsequent to the dissolution of his partnership with Dave Ball—singer Marc Almond assembled various associates to be the Mambas on his first two solo albums, both of them two-record sets. **'Untitled'** (an LP plus a three-song 12-inch) is a swell hodge-podge of originals, covers, collaborations and excesses, all sung in Almond's appealing but pitch-poor voice. With Ann Hogan and Matt (the The) Johnson as the main Mambas, Almond ventures into summery soul ("Angels"), ambient balladry ("Big Louise") and obvious source material (Lou Reed's "Caroline Says," Syd Barrett's "Terrapin," Jacques Brel's "If You Go Away"), covering a phenomenal variety of terrain. More an audio sketchbook than a coordinated album, **'Untitled'** is nonetheless a fine excursion outside the techno-pop corridors of Soft Cell.

Torment and Toreros, on the other hand, is a vile and pathetic attempt to ape '30s German cabaret decadence with mostly piano/orchestral backing and vulgar calculated-to-shock lyrics. A sleazy drag that elicits pity and disgust rather than any intended emotional response. And for two discs' worth, no less.

Almond's two subsequent albums with the Willing Sinners are far less offensive, and border on the amusing. He plays his gutter queen persona to the hilt, posing on the cover of **Vermin in Ermine** perched on a garbage can wearing a Liza Minelli spangled jacket and devil's horns. The songs typically reflect Almond's seamy, negativist taste ("Ugly Head," "Tenderness Is a Weakness," "Crime Sublime," "Shining Sinners," etc.), while the Sinners (and sidemen) provide theatrical, often sarcastically caricatured music to accompany his stylized singing. As such, **Vermin** isn't that involving—the jolly presentation works against the grungy intent, leaving a sense of aimlessness rather than artistic tension. (The cassette has three extra cuts.)

Stories of Johnny is more on track, matching moody, sometimes pretty atmospherics with Almond's disconsolate (but brightening) outlook. The backing sporadically includes slick synthesizer maneuvers, bringing him full circle and proving once again just how important Soft Cell was to that instrument's development in pop music. The title track sounds more like a hit single than anything he's recorded since "Tainted Love" without resembling that tune's simple presentation; it's a full-scale Spectorized production number with excellent singing. All told, **Stories of Johnny** is Almond's most enjoyable, least posey or willfully perverse record yet. [iar]

ALPHAVILLE

Forever Young (WEA/Atlantic) 1984

Obnoxious synthesizer rock from a German trio with English vocals making trite hit records for morons. Slickly polished and lyrically vapid ("Big in Japan," "The Jet Set"), Alphaville is at best inconsequential but more frequently overbearingly dumb. The title track comes within range of a bewitchingly textured Ultravox-like sound; otherwise this insipid fare is utterly resistible. [iar]

ALTERED IMAGES

Happy Birthday (Epic/Portrait) 1981
Pinky Blue (Epic/Portrait) 1982
Bite (Epic/Portrait) 1983
Collected Images (Epic/nr) 1984

Led by baby-voiced singer (and budding film actress) Claire Grogan, this twinky Scottish nuevo pop outfit hit high in the singles charts with catchy, uncomplicated tunes like "Happy Birthday" and "Dead Pop Stars." Grogan's cutesy-poo vocals, however, are not universally appreciated, and many found the group more precious than charming. The group's three albums feature four different producers, and clearly indicate how big an influence they wielded on these impressionable youngsters.

The first LP, produced mainly by Banshees bassist Steve Severin, shows no signs of life, except on the Martin Rushent-produced title track. The songs drag along, refusing to make any instrumental impression, relying on the singing, which just isn't enough.

Fortuitously, Rushent produced all of **Pinky Blue**, which revealed Altered Images to be a clever dance-pop force. With a gleaming, bouncy sound, the songs jump out in classic hit single fashion—"See Those Eyes" and "I Could Be Happy" especially provide the joyous setting that Grogan's voice needs to succeed. (The cover of Neil Diamond's cloying "Song Sung Blue," however, should have been nixed.)

Bite, the band's final album before splitting, is something of a departure. From the mature-young-sophisticate photo of Grogan on the front cover to the lush disco sound—strings, chorus, sax, wah-wah guitar, the works—of "Bring Me Closer," the album foolishly attempts to haul Altered Images out of their adolescent innocence and make them a Scottish Blondie. **Bite** suffers from serious schizophrenia induced by the equal division of production responsibilities between Tony Visconti and Mike Chapman. Visconti's tracks are basically heartless dance numbers—Abba gone funky; Chapman's trespass into the same terrain, but "Change of Heart," "Another Lost Look" and the memorable "Don't Talk to Me About Love" are attractive pop tunes that retain some of the band's winsome charm. (The English cassette release has extra tracks and bonus remixes.) **Collected Images** is a posthumous compilation. [iar]

See also *Hipsway*.

ALTERNATIVE TV

The Image Has Cracked (Deptford Fun City/nr) 1978
What You See ... Is What You Are (Deptford Fun City/nr) 1978
Vibing Up the Senile Man (Deptford Fun City/nr) 1979
Live at the Rat Club '77 (Crystal-Red/nr) 1979
Action Time Vision (Deptford Fun City/nr) 1980
Strange Kicks (IRS) 1981

The hipness and success of London punk-explosion photocopy fanzine *Sniffin' Glue* was almost totally due to the irreverent, pugnacious sincerity of its founder/sparkplug Mark P(erry). That Perry should form a band seemed a natural progression; that it was any good at all a surprise; that it maintained a stance utterly disdainful of compromise a small miracle. Unfortunately, Perry as a musical Diogenes had neither adequate vision nor foresight to avoid the pitfalls of Striving for Artistic Expression.

Live at the Rat Club '77 (an authorized bootleg) consists of messy-sounding live material taped before co-founder/guitarist Alex Fergusson split. He was replaced by the Police's then-road manager Kim Turner, but rejoined in time for **Strange Kicks**. By **The Image Has Cracked**, Perry's urge to experiment was taking intriguing turns (e.g., a half-studio, half-live attempt at meaningful audience participation) and—though the abstract stuff doesn't hold up so well—it's still an amazing document of a time and place. The straighter efforts are better: an early Buzzcocks/Clash sock is well-exercised on the band's rousing manifesto, "Action Time Vision." It's also why **Action Time Vision**, a compilation including non-LP singles sides (through '79) on which Perry's righteously vented spleen is effectively displayed, works better than **Image** as entertainment if not artifact.

What You See ... Is What You Are is also live, but shared half-and-half with tour partners Here & Now, a horrid hippie offshoot of Gong. Worse (even discounting the tinny sound) still, such disillusion had set in that Perry remade his song as "Action Time Lemon" in sheer disgust. While a move toward edge music could be seen

coming—further spurred by Mick Linehan (later in the Lines) replacing Kim Turner—ATV's tracks sound aimless and desperate. **Vibing Up the Senile Man** was made by an ATV consisting of just Perry and stalwart bassist Dennis Burns; while some of the lyrics are eloquently impassioned, Perry's tuneless vocals ride atop music that's up the pseudo-avant creek without a paddle.

Come 1981, Perry, Burns and the more pop-minded Fergusson reunited (adding a drummer and a keyboard player) for **Strange Kicks**, an album that's a different proposition altogether. The one-time quasi-nihilist says, "What the hey!" and rattles off smart, vernacular humor, easygoing if still reasonably cynical, thereby unifying ATV's snappy romp through an assortment of styles (ska, pop-punk, even electro-dance). Still, "There must be more to life than a heading in a record store." [jg]

See also *Mark Perry, Psychic TV*.

LAURIE ANDERSON

You're the Guy I Want to Share My Money With (nr/Giorno Poetry Systems) 1981
Big Science (Warner Bros.) 1982
Mister Heartbreak (Warner Bros.) 1984
The United States Live (Warner Bros.) 1984
Home of the Brave (Warner Bros.) 1986

Balanced on a high-wire above the designations "performance art" and "art pop," Laurie Anderson's **Big Science** is perhaps the most brilliant chunk of psychedelia since **Sgt. Pepper**. She combines sing-song narrative (often electronically treated) with a strong musical base that evokes, yet postdates, traditional musical forms. **Big Science**, featuring the surprise hit single, "O Superman," is a most enjoyable work of genius. (Anderson had previously appeared on several compilation albums, the most prominent being **You're the Guy I Want to Share My Money With**, a two-record set featuring Anderson, John Giorno and patriarch William S. Burroughs.)

On **Mister Heartbreak** Anderson continues merging not-readily-identifiable morsels of '60s psychedelia and '70s progressivism into a blinding studio-perfect maelstrom of oddity with the help of co-producers Bill Laswell, Roma Baran and Peter Gabriel (who sings on "his" cut). But this excellent record was over-shadowed in the year of its release by the five-record (!) **United States Live**, a summation of the state of Anderson's bewildering but popular performance art. Anderson and crew performed *United States* whole in London, Zurich and New York, where the Brooklyn Academy of Music, which commissioned the last of its four parts, provided the site (in February 1983) for recording it. Perhaps better suited for videotape, it mixes spoken-word monologues, music and noise (in that order) with snippets of film, slides, lighting and other visual effects that are inevitably lost here. Anderson's impressionistic multi-media portrait of the USA makes a good case for her talents as standup comedian ("There are ten million stories in the Naked City, but nobody can remember which is theirs"), yet reveals its

miscellany of truths slowly and coolly. Although it's a little like having an artsy friend over who always talks *at*, rather than *to*, you, **United States Live** remains a definitive statement of what a clever artist can get away with—and that's a compliment.

Home of the Brave is the digitally-recorded soundtrack to Anderson's performance film. Joined by an all-star collection of players (Adrian Belew, David Van Tieghem, Nile Rodgers, Bill Laswell), Anderson proffers technically exquisite versions of familiar items as well as new compositions, all imbued with her usual blend of dadaist humor and bemused social criticism. [jw/mf]

MARK ANDREWS AND THE GENTS

Big Boy (A&M) 1980

Keyboardist Andrews was Joe Jackson's bandmate in Arms & Legs during the latter's formative years in Portsmouth, England. Funnily enough, shortly after Jackson's initial success, Andrews wound up on the same label, playing a not terribly dissimilar style of music. Unfortunately for him, he's not Jackson's equal as a singer or songwriter. Some may find that **Bad Boy** shares many attributes with **Look Sharp**, though others may wonder why Andrews bothered, since he offers nothing new with the exception of a slow, reggae-tinged version of "Born to Be Wild." [ds]

ANGELIC UPSTARTS

Teenage Warning (Warner Bros./nr) 1979
We Gotta Get Out of This Place (WEA/nr) 1980
2,000,000 Voices (EMI/nr) 1981
Live (EMI/nr) 1981
Still from the Heart (EMI/nr) 1982
Reason Why? (Anagram/nr) 1983
Angel Dust (Anagram/nr) 1983
Last Tango in Moscow (Picasso/nr) 1984

With the commanding Mensi (Tommy Mensforth) as singer and spokesperson, the Upstarts came down from Newcastle in 1977 and found a patron in Sham 69's Jimmy Pursey, who produced their first album. Partly responsible for the continued strength of punk in England, it is to the Upstarts' credit that they have avoided the demagogic stupidity of other skinhead bands by maintaining a progressive attitude and speaking out against racism and fascism. Nonetheless, the Angelic Upstarts, like their London counterparts, the Cockney Rejects, make records that are generally just for fans of loud, fast and not-too-intellectual punk rock. Their albums are quite predictable.

Reason Why? takes a major step forward, however, blending the Upstarts' social observation/protest lyrics with a controlled and melodic rock attack (broken on the title track with a reggae digression and on the unaccompanied folk ballad, "Geordies Wife") that is punky only in Mensi's unpolished/accented bellow and the band's gang-shouted backing vocals. Otherwise, the guitars build an attractive base—like the Clash on **Give 'Em Enough Rope**—that is embellished by guest sax and keyboards. The songs are competent enough and the production, by guitarist Mond, captures it all with

clarity and energy. A surprisingly good record for all rock tastes.

Angel Dust, subtitled "The Collected Highs 1978—1983," is a two-record compilation recapping the band's prior career. [tr]

ANNABELLA

Fever (RCA) 1986

Having recovered from her traumatic youth with Malcolm McLaren and Bow Wow Wow, Annabella's (no last name, please) first solo album is basically high-gloss rubbish, despite the efforts of six very different producers (including Slade's Jim Lea, John Robie and Zeus B. Held). It's not that Annabella can't sing, it's just that she's foundering here without purpose or personality. Even a cover of Alice Cooper's "School's Out" goes appallingly wrong. [iar]

ADAM ANT

Friend or Foe (CBS/Epic) 1982
Strip (CBS/Epic) 1983
Vive le Rock (CBS/Epic) 1985

ADAM AND THE ANTS

Dirk Wears White Socks (Do It/nr) 1979 (CBS/Epic) 1983
Kings of the Wild Frontier (CBS/Epic) 1980
Prince Charming (CBS/Epic) 1981
Antmusic EP (Do It/nr) 1982

When Adam turned up with his Ants on the awful **Jubilee** movie soundtrack in 1978, you'd never have guessed he'd amount to anything. His two cuts were just ordinary meatgrinder punk, like much of the rest of the record. Nor was the ambitious **Dirk Wears White Socks** all that encouraging, despite the considerable effort Adam obviously expended on it. The LP's word-heavy tunes examine sexual excess ("Cleopatra"), bizarre visions ("Day I Met God"), alienation ("Digital Tenderness") and the like. Adam's dour, uncomfortable vocals find compatible backing from his band, which sounds nearly dead and far too slow. It's as if the nastiest portion of **Ziggy Stardust** had come to life full-blown. (After he'd made it big, Adam obtained the rights to the record, remixed and resequenced the tracks, added some early 45 sides, and had it reissued with a new cover.)

Adam's old Ants subsequently left for the employ of Malcolm McLaren, transmuting (more or less) into Bow Wow Wow. In their place, Adam recruited drummer/producer Chris Hughes (aka Merrick) and guitarist Marco Pirroni, who proved to be a significant collaborator. A single from this transitional period ("Cartrouble" b/w "Kick") was later included with three other early tracks on the **Antmusic** EP issued after his breakthrough.

Adam found his groove with **Kings of the Wild Frontier**. Goodbye heaviness and failure, hello hit parade. Dressed in flamboyant pirate gear, Adam and his merry crew bounce through a delightful program of modern bubblegum with shrewd under-pinnings. "Dog Eat Dog" uses the rampaging tribal drums Adam learned from McLaren. "Antmusic" shamelessly self-promotes (as do many of Adam's lyrics) to the accompaniment of an irresistible stop-start melody. The sourness of **Dirk** survives on **Kings**, but there's so much exuberant fun on the surface that it's hard not to have a good time.

Prince Charming is a letdown. Though "Stand and Deliver" offers more percussive entertainment à la "Dog Eat Dog" and the title track is florid melodrama, much of the LP seems forced, ill-tempered and silly. Adam hits bottom on "Ant Rap," an embarrassing rap tune filled with braggadocio.

After dumping the Ants (save Marco), Adam came up with his neatest LP yet. **Friend or Foe** has a surfeit of energy and plenty of variety. Adam and Marco touch on everything—soul, rockabilly and his usual weightless pop—with convincingly joyful results. Highlights include "Goody Two Shoes," a spirited, cheeky self- defense, and the Doors' "Hello, I Love You." This may be junk, but it's classy junk.

After that triumph, time for another bad album? No problem! **Strip** is pathetic. Adam's attempt to grow up was recorded at Abba's state-of-the-art studio in Stockholm and features two cuts produced by Phil Collins. By taking a less sensational approach, Adam exposes the weakness of his melodies and the inherent silliness of his sleazoid attitudes. Best suited for emotionally stunted *Playboy* readers.

For the next outing, Adam pulled in his horns and, with the production suss of Tony Visconti, made a big-league pop album even a mother could endure. **Vive Le Rock**'s title track is a perfect Electric Light Orchestra send-up; "Rip Down" likewise recalls Marc Bolan. Other songs ("Razor Keen," "Miss Thing") proffer Bolanesque lyrics but suffer from characterless backing. "Apollo 9," a wonderfully gimmicky single (an *a cappella* version is also included), proves that the old boy's still got it, whatever *it* may be. "Yabba yabba ding ding," indeed!

See also *Bow Wow Wow, Wide Boy Awake*. [jy/iar]

10

ANTI-NOWHERE LEAGUE

Anti-Nowhere League EP (nr/WXYZ) 1982
We Are . . . the League (WXYZ) 1982 (ID/nr) 1985
Live in Yugoslavia (ID/nr) 1983

It's hard to take this cartoonish punk quartet (now known simply as the League) seriously. The songwriting team of Animal and Magoo pens irate hardcore diatribes aimed at what they call the "nowheres" of the world: straights, nine-to-fives, etc. Although you don't dare doubt them when they spit "I Hate . . . People," they do manage to inject a sense of humor which can soften even the most potentially offensive song, such as the ragingly misogynist "Woman." And anyone who doubts their ingenuity should listen to their blazing (but surprisingly appropriate) treatment of Ralph McTell's folkie chestnut, "Streets of London." (That number also appears on the prior American EP, joined by two other tunes from the studio album and a bonus cut.) [ks]

ANTI-PASTI

The Last Call (Rondelet/Shatter) 1981
Caution in the Wind (Rondelet/nr) 1982
Anti-Pasti (Rondelet/nr) 1983

These five young Britons pound out loud and angry punk with a message—against war, nuclear testing, espionage, the army, Thatcher and the like. The playing is solid and straightforward; the songs may be simple, but at least they're songs, not merely riffs. Their lyrics, though rudimentary, are better than some of the competition's.

The Last Call is too typical of the genre to merit any serious notice. **Caution in the Wind**, which borrows liberally from the Clash's early stylings, is a much better record, employing three-dimensional arrangements that expand on the band's subtler assets without losing any power. The third album is a compilation of singles. [iar]

ANY TROUBLE

Where Are All the Nice Girls? (Stiff) 1980
Live and Alive EP (Stiff) 1980
Wheels in Motion (Stiff) 1981
Any Trouble (EMI America) 1983
Wrong End of the Race (EMI America) 1984

CLIVE GREGSON

Strange Persuasions (Demon/nr) 1985

Stiff Records had great commercial hopes for this Manchester quartet, led by balding, bespectacled singer/guitarist/ pianist Clive Gregson, whose songs—most about the unhappy side of love—have always shown real talent. It unfortunately took the group a long time to escape their basic facelessness and locate a sound, a slow start that may be why Any Trouble has remained underappreciated so far.

Their first LP suffers from (reasonable) comparisons to early Elvis Costello, and shows Any Trouble to be a pub band five years after the end of that era, playing competent, melodic rock with no special character. Only "The Hurt" and the stunningly derivative "Second Choice" (a retread of "Less than Zero") leave any lasting impression beyond their overall nice-guy swellness.

Live and Alive, recorded onstage in London, includes both aforementioned songs and a rendition of Bruce Springsteen's "Growing Up" (shades of Greg Kihn). The band shows a helpful increase in spunk and velocity, but still falls short of being exciting.

Wheels in Motion, produced by Mike Howlett (later a hitmaker for A Flock of Seagulls), evinces further improvement, adding impressive intricacy and dynamics to the arrangements. Gregson's singing is more confident, which helps put across his pessimistic (but not cynical) lyrics on songs like "Trouble with Love," "Another Heartache" and the album's standout, "Walking in Chains." **Wheels in Motion** still isn't a record to make you stop in your tracks, but nonetheless a likable collection of intelligently written and performed rock songs by a capable, unpretentious band.

Any Trouble, by a half-new lineup, is the band's first great album, a wonderful new blend of soul and pop strengthened by Gregson's sharpening melodic sense and lightening lyrical outlook. "Please Don't Stop," "Man of the Moment," "Northern Soul" and other tracks resemble a non-obnoxious Hall and Oates crossed

with Costello and recorded in Motown; production by David Kershenbaum provides the sonic variety and sophistication previously lacking. Gregson's development into a powerful, sensitive singer is merely the icing on the cake.

Any Trouble inexplicably re-recorded three early (and not timeless) songs for **Wrong End of the Race**, adding a rousing cover of "Baby Now That I've Found You," as well as a bunch of new Gregson compositions. Featuring an illustrious cast of guests (Richard Thompson, Billy Bremner, Geoff Muldaur), it's less stylized than its remarkable predecessor, but bristles with renewed vigor and rich arrangements filled with vocals and horns. [iar]

APB

Something to Believe In (Link) 1986
Cure for the Blues (Red River/Link) 1986

A popular component of Scotland's neo-funk movement, Aberdeen's five-man APB found a friend in American college radio, where its records have been very well-received. **Something to Believe In** is a compilation of singles—some effectively claustrophobic and offbeat, others trite and obnoxious. **Cure for the Blues** is a fine album of new tunes (not all in the band's basic mold—"Part of the Deal" is light pop that resembles Aztec Camera). Iain Slater's pressure-funk bass and mildly adenoidal vocals drive the dance songs, leaving the rest of the band to play a subsidiary role. [iar]

A POPULAR HISTORY OF SIGNS

A Popular History of Signs EP (nr/Wax Trax!) 1984
Comrades (Jungle/nr) 1985

This quartet plays generally boring arty dance music that is variously chilly, funky, humorless and clever. Save for a few exceptions on Side Two, the poorly structured songs on **Comrades** typically work one groove for several minutes and then fade out with the vocals still going. Despite the nicely spare arrangements, provocative subject matter ("Lenin," for instance), crystalline production and flawless playing, this is mighty boring music, only suited for utilitarian club play.

The American 12-inch consists of four tracks from pre-**Comrades** British singles that sound like bad O.M.D. "Ladder Jack" and "House" were remixed by Ministry's Al Jourgensen for the occasion, making them longer and heavier. [iar]

ARCADIA

See *Duran Duran*.

ARMOURY SHOW

Waiting for the Floods (Parlophone/EMI America) 1985

It's nice to see musicians with the courage of their convictions. After turning the Skids into a joke with his absurd pretensions, Richard Jobson pursued a career of poetry and preciousness, allying himself with assorted artsy types. Meanwhile, his one-time bandmate Stuart Adamson got on with Big Country, turning the Skids' anthemic Scottishness into a saleable guitar-rock commodity. Jobbo

ultimately abandoned his worthless posing and—with Russell Webb (ex-Skids), John McGeoch and John Doyle (both ex-Magazine)— formed the Armoury Show, whose resemblance to Big Country didn't escape notice. **Waiting for the Floods** is not a bad album, it's just a shame Jobson had to take such a long way 'round to get back to where he started. [iar]

ART & LANGUAGE

See *Red Crayola*.

ART BEARS

See *Henry Cow*.

ARTERY

Oceans EP (Red Flame/nr) 1982
One Afternoon in a Hot Air Balloon (Red Flame/nr) 1983
The Second Coming (Golden Dawn/nr) 1985

Sample: "Ghost of a Small Tour Boat Captain" is the story, theatrically declaimed (complete with rolling r's), of an adulterous chap murdered for his sins who comes back to haunt tourists on his dinghy. There's eventually lots of funny noises that take over from the narrative (including chalk-squeak violin). These guys aren't art school dropouts—**Oceans** sounds like a term project on new wave art rock. [jg]

ART ET TECHNIQUE

Climax (Fr. Hi-Tec) 1981

These Parisian progressives, with their radio-noise electronics, delayed-echo effects (used, among others, to process the minimal vocals) and contrapuntal, contra-rhythmic bass lines, make just the sort of avant-garde music that is most difficult to judge: Is it flim-flammery or are they making an unfathomable artistic statement? In the end, what's most important is that none of it is outrageous enough to make it matter one way or the other. [jg]

ART OF NOISE

Into Battle with the Art of Noise EP (ZTT-Island) 1983
(Who's Afraid of?) the Art of Noise! (ZTT-Island) 1984
In Visible Silence (China/Chrysalis) 1986

Originally a pop producer's idea of nouveau hip-hop instrumentals, the Art of Noise—a brilliant meld of studio/tape wizardry, floor-shaking dance percussion and adventurous audio experimentation—began semi-anonymously as a studio band under the guidance of Trevor Horn, who put out their records on his Zang Tuum Tumb label between editing Frankie Goes to Hollywood remixes. **Into Battle** has the aptly-named "Beat Box," with choral vocals and crazy effects (including, repeatedly, a car starting) punctuating typically booming drums. But it also has far lighter essays: "The Army Now," with cut-up Andrews Sisters-style vocals, and "Moments in Love," an obsessionally, lush backing track (for Barry White, perhaps?) that goes nowhere for an unconscionably long time. Produced to some incomprehensible blueprint, bits from one track often turn up in the midst of another.

The full-length AoN album, **Who's Afraid of?**—which was

available in the US for almost a year before being issued at home to enormous commercial success—contains some of the same cuts, but most notably adds the brilliant "Close (to the Edit)," a furious and unforgettable march of highly organized rhythm, effects and jagged musical/vocal ejaculations. Elsewhere, spoken-word collages commingle with the disjointed assemblages to create newsreel-inflected dance music of enormous vitality and originality. Remarkable and significant.

Disproving their reliance thereon, Art of Noise—Gary Langan, Anne Dudley and J.J. Jeczalik—split from Horn and ZTT, forming a label (China) on which they issued a single, "Legs," in November 1985. A full new album, **In Visible Silence**, followed several months later. Although no individual track is as gripping as "Close (to the Edit)," a semi- straightforward version of "Peter Gunn," with twang legend Duane Eddy providing guitar, became a substantial international hit, and other pieces are typically intriguing, aggravating and entertaining. Their talent and originality is unquestionable, but it's hard to discern what the consumer appeal is. Too challenging for ambience, yet not really suited for dancing, AoN's intellectual instrumental assault inhabits a genre all its own.   [iar]

ART ZOYD

Musique pour l'Odyssee (Fr. Atem) 1979
Generation sans Futur (Fr. Atem) 1980
Symphonie pour le Jour du Bruleront les Cités (Fr. Cryonic) 1981
Phase IV (Recommended/nr) 1982
Les Espaces Inquiets (Fr. Cryonic) 1984

THIERRY ZABOITZEFF

Promethee (Fr. Cryonic) 1984

French classical/jazz/avant-gardists who eschew drums for a primary reliance on strings, horns and piano, Art Zoyd have released a number of albums on European labels. **Phase IV** is generally acknowledged to be one of their best, a two-disc set of pieces that, to this untrained ear, sound like excellently recorded, unstructured blurts of evocative instrumental sound that ebb and flow in meter and volume and never stop resembling the unpleasant soundtrack to an unpleasant art film. **Les Espaces Inquiets** takes a more experimental tack but is essentially the same sort of affair, with polyrhythmic threads of various instruments weaving in and out of each other in seemingly unstructured hunks cut from one endless ramble. **Promethee**, a far simpler solo album from one of Zoyd's two string players, contains music from a theatrical production; it varies crazily from quiet/soothing to earsplitting/tense.   [iar]

ASSOCIATES

The Affectionate Punch (Fiction/nr) 1980 (Fiction/nr) 1982
Fourth Drawer Down (Situation 2/nr) 1981 (Beggars Banquet/nr) 1982
Sulk (Associates-WEA/Sire) 1982
Perhaps (Associates-WEA/nr) 1985

The Associates—Billy MacKenzie (most words and all vocals, eventually everything) and Alan Rankine (most music and all instruments except drums)—once attempted brilliance; then they settled for playing at being clever. **The Affectionate Punch** boldly tried to stake a claim for some of the no-man's land between Bowie's theatrical, tuneful rock and Talking Heads' semi-abstract, intellectual dance approach, with a slight flavoring of the pair's native Scottish traditional music. Not fully mature, and sometimes almost burying its own best points, the band seemed a promise of riches to come.

Unfortunately, the duo veered off into a more art-conscious—at times wilfully obscure—direction, with harsh musical textures often dominating the melodies. **Fourth Drawer Down**, a compilation of singles, gives the somewhat redeeming impression of determined experimentation that is, however, lessened by the exclusion of certain B-sides in favor of other, later tracks which make apparent MacKenzie's growing preference for pose over accomplishment.

By **Sulk**, such talent as comes through seems to strain under the weight of MacKenzie's self-consciousness. Rankine's emphasis on keyboards over guitar is symptomatic of the defection away from rock and toward a sort of neo-pop, but the melodies are hindered by tinny sound, arrangements that muddle rather than clarify, and vocal excesses that make Bowie's worst sound tame. The US edition subtracts three cuts, inserting instead a pair from **Fourth Drawer Down** and two subsequent singles. Net result: Associates (no article) are a shrill, non-synth Human League for emotional infants. The title's all too accurate; MacKenzie comes across as a callow, shallow poseur.

To write off **Perhaps** with a snide "perhaps not" would be a cheap shot, but still more than generous. The article is back in the name, but Rankine's gone, which makes MacKenzie the entire band. He does have associates, including guitarist Steve Reid—who co-wrote half the songs—yet whether any given track was produced by Heaven 17's Martyn Ware, the team of Billy Mac and Dave Allen, or Martin Rushent, it all sounds like Heaven 17 or the Human League—with synths, now—making undanceable dance music with a few ho-hum twists. The lyrics include strange, gratuitous, incomprehensible non sequiturs; the music is at best uninvolving, even if you listen for sheer sound and ignore the pose. The one all-around good track ("Waiting for the Love-boat," would you believe?) at 6:56 overstays its welcome by half. If you must, the cassette edition has extra tracks.   [jg]

VIRGINIA ASTLEY

From Gardens Where We Feel Secure (Happy Valley-Rough Trade/nr) 1983
Promise Nothing (Bel. Crépuscule) 1983

Astley is a classically trained pianist and flautist less known for her own work than for the illustrious company she keeps. She's played sessions for Siouxsie and the Banshees, Richard Jobson and Troy Tate, among others. Her father, Ted Astley, is an accomplished composer best known for television

themes; her brother-in-law is Pete Townshend. (She plays piano on his "Slit Skirts.") Astley's own pastoral and tranquil records are markedly different from those of family and friends.

Evoking images of summer afternoons in the countryside, **From Gardens Where We Feel Secure** is, superficially at least, sonic wallpaper to soothe the savage beast. Except for a few syllables, it's entirely instrumental and consists basically of piano, flute, clarinet and tape loops. Upon close scrutiny, the tapes (animal sounds, church bells, etc.) build subliminal tension, and show that there's more to Ms. Astley than initially meets the ear. **Promise Nothing** is a compilation including cuts from **Gardens** and various singles. The orchestration on the earlier works is thicker—synthesizers, sax and percussion place the material more in the rock realm—but her choir-boy soprano keeps things from getting too raucous. Standouts: the irresistible "Love's a Lonely Place to Be" and "Arctic Death," as haunting as any John Cale effort. An impressive record from an intriguing artist.

In 1985, Astley signed to Elektra and released a pair of singles, neither of which broke any new musical ground for her.   [dgs]

ASWAD

Aswad (Grove-Island/Mango) 1976
Hulet (Grove/nr) 1978 (Grove-Island/nr) 1979
Showcase (Grove-Island/nr) 1980
New Chapter (CBS/nr) 1981
New Chapter of Dub (Grove-Island/Mango) 1982
Not Satisfied (CBS/Columbia) 1982
Live and Direct (Island/Mango) 1983
Rebel Souls (Island/Mango) 1985

Though they've never really caught on in the States, Aswad is one of Britain's best, most popular reggae bands. Their work is characterized by consistently excellent musicianship (Aswad's horn section is superlative) and a sound that is modern yet authentic. Their easygoing groove may resemble UB40's, but Aswad is thoroughly individual and, after ten years, their continued growth and versatility are remarkable. Along with Linton Kwesi Johnson and Dennis Bovell, Aswad represents the flowering of British reggae. Their recording history, however, is disjointed and reflects shifts in personnel, musical direction and labels.

The first album (with "Back to Africa") is of mixed quality, but showcases the band's stylistic variety, featuring lovers rock, dub and Marley-inspired roots. **Hulet**, released two years later, is much better—assured and capable—but indecision about direction is clearly audible. Shortly after this release, bassist George Oban left; Tony "Gad" Robinson, who had played keyboards in the group, took over on bass. A stint with CBS yielded two albums, **New Chapter** and **Not Satisfied**, both rich with fine songs and performances, particularly the latter. **New Chapter of Dub**, while decent enough, is for fans only. **Rebel Souls** has a genial consistency and includes significant covers of Toots Hibbert's "54-46" and Marvin Gaye's "Mercy Mercy Me." Quite rightly, Aswad are linking themselves to tradition as they gear up for the future.

To some extent, Aswad's strongest releases have been their singles. No proper greatest-hits package exists, but two albums fill the gap. **Showcase**—remixes of their most popular non-LP numbers, including "Rainbow Culture," "Warrior Charge" and "Babylon" (the title theme of a film which starred Aswad's Brinsley Forde)—is both stunning and welcome, a fine place for novices to start. In addition, **Live and Direct** compiles some of Aswad's best-loved songs, and gives a hint of their live power. "Rockers Medley" stands out, but the whole LP is great.   [bk]

ATHLETICO SPIZZ 80

See *Spizz*.

ATTRACTIONS

See *Elvis Costello*.

AU PAIRS

Playing with a Different Sex (Human/nr) 1981
Sense and Sensuality (Kamera/nr) 1982
Live in Berlin (AKA/nr) 1983

Although the quartet was evenly divided between the sexes, Au Pairs' trademarks were singer/guitarist Lesley Woods' husky vocals and her feminist themes. They favored stripped-down, generally tuneless dance-rock, perhaps the better to drive home ironic messages like "We're So Cool," "Set-Up" (both on the first album), "Sex Without Stress" and "Intact" (on **Sense and Sensuality**). A female viewpoint is, unfortunately, still novel for pop music; Woods is humorless and sometimes oozingly graphic, but usually thought-provoking in her romantic analyses. Au Pairs' few overtly political songs ("Armagh," "America") are less successful.   [si]

AVANT GARAGE

Music (NZ Unsung Music) 1983

A jazzy-cum-classical nine-person ensemble with clarinets, cello, tuba and bassoon in addition to guitar, bass and drums. New Zealand's determinedly oddball Avant Garage sounds like something Zappa might have done in his dada orchestral phase. The music itself is generally pleasant (despite occasional skewed digressions, as on the instrumental "Funky Cockroach"); it's the lyrics and vocals on songs like "Garage Sale" and "Mr Granite" that give this its modern, boundary-breaking character. Intelligent, esoteric and fascinating.   [iar]

AVANT GARDENERS

Dig It (It. Appaloosa) 1980

I'm a bit unclear how this frivolous English wideboy new wave trio, known in the singular when originally signed to Virgin, ended up with an Italian album that mates all four tracks from a 1977 UK EP (like "Strange Gurl [sic] in Clothes" and "Bloodclat Boogie Baby") with a version of Roky Erickson's "Two Headed Dog," a porno pisstake called "Johnny Cash" and "Never Turn Your Back on a Silicon Chip," as well as other semi-inspired bits of doggerel. It's pretty funny—like Johnny Moped— and not badly played; an odd footnote to new wave's original explosion.   [iar]

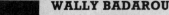

AZTEC CAMERA

High Land, Hard Rain (Rough Trade/Sire) 1983
Oblivious EP (WEA/Sire) 1983
Knife (WEA/Sire) 1984
Still on Fire EP (WEA/nr) 1984
Backwards and Forwards EP (nr/Sire) 1985

Young Glaswegian guitarist/singer/songwriter Roddy Frame is the creative force behind Aztec Camera, whose delicate pop conveys his poetic sensibility and rampant originality. **High Land, Hard Rain** is a magnificent debut, airy yet somehow lush, filled with Frame's lovely melodies and thoughtful, impressionistic lyrics. "Oblivious," "Walk Out to Winter" and "We Could Send Letters" are all memorable, distinguished by layered acoustic guitars, beautiful vocal arrangements and jazzy rhythm moves; "Down the Dip" displays a playful side.

The two **Oblivious** EPs include the same remix of the title tune, but different sets of accompanying tracks. The version issued in the US in 1984 has three British B-sides; the earlier UK edition has a B-side, an LP track and a live take.

Knife, produced by Dire Straits' Mark Knopfler, is a lot less ethereal, employing a stronger backbeat, sterner vocals and horns. Frame's lyrics continue to walk the line between profound and ludicrous, but for the most part manage to stay within the realm of lucidity. His writing shows the influence of Elvis Costello and also incorporates a mild R&B feel. Typical of the record's approach, the lead-off track, "Still on Fire," faintly recalls the Jackson 5's "I Want You Back." (That song's 12-inch release adds four live cuts.)

It's rare to encounter a marketing gimmick worthy of special mention, but the American **Backwards and Forwards** EP is brilliant. The folder that covers the 10-inch record contains the band's complete discography and history, plus profiles and photos, all avoiding hype and sales pressure. The record is additionally pretty neat: four live tracks (only two encores from the aforementioned EP) plus the band's languid acoustic cover of Van Halen's "Jump." [iar]

WALLY BADAROU

Echoes (Island) 1985
Chief Inspector EP (Island) 1986

Born in Paris, keyboardist Badarou is a veteran of Sly and Robbie's Compass Point All-Star band and has played behind such luminaries as Grace Jones, Black Uhuru and M (on "Pop Muzik"). He's also done significant production and playing for Marianne Faithfull, Level 42 and others. Moving into soundtracks, he's most notably been featured on *Kiss of the Spider Woman* and *Countryman*.

Following a debut solo single ("Chief Inspector," a hard synth-funk instrumental) that topped British dance charts, Badarou's first album under his own name reveals Indian, African and jazz influences, but the best track remains that single. Glossy, versatile and forgettable. The EP contains remixes of five tracks, including "Chief Inspector" and "Spider Woman." [bk]

BAD BRAINS

Bad Brains [tape] (nr/ROIR) 1982
Bad Brains EP (Alternative Tentacles/nr) 1982
I and I Survive/Destroy Babylon EP (Food for Thought/Important) 1982
Rock for Light (Abstract/PVC) 1983
I Against I (SST) 1986

H.R.

Its About Luv (nr/Olive Tree) 1985

In their quest to become a crossover band, these black jazz-rock fusionists from Washington, DC turned to orthodox speedpunk, and in 1980 released a memorable super-fast single, "Pay to Cum," that established their mastery of that genre. Bad Brains' hardcore is a more distinctively modulated roar than most, but what really sets them apart are their radically contrasting excursions into dub and rasta reggae. Hardcore's dogmatic streak makes it harder on chameleons than most rock subgenres; these guys almost get away with it.

On the cassette album (and the four-song **Bad Brains** EP excerpted from it), the quartet excels in both fields: loping, Jah-praising reggae and powerhouse slam-rock. The Ric Ocasek-produced **Rock for Light** includes newly-recorded versions of five songs from the tape and offers the same dualism, with subject matter covering everything from angry politics ("Riot Squad") to minor pop culturisms ("At the Movies"), stretching from rasta topics to "How Low Can a Punk Get" sociology. Throughout, Joseph I's (aka H.R.) reedy vocals set off the hardcore roar and sweetly color the reggae rumble. A fascinating and truly unique blend by a very special band. [mf/iar]

BAD MANNERS

Ska'n'B (Magnet/nr) 1980
Loonee Tunes! (Magnet/nr) 1980
Bad Manners (nr/MCA) 1981
Gosh It's . . . (Magnet/nr) 1981
Forging Ahead (Magnet/Portrait) 1982
The Height of Bad Manners (Telstar/nr) 1983
Klass (nr/MCA) 1983
Mental Notes (Portrait) 1985

This popular rollicking nine-piece London neo-ska nonsense ensemble is fronted by a cartoon character vocalist dubbed Buster Bloodvessel, an immense bald hulk. The rest of the lineup—three horns, guitar, bass, drums, keyboards and harmonica (played, but of course, by Winston Bazoomies)—churns out smooth, tight bluebeat like early Madness or Specials, while embracing all manner of musical silliness for humorous effect. Bad Manners is strictly entertainment; their records, juvenile though they may sometimes be, consistently provide smile-inducing, good-natured, toe-tapping value in every groove.

Ska'n'B (the band's original musical self-description) has fewer originals than subsequent LPs; versions of "Monster Mash," "Scruffy Was a Huffy Chuffy Tug Boat," the "Magnificent Seven" theme and "Ne-Ne Na-Na Na-Na Nu-Nu" are ludicrous but engaging. Their first American escape, **Bad Manners**, draws tracks from **Ska'n'B** as well as **Loonee Tunes!**, released in the meantime. **Gosh It's . . .** squeezes in a frisky instrumental rearrangement of "Can Can" amid pleasing originals like "Gherkin" (giddily described on the back cover as a "deeply moving tribute to Charles Aznavour") and "Ben E. Wriggle," plus some almost serious numbers that suggest insidious maturation.

Forging Ahead, the group's finest record, has a (thankfully instrumental) version of "Exodus," a cover of "My Boy (Girl) Lollipop," and an original called "Samson and Delilah (Biblical Version)." When released in the US two years later, a great subsequent single, "That'll Do Nicely," had been added.

With **Mental Notes**, B.M. pulls away from their original concept, managing to cover Todd Rundgren's "Bang the Drum All Day" without serious damage. Like Madness' transitional period (which came a lot earlier, careerwise), the bluebeat tempos remain, but they're under a slick coat of restraint, sophistication and—dare we say it—maturity. Bring back giddy stupidity!

Rounding off the discography to date are a pair of 1983 compilations. The American one has a truly disgusting pig-out cover and most of the band's best early tracks; the British release offers a different selection, with only six songs in common. [iar]

HENRY BADOWSKI

Life Is a Grand . . . (A&M/IRS) 1981

Badowski—who's played with Wreckless Eric, the Doomed and Good Missionaries—has a deep, pleasant, near-conversational voice that's almost always on key plus a dry and/or whimsical sense of humor. Henry plays almost every note here (even drums and sax), often with simple eloquence, on songs about getting married and swimming with fish in the sea. Could you ask for more? [jg]

CHRIS BAILEY

See *Saints*.

DAVE BALL

In Strict Tempo (Some Bizzare/nr) 1983

Without erstwhile Soft Cell partner Marc Almond supplying the sleaze, shy keyboard man Dave Ball is a cold-hearted bore. **In Strict Tempo**'s drab mood pieces strain for wry wit to leaven the pretentiousness but with little success and wind up just a jumble of undeveloped ideas. Genesis P-Orridge of Psychic TV warbles on two tracks. [jy]

BALLISTIC KISSES

Total Access (Don't Fall Off the Mountain/nr) 1982
Wet Moment (Don't Fall Off the Mountain/nr) 1983

Pseudo-streetwise lyrics tend to distract attention from the solidly danceable, cleanly produced synth-dominated pop on this New York band's first album. When their political stance turns to political role-playing, though, the result is oversimplification that borders on insincerity. Little wonder, then, that vocalist/wordsmith Michael Parker strives to sing like Joe Strummer (cough, cough), though he sounds more comfortable in his Brian Eno mode.

Wet Moment sounds like a tedious cross between the B-52's and Gang of Four: minimal melodies, propulsive rhythms and bleak vocals. It's easy to believe freaked-out tunes like "Emotional Ice" and "Everything Leaks," but how alienated do you really want to feel? [mf/jy]

AFRIKA BAMBAATAA & THE JAZZY 5

"Jazzy Sensation" (nr/Tommy Boy) 1981

AFRIKA BAMBAATAA & SOULSONIC FORCE

"Planet Rock" (21/Tommy Boy) 1982
"Looking for the Perfect Beat" (Tommy Boy) 1982
"Renegades of Funk" (Tommy Boy) 1983

AFRIKA BAMBAATAA & JAMES BROWN

"Unity" (Tommy Boy) 1984

TIME ZONE

"The Wildstyle" (Celluloid) 1983
"World Destruction" (Celluloid) 1984

SHANGO

Shango Funk Theology (Celluloid) 1984

AFRIKA BAMBAATAA & FAMILY

"Funk You!" (Tommy Boy) 1985

Bronx dj-turned-hip-hop-superstar Bambaataa not only created the record that thrust beat-box electro-funk into the '80s, he has made pioneering records with numerous performers and established himself as a major figure in contemporary music. Working mainly in the 12-inch format, Bam's ascent began with a routine boast rap, "Jazzy Sensation," but then got into gear with "Planet Rock," the Arthur Baker-produced (and co-written, with the band and John Robie) explosion of scratch cuts, electronic gimmickry, processed vocals and all-transistor rhythms. (Both tracks were later compiled on the Tommy Boy label retrospective, **Greatest Beats**.) "Looking for the Perfect Beat" is even better, with Baker mostly soft-pedaling the monolithic pounding in favor of a skittish, electronic metronome and tacking on fancier effects, vocals and mix tricks to create an ultra-busy urban symphony. The mega-rhythmic "Renegades of Funk" adds social/historical/political lyrics to the dance-floor dynamism and delivers a really bizarre blend of rap, synthesizers and oppressive electronic percussion.

In a fascinating cross-generational culture mix, Bambaataa teamed with the Godfather of Soul to record "Unity," a positive political message released in six alternate versions (connected by studio patter) on one disc. Hitting a funky compromise between classic soul and nouveau hip-hop, the record works on a number of levels, and is certainly a significant milestone in rap. Taking another startling detour, Bambaataa wrote and recorded "World Destruction" with Bill Laswell, sharing the vocals with John Lydon, jump-cutting the Englishman's no-wave keen into an intense, ominous funk-rock maelstrom for one of the most remarkable dance singles in recent memory.

Bambaataa also records as a member of Shango, a vocal trio that is supported by Material (for this purpose, Laswell and Michael Beinhorn). The album-length **Shango Funk Theology** offers five sophisticated party creations that also feature guitarist Nicky Skopelitis. The originals get no heavier, lyrically, than "Let's Party Down"; a version of Sly Stone's "Thank You" is utterly appropriate. Good for dancing but a bit dull and samey for listening.

During the wait for Bambaataa's long-promised album, his main release was the 12-inch "Funk You!," a corny idea delivered with Bam's typical panache and stretched out in four very different mixes, with borrowings from James Brown and Queen. [iar]

BANANARAMA

Deep Sea Skiving (London) 1983
Bananarama (London) 1984
True Confessions (London) 1986

Keren Woodward, Sarah Dallin and Siobhan Fahey first gained notoriety singing with the Fun Boy Three, who later returned the favor by producing and backing the female trio on their earliest singles. **Deep Sea Skiving** essentially compiles their first string of infectious 45s, encompassing a panoply of styles: percussive Afro-beat ("He Was Really Sayin' Somethin'"), girl-group soul ("Shy Boy"), '60s chart silliness ("Na Na Hey Hey Kiss Him Goodbye") and lush pop ("Cheers Then"). Additionally, **Deep Sea Skiving** offers Paul Weller's "Doctor Love," the charming, light "Hey Young London" and the morose "What a Shambles." With an assortment of producers involved there's little uniformity of sound, but the ensemble vocals provide the crucial character, regardless of setting.

For their first real album, Bananarama gave the ball to hitmakers Swain and Jolley (Spandau, Alison Moyet, Imagination) who, as is their custom, co-wrote the material. Over the lush, highly arranged backing, the ladies croon two wonderful singles—the evocatively tropical "Cruel Summer" (a hit, one year apart, in the UK and US) and "Robert De Niro's Waiting"—otherwise, the album deflects much of their engaging individuality and substitutes a formulaic, vacuous sheen that's too functional and defeats their ingenuous image. **Bananarama** isn't bad—the vocals are charming in any case—but it is forgettable. [iar]

BAND APART

Band Apart EP (Bel. Crammed Discs) 1982
Marseille (Bel. Crammed Discs) 1983

Centered around expatriate Frenchman Medak Mader (guitars, synth) and one Jayne Bliss (vocals, e-bow guitar), Band Apart make grimly impressive music: an intimidating bass'n'drums 4/4 laid down just faster than a stroll (but with vicious inexorability) and whining, gnashing guitars, plus scary vocals. One near-mesmerizing track of multiple guitar/synth washes on the EP is hampered only by the limits of recording and pressing quality. [jg]

BANGLES

Bangles EP (nr/Faulty Products) 1982
All Over the Place (CBS/Columbia) 1984
Different Light (CBS/Columbia) 1986

These four young women from Los Angeles—originally known as the Bangs—display an odd collection of influences on their five-track debut EP, neatly produced by Craig Leon. The swell harmonies on several cuts come straight from the Mamas and Papas, while the music alternates between evoking **Rubber Soul** and energetic, bantamweight Yardbirds-styled garage rock. The playing's fine and the vocals are great—the songs just aren't up to snuff.

Despite generating a lot of interest, the Bangles' career was temporarily derailed when Faulty Products went out of business and their bassist left to join Blood on the Saddle. Nonetheless, come 1984, the Bangles swung back into action, armed with a new member, a contract with a more reliable record company, the best American pop producer money can buy (David Kahne) and a passel of (mostly guitarist Vicki Peterson's) brilliant new songs, including Kimberley Rew's "Going Down to Liverpool," which indirectly led to his group, Katrina and the Waves, finally securing an American deal. **All Over the Place** has everything a pop album needs: exceptional harmony vocals, catchy, memorable and intelligent tunes and a full dose of rock'n'roll guitar energy. Unlike the Go-Go's, who never fully clarified their lyrical stance, the Bangles offer an adult play-fair-or-take-a-hike independence that is a lot more contemporary than their joyously evocative sound. The best cuts other than "Liverpool"—"Hero Takes a Fall," "Tell Me" and "James"—feature Susanna Hoffs' alluring vocals and are unassailable pop gems; the worst tracks only fall short of that by a smidge. Simply wonderful.

Prince became a fan, and ended up giving the Bangles a song, "Manic Monday" (written pseudonymously by "Christopher"), for **Different Light**. Despite trivial lyrics, it became a gigantic hit single, establishing the quartet's stardom, but causing many to overlook the LP's finer pieces—Jules Shear's "If She Knew What She Wants," Alex Chilton's classic "September Gurls," and bassist Michael Steele's harrowing "Following." Maybe not as consistently alluring as **All Over the Place**, but a thoroughly enjoyable (and often memorable) sophomore showing. These women know how to sing! [iar]

See also *Blood on the Saddle*.

RICHARD BARONE

See *Bongos*.

BARRACUDAS

Drop Out with the Barracudas (EMI/Voxx) 1981
Mean Time (Fr. Closer) 1982
House of Kicks EP (Flicknife/nr) 1983
Live 1983 (Fr. Coyote) 1983
Endeavor to Persevere (Fr. Closer) 1984
I Wish It Could Be 1965 Again (Fr. GMG) 1986

Despite a cheerfully self-deprecating stance, Britain's Barracudas offer quite an enjoyable sentimental journey through American traditions on **Drop Out**. Some tunes plunge headlong into dense, ringing folk-rock—see "We're Living in Violent Times" or "I Saw My Death in a Dream Last Night" for an update of the Byrds on a gloomy day. Surf tunes like "Summer Fun" and "His Last Summer" strive a little too hard for laughs to overcome fundamental lightweightness, but are fun and can't be faulted on attitude. (The UK and US versions of the LP differ by a track.)

After losing drummer Nicky Turner to the nascent Lords of the New Church, a new Barracudas lineup put together the more R&B-geared **Mean Time**. It's a losing proposition trying to keep up with their unpredictable recording career, but **House of Kicks** is a four-song 12-inch. The live album, packaged and recorded so amateurishly as to resemble a bootleg, finds them an older and far less innocent-sounding quintet, playing blues and rock cover tunes like "Seven and Seven Is," "You're Gonna Miss Me" and "Fortunate Son." [jy/iar]

SYD BARRETT

The Madcap Laughs (Harvest/nr) 1970
Barrett (Harvest/nr) 1970
The Madcap Laughs/Barrett (Harvest) 1974

One of rock's legendary living dead casualties, guitarist/songwriter Syd Barrett formed Pink Floyd in 1965 and made it one of the first art-school bands to abandon blues for druggified psychedelia. He fell out of Pink Floyd after a debut album that put the band on the verge of major international success; having grown erratic, withdrawn and unpredictable, he pretty much retired in 1968, and has since lived a private, reclusive existence—except for making two solo records in 1970. Despite his inactivity and disinterest with regard to rock music, Barrett has influenced many bands who have explored similarly detached concepts with like-minded laconic sounds. Fifteen years later, his unselfconscious looniness continues to set a style for artists to explore updated acid-rock with little more than an acoustic guitar. The Television Personalities have sung about him, and Robyn Hitchcock, Anthony More and others have been compared to him, and numerous art, psychedelic and neo-mod bands have invoked his name, recorded his songs and acknowledged his impact. Tormented but unquestionably brilliant, Barrett has left a musical legacy which is—excepting the Floyd's first LP—wholly contained on these two discs, issued separately but subsequently repackaged as a double album.

The Madcap Laughs sounds as though it was a difficult record to make. Having dragged Syd into a studio, ex-bandmates David Gilmour and Roger Waters had to get him organized enough to produce releasable tracks. False starts and between-take discussions included on the record make it obvious this was no mean feat. The songs are wonderful, and Syd's delicate but clumsy singing lends charm to the effort, which alternates between one-man performances and subtle group backing.

Barrett features an all-star trio of Gilmour, Richard Wright (Floyd's keyboardist) and drummer Jerry Shirley; Gilmour and Wright produced. It's a more consistent-sounding record—relatively confident and upbeat—yet it still offers Barrett's idiosyncratic view of life in songs like "Waving My Arms in the Air" and "Effervescing Elephant." Barrett's confusion and anger lurk just below the surface of misleadingly chipper bits of Carnaby Street flower-power music.   [iar]

B

14

WILD WILLY BARRETT

See *John Otway*.

BASEMENT 5

1965—1980 (Island/Antilles) 1981
In Dub (Island/nr) 1981

Basement 5 came out of Island Record's London art department playing a blend of reggae and synth-pop under the production auspices of Martin Hannett. **1965— 1980** waffles between both forms, never quite achieving the hoped-for marriage, but does sport a number of light ditties with heavy political overtones. The contrast between roots and futurism gives Basement 5 a fascinating, if ephemeral flavor. Even more interesting is **In Dub**, a paean to Hannett's control-booth genius, which naturally features dub versions of some material from the first LP.   [sg]

TONI BASIL

Word of Mouth (Radialchoice/ Chrysalis) 1981
Toni Basil (Virgin/Chrysalis) 1983

This veteran choreographer-turned-video director (who had a role in *Easy Rider*) skipped America for England, where she briefly became a glamourpuss pop star with the Chinn/Chapman-penned "Mickey," a simpleminded bit of new wave bubblegum that was an enormous hit in the States a year later. Unfortunately, the rest of her first album is disjointed, touching on more synth-dance rock and Pat Benatar-level mundanity, plus a trio of Devo songs on which Ms. B. is backed by the Akronites themselves. (The American release has

two track substitutions and different artwork.) Basil is clever, likable and sings well enough, but the album has a disconcerting lack of cohesion and believability.

Except for the hyperactive "Over My Head," Basil's follow-up is a drag, filled with banal, clichéd rock and none of the inspired lunacy or even personality that made **Word of Mouth** spottily diverting.   [iar]

STIV BATORS

Disconnected (nr/Bomp) 1980
The Church and the New Creatures (Fr. Lolita) 1983

So what does a typecast Dead Boy do when his band breaks up? He moves to Los Angeles, hires local musicians, and cuts a tremendous album of melodic rock tunes. Playing down his outrageous side, Bators' solo record keeps up an Iggy-like persona while replacing chaotic garage-punk with thoughtful music that owes power pop a sizable debt. Originals like "Evil Boy" and "The Last Year" mask their dark messages with pretty tunes; a great cover of the punk classic "I Had Too Much to Dream Last Night" clarifies Bators' roots and caps off the album nicely.

The French LP contains all of **Disconnected**, adding three sides from a pair of Bomp singles and one other cut.   [iar]

See also *Lords of the New Church, Wanderers*.

BAUHAUS

In the Flat Field (4AD/nr) 1980
Mask (Beggars Banquet/nr) 1981
The Sky's Gone Out (Beggars Banquet/A&M) 1982
Press the Eject and Give Me the Tape (Beggars Banquet/nr) 1982
Ziggy Stardust EP (Beggars Banquet/nr) 1982
Burning from the Inside (Beggars Banquet/A&M) 1983
The Singles 1981—1983 EP (Beggars Banquet/nr) 1983
4.A.D. EP (4AD/nr) 1983
1979—1983 (Beggars Banquet/nr) 1985

DAVID J

Etiquette of Violence (Situation 2/nr) 1983
Crocodile Tears and the Velvet Cosh (Glass/nr) 1985
Blue Moods Turning Tail (Glass/nr) 1985

In their prime the leading practitioners of gloomy angst-rock, Bauhaus combined guitars and electronics into a bleak backdrop for Peter Murphy's tortured vocals. Adding theatrical makeup, poseur lyrics and a nearly hidden but stubborn pop streak, Bauhaus were both popular (in the UK) and influential. Their biggest short-coming was a complete lack of irony; while promoting a somber image of deep seriousness, the band was an utter joke, a laughably pretentious attempt to be something way beyond its ken.

Bauhaus' self-produced debut, **In the Flat Field**, is a dense, disjointed patchwork of sounds and uncertain feelings, supported by a pressured, incessant beat. Delving deep into the dark side of the human psyche with chilling results, Bauhaus conjures up unsettling images of a world given over to death and decay. **Mask** attempts an exploration of styles, incorporating airs

of heavy metal, funk brass and Tangerine Dreamlike electronics into their work. Though still weighty, the lyrics make occasional (intentional) stabs at humor and show an increasingly romantic nature.

The Sky's Gone Out opens with a lively, bright version of Brian Eno's "Third Uncle" that signaled a more upbeat mood for Bauhaus, offsetting the continuing themes of damnation and destruction. Good production opens up the sound considerably, and Bauhaus draws even closer to the heavy metal frontier. Exposing an ongoing ambitious streak, the album includes a three-part mini-opera, "The Three Shadows." **Press the Eject and Give Me the Tape**, a live LP recorded in London and Liverpool, was first included as a bonus second disc in UK copies of **The Sky's Gone Out**, then reissued as a separate album.

In their role as a singles band, Bauhaus' late '82 release of a copy-cat live-in-the-studio version of "Ziggy Stardust" (joined on the 12-inch by "Third Uncle," a bizarre, funny original consisting of Faustian film dialogue over cool instrumental backing and a live recording of "Waiting for the Man" with guest vocalist Nico) supported their self-image as descendants of early '70s glam-rockers. (Typically, they had released a single of Marc Bolan's "Telegram Sam" in 1980.) A strange artistic dichotomy, to be sure.

The final Bauhaus album, **Burning from the Inside**, took them further into new realms of dark-spirited, mildly abrasive rock, with pounding drums, booming bass, buzzing guitars and some of the most ludicrous wanky lyrics you're ever likely to encounter. The nicest track is "King Volcano," an instrumental with skimpy chanting. Still, many took Bauhaus very seriously, and certainly a lot of bands have copied them, delving into the darkest, most pretentious corners of solemn rock.

The Singles EP consolidates six of their best-loved A-sides, including "Ziggy Stardust," "Kick in the Eye" and "Lagartija Nick." **4.A.D.** compiles several 1980 singles, including "Telegram Sam," "Dark Entries" and a rare version of John Cale's "Rosegarden Funeral of Sores." Bauhaus split up in late 1983; several of the members stuck together to form Tones on Tail. Pete Murphy teamed with ex-Japan bassist Mick Karn to form Dalis Car.   [sg/iar]

See also *Dalis Car, Jazz Butcher, Love and Rockets, Tones on Tail, This Mortal Coil*.

BEASTIE BOYS

Polly Wog Stew EP (nr/Rat Cage) 1982
"Cookie Puss" (nr/Rat Cage) 1983
"Rock Hard" (Def Jam) 1984
"She's On It" (Def Jam-CBS) 1985

New York's Beastie Boys began as a hardcore band in 1979; they broke up, reformed, cut a 7-inch EP (**Polly Wog Stew**, containing such punk creations as "Egg Raid on Mojo" and "Transit Cop") and then hit the big time as a hip-hop band. Their "Cookie Puss" single combines a tremendous beat pulsing with rock energy and sharp mix tricks with puerile spoken-word stuff, including crank telephone calls. It's a ridiculous record, but funny (and danceable). The 12-inch includes two demented remixes and

a bogus reggae song ("Beastie Revolution") that assaults Musical Youth and the entire rasta culture. The Al Jolson routine is fairly offensive, but the band seems more parodic than mean-spirited.

In 1984, the Beastie Boys became a credible rap band. "Rock Hard" (joined by three other tracks on the 12-inch) uses a backing track very reminiscent of Run—D.M.C.; their raps don't sound all that different either. Although unmistakably white and middle class, these guys are serious; their cultural heritage still leads producer Rick Rubin to toss hunks of guitar and AC/DC riffs into "Rock Hard" and "Party's Gettin' Rough" and shards of Led Zeppelin into "Beastie Groove." In 1985, the story of Def Jam Records—Rubin's partnership with rap mogul Russell Simmons—formed the basis of the plot of the film *Krush Grove*, in which both, as well as the Beasties, appeared. "She's On It" is a fun, dumb stomper, accompanied by (or as the sleeve says, soundtrack to) a great tongue-in-cheek T&A video. The song is so over the top that a couplet like "She'd get down on her knees/If we'd only say please" isn't that offensive.

With Run—D.M.C. working towards rock from the rap side and the Beasties giving rap a rock background, New York-produced dance music is busily hybridizing itself into the future.   [iar/dgs]

BEAT

I Just Can't Stop It (Go-Feet/Sire) 1980 (Fame/IRS) 1983
Wha'ppen? (Go-Feet/Sire) 1981 (nr/IRS) 1983
Special Beat Service (Go-Feet/IRS) 1982
What Is Beat? (Go-Feet/IRS) 1983

Although lumped in with the 2-Tone crowd upon emerging in 1979, the Beat (known in America as the English Beat) proved far more versatile than most of their skanking contemporaries. True, **I Just Can't Stop It** has its share of ska-influenced upbeats—a delightful reworking of Tears of a Clown" (on the US release only) and patois-tinged toasting ("Rough Rider") from Ranking Roger—but the band's furious drive and pumping bass ("Two Swords," "Click Click," "Twist & Crawl") relate more to the rock tradition. A recording of Andy Williams' "Can't Get Used to Losing You" is a nice gesture, regardless of the outcome. (The US release also includes another track not on the original album.)

By **Wha'ppen?**, the Beat had mellowed out, preferring mid-tempo grooves drawn from various Third World cultures. Loping music, playful combinations of voices (Roger and lead singer/guitarist Dave Wakeling) and Saxa's effervescent sax almost obscure the songs' depressing views of personal and social troubles ("Drowning," "All Out to Get You," "Cheated").

Special Beat Service is the band's slickest offering. The polished music generates more light than heat, but lyrics—dwelling more on romantic than political problems—depict believably complex scenarios. Ranking Roger's lighthearted showcases are now isolated from the group's main concerns, but the Beat here remains a fine band committed to pan-cultural understanding.

The band's farewell compilation, **What Is Beat?**, is actually three different records: a fourteen-track English album, a bonus disc's worth of extended remixes included with early copies and on the cassette of same, and an altogether different American release, with live takes and a Jellybean Benitez remix. Collect 'em all!

Following the Beat's much-lamented dissolution, Ranking Roger and Dave Wakeling stuck together to form General Public while David Steele and Andy Cox assembled Fine Young Cannibals. [si/iar]

See also *Fine Young Cannibals, General Public*.

BEAT

The Beat (CBS/Columbia) 1979
To Beat or Not to Beat EP (nr/Passport) 1983

PAUL COLLINS' BEAT

The Kids Are the Same (CBS/Columbia) 1982

Collins, once one-third of LA's fabled Nerves (the other two were Peter Case, later of the Plimsouls, and tunesmith-to-the-stars Jack Lee), writes songs calling to mind the early Hollies (except grittier and American) and a more down-to-earth, less poetic Byrds. Though never scaling the heights of either band, **The Beat** (issued prior to the name conflict with the English Beat) is simple, satisfying power pop, all meat and no filler. If anything, though, it may be too no-frills, with unimaginative production and a lack of idiosyncrasy or variation giving it a monotonous feel.

This problem was remedied somewhat on the Beat's second album, which is quite a bit heavier. Although they seem to run out of steam—and songs—halfway through, the good chunk generates more heat than many bands can manage.

Collins refurbished the Beat's lineup for the 1983 EP. The new combo includes ex-Patti Smith Group drummer Jay Dee Daugherty and guitarist Jimmy Ripp, both of whom have played on Tom Verlaine LPs. Although the band smokes and the songs are stylistically varied, this glorified demo surprisingly failed to get Collins a new major-label deal. [jg]

BEATNIKS

See *Yukihiro Takahashi*.

BEAT RODEO

Staying Out Late with Beat Rodeo (nr/IRS) 1985

STEVE ALMAAS

Beat Rodeo EP (nr/Coyote) 1982

CRACKERS

Sir Crackers! EP (nr/Twin/Tone) 1980

Following the breakup of the Suicide Commandos, Almaas formed the Crackers (not the New Mexico band with the same name), a trio whose EP is of little consequence except to vaguely indicate the direction he'd pursue: rough-hewn melodic rock. **Sir Crackers!** threatens to take off, but just fizzles. After leaving Minneapolis and

working with the Bongos, Almaas and boss Bongo Richard Barone headed down to visit with Mitch Easter at his Drive-In Studio in North Carolina, where the three of them whipped up an EP, **Beat Rodeo**, at last showing Almaas off to great advantage. If Marshall Crenshaw's treatment of the Buddy Holly legacy irks you for being wrapped in candy floss, this charming, rocking disc should be right up your alley—swell tunes, Almaas' straight-as-an-arrow vocals and Easter's clear production that adds no sugar but lets the natural sweetness shine through.

Almaas almost immediately formed a quartet named for the EP but not including any previous bandmates. Beat Rodeo leans toward the country orientation implicit in its name (but absent from the EP) and integrates it (countryish guitar sound, even a dash of fiddle) rather well into the already established pop-rock context. The problem is that none of the LP (originally issued in Germany in 1984) is involving or exciting. Light, pleasant, inoffensive —but Almaas' melodies seem bereft of inspiration, and their performance lacks snap. [jg]

ADRIAN BELEW

Lone Rhino (Island) 1982
Twang Bar King (Island) 1983

Having served with David Bowie, Talking Heads, Tom Tom Club and—most notably and recently—King Crimson, guitarist Belew echoes famous associates on his first solo LP without staking out any turf to call his own. The Kentucky native employs pre-stardom friends from Midwestern bands rather than big names, serving up a varied program of calculated weirdness, straight rock and semi-funk. Mildly charming and rather unfocused, the tenuous unifying thread is his David Byrne-influenced voice.

On his second outing, Belew is much more self-assured in putting over the same ingredients—an assurance that spills over into self-indulgence long before the album is over. But this record does underscore his contributions to Crimson: the distinctive vocabulary of extra-musical noises, the personality and especially the humor which is much more in evidence here than anywhere else. When it all works, it works incredibly well. [jy/mf]

BELFEGORE

Belfegore (WEA/Elektra) 1984

An American bassist, a Canadian drummer and a German guitarist comprise this unique crypto-metal band, a strange case of subversive musical activity. **Belfegore** was produced by Conny Plank, best known for his Ultravox and D.A.F. work; their first video was directed by Zbigniew Rybczynski right after Art of Noise. Musically dark and energetic, Belfegore avoids the clichés of metal for a sombre intelligence that has common ground with everyone from Motörhead to Joy Division. Fascinating. [iar]

BELLE STARS

The Belle Stars (Stiff/Stiff-Warner Bros.) 1983

Offering a self-contained, funkier alternative to Bananarama, the

seven-woman Belle Stars played and sang neo-soul and dance-rock. At their most glamorous (e.g., the excellent "Sign of the Times") they resemble an early ABC with added spunk and less chrome. Much of the material is, however, much plainer. Far more enjoyable than the band's originals are covers of "Iko Iko," "Mockingbird," "Needle in a Haystack" and "The Clapping Song," which provoke a good time largely through the band's own evident enjoyment. [iar]

BERLIN

Pleasure Victim (nr/MAO-Enigma) 1982 (Geffen) 1983
Love Life (Geffen) 1984

Los Angeles-based Berlin (has there ever been a Berlin band named Los Angeles?) had been active for several years—an almost totally different lineup issued a 1980 single on IRS—before bursting onto the national scene with an impressively slick seven-song mini-album commercializing routine synth-rock with singer Terri Nunn's audio pornography. The record's most blatant (and hence, best-selling) track, "Sex (I'm a . . .)," is tasteless and offensive, with crude lyrics and ridiculous moaning. There are two good, atmospheric tunes ("Masquerade" and "The Metro"), but the LP is otherwise bland heading towards inept.

Love Life offers more singles-bar smarm, while attempting to gain Berlin respectability as a techno-dance band. Unfortunately, leader John Crawford is too shallow a songwriter to make any lasting impact, and the best Berlin can manage is a slick, Mike Howlett-produced sound (Giorgio Moroder did a pair of tracks as well) to glamorize a vapid and depressing view of sex. Pathetic. [iar]

BERLIN BLONDES

Berlin Blondes (Odeon-EMI/nr) 1980

Their name notwithstanding, this band hails from Glasgow and plays undistinguished, danceable hybrid synth/bass/drums clichés, occasionally adding colorful Sparks-like vocals for character. Mike Thorne produced the album with skill, allowing the music to be heard loud and clear. Unfortunately, there really isn't much reason you'd want to. [iar]

BETHNAL

Dangerous Times (Vertigo/nr) 1978
Crash Landing (Vertigo/nr) 1978

On the strength of live performances during 1976, this multi-ethnic London band (named after Bethnal Green) was considered one of the most promising new groups in Britain. Admittedly different from the pack, lead singer George Csapo played keyboards and violin—both instruments not then in vogue among new wavers. Unfortunately, Bethnal was never able to properly translate its hard-driving mid-period-Who-influenced sound to vinyl. They came closest on **Dangerous Times**, but were thwarted by Kenny Laguna's thin, pop-oriented production which highlights the band's material and vocals (both spotty) over its superior musicianship and energy; covers of "Baba O'Reilly" (sic) and "We Gotta Get Out of This Place,"

while interesting choices, add nothing to the originals.

Crash Landing, produced by Phil Chapman and Pete Townshend's brother-in-law, Jon Astley, is a move into glossy, empty-headed arena-style terrain that effectively alienated the band's original supporters and failed to interest a new audience. [ds]

B-52'S

The B-52's (Island/Warner Bros.) 1979
Wild Planet (Island/Warner Bros.) 1980
Party Mix EP (Island/Warner Bros.) 1981
Mesopotamia EP (Island/Warner Bros.) 1982
Whammy! (Island/Warner Bros.) 1983

FRED SCHNEIDER AND THE SHAKE SOCIETY

Fred Schneider and the Shake Society (Island/Warner Bros.) 1984

Just when new wave seemed to be bottoming out, along came Athens, Georgia's B-52's to rev it back up again, with distinctive junk-store '60s visuals (the two women in the band sport bouffant wigs—"B-52's" in southern regional slang) and stark, highly danceable songs with appropriately surreal kitsch lyrics. The B-52's' wacky sense of humor made their self-titled first album a sleeper that was certified (US) gold in 1986. Now a cult classic, it contains such cornerstones of the repertoire as "52 Girls," "Dance This Mess Around," "6060-842" and the ever- popular "Rock Lobster."

The B-52's have been wondering what to do for an encore ever since. The eagerly awaited **Wild Planet** has its inspired moments: "Private Idaho" and "Devil in My Car" mesh a firm beat with dark and/or silly sentiments. "Give Me Back My Man" takes a new direction—a serious (!) showcase for Cindy Wilson's singing. (Vocalist Fred Schneider is usually up front for comic relief.) But too much of the album, with its short length and recycled ideas, comes across as a pale imitation of its predecessor.

Apparently the band felt the same way, staying away from the recording studio for the next year and a half. **Party Mix**, issued in the interim, takes three songs from each of the two LPs and—through the miracle of tape loops, overdubs and other studio tomfoolery—inflates them to nearly 30 minutes playing time. The result is functional for discos but antithetical to the B-52's' minimalist precepts.

The band was next "officially" heard from with another mini-LP, **Mesopotamia**, salvaged from sessions produced by Talking Head David Byrne. Whether under Byrne's humorless influence or not—he plays on the record and engages a couple of Heads-family percussionists to help out—the B-52's get serious with dire results. "Loveland" and "Deep Sleep" sacrifice élan for slickness—not a fair trade. "Cake" and the title cut (one of only two Schneider vocals) come off as self-conscious parodies of the old, carefree B-52's. Only "Throw That Beat in the Garbage Can" taps the zany reservoir that made the group popular in the first place.

B

15

After the curious abortion of **Mesopotamia, Whammy!** came as a reassuring return to form, or perhaps formula. On some cuts ("Whammy Kiss," "Trism," "Butterbean"), the band goes through the, by now, well-worn motions. Elsewhere ("Big Bird," "Queen of Las Vegas"), horns—introduced on **Mesopotamia**— and intriguing narratives show the B-52's are only on semi-automatic pilot. The drummer and guitarist play all the instruments (save horns) and the sound is more electronic than funky-human.

Fred Schneider's solo project hardly discouraged fears about the state of the B-52's. (Another member, Kate Pierson, helps Fred out with vocals.) The *pro tem* Shake Society is a fine stopgap for the parent band's looniness. Schneider's lyrics continue to dwell on campy sci-fi ("This Planet's a Mess," "Orbit") and campy fantasy ("Summer in Hell," "Boonga"), with campy sex ("Monster," "It's Time to Kiss") thrown in for good measure (and a bit of controversy). Whatever happens to the B-52's, Schneider at least has established himself as a fizzy pop presence.

In October 1985, guitarist Ricky Wilson died of cancer.   [si]

BIG AUDIO DYNAMITE

This Is Big Audio Dynamite (CBS/Columbia) 1985

The rote replay of **Cut the Crap** only underscores the accomplishment of Mick Jones' new band with filmmaker Don Letts. Joe Strummer attempted to purify the Clash by purging Jones, but wound up liberating the guitarist's muse and misplacing his own. BAD takes off from various things the Clash had tried on **Sandinista!** and **Combat Rock**, but goes much further with audio verite, sonic effects, and beat box funk. **This Is Big Audio Dynamite** is an adventurous, creatively ambitious crazy quilt of half-baked songs with fascinating lyrics, slathered over with shards of film dialogue and news reports. Although flimsy and gimmicky on first exposure, BAD's meandering dance grooves (especially "E=MC2" and "The Bottom Line") prove far more alluring and resilient with repeated exposure. Jones' monochromatic vocals can be a limiting factor in spots, but are generally adequate to the task, and occasionally perfectly suited. Where BAD can go with their unique hybrid of art and life remains to be seen, but this album is an impressive work in progress.   [iar]

BIG BALLS AND THE GREAT WHITE IDIOT

Foolish Guys (Ger. Strand) 1978

With some guidance by ex-Grapefruit George Alexander (né Alec Young, as in the family that gave us the Easybeats and AC/DC), the three Grund brothers play high-spirited punk in the style of the day (Pistols, Ramones, et al.). It's charming by dint of amusingly awkward attempts to translate their idea of punky aggro into English ("Hell So Neat," "Hang Yourself from an Apple Tree") and general goofiness.   [jg]

BIG BLACK

Lungs EP (nr/Ruthless) 1983

Bulldozer EP (nr/Ruthless-Fever) 1984
Racer-X EP (nr/Homestead) 1984
Atomizer (Homestead) 1986

"The only good policeman is a dead one/The only good laws aren't enforced/I've never hung a darkie but I've fed one/I've never seen an Indian on a horse." With these gentle words, acerbic fanzine writer Steve Albini began his extremely serious adventures in the rock'n'roll skin trade. For a while, Albini assembled makeshift lineups from other Chicago bands (Big Black has since stabilized a lineup of its own); regardless of who, they make music that's grating, angular, humorless and very intelligent—sort of a cross between Gang of Four, PiL and the Great Crusades (not a band). Albini's self-righteousness sometimes causes him to be as much unaccommodating as uncompromising, but his bile is generally well directed, and he's immune to corruption, except from within. All these records are challenging and rewarding.

Lungs is at once the most homegrown, overwrought and best Big Black release. Over a skeletal art-funk background, Albini creates bleak, tough images of recessioned industrial America. While "I Can Be Killed" is almost laughable for its delusionary self-importance, "Steelworker" is intensely muscular. **Bulldozer** goes for a chunkier sound and more violent imagery. The recording and playing are more sophisticated, making it less alluring than the spartan **Lungs**. "Cables" is about voyeurs at a slaughter-house; "The Pigeon Kill" is about poisoning birds; "Seth" is about a dog trained to attack black people. Overambitious, but sincere and scary.

Racer-X is less obsessively cranky than the first two records (a positive development). The basic elements remain: one-riff industrial funk grooves, coarse vocals, jagged guitar. But this EP fills out the sound without sacrificing any of its amateur appeal. The musicians, while skilled technicians all, keep the sound raw. And if Albini is still something of a cartoon curmudgeon in his boasts about being "The Ugly American," he at least includes a James Brown cover and a tribute to Speed Racer's cooler brother. Not as idiosyncratically brilliant as **Lungs**, but fine stuff nonetheless.

Atomizer comes thundering out of the starting gate like a wounded rhino, charging around madly with awesome, claustrophobic rock power. Albini leads his troupe through such angry slices of niho-philosophy, depravity and arson as "Big Money," "Stinking Drunk," "Fists of Love," "Jordan, Minnesota," "Kerosene" and "Bazooka Joe" (for which the liner notes note "part of the drum track is an M1 carbine being fired in a field exercise by a guy named Joe.") A magnificently rugged record.   [jl/iar]

BIG COUNTRY

The Crossing (Mercury) 1983
Wonderland EP (nr/Mercury) 1984
Steeltown (Mercury) 1984
The Seer (Mercury) 1986

Guitarist Stuart Adamson—the unsung hero and sound shaper of the Skids—survived that wonderful band's miserable end to form a much more down-to-earth rock quartet unhampered (at the outset, anyway) by grandiose artistic pretensions. Joined by guitarist Bruce Watson and the ace rhythm section of Tony Butler and Mark Brzezicki (who had played sessions individually and collectively for Pete Townshend and the Pretenders, and later Roger Daltrey), Big Country quickly jumped into the vanguard of resurgent guitar-hero bands. Retaining some of the Skids' pseudo-Scottish six-string-bagpipe effects, Big Country's first album, brilliantly produced by Steve Lillywhite, offers rousing anthems ("In a Big Country," "Inwards," "Fields of Fire," its riff cleverly lifted from "The Guns of Navarone") and moving romantic ballads ("The Storm," "Chance") that neatly intertwine folk traditions with blazing guitar riffs. (The UK tape edition has extra tracks.) The **Wonderland** EP presents four songs, including an early B-side and the uplifting, catchy title track, one of the band's best efforts.

Steeltown breaks no new ground and is basically a formulaic reprise, but the band is so unique, passionate and skilled at what they do that you don't really mind. Best selections: "East of Eden," "Where the Rose Is Sown" (a virtual rewrite of "In a Big Country," itself not all that different from "Fields of Fire") and "Just a Shadow." Even if they don't vary much, Big Country's records offer a very pleasing and invigorating brand of rock'n'roll.   [iar]

BIG SIDEWAYS

Big Sideways (NZ Unsung) 1983

You're not kidding big: this New Zealand band boasts twelve members, including four horn people, four guitarists and two drummers. Seven of them write songs, making this (not surprisingly) a pretty diverse record, fusing rock, jazz, funk and antipodean ethnic musics. Capped off with idealistic lyrics, **Big Sideways** is upbeat and intelligent; highly arranged but certainly not slick.   [iar]

BIG STAR

See *Alex Chilton*.

BIG YOUTH

Screaming Target (Trojan/nr) 1973
Dreadlocks Dread (Klik/nr) 1975 (Front Line/nr) 1978 (Virgin/nr) 1983
Natty Cultural Dread (Trojan/nr) 1976
Hit the Road Jack (Trojan/nr) 1976
Isaiah, First Prophet of Old (Front Line/nr) 1978
Everyday Skank—The Best of Big Youth (Trojan/nr) 1980
Some Great Big Youth (Blue Moon/Heartbeat) 1981
Live at Reggae Sunsplash (Sunsplash) 1984
A Luta Continua (nr/Heartbeat) 1985
The Chanting Dread inna Fine Style (Blue Moon/Heartbeat) 1985

His front teeth inlaid with red, green and gold gems, Big Youth is probably the best-known and most popular of all reggae djs, with a career that's been going strong for more than 15 years. Born Manley Buchanan, he began toasting in the early '70s, after working as a cabbie and a mechanic. His success was quick: records like "The Killer" and "S.90 Skank" (named after a motorcycle) scaled the charts with ease, demonstrating his power and versatility. Many years and albums later he remains a major reggae presence, an influence on an entire generation of toasters. (He's credited with coining the term "natty dread.") If U-Roy laid the foundation, Big Youth made it happen—he gave toasting style as well as something to say.

Eccentric and startling, all of Big Youth's early records sounded radical when they first appeared, and have held up marvelously. Featuring instrumental tracks from songs by Dennis Brown, Gregory Isaacs and others, **Screaming Target** boasts two versions of the wild title cut, along with "The Killer" and "Solomon a Gunday." **Natty Cultural Dread** features the amazing "Every Nigger Is a Star" and "Jim Squashy," which invokes John Coltrane. **Hit the Road Jack** has several loopy covers of American soul hits, including Marvin Gaye's "What's Going On," the Ray Charles song of the title and Teddy Pendergrass' "Wake Up Everybody." You've never heard these songs this way—offbeat and wonderful. Although all of the Trojan releases are worth owning, **Everyday Skank** is an invaluable compilation of LP tracks and early singles.

Dreadlocks Dread (reissued by Virgin in the **Crucial Cuts** series) features "Marcus Garvey Dread" (a toast of the Burning Spear classic), "Train to Rhodesia" and "House of Dread Locks." The LP marks Big Youth's development as a composer, and his increased reliance on Rasta subject matter. Side Two has a couple of filler instrumentals, but the record is widely considered his best.

Isaiah continues the evolution heard on **Dreadlocks Dread**. He does more singing (or sing-jaying, as it's called) than toasting and originals outnumber covers. The groove is steady and appealing. Big Youth's recent releases, available mostly on Heartbeat, are also marked by their able consistency. All three listed boast a variety of styles, tough and relevant protest lyrics and rootsy playing. Not as wild as his early sides, these records are nonetheless some of the best contemporary reggae—authentic and uncorrupted, personal and moving. He's mellowed a bit with age, but Big Youth remains as formidable an artist as ever.

Rounding out the canon, **Live at Reggae Sunsplash** (from a 1982 festival) proves he hasn't lost his ability to work a crowd, and provides a decent document of one of his better shows.   [bk]

BIJOU

Danse avec Moi (Fr. Philips) 1977
OK Carole (Fr. Philips) 1978
Pas Dormir (Fr. Philips) 1979
En Public (Fr. Philips) 1980
Jamais Domptés (Fr. Philips) 1981
Bijou Bop (Fr. Philips) 1981

Bijou is billed on the shrink wrap of its debut LP as France's top punk band. Considering how mild and derivative of basic rock'n'roll moves Bijou is—there are musical quotes all over the LP—this says little for the Gallic sense of rock in revolt. Bijou plays with no frills and few surprises; kind of poppy here (especially the earlier stuff), more boogieoid there, a token "arty" touch or bit of '60s nostalgia, a modest rockabilly orientation (**Bijou**

B

16

Bop), and so on. Very few tracks (aside from the live **En Public**) are as long as four minutes, with most barely reaching three.

What makes the trio likable is their almost naive enthusiasm, which is supported by confident playing ability that has strengthened with each album. Bijou loves what they're doing and don't want to change it, only to hone it; even cutting **Pas Dormir** in LA under the supervision of Sparks' Ron and Russell Mael made little difference, except to underline the melodies. The lyrics (for those conversant *en francais*) range from corny and jokey (especially the first LP) to flippantly snotty and angry-young-rocker, with an increasing degree of wit. **Jamais Domptes** is their best overall show of strength. Now if Dave Edmunds ever got to produce them . . . [jg]

BIRDSONGS OF THE MESOZOIC

Birdsongs of the Mesozoic EP (nr/Ace of Hearts) 1983
Magnetic Flip (nr/Ace of Hearts) 1984

Launched in 1980 as a side project for Mission of Burma guitarist Roger Miller (playing keyboards), with synthesizer and percussion help from local Boston legend Erik Lindgren, Birdsongs of the Mesozoic expanded to a four-piece with the addition of Rick Scott and fellow Burmite, Martin Swope. They remained a part-time hobby until Miller developed tinnitus and decided to continue his career at a lower volume, thus ending MoB. BoM's debut showed them taking quite a different tack from Burma's impassioned, chaotic noise-on-the-brink, with six instrumentals ranging from the achingly pretty romance of "The Orange Ocean" to juxtaposed chords played as much against as with each other.

On **Magnetic Flip** the flat production of the previous record was improved and the band's whole idea and execution became bolder and more aggressive. The opening of "Shiny Golden Snakes" is pure rock power chording, while the variations on "The Rite of Spring" piles one thundering dissonance over another, and the austere keyboard repetition starting off "Ptoccata" recalls Philip Glass. BoM are often compared to new minimalist composers like Glass and Terry Riley, who do a lot with a little, although Birdsongs seem to be doing a lot with more. And probably going right over the heads of many old Burma fans in the process. [ep]

BIRTHDAY PARTY

The Birthday Party (Aus. Missing Link) 1980
Prayers on Fire (4AD/Thermidor) 1981
Drunk on the Pope's Blood EP (4AD/nr) 1982
Junkyard (4AD/nr) 1982
The Bad Seed EP (4AD/nr) 1983
The Birthday Party EP (4AD/nr) 1983
Mutiny! EP (Mute/nr) 1983
It's Still Living (Aus. Missing Link) 1985
A Collection . . . (Aus. Missing Link) 1985 (nr/Suite Beat) 1986

BOYS NEXT DOOR

Door Door (Aus. Mushroom) 1979
Hee Haw EP (Aus. Missing Link) 1979 & 1983

This intensely challenging Australian band put everything it had into the pursuit of making inhospitable and unyielding records. With partial comparisons possible to such noisy free-formists as the Fall, Pere Ubu and Public Image Ltd., the Birthday Party's unique sensibility sprang from singer Nick Cave (who wrote most of the lyrics) and guitarist Rowland Howard, who took care of a good chunk of the songwriting.

Before relocating from Melbourne to London, the Birthday Party released several Australian-only records, some under their original name, the Boys Next Door. **Door Door** is surprisingly normal-sounding aggressive rock with traditional song structures and musical values. Cave's vocals invest the album with an ominous undercurrent, but the overall ambience hardly suggests the insanity that lay ahead.

That insanity began with their next release, **The Birthday Party** (the label credits the band under both monikers). Whatever their name, though, serious derangement was setting in fast. Cave's vocals and Howard's newly developed wall of feedback make **Door Door** sound inhibited; each track here is unsettling. The LP's opening kick, "Mr. Clarinet," presents an ultra-distorted organ sitting atop a stiff, martial goose-step beat. The second side is even more crazed: "The Friend Catcher" (relentless and hypnotic) and "Happy Birthday" both contain some of the most frenzied guitar work ever captured on vinyl.

After moving to the UK, the Birthday Party recorded and released their first international LP, **Prayers on Fire**, a raging vinyl beast filled with agonized howling, braying Cave vocals flung against a backdrop of violently attacked guitars and no-wave horn noise. Drums and bass alone toe the line of established patterns; everything else ignores the song at hand and goes flat out in competition with Cave's literate invective.

An EP, **Drunk on the Pope's Blood**, followed, coupling one side of live Birthday Party with a side of live Lydia Lunch (who later formed the Immaculate Consumptives with Cave and recorded with Howard). Recorded in London at the end of 1981, the disc is honestly described on the jacket as "16 minutes of sheer hell!" Drawing two of its four songs from **Prayers on Fire**, Cave and his ensemble growl and shriek through the slow pieces with stunning gruesomeness—incomprehensibility aside, no one has ever suffered with a more effective sonic display than is caught in these grooves. **Junkyard** has less energy to the sound, but still manages to lift blood pressure with such assaults as "Dead Joe," "Big-Jesus-Trash-Can" and "6-inch Gold Blade."

Four BP EPs were released in 1983 (one a reissue of a disc recorded four years earlier as the Boys Next Door), the same year the band broke up. The first was **The Bad Seed**, a concise four-cut disc of incredible visceral impact. Whether on the slow psycho-blues of "Deep in the Woods" or the frenzied blur of "Sonny's Burning," it leaves the listener helpless and enthralled. **The Birthday Party EP** and **Hee Haw** both contain material from **The Birthday Party** album, along with assorted singles and previously

unreleased tracks. The posthumous **Mutiny!** was released at the correct time: it wouldn't have been easy to follow. Like **The Bad Seed**, it mixes two furious numbers with a pair of funereal dirges. "Jennifer's Veil," a harrowing lament, is perhaps the band's finest song ever. Neither John Cale nor Alfred Hitchcock was ever this scary.

It's Still Living was released in Australia two years later. Recorded in Melbourne in 1982, it offers spirited performances of material from **Prayers on Fire** and **Junkyard** and, although decried by the band, is recommended for fans. **A Collection . . .** takes tracks from **Junkyard**, **Hee Haw** and some singles, with a few alternate versions unavailable elsewhere. For completists only. [iar/dgs]

See also *Nick Cave and the Bad Seeds, Crime and the City Solution, die Haut, Kas Product, Lydia Lunch.*

BISHOPS

See *Count Bishops.*

BITING TONGUES

Don't Heal (Situation 2/nr) 1981
Libreville (Paragon/nr) 1983
Feverhouse (Factory/nr) 1985

On **Don't Heal** a fellow named Capalula delivers monotonic spoken-word vocals over a no-wav-ish backing of sax (squealing, of course), guitar (noise, of course) and rhythm section (altered funk, of course)—none particularly distinguished. A pretender to the throne once occupied by Joy Division's late Ian Curtis (also from Manchester), Capalula seems to have acquired Curtis' psychic stomach ache, but lacks the dark depths of black feeling that made Curtis unique. **Feverhouse** is a soundtrack. [mf]

BLACKBEARD

See *Dennis Bovell.*

BLACK FLAG

Jealous Again EP (SST) 1980
Damaged (nr/SST) 1981 (SST/nr) 1985
Everything Went Black (SST) 1983
The First Four Years [tape] (SST) 1984
My War (SST) 1984
Family Man (SST) 1984
Slip It In (nr/SST) 1984
Live '84 [tape] (nr/SST) 1984
Loose Nut (SST) 1985
The Process of Weeding Out EP (SST) 1985
In My Head (SST) 1985
Who's Got the 10 1/2? (SST) 1986

D.C.3

This Is the Dream (SST) 1985
The Good Hex (SST) 1986

GONE

"Let's Get Real, Real Gone for a Change" (SST) 1986

OCTOBER FACTION

October Faction (SST) 1985
Second Factionalization (SST) 1986

SWA

Your Future if You Have One (SST) 1985

TOM TROCCOLI'S DOG

Tom Troccoli's Dog (SST) 1985

WURM

Feast (SST) 1985

Black Flag was the first hardcore band to emerge from Southern California and gain national prominence, touring enough to become a major attraction in virtually every city where a hardcore scene exists. Many revolving-door personnel changes later (spawning numerous other outfits), Black Flag continues, via their SST label, to fulfill an essential role in the development and popularization of American punk, although they themselves have wandered into the zone where punk and heavy metal intersect and overlap.

Jealous Again, five brief tracks by an early lineup on a 12-inch 45, offers a convincing but restrained primal punk roar; the ghost of the Sex Pistols comes floating through the brazen blare of guitars and vocals. **Damaged** features a superior cast (with Washington, DC singer Henry Rollins and stun guitarist Dez Cadena joining) and includes the wonderful Dictators-like "TV Party," as well as other goofy paeans to dissipated suburban life ("Six Pack," "Thirsty and Miserable") and the anthemic punk classic, "Rise Above." Rollins' hoarse shout grates painfully, but the barely-contained rock energy and tongue-in-cheek lyrics make **Damaged** a great rock'n'roll LP that isn't beholden to any cliched genre.

In the midst of a horrible legal dispute with Unicorn Records, Black Flag found themselves enjoined from using their name and logo on any new records, and were forced to release the double-album outtakes-and-more career retrospective, **Everything Went Black**, identified only by a listing of band members on the cover. The tracks date from 1978 to 1981 and feature various lineups attacking a motley collection of songs. ("Police Story," "Gimmie Gimmie Gimmie," "Damaged" and "Depression" all get done twice.) Collectors note: the European edition is very different. As a developmental Black Flag sampler, **Everything Went Black** is both illuminating and entertaining, but the real treat is Side Four, "Crass Commercialism," a hysterically funny collection of crazed radio spots for Flag gigs, most with music, that say a lot about the cultural milieu in which the band exists. **The First Four Years** is a tape-only reissue compilation of early releases, including **Six Pack** and **Jealous Again**.

Following the resolution of their litigation (Unicorn helpfully went bankrupt), a new and prolific Black Flag—Rollins, guitarist Greg Ginn, drummer Bill Stevenson and (briefly) bassist Dale Nixon—drifted vaguely towards metal on **My War**, a mediocre album with some interminably long songs. (One plodding side has a grand total of three!) There *are* some good punk tunes ("I Love You") but elsewhere, a heavy-bottomed, labored sound and appallingly bad guitar solos cross the line from sarcasm into sheer awfulness. Rollins' vocals are the same as ever, which makes the bad tracks even stranger.

Slip It In, with a woman named Kira taking over on bass, has far clearer sound, a grand total of eight tracks and a further blurring of the line between moronic punk and moronic metal. The songs are mostly built on trite riffs repeated endlessly (check your Black Sabbath records for elaboration). Krokus wouldn't have trouble singing the rude lyrics of the title song, which is performed here complete with female sex noises, in case anyone fails to grasp the point and/or be offended by it. Other songs are less tasteless but little more interesting. **Family Man** dissects Black Flag: half-and-half Henry Rollins reading his poetry and group instrumentals without him.

The cassette-only **Live '84** adds the band's recent creative output to selected oldies and puts it onstage for an hour of wanton loud fun. Black Flag concerts are typically an utter mess, which suits the songs perfectly, making this chaotic explosion naturally one of their best releases.

In 1985, Black Flag continued their torrid pace, releasing three new albums: **Loose Nut**, **In My Head** and **The Process of Weeding Out**. The first two, both using the Rollins-Ginn-Kira-Stevenson lineup, are fairly similar: nine songs each of varied but mostly medium-tempo guitar-based rock'n'roll that keeps a safe distance from metal, hardcore *and* sleazemongering. The best Black Flag LP of 1985 has to be **Loose Nut**, which has clean sound, Rollins' brutally self-hating "This Is Good," and lyrics on the inner sleeve, but both are reasonably indicative of Black Flag's current state.

The Process of Weeding Out is a Henryless instrumental EP: four lengthy improvisations displaying unexpected technical prowess (especially Kira on "Your Last Affront") and a new side to the band. There's a certain nostalgia factor for those who remember Canned Heat or Ten Years After in the old days, but on its own merits, there's precious little here you'd want to hear more than once.

With a new drummer, Anthony Martinez, Black Flag recorded **Who's Got the 10 1/2?** in Portland, Oregon on 23 August 1985. Besides a great cover photo of the band's actual tour calendar that says more about the rock'n'roll life than any half dozen magazine articles, the album features hot versions of 1984/1985 material, plus a genuine oldie, "Gimmie, Gimmie, Gimmie." (The cassette version adds 24 minutes more music.)

Present and former members of Black Flag have also been prolific with side projects. Guitarist Dez Cadena's D.C.3 has made two albums, to quote him, "in the style of the records that used to excite us when we were young." Unfortunately, the bands he remembers include Deep Purple and Humble Pie, and the albums resemble various '60s/'70s nightmares, from Blue Oyster Cult to Sabbath. There's actually some fine music and an amusing under-current to both, although I fear the subtle satirical aspect may be missed by those too young (or too old).

Three of Greg Ginn's side projects have already resulted in vinyl. Gone is a power trio that could use a vocalist as well as more organized power; the album (named after an Elvis Presley remark) often meanders aimlessly like a bad rehearsal session. Pass on Gone. Ginn plays bass in and produces another trio, Tom Troccoli's Dog, whose low-key, Neil Youngish album (cover drawn by D. Boon)

includes everything from a politely acoustic "Girl from the North Country" to occasionally anarchic meltdowns like "Suicide," "Slow Dancing" and "Davo's Boogie." Finally, there's October Faction, a twice-off ensemble. Recorded live in San Francisco, 26 August 1984, **October Faction** (also mistakenly referred to as **The Nazi Sex Doctor**) features Chuck Dukowski, other members of Black Flag and T.T.'s Dog, plus assorted SST family and friends. A second get-together will be issued in 1986.

Damaged-era Flag bassist Dukowski now fronts SWA, whose hard-driving, intelligent debut album was produced by Ginn. SWA's secret weapon is Merril Ward, a powerful rock singer who can really project. Wurm originally pre-figured Dukowski's tenure in Black Flag; he reformed the group temporarily in 1982 and cut a belated LP which SST issued a few years later. **Feast** features the gallingly awful singing of Dead Hippie's Simon Smallwood, but, to be fair, is pretty dire all by itself. I'm not sure, but I think it's an imitation of the Crazy World of Arthur Brown. Then again, it might have been more influenced by Atomic Rooster . . .

That's where things stand as of mid-'86. More will certainly follow.
[iar]

BLACK UHURU

Love Crisis (Third World/nr) 1977
Showcase (Virgin/Heartbeat) 1979 (Butt/nr) 1980
Sinsemilla (Island/Mango) 1980
Black Sounds of Freedom (Greensleeves/Shanachie) 1981
Red (Island/Mango) 1981
Black Uhuru (Virgin/nr) 1981
Tear It Up—Live (Island/Mango) 1982
Chill Out (Island/Mango) 1982
The Dub Factor (nr/Mango) 1983
Anthem (Island/Mango) 1983
Reggae Greats (Island/Mango) 1985
Brutal (Greensleeves/Ras) 1986

The leading second generation reggae vocal group, Black Uhuru was formed in Jamaica in 1974 by Duckie Simpson; after a couple of false starts, he enlisted Michael Rose, whose quivery voice makes him sound like a Rasta cantor, and recorded **Love Crisis**—competent but hardly distinctive (although the best track, "I Love King Selassie," survived to become a live staple). (**Black Sounds of Freedom** is a 1981 remix of the same album.) After American expatriate Puma Jones joined to add haunting high harmony, Black Uhuru joined forces with Sly and Robbie; their riddims pushed the singing along with the force of a tank. **Showcase** is a compilation of their early singles ("Abortion," "General Penitentiary," "Guess Who's Coming to Dinner," etc.)—an unqualified classic.

Sinsemilla firmly established Uhuru as an album act. The record delivers a level of consistency only Bob Marley himself had achieved. Their breakthrough, however, came with **Red**. From the first track, "The Youth of Eglington," listeners—even those not particularly interested in reggae—discovered Black Uhuru.

The band spent considerable time on the road. A live album (**Tear It Up**) recycles a lot of the material from **Showcase** and is only a so-so approximation of their in-concert

excitement. **Chill Out**, the next studio effort, is great. Rose had moved to New York and takes on the city in the title cut; "Darkness," "Emotional Slaughter" and others reveal a departure from Rasta subject matter. The American-only **Dub Factor** is a ferocious dub disc, more of which can be found on Sly and Robbie's **Raiders of the Lost Dub**.

The release of **Anthem** was troubled. The original issue was remixed and revised for America; that version was subsequently re-released in Europe. In any case, it's a spotty record, despite a couple of killer tracks ("Party Next Door" and Steve Van Zandt's "Solidarity"). Sly and Robbie's synthetics are more pronounced, perhaps to compensate for the weak material and convictionless performances. (Ironically, it won a Grammy award in the US.) A decent hit collection in the **Reggae Greats** series followed. Then Michael Rose left to go solo.

On **Brutal**, Black Uhuru unveiled their new lead singer, Junior Reid, who displays an awkward tendency to mimic Rose. Sly and Robbie still provide backup; Arthur Baker is among the producers. While the Reid/Simpson songs attempt a number of different styles, not all are successful.
[bk]

See also *Sly Dunbar and Robbie Shakespeare*.

BLAM BLAM BLAM

Blam Blam Blam EP (NZ Propeller) 1980
Luxury Length (NZ Propeller) 1982
The Blam Blam Blam Story (NZ Propeller) 1984

Reckoned by some to be New Zealand's top local group, Blam Blam Blam share a bit of their genealogy with the Swingers. An intriguing and somewhat strange trio, they have a sure-handed, full but uncluttered approach and oblique melodies, with a lot of indigenous references, as in "There is No Depression in New Zealand," a Top 20 hit there, and included on a revised edition of the EP. Guitars may chime like bells or whine sweetly like violins; drums aptly support muscular bass work; the vocals are a bit dry but deliver a pinch of tartness when needed. Not wildly spectacular, but definitely stimulating.
[jg]

BLANCMANGE

Happy Families (London/Island) 1982
Mange Tout (London/London-Sire) 1984
Believe You Me (London/London-Sire) 1985

One of the more individual and original synth-based duos, Stephen Luscombe and Neil Arthur mix dominant percussion with bizarre, often exotic seasonings to create tracks with abundant personality and enormous dance potential. There is one major and general drawback: Arthur has a rough, unpleasant singing voice which becomes riddled with melodrama when he gets excited.

On **Happy Families**, Blancmange offer typically (for them) eccentric concepts—"God's Kitchen," "Living on the Ceiling"—in varied settings that fall into two general styles:

1) Loud, rhythmic and derivative of Talking Heads. These tunes, especially "Feel Me," suffer from

extreme monochromatic tediousness.

2) Delicate and reserved. "I've Seen the Word" and others are quite lovely, resembling the spare grace of mid-period Orchestral Manoeuvres in the Dark.

Mange Tout (a brilliant bilingual pun that raises my estimation of the band a few notches) is simultaneously a bit sillier and grander overall, using more horns, woodwinds and strings than before. Largely neglecting option 2 but not sounding much like the Heads either, Blancmange opt to let the beat send the message, while thankfully maintaining better song quality and, thus, less boredom. The four major tracks—"Don't Tell Me," "My Baby," "Blind Vision" and "That's Love That It Is"—all offer different levels of melodiousness (most pretty high) with Arthur's vocals, though improved, still an occasional stumbling block in the way of enjoyment.

Believe You Me is an ambitious undertaking, recorded in seven different studios with four producers and zillions of guest musicians. The results are hardly as inconsistent as they might have been, and, in fact, the restrained album is quite agreeable, reasonably free of the overzealousness, busyness and absurdity that diminished some of their prior work. The songs aren't consistently wonderful, but simplicity and understatement make insquisitive tracks like "Don't You Love It All" (with flugelhorn played by Hugh Masekela), "What's Your Problem?" and "Why Don't They Leave Things Alone?" pleasant, if not immediately memorable. Gratuitous query: am I the only one finding it difficult to tell recent Blancmange and O.M.D. records apart?
[iar]

BLASTERS

American Music (nr/Rollin' Rock) 1980
The Blasters (F-Beat/Slash-Warner Bros.) 1981
Over There: Live at the Venue, London EP (WEA/Slash-Warner Bros.) 1982
Non Fiction (WEA/Slash-Warner Bros.) 1983
Hard Line (WEA/Slash-Warner Bros.) 1985

They say everything old becomes new again, and California's Blasters proved it in 1981 by jumping into the national spotlight with an utterly familiar brew of blues, rockabilly and rock'n'roll. Detractors might call them little more than an updated Canned Heat—as if anything were wrong with that—but such criticism ignores their strengths: tight ensemble work, swingin' original tunes in the classic mold and Phil Alvin's ageless, confident vocals.

American Music appeared on an independent rockabilly revival label which is probably one reason it didn't reach a larger audience. The band already had total control of R&B and rock conventions, fusing them into a supple, flowing style. Although there's not quite as much sting here as later on, Dave Alvin's guitar work displays plenty of spirit. Oldies like "Buzz Buzz Buzz" and "I Wish You Would" (Billy Boy Arnold via the Yardbirds) mingle with catchy new tunes like "Marie, Marie," later a big UK hit for Shakin' Stevens.

The Blasters established the quintet nationwide. Originally released on LA independent label Slash, it did so well that the company was able to strike a licensing/distribution deal with Warner Bros. No wonder: it smokes. The band is tighter than a drum, and Dave Alvin's songs—including "No Other Girl," a re-recorded "Marie, Marie" and "Border Radio"—have a joyous, irresistible momentum. R&B legend Lee Allen guests on sax. Highlighted by a crackling hot sound, the live London EP serves as a good introduction to the Blasters, but offers no new wrinkles. Definitely suitable for parties, though.

Any lingering suspicions that the Blasters were just an oldies band at heart were surely dispelled by the fine **Non Fiction**. Dave Alvin's essay on real life, the LP presents a series of well-crafted vignettes reminiscent of Robbie Robertson's work with the Band. Songs like "One More Dance" and "Fool's Paradise" depict the trials and tribulations of the little people, while "Long White Cadillac" laments Hank Williams. The playing on the self-produced record is smoother and not as quaint as before.

A shade less stirring than **Non Fiction**, **Hard Line** reprises that LP's formula, but also includes a blatant stab at commercialism. Although "Colored Lights," penned for the Blasters by John Cougar Mellencamp, isn't bad, other songs are more heartfelt. Highlights include "Trouble Bound" and "Help You Dream," both featuring the Jordanaires (of Elvis Presley fame for you young'uns).

Latest news: Dave Alvin left to join X, replacing Billy Zoom who had set off to form his own band. Alvin's replacement in the Blasters is someone called Hollywood Fats.
[jy]

See also *X*.

BLESSED VIRGINS

Blessed Virgins (Fr. Epic) 1982

Judging by the three laughing faces on the cover, you have to wonder how good the band can be. After playing the record, though, you know the joke in their moniker is funnier (and more joyful) than you thought: These guys have youth on their side. The musical forms are hardly new—a little revved-up blues, a little chugging punk and a whole lot of high energy rock'n'roll—and the songs won't change the world, even if these boys do have a passel of catchy chord progressions and riffs up their sleeves. (The lyrics are in slangy French, but what I could decipher indicates these garcons could be smart cookies.) What makes this album special is that the BV's make it all sound new and fresh—they even do an enjoyable, totally reworded (in French) version of "Summertime Blues"! The Virgins are vibrant, alive and enthusiastic, their commitment free of pose. It's enough to make you believe the folks going around saying rock's too young to die.
[jg]

BLONDIE

Blondie (Private Stock) 1976 (Chrysalis) 1977 (Hallmark/nr) 1982 (MFP/nr) 1985
Plastic Letters (Chrysalis) 1977
Parallel Lines (Chrysalis) 1978 (Fame/nr) 1983

Eat to the Beat (Chrysalis) 1979
Autoamerican (Chrysalis) 1980
The Best of Blondie (Chrysalis) 1981
The Hunter (Chrysalis) 1982

DEBBIE HARRY

KooKoo (Chrysalis) 1981

JIMMY DESTRI

Heart on a Wall (Chrysalis) 1982

Blondie's string of superior singles is extraordinary in itself, but the group's inability to extend that consistency to its albums proved something of a disappointment, always leaving the impression that even what's good somehow could have been better. Nonetheless, for a group whose ascendance detractors dismissed as due to little more than the projection of Debbie Harry's attractive image, a little luck and a lot of ethno-musicological pilferage, Blondie was remarkably successful at creating a widely identifiable and influential sound, and at incorporating many popular music genres (regardless of the color line) without losing its own sound—at least, not until the very end. Blondie's dabblings in other styles may not have always worked creatively, but they can't be criticized as dilettantes without acknowledging that few others wet their musical toes in the same exotic waters until after Blondie set the precedent. Additionally impressive is the fact that the group pursued its more commercial goals in its own nonconformist fashion, often to the dismay of its record company (and even some of its fans).

Blondie effervesces with exuberance which, at points, leads it to reach past the limits of its grasp. But no matter; a guileless classic, and arguably Blondie's best album. The band rampages with equal abandon through admixtures of salsa, funk, Broadway pop and thrill-flick soundtrack sounds, as well as their more typical girl-group/surf/Anglo-pop hybrid (as on the first single, "X Offender," included here). The sense of fun easily compensates for any gaps in expertise.

Plastic Letters reflects not only professional seasoning and closer work with producer Richard Gottehrer, but also the band's inner turmoil, due to management, label and personnel changes. The result is a fuller, tighter, more authoritative sound and the band's first two UK hits: "(I'm Always Touched by Your) Presence, Dear" and "Denis." It also resulted in tracks with a more brooding feel, whether hard, riffy stuff or thoughtful experimentation ("Cautious Lip"). Less adventurous than **Blondie**, and less exciting.

For **Parallel Lines**, the new lineup had already jelled, and hit maestro Mike Chapman moved in as producer, yielding an even more disciplined sound. The band seems totally in control of every form it attempts, from zombie metal to pop-abilly, quasi-avant spaciness to the hitbound electro-disco flirtation, "Heart of Glass." Compared to Gottehrer's first-take spontaneity, the LP might seem a tad clinical, but it's good enough to be considered America's answer to Nick Lowe's first solo album.

Eat to the Beat, surprisingly, proved less artistically and commercially successful than an album that recapitulates the band's strong points should have been, but it does include some of the best sheer rock'n'roll the group ever produced. **Autoamerican** went in precisely the opposite direction; breaking out of a stylistic cul-de-sac, Blondie jumped out in a number of new directions again (cocktail jazz, Eurodrama, country—sort of—and rap-funk). An "A" for effort, but Blondie's most uneven album.

With **The Hunter**, decay had set in: able to manipulate all sorts of stylistic devices in divergent genres, Blondie had pretty much run out of gas—bereft of things to say, or even ways to say nothing with style and grace. Aimless and/or elephantine, the impenetrably pretentious LP presaged the disintegration of the band several months later.

The Best of Blondie should really be called **The Singles Album**, since that's exclusively what's on it and what limits the view it gives of the group. It includes three special remixes and the otherwise non-LP hit, "Call Me." The American and English editions, reflecting the band's different chart successes, offer alternate selections.

Debbie Harry's collaboration with Nile Rodgers and Bernard Edwards of Chic (and, to a lesser extent, her usual partner Chris Stein) finds her somewhat out of her depth. Trying to insert herself into Chic's format—with few changes in it beyond some of the lyrical stances—she strains for vocal personae (serious romantic and quasi-politically streetwise) to which she is unsuited. About one-third of the record is moderately successful, infectious funk-pop. In retrospect, of course, the then-controversial selection of Rodgers to work on **KooKoo** is another example of the adventurous (and prescient) trailblazing typical of Stein and Harry.

Blondie keyboardist Destri's first solo outing, produced by Michael Kamen, takes traditional pop values and updates them with decidedly Bowiesque leanings. No tracks stand out as exemplary, but **Heart on a Wall** proves Destri to be a talented songwriter and musician (two things he had already confirmed within Blondie). He should, however, have hired someone else to provide vocals.

Harry broke a long professional silence in mid-1985 by recording a song for the soundtrack of *Krush Groove*.
[jg/iar]

See also *Chequered Past*.

BLOOD ON THE SADDLE

Blood on the Saddle (nr/New Alliance) 1984
Poisoned Love (Gates of Heaven/Chameleon) 1986

These California cow-punks are less concerned with revering C&W icons than trashing them at a furious pace: their country is Hank Williams OD-ing in the back of his car and western that of spaghetti flicks. On their debut, ragged harmonies, yodelled vocals and the slap of stand-up bass lend authenticity, making the record a rodeo where even the horses are doing speed. One of three lead singers in the band, ex-Bangle Annette Zalinskas vocalizes on the best songs, including "Do You Want to Dance?" and "(I Wish I Was a) Single Girl (Again)," where she sounds like a real down-home country singer trying to stay straight while her band, out of control, beats her to the finish.
[ep]

KURTIS BLOW

Kurtis Blow (Mercury) 1980
Deuce (Mercury) 1981
Tough (Mercury) 1982
Party Time? (Mercury) 1983
Ego Trip (Mercury) 1984
America (Club-Phonogram/Mercury) 1985

One of the earliest and most enduring stars of rap, New York's Kurtis Blow consistently makes solid records with workable grooves and lyrics that alternately address issues of social and socializing interest. In doing so, Blow has become something of a modern black culture maven, singing the praises of Harlem ("One-Two-Five (Main Street, Harlem, USA)" on **Party Time?**), waxing eloquent about hoops ("Basketball" on **Ego Trip**) and competing with "The Message" in discussing the urban challenge ("Tough" on the LP of the same name). All of Blow's records are state-of-the-art in a semi-mainstream way; **Ego Trip** makes a concerted effort to get hipper by having Run—D.M.C. do a guest rap on "8 Million Stories."

Taking a turn towards patriotism in the title cut of **America**, Blow (who produced the LP) shows off his dichotomous musical goals. In the same song he uses aggressive electronic percussion and mixing to mimic the Bambaataa/Lydon Time Zone sound (with Art of Noise effects) *and* sings like Kool and the Gang. The rest of the album is passable but only the catchy and soulful strut of "If I Ruled the World" is worth remembering. (And "Super Sperm" is well worth forgetting.)
[iar]

BLOW MONKEYS

Limping for a Generation (RCA) 1984
Forbidden Fruit EP (RCA) 1985
Animal Magic (RCA) 1986

Perhaps hoping to move in on the vapid-soul vacancy left by Culture Club during that band's lengthy creative drought, the Blow Monkeys whipped up "Digging Your Scene," a disturbingly familiar-sounding bit of fluff for their second album. While Dr Robert manages a passable imitation of George's vocals and songwriting, *his* subordinates are no match for the Clubbers, and the rest of **Animal Magic** is equally redundant and stupid. The title track is an appalling T. Rex knock-off; "Sweet Murder" attempts to rewrite Talking Heads' "I Zimbra." The album's most consistent feature is its pathetic lack of originality.

Forbidden Fruit mixes "Atomic Lullaby" and the Smithsy "Wild Flower" from the first LP with four foretastes of **Animal Magic**. The only items of note are a pair of crazed Eek-a-Mouse dub mixes that largely obscure the songs.
[iar]

BLUE AEROPLANES

Bop Art (Abstract/nr) 1984
Action Painting and Other Original Works EP (Fire/nr) 1985
Lover and Confidante and Other Stories (Fire/nr) 1986
Tolerance (Fire/nr) 1986

Aided by numerous friends, this eccentric Bristol quintet often has as many as a dozen people playing on its records, and the diversity of ideas shows in the rich sound. Referents such as the Velvets, Fall, Pere Ubu, Feelies and others ricochet from all sides, topped off by Gerard Langley's poetic lyrics. From the hard funk of "Pinkies Hit the Union" to the sonic landscape of "Owls," **Bop Art** has something for everyone. Along with a barrage of guitars, bass and percussion, the instrumentation includes saxes, bagpipes and several 16th-century guitar ancestors. The band is such an effective ensemble that—even with all the masterful diversity—the LP manages a logical progression.

The **Action Painting** EP builds some nice Velvets-cum-early Cabaret Voltaire drones; **Lover and Confidante**, another four cuts, is a trailer for **Tolerance**. Not quite as kaleidoscopic as **Bop Art**, **Tolerance** trades much of the oddness and idiosyncracy of previous work for some psychedelic touches, adding just enough characteristic embellishment to prevent deep identification with the paisley bandwagon. The Blue Aeroplanes' entire catalogue is highly recommended. [dgs]

BLUE ANGEL

Blue Angel (Polydor) 1980 (Polydor/Phonogram) 1984

As crass trash goes, you could certainly do worse than New York City's Blue Angel. Their painfully obvious mixture of '50s hokum, '60s girl-group theatrics and '70s detachment might have been more noteworthy if Blondie hadn't issued their own, more original version a few years earlier. The singer warbles and trills skillfully, but without much charm. The album was reissued in 1984, after said warbler, Cyndi Lauper, topped the charts with a song called "Girls Just Want to Have Fun." [jy]
See also *Cyndi Lauper*.

BLUEBELLS

The Bluebells EP (nr/Sire) 1983
Sisters (London/Sire) 1984

Although they've been recording since 1982, the rustic pure-pop Bluebells haven't made anything near their full impact yet. For one thing, they've concentrated far more on making singles than albums; additionally, they seem to change producers every time they go in the studio, and have had some lineup shuffles as well. But even if their output hasn't exactly been enormous—they've only got one LP to show for themselves—no matter: Guitarist and ex-fanzine publisher Robert Hodgens (aka Bobby Bluebell) writes memorable instant classics and sings 'em in a likably plain voice, making every track count. The five-song EP and the album have three songs in common (a moving folk classic, "The Patriot's Game," "Cath" and—re-recorded for the LP—"Everybody's Somebody's Fool"), all of them winners. **Sisters** also has "I'm Falling (Down Again)" and six others, all subtly shaded with country fiddles and mandolins, ringing guitars, a light bouncy beat and choruses that you'll be humming all the way home. Utterly wonderful. [iar]

BLUE IN HEAVEN

All the Gods' Men (Island) 1985
Head (Island) 1986

Although this young Irish quartet debuted on 45 with a fiery guitar anthem ("Julie Cries"), a poor choice of producer (gothic master Martin Hannett) for their first album turned them into bass-heavy doom mongers. A remix of the single on **All the Gods' Men** tells the whole sordid tale. A little light does shine through in "Sometimes," "Big Beat" and "In Your Eyes," but Hannett's lush atmospherics detract rather than complement the effect.

The second record (**Explicit Music** in the US) was co-produced by Island Records head Chris Blackwell, Eric Thorngren and Blue in Heaven to far more appealing effect. Guitars power the mostly melodic songs along without overly coloring them; Shane O'Neill's vocals provide the band's dominant character. Amidst the attractive pop, Shane's avowed Iggy fixation comes through on the grungy "Be Your Man" (which also mentions a familiar canine variation). [ag/iar]

BLUE NILE

A Walk Across the Rooftops (Linn-Virgin/Virgin-A&M) 1984

This unique Scottish trio has considerable creative depth, building atmosphere with lots of empty space and well-controlled conflicting musical maneuvers. The title track mixes strings, horns, drum and bass with a meandering, disjunct vocal for something like a blend of Robert Wyatt, Joni Mitchell and John Cale. Although the LP defies easy acceptance, at its most accessible point ("Stay," which actually has a chorus and more of a verse melody than the others), it's quite appealing. [iar]

BLUE ORCHIDS

The Greatest Hit (Money Mountain) (Rough Trade/nr) 1982
Agents of Change EP (Rough Trade/nr) 1982

This Manchester quartet includes two early members of the Fall and uses organ as its main instrument, but at times it sounds as if Una Baines is playing a different song from the rest of the band. There are many overlapping layers in the deceptively simple sound of the album: the long organ washes are interrupted by guitars lurching to the fore; bass and drums keep the steady beat, but the others don't necessarily fall in line behind them. Vocals are half-sung, half-spoken and full of poetic pretense, but it's the mesmerizing music that captures the listener in bright swirling folds. While **The Greatest Hit** can be simply tagged as neo-psychedelia, that doesn't cover the full scope of this fascinating band's music.

The EP, packaged in a printed plastic shopping bag, offers four subsequent tracks that are at once subtler and more conservatively structured, sounding like nothing so much as the pretty side of early Velvet Underground. Very nice, indeed. [iar]

BLUE RONDO A LA TURK

Chewing the Fat (Diable Noir-Virgin/nr) 1989

BLUE RONDO

Bees Knees and Chickens Elbows (Virgin/nr) 1984

It shows you how far and fast new wave traveled: five years earlier, Chris Sullivan might have been screaming lyrics in a punk combo; in 1980, he could have been skanking in front of some neo-ska bunch. But in 1982, he was singing in a quasi-salsa/cool-jazz group wanting, in his words, to bring back show biz. **Chewing the Fat** uses a number of big name producers (Langer and Winstanley, Godley and Creme, Mike Chapman), and the multi-ethnic London-based ten-piece turns in solid performances. But why bother settling for imitations when you can get the originals? (Sullivan did paint an attractive neo-Cubist album cover, though.) [jg]

BLURT

In Berlin (Armageddon/Ruby) 1981
Blurt (Red Flame/nr) 1982
Bullets for You (Divine/nr) 1984
Friday the 12th (Another Side/PVC) 1985
Poppycock (Tocblock/nr) 1986

Blurt's formula is simple and unvarying: Ted Milton alternately (over)blows alto sax and shouts hoarsely, all against Pete Creese's minimal guitar licks and brother Jake Milton's steady drumbeat. You either love it or press "reject" after 30 seconds.

Ted Milton was known as a poet before taking up sax, but his vocals, rampant with echo and distortion, are largely incoherent. Instead, Blurt operates on a more visceral wavelength. The pulsing drums and unvarying ostinatos anchor free-form sax squeals and (from what can be discerned) lyrical flights of fancy. The more variegated and upbeat **In Berlin** has an edge over **Blurt**. This band is really sayin' something.

Blurt returned after a two-year absence with **Bullets for You**. Recorded live in a wine cellar, it's not quite as manic as the first two albums, displaying instead a well-controlled, tight little noise. The overall sound—especially vocals—is clearer than before; this new precision shows Ted Milton's lyrics to be ugly, satirical views of politics and death, but then one wouldn't expect moon-june-party stuff from this bunch. As usual, the band plays with considerable heart—the guitar and drum interplay on tracks like "Sugar-Coated" and "Enemy Ears" makes it easy to miss the fact that they don't use bass.

Friday the 12th is a ten-track live album recorded in Belgium. [si/dgs]

BMOVIE

Forever Running (Sire) 1985

"Nowhere Girl," this trio's best-known effort, is a lame (although catchy enough) pop song employing a '60s sound somewhere near the Left Banke's. The rest of **Forever Running** attempts a collection of other styles, but proves neither as memorable nor as clever. And the lyrics are embarrassingly pseudo-intellectual as well. Competent but uninteresting. [iar]

BOLLOCK BROTHERS

The Last Supper (Charly/nr) 1983
Never Mind the Bollocks 1983 (Charly/nr) 1983
Live Performances (Charly/nr) 1983
'77 '78 '79 (Konexion/nr) 1985
The 4 Horsemen of the Apocalypse

(Charly/nr) 1985
Bollock Sisters (Konexion/nr) 1986

Led by singer/looner Jock McDonald, the semi-serious Bollock Brothers will try anything once, and make an art out of prole wideboy absurdity. **The Last Supper**, a double studio album, has the juvenile "Horror Movies," a Munsterized dance theme and a swipe at political criticism ("The Act Becomes Real," with regard to Reagan), plus lots more, all characterized by inept singing and inept playing.

The conceptually bizarre **Never Mind the Bollocks 1983** reprises the entire contents (and cover design) of the Sex Pistols' 1977 debut album. Rather than merely attempting to mimic the Pistols, however, the Bollock Bros. borrow the material, adding a few lyrics of their own, and employ synthesizers to convert most of the tunes into a sub-New Order update with McDonald's blandly artless vocals serving in lieu of Rotten's sneering bile. Not exactly a piece of timeless musical history, but an amusing novelty record made just a bit weirder by the guest vocal appearance of Michael Fagin, the nutter who was arrested for sneaking into Buckingham Palace, on "God Save the Queen" and "Pretty Vacant." Fagin also appears on one side of the **Live Performances** official bootleg, a two-record set of concert appearances which also reprises the band's (and the Pistols') catalogue. Ridiculous.

The 4 Horsemen employs three of the least likely songwriters you'd ever expect to find sharing one album—McDonald, the late Alex Harvey and Vangelis (!)—yet this well-produced (by the band) studio job isn't as bizarre as that might indicate. Jock still can't sing worth a damn (although his dumb B-movie lyrics remain as crazed and offbeat as ever); combined with the conservative rock backing, it makes for a regrettably tepid and laborious album. [iar]

BOLSHOI

Giants EP (Situation 2/IRS) 1986

Sounding like a cross between U2 and the Cult, this Leeds trio isn't exactly good (Trevor Tanner isn't much of a vocalist), but it's not dead in the water, either. **Giants**, a six-track mini-album, has some promising ideas and intriguing production qualities. [iar]

BONE ORCHARD

Jack (Jungle/nr) 1984
Princess Epilepsy EP (Jungle/nr) 1985
Penthouse Poultry (Vax/nr) 1985

The artwork on this Brighton quintet's debut LP employs the same scratchy/violent style as Batcave bands like Specimen and Alien Sex Fiend; the music on **Jack** is similarly gloomy and intense, but generally less cliched and more interesting. Credit is due singer Chrissy McGee (an original, intelligent lyricist—check the story-like "Five Days in the Neighbourhood" for details), whose deep, deadpan voice sounds a little like Siouxsie's, and the use of four guest musicians, who augment the band's guitar-based lineup with piano, strings and sax. Bone Orchard's other strength is a sense of dynamics—they can thunder oppressively or drop back for contrast. **Jack** may not be an overly pleasant disc, but it is a well-crafted one with some appealing features. [iar]

BONGOS

Time and the River (Fetish/nr) 1982
Drums Along the Hudson (nr/PVC) 1982
Numbers with Wings EP (RCA) 1983
Beat Hotel (RCA) 1985

RICHARD BARONE/ JAMES MASTRO

Nuts and Bolts (nr/Passport) 1983

Led by enthusiastic guitarist/ singer Richard Barone, this Hoboken, New Jersey pop band makes no effort to conceal its roots. On **Drums Along the Hudson** (an expanded version of the **Time and the River** mini-album, itself a compilation of singles), mixed among original songs is their breathy cover of T. Rex's "Mambo Sun"; elsewhere, Barone spins out streamlined Byrds guitar licks and maintains a brisk pace (a la Sparks) throughout. Tuneful originals like "In the Congo" and "Video Eyes" may trade a certain amount of substance for guaranteed immediate appeal, but there's no better musical equivalent of whipped cream anywhere.

The Bongos subsequently expanded from a trio with the full-time addition of guitarist James Mastro. In an interesting variation on the solo record concept, Barone and Mastro dropped down to North Carolina to record **Nuts and Bolts** in collaboration with Mitch Easter. The two Bongos each take a side to showcase their own writing and singing, and help the other out as well. Barone's results are bland and resemble unfinished band demos or outtakes, with dull sound matching uninspired material; Mastro takes a more idiosyncratic approach, using the opportunity to express some individuality and depict his contribution to the Bongos.

Recording for the first time as a quartet, the Bongos cut five new songs for **Numbers with Wings**, produced by Richard Gottehrer. "Barbarella" and the title track are prime, filled with swell harmonies, driving acoustic guitars and subtle structural tricks; the rest is adequate but dispensable.

Beat Hotel, produced by John Jansen (Lou Reed, Television), is the most rocking Bongos record to date, a sparkling explosion of guitar pop. "Space Jungle" has a nagging hook and a full-blown arrangement; "Apache Dancing" is similarly ambitious in a different vein; "Come Back to Me" and "A Story (Written in the Sky)" hark back to the band's simpler days; "Totem Pole" sounds a bit like the dB's except for the overblown big-band finale. Given the best audio treatment of their career, the Bongos prove their mettle, while simultaneously exposing their main inadequacy: inconsistent songwriting quality. [jy/iar]
See also *Beat Rodeo*.

BOOK OF LOVE

Book of Love (I Square-Sire) 1986

Produced by Ivan Ivan for his custom label, this New York art-school quartet's album is a clever synthesis of catchy electro-pop minimalism and dance-driven rhythmatics. Susan Ottaviano's breathy, almost spoken vocals on atmospheric tunes like "Boy" and "Happy Day" neatly offset the simple, spacious arrangements; others aren't quite as memorable. A little like Trio without the irony, or Dominatrix for the masses, **Book of Love** is an alluring if insignificant way to while away time in clubland. (Special note to aficionados of esoteric cover versions: the LP contains Liliput's "Diematrosen.") [iar]

BOOKS

Expertise (Logo/nr) 1980

Singer/synthesist/songsmith Stephen Betts uses the middle initials "F.X." and quirky electronic effects are predictably rife on this well-produced (by Colin Thurston) batch of hollow numbers that have substantially more flash than substance. The band plays well in a vaguely modern way, but with none of the originality or talent that characterizes Thurston's early success story, Duran Duran. Betts sings like a right poseur, and his songs don't even steal enough from others to resemble anything in particular. Intensely second-rate. [iar]

BOOMTOWN RATS

The Boomtown Rats (Ensign/ Mercury) 1977
A Tonic for the Troops (Ensign/ Columbia) 1978
The Fine Art of Surfacing (Ensign/Columbia) 1979 (Phonogram/nr) 1984
Mondo Bongo (Mercury/Columbia) 1981
Rat Tracks EP (Can. Vertigo) 1981
V Deep (Mercury/Columbia) 1982
The Boomtown Rats EP (nr/Columbia) 1982
Ratrospective EP (nr/Columbia) 1983
In the Long Grass (Mercury/ Columbia) 1985

Like Madness and the Jam, the Rats have generally matched considerable Anglo-European success with American obscurity. Despite a string of intelligent, unavoidable pop singles and intricate, skillful, unpredictable albums filled with assorted musical styles and sounds, the Rats have never sold many records in the US, with the exception of their morbid ballad, "I Don't Like Mondays." While the albums are not all equally excellent—two are self-indulgent and largely-impenetrable—the band's commitment to quality and growth, plus singer/ songwriter Bob Geldof's magnetic personality, help elevate even lesser efforts to listenability, and much of their work is downright brilliant.

The six future Rats left the unemployment lines in their hometown, Dublin, to enter the rock sweepstakes and had become a going concern on Irish concert stages by the time new wave came along. While the resulting upsurge in record-industry openness toward young, energetic bands undoubtedly helped them get a contract, it was clear from the start that the Rats were a different breed, musically. Produced in Germany by Mutt Lange, the first album is more tradition-minded than punky, but there's no mistaking the band's verve and independence, which tied them solidly to the less accomplished, more enraged outfits. From the Springsteenish "Joey's on the Street Again" to the Dr. Feelgoody "Never Bite the Hand that Feeds" to a Mott the Hoople-styled ballad, "I Can Make It If You Can," and the album's sarcastic standout, "Looking After No. 1," the ambience is different, but the rock is fairly routine. Geldof's incisive lyrics and the band's credible musicianship invest the stylistically diverse selections with character, making this a top-notch, timeless record.

Assumptions about the Rats' musical intent were dispelled with **A Tonic for the Troops**. Taking a giant step forward in terms of invention and sophistication, Geldof turned from a junior rock singer into a skilled vocalist with a recognizable style, and the band exhibited new-found intricacy and multi-faceted versatility, thanks in large part to Johnnie Fingers' keyboard cleverness and Mutt Lange's layered production. **Troops** is not a total departure—"Rat Trap" picks up exactly where "Joey" left off, and "She's So Modern" merely improves on "Mary of the Fourth Form"—but "Me and Howard Hughes," "Like Clockwork" and "Living in an Island" display great development on all fronts: writing, singing, performing, arranging. (The American version deletes "Can't Stop" and "Watch Out for the Normal People" in favor of two tracks retrieved from the first LP, which had sunk without a trace upon its release by the Rats' previous label.)

The Rats took another leap ahead on **The Fine Art of Surfacing**, but with less rewarding results. Substandard songs get unenthusiastic treatment, and an overwhelming sense of self-importance only highlights the ennui, despite impressive technical aptitude and obviously strengthened confidence and stylistic reach. The record does contain the stunning "I Don't Like Mondays" and a few other standouts—"Someone's Looking at You," which is clumsy but melodic and charming, and "When the Night Comes," a showstopper with ace Geldof lyrics and a swell arrangement that uses Latin-flavored acoustic guitar for color—but otherwise **Surfacing** is a slick drag.

On first listen, **Mondo Bongo** is even more outlandish, but a little application reveals a number of great tracks in a percussion-laden Afro-Caribbean style, delivered up in gonzo fashion by co-producer Tony Visconti. "Up All Night," "The Elephants Graveyard" and "Don't Talk to Me" are rollicking good fun, but "Mood Mambo" takes the genre detour too literally, and a totally unnecessary rewrite of an old Rolling Stones tune ("Under Their Thumb . . . Is Under My Thumb") adds to the record's shortcomings. Neither a triumph nor a disaster, **Mondo Bongo** is a half-baked but entertaining digression for the Rats. The Canadian-only **Rat Tracks** has a live cut, a remix of "Up All Night" and several otherwise UK-only obscurities; five tracks in all.

Total confusion as to the band's direction and frustration at the disinterest shown by the American audience may have been the reasons why Columbia tried to avoid releasing **V Deep**, opting instead for a 12-inch condensation of it. (The company eventually came around and issued the entire LP, including the EP's contents.) Although heavily stylized and partially overproduced, **V Deep** (so named because it's the band's fifth LP and their first as a quintet following the departure of guitarist Gerry Cott, who's since released a couple of solo singles) contains some of the Rats' strangest songs, but also some of their most evocative and moving efforts. Geldof is at his driven best, and the band keeps pace in a number of styles (including an encore of **Mondo Bongo**'s sound and a Dennis Bovell dub mix of one track) that don't neatly hang together, but paint the group in a most fascinating light. Controversial perhaps, but thoughtful and intriguing—a fine album to be savored repeatedly.

After **V Deep**, the Rats dropped out for several years, prompting the US issue of **Ratrospective**, a mini-album containing "I Don't Like Mondays," "Up All Night," "Rat Trap" and three other familiar cuts. In late 1984, Geldof surfaced as the instigator of Band Aid, the all-star fundraiser 45 that started a wave of similar ventures throughout the music world. (The following year, Geldof organized Live Aid and was mooted for Nobel Prize consideration, but it hardly aided the Rats, who met 1986 without an American label.)

The band's return was marked in 1985 with a single, followed several months later by a whole new album, **In the Long Grass**. Evidently back from the wars (the acknowledgments on the inner sleeve read "For making an unbearable year tolerable . . . "), the Rats look miserable and spent on the cover; the lyrics are unremittingly bitter, angry and defiant. Matching the verbal onslaught, the music is likewise as dense and rugged as any the band has ever made, yet uplifting in their refusal to buckle under whatever pressures they had to face. An extraordinarily powerful record.

In mid-1986, after enormous efforts on behalf of others, Geldof took a step in his own direction, signing a solo recording deal and promptly recording an album with Dave Stewart. [iar]

DUKE BOOTEE

Bust Me Out (nr/Mercury) 1984

Duke Bootee (Edward Fletcher) is one of the unsung heroes of rap. As a member of the Sugar Hill label's crack house band, he wrote the tune, "chorus" and half the raps for "The Message." Although that groundbreaking single came out under the name Grandmaster Flash and the Furious Five, the raps belong to Bootee and Melle Mel. The two paired up less successfully (and more formulaically) on "Message II" and "New York, New York," before Bootee rediscovered the urban claustrophobia groove on the title track of his solo LP. The album boasts aggressive playing and production from his old Sugar Hill friends, and the rap side (as opposed to the song side) smokes. [jl]

BOOTHILL FOOT-TAPPERS

Get Your Feet Out of My Shoes EP (Go! Discs/nr) 1984
Ain't That Far from Boothill (Mercury/nr) 1985

In yet another installment of "Musical Styles Traverse the Ocean," these seven rustic English lads and lassies play a charming and catchy version of old-timey folk (banjo, fiddle, guitar, washboard, accordion) on the wonderful title track of their five-song 12-inch. But it doesn't stop there; elsewhere, they essay a soulful choral arrangement of Curtis Mayfield's "People Get Ready" and a rousing assault on Margaret Thatcher called "True Blues." The only duff item is the rushed, tuneless "Milk Train."

Unfortunately, the album makes a crime of eclecticism: the band dabbles in everything from ska to country-western, connecting emotionally with none of it. Flat, insipid production (mostly by Dick Cuthell) matches the performances' lack of spunk; the net result is a record without depth or charm. Even a new version of "Get Your Feet Out of My Shoes" is tedious and contrived-sounding. What a shame.

The Boothill Foot-Tappers disbanded at the end of 1985. [iar]

DENNIS BOVELL

Brain Damage (Fontana-Phonogram/nr) 1981

BLACKBEARD

Strictly Dub Wize (Tempus/nr) 1978 (Ballistic-UA/nr) 1978
I Wah Dub (More Cut-EMI/nr) 1980

Dennis "Blackbeard" Bovell is a noted musician (mainly with Matumbi, one of England's top reggae bands—try their 1980 **Point of View** LP on EMI America) and reggae producer of high standing. Close school chum of jazz-popper Nick Straker and hit producer Tony Mansfield, his eclectic interests have also enabled him to bring fresh perspectives to production of new wavers like the Slits, Pop Group and others.

This same eclecticism informs his dub LPs in conceptual perspective and willingness to take chances, to go beyond the repetitiousness of the style's usual electronic overkill. Bovell creates strong reggae instrumentals written and arranged expressly to accommodate his dub technique, insuring that there are catchy melody lines that may be dissected but not disintegrated. **Strictly Dub Wize** (mostly performed by Bovell, but with some help from Matumbi mates and other musicians) exhibits cleverness and humor by the bagful: one track is even based on "Surrey with the Fringe on Top"! **I Wah Dub** carries Bovell's creation of aurally pungent tracks infused with musical witticisms from merely excellent to brilliant. Except for much of the drumming, the odd piano part here or melodica toot there, Bovell plays everything.

Brain Damage is also consistently enjoyable though less spectacular. Bovell uses dub sparingly in a mixed bag that includes boogie-woogie, rock'n'roll and R&B, as well as reggae, and his good-humored (if homely) vocals on several tracks. A bonus dub LP (not of the album's other tracks, but along similar lines to **I Wah Dub**) is included. Good grooves, lightweight material—solid summer music. [jg]

DAVID BOWIE

The Man Who Sold the World (Mercury) 1971
Hunky Dory (RCA) 1971
The Rise and Fall of Ziggy Stardust and the Spiders from Mars (RCA) 1972
Aladdin Sane (RCA) 1973
Pin-Ups (RCA) 1973
Diamond Dogs (RCA) 1974
Young Americans (RCA) 1975
Station to Station (RCA) 1976
Low (RCA) 1977
"Heroes" (RCA) 1977
Lodger (RCA) 1979
Scary Monsters (RCA) 1980
Let's Dance (EMI America) 1983
Tonight (EMI America) 1984

Throughout his lengthy career, David Bowie has worked in many widely disparate musical areas, and virtually all of them have proven enormously influential, even if sometimes it's taken years for the rest of the rock world to catch up with him. Nonetheless, Bowie mercurially continues to shift gears, styles and fashions almost as often as shirts and, by example, helps keep pop and rock developing and changing. Unfortunately, even long after he's abandoned some excessive dalliance or another, his camp followers trundle on, missing the transitory essence of Bowie's work. Even if only as the source of unreproachably hip songs to cover, Bowie has played an essential role in glam-rock, new wave, post-punk, neo-soul, etc.

Although he actually began recording in the late '60s, we join the show in progress at the dawn of the last decade when he dropped some of his more theatrical Anthony Newley affectations and got down to rock'n'roll cases. (Incidentally, the discography above omits compilations, reissues, repackages, soundtracks, EPs, spoken-word records, live albums and other extraneous items.)

The Man Who Sold the World begins Bowie's affair with guitar-heavy rock'n'roll, courtesy Mick Ronson. Tony Visconti's compressed production gives the album an utterly synthetic audio quality; few records this simply played sound as studio-created. The grim futurist imagery of "Saviour Machine," "The Super-men" and "Running Gun Blues" in retrospect seems far more prescient than the thrilling but hardly adventurous band's music. Still, a shockingly strong debut for the electrified Bowie.

Hunky Dory was a detour of sorts, briefly returning a seemingly innocent Bowie to his hippie/folkie/cabaret days for the catchy "Changes" and the obnoxiously precious "Kooks," plus such atypically direct tributes as "Song for Bob Dylan" and "Andy Warhol." But the album also contains the redemptive "Life on Mars," "Queen Bitch" and "Oh! You Pretty Things," all essential components in the burgeoning glam/sci-fi/decadence world Bowie was assembling.

Bowie began his fey alien role-playing in earnest on **Ziggy Stardust**, an unquestionably classic rock'n'roll album. He introduces this new persona via the pseudo-biographical title track; otherwise, songs paint a weird portrait of the androgynous (but sexy) world ahead. Armed with supercharged guitar rock and truly artistic production (Bowie and Ken Scott) and mixing rock'n'roll stardom imagery with a more general *Clockwork Orange* outlook, the peerless set of songs (including "Suffragette City," "Hang on to Yourself," "Rock'n'Roll Suicide" and "Moonage Daydream") outline some of the concerns that underpin much of '70s/'80s rock songwriting.

Having peaked so gloriously with a character that could not last indefinitely, Bowie adjusted Ziggy a bit on **Aladdin Sane** and came up with a weird set of tunes—some tremendous, some minor—and a distant, unpleasant left field studio sound. "Panic in Detroit," "Watch That Man," "The Jean Genie" and "Drive-In Saturday" are some of his greatest songs, painting bleak pictures of detached existences with cinematic strokes and killer riffs. Rather than singing about apocalypse, Bowie captures the barren feel of a dead world, and feeds it into the music. **Aladdin Sane** is also notable for allowing a serious crooner side to re-emerge—as on "Time"—a foreshadow of future developments. That said, it must be noted that Bowie's cover of "Let's Spend the Night Together" is utterly misguided and worthless.

In a surprisingly guileless gesture, Bowie's next album consisted exclusively of cover versions of material from mid-'60s English bands. Although hard to relate creatively to his own originals of this era, **Pin-Ups** is a wonderful, loving tribute that just happens to contain (almost all) ace renditions of great and, in America at least, largely unknown songs. Perhaps recognizing that his own records are destined to become more obscure to future generations, by recording these classics Bowie generated interest in his forebears, giving the bands he chose (Pretty Things, original Pink Floyd, Them, Mojos, Merseys, Kinks, Yardbirds, Easybeats and Who) much-deserved cachet in the new rock world.

Bowie jettisoned his band and drafted a new bunch of sidemen to further his trendily somber vision of the doomsday future on **Diamond Dogs**. Although the LP contains one of Bowie's most incredible and concise songs—"Rebel Rebel," perfectly describing his followers and their role in the new society—it also has an overblown and underdeveloped concept that falls under the wheels of mammoth pomposity. In retrospect, it's not so bad, but does suffer significantly from audio clumsiness and unpleasant, seemingly unfinished sound.

Dropping one set of gimmicky costumes and British players, Bowie made **Young Americans**, an album mainly of phony (but pleasant) Philadelphia soul/rock mixed with other oddities, like his truly awful collaboration with John Lennon, "Fame." It took five years for the British new wave, finally bereft of new ideas, to ape Bowie and start absorbing black American idioms into their work.

Following that brief infatuation, Bowie launched into an experimental phase that influenced many bands, especially the "new romantics" and arty minimalists. **Station to Station** is a strangely impersonal mixture of chilly show ballads, techno-pop and whatever was passing for disco that year. The album featured the hit "Golden Years," but also the experimental and challenging "TVC15." It also marked the beginning of Bowie's distancing himself from his former rock-idol role.

That trend was formally instigated with **Low**, on which Bowie arranged to co-opt the modernistic sensibility of Brian Eno (his collaborator on three consecutive studio LPs) and presented a selection of tracks—less songs than word-paintings, and in many cases simply mood pieces. From the grandiosity of **Young Americans** to the sketchy minimalist slices here, Bowie took heart from intellectual, bare-bones rock bands like Wire and, in turn, helped legitimize and promote such spartan stylings.

The follow-up to **Low**, **"Heroes"** has slightly fleshier production, though nearly one full side is comprised of whizzing synthesizers and amorphous textural noodling. Robert Fripp contributes lead guitar, and his presence adds a bit of sinew to the overall sound, something lacking in the less-forceful **Low**. The album leans heavily on chilly, European affectations (with a large debt owed to Kraftwerk), but also has room for a genuine pop single, the atmospheric title track.

Lodger finds Bowie drifting back into a solid song-oriented context and can be considered the third instalment of the Bowie-Eno trilogy. Though many of the songs seem to be stream-of-consciousness, there are a couple of pure poppers, such as "D.J." and "Boys Keep Swinging," that recall a more commercial time. Also of interest is Bowie's version of "Sister Moonlight," rewritten as "Red Money."

Scary Monsters is Bowie's most consistent LP since the pre-**Low** period, a culmination of the styles that had been individually showcased on previous discs. The tone is up-front, a confrontation with the real world of alienation Bowie always ascribed to his fictional settings. **Scary Monsters** contains two Bowie standards: "Ashes to Ashes" and "Fashion."

Having tired of years of acclaim and only sporadic and middling glimmers of the kind of success that usually befits a superstar (although Bob Dylan could teach him a few lessons about humility in that area), Bowie made **Let's Dance**, a calculated effort with the production assistance of Nile Rodgers to get in step with the sound of today (rather than tomorrow or yesterday, Bowie's far more common habitats.) Not surprisingly, as it usually happens, Bowie succeeds at whatever he sets his mind to, and the record was a worldwide smasheroonee. "Let's Dance," "Modern Love" and "China Girl" may not be the Thin White Duke's finest creations, but they do hit a solid compromise between art and commerce, and don't harm his reputation nearly as much as expand his audience (and bank balance).

After a mega-tour to consolidate the album's huge success, Bowie banged out a quickie, **Tonight**, which has all the earmarks of a casual, smug effort to create another big hit without even trying. (What other recording challenges are left for Bowie? He's tried self-indulgent art and jugular commercialism, scoring just what he wanted on both fronts.) The album includes a duet with Tina Turner and a remarkably swell pop hit, "Jazzin' for Blue Jean," that recalls far earlier sections of his career.

There's utterly no point in trying to predict Bowie's future. He's really done it all and still somehow remains in touch and in charge. The safest assumption? Whatever he

does, it won't be boring. [jw/iar]
See also *Iggy Pop, Lou Reed*.

BOW WOW WOW

Your Cassette Pet tape (EMI/nr) 1980
See Jungle! See Jungle! Go Join Your Gang Yeah! City All Over, Go Ape Crazy (RCA) 1981
The Last of the Mohicans EP (nr/RCA) 1982
I Want Candy (EMI/RCA) 1982
Twelve Original Recordings (nr/Harvest) 1982
When the Going Gets Tough the Tough Get Going (RCA) 1983

Bow Wow Wow may have been easily dismissed by some as entrepreneur Malcolm McLaren's creation, but the band deserved better. (McLaren and Bow Wow Wow parted company in 1982.) Formed by combining musicians lured away from Adam and the Ants (with whom McLaren was briefly involved) and a 15-year-old singer, Annabella Lwin, the ever-provocative McLaren launched the band via a 45, "C-30, C-60, C-90 Go," which espoused the virtues of home taping at a time when the band's record company (and virtually all others) were first bitterly fighting it. True to McLaren's precepts (although it should be noted that tapes are not as commonly copied as discs), **Your Cassette Pet** is a tape-only collection of eight songs. Except for "I Want My Baby on Mars" and a painful rendition of "Fools Rush In," the material is marked by Annabella's breathless ranting and incessant drumming "borrowed" from the African Burundi tribe. The results are cheerful if smarmy.

The band's first full-length album, **See Jungle! See Jungle!**, isn't as wound up as **Cassette Pet**, but shows artistic growth. By downplaying the leering football chants, Bow Wow Wow is able to investigate subtler lyrics and rhythms. Fueled by drummer Dave Barbarossa, they pack quite a wallop.

Last of the Mohicans is a four-song EP whose producer (Kenny Laguna of Joan Jett fame) and lead-off track (the Strangeloves' "I Want Candy") were chosen presumably for American commercial reasons. If nothing else, the sound is cleaner than before.

The discographical plot thickens with **I Want Candy**, released in two distinctly different versions. The American LP is comprised of the **Mohicans** EP, four tracks from **See Jungle!** (three of them remixed) and two "new" cuts. The UK album of the same title, on Bow Wow Wow's original label, makes **Your Cassette Pet** available on vinyl, except for "Louis Quatorze." It also includes a few British single sides and the US-only EP, with its re-recorded "Louis Quatorze." Got that?

Not to be outdone, EMI's American affiliate issued **Twelve Original Recordings**. This is essentially the British **I Want Candy** LP minus several tracks. Pay your money and take your choice.

For a change, **When the Going Gets Tough the Tough Get Going** was an all-new recording free of McLaren's machinations. On their final album, Bow Wow Wow delivered much the same musical barrage as before without any propagandistic pretense. The band subsequently ejected Annabella (who launched a solo career in 1985) and regrouped as the Chiefs of

Relief. [si]
See also *Annabella*.

THE BOX

The Box EP (Go! Discs/nr) 1983
Secrets Out (Go! Discs/nr) 1983
Great Moments in Big Slam (Go! Discs/nr) 1984
Muscle In EP (Doublevision/nr) 1985
Muscle Out (Rough Trade/nr) 1985

One of the few bands capable of effectively combining the spontaneity and musicianship of jazz with the urgency and rough-edged sound of rock, the Box are a five-piece spin-off from British industrial funksters Clock DVA. Comparisons to Captain Beefheart, Gang of Four, the Minutemen and Ornette Colemam are all appropriate; execution is first-rate (especially by ex-Clocks Paul Widger on guitar and saxophonist Charlie Collins), their material frantic.

The eponymous debut EP contains five manic cuts, setting instruments on wild collision courses behind Peter Hope's vocals. **Secrets Out** improves on that formula by injecting unexpected subtleties and an underlying murkiness that give even more impact to the hyperactive guitar/sax counterpoint. A solid, frenzied album guaranteed to keep any listener on his/her toes.

Great Moments in Big Slam, however, is quite a letdown. The pace is slower and the band really doesn't get a chance to cut loose, but that's not the problem so much as the heavy-handed percussion and grossly exaggerated vocals which dominate the production. After releasing the **Muscle In** EP, the Box announced a trial separation to pursue other projects. The posthumous **Muscle Out** was recorded live at the Leadmill in the Box's hometown, Sheffield. [dgs]

BOYS

The Boys (NEMS/nr) 1977
Alternative Chartbusters (NEMS/nr) 1978
To Hell with the Boys (Safari/nr) 1979
Boys Only (Safari/nr) 1981

YOBS

The Christmas Album (Safari/nr) 1979

Too unseriously pop-minded for the punks but too punky for the power-poppers, well received nearly everywhere in Europe except their homeland (England), beset with label woes in the UK and name confusion in the US, the star-crossed Boys were perenially in the wrong place at the wrong time.

Norwegian expatriate Casino Steel (the band's keyboard player and co-writer of much of their first three albums) was already a veteran of this sort of thing, having been a member of the Hollywood Brats, a London glitter band like the New York Dolls but with better musicianship. The Brats' self-titled album, recorded in '73, came out at the time in Scandinavia, was bootlegged in the US as **Grown Up Wrong** two years later, and finally appeared in 1980 on UK Cherry Red.

The first Boys album is an inconsistent (if promising) melange of Steel's Bratisms, standard punka-rama and the stirrings of a Beatle

(and other pop) influence. **Alternative Chartbusters**, though, presents infectiously rocking tunes played with irreverent elan, featuring Duncan "Kid" Reid's engagingly adolescent readings of the mostly humorous lyrics (often, as on **To Hell With the Boys**, playing the punk schlemiel), culminating in a pair of classic pop-punk singles, "Brickfield Nights" and "First Time." The third album (recorded in the tiny Norwegian town of the punny title) delivers more of the same, but with slicker and fuller sound—organ in addition to piano, more dual guitars—and more variety.

Sadly, reverses (among them, Steel's deportation) took their toll, and the Boys, as a quartet, made a fourth album that sounds flatter than stale soda tastes. Perhaps they knew they were recording their swan song.

Under the pseudonym of the Yobs, the Boys early in their career recorded an LP of Yuletide favorites, plus their own holiday compositions, in various variations on pop-punk, sometimes just cute, but mostly skipping irreverence and heading straight for sheer tastelessness, e.g., "Silent Night" by Nazi-punks and "Twelve Days of Christmas" translated by "Qi" brigands into locker-room scatology. Subsequently, Boys guitarist Honest John Plain cut an LP, **New Guitars in Town**, with Lurker Pete Stride, supported by other members of both bands, who had formed an alliance of sorts. [jg]
See also *Lurkers*.

BOYS NEXT DOOR

See *Birthday Party*.

BPEOPLE

See *Alex Gibson*.

BILLY BRAGG

Life's a Riot with Spy vs. Spy (Utility/nr) 1983 (Utility-Go! Discs/nr) 1983
Brewing Up with Billy Bragg (Go! Discs/CD Presents) 1984
Between the Wars EP (Go! Discs/nr) 1985
Life's a Riot Etc (nr/CD Presents) 1985
"Days Like These" (Go! Discs/nr) 1985

Bard of the '80s, young Billy Bragg is a rough-hewn modern troubadour playing a solitary electric guitar and singing his pithy compositions in a gruff voice. Although his tools are utterly simple, Bragg is capable of enormous strength and depth in his writing and performing, spinning off touching, warm love songs as well as trenchant social satire and political comment. On the seven tracks of **Life's a Riot** (recorded originally as demos), Bragg waxes tender ("The Milkman of Human Kindness"), bitter ("A New England") and sarcastic ("The Busy Girl Buys Beauty"), keeping things blunt and one-take spartan. The ultimate no-frills pop record. Combining the wordplay and strong emotions of Elvis Costello with the grumpy melodic charm of Paul Weller, it's a small, articulate masterpiece.

Brewing Up, a relatively ambitious full-length undertaking with a tiny bit of organ and trumpet (not to mention— gasp!— overdubbed guitars and vocals),

finds Bragg retaining all of his rugged pop appeal while sharpening his pen a bit. The songs focus on romance, offering nervous but perceptive angles on love and lust (e.g., "Love Gets Dangerous," "The Saturday Boy," "A Lover Sings"). He also shreds Fleet Street with "It Says Here."

More recently, Bragg's career has involved another traditional subject for angry young men with guitars: politics. He's done benefit concerts, helped found the Red Wedge and turned his songwriting to address serious issues in a tone that recalls the Wobblies. **Between the Wars**, an extraordinarily powerful 7-inch EP, is Bragg at his finest, singing of England's peacetime recessions ("Between the Wars"), chronicling a 17th century rebellion ("World Turned Upside Down") and reviving the 1940s union classic, "Which Side Are You On." "Days Like These," a subsequent three-song single shows Bragg's deepening commitment to socialist political activities. This latter-day Woody Guthrie belts out sincere (if occasionally awkward) constructs like "I see no shame in putting my name to socialism's cause/Nor to seek some more relevance than spotlight and applause."

Life's a Riot Etc is a handy American-only release that combines all of the first mini-album with **Between the Wars** for a Bragg then-and-now extravaganza, complete with lyric sheet. [iar]

BRIAN BRAIN

Unexpected Noises (Secret/nr) 1980

Although Brain—or, more accurately, Martin Atkins—was the drummer in Public Image for a time, his subsequent solo career has taken a much less dour direction. So while this record—mostly his own work—is of little consequence, at least it attempts to be anarchic and funny rather than anarchic and glum. Biggest problem here is the poor recording quality, which leaves the sound muddled and flat. In 1985, Brain/Atkins emerged from a period of inactivity and returned to the concert circuit. [iar]

BRAINS

The Brains (Mercury) 1980
Electronic Eden (Mercury) 1981
Dancing Under Streetlights EP (nr/Landslide) 1982

The Brains' story is typical of many independent bands who signed to not-so-swift big labels. Led by lanky Tom Gray, this Atlanta-based quartet first garnered widespread attention with a striking homemade single, "Money Changes Everything." The Brains subsequently recorded two LPs for Mercury, but neither sold a speck. Following a divorce by mutual consent, the group returned, poorer and wiser, to the indie label scene.

On both albums, producer Steve Lillywhite concocts a thick, heavy sound that subjugates Gray's synthesizers and Rick Price's aggressive guitars to the tunes themselves. And for good reason: Gray's songs are tart accounts of love and confusion perfectly suited to his dry, sardonic voice. The Brains offer a rougher and less glib variant of the Cars' ironic sensibility, which is probably why they haven't achieved widespread popularity. Gray and crew unsettle rather than divert.

The Brains includes a re-recording of the cynical "Money Changes Everything" and "Gold Dust Kids," a pithy, unsentimental portrait of decadence. **Electronic Eden** features the bitter romanticism of "Heart in the Street," covered (badly) by Manfred Mann and "Collision," a humorously tasteless look at a brain-damaged car-crash survivor.

The four-song EP is more of the same intense longing and hidden passion. If the Brains sound a bit weary, chalk it up to the record biz blues. **Dancing Under Streetlights** isn't the best starting point, but it's a worthy continuation. The Brains have since disbanded. (As an undoubtedly lucrative footnote, Cyndi Lauper covered "Money Changes Everything" on her first LP.) [jy]

GLENN BRANCA

Lesson No.1 (nr/99) 1980
The Ascension (nr/99) 1981
Symphony No.1 (Tonal Plexus) [tape] (nr/ROIR) 1983
Symphony No.3/Gloria (Crépuscule/Neutral) 1983

GLENN BRANCA/JOHN GIORNO

Who You Staring At? (nr/Giorno Poetry Systems) 1982

Many artists have had their music described as a wall of sound, but few have deserved it as much as New York composer/guitarist Glenn Branca. One of the first to realize that a classical-rock fusion need not be technique-crazed keyboardists soloing away to the accompaniment of rehashed Brahms or Stravinsky, Branca writes music of orchestral richness that retains—intact—all of rock's danger, urgency and impact.

With his roots in the downtown no-wave movement of the late '70s, Branca's **Lesson No.1** was the first release on the influential local independent 99 Records. Slow, repetitive harmonic changes and hidden sub-motifs invite comparisons to minimalists like Philip Glass, but Branca's music is more dissonant, primitive and— above all—loud.

The Ascension is the closest he's ever come to an out-and-out rock album. Atop pulverizing bass/drum combinations, Branca and three other guitarists build a thick, layered mass of shifting textures, sometimes all on one chord, sometimes in a dense cacophony of six-string clusters. Suffice to say, it packs quite a wallop. Branca's side of the joint disc with poet John Giorno is music commissioned for Twyla Tharp's dance, **Bad Smells**. Most of it is much like **The Ascension**, except for very brief sections of quiet.

Only two of Branca's five symphonies have been recorded and released commercially so far, and it is in this format that he is most effective. Played by large ensembles, the pieces incorporate a plethora of instruments of his own design (primarily dulcimer-like things strung with steel wire and hammered with mallets) in addition to guitars, horns and a battery of percussion. He builds intense drones and ear-shattering crescendos while exploring the sonic possibilities of large tonal clusters and the resultant overtones. **Symphony No.1** alternates between one relentless,

thundering chord and primal rhythmic pounding. As instrumental layers build, overtones clash to produce melodies of their own, and can even trick the listener into hearing instruments that aren't there. **Symphony No.3** adds home-made keyboards, giving an orchestral and almost Oriental sound to the piece—delicacy amidst the thunder. Both recordings are hindered in that it is impossible to capture the full effect of his live performances, where the volume generally runs around wake-the-dead level. [dgs]

BILLY BREMNER

Bash! (Arista/nr) 1984

Erstwhile Rockpile guitarist Bremner is far more talented than his low profile would indicate; one alleged reason this LP passed unnoticed (and wasn't even released in the US) was his unwillingness to tour. In many ways, it's the Dave Edmunds album Edmunds never made; it's certainly more consistent than anything Edmunds has done in years. Bremner's taste and style are similar, and there's some Rockpile/ Lowe band crossover over here as well. On the other hand, Bremner doesn't mind pursuing a more pop-rock feel, and is a better and more prolific songwriter. (Ex-Records drummer Will Birch produced and supplied the lyrics.) Bonus: previously-unrecorded donations (one each) from Elvis Costello (brilliant!) and Difford/Tilbrook (they should have finished writing it first). **Bash!** doesn't contain Bremner's Stiff 45, "When Laughter Turns to Tears," but still delivers the goods track after track. [jg]

BETTE BRIGHT AND THE ILLUMINATIONS

Rhythm Breaks the Ice (Korova/nr) 1981

Criminally underused in Deaf School, Bette Bright blossomed into an exciting performer on this solo effort, thanks partly to the help of clever friends. **Rhythm Breaks the Ice** was produced by fellow DS graduate Clive Langer and his partner, Alan Winstanley, the team behind Madness' phenomenal success. (Bright intertwined the family trees by marrying that band's singer, Graham McPherson, in 1981.) Here they balanced studio smarts with the need to emphasize Bright's plaintive tones, and came up with a canny modern-day variation on Phil Spector. The full, smooth sound has a kaleidoscopic quality, continually shifting to highlight the key element in the arrangement—guitar, marimba or whatever—and providing Bright with a perfect launching pad for her soaring style. [jy]

BRITISH ELECTRIC FOUNDATION

Music for Stowaways [tape] (Virgin/nr) 1981
Music for Listening to EP (Can. Virgin) 1981
Music of Quality and Distinction, Volume 1 (Virgin/nr) 1982

In search of more meaningful dance music, Martyn Ware and Ian Craig Marsh abandoned the about-to-be-enormous Human League in 1980 to form the more experimental (musically and structurally) British

Electric Foundation. The core members— Marsh, Ware and singer Glenn Gregory—also work as Heaven 17, a "division" of B.E.F. Confused? While Heaven 17 is geared for dance funk'n'soul, B.E.F. pursues intermittent one-off concept projects with a variety of other people.

Music for Stowaways—released only on tape—consists of moody instrumentals, ranging from funk rock to icy Germanic synth-garde to electro-bop and sound experiments. Much of it was reissued on a Canadian EP, **Music for Listening To**, which also includes an extra track, "A Baby Called Billy."

Music of Quality and Distinction is B.E.F.'s first venture into pop experimentation, as they brought in a number of people (including Tina Turner, Gary Glitter, Sandie Shaw and John Foxx) to perform cover versions of well-known and not-so-well-known oldies, from "These Boots Are Made for Walking" and "Wichita Lineman" to David Bowie's "Secret Life of Arabia" and Lou Reed's "Perfect Day." Older songs hold up better under this treatment than new ones but, overall, choices of singer and musicians are on the mark. Despite any social implications (or lack thereof), a good time. [sg]

See also *Heaven 17*.

BROKEN BONES!

Dem Bones (Fall Out/nr) 1984
Live at the 100 Club (Subversive Sounds/nr) 1985
Bone Crusher (Jungle/Combat Core) 1986

This quartet (Bones, Baz, Oddy, Nobby) may not be too good at spelling, but they certainly have a clear idea which end of a guitar to bash at. Playing at maximum stun volume, the band's lack of literacy seems no obstacle to creating blunt protest songs with clear and indomitable rock power. A very British center ground between parochial punk (BB generally play too slow) and modern metal (BB are far too topical and fiery), Broken Bones! could be the '80s answer to the MC5. Or just another would-be Black Sabbath. [iar]

BRONSKI BEAT

The Age of Consent (London/MCA) 1984
Hundreds & Thousands (London/MCA) 1985
Truth Dare and Double Dare (London/MCA) 1986

Playing only electronic instruments and singing unequivocal gay lyrics in an astonishing, somewhat grating falsetto, this English trio burst full-blown onto the scene. Jimmy Somerville (who left the band in early 1985 to form the Communards) has a piercing voice which he can modulate for greater appeal (as on "Junk"); the band plays a powerful and unique breed of techno-dance, with room for such digressions as George and Ira Gershwin's "It Ain't Necessarily So" and Giorgio Moroder-for-Donna Summer's "I Feel Love." Far more blunt and sexy (the cover image and sleeve notes are similarly plain-spoken) than Tom Robinson's old records, the Bronskis are a highly original entity, drawing on a wide

variety of sources to create an invigorating, courageous and memorable album of modern dance music.

Hundreds & Thousands is an album of six lengthy remixes, including the previous LP's "Why," "Smalltown Boy," "Junk" and "Heat Wave." Horns have been added, and all the tunes extended to the six-minute-plus range for maximum nightclubbing pleasure. The cassette and CD have extra tracks.

Replacing Somerville with a far less distinctive singer, Bronski Beat released **Truth Dare and Double Dare**, a peppy collection of adequate tracks that are, unfortunately, lacking a strong vocal identity. [iar]

BRYGADA KRYZYS

Brygada Kryzys (Polish Tonpress) 1982
Brygada Kryzys (Fresh/nr) 1982

This semi-underground (and I don't mean that figuratively) Polish quartet is not exactly in the mainstream of world punk rock, but does play a slightly-toned-down version of high-octane guitar (and sax) raunch that compares favorably to bands from Bauhaus to the Sex Pistols. While not breaking any new creative ground, Brygada Kryzys is a fascinating and credible example of stylistic transliteration from one culture to a rather different one. [iar]

HAROLD BUDD/BRIAN ENO

See *Brian Eno*.

BUGGLES

The Age of Plastic (Island) 1980
Adventures in Modern Recording (Carrere) 1982

After "Video Killed the Radio Star" changed the course of electro-pop forever, it was straight downhill for the Buggles as a group. The two members, however, proved a lot more durable on their own: Geoffrey Downes went on to enormous success with Yes and Asia; Trevor Horn became a hit record producer (for ABC and Malcolm McLaren) before founding ZTT Records and guiding Frankie Goes to Hollywood into the record books.

The Age of Plastic was a disappointment to fans of the Buggles' cogent 45s, while **Adventures** amounted to little more than a self-explanatory post-mortem. Both albums are technically stunning, reasonably catchy and crashingly hollow. [iar]

See also *Art of Noise, Frankie Goes to Hollywood, Bruce Woolley*.

RICHARD JAMES BURGESS

See *Landscape*.

J.J. BURNEL

See *Stranglers*.

KATE BUSH

The Kick Inside (EMI/Harvest) 1978
Lionheart (EMI/EMI America) 1978
On Stage EP (EMI/nr) 1979
Never for Ever (EMI/EMI America) 1980
The Dreaming (EMI/EMI America) 1982
Kate Bush EP (nr/EMI America) 1983

Hounds of Love (EMI/EMI America) 1985

Falling somewhere between Joni Mitchell, Laura Nyro, Peter Gabriel and Laurie Anderson, Kate Bush's literate, masterful, enchanting (if occasionally overbearingly coy and preciously self-indulgent) records have won her enormous popularity in Great Britain. America has never really known what to make of her, although pockets of enthusiastic support do exist. Over the years, she has become increasingly independent and ambitious, turning what might have been a career dominated by others into a singleminded pursuit of her own muse. From the young piano-playing singer on **The Kick Inside**, Bush has bloomed into a fully autonomous artist.

The Kick Inside is dominated by Bush's startling falsetto and such imaginative songs as "Them Heavy People," "Wuthering Heights" and "Kite." Top-notch sessionmen and Andrew Powell's sparkling production provide a rich setting for the songs. The record's huge popularity didn't seem to faze Bush, who returned before the end of the same year with another well-crafted album, **Lionheart**. More subtle, jazz-inflected arrangements keep it less immediate, but the cinema-minded "Hammer Horror" and theatre-minded "Wow," as well as the fondly nationalistic "Oh England My Lionheart," make it memorable.

Bush's next release was a 7-inch EP smartly reproducing four songs from the first two albums in a concert setting. She then arranged and co-produced **Never for Ever**, which yielded three singles ("Babooshka," "Breathing" and "Army Dreamers") and provided further evidence of her compositional depth. Songs about dead rock stars ("Blow Away"), a murder ("The Wedding List"), and a tribute to the "Violin" are among her strangest lyrical concerns. A credit line thanking Richard Burgess and John Walters for "bringing in the Fairlight" gains significance in hindsight, given how integral the sampling device subsequently became to her music-making.

Self-produced, **The Dreaming** offers Bush's first truly rock-oriented work, tinted with strong rhythms and clever Fairlight sounds. Almost free of her little-girl voice, Bush is by this record a highly skilled, controlled singer with abundant drama and personality to draw on. The Peter Gabriel resemblance—in terms of what can be done artfully within the song form—is obvious here; still, it's all Kate Bush and perhaps her first really extraordinary album.

Kate Bush is an American-only mini-album: one track from the live EP plus a pair of cuts from **The Dreaming** and one each from the two preceding LPs.

Hounds of Love is divided into separately titled halves. The "Hounds of Love" side contains one of Bush's most impressive singles, "Running Up That Hill (A Deal with God)," as well as other similarly complex and enticing creations; on the back, "The Ninth Wave" is an overextended side-long contemplation on drowning—impressive, but not really enjoyable. [tr]

BUSH TETRAS

Rituals EP (Fetish/Stiff) 1981

Wild Things [tape] (nr/ROIR) 1983

Arising from the New York post-rock scene, the Bush Tetras attempted a synthesis of African sensibilities (as perceived by white Americans) with the modern dance to form a global tribal music. The 12-inch **Rituals** (produced by then-Clash drummer Topper Headon) sets songs against a funk/reggae beat with horns and punchy guitar work tossed in liberally. "Can't Be Funky" and its doppelganger, "Funky Version," are the most explicitly Third World tunes, while "Cowboys in Africa" rushes along with punk intensity and "Rituals" employs a threnody pace. The **Wild Things** cassette is a concert recording compiled from late 1982 performances in and around New York. The band is in fine, ferocious form, and Cynthia Sley spits and scowls her vocals as if the songs really meant something. The material reprises most of the Tetras' slim recorded repertoire, plus a couple of appropriately savage covers. [sg/iar]

BUTTHOLE SURFERS

Butthole Surfers (Alternative Tentacles) 1983
Live PCPPEP (Alternative Tentacles) 1984
Psychic . . . Powerless . . . Another Man's Sac (Fundamental/Touch and Go) 1985
Cream Corn from the Socket of Davis EP (Pray/Touch and Go) 1985
Rembrandt Pussyhorse (Red Rhino/Touch and Go) 1986

There are few experiences in this life that leave one feeling as sullied as a spin through the grooves of a Butthole Surfers record. Unlike so many nouveau scuzzbos, when the Buttholes descend into the depths of squalor, they don't do so to make a point about the human condition—they just like it down there. Pus-tinged splotches of guitar noise and tortured screams are their bread and butter. When their noise revs up really fast, it sounds almost like hardcore, but this band relies more on filth than speed or power. The Buttholes inflict and exorcise pain like other people eat potato chips, and whatever debts they owe to Flipper and PiL would probably be forgotten if they'd just go away. There's clearly no one like 'em.

The debut mini-LP poses its threat to the social order through a varied thrash-to-Beefheart-blues attack and an inspired/inspiring set of lyrics. "The Shah Sleeps in Lee Harvey's Grave" is the obvious anthem, while on "Suicide" singer Gilley leaves aside political matters for an intensely political statement: "I'm not fucking kidding man, it hurts!" "Hey Hey," on the other hand, is almost subdued, Feelies-style material.

The seven-song **Live PCPPEP** disc offers denser and dirtier treatments of some of the first record's hits. The biggest improvement is the new brother and sister standup drumming team. **Another Man's Sac** shows an addled creative sensibility—you were expecting them to develop into Hall and Oates? The faint-at-heart may not survive this long-playing assault, but then they probably don't deserve to.

Cream Corn is a four-track EP which hauls more sediment and sludge up from the gutter and onto the turntable. Mixing deranged blues with metal-punk and playing both with anarchic sensibility, these looneys don't make guitars scream, they make 'em vomit and choke on it. **Rembrandt Pussyhorse** goes for a gonzo psychedelic approach that is (dare we say it) downright arty in its bizarre sonic experimentation. With some of the bowel-grinding dregs toned down, piano, organ, violin and a plethora of guitar techniques make the album a real diversion. Of special note is a cover of the Guess Who's "American Woman," which, in the Butts' hands, sports a huge drum sound and metallic guitar, with tinny, atonal voices—imagine Nile Rodgers producing the Residents. Love 'em or hate 'em, reactionary times demand more rebels like these. [jl/dgs]

BUZZARDS

Jellied Eels to Record Deals (Chrysalis/nr) 1979

Although the Buzzards (originally the Leyton Buzzards) appeared on the surface to be another London-area group of punk/reggae dilettantes, closer examination revealed them to be a subversive vehicle for satiric songwriters Geoff Deane (vocals) and David Jaymes (bass). Comprising all their recorded output, this seventeen-track retrospective is jammed with lively (if heavy-handed) potshots at everything from Pink Floyd ("No Dry Ice or Flying Pigs") to modern mores ("Disco Romeo") to punk itself ("We Make a Noise"). And be sure not to miss "Saturday Night Beneath the Plastic Palm Trees." The tone throughout is cheerfully abusive; it's appropriate that two Monty Pythoners get thanked on the cover.

Underscoring the band's undiscovered assets, Deane and Jaymes went on to major commercial stardom playing dance music as Modern Romance. [jy]

See also *Modern Romance*.

BUZZCOCKS

Spiral Scratch EP (New Hormones/nr) 1977 & 1981
Another Music in a Different Kitchen (UA/nr) 1977
Love Bites (UA/nr) 1978
Singles Going Steady (Liberty/IRS) 1979
A Different Kind of Tension (UA/IRS) 1980
Parts One, Two, Three EP (nr/IRS) 1984

Inspired by the Sex Pistols, Howard Devoto and Pete Shelley formed the Buzzcocks in Manchester in 1975, specializing in high-energy, staccato delivery of stripped-down pop songs. With John Maher (drums) and Steve Diggle (bass), the Buzzcocks released **Spiral Scratch**, one of the earliest new wave EPs, and a pioneering independent label release. Though ragged and rudimentary, the 7-inch features the frantic, minimalistic pop stylings that would characterize the Buzzcocks and, with songs like "Breakdown" and "Boredom," remains the most exciting version of the band on record.

Devoto departed shortly thereafter to form Magazine, and Steve Garvey joined, taking over bass while Shelley switched to vocals (in addition to guitar) and Diggle to lead guitar. **Another Music in a**

Different Kitchen expands on the stark three-minute pop song and themes of confusion, alienation and betrayal, with a new emphasis on harmony and humor and a growing coordination of the players in contrast to the earlier inspired chaos.

Love Bites demonstrates both the Buzzcocks' perfection of their particular brand of pop and their disillusionment with its restrictions. Producer Martin Rushent clarifies the elements of the sound even further, and Shelley's songwriting reaches its peak, but the strongest numbers—"Ever Fallen in Love" and "Just Lust"—are essentially singles as opposed to album tracks, underscoring a problem that plagued the band.

A Different Kind of Tension makes tentative manoeuvres into the new, as the Buzzcocks attempt to throw off the yoke of pop music. This schizophrenic album features some of Shelley's finest songs, notably "You Say You Don't Love Me" and "I Believe." Diggle provides some of the songwriting, and the band reaches a zenith of effortless craft. The aptly named **Tension** marked the end of the Buzzcocks, with Shelley pursuing a productive and fascinating solo career and the others working in a number of outfits, including the Teardrops and Flag of Convenience.

Singles Going Steady is a compilation of stunning, classic singles, proving conclusively that the Buzzcocks **were** a singles band, and a great one at that. From the teen angst of the Devoto/Shelley "Orgasm Addict" to the 20th century malaise of "Something's Gone Wrong Again," the songs are across-the-board great, and the album comes as close to art as new wave can. **Parts One, Two, Three**—another compilation of sorts—reprises a conceptual sequence of three singles released in 1980: "Are Everything" and "What Do You Know?" are prime; the other four cuts less essential. [sg/iar]

See also *Howard Devoto, Flag of Convenience, Magazine, Pete Shelley, Teardrops.*

DAVID BYRNE AND BRIAN ENO

My Life in the Bush of Ghosts (EG-Polydor/Sire) 1980

DAVID BYRNE

Songs from the Broadway Production of "The Catherine Wheel" (Sire) 1981
Music for The Knee Plays (EMI/ECM) 1985

In the Heads, David Byrne—guitarist, songwriter, singer—has long shown an inquisitive, intelligent interest in unusual applications of pop music. His solo musical work (Byrne also creates in video and film) revolves around transfiguring pop through the infusion of alien elements or by injecting it into foreign situations. **My Life in the Bush of Ghosts**, a continuation of his (and the band's) collaboration with Eno, blends found vocal tapes with electronic music centering around Third World, notably African, rhythms to interesting effect and uneven results.

Byrne created the music on **The Catherine Wheel** for a dance production by the renowned Twyla Tharp. Listeners can get either a selection of tracks on the album, or the complete score on the cassette version. The pace and instrumenation on the more pop material bears a strong resemblance to Talking Heads' work of the **Remain in Light** period, with volatile rhythms and jazz inflections, while other songs are more experimental, drawing heavily on Eno's ambient and tape-editing techniques.

The Knee Plays is music for a portion of an as-yet unproduced Robert Wilson piece.   [sg]

CABARET VOLTAIRE

Extended Play EP (Rough Trade/nr) 1978
"Mix-Up" (Rough Trade/nr) 1979
Voice of America (Rough Trade) 1980
Live at the YMCA 27-10-79 (Rough Trade/nr) 1980
Three Mantras EP (Rough Trade/nr) 1980
1974—1976 tape (Industrial/nr) 1980
3 Crepuscule Tracks (Rough Trade) 1981
Red Mecca (Rough Trade) 1981
Live at the Lyceum [tape] (Rough Trade/nr) 1981
2 X 45 (Rough Trade/nr) 1982
Hai! Live in Japan (Rough Trade) 1982
The Crackdown (Some Bizzare-Virgin/nr) 1983
Johnny YesNo (Doublevision/nr) 1983
Micro-Phonies (Some Bizzare-Virgin/nr) 1984
Drinking Gasoline (Some Bizzare-Virgin/Caroline) 1985
The Arm of the Lord (Some Bizzare-Virgin/Caroline) 1985

PRESSURE COMPANY

Live in Sheffield 19 Jan 82 (Paradox/nr) 1982

RICHARD H. KIRK

Disposable Half-Truths [tape] (Industrial/nr) 1980
Time High Fiction (Doublevision/nr) 1984

STEPHEN MALLINDER

Pow-Wow EP (Fetish/nr) 1982
Pow-Wow Plus EP (Doublevision/nr) 1985

With the exception of Throbbing Gristle the most prolific group to emerge via the new wave, Cabaret Voltaire is also one of the most energetic, progressive and dissonant. Working primarily in the electronic form, specializing in found sounds and tape manipulations, Cabaret Voltaire has relentlessly pushed at the outer edges of music, shedding an early primitivism for a subsequent accessibility that plays on the (almost) familiar. Coming from the industrial city of Sheffield, they have spent years attempting to make a music that reflects their experience and perceptions.

Extended Play virtually launched both Cabaret Voltaire and the Rough Trade label (it was the label's third single) and highlights the Cabs' main features: unpredictable sounds and eerie, disembodied vocals manipulated over a very physical beat. It is particularly notable for a distorted cover version of Lou Reed's "Here She Comes Now."

More professionally produced, **"Mix-Up"** shows more coordinated use of electronics, increasing the bizarre intensity of the sound. Bass, guitar and flute are evident (but deformed) in the mix, and Cabaret Voltaire makes visible use of other people's material, as with the Seeds' "No Escape."

Live at the YMCA (as well as the later **Live at the Lyceum** tape) dispels any notions of Cabaret Voltaire as a sterile studio group. Wisely, they don't seek to precisely duplicate their recorded sound, but convert it into outré-populist dance music that is almost improvisational in nature. Though the live recordings are more fragmented than their studio counterparts, they

compensate for that in energy.

Three Mantras is Cabaret Voltaire's first explicit venture into non-Western musical forms. The Arabic material used is successfully developed into a chant, and then its structure is applied to a new work. It also features a shift in Cabaret Voltaire's technique, with musical demands taking precedence over production, to strange and beautiful effect.

Voice of America is an uneven release, combining older material with much more assured newer work, such as the political "The Voice of America/Damage Is Done," which uses found tape and sparse electronics to juxtapose the repressive and libertarian aspects of American life. The new material shows much greater focus and cleaner production than the older, with the mantra technique rising in place of the former chaotic electro-noise.

For completists and/or fanatics, **1974—1976** is a series of curious and intriguing false starts and experiments from the band's earliest days.

3 Crépuscule Tracks shows the band in transition between their found-vocals/art-noise period and a commitment to dance-floor electronics. "Sluggin' fer Jesus (Part One)" is a masterful combination of the two, as a right-wing TV preacher demands large cash contributions over a powerful, trance-inducing synth beat.

On **Red Mecca**, Cabaret Voltaire tightens the focus to produce an album more coherent than its predecessors, underscored by a reworking of Henry Mancini's score for Orson Welles' **Touch of Evil.** As their music reaches a new level of maturity and polish in both production and performance, Cabaret Voltaire focus and extend their film noir theme through all the material, making this an odd, deceptively accessible record.

Two 12-inch EPs packaged as an album, **2 X 45** picks up the trends begun on **Red Mecca** and compresses them into a new form. Also interesting is the move away from obvious electronics and manipulations to a more naturalistic sound, with emphasis on acoustic instruments like saxophone and clarinet. This is the closest the group has come to making a rock'n'roll album.

Like earlier live albums, **Hai! Live in Japan** marks time, playing with the band's recent development, funky in nature and far more coherent than **Live in Sheffield.** The latter was a one-off show to raise funds for the Polish Solidarity union, and was released under the Pressure Company name for contractual reasons. Disordered and trenchant, it is a reminder that the band is still capable of electrifying cacophony.

In 1983, Cabaret Voltaire signed with that noted asylum for eccentrics, Some Bizzare (here in consort with Virgin), a move criticized by some as a sell-out. The resulting LP, **The Crackdown,** is perhaps the most left-field record ever accused of commercial compromise. Sticking mostly to a funk format, the songs are more structured than those on **2 X 45,** and the band displays a plethora of high-tech but dark electronic textures. Probably the strongest of their many albums.

Johnny YesNo is a soundtrack to Peter Care's film about a junkie. Released on the band's own Doublevision label, it was recorded in 1981, prior to co-founder Chris Watson's departure. Like most soundtracks, it's not designed for careful listening, consisting primarily of eerie electronic noodling. **Micro-Phonies** is similar to **The Crackdown**, except the sound is a bit sparser and decidedly more rhythm-conscious. Much of the material would be very much at home coming from a beat-box, particularly "Sensoria" and "James Brown," the 12-inch remixes of which are both highly recommended.

Drinking Gasoline is a double 12-inch (running over 30 minutes) recorded primarily as a video soundtrack. The four numbers are entirely interchangeable, the sort of hard electro-funk found on previous LPs. Fans will enjoy it, but the Cabs seem stuck in a rut, an unsurprising problem after so many releases. **The Arm of the Lord** proves that no band could be so productive without a few tricks up its sleeve. Titled after an American neo-Nazi religious zealot organization, the record crossbreeds trademark electro-rhythm attack with odd breaks, varied tempos, the return of eerie found voices, unpolished production and harsh dissonances. "I Want You" and "Motion Rotation" actually have catchy melodies—a first for the band! In early '86, Cabaret Voltaire suddenly and angrily left Some Bizzare, announcing they would release their own records in the future.

The two remaining members of Cab Volt maintain low individual profiles, but have each done solo work, especially interesting for providing identification of who brings what to the band. Stephen Mallinder's **Pow-Wow** mini-album is dominated by muscular bass and drum combinations, tapes and his husky voice. On his own, he seems to prefer electronically treated acoustic instruments rather than synthesizers. **Pow-Wow Plus** repackages that record with the addition of 1981's "Temperature Drop" single. Richard Kirk's **Time High Fiction** is a one-man double album recorded over a three-year period; it's richer in texture (mostly electronic) and less rhythmic than his partner's work. The two-side-long "Dead Relatives" is even more dissonant than anything the two have done together.   [sg/dgs]

JOHN CALE

Fear (Island) 1974
Slow Dazzle (Island) 1975
Helen of Troy (Island/nr) 1975
Animal Justice EP (Illegal/nr) 1977
Guts (Island) 1977
Sabotage/Live (Spy) 1979
Honi Soit (A&M) 1981
Music for a New Society (ZE-Island/ZE-Passport) 1982
Caribbean Sunset (ZE-Island) 1984
John Cale Comes Alive (ZE-Island) 1984
Artificial Intelligence (Beggars Banquet/Beggars Banquet-PVC) 1985

KEVIN AYERS/JOHN CALE/ENO/NICO

June 1, 1974 (Island) 1974

John Cale's musical career since leaving the Velvet Underground—after two albums on which his viola-scraping and genuine musical training played a pivotal role—has been diverse and unpredictable, exploring both classical/avant-garde "serious" music as well as more shoot-from-the-hip rough rock. Throughout, the inscrutable Welshman has surrounded himself with able and distinguished cohorts, and has produced some music of real challenge and quality.

His first solo efforts after the Velvets were effectively collaborations: **Vintage Violence**, with low-key backing by a New York rock group, Grinderswitch; **Church of Anthrax**, with avant-garde titan Terry Riley; **Academy in Peril**, with the Royal Philharmonic Orchestra. Also in much the same vein, Cale made **Paris 1919** with backing by members of Little Feat. It wasn't until he signed to Island that his music became weird and abrasive, signifying a partial return to the chaos of his Velvet days.

His first such release was as a member of the **June 1, 1974** project, a one-off concert documented on an LP and featuring Kevin Ayers, Brian Eno and Nico as well as Cale, Robert Wyatt and others. It's a wonderful album, with Cale taking a vocal on "Heartbreak Hotel" and elsewhere contributing viola and piano.

Cale emerged into pre-new wave weirdness with **Fear**, an aggressively wild record made with assistance from the likes of Eno and Roxy Musician Phil Manzanera. Clean production only heightens the anxiety inherent in Cale's voice and created by the skittering, modified guitar sounds. "Fear Is a Man's Best Friend" and "Gun" build a claustrophobically intense aura; quieter efforts like "Ship of Fools" only slightly diminish the queasiness level. A brilliant record full of neat surprises and great, unsettling songs.

Slow Dazzle adds Chris Spedding to the lineup and pursues some curious pathways: "Heartbreak Hotel," recast as a haunted-house dirge; "Mr. Wilson," an homage to the Beach Boys' Brian; "The Jeweller," a recitation reminiscent of the Velvets' "The Gift." More restrained, but no less entrancing than **Fear**.

Helen of Troy, featuring Phil Collins as well as Spedding and Eno (but not Manzanera), is a gripping, morbid collection of songs, including Jonathan Richman's "Pablo Picasso," powered by Cale's commanding vocals and whining slide guitars, and "Leaving It All Up to You" which has a reference to Sharon Tate that caused it to be removed from the album when first issued; it was subsequently replaced. A dark and pained album.

The **Animal Justice EP**—three cuts on a 12-inch disc—features what remained of a touring band after half had quit in protest of a legendary onstage chicken-chopping incident. The EP's leadoff track ("Chicken Shit") concerns that brouhaha; the other songs are a pointless version of Chuck Berry's "Memphis" and a stunning Cale original, "Hedda Gabler." **Guts** is an excellent collection of tracks from the three preceding LPs and is very highly recommended.

Sabotage, recorded onstage at New York's CBGB in June 1979, presents almost all new material. The sound's just passable, and the album never jells. **Honi Soit** used an outside producer (Mike Thorne) for a change and a totally new band as well; some tracks are good, but it's not on a par with Cale's best. With **Music for a New Society**, Cale retreated from nakedly aggressive music and turned to a more orchestrated style that owes something to his early pre-punk efforts, like **Paris 1919**. Cale's lyrics, however, have rarely been as grim or violent as they are here. The arrangements prominently feature keyboards and the music effectively matches the darkly moody subject matter.

Caribbean Sunset is Cale's least interesting album to date. Even if his puzzlingly muddy self-production hadn't stifled everything but his jagged-edged vocals, the songs themselves are too flimsy to support his words or passion.

Perhaps realizing this, Cale released **Caribbean Sunset** back-to-back with another LP showcasing his in-concert strengths with the same band. Though he self-defeatingly begins **and** ends **Comes Alive** with half-assed studio efforts, the disappointment ends there and the virtuosity begins. Forming the live core of the album are gripping versions of vintage material like "Fear" and "Leaving It All Up to You"; a death-rattling "Heartbreak Hotel" performed solo at the electric piano; a bouncily tongue-in-cheek "Waiting for the Man" as a tip of the hat to Lou Reed, now that he can be taken seriously again; and a couple of **Sabotage Live** songs minus the overly metallic sound that made them almost unlistenable on that LP. Cale should record _all_ his material this way: live and with a solid band.

Artificial Intelligence has the solid band, a trio of James Young, Graham Dowdall and David Young. It also has Cale co-writing lyrics with journalist Ratso Sloman, whose Dylan fixation comes through clearly on the articulately verbose "Everytime the Dogs Bark" and other songs. Elsewhere, a mild island lilt suggests a well-read Jimmy Buffett. Moody and contained, but energetic and occasionally stimulating, **A.I.** is a reasonable if unspectacular addition to Cale's extensive catalogue.   [iar/mf]

CALL

The Call (Mercury) 1982
Modern Romans (Mercury) 1983
Scene Beyond Dreams (Mercury) 1984
Reconciled (Elektra) 1986

A dark fascination with the effect of politics on both a personal and world level preoccupies Call leader-singer-guitarist-bassist-producer Michael Been. The California band's Anglofied music, with the Band's Garth Hudson guesting on the first three LPs (Robbie Robertson took over that chore on **Reconciled**), evokes the mainstream guitar sounds of Dire Straits or the Rumour—compelling and occasionally ominous. But the instruments on the promising debut take a backseat to Been's eventually overbearing lyrical concerns; if his songs were not delivered from atop a soapbox, their impact might be far greater.

Modern Romans contains the Call's only great song—"The Walls Came Down"—as well as a reasonably clever cover design. Otherwise it's a pretty tiresome didactic exercise. **Scene Beyond Dreams** is more of the same with fleeting moments of entertainment (like the title song) hiding amidst items like "The Burden" and "Heavy Hand." (Hey, maybe this guy isn't so nearsighted about his work after all . . .)

Reconciled has more optimistic song titles, plus guest vocals by Jim Kerr and Peter Gabriel. Unfortunately, it still has Been's overweening emotionalism and pompous self-importance. Just how much angst should one invest in a line like, "I look for you everywhere I go"? What a bore.   [wk/iar]

CAN

Monster Movie (UA/nr) 1969
Soundtracks (UA/nr) 1970
Tago Mago (UA/nr) 1971
Ege Bamyasi (UA) 1972
Future Days (UA) 1973
Limited Edition (UA/nr) 1974
Soon Over Babaluma (UA) 1974
Landed (Virgin/nr) 1975
Unlimited Edition (Caroline/nr) 1976
Flow Motion (Virgin/nr) 1976
Opener (Sunset/nr) 1976
Saw Delight (Virgin/Harvest) 1977
Out of Reach (Lightning/Peters Int'l) 1978
Cannibalism (UA/nr) 1978
Can (Laser/nr) 1979
Incandescence (Virgin/nr) 1981
Delay 1968 (Ger. Spoon) 1982
Prehistoric Future—June, 1968 [tape] (Fr. Tago Mago) 1984

HOLGER CZUKAY

Movies (EMI/nr) 1980
On the Way to the Peak of Normal (EMI/nr) 1982
Der Osten Ist Rot (Virgin/nr) 1984

HOLGER CZUKAY/ROLF DAMMERS

is (Ger. Spoon) 1982

IRMIN SCHMIDT

Canaxis Filmmusik Vol. II (Ger. Spoon) 1982

A German group that arose during the psychedelic movement of 1968 from jazz, avant-garde and rock sources, Can (essentially Holger Czukay, Irmin Schmidt, Jaki Liebezeit, Michael Karoli) developed (and perfected) electronic collage in rock music and actively absorbed a number of musical traditions into their eclectic work. In addition to providing an example of individualistic behavior remote from commercial music, Can's output influenced a number of more modern figures, including Pete Shelley and John Lydon, while Can's Holger Czukay has worked with musicians as disparate as Eurythmics and Jah Wobble.

Monster Movie and **Soundtracks** are interesting but forgettable excursions into psychedelia, the latter compiling actual film work the band had done, but **Tago Mago** features a full-blown burst into electronic collage and tape effects, continued on **Ege Bamyasi**, which has reverberations in music as late as Public Image's **Metal Box**. These new techniques are pared down and subdued in the minimalistic **Future Days** and **Soon Over Babaluma**, but make a reappearance in superior form on the darkly perverse **Landed**.

Limited Edition, meanwhile,

exposed Can's fascination with non-Western musics by unveiling several pieces in the Ethnological Forgery Series, more of which appear on **Unlimited Edition**, **Flow Motion** and **Can**. The inclusion of Rosko Gee and Reebop Kwaku Baah in the group gave a Jamaican voodoo flair to **Saw Delight** that prefigured the reggae absorption of the Clash, the Police and other groups.

Relative popular success with "I Want More" from **Flow Motion** strained the group to the point where they opted to break up, but Holger Czukay continues his tape collage experiments on the excellent **Movies** and **On the Way to the Peak of Normal**, the latter with Jah Wobble guesting. Similarly, **Der Osten Ist Rot** ("The East Is Red"), with Liebezeit and Conny Plank helping out, takes a lighthearted and often amusing tack, splicing found tapes to fairly straightforward songs that run the gamut from cabaret crooning to demented instrumentals. A wonderfully foolish excursion with serious undercurrents of political satire.

Opener and **Cannibalism** both anthologize work from 1968 to 1973, with the latter featuring several songs in re-edited versions. **Delay 1968** features heretofore unreleased work by the original group—including highly inappropriate singer Malcolm Mooney—from 1968/69. **Incandescence** (enough with the corny puns already!) is also a compilation.

Canaxis—dating from 1969 (when it was released in a tiny private pressing) consists of two long pieces of environmental mood music incorporating various ethnic components. Schmidt's album contains excerpts from his music for films; on the whole, inobtrusive audio wallpaper.   [sg/iar]
See also *Jah Wobble*.

CAPTAIN BEEFHEART AND THE MAGIC BAND

Safe as Milk (Pye/Kama Sutra) 1965 (nr/Buddah) 1970
Dropout Boogie (Buddah/nr) 1967
Strictly Personal (Liberty/Blue Thumb) 1968 (UA/nr) 1969 (Sunset/nr) 1970
Trout Mask Replica (Straight) 1969 (Reprise) 1970
Lick My Decals Off Baby (Straight) 1970 (Reprise) 1970
Mirror Man (Buddah) 1971 & 1974
The Spotlight Kid (Reprise) 1972
Clear Spot (Reprise) 1972
Unconditionally Guaranteed (Virgin/Mercury) 1974
Bluejeans and Moonbeams (Virgin/Mercury) 1974
The Captain Beefheart File (Pye/nr) 1977
Shiny Beast (Bat Chain Puller) (Virgin/Warner Bros.) 1978
Doc at the Radar Station (Virgin) 1980
Ice Cream for Crow (Virgin/Virgin-Epic) 1982
Top Secret (nr/Accord) 1982
The Legendary A&M Sessions EP (A&M) 1984

CAPTAIN BEEFHEART WITH FRANK ZAPPA AND THE MOTHERS

Bongo Fury (Discreet) 1975

Possessor of a five-octave vocal range, fluent on saxophone and harmonica, intuitively musical enough to compose for, play (after a fashion) and even teach other instruments so as to enable sidemen to function in his rarefied musical world, Captain Beefheart (alias Don Van Vliet) is one of rock's genuine geniuses. He's also an accomplished poet, sculptor and painter. Starting with a mixture of blues and rock, Beefheart has dismembered and reassembled rhythms, song structure, harmony and tonality, adding in quantities of free jazz—all without getting academic, flashy or self-consciously pompous about it.

Beefheart's awesome yet idiosyncratic (as well as groundbreaking) talent has deeply influenced bands like Devo, Pere Ubu, the Residents, Public Image and others, each in a different way. Bridging the worlds of free-form jazz and modern rock, Beefheart has demolished conventions and paved the way for much of rock's recent adventurousness.

After winning a two-single record contract with A&M as the grand prize in a Vox battle of the bands, Californian Captain Beefheart produced a regional hit with his version of "Diddy Wah Diddy"—but the company turned down his album demos as too unsettling. (Nearly 20 years later those two singles were reissued, along with a theretofore unreleased track from the period, as **The Legendary A&M Sessions**. **Top Secret** also compiles early, bluesy tracks.) Another label gave him a shot, and **Safe as Milk** (also known in the UK as **Dropout Boogie**) emerged to redefine what white boys could do with the blues. This wasn't "good" enough, either (although much later Buddah would release **Mirror Man**, an album consisting of four extended live semi-jams that show just how far ahead of his time the Captain was, even in 1965), and the label simply dropped him. Another recording deal arose and Beefheart came up with **Strictly Personal**, adding a healthy dose of free jazz to the musical stew.

Frank Zappa—Beefheart's old friend, long-time admirer and former bandmate—had wrangled a custom label deal with Warner/Reprise, and provided the Captain's next recording opportunity, with no artistic restrictions. Beefheart took the occasion to recruit two new musicians and cut what is generally agreed to be his first masterpiece, **Trout Mask Replica**. The two records allowed him to expand his creative horizons on vinyl as never before, and his musical experimentation (minimalist rock and free jazz) and lyric-writing blossomed. **Lick My Decals Off Baby** further consolidated these artistic gains though, like **Trout Mask Replica**, it was a commercial bust.

The Spotlight Kid reverted to a simpler, bluesier sound akin to **Safe as Milk**, albeit considerably enriched by the exploration Beefheart had done since 1965. Further changes and commercial pressures resulted in some of **Clear Spot's** harder rock (and an excellent though uncharacteristic Memphis soul-type number).

Beefheart's next two LPs—the second allegedly consisting mostly of outtakes from the first—are simplified to the point of occasional inanity. Though gaining him some new European fans, this pair partially alienated his old following.

With a new band that included ex-Mothers trombonist Bruce Fowler, Beefheart came up with **Shiny Beast**—a progression from **Decals**, as if the intervening albums had never happened. The words are more direct than on **Decals** and the music more orchestral and much smoother—even a bit *too* smooth—yet it stands as one of Beefheart's best. He proceeded to top himself with **Doc at the Radar Station**; a minor shift in lineup had toughened the band, and the LP combined Beefheart's cumulative musical refinement with a touch of **Clear Spot's** hard-nosed attack.

How can Beefheart keep getting better? **Ice Cream for Crow** represents the current height of the most definite, sustained upward creative curve of his career. This despite (because of?) the lineup almost completely turning over soon after **Doc's** recording. **Ice Cream for Crow** is Beefheart at his most distinctively and beautifully melodic, and most frightening ("The Thousandth and Tenth Day of the Human Totem Pole")—even most danceable, thanks to the rock-a-boogiesque title track.

As music progresses further into and past the outer reaches of convention, Captain Beefheart's trailblazing efforts seem ever more important and impressive.   [jg]
See also *Robert Williams*.

CAPTAIN SENSIBLE

Women and Captains First (A&M/nr) 1982
The Power of Love (A&M/nr) 1983
A Day in the Life of . . . Captain Sensible (nr/A&M) 1984
One Christmas Catalogue EP (A&M/nr) 1984
Sensible Singles (A&M/nr) 1984

When he's not playing guitar and keyboards in the Damned, this good Captain (Ray Burns to his parents) makes lighthearted hit records with producer Tony Mansfield. His two best weird'n'wonderful chart-toppers— the joke-rapping "Wot" and "Happy Talk" (from the musical *South Pacific*, no less)—are included on **Women and Captains First** alongside other equally ridiculous concepts, ranging from country-western to cabaret. Aided and abetted by such divergent talents as Robyn Hitchcock and female vocal trio Dolly Mixture, Sensible's homely singing is invariably ingratiating (if not always on key).

His second English album, **The Power of Love** is less varied and novelty-filled, but nonetheless contains a few subtler gems: "It's Hard to Believe I'm Not" and "Secrets," both co-written with Hitchcock; as well as "Stop the World" and "The Power of Love," all distinguished by Sensible's engaging wideboy vocals and silly/serious lyrics.

In a vain attempt to introduce Sensible to America, **A Day in the Life** compiles tracks from both English albums (plus a previously non-LP single) and has most of what you would want to hear by the lad. But you should also be aware of the seasonal EP, **One Christmas Catalogue**, which came complete with a plastic Santa beard and, amidst three great originals, Sensible's puzzling *nearly* straight version of "Relax." And for completists, there's **Sensible Singles**, a thirteen-cut collection that largely overlaps the albums.   [iar]

BELINDA CARLISLE

Belinda (IRS) 1986

Following the Go-Go's' breakup, Belinda Carlisle stuck with guitarist Charlotte Caffey and recorded this mixed-up album, whose stylish cover shows the glamorized singer striking a stylish Cyd Charisse/Ann-Margret pose. Inside, however, the mock-girl groupisms, misbegotten Motown take-offs and lush quasi-Ronstadt rock are easy on the ears, but never convincing or compelling. Carlisle's voice was never the Go-Go's' strongest feature; her skills have improved over the years, but she still isn't a very interesting vocalist. Dull material and unimaginative production adds little to this bid for acceptance as an adult artist.   [iar]

CARMEL

The Drum Is Everything (London/Warner Bros.) 1984

Brassy belter Carmel McCourt and her two-man band (drummer Gerry Darby and stand-up bassist Jimmy Paris) plus various organists, singers, drummers and hornmen make **The Drum Is Everything** (produced by Mike Thorne) a joyous and raucous outing that has a bit in common with nouveau jazzpop crooners like Sade, but is far more adventurous and ambitious in scope. "More, More, More" and "Willow Weep for Me" are inspiring, near-gospel outbursts of enthusiasm; "Tracks of My Tears" (no, not that one) and "Stormy Weather" (yes, that one) show a bluesier, more reserved side that isn't as appealing in this setting. Carmel doesn't modulate all that well—for her, singing is a full-blooded pastime with no room for pussyfooting—and tends to overpower the more subtly played songs.   [iar]

CARPETTES

Cream of the Youth EP (Small Wonder/nr) 1978
Frustration Paradise (Beggars Banquet/nr) 1979
Fight Amongst Yourselves (Beggars Banquet/nr) 1980

This trio may have personified modest, no-frills rock'n'roll, almost singlehandedly defining the area just above mediocrity. The competent Carpettes were new wave by association, and by the goodly speed of their tempos, notwithstanding an occasional foray into reggae territory. In fact, the closest musical analogue is probably early Kiss, with brighter tunes replacing the show-biz snarl, and without the dumb macho/sleazoid pose.

Following a ragged 7-inch EP, the Carpettes made two albums in the same style, despite very different producers—Bob Sargeant (the Beat, early Fall, Haircut One Hundred) and Colin Thurston (Duran Duran, Thompson Twins, Magazine). Sargeant's **Paradise** has the edge for containing more of those songs you'll be surprised to find yourself remembering.   [jg]

PAUL CARRACK

Nightbird (Vertigo/nr) 1980
Suburban Voodoo (Epic) 1982

. . . or the story of how a man belatedly found himself through the auspices of the musical changes that disenfranchised him.

28

Carrack was the lead-singing keyboardist in Ace, a rootsy pub-rock outfit that hadn't the faintest idea what to do when Carrack's "How Long" became a worldwide hit, and they proved same with three boring albums of near-filler-quality tracks. Carrack later surfaced with **Nightbird**, an all-too-pat solo LP, but got his next grab at the ring by joining Squeeze as Jools Holland's replacement. Carrack appeared on only one of that group's LPs, taking lead vocal on "Tempted," one of their most popular numbers.

After a short spell in Carlene Carter's backing band, Carrack and Nick Lowe formed Noise to Go, a Rockpilish arrangement in which the two alternate top billing. As a result, **Suburban Voodoo** sounds like a souled-up version of **Nick the Knife** (not to mention that much of the material was written with Lowe and his then-missus, Carlene). It's also why Carrack has found a niche in rock'n'roll; his Lowe point is also his high point, surrounding a fine voice with the kind of pop smarts and snap that brings out its best.

[jg]

JOE "KING" CARRASCO AND EL MOLINO

Joe "King" Carrasco and El Molino (Chiswick/Lisa) 1978

JOE "KING" CARRASCO AND THE CROWNS

Joe "King" Carrasco and the Crowns (Stiff/Hannibal) 1980
Party Safari EP (Hannibal) 1981
Synapse Gap (Mundo Total) (MCA) 1982
Party Weekend (MCA) 1983
Tales from the Crypt [tape] (nr/ROIR) 1984
Bordertown (Big Beat/nr) 1984
Viva San Antone EP (Big Beat/nr) 1985

Joe "King" Carrasco grew up in Texas under the spell of Tex-Mex border music. El Molino, his first band, straddled this tradition (with horns and marimba) and rock (with Doug Sahm's keyboard player, Augie Meyers, and songs like "Rock Esta Noche"). El Molino's only album is pleasant enough, but sounds pale compared to what followed.

Whether influenced by new wave or reverting to more adolescent taste, Carrasco traded in El Molino for the Crowns. This no-nonsense backing trio, dominated by Kris Cummings' cheesy organ, is built for speed. The Crowns' debut album touches on rockabilly ("One More Time"), polka ("Federales") and border influences ("Buena," "Caca de Vaca"). Their forte, though, is performing "96 Tears" under a variety of thin guises, all of them delightful ("Let's Get Pretty," "Betty's World," you name it). The tempos are revved-up punk, the feeling, Southwestern *mestizo*. (The Stiff LP has two numbers not on the American album, but Hannibal's release has three songs not on the English version, and a funnier cover as well.)

Party Safari is a four-song EP further displaying Carrasco's cultural dementia; the Crowns' next album, **Synapse Gap**, finds them only slightly more subdued. Besides re-recording two of **Party Safari's** songs, Carrasco dabbles in reggae rhythms and somehow got Michael Jackson (!) to sing along on "Don't

Let a Woman (Make a Fool Out of You)."

In a last-ditch effort to sell out (well, to sell a few records at least), Carrasco made **Party Weekend**, a non-stop heap o' fun. Richard Gottehrer produced it, and tunes like "Let's Go" and "Burnin' It Down" (not to mention a spiffy reprise of "Buena") perfectly crystallize all of the group's strengths. Murderously infectious and upbeat—attitudinally the Southwest's answer to the Ramones—**Party Weekend** seemed perfectly designed to introduce the world to Carrasco's abundant talent and charm. But it didn't take off, and so Carrasco unceremoniously returned from his safari in the majors.

Carrasco's next release was the tape-only **Tales from the Crypt**, a marvelous set of demos from 1979 with embryonic (read raw and exciting) versions of many of Carrasco's best tunes, from "Let's Get Pretty" to "Caca de Vaca" to "Federales." Although not intended as such, it's an ideal introduction to a world of boundless spirit and infectious fun.

By **Bordertown**, Carrasco's act is getting kind of, er, familiar: too many of the songs employ not only the same chords and melody, but a lot of 'em stick to the same Spanglicized rhyming patterns. Adding to the fatigue is a new-found political sensibility, yielding well-intentioned mistakes like "Who Buys the Guns" and "Current Events (Are Making Sense)." If you haven't been following the Carrasco saga for long, **Bordertown** is as good as any of his prior records; however, those with a Carrasco collection will likely live happier without owning this one.

[si/iar]

CARS

The Cars (Elektra) 1978
Candy-O (Elektra) 1979
Panorama (Elektra) 1980
Shake It Up (Elektra) 1981
Heartbeat City (Elektra) 1984
Greatest Hits (Elektra) 1985

RIC OCASEK

Beatitude (Geffen) 1982

GREG HAWKES

Niagara Falls (Passport) 1983

ELLIOT EASTON

Change No Change (Elektra) 1985

For an example of shifting perceptions, consider the Cars. When their debut LP appeared in 1978, the Boston-based quintet was tagged as a prime commercial *and* critical prospect of the emerging post-punk phenomenon called new wave. In other words, they were cool and potentially popular. Then, presto! Upon release of an album, the Cars became an immediate smash and entered the ranks of platinum-sellers, where they remain today. Quickly, they lost all artistic credibility among critics despite the fact that they've been remarkably consistent on disc.

The Cars have changed little since that first record established the ground rules. On their debut, singer/songwriter Ric Ocasek pursues the trail of ironic, sometimes wistful romanticism blazed by David Bowie and especially Bryan Ferry.

"Good Times Roll," "My Best Friend's Girl" and other tunes contradict blithe surfaces with nervous undercurrents. As sparely produced by Roy Thomas Baker, virtually interchangeable lead singers Ocasek and bassist Ben Orr ride a slick, pulsing current generated by Elliot Easton's skittish guitar, Greg Hawkes' poised synths and ex-Modern Lover David Robinson's booming drums. Here, and on subsequent albums, the alluring glibness serves as a gateway to underlying emotional anguish.

Candy-O's main flaw is that it offers the same accomplished style. Emotions are more directly expressed on the title track and the frankly sentimental "It's All I Can Do," but the polish remains. "Let's Go" and "Dangerous Type" express a muted ambivalence that allows the Cars to continue pleasing superficial listeners. **Panorama** tampers with the formula slightly, though not enough to jeopardize the band's enormous popularity. Many tunes are murkier and less immediate, giving greater play to the creeping desperation that permeates Ocasek's writing. More unsettling, though still highly listenable.

Shake It Up is the Cars' lightest album so far. The title track comes the closest they've gotten to a conventional good-time tune, and others are less haunting than you might like Ocasek's songs to be. Highlight: the feverish, blatantly Roxyesque "This Could Be Love."

After dallying as a solo artist with middling results, Ocasek reconvened the Cars for **Heartbeat City**, a more substantial LP than **Shake It Up** and the band's most commercially potent record to date. The disc produced no less than three major hits: the dreamy "Drive," the ebullient "You Might Think" and "Magic," which might best be described as the Cars meet the Electric Light Orchestra. The album's lyrics are Ocasek's usual neurotic doodlings, though he shows more compassion for his "lost generation" characters than before.

For his solo album, Ocasek enlisted Cars keyboardist Greg Hawkes, handpicked musicians from various semi-underground bands (Bad Brains, New Models, Ministry, Dark, Reflectors) and created a moody collection of stimulating but only semi-commercial new songs. Because of Ocasek's dominant role within the Cars, **Beatitude** bears an unavoidable resemblance to the group's sound, but the prevalence of synthesizer over guitar and an avoidance of the choppy, driving rhythms that characterize the Cars' music make it different enough. While several Cars tracks have worked similar languid terrain ("Since You're Gone" on **Shake It Up** and "You Wear Those Eyes" on **Panorama** are two), Ocasek's solo approach is subtler and texturally richer; his lyrics here are also exemplary. Best track: "jimmy jimmy," a sympathetic portrait of a troubled teen.

Niagara Falls, keyboardist Hawkes' solo outing, confirms his role in shaping the Cars' instrumental sound, but it's mighty dull fare all the same. Take away the band's lyrics, vocals and tension and you get this sort of muzak. Easton's solo shot, **Change No Change**, is a minor work to be sure, but a surprisingly

good record nonetheless. A more immediate and electric record than the band would dare to make, it contains some pithy harmonies, some snarling boogie and even a Costello soundalike. Irrepressible Jules Shear co-wrote all the tunes.

[jy/iar]

CASINO MUSIC

Jungle Love (ZE-Island/nr) 1979

Blondie's Chris Stein produced this French quartet's album in New York; Island Records chief Chris Blackwell mixed the tapes in the Bahamas and released the LP in England—all for no audible reason. While the cool ambience of relaxed disco (complete with a female vocal trio and Cristina guesting on one track) may be soothing to tired dancers, the music is too bland to avoid instant forgettability, notwithstanding the suave French vocals. [iar]

NICK CAVE

From Her to Eternity (Mute/nr) 1984
The Firstborn Is Dead (Mute/Homestead) 1985
Tupelo EP (nr/Homestead) 1985

Following the Birthday Party's self-destruction, singer/lyricist Nick Cave formed the Bad Seeds as a new vehicle for his foreboding visions of love and death. As well as his passionate bellowing fit in with his former mates' wall of noise, **From Her to Eternity** sounds like the record he always wanted to make. The Bad Seeds—an all-star unit including ex-Magazine bassist Barry Adamson, ex-Birthday Party drummer Mick Harvey and guitarist Blixa Bargeld on loan from Einstürzende Neubauten— provide a sparse twisted blues setting that gives Cave plenty of room for his vocal pyrotechnics. The guitars are bizarre but subdued, bass and drums slow and deliberate; rudimentary piano fills the gaps. While the album relies less on shock effects than any the Birthday Party ever made, the explosive parts are resultingly much more effective, and the title track, "A Box for Black Paul" and a chilling rendition of Leonard Cohen's "Avalanche" stand up to anything Cave did with the Birthday Party. (A contemporaneous single not included here of "In the Ghetto" is also highly recommended.)

Cave's follow-up, **The Firstborn Is Dead**, takes his fixations with the blues and Elvis Presley one step further, this time with somewhat mixed results. A resident of London and Berlin, the Melbourne native leaves himself open to accusations of romanticizing a culture he's never known, but this doesn't sound like a man singing out of ignorance. Slow moving and perhaps as self-indulgent as it is heartfelt, **The Firstborn** is a mature work which may at first disappoint those awaiting another "Big-Jesus-Trash-Can," but the patient listener will find Cave's emotional range intact, albeit in a subtler setting. The American EP takes the album's opening track as its title and adds "In the Ghetto," "The Moon Is in the Gutter" and a drastically different version of the old Birthday Party live staple, "The Six Strings That Drew Blood."

Nick Cave is a unique artist who figures to be in the forefront of rock's fringe for some time to come.

[dgs]

See also *die Haut, Lydia Lunch.*

CELIBATE RIFLES

Quintessentially Yours (What Goes On) 1985

This excellent garage-punk outfit from Sydney has released several records in Australia since forming in 1982; this Anglo-American compilation distills their work into a red-hot onslaught of sharp-edged guitar rock'n'roll. "Let's Get Married" may not be your typical punk sentiment, but is indicative of the Celibate Rifles' avoidance of clichés.   [iar]

EXENE CERVENKA

See *X*.

EUGENE CHADBOURNE

There'll Be No Tears Tonight (nr/Parachute) 1980
The President: He Is Insane (nr/Iridescence) 1985
Country Music of Southeastern Australia (nr/RRRecords) 1986
Country Protest (Fundamental Music) 1986

On his compulsive own, Eugene Chadbourne, guitarist and leader of the late Shockabilly, has spewed forth a stream of records and cassettes (the latter all on his own Parachute label) that easily represent the oddest version of country and folk music ever. While his guitar playing is as loose as clams, it has a unique energy. He's also the master of several different voices, some of them deceptively sincere. Harsh, funny, irritating, packed with ideas, Chadbourne's work often suggests a politically correct Frank Zappa.

There'll Be No Tears Tonight lovingly takes on thirteen C&W standards, from Carl Perkins' "Honey Don't" to Merle Haggard's "Swingin' Doors," acting out his "free improvised country & western bebop" with several game free-music experts. The results are hilarious and touching.

The President contains Chadbourne's own politically charged ditties (often in a decidedly Phil Ochs-ish bag.) His targets include Reverend Jerry Fallwell, Women Against Pornography and his arch-nemesis, ultra-right-wing Senator Jesse Helms.

Country Music of Southeastern Australia mixes ten country standards with ten originals, played free-form style with such noted noisemongers as Rik Rue, John Rose and David Moss. **Country Protest** features the quintessential Chadbourne cover-version collage, "Medley in C," where he is joined by Lenny Kaye and the Red Clay Ramblers for 11:25 of everybody from John Lennon to Black Flag to Rod Stewart to the Butthole Surfers.   [rg]

CHAMELEONS

Script of the Bridge (Statik/MCA) 1983
What Does Anything Mean? Basically? (Statik/nr) 1985
The Fan and the Bellows (Hybrid/nr) 1986

Somehow, this atmospheric British pop quartet manages to bring something of their own to this much-traveled terrain, making songs like the melodic "Up The Down Escalator" and the far denser "Don't Fall" moody and memorable. Bassist Mark Burgess recalls Psychedelic Fur Richard Butler's world-weariness in his singing; the band's playing is, however, generally lighter in tone and simpler in design than that band's. **Script of the Bridge** isn't a great album, but it has very appealing moments. (US and UK editions differ. **The Fan and the Bellows** is a compilation.)   [iar]

JAMES CHANCE

Theme from Grutzi Elvis EP (ZE) 1979

JAMES CHANCE AND THE CONTORTIONS

Live aux Bains Douches (Fr. Invisible) 1980
Live in New York [tape] (nr/ROIR) 1981

CONTORTIONS ET AL.

No New York (nr/Antilles) 1978

CONTORTIONS

Buy (ZE-Island/ZE-Arista) 1979

JAMES WHITE AND THE BLACKS

Off White (ZE-Island/ZE-Buddah) 1979
Sax Maniac (Animal) 1982

JAMES WHITE AND THE CONTORTIONS

Second Chance (ZE/ZE-PVC) 1980

JAMES WHITE

Flaming Demonics (ZE-Island/nr) 1983

Coming from Milwaukee with a saxophone on his knee, James (Siegfried) Chance/White/Black quickly became the linchpin of the budding New York no wave movement, appearing in Teenage Jesus and the Jerks with Lydia Lunch. More than any of his contemporaries, Chance turned harsh, abrasive music into an art form, and at one time or another almost everyone of any importance on the New York art music scene was in the Contortions.

No New York, produced by Brian Eno and shared by three other bands, features Chance and the Contortions at their most cacophonous, shattering the limits of taste and anti-commerciality with a mixture of punk and jazz. Recommended in all its jangle. **Buy** lacks the jagged edge of the **No New York** material, but expands the Contortions into a first-class, no-holds barred act, with every note and vocal oozing out Chance's deranged contempt for man and society with passionately cold renditions of normally pleasant dance music, epitomized by his then-anthem, "Contort Yourself."

Theme from Grutzi Elvis separates Chance's haranguing, bitter vocals from what turns out to be unusual if colorful music. Notably, Chance sings a subdued, oddly touching version of "That's When Your Heartaches Begin."

The very rare **Live aux Bains Douches** features Chance and the Contortions live in Paris, but the more readily available **Live in New York** demonstrates that there is real emotion energizing Chance's savage, solipsistic music.

Off White is a set of funky, demented disco tunes performed with the help of New York luminaries George Scott, Jody Harris, Don Christensen and Pat Place. Though milder and more accessible than White's Chance-work, **Off White** plays freely with his attempts at sexual ennui ("Stained Sheets") and racial ambiguity ("Almost Black") and features a wonderfully weird and erotic version of Irving Berlin's "(Tropical) Heat Wave." Recommended.

After White/Chance left the label, ZE compiled material from **Off White** and **Buy** to make **Second Chance**. **Sax Maniac**, which he produced, proved that several years' absence hadn't harmed White at all, and that he is a wonderful, inventive sax player. Similar in all respects except personnel to **Off White**, **Sax Maniac** (complete with a cover of "That Old Black Magic") is a fevered masterpiece of white funk.   [sg]

See also *Jody Harris*.

SHEILA CHANDRA

Out on My Own (Indipop/nr) 1984
Quiet! (Indipop/nr) 1984
Nada Brahma (Indipop/nr) 1985
The Struggle (Indipop/nr) 1985

It's hard to figure out why Sheila Chandra's post-Monsoon solo career, also masterminded by Steve Coe and Martin Smith, is less compelling than the band's one stunning album. The blend of Indian instrumentation with standard Anglo-pop maneuvers keeps the music from being mistaken for anyone but Chandra, and all are utterly listenable, with some fine moments scattered throughout, but none are as hypnotic or memorable as **Third Eye**.   [iar]

CHANNEL 3

CH3 EP (nr/Posh Boy) 1981
Fear of Life (nr/Posh Boy) 1982
I've Got a Gun (No Future/nr) 1982
After the Lights Go Out (No Future/Posh Boy) 1983
Airborne EP (nr/Enigma) 1984
Last Time I Drank (nr/Enigma) 1986

Channel 3 (aka CH3) hailed from Cerritos, one of many Southern California suburban hardcore bands signed to local label Posh Boy. A mixture of Black Flag and early Ramones, CH3's first EP and album are fairly typical genre fare, and not very inspired at that. The lyrics predictably concern school, girls and the angst of growing up middle-class, making CH3 of potential interest only to the least discerning element of hardcore fandom. Although they have never become indispensably wonderful, the lineup on **Airborne** is a far more musically proficient and creatively developed unit, and the songs—written by singer Mike Magrann with ex-Stepmother Jay Lansford (who likely has a lot to do with the band's improvement)—are strong aggrofolk of some note.   [iar]

CHARLES DE GOAL

Algorhythmes (Fr. New Rose) 1980
Ici l'Ombre (Fr. New Rose) 1983
3 (Fr. New Rose) 1985

Stylish but awkward, this French band does best on weird, moody and quirky synthesizer workouts—the songs that rely on choppy guitar and weak singing aren't as successful. A version of Bowie's "Hang on to Yourself" on **Algorhythmes** is skittish and tense, but not especially different from the original, and its inclusion seems purposeless.   [iar]

CHELSEA

Chelsea (Step Forward/nr) 1979
Alternative Hits (Step Forward/nr) 1980
No Escape (nr/IRS) 1980
Evacuate (Step Forward/IRS) 1982
Just for the Record (Step Forward/nr) 1985
Original Sinners (Communique/nr) 1985

Dismissed by more than a few as a bad joke, the never-say-die Chelsea was one of the few original punk groups to forge a unique sound *and* survive. Their distinctiveness stems from the grunt'n'groan vocals of Gene October, the guiding force and only constant member through numerous lineup changes.

Even in the early days, Chelsea didn't pursue the buzzsaw punk stereotype, instead favoring a less-fevered, sometimes lumbering intensity suggestive of an ignorant, lower-class background. **Chelsea** does offer plenty of thrills, however. James Stevenson's guitar enlivens slashing rockers like "I'm on Fire," and October constantly seems about to burst from the pressure. On the cover of Jimmy Cliff's exquisite "Many Rivers to Cross," he renders a vivid portrayal of someone suffering extreme pain who can't articulate it properly. It's poignant.

Alternative Hits (aka **No Escape**) consists largely of tracks originally (and better) heard on singles. Collected on an album, these songs betray the band's lack of versatility. But at least it includes Chelsea's electrifying debut 45, "Right to Work."

Evacuate brings Gene October about as far into the modern age as he can go. The bull-in-a-china-shop approach is toned down somewhat in a bid for relative respectability. Somehow, it just doesn't seem right.   [jy]

CHEQUERED PAST

Chequered Past (Heavy Metal America/EMI America) 1984

Although listening to this run-of-the-mill Bad Company arena rock may not, a glance at the credits indicates why Chequered Past was one of the most depressing groups/albums of recent years. Clem Burke and Nigel Harrison (both ex-Blondie) and Steve Jones (ex-Pistols) formed three-fifths of the band, proving conclusively that even talented new wavers, no matter how idealistic and rebellious, were merely a few years away from becoming just as bogus as the musicians they originally served to dethrone. Disgusting.   [iar]

ALEX CHILTON

Singer Not the Song EP (nr/Ork) 1977
Like Flies on Sherbert (Aura/Peabody) 1980
Bach's Bottom (Ger. Line) 1981
Live in London (Aura/nr) 1982
Feudalist Tarts EP (New Rose/Big Time) 1985
Document (Aura/nr) 1985
The Lost Decade (Fr. Fan Club) 1986

BIG STAR

#1 Record (nr/Ardent) 1972

Radio City (nr/Ardent) 1974
#1 Record/Radio City (Stax-EMI/nr) 1977
3rd (Aura/PVC) 1978
Sister Lovers (nr/PVC) 1985

A seemingly unlikely figure for a new wave progenitor, Memphis-born ex-Box Tops singer Chilton nonetheless exerted tremendous influence on many groups via his unconventional early '70s recordings with Big Star. **#1 Record** is the most cohesive of Big Star's three LPs, if not the best. Recorded in 1972, when its Beatlesque four-part harmonies, early Byrds/Kinks guitar sound and crisp, tight, live-sounding production were decidedly out of vogue, it signals an early rejection of then-dominant bloated "progressive" rock, which had already fallen victim to the giant ego-tripping of not-so-giant talents.

Whereas **#1 Record** is a collaborative effort in every sense of the word (Chilton co-wrote and shares lead vocals with the talented Chris Bell; all four members sing), **Radio City** is more a showcase for Chilton's increasingly quirky talents. Bell had left the group (he died in a 1978 car crash), and Chilton, whose gruff tenor epitomized the Top 40 sound of the Box Tops, sings at the very top of his range, straining at times to reach high notes of his own songs. The well-organized production values of **#1 Record** give way to a more emotional and spontaneous sound, a middle ground between Lennon's **Plastic Ono Band** and early Sun records. If the material on **Radio City** is spotty, it's never uninteresting, and the best songs—"September Gurls" and "Back of a Car"—are as good as any rock'n'roll produced in the first half of the '70s.

Recorded in 1974 but unreleased until 1978, by which time Big Star had broken up, **3rd** (reissued much later under its original title, **Sister Lovers**) is almost a Chilton solo album: Alex, drummer Jody Stephens and a host of Memphis friends and sessioneers (Jim Dickinson and Steve Cropper among them) comprise the band. It's an eclectic mix, alternately depressing and uplifting, ugly and beautiful. Though a bit of a pastiche, it's quite often brilliant, if strangely so. (The American LP contains a larger and better track selection than the British.)

Between the release of **Radio City** and **3rd**, Chilton had recorded an album's worth of material in a series of stormy sessions in Memphis with rock critic/musician Jon Tiven producing. Chilton was reportedly so out of it during the recording that Tiven ended up playing all the guitar. The results of the sessions were released in 1977 on an Ork Records EP. **Singer Not the Song** includes versions of the Stones song of the title and a 59-second "Summertime Blues," plus a couple of decent Chilton co-compositions that might have sounded better under other circumstances. In 1981, the EP's contents plus more material from the same wild sessions (including five more minutes of "Summertime Blues") were released in Germany as **Bach's Bottom**. Only the really faithful will want to know.

Despite leading bands in New York and Memphis between 1975 and 1980, the years when he was rediscovered and lionized by critics and musicians alike, Chilton has no extant studio recordings from that period. Live shows did serve to increase his reputation as an erratic and eccentric performer, and 1980's **Like Flies on Sherbert** painfully confirms the degradation of a once-major talent. The LP sounds like a bunch of drunken louts running amok in a studio with no producer to restrain or guide them. Sadly, some potentially good Chilton material is trampled to death in the process, as well as some covers. In short, it stinks.

Live in London captures a 1981 performance at Dingwalls on what is, for Chilton, a fairly good night. Backed by the Soft Boys rhythm section (Matthew Seligman and Morris Windsor) and Vibrator Knox on guitar, Chilton runs through material from all three Big Star LPs and **Like Flies on Sherbert**. Although characteristically sloppy and erratic, the album has moments that indicate there may be life in the old boy yet. As such, it's his best solo LP to date.

After a long period spent drying out and laying low in New Orleans and Memphis, a revived Chilton returned to active duty in late 1984, touring with a new pair of sidemen and recording his first new studio release in many years. **Feudalist Tarts** is a delight, six sides marked by control, easy confidence and entertaining variety. Chilton even sounds like he's enjoying the work for a change. Among Alex's originals are a humorously raunchy blues, "Lost My Job," and the absurdist jivey "Stuff" (with horns); covers include a slow, lazy take on "B-A-B-Y" (remember Rachel Sweet's version?) and a funky slide from the Slim Harpo songbook. The EP is a bit insubstantial, but most encouraging and a fine slice of Chilton.

Document is a 1985 compilation covering both Big Star and solo tracks; **The Lost Decade** packages one disc of Chilton's solo work as a performer with one as producer of various obscure records.   [ds/iar]
See also *Panther Burns*.

CHINA CRISIS

Difficult Shapes & Passive Rhythms, Some People Think It's Fun to Entertain (Virgin/nr) 1982
Working with Fire and Steel EP (nr/Warner Bros.) 1983
Working with Fire and Steel Possible Pop Songs Volume Two (Virgin/Warner Bros.) 1983
Flaunt the Imperfection (Virgin/Virgin-Warner Bros.) 1985

The title of the first album by this Liverpool group—essentially a duo at the outset—does convey a sense of what China Crisis is about. Using keyboards, guitar and percussion, with occasional augmentation, the rhythms—R&B, funk, reggae, Afro-gypsy, bossa nova—are so gently, modestly, melodiously proffered that it goes down *too* smoothly. Then you notice that, however dreamily enunciated, the sentiments conveyed are disquieting admissions of self-doubt and inner struggle. China Crisis' sturdy intellectual backbone becomes visible often enough to avoid mere wimpiness. The second album has just as much going for it musically, and with more snap—yet lyrically it's less tortured, if often as thoughtful/melancholic. (The American EP combines two versions of the title track with two British B-sides that are pretty, wistful instrumentals.)

Recorded as a quartet with instrumental assistance from producer Walter Becker, **Flaunt the Imperfection** shows the extent of China Crisis' development. Their delightfully lighter-than-air creations are now astonishingly delicate, but not insubstantial. The finely-honed commercial collection includes "The Highest High" and "Black Man Ray," both memorable pieces of modern art-pop that display obvious Steely Dan tendencies.   [jg/iar]

CHORDS

So Far Away (Polydor/nr) 1980

It is impossible to describe the Chords without referring to the Jam's early albums. In essence a copy of a copy, these four earnest young Englishmen weren't half bad, merely redundant. **So Far Away** manages one truly great song ("Maybe Tomorrow") that out-Jams Paul Weller's power pop concoctions and two properly reverent oldies ("She Said, She Said" and "Hold On, I'm Coming"); otherwise, the LP belongs in the dustbin. The talent was there to some measure; his chronic lack of individuality prevented singer/guitarist Chris Pope from achieving anything lasting.   [iar]

CHRIS AND COSEY/ CREATIVE TECH-NOLOGY INSTITUTE

Heartbeat (Rough Trade/nr) 1981
Trance (Rough Trade/nr) 1982
Flow Motion (Integrated Circuits/nr) 1982
Songs of Love and Lust (Rough Trade/nr) 1984
Elemental 7—The Original Soundtrack (Doublevision/nr) 1984
European Rendezvous (Doublevision/nr) 1984

CHRIS CARTER

Mondo Beat (Conspiracy International/nr) 1986

Rising from the corpse of Throbbing Gristle, Chris Carter and Cosey Fanni Tutti (also using the Creative Technology Institute moniker) infuse their electronic mantras with the beat of the factory to create a desolate industrial vision. Much of the work on **Heartbeat** follows solidly in Throbbing Gristle's footsteps, with found voices playing over pulsating synthesizer sounds, while the remainder strives toward lightweight Kraftwerkian metal pop.

Trance's songs unfold more slowly and deliberately, only reaching their final rock forms after passing through stages that frequently bear an uncanny resemblance to Gregorian chant warped into the future. As the title suggests, the mood is dark and contemplative; within the inventive and apparently emotionless electronics lie deep wells of terror and claustrophobia. Worth looking into.

Songs of Love and Lust has a distinctively icy sound with precise, percussive synths not very far to the left of Depeche Mode. Cosey's cold, distant voice, paying only passing attention to intonation at times, fits in perfectly amidst the machines. The problem is the songs—they're highly repetitive and go nowhere. (Five of the LP's nine tracks exceed five minutes.) Considering the pair's background, this record takes few chances.

CTI's **Elemental 7**, the soundtrack to a long-form video, consists primarily of tempoless washes of synthesizers, bordering on '70s-style space rock. Not very listenable as an album. **European Rendezvous** is a live set recorded throughout the Continent in 1983.   [sg/dgs]

CHRIS D./DIVINE HORSEMEN

See *Flesh Eaters*.

CHROME

The Visitation (nr/Siren) 1977
Alien Soundtracks (nr/Siren) 1978
Half Machine Lip Moves (Beggars Banquet/Siren) 1979
Read Only Memory EP (Red/Siren) 1979
Red Exposure (Beggars Banquet/Siren) 1980
Inworlds (nr/Siren) 1981
Blood on the Moon (Don't Fall Off the Mountain/Siren) 1981
3rd from the Sun (Don't Fall Off the Mountain/Siren) 1982
No Humans Allowed (nr/Siren) 1982
Chrome Box (nr/Subterranean) 1982
Raining Milk (Fr. Mosquito) 1983
Into the Eyes of the Zombie King (Fr. Mosquito) 1984
The Lyon Concert (Ger. Atonal) 1985

DAMON EDGE

Alliance (Fr. New Rose) 1985
The Wind Is Talking (Fr. New Rose) 1985

HELIOS CREED

X-Rated Fairy Tales (nr/Subterranean) 1985

Under the innocent name of Chrome, two San Franciscans—Damon Edge and Helios Creed—created an awesome (some would say awful) series of LPs that explore a dark state of mind only hinted at by '60s psychedelia. Their dense, chaotic science-fiction epics are vivid vinyl nightmares—a thick blend of mechanical noises, filtered, twisted voices and fantastic, bizarre lyrics—that flesh out a frightening world both absorbing and repellent. Though conventional song structures are preserved to the point where tracks can be distinguished, Chrome's strength is its ability to create sounds of horrible beauty that transcend discrete musical units. Apart from refinements, Edge and Creed have stuck to the same uniquely nerve-shattering style—metal-drone-punk—throughout. If you want to go whole hog, try the **Chrome Box**, a limited-edition set of six albums, including two otherwise unreleased LPs.   [jy/iar]

CHRON GEN

Chronic Generation (Secret/nr) 1982
Apocalypse Live Tour (Chaos/nr) 1984
Nowhere to Run EP (Picasso/nr) 1984

A top-notch hardcore band, rippling with strength and clarity. Played at reasonable speed with a generally high level of comprehensibility, **Chronic Generation** offers songs about the expected subjects (drugs, rock'n'roll, kids, fighting) that take a mature stance against mindless violence and substance abuse. Perhaps a little tame for true thrash aficionados, Chron Gen has much greater potential for growth than most of their punk contemporaries. [iar]

CH3

See *Channel 3*.

CHURCH

Of Skins and Heart (Aus. Parlophone) 1981
The Church (Carrere/Capitol) 1982 (Carrere/nr) 1985
Temperature Drop in Downtown Winterland EP (Carrere/nr) 1982
The Blurred Crusade (Carrere/nr) 1982
Sing-Songs EP (Aus. Parlophone) 1982
The Unguarded Moment EP (Carrere/nr) 1982
Seance (Carrere/nr) 1983 & 1985
Persia EP (Aus. Parlophone) 1983
Remote Luxury EP (Aus. Parlophone) 1984
Remote Luxury (EMI/Warner Bros.) 1984
Heyday (EMI/Warner Bros.) 1986

Of all the comparisons this Australian foursome's music may conjure up, the most helpful is perhaps that the Church is to the Beatles (musically) and early Bowie (lyrically and vocally) what Dire Straits is to Bob Dylan, circa '65-'66. Such a simplification is less unfair than you'd think; Marty Wilson-Piper explores the guitar territory first mapped out by George Harrison and John Lennon but in greater detail and with a more practiced hand, while Steve Kilbey chants/talks/sings articulate lyrics with a world-weary melancholy, like early Bowie, but drier and more forceful.

The Church, consisting of most of the first Australian LP plus the best of a subsequent double-45 release, has much to offer in its gorgeous guitar soundscapes and evocative verbal imagery, but **The Blurred Crusade** displays dangerous tendencies toward confessional long-windedness amid melodies stretched too thin. **Seance** never found its way to America, but the band finally got a proper shot with **Remote Luxury**, a combination of the two preceding Australian EPs. It's an attractive, often Byrdslike album of shimmering folk-rock hampered a bit by Kilbey's overly oblique lyrics.

Heyday, seemingly recorded as an album for a change, is really good; well-produced, straightforward guitar pop housed in an ironically paisleyfied cover. Although titles like "Tristesse" and "Myrrh" suggest otherwise, Kilbey's lyrics are more tangible, albeit in an engagingly vague manner, than usual. Strong, memorable melodies also add to what is easily the Church's best album so far. [jg/iar]

CIRCLE JERKS

Group Sex (nr/Frontier) 1981
Wild in the Streets (Step Forward/Faulty Products) 1982
Golden Shower of Hits (nr/LAX) 1983
Wonderful (Rough Justice/Combat Core) 1985

Keith Morris formed this popular LA slam band after leaving Black Flag, having appeared only on that group's debut single, "Nervous Breakdown." First immortalized on celluloid in *The Decline of Western Civilization* hardcore documentary, the Jerks' vinyl success (via the film soundtrack and their own releases) came later. Typically crude and undisciplined, despite occasional offbeat choices of material (**Wild in the Streets** contains a hyper remake of Jackie DeShannon's "Put a Little Love in Your Heart"), the Circle Jerks have managed to become a live success; their shows generate some of the most intense slam-dancing and stage-diving to be found anywhere on the face of the earth.

With a joyously tasteless urinal cover photo, **Golden Shower of Hits** offers a new batch of tuneless kinetic guitar rock, built around the titular centerpiece (subtitled "Jerks on 45"), which dismembers a number of well-known wimp tunes ("Along Comes Mary," "Afternoon Delight," "Having My Baby," "Love Will Keep Us Together," others) in a parodic five-minute medley that's funnier in concept than execution.

Joined by a new rhythm section, Morris and guitarist Greg Hetson cut **Wonderful**, a tepid imitation of a punk record by a band that, while bearing a passing resemblance to the Dictators, sounds old, tired and bored. [rnp/iar]

CIRCUIT II

Can't Tempt Fate (WEA/Elektra) 1985

With Arthur Baker producing, this inter-racial Detroit trio plays a different combination of rock and funk, avoiding all the contemporary stereotypes to forge a blend quite their own. The balance shifts from song to song, electronically syncopated beats sharing the grooves with rock-inflected guitar; overlaid tape effects (edits by the Latin Rascals) color some of the tracks a hip-hop hue. A solidly played, interesting record. [iar]

JOHN COOPER CLARKE

Où Est la Maison de Fromage? (Rabid/nr) 1978
Disguise in Love (CBS/nr) 1978
Walking Back to Happiness EP (Epic/nr) 1979
Snap, Crackle [&] Bop (Epic/nr) 1980
Me and My Big Mouth (Epic/nr) 1981
Zip Style Method (Epic/nr) 1982

The first acknowledged new wave poet, Manchester's John Cooper Clarke created a genre all on his own, reciting trenchant, often hilarious poetry in a thickly accented, adenoidal voice; a deviant British precursor of rap. Looking like **Blonde on Blonde**-era Dylan (but skinnier) and suggesting a mindset lifted from Jack Kerouac or Lenny Bruce, Clarke exists with one foot in literature and the other in rock music, using both but succumbing wholly to neither. On most of his recordings, musical backing is provided by a nebulous organization known as the Invisible Girls, which—besides a nucleus of keyboardist Steve Hopkins and producer Martin Hannett—has included such name-brand players as Pete Shelley and Bill Nelson. When combined on vinyl, the two

forces—Clarke as satiric commentator and the Invisible Girls as musical adventurers—make for a unique listening experience.

Où Est la Maison de Fromage?, released on a Manchester independent label, is a sloppy, ragged, (almost) unaccompanied, poorly-recorded but enthralling hodgepodge—demos, rehearsals and recitations—of pieces that wound up on later albums. Clarke's major-league debut, **Disguise in Love**, contains such classic inventions as "(I Married a) Monster from Outer Space," "Psycle Sluts 1 & 2" and "I Don't Want to Be Nice." The collaboration between words and music works splendidly, although it should be noted that Clarke's approach doesn't vary on two tracks performed **a cappella**. The music leans heavily to electronics, but varies the sound with guitar and weird noises.

Walking Back to Happiness is a live recording released as a 10-inch EP on clear vinyl. For over 20 minutes, Clarke goes one-on-all against a generally appreciative but partially hostile audience, reciting, jousting, cracking deadly one-liners, dealing with hecklers and being captivating with scathing, funny numbers like "Majorca" (an attack on tourists) and "Twat." As a bonus, the EP closes with a studio track called "Gimmix."

Snap, Crackle [&] Bop matches impressive packaging (the front cover is a photo of a sports coat with working pocket containing a lyric book) with awesomely powerful songs like "Beasley Street," recalling nothing so much as Dylan's "Desolation Row." And while "Conditional Discharge" is a cheap pun about venereal disease, the notable "Thirty Six Hours" is his most songlike effort to date. On it, the Invisible Girls' backing matches the bard's intensity dram for dram, creating dense waves of electronics and electrics that fit the words perfectly.

Me and My Big Mouth collects Clarke's greatest non-hits, drawing equally from the three previous records, and suffices as an ideal introduction and overview.

Zip Style Method, still Clarke's most recent release, finds him in a more upbeat humor, and includes a pair of love songs amidst the remorseless satire. The Invisible Girls are at their best, working in a number of idioms. More than any of the other albums, this seems to be a cooperative venture—more organically entwined than autonomous—between poet and players. That's a major development, because it makes Clarke's words stand out less, but convey more. There aren't any bad tracks; although the intensity level isn't up there with "Beasley Street," songs like "Midnight Shift," "The Day the World Stood Still" and "Night People" present different, entertaining sides to Clarke's musical persona.

Clarke has continued to perform as a poet, but regrettably has not recorded anything of late. [iar]

See also *Pauline Murray and the Invisible Girls*.

CLASH

The Clash (CBS/nr) 1977
Give 'Em Enough Rope (CBS/Epic) 1978
The Clash (nr/Epic) 1979
London Calling (CBS/Epic) 1979
Black Market Clash (nr/Epic) 1980

Sandinista! (CBS/Epic) 1980
Combat Rock (CBS/Epic) 1982
Cut the Crap (CBS/Epic) 1985

TOPPER HEADON

Waking Up (Mercury/nr) 1986

That the Clash survived as long as they did and in fact proved commercially viable in both the UK and US is a clear testament to the band's rugged integrity and stubborn refusal to buckle, despite enormous adversity, much of it self-induced. In the great Who tradition, the Clash were formed to fall apart, but it took better than seven years for the Joe Strummer-Mick Jones bustup to finally take place.

If any rock band ever insisted on doing it their way, the Clash deserves first-place honors, despite the price their nonconformity exacted. Nonetheless (or as a result), they became enormously popular, even in America, where their Top 20 chart success stands as proof of an indomitable spirit. The Clash received no small amount of criticism over the years: damned for their integrity (or lack thereof); assailed for absorbing black musical styles; attacked for injecting politics into their songs; blamed for changing; blamed for not changing; ridiculed for having ideals; branded sell-outs, hypocrites, rockists, opportunists and worse. Through it all, the Clash consistently proved equal to the task of confounding everyone that ever followed or dealt with them, offering contradictory and inconsistent statements in classic Bob Dylan obfuscatory oratory fashion and generally failing to act in their own self-interest.

With all of this controversy swirling around them, the Clash still managed to make some of the most brilliant, absorbing, potent and staggering rock'n'roll of all time. Alone save for Elvis Costello, Joe Strummer, Mick Jones and Paul Simonon (plus various drummers) stand as new wave's original and most significant trendsetters; like Costello, the original Clash never made an album that isn't worth owning.

The Clash, 1977's finest LP bar none, was not issued in the US until 1979, and then in radically altered form, adding subsequent single sides and deleting four original tracks, making it fragmentary but stronger. In the album's original form, the fourteen songs explode in a scathing frenzy of venom and sardonic humor, ranging in subject from unemployment ("Career Opportunities") to the underground music scene ("Garageland") to cultural imperialism ("I'm So Bored with the U.S.A.") to rebellion ("White Riot," "London's Burning," "Hate and War"). Strummer's incomprehensible bellow exudes focused rage and Mick Jones' flaming guitar work both sets and supersedes the style for countless derivative bands who followed. Since the original album lacks a lyric sheet (the US label couldn't resist adding one), the exact words are—as is appropriate— undiscernible, but there's no missing the power of the music. A full disc of classics, including the Clash's first stab at reggae, a brilliant rendition of Junior Murvin's "Police and Thieves." (The American LP also included a bonus 45 with two odd numbers recorded a few years later: "Groovy Times" and "Gates of the West.")

The pairing of the fiercely English and (then) anti-commercial Clash with American big-shot hit producer Sandy Pearlman (Blue Oyster Cult, but also the Dictators) proved controversial but fruitful on **Give 'Em Enough Rope**. By exchanging the band's garageland raunch for heavily overlaid (but crystal-clear) guitars and drums, Pearlman delivered a supercharged rock sound, while Strummer and Jones came up with some of their best songs—"Safe European Home," "Tommy Gun," "English Civil War," "Stay Free" and "All the Young Punks." The band's new-found studio sophistication did nothing to blunt their power—quite the opposite, especially in terms of Topper Headon's crisp, authoritative drumming—and their defiant confidence to mix in more liberal amounts of sensitivity and cleverness add to the album's appeal. Jones' vocal on "Stay Free" casts him as the tender side of the band, but his guitar work throughout goes against punk's early egalitarian precepts, proudly standing up as a genuine guitar hero for the new age.

London Calling established the Clash's major-league stature, regardless of commercial considerations. The two records, produced by the legendary Guy Stevens (Mott the Hoople), stretch over an enormously expanded musical landscape with few weak tracks. Unlike most double albums, **London Calling** needs all four sides to say its piece; while not especially coherent or conceptual, the tracks share a maturity of vision and a consistency of character. Whichever way the band turns, the record bears their unique stamp—from the anti-nuclear throb of the title track to the updated blues oldie, "Brand New Cadillac," to the bebop of "Jimmy Jazz" and the anthemic "Rudie Can't Fail." And that's just the first side! Some of the other stunners are "Death or Glory," "Koka Kola," "Lost in the Supermarket" (Jones' spotlight), "Guns of Brixton" (a powerful reggae rumble featuring Simonon), "Spanish Bombs," "The Right Profile" (about actor Montgomery Clift—how's that for a change of direction?) and "Working for the Clampdown," collectively proof positive that the Clash would not be limited by anyone's expectations. A masterwork.

The Clash's many singles contained as much exciting music as their albums, and a lot of non-LP tracks were issued along the way. Since very few of their early 45s were even released in the US, Epic assembled an odds-and-ends collection, **Black Market Clash**, gathering nine tracks on a 10-inch platter (subsequently reissued as 12-incher). Tracks appended to the US release of the first album were left off here; the two records collectively fill in the non-LP gaps through 1980. Essential items like "Capital Radio One," "Armagideon Time," "The Prisoner" and "City of the Dead" join interesting but less exciting things like versions of "Time Is Tight" and "Pressure Drop." **Black Market Clash** is a worthwhile and entertaining record, not a collection of inferior scraps.

Whatever self-restraint the Clash might once have had evaporated on **Sandinista!**, six sprawling sides of wildly varied styles and, to put it mildly, uneven quality. There are proper songs, kiddie renditions,

guest artists coming and going, utter self-indulgent rubbish—you name it, it found its way onto vinyl here, with neither rhyme, rhythm nor evidence of editing. While it may be nice to give the Clash high marks for iconoclasm, much of **Sandinista!** is indefensible, burying one album's worth of sheer excellence in a towering heap of endurance-defying nonsense.

In fairness, the guff doesn't diminish the LP's greatness, it just makes the gems harder to find. Kudos for Side One ("The Magnificent Seven," "Hitsville U.K.," "Ivan Meets G.I. Joe," "Something About England") and Side Four (Eddy Grant's ace oldie "Police on My Back," "The Call Up," "Washington Bullets") and a few other things. The wide stylistic swath is hypothetically interesting though not musically rewarding; a better-focused album would have been much more powerful and politically meaningful, as the enormous catalogue of social and international concerns dilutes the tracks' effectiveness. If pared down to a single LP (as many fans probably did with their tape recorders), **Sandinista!** would have been truly worthy of the Clash.

Returning to a manageable one-disc format, **Combat Rock** found the Clash taking a new musical detour, absorbing and regurgitating rap and funk with more conviction than ever before (**Sandinista!** had a few test runs) and also becoming arty enough to invite poet Allen Ginsberg to appear on the record. A bizarre collection of material that seems to be diverging at a blinding rate, the twelve tracks proved extremely popular, yielding two bona fide American chart hits (the moronically simple "Should I Stay or Should I Go?" and the ultra-danceable if topical "Rock the Casbah"). Despite slick production possibilities (ace studio hand Glyn Johns "mixed"), the Clash sound even more ragged than ever, getting dolled up only for the dance numbers like "Overpowered by Funk," which features a guest rap by Futura 2000. A perplexing but partially entertaining set of sounds from the world's most unpredictable rock band.

Although it wasn't well known at the time, the Clash had become divided into two musical camps. With commercial success tugging on one side, abiding fascination for "black" music on the other, and problematic idealism presenting a genuine challenge up the middle, the Clash finally rended, with Strummer and Simonon booting Jones out of the band. Joined by three young players, the remaining pair later toured and recorded **Cut the Crap**, ostensibly a Clash album. With one notable exception (the mournful anthem, "This Is England"), **Crap** is just that, a painfully tired and hopelessly inept attempt to catch up with an elusive, fading legend. Strummer and Bernard Rhodes co-wrote the songs (a dead giveaway of major creative problems right there), but they needn't have bothered: Sham 69 outtakes would've been preferable to these prosaic, forgettable shouters. "We Are the Clash," indeed. Shortly after the album appeared, the lineup dissolved. Jones played with General Public in the studio during that band's formative months, and unveiled his new group, Big Audio

Dynamite, to great critical acclaim, in late 1985.

Topper Headon, who vanished from the Clash and the music business soon after the release of **Combat Rock**, reportedly because of drug problems (Terry Chimes—"Tory Crimes" of the first LP—replaced him for live work), launched a solo career in 1986 with **Waking Up**. Ambitious and plucky but surprisingly underwhelming, this horn-soul album is so humble his drums aren't even mixed high enough. Despite an impressive talent roster (including Mickey Gallagher and ex-Beck guitarist Bobby Tench), Headon's songs are amateurish, and the arrangements routine and uninvolving; even another version of Booker T's can't-miss "Time Is Tight" doesn't hit a nerve. (Chimes went on to form the Cherry Bombz with former members of Hanoi Rocks and Toto Coelo.) [iar]

See also *Big Audio Dynamite, Mikey Dread, Ellen Foley, Ian Hunter, 101ers.*

CLASSIX NOUVEAUX

Night People (Liberty/nr) 1981
Classix Nouveaux (nr/Liberty) 1981
La Verité (Liberty/nr) 1982
Secret (Liberty/nr) 1983

This quartet of poseurs, led by singer/multi-instrumentalist Sal Solo (whose totally bald pate and permanently serious expression make him resemble a constipated Yul Brynner), uses both synthesizers and regular rock tools (guitar, bass, drums, sax) to turn out talented if shallow dance rock that's utterly pretentious but not unattractive.

Night People (retitled **Classix Nouveaux** in the US) actually includes a couple of enjoyable tracks ("Guilty" stands out) that are straightforward and melodic enough to be recognizable as songs; the remainder of the record consists of windy instrumentals and foolish sci-fi tales. Their second effort, **La Verité**, goes over the edge, being far too intricate and overblown. Turn down the volume and the music serves as subtle ambient noise.

Produced by Alex Sadkin and employing guest musicians to add horns and other embellishments, **Secret** takes a more aggressive and rhythmic attack, aiming straight for the dance-floor with loud, energetic numbers like "All Around the World" and "No Other Way." They still find room to include refined and textured creations (à la Japan) and even an engaging pop song, "Forever and a Day." Although Solo's singing remains the band's least enticing feature, the impressive variety and sophistication makes **Secret** the band's best album, one well worth repeated playings.

Sal Solo has most recently fashioned a career in keeping with his surname. [iar]

CLOCK DVA

White Souls in Black Suits [tape] (Industrial/nr) 1980
Thirst (Fetish/nr) 1981 (Doublevision/nr) 1985
Advantage (Polydor/nr) 1983
Breakdown EP (Polydor/Relativity) 1983

Appearing in 1980 and allied with industrial bands like Throbbing Gristle and Cabaret Voltaire, Sheffield's Clock DVA aped the sound of British white soul groups

of the day on **White Souls in Black Suits**, though the mock-soul energy is strangely vitiated by urban metal noise that distorts the songs around the edges. Eerie but captivating, with a punchy beat. (Although available in England only on cassette, **White Souls** *was* released on disc in Italy.)

On **Thirst**, the band maintained an interest in dance music, but abandoned soul pretensions for electro-noise, and the album is a playground of startling, unearthly machine chants. **Advantage** is their strongest, most powerful LP, a funky concoction of intense dance-powered bass/drums drive with splatters of feedback, angst-ridden vocals by mainman Adi Newton, tape interruptions and dollops of white-noise sax and trumpet. The band also digresses into devolved be-bop. Released as a British single from **Advantage**, "Breakdown" was also issued on an American EP, joined by an extended version, another great LP cut and a mesmerizing take on the Velvet Underground's "Black Angels Death Song."

Clock DVA's often-shifting lineup provided members for the Box as well as Siouxsie and the Banshees. After Clock DVA broke up, Newton formed the Anti-Group, who've done a single produced by Cabaret Voltaire. [sg/iar]

See also *Box.*

CLUSTER

See *Brian Eno.*

COCKNEY REJECTS

Greatest Hits Vol. 1 (EMI/nr) 1980
Greatest Hits Vol. 2 (EMI/nr) 1980
Greatest Hits Vol. 3 (EMI/nr) 1981
The Power and the Glory (EMI/nr) 1981
The Wild Ones (a.k.a./nr) 1982

This bunch of London skinheads was discovered by Sham 69 leader Jimmy Pursey, who co-produced their first album. The Rejects gained immortality of a sort on **Vol. 2** by coining a name for the punk resurgence with the chant "Oi Oi Oi." **Vol. 3** (logically subtitled **Live and Loud**) was recorded in a studio with a vociferous audience of fans adding background vocals to the band's fast rock'n'roll noise.

While retaining the aggressiveness and spunk, **The Power and the Glory** took a big chance by trying such experimental ventures as acoustic guitar, melodies, musicianship and semi-tasteful artwork. The album contains impressive moments, especially noteworthy given the Rejects' prior blitzkrieg approach. Not stunning, but their best effort, and an LP of interest not solely to punk aficionados.

Having gotten "art" out of their systems (and switching labels), the Rejects' next move (subsequently not an uncommon gambit for punk bands) was a heavy metal album. Produced by UFO bassist Pete Way, **The Wild Ones** is a terrible record; although the distance from teen punk sludge to adult metal sludge is not very far, this lot was much better at doing numbers like "Greatest Cockney Rip-off." [iar]

COCONUTS

See *Kid Creole and the Coconuts.*

COCTEAU TWINS

Garlands (4AD/nr) 1982
Lullabies EP (4AD/nr) 1982
Head Over Heels (4AD/nr) 1983
Sunburst and Snowblind EP (4AD/nr) 1983
Pearly-Dewdrops' Drop EP (4AD/nr) 1984
Treasure (4AD/nr) 1984
Aikea-Guinea EP (4AD/nr) 1985
Treasure/Aikea-Guinea (Can. Vertigo) 1985
The Pink Opaque (4AD/Relativity) 1985
Tiny Dynamine EP (4AD/nr) 1985
Echoes in a Shallow Bay EP (4AD/nr) 1985
Tiny Dynamine/Echoes in a Shallow Bay (Can. Vertigo) 1985
Victorialand (4AD/nr) 1986

The Cocteau Twins are actually a Scottish trio who, on their first album, add a borrowed drum synthesizer to vocals, bass and heavily treated guitar, producing atmospheric dirges with rich textures and little structure. Elizabeth Fraser's vocals are essentially tuneless, and the backing goes nowhere, but it's all artily agreeable enough for those with the patience to wade through the murk and mire.

Head Over Heels shows marked improvement, both in terms of songwriting technique and vocal performances. "Sugar Hiccup" (a different version of which appears on **Sunburst and Snowblind**) exhibits a stronger melodic sense, and Fraser's voice soars on songs like "In the Gold Dust Rush" and "Musette and Drums." The record also offers more varied tempos: the rather Bansheelike "In Our Angelhood" rocks more than anything previous. **Sunburst and Snowblind** is a strong four-song EP, well-honed for those who'd rather meet the Cocteau Twins in smaller doses. Delicate and precious yet accessible, the instrumental backing is a little thinner and the vocals more confident. **Pearly-Dewdrops' Drop** strips down the sound a little further; "The Spangle Maker" and the title track even forego much of the reverb that permeates their records.

By this point, the Cocteau Twins had become ubiquitous figures in the alternative record charts and a major live attraction as well. **Treasure** stands as their finest vinyl presentation to date. It contains no black and white sounds—just intriguing shades of gray— immersing the listener in a full range of emotions, with Fraser's now-powerful voice alternately full of sorrow, joy, calm and fury. The production is meticulously detailed; increased use of keyboards and drums provides a wider range of tone colors. All ten diverse tracks work well, with "Persephone" and "Ivo" particularly noteworthy.

Since **Treasure**, the Cocteaus have been running a little short on new ideas. In 1985, they released three four-song EPs. **Aikea-Guinea** could pass as outtakes from previous albums, while **Tiny Dynamine** and **Echoes in a Shallow Bay** are virtually identical, in sound and cover art. The following year, they issued an LP, **Victorialand**. Almost all the instrumental backing is psychedelic-tinged treated acoustic guitar; while it opens things up and gives Fraser's voice more room, the material again recalls earlier records. All of these recent works, if heard individually, are pleasant,

effective mood music; taken as a whole, however, they're all cut from the same cloth.

The Pink Opaque is a career-spanning compilation, released on compact disc in the UK. (The vinyl version served as the band's first American record.) The Cocteau Twins have recorded some of the '80s most rewarding records; here's hoping they have some more tricks up their sleeves. [dgs]

See also *This Mortal Coil*.

LLOYD COLE AND THE COMMOTIONS

Rattlesnakes (Polydor/Geffen) 1984
Easy Pieces (Polydor/Geffen) 1985

Scotland's Lloyd Cole has the post-beatnik lyrical outlook of a young Bob Dylan. The strength of **Rattlesnakes** is contained in his folk-rock songs and casually emotive singing. The four Commotions make a tight, talented unit capable of subtlety and power in many voices. Cole's prose occasionally overreaches, but never by much, and lyrics that hit their mark do so sharply. Those hypersensitive to folky Dylanitis will find **Rattlesnakes** a bit much; open-minded adventurers will be immediately engrossed.

Easy Pieces, smoothly produced by Langer/Winstanley, succumbs to the hazards threatened on the first LP. While the band remains solidly unprepossessing, Cole's vocals are overly stylized; his lyrics veer towards meaningless self-importance, quoting Bolan and the Beatles. Not all that different from **Rattlesnakes**, **Easy Pieces** makes you wonder why you liked the best in the first place. (The CD has three extra tracks.) [iar]

PAUL COLLINS' BEAT

See *Beat*.

COLOR ME GONE

See *Marti Jones*.

COLOURBOX

Colourbox EP (4AD/nr) 1984
Colourbox (4AD/nr) 1985

Although this London trio's music is not particularly avant-garde, the group does fit in with the uncompromising 4AD family due to their steadfast determination to totally redefine a musical style. Instrumentalists Martyn and brother Steven Young, along with vocalist Lorita Grahame, take soul places it's never been (and is unlikely to go again).

The eponymous EP—three hours of sessions edited down to a half-hour of hip-hop/scratch and reggae/dub experiments, with a graphic depiction of horses mating on the cover—largely deserved the disregard it received. The LP, however, is a vast improvement, an eclectic display that embraces the entire realm of dance music: reggae, vibrant industrial dance, hard'n'heavy funk, '50s R&B. Screeching guitar on the almost-metal "Maniac" segues into the highlight, a sparkling remake of the Supremes' "You Keep Me Hanging On." (Footnote: the cassette of **Colourbox** is double-length, adding an LP's worth of remixes; some copies of the LP have the same on a bonus disc.) [ag]

COLOUR FIELD

Virgins and Philistines (Chrysalis) 1985
The Colour Field EP (Chrysalis) 1986

Terry Hall's post-Fun Boy Three band started out slowly, with just an eponymous single in 1984, but the trio's first album a year later was well worth the wait. The LP kicks off brilliantly with the mock-"96 Tears" organ intro to "Can't Get Enough of You Baby," itself a fine version of Georgie Fame-era beat music. The music mixes metaphors, from stripped-down Fun Boys rock to samba, folk and jazzy '60s R&B; Hall's sharp tongue and the band's intelligent creativity makes each track different. Of special note: a shimmering acoustic version of the Roches' "Hammond Song" and "Pushing Up Daisies," a vicious condemnation of celebrity. Drama, beauty, ideas and energy make **Virgins and Philistines** provocative, stylish and memorable.

The EP portrays the Colour Field as a quartet and features a pair of live takes plus four excellent non-LP tracks, including the memorable "Faint Hearts," an almost psychedelic folk tune, and "Things Could Be Beautiful," a soulful rocker. [iar]

COMATEENS

Comateens (nr/Cachalot) 1981
Pictures on a String (Virgin/Virgin-Mercury) 1983
Deal with It (Virgin/Virgin-Mercury) 1984

This New York trio plays a bouncy brand of dance rock rooted in chintzy '60s Farfisa organ pop and spooky horror-movie soundtrack music. The group first gained recognition in 1979 with a home-made single that featured a stripped-down version of Bowie's "TVC 15," which they re-recorded for their first LP. After a number of personnel changes, the lineup solidified at Lyn Byrd (keyboards), Oliver North (guitar), Nic North (bass) and synthetic drums. Their debut album is a delightful distillation of the aforementioned influences, with neat contrasts between the thin-sounding synth fills and the chunky, rhythmic guitar. There's also a three-track 12-inch—on the same label—of the hypnotic "Ghosts," the pure pop "Late Night City" and the theme for TV's *Munsters*, which pretty much sums up the Comateens music.

Signed to a major label, the Comateens made **Pictures on a String**, which diverges into rock quirkiness and danceable commercialism, pushing a powerful disco beat on "Get Off My Case," "Cinnamon" and other numbers. The rock-oriented material, especially the Beatlesque "Comateens," with its awesome fuzz-blizzard guitar solo, and a weird overdrive cover of the oldie "Uptown," are more intriguing; the dance tracks don't really go anywhere.

With a guest drummer and veteran hitmaker Pete Solley producing, **Deal with It** sublimates the big beat into various styles, much the way Blondie often did. Rather than base tunes on rhythms, these songs explore widely differing pop modes, welded to strong, emphasized drum tracks, resulting in a fascinating mix full of unexpected, delightful juxtapositions. This is the

album that finally and fully realizes the Comateens' hybridizing potential. [ds/iar]

COMSAT ANGELS

Red Planet EP (Junta/nr) 1979
Waiting for a Miracle (Polydor/nr) 1980
Sleep No More (Polydor/nr) 1981
Fiction (Polydor/nr) 1982
Land (Jive) 1983
Independence Day EP (Jive/nr) 1984
Enz (Polydor/nr) 1984
7 Day Weekend (Jive) 1985

Like Joy Division and the Cure, Sheffield's Comsat Angels have mastered the art of atmospherics; only nominally involved in rock'n'roll at the outset, they were actually interested in creating haunting mood music. Firm beats play against melancholy melodies and hushed vocals to create the impression you're spying on someone's inner turmoil, an approach which is morosely fascinating on **Waiting for a Miracle** and tunes like "Total War" and "Independence Day" (both included on the 1984 EP). It sours on **Sleep No More** because the tone is too uniformly somber to avoid monotony. "Our Secret," "Dark Parade" and others would be more memorable if they contrasted with less downbeat material.

Fiction is a full-fledged recovery, with an unsettling sense of tension underlying Stephen Fellows' dejected vocals and guitar on "Ju-Ju Money" and "Zinger." However, even this success raises questions about how much longer the band could prosper working in such a restricted style.

They did attempt to expand. Switching labels and getting American release for the first time, the Comsat Angels ran into name problems and had to be billed as the C.S. Angels for the US. **Land**, produced by Mike Howlett, fails in an effort to cast them as a variant on A Flock of Seagulls, but does contain a number of upbeat, memorable tunes that resemble a poppier, less serious Simple Minds. The first side especially is one of the band's finest hours (well, quarter-hours). The subsequent EP takes two good songs off the LP and adds three early tracks; **Enz** is a pre-Jive compilation.

The liner notes on the back cover of **7 Day Weekend** are downright sad ("We had a stretch of good luck, which rapidly turned into bad . . . "); the music itself is more self-assured and dignified. Produced variously by Mtume, Chris Tsangarides and Mike Howlett, there is scant sonic continuity, but for a band with no recognizable character, little damage is done.

For a group that still seems uncertain about what to be when they grow up, this lot have sure made a lot of records. [jy/iar]

CONFLICT

It's Time to See Who's Who (Corpus Christi/nr) 1983
Increase the Pressure (Mortarhate/nr) 1984

I'm not sure what to think about the music of a band that informs me that "three members are vegetarians" and then tattles on the one—Paco—who isn't. The sleeve of the second album by these Crass-family anarchists also notes that the band "still wear articles of leather" but they've gotten down to "just boots," which "they will continue to wear until they are useless" but "will not buy more." I have nothing against people with a highly developed and self-disciplined political consciousness, but I can't shake the feeling that a record album should do more than announce how deep the musicians' commitment runs. In the rock world, only the young and the gullible expect their favorite bands to abide by any personal standards.

All that aside, Conflict is a pretty good punk band, powered with fire and intelligence. The first album has incredibly ornate artwork and songs about media, Viet Nam, vegetarianism (Smiths fans should note Conflict's "Meat Means Murder" here) and other proto-anarchist issues. **Increase the Pressure** is a more proletarian production with black and white artwork; the LP itself is half-studio (dynamic), half-live (raucous). This time out, the prominent issue illustrated on the graphics is Save the Seals; songs attack cruise missles, the music press, the police, etc. with undiminished zeal and venom.   [iar]

CONTORTIONS

See *James Chance*.

JULIAN COPE

World Shut Your Mouth
    (Mercury/nr) 1984
Fried (Mercury/nr) 1984
Sunspots EP (Mercury/nr) 1985

Ex-Teardrop Explodes leader Cope has done some strange projects in his career—from assembling a reverent compilation (**Fire Escape in the Sky—The Godlike Genius of Scott Walker**) to his own idiosyncratic records. **World Shut Your Mouth** is a highly inventive take on '60s psychedelia, mainly blending weird sounds with charming pop, his acceptably inelegant voice and period organ playing adding substantial personality to the non-nostalgic venture. His humorous and sensitive lyrics may be a touch *too* sensitive in spots, but Cope has an openness and a fanciful streak that undercuts any semblance of pretentiousness his work may engender.

Fried is a more energetic, less stylized effort that gains appeal from its rocking forthrightness and a strong backing quartet. Affecting a self-conscious Syd Barrett-ish pose on the sleeve (where he is pictured hiding in a tortoise shell) seems a bit gratuitous, but the music more than compensates. A fine record with many intriguing aspects. "Sunspots," an LP track, was subsequently issued on a twin-pack single with three other songs. [iar]

STEWART COPELAND

See *Klark Kent, Police*.

HUGH CORNWELL & ROBERT WILLIAMS

See *Stranglers*.

CORTINAS

True Romances (CBS/nr) 1978
The Cortinas' pounding, belligerent independent singles ("Fascist Dictator," "Defiant Pose") offered no clue that they'd cut such a mild-mannered album for a major

label, on which the few confrontational gestures sound forced. On **True Romances**, the Cortinas are revealed as simple rock'n'rollers with a taste for primitive, good-time R&B/pop-rock and endearingly yobbish vocals (e.g., "Heartache" and the jolly "Ask Mr. Waverly"—remember *The Man from U.N.C.L.E.?*). Nonetheless, halfway through, the record decays into bland forgettability.   [jg]

ELVIS COSTELLO

My Aim Is True (Stiff/Columbia) 1977

ELVIS COSTELLO AND THE ATTRACTIONS

This Year's Model (Radar/
    Columbia) 1978 (F-Beat/nr) 1981
    (Imp/nr) 1984
Armed Forces (Radar/Columbia)
    1979 (F-Beat/nr) 1981 (Imp/nr)
    1984
Get Happy!! (F-Beat/Columbia) 1980
    (Imp/nr) 1984
Taking Liberties (nr/Columbia)
    1980
**Ten Bloody Marys & Ten How's
    Your Fathers [tape]** (F-Beat/nr)
    1980 (Imp/nr) 1984
Trust (F-Beat/Columbia) 1981
    (Imp/nr) 1984
Almost Blue (F-Beat/Columbia)
    1981 (Imp/nr) 1984
Imperial Bedroom (F-Beat/
    Columbia) 1982 (Imp/nr) 1984
Punch the Clock (F-Beat/
    Columbia) 1983
Goodbye Cruel World (F-Beat/
    Columbia) 1984
**The Best of Elvis Costello and the
    Attractions Vol. 1** (F-Beat/
    Columbia) 1985
Elvis Costello EP (Stiff/nr) 1985

THE COSTELLO SHOW

King of America (F-Beat/
    Columbia) 1986

ATTRACTIONS

Mad About the Wrong Boy
    (F-Beat/nr) 1980 (Demon/nr) 1984

STEVE NIEVE

Keyboard Jungle (Demon/nr) 1983

Elvis Costello has become the King Kong of contemporary music, looming so large over everything that admirers and detractors alike feel compelled to take note of his most trivial actions. A remarkable performer with a cutting voice, he's charted a consistently interesting course in an intensely productive decade and shows no sign of fatigue. Amazingly, Costello may be just entering artistic maturity. In any case, he's arguably the most significant individual creative voice to emerge in rock'n'roll since Bob Dylan, and definitely one of music's most unforgettable characters.

My Aim Is True quickly established Elvis as an angry young man armed with cleverly worded insults and taut melodies. Although the backing (by American band Clover, *sans* future star Huey Lewis, the group's harmonica player) lacks his intensity, the bespectacled one's passion comes through full force. Many of the songs are already standards: "Watching the Detectives," a sizzling, disorienting excursion into reggae (not included on the original UK version of the LP); "Alison," a searing ballad later ineptly covered

by Linda Ronstadt, and "Less Than Zero," Elvis' first single and a wry attack on one of his preferred targets, fascism. The overall effect is that of an updated Buddy Holly, neurotic and tormented by sexual insecurity. For more information, consult "Miracle Man" and "No Dancing."

This Year's Model actually improves on Costello's stunning debut by winding the music uncomfortably tight. Elvis gained confidence from the addition of a permanent backing band of outstanding musicians: Bruce Thomas on bass, Pete Thomas (no relation) on drums and Steve Nieve, whose piano and organ, rather than Elvis' guitar, fill in melodies. The album finds Costello's anger and insecurity grown harsh and nasty. The surging "No Action," "Pump It Up" (something of a rewrite on Dylan's "Subterranean Homesick Blues") and "Lipstick Vogue" fairly bristle with ingeniously stated, hard-rocking vitriol. "Radio Radio" (not on the UK edition) became Costello's unofficial theme song, a daring and snotty put-down of the powers that rule the airwaves.

On **Armed Forces** Costello avoids sneering himself into a dead end. With the help of producer Nick Lowe, he fashions a prettier, less demanding and more varied sound that still allows him freedom of expression. "Oliver's Army" borrows from Abba's pop lushness; "Accidents Will Happen" mixes a beautiful melody with a driving arrangement; Lowe's "(What's So Funny 'Bout) Peace, Love and Understanding" offers an unironic, unexpected and agitated plea for tolerance. **Armed Forces** was the "nicest" of Costello's first three LPs.

Get Happy!! marks the beginning of Elvis' concerted stylistic fiddling and his first serious attempt to shift the emphasis to the music and away from the overpowering persona. The watchword here is simplicity, with 20 short songs and borrowings from such soul greats as Booker T & the M.G.'s and Sam and Dave, whose "I Can't Stand Up for Falling Down" gets disheveled but earnest treatment. Other highlights include "Motel Matches," an early flirtation with Nashville country; the moving "King Horse" and a rip-snorting version of the Merseybeats' "I Stand Accused." By lessening the intensity somewhat, Elvis comes up with a most personable LP.

Reflecting Costello's prolific nature, **Taking Liberties** collects an amazing 20 previously non-LP odds and ends in wildly divergent styles. (The UK counterpart, **Ten Bloody Marys & Ten How's Your Fathers**, has altogether different tracks, thanks to the wilful creation of alternate international releases. Originally issued only on cassette, the album was put out in disc form four years later.) Despite a few dull entries, there's plenty of remarkable stuff: The classic "My Funny Valentine," a harbinger of **Imperial Bedroom**; "Talking in the Dark," gaily recalling "Penny Lane"; "Stranger in the House," dating from the period of **This Year's Model**, masterfully reflecting his growing obsession with country music. Chaotic and marvelous.

Trust exhibits new self-confidence, blending some of the polish of **Armed Forces** with the straightforward delivery of **This**

Year's Model. Though few tracks stand out individually, the LP packs a powerful, coherent punch. "Clubland" is an impassioned lament while "Lovers Walk" overlays a Bo Diddleyish motif with Latin piano and heaps of anxiety. On the fierce "From a Whisper to a Scream," Costello engages in a spirited dialogue with Squeeze's Glenn Tilbrook, reaffirming his presence in the real world.

Elvis was bound to goof eventually, and **Almost Blue** is a real stinker. This album of country cover versions, recorded in Nashville with veteran producer Billy Sherill (Tammy Wynette, George Jones, just about everyone else), is surprisingly clumsy given Costello's previously demonstrated ability to come up with fine originals in the same genre. Curiously, he succumbs to the urge to over-sing instead of finesse the vocals, a mistake his obvious model, the late Gram Parsons, never made.

Imperial Bedroom is a resounding return to form, and indicates Costello's interest in becoming a classic tunesmith in the Tin Pan Alley tradition instead of just a venerated rocker. This is certainly his most subdued LP, with songs such as "Beyond Belief," "Kid About It" and "Town Cryer" more suitable to a cocktail lounge torch singer than a garage band. How time flies.

Punch the Clock constitutes yet another tour de force. Produced by Madness architects Clive Langer and Alan Winstanley, the disc continues in the pop vein of **Imperial Bedroom**, with considerably more attention paid to mixing up styles and textures. Hence you get politically motivated ballads like the brooding "Pills and Soap" and the ethereal, but desperately angry "Shipbuilding," as well as swaggering rave-ups ("The World and His Wife"), classic Costello angst ("Charm School") and much more. Best of all is the lilting "Everyday I Write the Book," a winning tune worthy of being sung by Aretha Franklin and the closest he's gotten to a US hit single yet.

By contrast, **Goodbye Cruel World** seems awkward and forced. The playing's overly baroque, the melodies mild and too much of Costello's edge is sublimated by the Langer/Winstanley cushion of sound. However, "Sour Milk-Cow Blues" has a cranky charm and "Peace in Our Time" brilliantly captures the chilling madness of nuclear politics. Otherwise, Costello sounds like he needs a vacation.

Perhaps The Best Of LP did the trick. Or maybe it was his decision to put the Attractions on the shelf for awhile. Then again, maybe it was his burgeoning romance with Cait O'Riordan of the Pogues. In any case, **King of America**—billed to The Costello Show and recorded with a bunch of top American sessioneers, including Elvis P's old sidemen and co-producer T-Bone Burnett—proved a return to masterful form. McManus (as he now wishes to be known) banged together fifteen intelligent, mature creations in a variety of idioms, many recalling styles he had already tried and abandoned (country, R&B, nightclub sophistication) and some (folk, blues) not so familiar. The sound often recalls the Band in its unique blending of country and urban traditions; elsewhere, it's latter-day Elvis Presley, played by his musicians. As articulate and clear-headed as he's ever been, McManus dissects several major themes—the British perception of America, alcoholism, his own stardom—each from more than one vantage point. Not only do all these forays work individually, the songs fit together with surprising ease. In addition, he's never sung better, with such subtlety and control. A career highlight.

On their own, the Attractions sound more like Nick Lowe than their boss. The sixteen snappily-executed ditties on **Mad About the Wrong Boy** feature bright, breezy surfaces and very little depth, which isn't so bad in light of the cheerful atmosphere. The title cut, "La-La-La-La-La Loved You" and others offer agreeably washed-out harmonies reminiscent of UK flower-power pop of the late '60s. Decent.

Steve Nieve's **Keyboard Jungle** is a cute set of miniatures crafted at the keyboard of a Steinway. Contents: fake film and classical music, none of it taken (or given) particularly seriously. Quite agreeable.

The 1985 Stiff EP consists of four early sides, all previously available.
[jy/iar]

See also *Twist*.

COUNT BISHOPS

Speedball EP (Chiswick/nr) 1975
Good Gear (Fr. Dynamite) 1977 (Fr. Lolita) 1982
The Count Bishops (Chiswick/nr) 1977

BISHOPS

Bishops Live (Chiswick/nr) 1978
Cross Cuts (Chiswick/nr) 1979

Although they never attained major popularity, hits or even a US release, the Bishops played a small but important role in the development of British punk. First, they provided a stylistic and chronological link between the raw R&B revivalism of Dr. Feelgood and early demi-punk flailings of Eddie and the Hot Rods. Second, their four-cut 7-inch **Speedball** EP was the debut release by the first independent new wave label in England, Chiswick, preceding Stiff by a matter of months.

The group's only recording with American (Brooklyn, no less) singer Mike Spencer (replaced by the gravel-throated Dave Tice soon after, for reasons that are audibly obvious), **Speedball** clearly defines the group's style. Combining rock-a-boogie rave-ups of mid-'60s style material with mid-'70s chops and energy, the Bishops re-cover the same R&B and rock'n'roll songs favored by the first wave of British beat groups (Stones, Yardbirds, Kinks) and American punks (Standells, Strangeloves). The idea was obviously to recapture the rawness and spontaneity of that period, and although the concept is both limited and doomed almost by definition, **Good Gear** (probably drawn from live-in-the-studio demos) is so raunchy and spirited that it succeeds, even if it is essentially a copy of a copy.

Trouble set in with their first *real* album, **The Count Bishops**. How do you convey a style that works best after a few beers and really offers nothing new to vinyl? Even with two solid guitarists and a fine rhythm section, the Bishops never were

quite able to resolve the problem. Though it sounds nasty as hell on **Bishops Live** (available as both a 12-inch and 10-inch LP), Tice's growl is hard to take over two sides of a recording made in the rarefied atmosphere of the studio. And where most bands use cover versions to fill space, the filler here is the Bishops' self-penned stuff. With rare exception, their originals are sub-Status Quo boogie, which just about destroys most of **Cross Cuts**. Following the death of guitarist Zenon deFleur in an auto accident just prior to the release of **Cross Cuts**, the Bishops called it a day.
[ds]

WAYNE COUNTY AND THE ELECTRIC CHAIRS

The Electric Chairs (Safari/nr) 1978
Storm the Gates of Heaven (Safari/nr) 1979
Things Your Mother Never Told You (Safari/nr) 1979
The Best of Jayne/Wayne County and the Electric Chairs (Safari/nr) 1982

JAYNE COUNTY

Rock 'n' Roll Resurrection (Safari/nr) 1981

Transsexual County was a (male) fixture on the budding New York club scene in the early '70s, stretching the limits of vulgarity and outrage on stages alongside the New York Dolls. After writing and recording the theme song for Max's Kansas City, County migrated to England, just as the London punk scene was getting underway. Having been commercially unappreciated at home, County found a sympathetic British label and recorded a series of albums, none of which were ever released Stateside.

High camp posturing and foul-mouthed (but not unfunny) lyrics form the basis of County's work. Along with a skillful trio playing routine rock, County sings (with more enthusiasm than talent) touching ballads ("Eddie and Sheena," a minor hit single recounting a love story between a Ted and a punk), catty putdowns ("Bad in Bed") and narcissistic scene celebrations ("Max's Kansas City") on the first album. **Storm the Gates of Heaven** has a great cover, was pressed on sickly-colored lavender vinyl and showcases two new guitarists hired to replace one left behind. The songs are less contrived and more interesting; the beginnings of a band sound can be discerned. All in all, a vast improvement that even includes a smoking version of "I Had Too Much to Dream Last Night." Flying Lizard David Cunningham produced the subsequent **Things Your Mother Never Told You** with the same lineup, but came up with a flat-sounding, dull LP.

A New Year's Eve gig in Toronto yielded the live **Rock'n'Roll Resurrection**. Fronting a largely new band, Jayne (following the surgery) belts out a shambling selection of non-hits, including such gutter faves as "Cream in My Jeans" and "F . . . Off." Pretty dire. A nicely packaged best-of collection (pressed on white vinyl) brought together everything you'd ever want to hear by Wayne or Jayne.
[iar]

COWBOYS INTERNATIONAL
See *Ken Lockie*.

CRACKERS
See *Beat Rodeo*.

CRAMPS

Gravest Hits EP (Illegal) 1979
Songs the Lord Taught Us (Illegal) 1980
Psychedelic Jungle (A&M/IRS) 1981
Off the Bone (Illegal/nr) 1983
Smell of Female EP (Big Beat/ Enigma) 1983
Bad Music for Bad People (IRS) 1984
A Date with Elvis (Big Beat/nr) 1986

Predating and never quite participating in the early '80s rockabilly revival, the Cramps used that genre's primal sound as a jumping-off point for their own weird pastiche of rock'n'roll, psychedelia and a monster movie/junk food/swamp-creature aesthetic.

The band—which had its roots in Cleveland but was actually formed in New York—crashed the 12-inch barrier with **Gravest Hits**, reissuing two 1977 self-released 45s plus a fifth track from the same time. Like a seance or voodoo session, the Cramps' music needs time to work its spell, and so the albums make a better introduction. **Songs the Lord Taught Us** is a delirious invocation to the demons behind rock'n'roll. Besides horror-comic originals like "TV Set," "The Mad Daddy" and "Zombie Dance," the band overhauls classics like "Tear It Up" and "Strychnine" to emphasize their Dionysian inheritance. A minimal approach—no bass, rudimentary drumming, Lux Interior's monotonous vocals—underlines the music's incantatory power. **Psychedelic Jungle** is not quite as intense, due to slower tempos; still, it contains prime Cramps psychobilly ("Voodoo Idol," "Can't Find My Mind") as well as related phenomena ("The Crusher," "Rockin' Bones").

On **Smell of Female**, a six-song live EP recorded at New York's Peppermint Lounge, the group's maniacal sense of humor comes through loud and clear on well-recorded mung like "Thee Most Exalted Potentate of Love" and "I Ain't Nuthin' but a Gorehound."

Amid rotating guitarists and disputes with their record label, the Cramps then temporarily submerged. IRS issued **Bad Music for Bad People**, a kiss-off collection of singles sides (both LP and non-LP) and other obscure gems, like the hilariously offensive "She Said." Meanwhile, the Cramps' foreign cult following was temporarily sated by **Off the Bone**, a fifteen-track compilation including all of **Gravest Hits** and the contents of **Bad Music for Bad People**, with two earlier album cuts replacing the latter's "TV Set" (originally from **Songs the Lord Taught Us**) and "Uranium Rock."

The Cramps returned to the living dead in late '85 with a wonderfully smarmy single ("Can Your Pussy Do the Dog?"), followed by an all-new sex-crazed studio album, **A Date with Elvis**. A bit more professional and less stylized than usual, but as happily crazed as ever, **Elvis** contemplates such Interior designs as "What's Inside a Girl?,"

"(Hot Pool of) Womanneed" and "The Hot Pearl Snatch."

Visually and musically, the Cramps are the Addams Family of rock.
[si/iar]

CRASS

The Feeding of the Five Thousand, The Second Sitting (Crass/nr) 1978
Stations of the Crass (Crass/nr) 1980
Penis Envy (Crass) 1981
Christ—The Album (Crass/nr) 1982
Yes Sir, I Will (Crass/nr) 1983

PENNY RIMBAUD & EVE LIBERTINE

Acts of Love (Crass/nr) 1985

Lords of English punk's extreme left, Crass don't just sing about anarchy in the UK—they *do* something about it. Formed in 1977 as a band much in the Sex Pistols/Sham 69 image, they have evolved into an anarchist commune, several record labels and an information service. They espouse all the proper causes—anti-war, anti-nuclear, feminism, flushing out hypocrisy in organized religion—with blood-curdling vehemence on their own records and on the numerous singles and albums by like-minded bands they've released (or inspired). The group has found itself embroiled in legal battles with various government agencies, but in an era largely typified by apathy, Crass stand as a successful model of dead-serious political commitment in rock.

The Feeding of the Five Thousand is a reissue of the group's debut EP on Small Wonder. Fitting eighteen songs on a 12-inch 45, it is typical of Crass' shock tactics: The first cut is a sneering recitation of "Asylum," an irreverent dismissal of Christ as anybody's lord over droning guitar feedback. The rest is mostly raw faster/louder punk spiked with protest demagoguery, four-letter words and harsh cockney ranting.

Stations of the Crass is even harder going—three studio sides and a live side containing a full seventeen songs. Almost in spite of the oppressive, relentless punk bluster, Crass often write anthemic songs (like the ironic "Banned from the Roxy" and "Do They Owe Us a Living?" from **Five Thousand**), but over the course of this album (all of the studio material was cut in one day!), they blur into white noise. "White Punks on Hope" forcefully summarizes their scorn of punk as fashion and the Sham 69 parody, "Hurry Up Garry," is a wicked snipe at the music press.

Better production and more expansive arrangements distinguish **Penis Envy**. Drawing an ugly parallel between rampant sexism and man's rape of nature and society, the album bounces vibrantly from the strident bash of the ironic rape fantasy "Bata Motel" to the LP's unsettling church-organ coda.

Christ—The Album is quintessential Crass. A boxed two-record studio and live set, it comes with a 28-page booklet packed with emotional small print about the revolution and one man who died for it. Musically, it builds on the daring of **Penis Envy**, even including a mock string arrangement in "Reality Whitewash," without tempering the band's brute punk rage. The severity of their sound and their belligerent politics can be predictable, even petulant, but **Christ-The Album** and the other records prove that Crass at least have the courage and strength of their convictions. **Yes Sir, I Will** is Crass' response to the Falklands' War, a series of musical speeches covering the conflict and indicting Prime Minister Thatcher for the deaths. Although most of the backing is typically abrasive, a couple of passages are quite beautiful. [df]

CRAWDADDYS

Crawdaddy Express (Bomp-London/Voxx) 1979
Still Steamin' (Ger. Line) 1980

This San Diego band delivers a 1979 record straight from 1964. Taking their name from the London R&B club where the Stones and Yardbirds started out, the Crawdaddys copy those and other like-minded period groups like the Pretty Things and Downliners Sect. Unfortunately, their lame renditions of various blues obscurities and originals from the same mold make this well-intentioned tribute to the genre little more than nostalgia-mongering. [wk]

ROBERT CRAY BAND

Who's Been Talkin' (nr/Tomato) 1980
Bad Influence (Demon/HighTone) 1983
False Accusations (Demon/HighTone) 1985

The most acclaimed new American blues artist in years, Robert Cray comes from Georgia by way of Washington. The young singer/guitarist has been leading bands for over a decade, and got a commercial break by appearing as a bassist in *Animal House*. Cray's first album was generally overlooked, with critics discovering him on both sides of the Atlantic only upon the release of **Bad Influence**. A smooth singer with a bit of Albert King's intonation and soul phrasing that recalls Otis Redding and Al Green, Cray has a deft guitar touch—a mix of Buddy Guy's jazzy leads and Albert Collins' driving raunch—and an enlightened way with songs built on traditional blues concerns. Both HighTone albums rely largely on familiar-sounding originals, with a supple quartet providing appropriate support. (Besides these three records, Cray plays and sings on **Showdown**, a joint album with Albert Collins and Johnny Copeland.) [iar]

CREATIVE TECHNOLOGY INSTITUTE

See *Chris and Cosey*.

CREATURES

Wild Things EP (Polydor/nr) 1981
Feast (Wonderland-Polydor/nr) 1983

Soon after the Banshees released their **Juju** album, Siouxsie Sioux and drummer Budgie, under the sobriquet Creatures, collaborated on a five-song double-45 of voice-and-percussion pieces, including a nasty reworking of the Troggs classic, "Wild Thing." The full-length **Feast**, however, is a dilettantish excursion into the only previously untested flavor-of-the-month: Hawaiian. The instrumentation incorporates marimba, while an ethnic choir adds bogus authenticity to the messy proceedings. Even worse, the lyrics are bad acid visions written by people evidently unfamiliar with their subject matter. The Creatures did make one great 1983 single, "Right Now," which is fortunately (for it) not on the LP. [rnp/dgs]

HELIOS CREED

See *Chrome*.

MARSHALL CRENSHAW

Marshall Crenshaw (Warner Bros.) 1982
Field Day (Warner Bros.) 1983
Our Town EP (Warner Bros./nr) 1984
Downtown (Warner Bros.) 1985
The Distance Between EP (Warner Bros./nr) 1986

Detroit native Crenshaw spent some time in a road company of *Beatlemania* before moving himself (and musician brother Robert) to New York, where he became a critical fave, following a local indie 12-inch with a major-label recording contract. Notwithstanding the Buddy Holly and Rick Nelson comparisons, Crenshaw's main strength lies in his bland, scrubbed presence—the first album sounds like an audio test for studio sound quality. Clean, crisp, neat and simple, free of frills and pretense, what makes **Marshall Crenshaw** great are the songs— "Someday, Someway," "She Can't Dance," "Cynical Girl," "Brand New Lover"—sparkling, tuneful gems that are instantly memorable and steadily enjoyable.

Field Day, rather bombastically over-produced by Steve Lillywhite, has a walloping drum sound, lots of sonic holes and a few of Crenshaw's best songs. Although artistically not a good LP, joyous numbers like "Whenever You're on My Mind," "All I Know Right Now" and "Our Town" mine Crenshaw's shuffle-pop resources effectively and salvage it from disaster. A clumsy piece of studio madness, it didn't help Crenshaw's career much. To counter some of the criticism the record engendered, "Our Town" and two other tracks from it were given a simplifying remix by John Luongo, attached to a live oldie ("Little Sister") and issued as an impressive second-chance 12-inch in the UK.

With production assistance by T-Bone Burnett and a large bunch of savvy sidemen in place of his usual band, Crenshaw filled **Downtown** with an extraordinary collection of intelligent, memorable pop songs in a number of musical veins. Easily his finest, most mature record, **Downtown** swings with easy confidence through heartbreakers ("The Distance Between," "Like a Vague Memory"), lovemakers ("Yvonne," "Terrifying Love"), country laments and blues struts. It also features Ben Vaughn's hauntingly wistful "I'm Sorry (But So Is Brenda Lee)." [iar]

CRIME AND THE CITY SOLUTION

The Dangling Man EP (Mute/nr) 1985
Just South of Heaven EP (Mute/nr) 1985

Growing out of the Birthday Party's debris, this oddly-named outfit is led by guitarist Rowlan S Howar and drummer Mick Harvey (also one of Nick Cave's Bad Seeds). Howard's brother Harry plays bass and Simon Bonney (another Australian) does the singing. On the second EP, former Swell Map Epic Soundtracks took over on drums, allowing Harvey to reclaim his original BP role as multi-instrumentalist.

The Dangling Man is a four-track disc that picks up where the Party ended—a slow, stripped-down, blues-flavored horror show. (Considering that Cave did much the same on his first solo recordings, one wonders if the band didn't break up out of boredom rather than any musical differences.) None of the songs really take off, but it does show promise.

Just South of Heaven is cleaner and more powerful, with all six tracks working well. Howard's guitar is as strong as ever, but piano and organ figure just as prominently. A hauntingly beautiful record by a well-integrated band. [dgs]

CRISTINA

Cristina (ZE-Island/ZE-Buddah) 1980
Sleep It Off (ZE/ZE-Mercury) 1984

August Darnell wrote five and produced all of the six long rhythmic romps on Cristina Monet's first album, but her impassive, inelegant singing ankles them, leaving it a botched mess of colliding styles and sensibilities. At its best, in "Mama Mia," Darnell effectively buries her in an active mix.

Sleep It Off, produced by Don Was, plays up the satirical possibilities of Cristina's pre-Madonna ultra-bitch pose (?), having her coolly pronounce witty songs (all her own lyrics) like "Don't Mutilate My Mink" and "What's a Girl to Do?" over richly executed multi-styled backing tracks. The musicians—the unofficial Friends of ZE/Was—include erstwhile Knackman Doug Feiger, James Chance, Barry Reynolds, Howie Wyeth and the two Was Bros. themselves. Cristina's deadpan voice perfectly suits this setting and the record is excellent, from the disconcertingly sadistic cover, until the last strummed guitar chord of "He Dines Out on Death" gives way to a brief snippet of restaurant noise. [iar]

CROOKS

Just Released (Blueprint/nr) 1980

Following the Jam came an onslaught of mod/pop bands boasting great songs and not a shred of individual character. The Crooks, in fact, were a significantly superior outfit with better songs, less derivative stylization and more overall inventiveness than their skinny-tie competitors. A shame really—if there hadn't been such a glut, the Crooks would have stood out and might have been noticed. [iar]

CROWN OF THORNS

Crown of Thorns EP (Illegal/nr) 1983

Despite the ominous cover photograph, this outfit has an almost chipper anthemic pop sound with heavy-on-the-tom-tom drumming, interestingly ragged guitar, reedy organ and shouted, echoed melodic vocals. A strange stylistic mix to be sure, but a workable one—kind of a weird detour from mid-period Adam and the Ants. [iar]

CRUZADOS

Cruzados (Arista) 1985

Despite the impressive backgrounds of three of the quartet's members—Tito Larriva and Chalo Quintana of the (LA) Plugz, and Steven Hufsteter of the (LA) Quick and other Kim Fowley-related ventures—Cruzados is a rather familiar-sounding melodic rock album with few distinguishing characteristics and no audible street-level credibility or evidence of southwest influences. Perhaps it's the fault of producer Rodney Mills, veteran of countless .38 Special albums. Or maybe the work these guys did on film scores or backing Bob Dylan on TV made them too slick. In any case, **Cruzados** is nothing to get excited about. [iar]

CUBAN HEELS

Work Our Way to Heaven (Cuba Libre-Virgin/nr) 1981

These four young Glaswegians make impressive ragged pop noise in a style that recalls both XTC and the Skids. Despite a somber back cover pic, this is infectious, quirky music; witty and wily. [iar]

CUDDLY TOYS

Guillotine Theatre (Fresh/nr) 1981
Trials and Crosses (Fresh/nr) 1982

As an early punk band, these gits called themselves the Raped; changing their name to Cuddly Toys, they also dyed their hair, dressed in androgynous threads and began playing Bowie-style glam-rock. Despite an auspicious debut 45 ("Madman," a curiosity piece—the only song co-written by Bowie and Marc Bolan), their first album is merely a pathetic attempt to clone **Ziggy Stardust**; lacking anything original or clever to add, it's a total flop. **Trials and Crosses**, by a revamped lineup (retaining only singer Sean Purcell), tries to be more modern by adding '80s rhythms and keyboards, but comes up similarly devoid of creativity and substance. [iar]

CULT

Dreamtime (Beggars Banquet/nr) 1984
Love (Beggars Banquet/Sire) 1985
Revolution EP (Beggars Banquet/nr) 1985

SOUTHERN DEATH CULT

The Southern Death Cult (Beggars Banquet/nr) 1983

DEATH CULT

Brothers Grimm EP (Situation 2/nr) 1983

The saga of the band with the diminishing name: for a while, every time these guys made a record, they lost part of their handle. The original Southern Death Cult had, in fact, disbanded without releasing an album; the eponymous LP was posthumously compiled from various sessions and live takes. As such, it paints an inconsistent picture of an ominous, dense doom-punk band with a serious power supply and a few original ideas. The songs aren't much to brag about—drum-dominated drones at various tempos—and the performances, given their mongrel origins, are too muddy to really judge what the original band was actually like. Pass on this one.

Singer Ian Astbury then formed a new band called Death Cult and released two 12-inch singles, including the four-song **Brothers Grimm**. Titularly reduced to the Cult, they finally got around to making a proper LP, **Dreamtime**, an extremely well-produced and intense outing that reveals their true intentions. Essentially a hip heavy metal band, the Cult blends domineering drums with layered lead guitar figures and Astbury's drama-drenched vocals on pseudo-poetic songs that oddly connect with the Doors and other bands of the first psychedelic era. Impressive in its clear-headed strength and attractive for its electric sound, **Dreamtime** is, like a lot of metal, exciting but ultimately empty and not a little stupid.

The well-produced **Love** chugs along like second-rate old Banshees, awash in William Duffy's guitars and Astbury's sweeping vocals. The material—except for the atmospherically powerful and (yes!) catchy **She Sells Sanctuary**—is pretty naff, with simple chord riffs providing a loud bed for draggy melodies and too much pointless riffing. (To be fair, drummer Mark Brzezicki, on loan from Big Country, adds a lot of the drive and precision.) The invocation of '60s hard-rock and grunge-punk bands is subtle enough not to be obnoxious, but the Cult's relevance to modern times (except for those too young to know better) remains marginal at best. A subsequent EP adds non-LP tracks to **Love**'s "Revolution" (not the Beatles tune). [iar]

SMILEY CULTURE

"Cockney Translation" (Fashion/nr) 1984
"Police Officer" (Fashion/nr) 1984

A recent arrival on the British reggae scene, toaster Smiley Culture is a fresh, smart comic who scored a left-field hit with "Cockney Translation," a bright and funny number comparing cockney with West Indian slang. The follow-up, "Police Officer," which pokes fun at the local constabulary, also topped the pop charts for weeks.

Smiley Culture's records speak directly to and for Britain's black people. "Cockney Translation" jokes about the confusing dialects that exist side-to-side in London but makes a point about how separate the groups that use them really are. Similarly, "Police Officer" is about racist treatment. Smiley gets off easy in the song when he's recognized, but the suggestion remains that not all blacks enjoy the same protection. [bk]

CULTURE CLUB

Kissing to Be Clever (Virgin/Virgin-Epic) 1982
Colour by Numbers (Virgin/Virgin-Epic) 1983
Waking Up with the House on Fire (Virgin/Virgin-Epic) 1984
From Luxury to Heartache (Virgin/Virgin-Epic) 1986

For a time England's biggest pop sensation, ludicrously heralded in the States as leaders of a second British Invasion (but only by those too disinterested to have been paying music any close attention for the past decade or two), Culture Club originally capitalized on singer Boy George's outrageous nightlife

cross-dressing and aimed-to-shock intelligent interviews to slip their mushy mainstream pop into respectable homes the world over. Phenomenology aside, the quartet is hardly as bizarre-sounding as they (actually just George—the other three have no fashion sense at all) originally appeared, and if their four albums are considered in coldly critical terms, they're nice but meaningless slices of sophisticated fodder, guaranteed to be memorable but in fact utterly disposable, in true pop tradition.

Kissing to Be Clever has such Club standards as "Do You Really Want to Hurt Me," its warm reggae pulse supporting a catchy melody, and "I'll Tumble 4 Ya," a somewhat boppier dance number. Spurred by the American success of the former as a single, the US label switched the track order around totally to highlight it, and later reissued the LP with a subsequent 45, "Time (Clock of the Heart)," appended. Dropping the silly "white boy" crypto-sociology that threads through the first album, **Colour by Numbers** gets right to the business at hand, which is the creation of unavoidable pop hits in a variety of molds. And in that regard, the album is a real success, containing as it does the mildly folk-rock-psychedelicized "Karma Chameleon" and "Church of the Poison Mind," as well as the more soul-oriented "Miss Me Blind" and "Black Money." Easily the best of the four albums, and the one that most prominently features singer Helen Terry providing a powerful foil to George's smooth crooning.

Riding high on stardom, Culture Club blew their rock credibility and career momentum totally with the ultra-dull **Waking Up with the House on Fire**. Although George has a fine soul voice and the band plays with maximum slickness and sophistication, the songs are irredeemably awful, from the torpid velveeta of "Mistake No. 3" (apt title, that) to the juvenile stupidity of "The War Song" ("War is stupid . . . ") and the inane stop-start mess of "Hello Goodbye." Having created the album with significantly misguided intentions of achieving political relevance *and* added middle-of-the- road acceptance, it's an unmitigated disaster.

At that point, it seemed likely that the Club was on the verge of disbanding, and the lengthy delay in producing a new album only fueled pessimistic speculation about the group's future. Nonetheless, they managed to deliver **From Luxury to Heartache**, which isn't awful at all. Culture Club's new problem is utter irrelevance: lacking controversy, a style to call their own, or truly catchy songs, there's nothing to hold onto here, just a bunch of well-produced (by Arif Mardin and Lew Hahn) mild soul/funk MOR disposables. Basically the same group they always were musically, **From Luxury to Heartache** underscores the inexplicability of their original reception: it was ever thus. [iar]
See also *Edge, London, Mood.*

DAVID CUNNINGHAM

See *Flying Lizards.*

CURE

Three Imaginary Boys (Fiction/nr) 1979

Boys Don't Cry (Fiction/PVC) 1980
Seventeen Seconds (Fiction/nr) 1980
Faith (Fiction/nr) 1981
Carnage Visors [tape] (Fiction/nr) 1981
. . . Happily Ever After (nr/Fiction-A&M) 1981
Pornography (Fiction/Fiction A&M) 1982
The Walk EP (Fiction/Fiction-Sire) 1983
Japanese Whispers: The Singles (Fiction/Fiction-Sire) 1983
The Top (Fiction/Fiction-Sire) 1984
Concert/The Cure Live (Fiction/nr) 1984
The Cure Anomalies 1977-1984 [tape] (Fiction/nr) 1984
The Head on the Door (Fiction/Elektra) 1985
Quadpus EP (nr/Elektra) 1986
Standing on a Beach: The Singles (Fiction/Elektra) 1986

Though catapulted to some success with the pop hit "Boys Don't Cry," the Cure—led by obsessive singer/guitarist Robert Smith, originally with Michael Dempsey on bass (replaced after one LP by Simon Gallup) and Laurence (Lol) Tolhurst on drums—generally specializes in the presentation of a gloomy, nihilistic world view. **Three Imaginary Boys** (released in America—and later England—as **Boys Don't Cry**, with several songs replaced by early singles) shows the Cure to be masters of the three-minute form, and includes some amazingly terse and effective musical dissertations on loneliness ("10:15 Saturday Night"), war and hatred ("Killing an Arab," "Fire in Cairo"), the precariousness of urban life ("Subway Song") and addiction to fashion ("Jumping Someone Else's Train"). An intelligent, unique halfway point between Gang of 4 and the Jam.

Seventeen Seconds moved the Cure further into terra incognita, away from the pop song and into the angst epic. Some songs ("Play for Today," "In Your House") still offer a fading element of hope, but the title track, "The Final Sound" and "A Forest" all take a turn toward disconsolateness.

Faith shows the arrival of despair as an element of style. Sacrificing any pretense of fun, the music is strengthened by an impassioned but sedated mood, its themes as powerful and defiant as any in recent music. (**Carnage Visors**, which appears only as a bonus on the UK cassette version of **Faith**, is the instrumental soundtrack of a short film, and provides even stronger reasons for locking up the razorblades while listening.) The sarcastically titled **Happily Ever After** combines **Seventeen Seconds** and **Faith** whole into a double album for American release.

Pornography seems to be the climax of Smith's obsessions, by now coalesced into resigned paranoia; the music firmly establishes the group as superior if idiosyncratic. As usual, the true star here is the phobic, morbid atmosphere. Recommended, but not for the suicide-prone.

With Smith splitting his time between Siouxsie and the Banshees and his own band (which by this point had essentially become a core duo with Tolhurst), a far different Cure emerged. The playful "Let's Go to Bed" heralded a new era of stylistic innovation and sporadic whimsy, played out on a series of

singles beginning in late 1982. **The Walk EP**—four songs of New Order-ish synth-based music that's more solemn than miserable—was also issued in the US with the earlier "Let's Go to Bed" and its flipside added. A compilation of recent 45s, **Japanese Whispers**, then appeared in both countries, reprising the entire American EP plus a subsequent bit of jazzy froth, "The Lovecats," and its similar B-side, "Speak My Language."

Having almost fully exercised their dalliance with light relief, Smith and Tolhurst, joined by a drummer and sax player, recorded an all-new album, **The Top**, which basically returns them to more familiar corners of gloomy self-indulgence. Except for "The Caterpillar," which is upbeat and likable pop, the record is not one of their best, with disconnected excursions into psychedelia, heavy rock and dance rhythms to punctuate it.

Over the course of the following two years, the Cure issued a lot of music, although only one new studio album was among the onslaught of "product." The UK-only live record is most notable in its cassette version, which adds a bonus album's worth of outtakes and esoterica under the name **The Cure Anomalies 1977-1984**. Ditto the fine career-long (thirteen) singles compilation, **Standing on a Beach**: various formats (US and UK) contain extra items. (Specifically, the CD adds four tracks; the tape a dozen B-sides.)

With "In Between Days," **The Head on the Door** opens sounding exactly like New Order. By the second song, of course, Smith's fickle idiom dabbling returns the band—here a revamped quintet, with Simon Gallup back in the fold—to an entirely different world, via the mildly oriental "Kyoto Song," and follows in flamenco style with "The Blood." Toeing a line here between pop and sullenness keeps the Cure from achieving maximal creative impact, but it's an altogether listenable album that is sporadically ("Push" and "Close to Me," for example) as eclectically brilliant as can be. The **Quadpus EP** joins two B-sides—including the bizarre "A Man Inside My Mouth"—to "Close to Me" and "A Night Like This" from the album. [sg/iar]
See also *Glove, Siouxsie and the Banshees.*

CYANIDE

Cyanide (Pye/nr) 1978

This band deserves credit for reducing the punk sensibility to a mindless cliché of aggression and speed. Made to burn. [jy]

ANDRE CYMONE

Livin' in the New Wave (nr/Columbia) 1982
Survivin' in the 80's (CBS/Columbia) 1983
AC (CBS/Columbia) 1985

An early member of Prince's touring ensemble, Cymone did his own "look ma, no band" musical crossover LP in 1982. Less horny and inspired than his former employer's contemporary approach, Cymone is nonetheless a strong contender in his own right and seems exhilarated (note the title of his first album) by the possibilities inherent in the same area of musical commingling.

Although **Survivin' in the 80's** still shows a lot of Prince's influence (especially imagewise—check the costumed male/female black/white band photo on the cover), Cymone is working more typical dance-floor terrain than the Purple One, with processed vocals and mild scratch production adjusting the slow funk grooves of numbers like "Make Me Wanna Dance" and "Body Thang." Slick and functional, but no creative biggie.

Back on his own in the studio, Cymone created **AC** with only skimpy outside assistance. Prince wrote and co-produced one easily recognizable track ("The Dance Electric") that also features backing vocals by Lisa and Wendy of the Revolution; he allowed others to add a few jots of percussion and vocals as well. Otherwise, Cymone remains perfectly capable— like his ex-boss—of working easily and independently in a number of styles, from languid reflection ("Pretty Wild Girl") to pretty balladry ("Sweet Sensuality") to kinetic dance music ("Book of Love," "Satisfaction"). [jg/iar]

HOLGER CZUKAY

See *Can, Jah Wobble*.

D

DALEK I

Compass Kum'Pas (Back Door/nr) 1980
Dalek I Love You (Korova/nr) 1983

Following several different line-ups during 1977 and 1978, Dalek I Love You's name was shortened to Dalek I and the band reduced to a duo by the time their first album was recorded. Alan Gill and Dave Hughes (the former was subsequently guitarist in The Teardrop Explodes; the latter, drummer for Orchestral Manoeuvres in the Dark) play a multitude of synths, guitars and percussion instruments on **Compass Kum'Pas**, an LP that should have been subtitled **Yet Another Green World**, what with its unabashedly Eno-esque soundscapes (not to mention a reading of "You Really Got Me" that owes its existence to Eno's **801 Live** arrangement). Still, any group that can segue the dirgelike "A Suicide" into a bouncy, poppy ditty like "The Kiss" is quirky enough to warrant investigation; also, as an exercise in stereo recordmaking, **Compass Kum'Pas** is a gem. A reformed Dalek I made a second album in 1983. [ds]

DALIS CAR

The Waking Hour (Paradox-Beggars Banquet/nr) 1984

Peter Murphy (ex-Bauhaus) and Mick Karn (ex-Japan) plus a less illustrious drummer comprise Dalis Car, mixing Japan's sensuous sound with Bauhaus' obsequious lyrical constructs. As a mellifluous noise, **The Waking Hour** is fine if a bit heavy on the bass; dig any deeper, however, and what you get is a hollow attempt to create art without any redeeming artistry. [iar]

ROLF DAMMERS

See *Can*.

DAMNED

Damned Damned Damned (Stiff/nr) 1977
Music for Pleasure (Stiff/nr) 1977
Machine Gun Etiquette (Chiswick/nr) 1979
Black Album (Chiswick/IRS) 1980
Friday the 13th EP (NEMS/nr) 1981
Best of the Damned (Chiswick/nr) 1981
Strawberries (Bronze/nr) 1982
Live Shepperton 1980 (Big Beat/nr) 1982
Live in Newcastle (Damned/nr) 1983
Damned EP (Stiff/nr) 1985
Damned but Not Forgotten (Dojo/nr) 1985
Is It a Dream? EP (MCA/nr) 1985
Phantasmagoria (MCA) 1985
Damned Damned Damned/Music for Pleasure (Stiff/nr) 1986

NAZ NOMAD & THE NIGHTMARES

Give Daddy the Knife Cindy (Big Beat/nr) 1984

Holding the distinction of being the very first British punk band to issue an album (also, notably, Stiff's first LP) as well as the first to tour America, the Damned hold a special position, historically if not always musically. Over an exceedingly checkered multi-label career—breakups, reformations, side projects, farewell gigs, a spell as the Doomed, vast popularity, near obscurity—the Damned have consistently managed to shatter expectations and defy the odds, wreaking havoc and nonchalantly tweaking convention. Getting a cogent critical perspective on their recorded oeuvre is as elusive as attempting to read the label on a spinning 45.

Damned Damned Damned was a major groundbreaker—a stripped-down punk album of high-speed songs filled with raunchy guitar rock and equally aggressive sentiments. With Nick Lowe producing, the Damned trounced such traditional recording values as musical precision and studio-quality sound. Unfailingly energetic and vital, it's the only Damned album to feature the original lineup of Dave Vanian (vocals), Brian James (guitar), Rat Scabies (drums) and Captain Sensible (bass). Just to heighten the bratty iconoclasm, early copies of the sleeve "goofed," picturing rivals Eddie and the Hot Rods in lieu of the Damned on the back cover.

In just one of many surprising career turns, the Damned's second opus was produced by Nick Mason of Pink Floyd. With added guitarist Lu, and no definite direction, the attack sounds blunted, and there aren't as many great songs as on the first. Despite its great cover, **Music for Pleasure** doesn't live up to the title. (Stiff reissued both LPs as a mail-order-only double in 1986.)

The Damned broke up and re-formed several times before cutting **Machine Gun Etiquette** with a new lineup. Sensible had traded bass for guitar, Lu had departed and ex-Saints bassist Algy Ward had joined. Despite the tumult, the band is totally revitalized and on top of things—more mature, but no less crazy—tearing through great numbers like "Love Song," "I Just Can't Be Happy Today" (both UK hits) and the anthemic "Noise Noise Noise." A great record by a band many had counted out.

With new bassist Paul Gray, formerly of Eddie and the Hot Rods, the **Black Album**—a two-record set in the UK, one disc in America—takes off in a totally different direction, displaying unexpected aspects of the Damned's character. The first two sides (the entire US release) are packed with melodic rock verging on power pop, using acoustic guitar, vocal harmonies, mellotron and synthesizers, as well as other seemingly inconceivable (for the Damned) components. "Wait for the Blackout" and "Dr. Jekyll and Mr. Hyde" indicate how far the debonair Damned had travelled; other tracks prove that they had not abandoned the roar'n'roll with which they began. Sides Three and Four are weird. One is a single composition—strung together by church organ—that doesn't work; the other a live best-of that's impressive but half-baked. (**Live Shepperton 1980** comes from the same gig but runs for two sides, not one, offering such bonuses as "Neat Neat Neat" and "Help.")

Best of the Damned consolidates the standout tracks from all the abovementioned albums, plus a couple of welcome non-LP sides that balance the bill nicely. A winning collection of great and diverse music. Stiff's 1985 **Damned** EP reissues 5 early cuts.

Strawberries, despite a humorous porcine cover shot, is a toothless, old-sounding affair that drags itself along with neither bite nor character, a few good songs notwithstanding. It's not terrible, merely forgettable.

Phantasmagoria is mainly Vanian's show. His imposing singing on graveyard items like "Grimly Fiendish" and "Sanctum Sanctorum" provides the character the songs themselves lack. Jon Kelly's production (complete with horror film effects and phantom-of-the-opera organ) is adequate, but the Damned no longer has a unique sound outside of Vanian, so it's fairly academic. (The LP was also issued in the UK with a bonus blue vinyl 12-inch of the subsequent "Eloise," a drippy Paul Ryan song.) An EP of the album's "Is It a Dream" adds four live tracks.

Released pseudonymously by Naz Nomad & the Nightmares, **Give Daddy the Knife Cindy** is the Damned's imaginary '60s psychedelic film soundtrack, filled with covers of such classics as "I Had Too Much to Dream (Last Night)," "Kicks," "Nobody But Me," Kim Fowley's "The Trip," plus a pair of originals. The material is great, but the unembellished studio performances are merely functional. It was a nice thought anyway.

For those keeping track of such things, the 1986 lineup (besides Dave and Rat) includes a pair of Welshmen: Roman Jugg (who joined in 1981) and Bryn Merrick ('82). [iar]
See also *Captain Sensible, Lords of the New Church.*

D

DANCE

Dance for Your Dinner EP (nr/GoGo) 1980
In Lust (Statik/nr) 1981
Soul Force (Statik/nr) 1982

Dance for Your Dinner introduced a promising New York funk outfit heavy on rhythmic interplay, fronted by the seductive Eugenie Diserio, who veers cuts like "She Likes to Beat" closer to Donna Summer than authentic funk. Helped on drums by Material's Fred Maher, the four songs live up to the band's intricate intentions.

In Lust finds the Dance stiff and stifled in the studio; the band never stretches out its bass lines and there's not really enough material to fill an album. Diserio's softcore eroticism, so appealing on the EP, is held in check.

Soul Force has a similar lack of inspiration. Except for a stirring cover of Stevie Wonder's "Do Yourself a Favor," the album never hits a groove, though not for lack of effort. Diserio is the sexiest she's been, and the production is uncluttered, but the Dance has yet to record anything memorable. [gf]

DANNY & DUSTY

The Lost Weekend (Zippo/A&M) 1985

This one-off studio bender assembles the cream of LA's cowpunk society for a batch of rowdy tunes about drinkin', lovin', gamblin' and losin'. The cast: Dan Stuart and Chris Cacavas of Green on Red, Steve Wynn and Dennis Duck of Dream Syndicate and most of the Long Ryders. Produced by Paul Cutler, **The Lost Weekend** offers a saucy good time, short on significance, but long on ambience

and spirit. For reference, a version of Dylan's "Knockin' on Heaven's Door" typifies the tenor of Wynn/Stuart's collaborative songwriting. [iar]

DANSE SOCIETY

Seduction EP (Society/nr) 1982
Heaven Is Waiting (Society-Arista/Arista) 1984
Heaven Again (Society-Arista/Arista) 1985

Arty and willfully obscure, Danse Society occasionally mixes almost-straightforward rock into dense dance rhythms, yielding a good song now and again. **Seduction** is a longwinded six-song effort with busy Bauhaus-strength mud supporting sporadic vocals and gimmicky sound effects. Tuneless and tedious. The first album contains additional plodding nonsense, but at least boasts the abrasive but catchy dance-rock of the title track and a weirdly modernized reading of the Stones' already spacey "2000 Light Years from Home." [iar]

DARK

Chemical Warfare (Fresh/nr) 1982
The Living End (Fall Out/nr) 1982

Two things probably kept England's Dark (not to be confused with a Boston band) from finding commercial success. First, they didn't fit the trendy punk image of the early '80s—just not fashionable compared to the mohawk haircut breed. Second, Fresh Records was going out of business at the time of their first album's release, and gave it little promotion. Still, **Chemical Warfare** showcases a fine punk band, rough and aggressive, yet intelligent. **The Living End** consists of eight songs from the band's final concert. The sound quality is uneven, but one can discern that the Dark were an entertaining band in front of an audience. [cpl]

DARK DAY

See *DNA.*

DATA

Elegant Machinery (Sire) 1985

The unpredictable career of Georg Kajanus (once leader of the ridiculous but entertaining Sailor) continues on a bizarre path with this appealing electro-pop duo. Joined by a femme singer named Frankie, with ex-Sailormate Henry Marsh and ex-Advertising man Simon Boswell providing added keyboards, Kajanus spins out technically facile but emotional numbers with enough formulaic pop sensibility to make them all likely hit singles. [iar]
See also *Peter Godwin.*

DAWGS

My Town (nr/Star-Rhythm) 1982
On the Road to You (Fr. New Rose) 1983

Boston bar-rockers the Dawgs play ingenuous '60s Stones-styled original rock'n'roll tunes with choogling guitars and vocal panache on **My Town**. Produced by Cub Koda, the sound is muddy and the energy level only about half of what it might be, but a refreshing lack of pose and nostalgia-mongering redeems the project. **On the Road to You** reprises two of those tracks (which sound far better—must have been

the mastering), adds three produced atmospherically by Elliot Easton of the Cars and five more; the audio results are far crisper and the playing significantly hotter. [iar]

MORRIS DAY

Color of Success (Warner Bros.) 1985

Morris Day's relationship with Prince is the stuff of *Dynasty* or *Dallas*—a longstanding friendship marred by rivalry, jealousy, public one-upsmanship and other professional feuding. Prince helped raise Morris to stardom by helping his band, the Time (hypothetically—and apparently—not one of Prince's puppet outfits). He even gave Day a starring role as his musical archenemy in *Purple Rain*, resulting in extravagant praise for Day's performance as the Kid's foppish, cruel competitor. Soon after, the Time collapsed and Day went solo, issuing an album with a thinly veiled title and a mock radio announcement on the first track explaining his situation and promising great things ahead. **Color of Success** has less of Day's personality than the final Time LP, pointing him in a rather familiar-sounding pop-soul direction. At the record's most ridiculous, Morris introduces a new dance, "The Oak Tree," in a seemingly endless display of self-amusement; on stronger footing, he rocks steady with "Love Sign" and waxes smoothly romantic on "Don't Wait for Me." [iar]

DB'S

Stands for Decibels (Albion/nr) 1981
Repercussion (Albion/nr) 1982
Like This (nr/Bearsville) 1984

WILL RIGBY

Sidekick Phenomenon (nr/Egon) 1985

It's difficult to understand why the dB's' first two albums—both well-conceived and accessible—were never released in the band's own country. On the first, the four New York-based North Carolina refugees draw inspiration from '60s pop psychedelia and quote freely from sources such as the Beatles, Move, Nazz and even the Beau Brummels. However, the group's two singer/guitarist/songwriters, Peter Holsapple and Chris Stamey, each have too individual a style to merely parrot, and nearly every song has some new twist, whether through production effects (few pop records are as consistently aurally interesting as this without resorting to gimmickry), or through an unusual instrumental or lyrical approach. It's not a happy record—often as not the songs are about deteriorating relationships—but played with such exuberance it's uplifting.

Repercussion adds a number of flourishes to the group's style. Producer Scott Litt achieves a fuller, more modern overall sound; on many of the tracks, instrumentation is denser than anything on its predecessor. The Rumour Brass makes an appearance on "Living a Lie." In addition, drummer Will Rigby—one of a mere handful of current rock drummers with a sound of his own beyond mere beat-keeping—is brought more to the fore on numbers like "Ask for Jill" and "In

Spain." Depending on one's preferences in production style, **Repercussion** can be seen either as a great advance from **Decibels** or as a glossing-up of the group's sound.

Just as the dB's *finally* signed to an American label, Chris Stamey left the band. With a little instrumental realignment, they recorded **Like This** as a trio, adding a new bassist afterwards. Although the reliance on Peter Holsapple's songwriting cuts down on the band's eccentricities, unpretentious intelligence, wit and ineffable pop smarts make it a wonderful album with no weak spots or inadequate songs. Dropping much of the British influence in favor of an Americanized, countryfied air, tunes like "Love Is for Lovers," "Lonely Is (as Lonely Does)" and "White Train" carry the banner of romance disappointed in memorable settings. An instantly lovable gem. [ds/iar]
See also *Kimberley Rew, Sneakers, Chris Stamey.*

D.C.3

See *Black Flag.*

DEAD BOYS

Young Loud and Snotty (Sire) 1977
We Have Come for Your Children (Sire) 1978
Night of the Living Dead Boys (nr/Bomp) 1981

Although originally from Cleveland, the Dead Boys made their international reputation in New York starting in early '77 by out-punking everyone else on the Bowery circuit. Having absorbed what had already happened in England (the Sex Pistols, Damned) and America (the Stooges), the Dead Boys took it a dozen steps further, uncovering new levels of violence, nihilism, masochism and vulgarity. Their two studio albums have improved considerably with age, and now undoubtedly serve as guideposts to younger fans and players.

Young Loud and Snotty, one of the earliest punk albums released on a US label, benefitted from the production skill of Genya Ravan, who made it loud and raw—an onslaught of sizzling guitars and Stiv Bators' sneering whine. Classic tracks include tasteless originals like "Sonic Reducer," "All This and More" and "Caught with the Meat in Your Mouth," as well as a dynamic rendition of the Syndicate of Sound's prototypical "Hey Little Girl."

We Have Come for Your Children, produced by Felix Pappalardi, has inferior sound, but equally strong playing. The material suffers from second-LP drought and an onset of self- parodic punk typecasting, leading to such dumb tunes as "Flame Thrower Love," the topical "Son of Sam" and "(I Don't Wanna Be No) Catholic Boy." The record's best track is the reflective "Ain't It Fun," co-written by guitarist Cheetah Chrome and Peter Laughner.

Night of the Living Dead Boys was recorded live at CBGB in New York in 1979, and captures the end of the band, flaying their way through their best numbers in ultimate ragged-but-right fashion. The mix is trebly and muddled (a rare combination), but it is still a punk documentary of some merit. [tr]
See also *Stiv Bators, Lords of the New Church, Wanderers.*

DEAD CAN DANCE

Dead Can Dance (4AD/nr) 1984
Garden of the Arcane Delights EP (4AD/nr) 1984
Spleen and Ideal (4AD/nr) 1985

Mesmerizing if a bit laborious, Australian quintet Dead Can Dance spin slow webs of drum-driven but mostly shapeless guitar music, with chanting, singing and howling by the two (male and female) singers. Possibly of interest to undiscriminating fans of moody psychedelia and/or the Cocteau Twins. The more intriguing four-song **Garden of the Arcane Delights** EP has crisper production than the album, although roughly the same musical stylings.

By the time **Spleen and Ideal** was released, DCD were down to a duo of vocalists Brendan Perry and Lisa Gerrard. Some of the guitars have given way to ethereal keyboards, with tympani, cellos and trombones blended in; much of the LP sounds as though it belongs in a cathedral rather than a concert hall. The songs are more structured than before, but things do get a bit precious, and the first three, hymnalesque cuts are pretty tough to sit through. The album gets meatier as it progresses, though, and the end result is a record of haunting and solemn beauty.   [iar/dgs]

See also *This Mortal Coil*.

DEAD FINGERS TALK

Storm the Reality Studios (Pye/nr) 1978

Dead Fingers Talk, although never very well known, was an important band ahead of its time. Tom Robinson, for one, reportedly took heart from BoBo Phoenix's frank discussions of gay life on this record before taking the militantly gay stance that first won him recognition. On this lone album, DFT play with a gritty recklessness reminiscent of the early Velvet Underground, a resemblance heightened by Mick Ronson's audio verite production. (Forget overdubs!) Singer/songwriter Phoenix's tunes don't mince words: "Nobody Loves You When You're Old and Gay" is simultaneously cutting and hilarious, while "Fight Our Way Out of Here" mixes desperation and anger. Elsewhere, he offers optimistic tunes just to show he's well rounded, but these too have a harsh intensity. Not to be missed, if you can find it. [jy]

DEAD KENNEDYS

Fresh Fruit for Rotting Vegetables (Cherry Red/IRS) 1980 (Cherry Red/nr) 1985
In God We Trust, Inc. EP (Statik/Alternative Tentacles) 1981
Plastic Surgery Disasters (Statik/Alternative Tentacles) 1982
Frankenchrist (Alternative Tentacles) 1985

KLAUS FLOURIDE

Cha Cha Cha with Mr. Flouride EP (Alternative Tentacles) 1986

It took a while, but in the Dead Kennedys, America finally produced a powerful, self-righteously moral band to match the fury of the Sex Pistols. Led by audacious and inimitable singer Jello Biafra (who once stood—and received a substantial number of votes—for mayor in San Francisco, the band's base),

the DKs combine blunt and sardonic discussions of touchy issues with crushing, high-speed guitar and drums. Generally acknowledged as the main pioneers of American hardcore, the Kennedys have been influential, not only by setting the style, sensibility and commendable standards, but through their Alternative Tentacles label and continued vocal/active support for grassroots rock activity.

Despite a few weak songs, **Fresh Fruit** is explosive and gripping (also controversial—a borrowed photo used on the back cover led to some unpleasant, but funny, legal trouble). Jello's political sarcasm erupts on "Kill the Poor" and "California über Alles," offering a funny but chilling condemnation of then-governor Jerry Brown and "zen fascists" in the latter. "Holiday in Cambodia" echoes the Pistols' "Holidays in the Sun." Jello picks another popular target for "Let's Lynch the Landlord" in typically unsubtle broadside fashion. (The 1985 reissue is on compact disc. Whatta concept!)

In God We Trust, Inc. makes more needed statements, but the music has been stripped of dynamics and reduced to routine hyperactive punk. Scrap the record and keep the lyric sheet.

Plastic Surgery Disasters, with its gruesome mock-*E.T.* cover, improves the musical blend to include more three-dimensionality while retaining the Kennedys' typical rock energy. Songs like "Terminal Preppie," "Winnebago Warrior," "Trust Your Mechanic" and "Well Paid Scientist" mix humor with political activism and offer pointed and intelligent observations on social absurdity. An impressive album from an increasingly important band.

The DKs stopped recording for several years while the members worked on outside projects (producing a number of bands released by Alternative Tentacles). In early 1985, they hit the road again. **Frankenchrist** repeats much of the same psycho-punk style as **Plastic Surgery Disasters**. Some songs are a little weak, with forced, awkward lyrics, but the LP does contain two of the DKs' finest moments: "MTV Get Off the Air" and "Stars and Stripes of Corruption," one of the most powerful political statements ever committed to vinyl. Instead of just bellyaching about problems (a common habit of politico-punks), Biafra offers possibilities for constructive change, demonstrating real American patriotism as opposed to the commie-bashing Rambo jingoism so prevalent these days.

Despite their sparse and spotty recorded output, the Dead Kennedys will always hold an important spot in the annals of punk and independent music. However, their greatest strength—undying conviction and sense of purpose—is at the same time their achilles heel. Biafra is a true champion of all the right causes, but his extreme stance (not to mention the band's perenially uncommercial sound) guarantees that he'll spend his days merely preaching to the converted.

[jy/dgs]

See also *Witch Trials*.

DEAD OR ALIVE

Dead or Alive EP (Black Eyes-Rough Trade/nr) 1982

Sophisticated Boom Boom (Epic) 1984
"Youthquake" (Epic) 1985

Dead or Alive's leader/singer—cross-dressing ultra-poseur Pete Burns—can claim historical credit in the second Liverpool explosion —he was in a brief band with Julian Cope and Wah! man Pete Wylie—before founding Dead or Alive's developmental predecessor, Nightmares in Wax. The early EP finds him searching for meaning and truth while attempting to appropriate the vocal style of Jim Morrison; murky, to say the least. **Sophisticated Boom Boom** includes a totally horrible and gratuitous remake of KC and the Sunshine Band's "That's the Way (I Like It)," and that's as good as the album gets. Burns sings like his urges ("What I Want," "You Make Me Wanna," "I'd Do Anything") are the stuff of Shakespearean drama; the backing is slickly competent dance-rock bereft of any personality.

Dead or Alive subsequently issued several much improved 45s, including "You Spin Me Round (Like a Record)," that cut a lot of the crap and substituted a kinetic, catchy pop sensibility. **"Youthquake"** contains that track, as well as the equally substantial "Lover Come Back to Me" and a few others that show how much fun the band can be. On the other hand, the record has its bad patches as well, proving the impossibility of pinning down DoA to any consistent style or quality level. Proceed with caution.

[jg/iar]

DEAF SCHOOL

2nd Honeymoon (Warner Bros.) 1976
Don't Stop the World (Warner Bros.) 1977
English Boys/Working Girls (Warner Bros.) 1978

A sprawling nine-piece (later eight), Liverpool's Deaf School seemed like an ideal candidate for success in the quiet pre-punk doldrums of 1976. Visually, the group had more than enough going for it to guarantee a high profile in the British press: The cast included pasty-faced guitarist Clive Langer, who sported wire-rims and wrote most of the melodies; the Rev. Max Ripple, a keyboardist done up like a parson; and no less than *three* lead vocalists: mustachioed Enrico Cadillac, a Bryan Ferry disciple; Bette Bright, who suggested a somewhat frumpy torch singer; and the suave, acid-voiced Eric Shark, who sang as Bogart might have.

Despite its slick, full sound, **2nd Honeymoon** has the clear markings of a first effort. The band cleverly mixes the melodrama of Roxy Music with the music hall vivacity of middle period Kinks, but many of the songs are bloated and their intent unclear. As on later LPs, crooner Cadillac takes the lion's share of the vocals, making tales of modern desperation ("What a Way to End It All") and lost love ("Room Service") into intriguing, if incomplete, exercises in style.

Deaf School came into its own on **Don't Stop the World**, trimming the excesses of **2nd Honeymoon** and adding impressive new elements to the mix. While Cadillac continues to warble romantically, Shark belts out a vicious rocker ("Capaldi's Cafe") and Bright shines

in a rare solo spot, the after-hours ballad, "Operator." (The two LPs were issued in the US as a double-pack in 1977.)

Although **English Boys/Working Girls** offers more of the same, it's the product of a band running out of steam. In a return to the clutter of their debut, Deaf School favors theatrics over substance; acounts of modern violence like "Ronny Zamora (My Friend Ron)" and "English Boys (with Guns)" are more exploitation than insight.

Deaf School's alumni remained busy after the band folded, making it—in retrospect—a startling fount of promise. Enrico Cadillac formed the Original Mirrors under his civilian name, Steve Allen, and recorded two albums. Bassist Steve "Average" Lindsey founded the Planets and did the same. Bette Bright cut a delightful solo record, produced by Clive Langer, who earned additional production credits (not to mention scads of money, no doubt) with Madness, Elvis Costello and Dexys Midnight Runners. Langer also formed a band and released records.   [jy]

See also *Bette Bright, Clive Langer and the Boxes, Original Mirrors*.

DEATH COMET CREW

See *Dominatrix*.

DEATH CULT

See *Cult*.

DEFUNKT

Defunkt (Hannibal) 1980
Thermonuclear Sweat (Hannibal) 1982

Led by singing trombonist Joe Bowie, the seven-man Defunkt peddles black funk with dry bounce. Their first album isn't a revolutionary breakout, but does include the super-catchy (if obtusely titled) "Blues," which was extremely popular in and around New York. **Thermonuclear Sweat**, named for a track from the first LP, is sweeter-sounding and jazzier, smoothed out by Joe Boyd's sage production. [jw]

DEL AMITRI

Del Amitri (Chrysalis) 1985

This Glasgow quartet fell victim to excessive hype before its debut album release. Many who went overboard praising the group on the strength of two singles and a few live performances unjustly criticized the LP—ten quirky, country-flavored tracks, drenched in crystalline Rickenbacker guitar and Hugh Jones' spare production—for being too traditionalist. Although admittedly a conventional construct, few play this style with as much heart as Del Amitri. These boys love what they do, and you can hear (and feel) it in such rollicking songs as "Crows in the Wheatfield" and "Sticks and Stones Girl."   [ag]

DEL-BYZANTEENS

Del-Byzanteens EP (Don't Fall Off the Mountain/nr) 1981
Lies to Live By (Don't Fall Off the Mountain/nr) 1982

Up from the murky pit of New York's art-punk scene came the Del-Byzanteens, a band with stylistic threads running back through Television and the Velvet Underground and the ability to give their dark, urgent arrangements a cinematic pan. An unsettling cover of the Supremes' "My World Is Empty (Without You)" on the three-track EP is a slice of jungle paranoia with voodoo percussion, ominous group vocals that sound like a satanic mass and a guitar quotation from *Perry Mason*.

The group's inventive resources are spread a little thin, though, on **Lies to Live By**. The quirky B-52's guitarisms and hyper-disco thump of "Draft Riot" and dour facelessness (Joy Division variety) of the title track dull the impact of both "War," a clever union of funk-punk drive with protest lyrics from Caribbean calypso records, and the gray soul of the old Jaynettes' shuffle, "Sally Go Round the Roses." Both "Lies to Live By" and a new version of "Girl's Imagination" (from the EP) were used by German filmmaker Wim Wenders in his movie *The State of Things*. [df]

DEL FUEGOS

The Longest Day (Rough Trade/ Slash) 1984
Boston, Mass. (London/Slash) 1985

A solid album from a great Boston band, **The Longest Day** is bursting with high-energy beat'n'billy-inflected guitar rock. The songs are memorable without pandering; the playing is simple but never simpleminded. From the quivering "Nervous and Shakey" (which opens the LP) to the ominous hipshake, "Call My Name," which ends it, this is a full therapeutic dose of mature, unaffected rock'n'roll from the '50s and '60s built strictly in and for the '80s.

Following a dubious linkup with a beer company that resulted in a reasonably cool TV ad, the group's second LP is just a hair more self-conscious. In light of the American popularity of "working class" rock (Springsteen and Mellencamp), **Boston, Mass.** (which interestingly recalls the old Animals more than anything else) sounds a bit too much like it was made to please a wide audience. On the other hand, the Del Fuegos were never far from that in the first place; it would be foolhardy to expect them to abandon a style simply because it had accidentally become the radio vogue. Still, this record's not as much fun as the first. [iar]

GABI DELGADO

Mistress (Virgin/nr) 1983

Formerly the singing half of Deutsche Amerikanische Freundschaft, Delgado enlisted some top names in modern German music—Conny Plank, Jaki Liebezeit and others—to make this slick but expendable album of disco music topped off with obsequious lyrics, mostly about sex. [iar]

DEL-LORDS

Frontier Days (Enigma-EMI America) 1984
Johnny Comes Marching Home (EMI America) 1986

Pioneers at the East Coast's westernmost boundaries, New York's Del-Lords stand in the forefront of back-to-the-roots countryfied rock'n'roll, eschewing any particular stylistic imitation to enthusiastically bang out well-written tunes of hard times and true love. With guitarist Scott Kempner

(once "Top Ten" of the Dictators) penning all the material but occasionally relinquishing vocals, the Del-Lords return to rock's basic components, but with so much skill and verve that they outshine most everyone else on the scene. Best tracks on **Frontier Days**: "Burning in the Flame of Love," "Feel Like Going Home" and a cover of "How Can a Poor Man Stand Such Times and Live." True-blue and brilliant.

Johnny Comes Marching Home was produced by Pat Benatar's husband, Neil Geraldo, with no ill effects whatsoever: the songs are better, the playing even more confident and enthusiastic. Lyrical topics stretch from the sunny optimism of "Heaven" to the misery of "Love Lies Dying," with stops along the way for a kidnapped victim of terrorism ("Against My Will"), a love letter to a real-life '60s radio dj ("Saint Jake"), and a wistful view of militarism from a veteran's perspective ("Soldier's Home"). The music runs the gamut from a greasy Link Wray instrumental to a brilliant re-write of "If I Had a Hammer." Not trendy, twangy, corny or self-conscious like other neo-realist rockers, the Del-Lords simply play the old-fashioned way, with a sharp ear for melody and choruses that don't evaporate. Considering that their roots are essentially a quarter-century old, they sure make it sound fresh and young. [iar]

DELTA 5

See the Whirl (Pre/nr) 1981

Their name sounds like a 1920s jug band, but Delta 5's album displays up-to-the-minute beat consciousness welded to songs of emotional discontent. Double female vocals in pronounced British accents are backed by whomping rhythm (two guitars, two basses) and occasional splashes of musical color (brass, keyboards, pedal steel guitar). Semi-cryptic lyrics, full of striking images, are worth the strain needed to pull them out of the seething mass. Jagged music for jagged times. [si]

DEPECHE MODE

Speak and Spell (Mute/Mute-Sire) 1981
See You EP (nr/Mute-Sire) 1982
A Broken Frame (Mute/Mute-Sire) 1982
Construction Time Again (Mute/Mute-Sire) 1983
Everything Counts EP (Mute/nr) 1983
Get the Balance Right! EP (nr/Mute-Sire) 1983
People Are People (nr/Mute-Sire) 1984
Some Great Reward (Mute/Mute-Sire) 1984
The Singles '81—'85 (Mute/nr) 1985
Catching Up with Depeche Mode (nr/Mute-Sire) 1985
Black Celebration (Mute/Mute-Sire) 1986

Born in the midst of the new romantic movement, Depeche Mode proved themselves capable of making flawlessly captivating electro-pop tunes with simple formulae. What set them apart was reliance on synthesizers for the entirety of their sound, offering post-modernistic gloss to comfortably familiar (but new) material.

Not coincidentally, the best songs on **Speak and Spell** were hit singles: "New Life," "Dreaming of

Me" and the smash "Just Can't Get Enough." Oblivious to innovation or deep thinking, the album is nonetheless a good collection of modern dance tunes.

Despite dire predictions following songwriter Vince Clarke's departure to form Yazoo, Depeche Mode pressed on essentially unhampered as a trio to make **A Broken Frame**, which has similar virtues, tempered with some deviation from course. The vocals are stronger, and while funk forms the rhythmic base of "My Secret Garden," a Japanese tinge is given to "Monument" and "Satellite" centers around a ska beat. The rest of the album varies to a small degree from the dance-mania of earlier work without abandoning it—a characteristic middle ground between experimenting and playing it safe.

Expanding to a quartet, but with Martin Gore continuing as the band's main songwriter, **Construction Time Again** exposes a mature outlook, dropping the simplistic pop tunes for a more intellectual, challenging approach. It's not an altogether smooth transition, so while "Everything Counts" offers a bitter denunciation of the (presumably, music) business world and "Shame" is a heartfelt confrontation with responsibility, other tunes ("Pipeline," "More Than a Party") are less probing, although the former has interestingly industrialized music and chanted vocals. Both the English **Everything Counts** EP and the American **Get the Balance Right!** maxi-single have live cuts in addition to remixes of the title tracks.

Although the reason for its assembly is unclear, **People Are People** is a compilation of post-Clarke tunes, drawing five of its tracks from the two preceding albums and the rest from singles. Not a cohesive album, but it does contain prime songs blending synth-rock with real-life and industrial noises to make truly modern pop music for the new age.

Some Great Reward is Depeche Mode's best record, containing everything from the bitter religious doubt of "Blasphemous Rumours" to the societal/sexual role-playing of "Master and Servant" and the egalitarian-minded "People Are People." The seamless incorporation of unsettling concrete sounds fits synthesized factory din (or clanking chains, or whatever else) into the music, achieving a music/life mix mastery few bands with the same goal have approached.

As Depeche Mode's international stature grew to awesome proportions, two compilation albums were released in 1985: **The Singles** and **Catching Up**. The former, issued in the UK, is a fine collection of thirteen familiar 45 sides; the cassette and CD add two more cuts. The American release has most of the same tracks (excluding those already compiled on **People Are People**), but includes "Fly on the Windscreen" (which also turns up on **Black Celebration**, the subsequent album of new material) and "Flexible."

Depeche Mode have tackled many different lyrical concerns in the past, but never have they done such a consistently downcast record as **Black Celebration**. Except for intermittent bouts of romanticism and a bluntly political protest

("New Dress"), the songs are filled with doubt, disgust and depression, an attitude their dirgelike, minor-chord constructions reinforce. The big problem is that the tunes mostly sound like each other; the same shards of melody turn up repeatedly. There's a certain demented power to this work, but it's one of their less appealing and accomplished albums. [sg/iar]

See also *Erasure, Yazoo.*

DEPRESSIONS

The Depressions (Barn/nr) 1978

DP'S

If You Know What I Mean (Barn/nr) 1978

In their first incarnation, this quartet was an awful fake-punk band. To the group's credit, the playing on their first LP isn't strictly inept, but the material is utterly detestable (a concept of punk as misogyny so ugly it would offend the Stones) and the pose so transparent that you have to hate them. Perhaps the embarrassment of this record caused the band's name change shortly after its release.

Switching from pseudo-punk to pseudo-power pop, the Depressions became the DP's and made a second record not nearly as offensive as their first. They still couldn't write a memorable song and their playing never surpassed adequate, but at least nil-content is innocuous compared to their earlier cretinous outlook. [ds]

DESPARATE BICYCLES

Remorse Code (Refill/nr) 1979

Along with the far more heralded Soft Boys, this post-punk Chocolate Watch Band predated the neo-psychedelic movement by several years with this LP of ten pop gems. The interplay of agile bass and near-perfect guitar helps kick things along, and songs like "Sarcasm" and "It's Somebody's Birthday Today" are utter classics. Sly humor is exhibited with silly tape and sound effects, not to mention the guitarist's savvy pseudonym: Dan Electro. [dgs]

JIMMY DESTRI

See *Blondie.*

DEUTSCHE AMERIKANISCHE FREUNDSCHAFT

Ein Produkt der D.A.F. (Ger. Warning-Atatak) 1979
Die Kleinen und die Bosen (Mute/nr) 1980
Alles Ist Gut (Virgin/nr) 1981
Gold und Liebe (Virgin/nr) 1981
Für Immer (Virgin/nr) 1982

Originating as art-punk cacophony cultists in the holdout hippie culture of late 1970's Germany, D.A.F.—originally a group, but known generally as the duo of Robert Görl and Gabi Delgado—broke away to find success in Europe as a synthesizer-and-dance band.

Ein Produkt der D.A.F. is an apocalyptic eruption of sound announcing the end of the German Republic, with shrieking, colliding overdubbed synths and guitars. The electro-metal avant-hardcore is simultaneously repellant and compelling. **Die Kleinen und die Bosen,**

D.A.F.'s first international release, modifies the electronic chaos with an eye towards the modern dance. Material is more polished, with anarchic synthesizer work slowly integrating a solid, defined beat.

Alles Ist Gut abandons D.A.F.'s Faustian tendencies for cerebral dance music, polished to a metallic shine by producer Conny Plank. Typical funk rhythms are replaced by industrial pulses (trains, etc.); some vocal experimentation casts the band onto shrewd pop turf, despite decidedly libidinous lyrics. **Gold und Liebe** perfects the advances of **Alles Ist Gut**, emphasizing the punchy use of drum-box and de-emphasizing other instruments, creating a robot void that eerily strands the guttural vocals.

D.A.F.'s final album, **Für Immer**, breaks the pattern, with a variety of styles from funk to rock'n'roll to distorted metal drone before returning to a dance blowout for the final track. While it's all interesting, none of these excursions are displayed long enough to be truly impressive. The inner spaces of earlier work are filled by a range of instruments, including very gentle bells. Like all of D.A.F.'s LPs, it is sung in German.

Delgado and Görl each pursued solo careers following the breakup of their partnership but reunited in 1985. [sg]

See also *Gabi Delgado, Robert Görl*.

DEVO

Q: Are We Not Men? A. We Are Devo (Virgin/Warner Bros.) 1978
Be Stiff EP (Stiff/nr) 1979
Duty Now for the Future (Virgin/Warner Bros.) 1979
Freedom of Choice (Virgin/Warner Bros.) 1980
Devo Live EP (Virgin/Warner Bros.) 1981
New Traditionalists (Virgin/Warner Bros.) 1981
Oh No! It's Devo (Virgin/Warner Bros.) 1982
Shout (Virgin/Warner Bros.) 1984

From their first independent 45, Devo has been one of the most entertaining new bands. Their records, short films/videos and live appearances are planned carefully to propagate a cynically offbeat view of humanity. Indeed, music sometimes seems like only one component of Devo's media mix.

Their first album is the most concentrated presentation of the band's nebulous "devolutionary" theories. "Jocko Homo," "Mongoloid" and "Shrivel Up" have a cold, assembly-line jerkiness to drive home their defeatist attitudes. The same nervous energy fuels more emotional messages like "Uncontrollable Urge," "Gut Feeling," "Sloppy (I Saw My Baby Gettin')" and a hilarious version of the Rolling Stones' "Satisfaction."

Be Stiff collects Devo's two indie 45s—four tunes that had been re-recorded for **Are We Not Men?**—and their third single, done for Stiff.

The second full-length album, **Duty Now for the Future**, doesn't score as many bullseyes as the first, but includes two Devo anthems of malaise, "Blockhead" and "S.I.B. (Swelling Itching Brain)." Amid disturbing signs of portentousness, Devo turns their bemused eyes to the mating ritual on "Strange Pursuit," "Triumph of the Will" and "Pink Pussycat."

Freedom of Choice is the band's most evocative pairing of words and music. Setting aside metaphysical foofaraw, they contrast choppy keyboard licks ("Girl U Want," "It's Not Right," "Snowball") and ironic but unalienated perceptions ("Gates of Steel," "Planet Earth," "Freedom of Choice"). Their tolerance was rewarded with a hit single from the LP, "Whip It."

Milking the success of "Whip It," **Devo Live** is thoroughly redundant. Five of the six songs, including you-know-what and an instrumental version of "Freedom of Choice," are from the preceding LP; only "Be Stiff" is new to album buyers. Hardly a jamming band, Devo live sounds just like Devo in the studio, except maybe sloppier.

Devo's been soft-pedalling their philosophy (on record, at least) since **Freedom of Choice**'s breakthrough. Musically they're still held back by a stunted sense of melody, although the dance-rock movement created a favorable climate for a rhythmic orientation and probably led to Devo's increasing emphasis on a whomping beat.

New Traditionalists has a couple of attention-getting songs ("Going Under," "Beautiful World"). Most of it, though, is laissez-faire techno-dance stuff, less than compelling lyrics set to a metronomic 4/4 beat. The same can be said of **Oh No! It's Devo**, while **Shout**'s only memorable contribution is a version of the Jimi Hendrix oldie, "Are You Experienced?" Songwriters Mark Mothersbaugh and Gerald Casale are evidently going through a dry spell of drought proportions, substituting clichés for the razor-sharp observations that used to keep Devo listenable as well as danceable. Has Devo succumbed to its own devolution? [si]

HOWARD DEVOTO

Jerky Versions of the Dream (Virgin/IRS) 1983

Following influential and estimable careers with the Buzzcocks and Magazine, singer/writer Devoto continues his quest for independence as a solo artist. Using Dave Formula and Barry Adamson from Magazine, as well as other players, Devoto offers his idiosyncratic worldview and original musical outlook on ten tunes that range from funky ("Topless," "Way Out of Shape") to ethereal ("Rainy Season") to playful ("I Admire You") and beyond. Full appreciation of Devoto's work requires a bit of forbearance and effort, but few artists make music that is as careful and intelligent. [iar]

DEXY'S MIDNIGHT RUNNERS

Searching for the Young Soul Rebels (Parolophone-EMI/EMI America) 1980 (Fame/nr) 1982
Don't Stand Me Down (Mercury) 1985

KEVIN ROWLAND AND DEXYS MIDNIGHT RUNNERS

Too-Rye-Ay (Mercury) 1982
Geno (EMI/nr) 1983 & 1986

Although changing Dexy's from a nouveau American-soul band to an ethnic Irish folk group may make singer/mastermind Kevin Rowland seem a tad fickle, his single-minded devotion to a chosen direction gives the group's first two albums a powerful sense of care and dedication that many infinitely more consistent musicians never achieve.

Searching for the Young Soul Rebels, recorded by the original eight-man lineup, boldly challenged the direction new wave had taken music in 1979 and '80, long before soul music and horns became trendy. Taking inspiration from soul men like Sam & Dave and Geno Washington, one-time punk singer Rowland anted up a batch of emotionally powerful songs that work equally well as heartfelt tributes and modern creations. Despite the enormous amount of image-building that surrounded it, **Searching** is a fine, expressive album with no bad tracks.

Too-Rye-Ay, overalls and country instruments notwithstanding, is not as radically different at its core from **Searching** as it might first appear. Fronting a totally new band (including Seb Shelton, one-time Secret Affair drummer), plus a two-piece fiddle section and a vocal trio, Rowland retains some of the earlier throaty horn work to make a few tracks (one a spot-on cover of Van Morrison's "Jackie Wilson Said") sound a lot like the first LP. Elsewhere fiddles, banjos, accordion and tin whistle take over to make jolly, rollicking jug band fare—the enormous worldwide hit "Come On Eileen" and "The Celtic Soul-brothers," for instance. Other songs mix metaphors and become something more indescribable. Truly a weird smorgasbord, the clever melodies and arrangements keep it consistently entertaining.

Dexys' only album release in either 1983 or 1984 was **Geno**, a worthwhile compilation of early singles (A- and B-sides) assembled by the band's former label. To everyone's discredit, the band didn't evaporate then and there: **Don't Stand Me Down** (forever to be recalled, if at all, as the "accountants" album due to a change of image—into pinstripes) is a torpid snore that denies entertainment on every level. With titles like "Knowledge of Beauty" and "Reminisce Part Two," the seven lengthy songs with absurd lyrics aim for a literate Van Morrison-like looseness, but end up just falling asleep or apart. Never mind the Dexys. [iar]

DIAGRAM BROTHERS

Some Marvels of Modern Science (New Hormones/nr) 1981

Something like XTC (but lacking their musical smarts or stellar wit), the Diagram Bros.—of the Manchester art-noise family encircling New Hormones—play dissonant weirdness with lyrics about current events. While the poorly-produced music only hints at talent hidden behind the anti-music self-indulgence, it's actually the four-sheet insert, containing detailed fold/cut/paste directions for assembly into a portfolio about the record, that indicates the presence of real cleverness. [iar]

MANU DIBANGO

Electric Africa (Celluloid) 1985

Manu Dibango is the foremost international practitioner of Cameroon's traditional makossa rhythm. He's played variations on it—along with the jazz and R&B he often prefers—since the mid-'50s, achieving world notoriety in 1972 with the hit single, "Soul Makossa." His albums have been released fairly consistently in America and England ever since. Dibango's vocal chants and choppy saxophone make an unlikely foil for producer/technophile Bill Laswell's revved-up keyboards and drum machines; the resultant LP, **Electric Africa** (featuring keyboardists Herbie Hancock and Bernie Worrell) is neither as soulful or as interesting as those involved probably hoped it would be. [rg]

DICE

Broken Rules (Fr. CBS) 1980
The Dice (Fr. CBS) 1982

This French quartet comes off insouciant, snotty and clever on **Broken Rules**. Maybe a touch too careful, enough to undercut the urgency that would have made more than a few of the songs memorable. By **The Dice**, the band consisted of the two prime movers (keyboardist Pascal Stive and singer J.M. Devlin) plus three backing vocalists (their soundman, manager and lyricist) and a few session players. While Elaine Rowen may have added to the band's image, her lyrics rework every old rock chestnut in the book. If anything, the cleaned-up music, while shiny and "new," is nothing more than a polished lemon without an engine. [jg]

DICKIES

The Incredible Shrinking Dickies (A&M) 1979
Dawn of the Dickies (A&M) 1979
Stukas Over Disneyland (nr/PVC) 1983
We Aren't the World! [tape] (nr/ROIR) 1986

For some reason, the lovable Dickies—a *Mad* magazine-flavored punk self-parody—never endeared themselves to a large cult the way the Ramones have. Perhaps this West Coast mob of zanies is too unserious and knowing of their own idiocy, while their New York counterparts may well be playing it straight. (That's cooler, apparently).

The Incredible Shrinking Dickies is a burst of generic hyper-active punk, California style, ca. 1979. Giddy good humor dominates, in blithe contrast to the surly conviction of more earnest bands. Seven of the thirteen tracks clock in at under two minutes (each, not all told), and everything sounds the same, from covers of "Eve of Destruction," the Monkees' "She" and Black Sabbath's "Paranoid," to originals like "Mental Ward" and "Rondo (The Midget's Revenge)." Disposably nice.

On **Dawn of the Dickies**, the title of which, like that of its predecessor, alludes to a junk-movie classic, something wonderful happens: the Dickies get genuinely good. By slowing down the tempo a half step and coming up with strong melodies, guitarist Stan Lee and crew manage to reel off one maniacally catchy gem after another. The pop-culture slant is the same as before, as "Manny, Moe and Jack" and "Attack of the Mole Men" aptly demonstrate, and the mood is equally flippant, but this is a record with staying power.

After a prolonged absence, the

boys next popped back into view with a frisky eight-song mini-album. Half of **Stukas Over Disneyland** dates from 1980, including a delightfully garbled version of Led Zeppelin's "Communication Breakdown." Of the others (cut around 1983), the highlight is "Pretty Please Me," a power-pop pearl. Not a work of demented genius like **Dawn**, but good fun.

More oddities and endities can be found on the cassette-only **We Aren't the World!**, 21 doses of live Dickiedom (many of them covers) done between 1978 and 1985, plus the raw 1977 four-song demo that, according to Lisa Fancher's belligerent liner notes, got them signed to A&M. Although the recording quality is as varied as the locales, this just might be **Dark Side of the Moon** for fans of chaotic smartassitude. [jy/iar]

DICTATORS

Go Girl Crazy (Epic) 1975
Manifest Destiny (Asylum) 1977
Bloodbrothers (Asylum) 1978
Fuck 'Em If They Can't Take a Joke [tape] (nr/ROIR) 1981

Considering that the Dictators' first album came out in 1975, scads of credit is due these hearty prepunk New Yorkers for being there first. The idea of melding junk culture—wrestling, fast food, television, beer, cars, scandal sheets—with loud/hard/fast rock'n'roll has been subsequently adopted and adapted by dozens of bands, from Black Flag to Cyndi Lauper, who revel in the same indulgent mentality. All four of the Dictators' albums (including the posthumous live tape) are great and, although wavering wildly in terms of style and track-to-track consistency, serve as memorable cornerstones for much of what followed. As protégés of genius music journalist Richard Meltzer, the Dictators helped translate a lot of intellectual fandom's crazed hypothetical theorizing about rock'n'roll's possibilities into wretchedly wonderful reality.

The Dictators were originally a quartet: former rock writer/*Teenage Wasteland Gazette* publisher Adny Shernoff (vocals/bass), monster guitarist Ross the Boss, Scott "Top Ten" Kempner (rhythm guitar) and Stu-Boy King (drums). On their first LP, crazy-roadie-turned-crazy-singer Handsome Dick Manitoba was photographed in wrestling regalia for the cover, guested on some of the tracks and was listed in the credits as "secret weapon." The album itself is a wickedly funny, brilliantly played if hopelessly naive masterpiece of smartass rock'n'roll. An absolute classic that was utterly ignored at the time.

Right after the release of **Go Girl Crazy**, King took a hike and various troubles beset the band, resulting in a two-year delay before a follow-up was issued. By then, Manitoba had become a full-time vocalist, drummer Ritchie Teeter had come on board and bassist Mark "The Animal" Mendoza had joined, allowing Shernoff to switch from bass to keyboards. Although the sonic quality was mortally damaged somewhere along the way, **Manifest Destiny** contains another helping of brilliant songs, like "Science Gone Too Far," "Sleepin' with the TV On" and a stunning rip through the Stooges' seminal "Search and Destroy." The musical approach is

less tongue-in-cheek and sounds nearly adult, but any band fronted by Handsome Dick Manitoba could hardly become pretentious.

Falling in with novelist Richard Price, the Dictators' third album, **Bloodbrothers**, made some concessions, hoping for mass appeal in a last-ditch attempt to turn the band into a commercially viable proposition. Mendoza had already left for greener metal pastures (specifically Twisted Sister, with whom he became a huge star on several continents in 1984); the five-man lineup sent Shernoff back on bass. Despite the halfhearted sell-out attempt, the record has its share of great tracks—a tribute to Meltzer ("Borneo Jimmy"), a seamy tale of teenage prostitution ("Minnesota Strip") and an electric statement of purpose ("Faster and Louder"). A blinding cover of the Flamin' Groovies' "Slow Death" closes the album, and put a lid on the Dics' studio days as well. They were soon without a label, and fell apart several months later.

A few reunion gigs played around the New York area in late 1980 and early '81 resulted in the album-length live cassette, which presents the Dictators in fine form, playing old and new material as well as they ever did, and with Manitoba doing a riotous bravado star turn as singer, ring-leader and MC. In January 1986, the Dictators played a one-off tenth anniversary reunion concert in New York. [iar]

See also *Del-Lords, Shakin' Street*.

DIFFORD & TILBROOK

See *Squeeze*.

DIF JUZ

Huremics EP (4AD/nr) 1981
Vibrating Air EP (4AD/nr) 1981
Who Says So EP (Red Flame/nr) 1983
Extractions (4AD/nr) 1985

The cover of **Huremics** offers no information on the band whatsoever; the disc consists of four mood-setting improvisational guitar/drums/bass instrumentals. **Vibrating Air** maintains the enigmatic graphic pose and style, featuring four new diminutive atmospherics. While not exactly captivating fare, these slight records are actually quite nice. I wonder if anyone's ever thought of using these records for scratch mixes, or as backing tracks for unwritten songs.

On Dif Juz's first full-length LP, **Extractions**, the Cocteau Twins help out, with Robin Guthrie producing and Liz Fraser becoming the first to vocalize on a Dif Juz record. With the addition of prominent keyboards and sax, it's not as atmospheric as prior work, shooting instead for a big, echoey sound, not unlike Simple Minds. As an instrumental band, Dif Juz must be vigilant not to fall into the nice-sound-few-ideas trap. On **Extractions** they get by, but just barely. [iar/dgs]

DIODES

The Diodes (Can. Columbia) 1977
Released (Can. Epic) 1979
Action-Reaction (Can. Orient) 1979
Survivors (Can. Fringe) 1982

This Toronto quartet got on the map with an inoffensive cover of the Cyrkle's hit, "Red Rubber Ball," but

never made much of an international impression afterward. Their albums—three studio forays and one assemblage of unreleased odds and ends—proves the Diodes to be a competent but mundane rock group with faint punky instincts. Too mild-mannered to be aggressive but too energized to be wholly bland, the Diodes stuck close to the conservative rail, which keeps their albums from being very interesting.

The Diodes bears the marks of a first-time band anxious not to offend anyone. **Released**, which actually reprises "Red Rubber Ball" (on the first album as well), contains the band's best work—melodic power pop, including a fine original, "Tired of Waking Up Tired." Unfortunately, the Diodes don't sustain that cut's vitality, and some of the other material here drags tediously. **Action-Reaction** is the final album by the original lineup; the band subsequently replaced its bassist and drummer and relocated to England. A collection of previously unreleased tracks—outtakes, demos and a live version of the Stones' "Play with Fire"—was issued in 1982, named after its lead-off song, "Survivors." [iar]

DIRTY LOOKS

Dirty Looks (Stiff/Stiff-Epic) 1980
Turn It Up (Stiff/nr) 1981

If you can get past the flat, brittle production (try cranking it up loud), you'll find this Staten Island, New York trio playing power pop with a vengeance. Chief assets: good melodic instincts coupled with tight, lean drive, like an adolescent Cheap Trick gone new wave. Moodily ranging through taut reggae ("Disappearing"), crazed quasi-rockabilly ("Drop That Tan"), even an emotionally masochistic ballad ("Lie to Me"), they may seem to let their depression run away with them, but when Dirty Looks soar, you might even be convinced that "rock'n'roll is still the best drug" (from the memorable "Let Go").

What a shock, then, to hear the trio descend into mediocrity on their second LP, despite production by Nick Garvey. Half-baked, full of misguided ideas and sputtering when it should smoke, **Turn It Up** slithers all too slickly. [jg]

DISCHARGE

Hear Nothing See Nothing Say Nothing (Clay/nr) 1982
Warning-H.M. Government EP (Clay/nr) 1983
Never Again (Clay/nr) 1984

Hear Nothing See Nothing Say Nothing is a great punk album, well played and produced. Bones' guitar buzzes with electricity and the drums are loud and powerful, driving Discharge with as much energy as early Sex Pistols or Clash. The words are difficult to understand, but Cal's voice is an important ingredient to the frenzy of Discharge. [cpl]

DISLOCATION DANCE

Slip That Disc! (New Hormones/nr) 1981
Music Music Music (New Hormones/nr) 1981
Midnight Shift (Rough Trade/nr) 1984

At the time of its inception, dance-oriented rock was a good

idea that quickly turned formulaic and mundane. But the irreverent genre-busting of Dislocation Dance, a skillful Manchester outfit, redeems early DOR almost single-handedly.

Slip That Disc!, an eight-song 12-inch, couches its peppy rhythms and schematic trumpet and guitar parts in kitchen-clean production. Only the cover of Lennon/McCartney's "We Can Work It Out" (which renders the hopeful outlook of the original dark and doubtful) and "Clarinetsource" (subversive dub with neurotic processed clarinet sounds) hints at DisDance's promise.

The **Music Music Music** LP fulfills the promise and then some, with busier, more stylized production and an eclectic brew of pop, funk and jazz. One of the many highlights is "Take a Chance (on Romance)," setting the demented '40s swing of the tune against the wistful "sadness that just won't go away" of the lyrics. Dislocation Dance's whimsical humor makes modern "dislocation" easier to take, and its use of varying jazz styles in a rock context is the widest and most effective since the Bonzo Dog Band held sway. [mf]

DISTRACTIONS

Nobody's Perfect (Island/nr) 1980

Decades from now, rock historians will scratch their heads in bewilderment that the Distractions' one fine album didn't ensure the quintet a longer lifespan. A lot of records belong to a specific time, but **Nobody's Perfect** continues to measure up as an ace slab of educated pop rock, right in tune with the ground rules laid down by Blondie, Squeeze and others of that ilk. Part of the problem may be that **Nobody's Perfect** is too weighty to be passed off as a simple diversion. The band's eclecticism draws on everything from Chuck Berry to Phil Spector to psychedelia—often within the same song—and the vocals tend to be more somber than carefree. "Boys Cry" comes on like a Ronettes tune but delivers none of the upbeat emotional release seasoned pop listeners are trained to expect. Regardless, **Nobody's Perfect** very nearly is. [jy]

DIVINYLS

Monkey Grip EP (Aus. WEA) 1982
Desperate (Chrysalis) 1983
What a Life! (Chrysalis) 1985

Christina Amphlett, singer in Australia's Sydney-based Divinyls, appeared in the movie *Monkey Grip*, for which her group recorded the six songs contained on the EP. Amphlett's unusual vocal mannerisms, coupled with the band's strong hard-pop (at times sounding like a blend of AC/DC and the Pretenders, with subtle, unexpected chord-progression shifts), are delivered with an expert punch—thick textures of dual guitars and keyboard.

Divinyls' first album, recorded in New York, contrasts Amphlett's generally alluring voice with the band's driving arena-rock arrangements. A few numbers offer something better—the clear standout being "Science Fiction," in which restraint and quirky vocal characterizations replace the otherwise routine bombast.

Produced by Mark Opitz, Mike

Chapman *and* Art of Noise's Gary Langan, **What a Life!** maintains roughly similar commercial and artistic appeal, but increased self-confidence engenders relative understatement for spots of considerable improvement. The Chapman-co-written hit, "Pleasure and Pain," sounds uncomfortably like Pat Benatar, but other tracks ("Good Die Young," "Dear Diary") suggest alternative paths which Divinyls might pursue.   [jg/iar]

DON DIXON

Most of the Girls Like to Dance but Only Some of the Boys Like To (Demon/nr) 1985
Praying Mantis EP (Demon/nr) 1986

Before his name started showing up as a producer on albums by R.E.M., Let's Active and many others, Don Dixon spent 14 years as bassist/singer/songwriter in a hot North Carolina band called Arrogance. On the 14-song solo debut from this jack-of-all-musical-trades, Dixon offers an uneven but engaging patchwork of singles and demos from his personal archives—some from the Arrogance days, others done at home on his 4-track and one recorded at Mitch's Drive-In Studio. The tracks span five years (and nearly as many studios), displaying Dixon's affection for '60s pop and R&B. Sometimes cynical, sometimes whimsical, his views of love and lust are delivered with a soul man's vocal passion. The wonderfully oddball images of kissing insects and claw action in "Praying Mantis" make it an instant gem. Easter contributes lead guitar to a cover of Nick Lowe's "Skin Deep." Although the album has some forgettable items, it leaves you anxious to hear what Dixon might do when he takes the time to record a fully-developed LP.

The four-song EP packages the title song with another album track and two more from the Arrogance library, including a sweat-drenched live version of Percy Sledge's "When a Man Loves a Woman."

[kh]

See also *Marti Jones*.

DMZ

DMZ (Sire) 1978
Relics (nr/Voxx) 1981

One of Boston's primary punk bands, DMZ was led by the maniacal Mono Mann (aka Jeff Conolly), an organist/singer whose '60s roots (British and American garage punk, psychedelia) and Iggy Pop fixation formed the basis for the group's influential stylings. Their first album, produced by Flo and Eddie, has bad sound, sloppy playing and little character, despite the rave-up playing and general enthusiasm. On the other hand, **Relics**—released four years after being recorded on a 4-track by Craig Leon—has the intensity and cutting sonic attack to effectively recreate the weird sounds of Mann's idols. Anyone that can do justice to a Roky Erickson number (as in the 13th Floor Elevators' "You're Gonna Miss Me") is okay by me. (Bomp had previously issued four of these cuts on a 1977 EP; the other five had never been released.)

Conolly eventually metamorphosed DMZ into the Lyres, and took his absolute commitment to garage rock even further.   [iar]
See also *Lyres*.

DNA

A Taste of DNA EP (Rough Trade/ American Clavé) 1980

DNA ET AL.

No New York (nr/Antilles) 1978
The Fruit of the Original Sin (Bel. Crépuscule) 1981

DARK DAY

Exterminating Angel (nr/Lust/ Unlust) 1980
Dark Day EP (nr/Lust/Unlust) 1981
Window (nr/Plexus) 1983
Beyond the Pale [tape] (nr/Nigh Eve) 1985

This controversial "noise" trio was a fixture on the New York scene for several years, initially tagged as part of the avant-garde no-wave wing of the city's punk movement. Despite a minuscule recorded output, DNA was a major presence of startling originality.

DNA's genius and power were immediately evident when the group entered four cuts on the **No New York** compilation album. Arto Lindsay—once described as James Brown trapped in Don Knotts' body—pits scratch-slash-kill guitar against Robin Crutchfield's sinister Suicidal electric piano and contributes two vocals showing his unique (if unintelligible) singing style in embryonic form. On "Not Moving," his playing approximates Syd Barrett with an amphetamine edge.

It was on **A Taste of DNA** that the band matured. Six pithy, polished statements show Kabuki-painted drummer Ikue Mori coming into her own as a tight, tireless master of shifting asymmetrical rhythm; Lindsay drawls, yells, yelps, gulps, burbles and gurgles his way to left-field legend. Replacing Crutchfield's monolithic riffing is the sensitive, painterly bass of Tim Wright. This is no formless anarchic blare—each piece is a painstakingly crafted kernel of ideas organized with fearless unorthodoxy.

The three live performances ("Taking Kid to School," "Cop Buys a Donut," "Delivering the Goods") on **The Fruit of the Original Sin** compilation are a poor epitaph. They suffer from crummy sound quality—one shifts from stereo to mono right in mid-song!—and bizarre editing, though Wright's bass solo on "Delivering the Goods" is typically exquisite.

For the final encore of its swan-song performance, DNA did Led Zeppelin's "Whole Lotta Love," fittingly capping an iconoclastic career with the utterly unexpected. Its members continue to be important members of the Manhattan music scene.

Keyboardist Robin Crutchfield formed Dark Day as a trio after his departure from DNA; **Exterminating Angel** uses machine-like riffs as the foundation for moody, Teutonic music. By the release of **Dark Day**, Crutchfield had jettisoned his backing band, and his music had shifted into the twilight of ambient Eno or Dome. Never a complete original, Crutchfield manages to get extra mileage out of the styles he borrows.   [mf/rnp]
See also *Golden Palominos, Arto Lindsay, Lounge Lizards*.

D.O.A.

Triumph of the Ignoroids EP (Can. Friend's) 1979
Something Better Change (Can. Friend's) 1980
Hardcore 81 (Can. Friend's) 1981
War on 45 EP (Alternative Tentacles) 1982
Bloodied but Unbowed (Alternative Tentacles/CD Presents) 1984
Don't Turn Yer Back (on Desperate Times) EP (Alternative Tentacles/nr) 1985
Let's Wreck the Party (Alternative Tentacles) 1985

Despite personnel changes (like the original drummer leaving to join Black Flag), Vancouver's top-dog punk band has never left behind their crusading but slyly hedonistic spirit as embodied by guitarist/vocalist/songwriter Joey Shithead (Keighley), the lineup's only constant. **Triumph of the Ignoroids** is raw and live, like a stripped-down Dead Boys; **Something Better Change** is tighter, with more anthemic material fleshed out by two guitarists; **Hardcore 81** is faster and looser. The sound of **War on 45** is akin to a keyboardless Stranglers playing punk, with humorous (not to mention highly charged) reworkings of Edwin Starr's "War" ("good god y'all!!") and other tunes. Listenable and—even at its most aggressively offensive—above-average punk. (The UK version of **War on 45** substitutes two tracks from **Something Better Change**.)

Subtitled "The Damage to Date: 1978—1983," **Bloodied but Unbowed** compiles nineteen tracks (remixed and remastered) from D.O.A.'s career, powerfully confirming their status as Canada's preeminent punk outfit, a raging behemoth of tightly organized high-compression rock aggression and four-letter-word titles. Incredible, intense and essential.

Don't Turn Yer Back is a 12-inch—four songs running under ten minutes total—recorded in 1984 for a John Peel session. More angry and political than ever, it's dedicated to striking miners. Despite sharing two songs—"General Strike" and "Race Riot"—in common with the EP, for the most part, **Let's Wreck the Party** is more lighthearted. Clean, professional sound and occasional slowish tempos may turn off hardcore fanatics, but it's a cutting and witty record nonetheless.

[jg/dgs]

See also *Randy Rampage*.

DR. FEELGOOD

Down by the Jetty (UA/nr) 1975 (Fame/nr) 1982
Malpractice (UA/Columbia) 1975
Stupidity (UA/nr) 1976 (Liberty/nr) 1985
Sneakin' Suspicion (UA/Columbia) 1977
Be Seeing You (UA/nr) 1977
Private Practice (UA/nr) 1978
As It Happens (UA/nr) 1979
Let It Roll (UA/nr) 1979
A Case of the Shakes (UA/Stiff America) 1980
On the Job (Liberty/nr) 1981
Casebook (Liberty/nr) 1981
Fast Women and Slow Horses (Chiswick/nr) 1982
Doctors Orders (Demon/nr) 1984
Mad Man Blue EP (ID/nr) 1985

To suggest that all of Dr. Feelgood's records sound alike would be less than generous; there are, however, groups that have explored varying modes of musical expression with greater diligence. Yet, the band has been utterly true to its original aims; few contemporary groups can challenge this veteran outfit when it comes to playing basic, energetic R&B. Over the course of more than a dozen albums in a decade (comprising studio LPs, live sets and compilations), the Feelgoods'—or, more precisely, singer/harmonicat Lee Brilleaux, for it is he who has kept the group going through various lineups—dedication to preserving the gritty spirit of groups like the early Rolling Stones has scarcely wavered.

Regardless of inventiveness (or lack thereof), Dr. Feelgood deserves a place of respect in modern music annals by being the commercially successful leader of English pub-rock at its zenith, drawing huge crowds into small clubs all over Europe in the mid-'70s. By playing grassroots music that pleased not only critics but fans in large numbers, the Canvey Island quartet helped set the stage for the transitional—younger, more rock-oriented— Eddie and the Hot Rods, as well as the more radical punk outburst that followed *them*. Without Dr. Feelgood, there would have been fewer venues for these populist groups to play, less likelihood of a successful indie label scene (Stiff's founding was financed, in part, by Brilleaux) and a much smaller audience receptive to groups without dry ice and laser beams.

The original Dr. Feelgood lineup—Brilleaux, singer and shock-guitarist extraordinaire Wilko Johnson, drummer "The Big Figure" and bassman John Sparks—made four albums together. Johnson left the band in 1977; Sparks and the Figure in 1982. Mixing Johnson's original tunes with a hefty selection of classics from the catalogues of Chuck Berry, Willie Dixon, Rufus Thomas, Leiber and Stoller, Sonny Boy Williamson and Muddy Waters, the first three studio albums had the same R&B/ primal rock/blues character as the original Stones. The band's fanatic devotion to the past led them to release the first album only in mono! While **Down by the Jetty** has a certain amateurish charm, **Malpractice** has a stronger, more confident sound, and includes better material, like "Back in the Night," "Riot in Cell Block £9" and "You Shouldn't Call the Doctor (If You Can't Pay the Bills)." Johnson's playing—a frantic, choppy, rhythm/ lead style adapted from Mick Green and John Lee Hooker mixed with a spasmodic, Devoesque stage presence—and Brilleaux's hoarse singing may sound a bit out-of-date, but there's no mistaking the energy and honesty they bring to their work.

The live **Stupidity**, although an effective representation, suffers from its similarity to their studio work and lack of the exciting visual factor that made their early gigs so great.

Sneakin' Suspicion is the last LP to feature Johnson; although he appears on the whole thing, a disagreement over musical purity led to a split during the recording. In fact, it's equally good as **Malpractice**, with strong originals ("Walking on the Edge" in particular) and nifty covers ("Nothin' Shakin' (But the Leaves on the Trees)," "Lights Out"). The next Dr. Feelgood album, **Be Seeing You** (title and graphics borrowed from *The Prisoner* TV series), features new six-stringer

John Mayo—a strong player with his own sound, but not an even swap for the inimitable Johnson—and Nick Lowe as producer. The change in guitarists is obvious; the band's overall style, however, survives nearly intact, and some of the tracks are good enough to carry the day.

Private Practice, a studio LP produced by Richard Gottehrer, has nothing on the ball, and is played too slow to avoid tedium. **As It Happens**, another live outing, is a *real* stiff, drawing its material almost totally from **Private Practice** and **Be Seeing You**. Completing this naff trilogy is **Let It Roll**, an inconsistent (not worthless) collection produced by blues veteran Mike Vernon.

Proving that they could still cut it, Dr. F. reunited with Lowe for **A Case of the Shakes**, a wholly revitalized effort that brings the group up-to-date (relatively speaking) and in line with the likes of Rockpile, giving their traditionalist approach a more modern setting. Mayo's playing is great and the songs are surprisingly impressive and enjoyable.

On the Job is a needless concert rehash with all but one number drawn from the two preceding albums. **Casebook** is a compilation containing enough of the Feelgoods' best to make it worthwhile. **Fast Women and Slow Horses**, produced by Vic Maile, is the last LP to feature the original Figure/Sparks rhythm section. The follow-up, **Doctors Orders**, puts the Feelgoods—Brilleaux, guitarist Gordon Russell, bassist Phil Mitchell and drummer Kevin Morris—back in league with producer Mike Vernon for a program that includes Eddie Cochran's "My Way" and Muddy Waters' "I Can't Be Satisfied." [iar]

See also *Solid Senders*.

DOCTORS OF MADNESS

Late Night Movies, All Night Brainstorms (Polydor/UA) 1976
Figments of Emancipation (Polydor/UA) 1976
Sons of Survival (Polydor/nr) 1978
Revisionism 1975—1978 (Polydor/nr) 1981

This odd excuse for a rock group was essentially the warped musical vision of Kid (Richard) Strange, as realized in posh, over-the-top pretentious style by a manager who spent scads of money in an unsuccessful attempt to make them the Next Big (Ultra-Outrageous) Thing. Although the blue hair, silly theatrical gear and transparent glam pose were awfully out-of-step with the younger and faster safety-pinned hordes who stole their thunder, the Doctors did possess a unique style, thanks in large part to Urban Blitz's (no kidding) eerie violin work, an unlikely instrument in a band hoping to be perceived as Bowie's post-Ziggy disciples.

Late Night Movies (released in the US only as a double-record set with **Figments of Emancipation**) is the wildest and freshest of the group's three albums, going all out to be—or at least seem—weird and exciting. It's hard to take seriously, but there is something worth hearing in terms of the creepy ambience, substantial songs and subtle musical shadings. **Songs of Survival** and **Figments** refine the approach but lack the gonzo originality of the first record. **Revisionism** is an adequate

career summary.

After a stint that saw Dave Vanian (on furlough during one of the Damned's collapses) a member, public response—a mixture of apathy and ridicule—proved terminal, and Strange embarked on a solo career. Whatever the verdict on the Doctors of Madness while they were in business, the fact that the new romantics later shouldered the same foolish mantle of narcissism, ludicrous costumes and stage names—an aberration also adopted by American nouveau-glam-metal bands like Mötley Crüe—proves that this band was indeed ahead of its time. [iar]

See also *Richard Strange*.

DOGS

Different (Fr. Phonogram) 1979
Walking Shadows (Fr. Phonogram) 1980
Too Much Class for the Neighborhood (Epic/nr) 1982

There have been several American bands with the same name; this combo from Normandy, however, is one of the French new wave's minor legends. Their '77-'78 indie maxi-singles displayed a quartet made of tougher, rawer but more authoritative fiber than more commercially successful Gallic neo-rockers like Bijou and Telephone. As a trio, they chopped out a pair of punchy LPs, the second with more savvy and polish than the first.

Once again a two-guitar quartet, the Dogs cut a third LP with ex-heavy metal engineer Tony Platt producing, and consequently achieved the cutting yet resonant guitar sound they deserve. They're like an amped-up, French-accented, late-'70s Flamin' Groovies (see "Death Lane") but not nearly as wimpy, and influenced more by the early Stones (e.g., the "Last Time" chord cops—with Byrds/Leaves vocals— on "Wanderin' Robin"). [jg]

THOMAS DOLBY

The Golden Age of Wireless (Venice in Peril-EMI/Capitol) 1982
Blinded by Science EP (nr/Capitol) 1983
The Flat Earth (Parlophone-Odeon-EMI/Capitol) 1984

After years of session work with Foreigner, Joan Armatrading, Lene Lovich and the early Thompson Twins, Thomas Dolby revitalized a largely moribund and redundant synth-pop scene with his own recordings. **The Golden Age of Wireless** avoids the usual error, and gives the songs prominence over the instruments. Besides demonstrating an unfailing flair for sharp, snappy compositions, Dolby shows himself unusually capable of getting warm, touching feeling out of his synthesizers and his voice, creating an evocative sound that magnificently straddles nostalgia and futurism. Although the album contains some really lovely tunes, like "Radio Silence" and "Europa and the Pirate Twins," Dolby followed it with an execrable moronfunk single, "She Blinded Me with Science," which mystically made him a huge star. After the album was reissued with that song added on, a five-track mini-album appeared, combining it again with three LP tracks and another lovely

new song, "One of Our Submarines." *That* was subsequently appended to the album for its third American variation.

Dolby ultimately got around to making a whole new record, **The Flat Earth**, which offers nothing really memorable, but does feature nicely restrained pieces of inviting atmospheric charm ("The Flat Earth," "Screen Kiss," others). Unfortunately, **The Flat Earth** also contains an utterly appalling low point: Dolby duetting with Adele Bertei on the strident "Hyperactive!"

Dolby has since worked mostly on other people's projects: he co-produced and played on George Clinton's **Some of My Best Jokes Are Friends** album, Joni Mitchell's **Dog Eat Dog** and Prefab Sprout's **Steve McQueen**. He also collaborated with Ryuichi Sakamoto on an EP. [sg/iar]

DOLL BY DOLL

Remember (Automatic/nr) 1979
Gypsy Blood (Automatic/nr) 1979
Doll by Doll (Magnet/MCA) 1981
Grand Passion (Magnet/nr) 1982

The one constant on these four albums is singer/guitarist/songwriter Jackie Leven, who started out the group's leader and wound up its sole member. On the first three records, his presence is so commanding—thanks to a deep, rich, expressive voice that leaps into falsetto or descends to an ominous whisper as the moment dictates—that everyone around him takes a back seat. Although the group began as a quartet, the fourth album followed a total upheaval that left the band nothing more than Leven solo.

An impressive but flawed debut, **Remember** needlessly limits Doll by Doll's obvious rock strength. Although some tracks go flat out, the group's folk roots place the song before the performance, occasionally blunting the excitement. Still, it's a sophisticated work that serves mainly to introduce Leven's startling voice.

After some personnel changes, a reconstituted Doll by Doll made the fine **Gypsy Blood**. With all restraint lifted and the emotional intensity turned up high, tunes like "Human Face" and "Teenage Lightning" are simply magnificent—crystal clear, intricately arranged and full of rock fire. Leven's voice and poetic lyrics invest the record with drama and grandeur. A bit overblown to be sure, but a real stunner nonetheless.

Long delayed by contractual problems, **Doll by Doll** suffers from creeping relaxation. The flame burns less brightly; although songs are strong and affecting, the reach isn't as expansive, and the results not as attention-grabbing.

In partnership with newcomer Helen Turner, Leven made **Grand Passion** using studio sidemen, attempting something in a different vein. Unfortunately, the experiment —whatever it may have been— failed. Turner's singing is like bad Nico and the songs are filled with pretentious and obnoxious lyrics. Musically adequate but totally unappealing. [iar]

DOME

Dome (Dome-Rough Trade/nr) 1980
3R4 (4AD/nr) 1980
Dome 2 (Dome-Rough Trade/nr) 1981

Dome 3 (Dome-Rough Trade/nr) 1981
MZUI/Waterloo Gallery (Cherry Red/nr) 1982
Will You Speak This Word (Nor. Uniton) 1983

BRUCE GILBERT

This Way (Mute/nr) 1984

DUET EMMO

Or So It Seems (Mute/nr) 1983

Upon splitting from Wire, Graham Lewis and B.C. (Bruce) Gilbert continued their partnership—under the name Dome—to explore the outer reaches of studio technique and synthetic sound, sidestepping Wire's arcane hitmaking tendencies and the more classical aspirations of former bandmate Colin Newman.

Dome abandons conventional song form for a hodgepodge of treated instruments and voices, with lurching mechanical noises infrequently keeping a vague beat. Melodies fragment under studio manipulation. Eerie. **3R4** moves into the ambient drone music pioneered on Brian Eno's later works, and its four tracks achieve an almost symphonic effect. **Dome 2** continues the ambient/minimalist experimentation of the first two albums, painting audio expressions of modern ennui, but **Dome 3** breaks stride, lifting the beats of other cultures and mixing them with abstracted bits of psychedelia and disembodied noises.

MZUI/Waterloo Gallery, done in conjunction with Russell Mills, makes extensive use of found noises and self-made instruments. Microphones placed around a London art gallery collected intentional and unintentional sounds from inside and out. The arhythmic result isn't music per se, but a curious examination of the relationship between environment and sound.

Will You Speak This Word, released on experimental Norwegian label Uniton, combines some of **Dome 3**'s ethnic borrowings with the repetitive minimalism of earlier works. The suite-like "To Speak" takes up all of one side; it begins with quasi-Arabic violin and random, atonal sax, moving into an acoustic guitar/sax/pseudo-African drum drone with slowly shifting textures before ending with extraterrestrial electronics. An interesting and well-composed piece. The other side's six tracks mix primal drum rhythms with light touches of art-noise generated on a variety of instruments, building intriguing trances. A progressive album in the truest sense of the term.

Duet Emmo was a one-off project by Gilbert, Lewis and Mute Records chief Daniel Miller (the Duet Emmo name is an anagram of Dome and Mute). The resultant LP, **Or So It Seems**, fluctuates between atonal, electronic sound collages and stiff, monotonous synth-funk reminiscent of D.A.F., with no track ever getting off the ground. Fun studio noodling no doubt, but little here of lasting import. [sg/dgs]

See also *Desmond Simmons*.

DOMINATRIX

"The Dominatrix Sleeps Tonight" (WEA/UpRoar) 1984

DEATH COMET CREW

At the Marble Bar EP (Beggars Banquet/nr) 1984

Charming and catchy, Dominatrix's one New York club hit consists of passionless dada femme recitation over light atmospheric music by Stuart Arbright (ex-Ike Yard) and Ken Lockie (ex-Cowboys International) with scratch mix effects by Ivan Ivan and Lockie. The 12-inch offers two full-scale versions plus two additional remixes ("Chants" and "Beat Me").

Collaborating again with Lockie as co-producer and joined by a few other musicians, Arbright became the Death Comet Crew for a 12-inch electro-funk exercise that's not as extraordinary as Dominatrix, but interesting nonetheless. "At the Marble Bar" offers a varied collection of percussion sounds; "Exterior St." has rap vocals by Rammellzee; "Funky Dream" is an amusingly reductionist cut-up edit of the word "funky." [iar]

DP'S

See *Depressions*.

DRAGONS

Parfums de la Revolution (Fr. Blitzkrieg) 1982

A piece of punk exotica: three underground musicians from mainland China recorded in secret by a visiting Frenchman. (Done, thankfully, before the brief 1985 tour there by Wham!) Using only vocals, electric guitar, rudimentary drums and Chinese violin, the trio attempts "Anarchy in the UK" and "Get Off My Cloud" with truly bizarre results; the remaining seven tracks are originals in a more traditional Oriental vein. A fascinating transliteration of rock from a country not generally considered in terms of modern music. [iar]

DRAMATIS

For Future Reference (Rocket/nr) 1981

Gary Numan's post-Tubeway Army backing group gone solo, Dramatis tries a little of everything—mock symphonics, electro-disco, mainstream pop—in a vain effort to accomplish something on their own. Predictably, the only track worth a toss is the one on which former employer Numan sings, adding his deadpan signature to an otherwise faceless outfit. [iar]

MIKEY DREAD

Dread at the Controls (Trojan/nr) 1979
World War III (Dread at the Controls/nr) 1980
Beyond World War III (nr/Heartbeat) 1981
S.W.A.L.K. (Dread at the Controls/Heartbeat) 1982
Pave the Way (nr/Heartbeat) 1984
Pave the Way (Parts 1 & 2) (DEP Int'l/nr) 1985

A former disc jockey for Jamaican radio, Michael Campbell changed his name, moved to England and made it as a recording artist. **Dread at the Controls** (the name of his radio show and, later, record label) is a modest debut, but **World War III** is an out-and-out sonic adventure. Mixed up (and down) by Scientist, the LP features Dread's dance-hall-style toasting,

beefed up with ultra-heavy production and sonic effects. The album tied into punk's enthusiastic acceptance of reggae ideology and techniques and Dread was thus considered a new wave reggae artist, a link he affirmed when he recorded (on **Sandinista!** and singles) and toured with the Clash. (**Beyond** is a slightly revised American edition.)

Unfortunately, none of his later releases are as impressive as **WWIII**. **S.W.A.L.K.** is a half-hearted imitation filled with unconvincing lovers rock made worse by Dread's nasal singing. **Pave the Way (Parts 1 & 2)** is just as inconsistent—although it offers stylistic variety, Dread's capable production and Paul Simonon on background vocals, the LP's best tracks are chant-down cuts like "Roots and Culture," the theme of a UK children's show. The two-LP British version is impressive at least for its ambition; the prior American single record seems spare in comparison. [bk]

DREAM ACADEMY

The Dream Academy (Blanco y Negro/Warner Bros.) 1985

The year's surprise success story, Dream Academy's easy-listening, generally dull pop found its way to the top of America's record charts in 1985. "Life in a Northern Town," the atmospheric Association-like '60s novelty tune (acoustic guitars, chanted vocals, cellos, tympani), though pretentious and shallow, is pleasant enough, but nothing else on the LP comes close to being as catchy or characteristic. Nick Laird-Clowes, who once led an act called the Act, is at best a bland vocalist; his partners (Gilbert Gabriel/keyboards, Kate St. John/woodwinds and horns) are equally inadequate to his transparent Thompson Twins fantasies. The LP employs many guest musicians; David Gilmour co-produced most of the tracks. Big hairy deal. [iar]

DREAM SYNDICATE

The Dream Syndicate EP (Rough Trade/Down There) 1982 (Zippo/Enigma) 1984
The Days of Wine and Roses (Rough Trade/Ruby) 1982
Tell Me When It's Over EP (Rough Trade/nr) 1983
Medicine Show (A&M) 1984
This Is Not the New Dream Syndicate Album . . . Live! (nr/A&M) 1984

Dream Syndicate was one of the first bands from the Los Angeles psychedelic revivial misleadingly known as the "paisley underground" to reach a national audience. While many of the movement's bands plumbed the Byrds/Buffalo Springfield or Pink Floyd archives for inspiration, Dream Syndicate's weird, obsessive lyrics, relentless noise maelstroms—mixed with eerie/ pretty otherworldly dirges and ballads—and singer Steve Wynn's nasal rasping and ranting recalled the Velvet Underground, though (of course) they steadfastly denied that to be their intent. With driving, feedback-drenched guitars and stream-of-consciousness spume, **The Days of Wine and Roses**, rawly produced by Flesh Eater Chris D., appealed to sensitive English major college radio programmers too young to

shoot up to the Velvets the first time around.

Following the departure of bassist Kendra Smith, the band signed to A&M and recorded a second album, produced by Sandy Pearlman. Wynn's songs remain driven and obsessive, but he seems more inclined to ape Mick Jagger than Lou Reed this time. Also, guitarist Karl Precoda cut back on the feedback and the entire album has more of a traditional rock'n'roll feel. Early fans cried sell-out, but with eight-minute jam/raps like "John Coltrane Stereo Blues" included, that accusation doesn't hold much water.

This Is Not the New Dream Syndicate Album . . . Live! is a dismal document recorded live on the national tour that followed **Medicine Show**.

In mid-'86, the Dream Syndicate returned with Paul Cutler (ex-45 Grave) in the lineup, releasing a new LP on the Big Time label. [ep]

See also *Danny & Dusty, Kendra Smith*.

DRINKING ELECTRICITY

Overload (Survival/nr) 1982

In keeping with rock's prevalent organizational trend of the '80s, Drinking Electricity is a duo: he plays synth and guitar, she sings. Joined by a guest bassist, these Londoners play simple, rather plain synth-rock with a strong electronic beat and thin ancillary instrumentation. Unlike successful proponents of the genre (Eurythmics, Soft Cell, Blancmange), however, their songs are dull and the vocals colorless, which leaves virtually nothing of value. [iar]

DRONES

Further Temptations (Valer/nr) 1977

Featuring the effervescent Gus Gangrene on guitar, this Manchester quartet sounds like all of the other early punk bands reveling in the flush of enthusiasm that swept them along into careers that only the creative or crass survived. This album shows a few signs of life, but is generally a fairly uninspired and poorly produced example of the genre. [iar]

DRONGOS

The Drongos (nr/Proteus) 1984
Small Miracles (nr/Proteus) 1985

A folky rock-pop quartet originally from New Zealand, the Drongos' eponymous debut (recorded in different sessions between 1981 and 1983) consists of unassuming songs about nebulous topics—nicely energized but a bit dull to make any serious impact. A few show melodic flair, and enthusiastic guitar strumming doesn't hurt the effort. **Small Miracles** was recorded live one day in September 1984 at four locations on the streets of New York, providing a unique audio experience. Although they've got a lot of pluck (not to mention guts), the Drongos are too plain to attract notice, especially in such a jaded town as New York, where pedestrians have seen (and heard) just about everything. [tr]

DROOGS

Heads Examined (nr/Plug-n-Socket) 1983
Stone Cold World (Making Waves/Plug-n-Socket) 1984

On their EP, LA's Droogs play bluesy garage rock and variously resemble the early Stones (thanks mostly to the harmonica wailing in "99 Steps"), the Yardbirds and the Seeds; a faithful cover of "Born to Be Wild" is both obligatory and superfluous. The album, well-produced by Earle Mankey, sets a more ambitious course, relying on period-evocative psychedelic originals and mixing in different instrumental flavors and textures, while never straying far from recognizable clichés. The Droogs benefit by avoiding genre slavishness but, with a few notable exceptions (the solid title track, for instance), are still a few quarts shy of being exciting on their own recorded merits. (Footnote: the album's UK release was in 1986.) [iar]

DUBSET

Flesh Made Word (WEA/Elektra) 1984

Bassist/writer/guitarist/singer Nigel Holland waxes ultra-funky on this collection of energetic dance grooves, recorded with various musicians. If not for his upper-class-twit accent on laughable pronouncements like "Promiscuity is boring and dangerous . . . " this would be a highly satisfying dance record. [iar]

DUB SYNDICATE

One Way System [tape] (nr/ROIR) 1983
Tunes from the Missing Channel (On-U Sound) 1985

Like the New Age Steppers, Dub Syndicate is a loosely assembled project under the creative auspices of English dub/reggae producer Adrian Sherwood. The ad hoc cast on the compilation cassette includes members of Aswad, Roots Radics and Creation Rebel, playing languid, instrumental reggae that is more repetitive and elongated than invigorating. The subsequent album on Sherwood's own label has Keith Levene and others providing fodder for his wild studio assemblies. [iar]

See also *New Age Steppers, Judy Nylon*.

DUCKS DELUXE

Ducks Deluxe (RCA) 1974
Taxi to the Terminal Zone (RCA/nr) 1975
Don't Mind Rockin' Tonite (RCA) 1978
Last Night of a Pub Rock Band (Blue Moon/nr) 1981

Heard in the cold light of the '80s, England's pub-rockin' Ducks Deluxe sound rather inconsequential (if amiable). Back in the dark ages of 1974, however, they were manna from heaven. Along with Brinsley Schwarz and Dr. Feelgood, the Ducks championed a much-needed return to basics by playing in traditional American styles diametrically opposed to the glitter and art trends then in vogue. And that paved the way for punk.

The Ducks' first and best LP captures the ultimate pub-rock band in all its glory—great for dancing and drinking, not critical analysis. Bursting with boisterous pride and spirit, the quartet careens through covers of songs by Eddie Cochran and the Stones, plus "originals" that borrow heavily from Chuck Berry, Lou Reed's "Sweet Jane," Otis Redding and so on. Three of the four sing:

D

Nick Garvey is the rough-hewn romantic and Martin Belmont the awkward crooner, but it's Sean Tyla's growling boogie that sets the tempo.

Taking its title from a line in Chuck Berry's "Promised Land," **Taxi to the Terminal Zone** beats the sophomore jinx but also exposes the band's limitations. Many of the tracks are simply rewrites of songs from the first LP, which themselves were hardly groundbreakers. A cover of the Flamin' Groovies' "Teenage Head" is inspired, however. The album benefits from Dave Edmunds' production and from the addition of keyboardist Andy McMaster, who contributes the surprisingly poppy "Love's Melody," foreshadowing the work he and Garvey would pursue in one of the Ducks' many subsequent outgrowths, the Motors.

In 1978, RCA sensed that the Ducks could be tied to the growth of new wave, and released **Don't Mind Rockin' Tonight**, a collection titled after one of the standout boogie tracks on the first album. A must for the band's fans, as it contains some previously non-LP B-sides; expendable for everyone else.

Last Night of a Pub Rock Band—that is, July 1, 1975—is so abysmally recorded that even aficionados should skip it. [jy]

See also *Nick Garvey, Motors, Graham Parker, Rumour, Sean Tyla*.

DUET EMMO

See *Dome*.

D DUFFO

Duffo (Beggars Banquet/nr) 1979
The Disappearing Boy (PVK/nr) 1980
Bob the Birdman (PVK/nr) 1981

Australian oddball Duffo—a wan-looking androgynous waif—relocated to the UK before finding a record company that would sign him. A good move, since he proved to be a witty writer/singer (if a bit smutty at times), poking impish fun at the music industry and other targets. His eponymous first album, which bears the legend "Maybe god's a genius too!," has hints of the Bonzos, Bowie (in his guise as Anthony Newley), Tubes and Kinks. Duffo sings well and invests the entire disc with a self-deprecating sense of absurdity. A facile backing quartet follows him neatly into a variety of musical styles to support the diverse songs. [iar]

STEPHEN "TIN TIN" DUFFY

The Ups and Downs (10-Virgin/nr) 1985

STEPHEN DUFFY

Because We Love You (10-Virgin/nr) 1986

If awards were handed out for foresight, Stephen Duffy would not likely be considered for one. At the turn of the decade, he parted company with a trendy young new romantic band, saying they were just too reliant on synthesizers for his taste. Never mind that his own subsequent work has included plenty of electronics; the band he left was Duran Duran.

It took a little while, but Duffy did eventually get his own career

off the ground. Using the ludicrous nom de rock Tin Tin, he had big international dance hits with "Kiss Me" and "Hold Me," both annoying, stereotypical synth-pop ditties. The former was re-released several times and (two years later) included on **The Ups and Downs**, his long-delayed solo debut.

Because We Love You drops the Tin Tin tag and much of the electronic orchestration, replacing the latter with generic pop/rock/soul from the Wham!/Spandau school. With such ingenious titles as "I Love You," "Love Station" and "Unkiss That Kiss," almost every track is a predictable melange of horns and standard bass/drums patterns, topped with Duffy's wimpy, emotionless voice. He can write good hooks, but neither of these albums offers anything you haven't been hearing more than enough of already. [dgs]

DUKES OF STRATOSPHEAR

See *XTC*.

SLY DUNBAR AND ROBBIE SHAKESPEARE

Sly and Robbie Present Taxi (Island/Mango) 1981
The Sixties, Seventies & Eighties =Taxi (Island/Mango) 1981
Raiders of the Lost Dub (Island/Mango) 1981
Crucial Reggae Driven by Sly & Robbie (Island/Mango) 1982
A Dub Encounter (Island/Mango) 1985
Language Barrier (Island) 1985

SLY DUNBAR

Simple Sly Man (Front Line/nr) 1976
Sly, Wicked and Slick (Front Line/nr) 1977
Sly-go-ville (Island/Mango) 1982

The cornerstone of contemporary roots, this nonpareil rhythm section has probably played on more reggae records than anyone else. Musical partners for well over a decade beginning in various Jamaican studio bands, in the late '70s the pair founded Taxi, a production company and label that worked with many of the top Jamaican singers, including Black Uhuru. The Taxi sound was characterized by Robbie's clean, monolithic bass lines and Sly's tasteful use of syndrums, decorating the reggae backbeat with state-of-the-art zing. The team went on to produce and play with such non-reggae artists as Grace Jones, Joan Armatrading and Ian Dury. Their trademark high-tech style has become familiar (some say tired), but Sly and Robbie's modern treatments have been a significant factor in reggae's development and popularity.

Many of their own albums are surprisingly unexciting. Sly's solo records sound like dry runs, uneventful groove collections (**Sly-go-ville** does have one Delroy Wilson vocal). **Sixties, Seventies & Eighties** is not much better. Their reworkings of past and present hits (including "El Pussy Cat Ska") demonstrate why they don't sing more often. **Language Barrier**, a superstar fusion jam produced by Bill Laswell, features everyone from Afrika Bambaataa to Bob Dylan;

danceable enough, but utterly unrelated to reggae.

Sly and Robbie are much more effective on the various Taxi compilations. **Crucial Reggae**, which has the Mighty Diamonds' original "Pass the Kouchie," is not quite as good as **Sly and Robbie Present Taxi**, but both are fine introductions to the duo's playing and the Taxi roster of singers. (The British and American editions of the latter differ slightly.) Similarly, **A Dub Encounter** (released in the **Reggae Greats** series) and **Raiders of the Lost Dub** are remix collections of backing tracks originally done for Black Uhuru, Burning Spear and others. Both are supersonic headcharges that shouldn't be missed. [bk]

KEVIN DUNN AND THE REGIMENT OF WOMEN

The Judgement of Paris (Armageddon/DB) 1981

KEVIN DUNN

C'est toujours la même guitare. EP (nr/Press) 1984
Tanzfeld (Press) 1986

The Judgement of Paris is a striking modern-music pop album by this onetime member of Atlanta's great pioneering independent band, the Fans. In reality a solo album, with lots of synths and guitars, Dunn mixes technical flash with semi-demented musical ideas, camouflaging nutty lyrics in engaging melodies and closing out the proceedings with an instrumental "Somewhere Over the Rainbow," complete with devolving rhythms.

Dunn's next release, a six-song EP, is far more ambitious but less adventurous, using guitar (adjusted with effects and varied playing styles) as a textural device to create fascinating, highly arranged clever avant-pop songs. (The cassette has two extra tracks, including one re-recorded from *Paris*.)

Tanzfeld is simply brilliant, a collection of adroit pop tunes wrapped with perceptive, informed lyrics. Besides such inspired originals as "Nam," "Giovenezza" (also on the first LP) and "Clear Title" are wickedly satirical covers of "Burning Love," "Louie Louie" and other classics. Great! [iar]

DURAN DURAN

Duran Duran (EMI/Harvest) 1981 (EMI/Capitol) 1983
Rio (EMI/Harvest) 1982
Carnival EP (nr/Harvest) 1982
Seven and the Ragged Tiger (EMI/Capitol) 1984
Arena (EMI/Capitol) 1984

ARCADIA

So Red the Rose (Parlophone-EMI/Capitol) 1985

Although conceived as a mix of the Sex Pistols and Chic, Duran Duran was in fact launched as another pretty-boy-new-romantic-clothes- horse-synth-pop-dance ensemble. Duran Duran surprisingly became an unimaginably popular teen sensation, drawing young fans into the otherwise unlikely world of techno-dance music. Taking cues (sound and image) from early Roxy Music and using simple electronics to flavor the lush but powerful rock sound, Duran Duran crossbreeds pop craft with a strong visual consciousness

(using videos as a major strategic weapon) to create records that are at once high-veneer pop disco and semi-inventive rock, even if that's not how the band and their fans view it.

Duran Duran introduced the band's dance attack, given a remarkable sonic setting by producer Colin Thurston. Tracks like "Planet Earth," "Girls on Film" and "Is There Anyone Out There," take the attributes of '70s disco—preeminent beat, repetition and studio gimmickry—and meld them to a variant on post-Ultravox rock to create something fairly original (at the time, at least). The elongated strains of synthesizer and syncopated tempos cover a multitude of creative shortcomings, but it's still an extraordinary album filled with now-classic songs.

Rio fulfills the band's potential, displaying stronger songwriting and far more intricate arrangements. The music's clearly danceable, but brilliantly listenable as well. Singer Simon Le Bon handles tantalizing melodies and obtuse lyrics with blithe confidence (if not profound ability), while honestly proficient musicianship by the other four defines each song's character differently. There isn't anything less than good, and "Rio," "Last Chance on the Stairway" and "New Religion" are downright astonishing in their melodic excellence. A top-notch album. "Hungry Like the Wolf," thanks to a remix that features prominent female moaning (and an exotic video), caught American radio programmers' attention, and lofted the band high into the charts, from which they have not since been dislodged.

Quick to recognize both their essential role as a dance band and rising commercial appeal, Duran's US label released **Carnival**, four remixes ("Hungry Like the Wolf," "Girls on Film," "Hold Back the Rain" and "My Own Way").

Parting ways with Colin Thurston, Duran attempted to expand their musical horizons from the lush ambience of **Rio** and developed a herky-jerky rhythmic style aimed at creating catchy singles in a variety of modes. Unfortunately, this led them to make the utterly detestable **Seven and the Ragged Tiger**, a sorry collection of half-baked melodies, meaningless lyrics (their earlier work may not have been poetry but it at least *sounded* clever) and over-active studio foolishness. Basically, the songs ain't no damn good. And even a passable item like "The Reflex" gets twisted with exaggerated, comical vocals; "Union of the Snake" sounds only half-written. The only truly noteworthy song, "New Moon on Monday," sounds like an outtake from **Rio**. A really sorry album which was nonetheless extremely successful among the audience who cheered the video monitors, not the band, during the tour that followed it.

Arena, the audio documentary of the group's mammoth coast-to-coast trek, features surprisingly good playing (but extremely bad singing) on nine hits; additionally, the package (and I do mean package) includes a studio cut, "The Wild Boys," which was produced by Nile Rodgers and resembles a possible theme song for *Lord of the Flies*. This album is unessential for anyone over the age of fifteen.

Duran Duran have abandoned

their commitment to music as a developmental enterprise, and now seem doomed to merely keeping up with the fickle tastes of their juvenile flock. An ongoing flirtation with "black music" may continue to provide them with hits, but unless they get hip to the soul, not just the lexicon, they're going to run themselves up a creative tree mighty soon.

Duran Duran spent the next two years split into two camps. Andy and John formed Power Station, while Simon, Nick and Roger stuck together, dubbing their sub-group Arcadia. Not surprisingly, with the artistic troublemakers out of the picture, Arcadia's **So Red the Rose** (produced by Alex Sadkin and featuring guest spots by Sting, Herbie Hancock, David Van Tieghem, David Gilmour, Andy Mackay and others) is virtually an old-fashioned Duran Duran album. Not an especially good one, mind you, but it does sound a lot more like **Rio** than **Seven and the Ragged Tiger** does. [iar]

See also *Power Station*.

DURUTTI COLUMN

The Return of the Durutti Column (Factory/nr) 1979
LC (Factory/nr) 1981
Another Setting (Factory/nr) 1983
Live at the Venue, London (VU/nr) 1983
Amigos in Portugal (Portuguese Fundacio Atlantica) 1984
Without Mercy (Factory/nr) 1984
Say What You Mean Mean What You Say EP (Factory/nr) 1985
Domo Arigato (Factory/nr) 1985
Circuses and Bread (Bel. Factory Benelux) 1986

Unlike Blondie, Durutti Column is not a group, but a single musician. Guitarist Vini Reilly is all there is, although, on his first album, producer Martin Hannett deserves equal credit. **The Return of the Durutti Column** is an album of evocative guitar instrumentals, often multi-tracked and backed with environmental, synthetic and studio-created percussive effects. Occasionally reminiscent of Mike Oldfield's **Tubular Bells** and some of the Frippertronics recordings, Reilly pretty much creates his own style—a gentle, uncluttered amalgam of acoustic and electric guitar textures.

Hannett is absent from **LC**, there's a drummer in spots and Reilly, regrettably, "sings" on a couple of the tracks, all of which makes it the lesser of Reilly's first two works, although the instrumentals still provide pleasant listening.

While hardly raucous, Reilly moves away from the ambient approach a bit on **Say What You Mean**; deep, heavy electronic (or treated) percussion is annoyingly high in the mix on most of the six tracks. The standout is "Silence," which starts out sparsely with electronic piano and marimba and builds nicely with the addition of drums, trumpet, slide guitar and Reilly's now much-improved voice. Although his vinyl output is perhaps more prolific than his creativity, Reilly is capable of producing rewarding music.

Domo Arigato is a live album released only on compact disc. [ds/dgs]

IAN DURY

New Boots and Panties!! (Stiff) 1977 & 1980
Lord Upminster (Polydor) 1981

IAN DURY AND THE BLOCKHEADS

Do It Yourself (Stiff/Stiff-Epic) 1979
Laughter (Stiff/Stiff-Epic) 1980
Jukebox Dury (Stiff/Stiff-America) 1981
Greatest Hits (Fame/nr) 1982

IAN DURY AND THE MUSIC STUDENTS

4000 Weeks' Holiday (Polydor/nr) 1984

Stunted in growth, crippled by polio and unrepentantly cockney, Ian Dury is one of rock's most memorable (and certainly lovable) figures. Hardly a newcomer in 1977—having been around with Kilburn and the High Roads—Dury came into his own with **New Boots and Panties!!**, an album whose energy almost defies it to stay on the turntable. With his motley but talented backing band, the Blockheads, Dury trounces merrily through outrageous odes like "Plaistow Patricia," "Billericay Dickie," "Blockheads" and the anthemic "Sex & Drugs & Rock & Roll." But a more sensitive side emerges lyrically on "Sweet Gene Vincent," "My Old Man" and "If I Was with a Woman" and musically on "Wake Up and Make Love with Me."

Dury and the Blockheads' disco leanings came to the fore on the dazzling **Do It Yourself**. The band's rich interweaving behind Dury's playfully obscure vocals may have meant sensory overload for some, and the more sophisticated music (compared to **New Boots**' often raucous blare) must have turned away the punk cadres. With hindsight, though, **Do It Yourself** can be heard as a trailblazing fusion of dance musics, in both upbeat ("Sink My Boats," "Dance of the Screamers") and relaxed ("Inbetweenies," "Lullaby for Francies") modes.

Blockhead musical director Chas Jankel left after **Do It Yourself**, but the band carried on with thinner textures and ex-Feelgood guitarist Wilko Johnson. (Jankel subsequently pursued a dull solo career as a pianist/singer.) **Laughter** is an uneasy and uneven mix of whimsical concepts like "Yes & No (Paula)," "Dance of the Crackpots" and "Over the Points" as well as less-inspired funk-rock like "(Take Your Elbow out of the Soup You're Sitting on the Chicken)" and "Sueperman's Big Sister."

Dury next abandoned Stiff and scuttled the Blockheads, but reunited with Jankel for **Lord Upminster**, recorded in the Bahamas with reggae rhythm king-pins Robbie Shakespeare (bass) and Sly Dunbar (drums). After the Blockheads' joyful noise, **Lord Upminster**'s funk sounds ascetic. (Keyboard player Tyrone Downie is the only other musician.) Disappointingly, Dury scales down his writing for the occasion, approaching minimalist levels on "Wait (for Me)" and "Trust (Is a Must)." Aside from the notoriously frank "Spasticus (Autisticus)," the record amounts to a creative holding pattern.

It took Dury three years to bang out another record, this time with a mostly unfamiliar set of sidemen working under the ironic Music Students moniker. The homemade-look cover of **4000 Weeks' Holiday** belies the slickly-produced soul tracks inside; only Dury's homey speak-singing connects the songs to a non-mainstream aesthetic. Lyrically conservative as well, Dury waxes romantic ("You're My Inspiration"), treacly ("Friends"), political ("Ban the Bomb"), noirish ("The Man with No Face") and whimsical ("Take Me to the Cleaners").

Dury seems to work best outside the album format. "Hit Me with Your Rhythm Stick" was hastily added to **Do It Yourself** as a bonus 45; "Reasons to Be Cheerful (Part 3)" fell between **Do It Yourself** and **Laughter**. Although it could be ungenerously interpreted merely as Stiff's last chance to cash in, **Juke Box Dury** is also the best and most consistent Dury LP. Besides the two hits just mentioned, it has other fine 45 sides ("What a Waste," "Razzle in My Pocket," "Common as Muck") and a few choice album cuts. Dury's humanism comes through loud and clear, and the record is programmed swell. [si/iar]

49

E

EARTHLING

Dance (Jap. King) 1981

This Japanese trio, led—believe it or not—by John (no last name) on vocals and guitar and Yoko (Fujiwara) on bass, toured both American coasts in 1981. Despite its title, the album is less influenced by current trends in terpsichore than by the group of performers that participated in the famous **June 1, 1974** concert/LP—Kevin Ayers, John Cale and pre-ambient Eno—with a healthy dollop of Roxy Music thrown in as well. The third Earthling, Jin Haijima, plays keyboards and synths à la Eno; there's even Andy Mackay-like sax on a couple of songs. Cale's influence is felt in the prevalent droning intensity; John's voice occasionally bears a striking resemblance to Ayers'. A strangely evocative combination.

[ds]

ELLIOT EASTON

See *Cars*.

EATER

The Album (The Label/nr) 1977
Get Yer Yo Yo's Out EP (The Label/nr) 1978
The History of Eater Vol. One (De Lorean/nr) 1985

One of Britain's primordial punk bands, Eater boasted a drummer too young to legally enter the clubs where they played, good taste in selecting songs to record ("Sweet Jane," "Queen Bitch," "Waiting for the Man," a rejuvenated adaptation of an Alice Cooper song: "Fifteen") but little else. Primeval hardcore.

[tr]

ECHO AND THE BUNNYMEN

Crocodiles (Korova/Sire) 1980
Shine So Hard EP (Korova/nr) 1981
Heaven Up Here (Korova/Korova-Sire) 1981
Porcupine (Korova/Korova-Sire) 1983
Echo and the Bunnymen EP (nr/Korova-Sire) 1983
Never Stop EP (Korova/nr) 1983
Ocean Rain (Korova/Korova-Sire) 1984
Songs to Learn & Sing (Korova/Korova-Sire) 1985

WILL SERGEANT

Themes for Grind (92 Satisfied Customers/nr) 1982

This vanguard foursome—at its 1978 inception, a trio plus Echo the drum machine—emerged from the Liverpool renaissance with a debut album stunning in its starkness and power. Unlike also-rans with the same idea, Ian McCulloch's specter-of-Jim Morrison vocals are no mere pilferage; where Morrison would have ordered you on your knees, McCulloch does it himself, alternately writhing in resistance or slumped in resignation to the agonies of a whole 'nother decade. On **Crocodiles**, the scratchy, yet ringing, guitar and unhurriedly relentless, pounding drums set the sonic scene for McCulloch's sometimes ambivalently delivered existential crises. (The US release adds a subsequent single track.)

Shine So Hard is actually part of the soundtrack to a half-hour film (same title) of a specially-staged concert (admittedly a logistic and musical disappointment), and mostly serves to preview the upcoming LP in lackluster fashion. But in its own right, the gloom engulfing **Heaven Up Here** seems to have smothered the band's cogency, with McCulloch less a fist-shaker than a whiner. The old potency is still audible at times (mainly on Side One), but—like McCulloch—the guitars sound fragile, even brittle, and overall it's a dreamy, depressed and depressing effort.

Echo's third LP is a far more enthralling proposition, a killer collection of bizarre, challenging songs given surprising but fitting color by Shankar's offbeat violin wailings. Sweeping creations like "The Cutter" and "The Back of Love" are tremendously exciting; the rest of **Porcupine**, if not as consistently memorable, captures the band's unique essence with grace and style. Also working in their favor is newfound efficiency that keeps them from being as self-indulgently inaccessible as in the past.

The even-better **Ocean Rain** exchanges Shankar's unique contribution for more routine string accompaniment, but offers an amazing skein of great songwriting. "Silver," "Crystal Days," "Seven Seas" and "The Killing Moon" all achieve the ideal marriage of pop with drama, using McCulloch's strong vocal presence and Will Sergeant's varied and textural guitar work to imbue the songs with majesty and subtlety.

Songs to Learn & Sing is a brilliant career retrospective, adding one new tune ("Bring on the Dancing Horses") to a bunch of familiar faves. The eponymous EP is a 12-inch released after **Porcupine**, containing the album's two best tracks plus a live oldie and two other cuts; **Never Stop** is similar, with some overlap. Sergeant's instrumental solo album is a weird, experimental effort that defies easy comprehension.

[jg/iar]

EDDIE AND THE HOT RODS

Live at the Marquee EP (Island/nr) 1976
Teenage Depression (Island) 1976
Life on the Line (Island) 1977
Thriller (Island/nr) 1979
Fish 'n' Chips (EMI/EMI America) 1980
One Story Town (Waterfront/nr) 1985

It may be difficult to hear now, but London's Eddie and the Hot Rods played a crucial role in the birth of new wave. If the Rods hadn't been out there, playing wild-and-fast rock'n'roll in the clubs at a time when superstar pomposity was the currency of pop music, bands like the Sex Pistols would never have had the opportunity to join, intensify and broaden that rebellious spirit into a national—and international—musical upheaval.

Today, **Teenage Depression** sounds like a fairly tame set of R&B-influenced simple rock tunes, like early Flamin' Groovies or Dave Edmunds, but at the time of its release had major impact on the British music scene. The title track (a hit single) is the record's finest moment. (The American album replaced two soul covers with four tracks that had appeared on the live EP.)

For **Life on the Line**, the Rods expanded to a five-piece with the addition of ex-Kursaal Flyer Graeme Douglas. It was a wise move, as Douglas gave the band a smart kick in the pop direction, best exemplified on the wonderful "Do Anything You Wanna Do," which he co-wrote. Overall, a strong album (thanks to good songs and enthusiastic playing) that stands up much better than its predecessor.

By the time of **Thriller** (is Michael Jackson a fan?), the Hot Rods were a thing of the past, culturally speaking. They hadn't been able to keep pace with the changes; rendered redundant by the bands they had inspired. The album reeks with bitterness; although competent, it has neither the freshness of **Life on the Line** nor anything substantial to replace it. As a sign of the band's "maturity," Linda McCartney sang some backup parts.

With Al Kooper producing, a revised lineup (without Douglas or bassist Paul Gray) turned out an unnecessary fourth album that is best forgotten. **One Story Town** is a live LP.

[iar]

See also *Damned, Inmates*.

EDGE

Square One (Hurricane/nr) 1980

The Edge came about when guitarist Lu and drummer Jon Moss (formerly of punk slouches London) left a brief and unrecorded incarnation of the Damned in 1978. With the addition of keyboardist Gavin Povey (who had played with Lew Lewis) and bassist Glyn Havard (whose long career has included stints with the Yachts and, er, Jade Warrior), the Edge was formed. They played behind Jane Aire as the Belvederes on her album and also appeared, nearly intact, on Kirsty MacColl's first album. Subsequent to the Edge, Lu has worked in a number of bands, including Shriekback and the Spizzles, while Jon Moss went on to fame and fortune in Culture Club.

Oh yeah—about the music. Never quite blending into any particular style, the Edge's eclectic, melodic rock has flashes of the Jam, Boomtown Rats, Deep Purple, Police and Stranglers—all united by the satirical outlook of amusing lyrics.

[iar]

DAMON EDGE

See *Chrome*.

EDITH NYLON

Edith Nylon (Fr. CBS) 1979
Quatre Essaies Philosophique EP (Fr. CBS) 1980
Johnny Johnny (Fr. CBS) 1981
Echo, Bravo (Fr. Chiswick) 1982

This French band went from a singleminded obsession with machines and bio-robotics on their first album, in a style toning down Gary Numanisms to suit a somewhat high-tech Blondiesque approach, to an everything-but-the-kitchen-sink melange on **Echo, Bravo** (an LP plus a 12-inch EP), incorporating all sorts of English and American influences along the way. As with Blondie, the name refers not to the female lead singer (Mylène Khaski) but the group itself; also like Blondie, the lineup expanded (from a quintet to a keyboards-plus-two-guitars sextet) while the founder members retained control of production as well as songwriting.

There's plenty of zip and charm to the CBS recordings. (**Echo, Bravo** is the most entertaining.) Khaski's French lyrics display moderate intelligence, and they're complemented by lighter-hearted humor as well as a mix-and-match stylistic grab-bag blending dance rock, '60s pop and bits that call to mind everyone from the Pretenders to Adam and the Ants. Sure, it's a stew, but more often than not they come out sounding like nobody so much as themselves, and that on some pretty fair numbers. A smart producer could have worked wonders with 'em. [jg]

DAVE EDMUNDS

Rockpile (Regal Zonophone/MAM) 1971
Subtle as a Flying Mallet (RCA) 1975
Get It (Swan Song) 1977
Tracks on Wax 4 (Swan Song) 1978
Repeat When Necessary (Swan Song) 1979
Twangin . . . (Swan Song) 1981
The Best of Dave Edmunds (Swan Song) 1981
D.E. 7th (Arista/Columbia) 1982 (Fame/nr) 1984
Information (Arista/Columbia) 1983
Riff Raff (Arista/Columbia) 1984

DAVE EDMUNDS ET AL.

Stardust (Ronco/Arista) 1974
Porky's Revenge (CBS/Columbia) 1985

Can traditional rock'n'roll survive in the modern world? As long as Dave Edmunds is around, the answer will be yes. A rousing singer, superlative guitarist and wizard producer, Edmunds has preserved the simplicity and directness of '50s rock without ever sounding like a slavish revivalist. Along the way, he's also performed tricks with country music and even Phil Spector's elaborate constructions. Edmunds has had his ups and downs on record, but the one thing he's never been is pretentious.

Dave prefaced his solo career with two LPs as the leader of manic blues-psychedelic trio Love Sculpture. Those days are well documented on numerous compilations, the best being the French twin-disc set, **Dave Edmunds, Rocker.**

Rockpile was recorded because Edmunds needed to make an LP to capitalize on his worldwide smash single, a one-man remake of "I Hear You Knockin'." This LP established the boundaries of the first phase of his solo career: a Chuck Berry tune, a Willie Dixon blues, a country stomp (by Neil Young, no less) and so on. **Rockpile** is a mishmash in terms of recording dates—one track dates from 1966—and creation, with Edmunds playing almost all the instruments himself. Nevertheless, it rocks like crazy.

Of the 40 cuts on the two-LP soundtrack/compilation for the David Essex film **Stardust**, seven are fine covers of oldies by Edmunds. A point of note here is that six of those tracks are credited to the Stray Cats—years in advance of Brian Setzer's group.

By 1975, the unprolific Edmunds had a few more UK hits and enough other odds and ends to assemble another LP; unfortunately **Subtle as a Flying Mallet** doesn't hold together. The Everly Brothers' "Leave My Woman Alone" and a few other individual tracks work,

but this is otherwise a largely lifeless record. The intricate one-man Spector homages ("Maybe," "Baby I Love," etc.) are pretty but strained. Two tracks recorded live with Brinsley Schwarz point to the end of Edmunds' hibernation in the studio.

Get It lets air into the musty, old room of Edmunds' musical mind. Dave still laid down a lot of the tracks unaided, but also utilized the services of members of the Rumour and the defunct Brinsleys, forming a significant partnership with the latter's Nick Lowe. This is Edmunds' brightest-sounding LP to date. Highlights include Lowe's Chuck Berry rewrite, "I Knew the Bride" and the Lowe/Edmunds salute to the Everly Brothers, "Here Comes the Weekend."

Tracks on Wax 4 hardens and intensifies the attack, fully freeing Edmunds from the negative aspects of his nostalgic leanings. Give credit for that to the formation of Rockpile, a hard-working band composed of Edmunds, Lowe on bass, guitarist Billy Bremner and drummer Terry Williams; over the following few years, Rockpile recorded both Lowe's and Edmunds' solo albums, then cut one of their own before splintering. On **Tracks on Wax 4** they drive Dave to new heights of rock'n'roll glory.

Perhaps his best effort, **Repeat When Necessary** follows the course set by **Tracks**, with a bit of country sweetening. Standouts: "Girls Talk," penned by Elvis Costello, "Queen of Hearts," later a hit for the wretched Juice Newton, and the sultry "Black Lagoon."

Following the acrimonious breakup of Rockpile, Edmunds rushed out **Twangin . . .**, a resounding disappointment. Despite the presence of a few pearls, this is clearly a patchwork of odds and ends. Outtakes deserve to remain outtakes. The return to the claustrophobic one-man-band sound of his early days is particularly disheartening.

Best Of, thirteen tracks drawn from the four Swan Song LPs, makes no chronological sense, but offers an impressive musical overview.

D.E. 7th marks a return to form. Edmunds corrals a hot new supporting cast and boogies like a happy man again. A new Springsteen song, "From Small Things (Big Things One Day Come)," and a rip-roaring version of NRBQ's "Me and the Boys" lead the parade.

Information and **Riff Raff** comprise Edmunds' Jeff Lynne period; a disastrous attempt to concoct slick, saleable contemporary product that'll sell. Though both albums have some good moments (generally those Lynne didn't collaborate on), they're largely characterized by a glib, crass sensibility.

The **Porky's Revenge** soundtrack, believe it or not, is a fine platter. In addition to some sharp cuts of his own, Edmunds produced tracks by Jeff Beck, George Harrison (a new Dylan song) and Clarence Clemons. Boogie one more time!

Edmunds' career as a producer heated up significantly in the '80s, guiding the latter-day Stray Cats to the top of the charts and fulfilling a longstanding ambition of working with the Everly Brothers by producing their 1984 comeback album. [jy]

EEK-A-MOUSE

Wa-Do-Dem (Greensleeves/ Shanachie) 1982
Skidip! (Greensleeves/Shanachie) 1982
Assassinator (nr/Ras) 1983
The Mouse and the Man (Greensleeves/Shanachie) 1983
Mouseketeer (Greensleeves/ Shanachie) 1984
King and I (Original Sounds/nr) 1985

Probably the biggest new solo reggae star of the '80s, Eek-a-Mouse (Ripton Joseph Hylton) has no trouble keeping a high profile. Not only is he six-foot-six, his distinctive voice is easily recognized. He sings with a nasal twang (like a higher-pitched version of Michael Rose), but punctuates his vocals with all sorts of syllabic thrusts, like reggae's answer to scat. The effect is melodic, but also percussive—it keeps the groove moving forward. Eek's success is also attributable to the high quality of his records. He works primarily with Roots Radics, a popular Jamaican session band that's played behind Gregory Isaacs and countless others. With Eek, however, the chemistry is unique—they seem to play better with him. The power of their collaboration helps keep his albums consistent and special.

Above all, Eek is funny, a comic as well as social critic. **Wa-Do-Dem**, a smart debut, features the hit single of the same name. ("Wa do dem stare? Because she's too short and he's too tall.") **Skidip!** also has its share of hits ("Modelling Queen" and "You Na Love Reggae Music"), though the second side is a little thin. **Assassinator** is steady and strong, but boasts no outstanding tracks.

The Mouse and the Man and **Mouseketeer** are his best albums, assured and versatile. The first includes the epic tale of Eek's meeting with Mickey Mouse, "Modelling King" (a followup to his earlier hit) and a curious ditty called "Hitler." **Mouseketeer** features "Star, Daily News or Gleaner," a song about anorexia and, for all who wondered, "How I Got Me Name." Not to be missed.

Eek's reign continues on his latest, but he's stretching out a bit. Working with a number of musicians besides Roots Radics, the instrumentation on **King and I** is fuller (and includes some synthesizer), but it's hardly a drastic departure from his successful formula. [bk]

8-EYED SPY

Live [tape] (nr/ROIR) 1981
8-Eyed Spy (Fetish/nr) 1981

Perhaps the acme of New York no-wave groups, 8-Eyed Spy collected the talents of Lydia Lunch, drummer Jim Sclavunos, ace bassist George Scott, sax player Pat Irwin and guitarist Michael Paumgarden. Considerably less shrill than other similarly conceived groups, 8-Eyed Spy was nonetheless dominated by Lunch's confrontational vocals and lyrics and Irwin's insistent quasi-jazz sax. On **Live**, it becomes apparent that Lunch's style is mutilated blues (especially on the Beefheart-inspired opener, "Diddy Wah Diddy"), and that Sclavunos and Scott's flawless rhythm/bass collaboration is the band's axis. The blend of influences (jazz/blues/ rock) creates exciting music that is beyond

description.

8-Eyed Spy reproduces much of the material from the cassette and is split into a live side and a studio side. While the former (which includes a hilarious version of "White Rabbit") shows the same gifted chaos apparent on **Live**, the latter proves 8-Eyed Spy capable of considerable restraint and polish. While the tone of the studio work implies an increasing reliance on jazz, the drumming rivets it to danceable rock. There is the hint of an impending breakthrough in these recordings; unfortunately, the band dissolved in the wake of George Scott's death. [sg]
See also *Lydia Lunch.*

EINSTÜRZENDE NEUBAUTEN

Kollaps (Ger. Zick Zack) 1982
Drawings of Patient O.T. (Some Bizzare/ZE-PVC) 1983
80-83 Strategies Against Architecture (Mute/nr) 1984
2 X 4 [tape] (nr/ROIR) 1984
Halber Mensch (Some Bizzare/ Rough Trade) 1985

Words such as "noisy," "raw," "primitive" and "radical" have been used to describe many a band, but few have earned these labels more than Berlin conceptual anti-artists Einstürzende Neubauten (translation: "Collapsing New Buildings"). Their instrumentation includes power tools and large metal objects beaten with hammers, pipes, wrenches and axes. What traditional musical implements they use receive similar treatment; Blixa Bargeld supplies pained vocals and guitar often blurred to the point of white noise. Their live shows are even more daring, and many a club owner has stopped performances and/or barred them from returning after watching a stage practically demolished under Einstürzende Neubauten's creative supervision.

Having built a reputation in the German underground avant-garde, the band released **Kollaps** in 1982, combining guitar and bass drones with a barrage of metallic pounding, both rhythmic and random. Topped off with tortured howls (and titles like "Hear with Pain"), it is one of the most shocking visions ever committed to vinyl. Not recommended for dancing or romantic interludes.

Neubauten soon became the darlings of the UK press. In 1983, they signed to Some Bizzare and released **Drawings of Patient O.T.** While no more melodic than **Kollaps**, the production is less primeval and the band shows a wider degree of textural variety. At times the sound is rather stripped down, and a few of the cuts are actually songs. (The title track *even has a chord progression!*) Two years later, the record was released in the US, adding four non-LP items on a bonus EP.

Strategies Against Architecture is a compilation of five tracks from **Kollaps**, an early single and some brilliant previously-unreleased works, three of them live. The itemization of instrumentation is amusing, including as it does an air conditioning duct, smashing glass, an amplified spring and a bridge. For more live material, try the cassette-only **2 X 4**, an admirable attempt to capture the mood of Neubauten on stage, recorded throughout Europe between

E

1980 and 1983. Like **Drawings**, it leaves more space in the sound, which makes the shock effects that much more shocking. "Armenisch Bitter" is, by their standards, a ballad, with plaintive sax warbling along with Bargeld's voice in a quasi-Middle Eastern style.

Halber Mensch ("Half Man") is the band's strongest record yet, displaying a wide range of creative compositional technique. Putting some of the junkyard orchestration aside, the title track is *a cappella*, sounding like some avant-garde opera; "Letztes Biest (am Himmel)" uses quiet bass harmonics as its only pitched instrument. Add such things as grand piano, inside-out dance beats and Neubauten's characteristic thunder, and **Halber Mensch** is truly remarkable.

With such an extreme sound and stance, it would be easy for this troupe to degenerate into self-parody, something they have yet to do. Not really rock music, and definitely not for the weak of stomach, Einstürzende Neubauten is one of the most original and challenging music bands in the world today. [dgs]

See also *Nick Cave*.

ELECTRIC CHAIRS

See *Wayne County and the Electric Chairs*.

ELECTRIC GUITARS

Electric Guitars EP (Stiff/nr) 1982

Yes, this septet of girls and boys from Bristol have all the chic moves: bi-sex vocals, fashionably funky beat, arty/clever lyrics and they even use electric guitars! (In between lots of percussion and some synth.) "Beat Me Hollow," or is it "Beat Me, I'm Hollow"? [jg]

DANNY ELFMAN

See *Oingo Boingo*.

ELVIS BROTHERS

Movin' Up (Portrait) 1983
Adventure Time (Portrait) 1985

This trio from Champaign, Illinois has roots in many local bands of that area (some credible, others cringeable); together, they play a marvelous (and deceptively simple) concoction of slicked-up rockabilly, stripped-down Cheap Trick-tinged melodic rock'n'roll and pristine pure pop that boasts superbly articulated energy, occasionally goofy lyrics and enough hooks to catch a school of minnows. **Movin' Up** traverses a panoply of mildly bent styles, from mock-Stray Cats ("Fire in the City") to Dave Edmunds-ish rock'n'roll ("Hey Tina") to Anglo-pop ("Hidden in a Heartbeat") to countryfied rock ("Santa Fe") and much more. Sure they futz around a lot (especially onstage), but their silliness never interferes with the serious task—playing catchy pop with maximum gusto. It may not mean a lot, but the album is truly mega-fun.

Adrian Belew produced **Adventure Time**, but didn't do too much damage to the E-Bros.' essentially lighthearted spirit. There are a couple of socially responsible messages about gun control and insanity in the modern world, but by and large, the Elvises go about their business with typical happy-go-lucky aplomb. From the high-powered rock of "Burnin' Desire"

and "Somebody Call the Police" to the beauty of "Crosswinds" and "Akiko Shinoda" they effortlessly toss off tune after tune of infectious should-be-hits. [iar]

EMPIRE

Empire (Dinosaur/nr) 1981

During their tenure in Generation X, guitarist Bob Andrews and drummer Mark Laff regularly suffered charges of being heavy metal musicians in disguise. In the foreground of Empire, they do indeed play with a metallic lack of subtlety, but the results aren't nearly as explosive as you might expect. Attempting their version of pop music, Andrews and Laff slow down the tempo to a pace that renders **Empire** labored and drab. [jy]

BRIAN ENO

Here Come the Warm Jets (Island) 1973
Taking Tiger Mountain (by Strategy) (Island) 1974
Another Green World (Island) 1975
Discreet Music (Obscure/Antilles) 1975 (EG) 1982
Before and After Science (Polydor/Island) 1978
Music for Films (Polydor/Antilles) 1978 (EG) 1982
Ambient 1: Music for Airports (Ambient) 1979 (EG) 1982
Ambient 4: On Land (EG) 1982
Apollo Atmospheres & Soundtracks (EG) 1983
Music for Films Volume II (EG) 1983
Working Backwards 1983-1973 (EG) 1984
Thursday Afternoon (EG) 1985
More Blank Than Frank (EG) 1986

ENO AND CLUSTER

Cluster and Eno (Ger. Sky) 1978

ENO WITH MOEBIUS AND ROEDELIUS

After the Heat (Ger. Sky) 1979

CLUSTER & BRIAN ENO

Old Land (nr/Relativity) 1985

HAROLD BUDD/BRIAN ENO

Ambient 2: The Plateaux of Mirror (EG) 1980
The Pearl (Editions EG) 1984

KEVIN AYERS/JOHN CALE/ENO/NICO

June 1, 1974 (Island) 1974

BRIAN ENO & ROGER ENO

Voices (EG) 1985

From his original role as electronics dabbler and art rocker with the fledgling Roxy Music in the early 1970s, Brian Eno has become the epitome of the independent artist—articulate, intelligent, serious and intent on following his own impulses. He has progressed from a tight, wry pop music into more difficult forms, incorporating aspects of many different disciplines. As well as a solo artist, Eno has collaborated with many people; he became a major force in the emerging music of the '80s as producer of Ultravox, Talking Heads,

New York no wave bands, Devo, U2 and others.

Here Come the Warm Jets, Eno's first foray as a solo artist, featured sharply crafted, cerebral pop songs that put equal emphasis on quirky music and chatty, surrealistic lyrics—an endearing novelty record that no one else could have made.

Taking Tiger Mountain (by Strategy) saw Eno flirting with Chinese communism and dream psychology as grist for his lyric mill. The tone of the music is darker overall than on the first album, but though Eno was already beginning to show a mistrust of pop forms, the songs here are filled with humor and joy and his continuing taste for experimentation.

By **Another Green World**, Eno was enhancing his work with crystal-clear production. Much of the album features beautiful, fragile instrumentals, leaving the manic rock tone of the first two albums behind. Electronics play a greater role, and Eno all but abandons standard pop forms for a less-formulaic sound that presages his future ambient work. Highly recommended.

Discreet Music (as well as his two collaborations with Robert Fripp) was first devised while Eno was recovering from an auto accident, and it marks his experimental break from pop forms, using classical structures as the basis for tape loops and manipulations. The result is striking and haunting, filled with beauty and apprehension, paralleling the minimalist music being made by Steve Reich and Philip Glass. Recommended.

Before and After Science was the apex of Eno's pop work, a collection of ten lyrical songs that ranged from bouncy, eccentric pop ("King's Lead Hat") to wistfully pastoral songs ("Spider and I," "Through Hollow Lands") that smack of vast distances. The pivotal work of Eno's career, it sees him spanning whole musical worlds, but from this point on, his involvement with pop music was relegated to production work.

Music for Films introduced Eno's subsequent focus, and consists of fragments done over the years as possible soundtracks for imaginary movies. (Eno's work has since appeared on several actual soundtracks.) Totally instrumental, the album features a return, with greater sophistication, to the work of **Discreet Music**—a conscious attempt to imply subtle moods and settings through electronically manipulated sound.

Ambient music, which goes directly against Western tradition by not demanding explicit attention from the listener, was introduced on **Music for Airports**, a stark but hypnotic collection of sounds especially composed for airport sound systems to inure passengers to flying and death. Whether successful (or even ever used) in that setting or not, the album's spare and delicate sounds open up the meditative possibilities of music.

Through numerous collaborations (with 801, Ayers/Cale/Nico, Bowie, Cluster, Jon Hassell, Talking Heads, etc.), Eno has dabbled in and influenced various strains of popular music, from fusion rock to electro-pop. **The Plateaux of Mirror**, with Harold Budd, found Eno expanding his ambient work to

multi-dimensional proportions, while **My Life in the Bush of Ghosts**, with David Byrne, allowed him to indulge his fascination with African and other Third World rhythms, with the latter made more intriguing through the mixture of these rhythms and found speech and music tapes. Eno continues to work occasionally with one of his earliest collaborators, Cluster. **Old Land** (another German Sky release, this one licensed for America) surprisingly has some vocals on it.

By **On Land**, Eno had polished his ambient music into a dense, evocative representation of terra incognita. Though sometimes obscure and always devoid of lyrics, the work shows Eno at his most expressive, with sound paintings that exist somewhere between ancient mantra and avant-garde. Highly recommended.

Invited to do the music for a film about the Apollo space missions, Eno used all of his inspiration about the grandeur and mystery of man's walking on the moon to create **Apollo Atmospheres & Soundtracks**, recorded in conjunction with his brother Roger and longtime collaborator, Daniel Lanois (also known for his production work with Martha and the Muffins and others). Avoiding any sensationalistic (or even typical space/rocketry) sounds, it's another hauntingly poetic collection of ambient pieces, written and played variously by all three musicians.

Eno's most recent release of new material came via a record issued only on compact disc, **Thursday Afternoon**.

Working Backwards 1983-1973 is the ultimate Eno collection—an eleven-disc boxed set containing all of his solo albums through **Music for Films Volume II** plus an otherwise unavailable album of **Rarities**, featuring such items as "Seven Deadly Finns" and "The Lion Sleeps Tonight." **More Blank Than Frank** is a more modest compilation—ten of the artist's own faves from his early records. Discographical footnote: Eno's albums have been reissued, unchanged, numerous times due to label rearrangements in both England and America. [sg/iar]

See also *David Bowie, David Byrne, Fripp & Eno, Jon Hassell, Talking Heads*.

EPIDEMICS

Shankar/Caroline (nr/ECM) 1986

Indian violinist Shankar—star of Echo and the Bunnymen's "The Cutter" and notable records by Peter Gabriel, Talking Heads, etc.—takes a break from sessions and jazz to try his hand at leading a crypto-rock group on this exciting, offbeat rock-pop experiment. The Epidemics' record tends to drone, but in a pleasant, Monsoonish sort of way, with bouncy synthesized percussion driving Shankar's weedy vocals and unique violin sound, which neatly contrast Percy Jones' agile bass work. The songs are simple and their construction familiar, but artificial-sounding production and uncommon arrangements keep the album well outside the pop mainstream. [iar]

EQUATORS

Hot (Stiff/Stiff America) 1981

The Equators' well-integrated

(no pun intended) hybrid of ska, reggae and rock (check the rhythm section), produced by then-Rumour member Bob Andrews, is musically if not lyrically similar to much of the output of the 2-Tone bands from the same era. This all-black quintet leaves out the heavy messages and aims for the feet, making **Hot** refreshingly unpretentious—danceable as well as listenable. [ds]

ERASURE

Wonderland (Mute/Sire-Mute) 1986

Vince Clarke's first steady post-Yazoo band, Erasure is a duo with singer Andy Bell, a soulful tenor who bears a creepy vocal resemblance to Alison Moyet. Clarke's backing tracks likewise sound a lot like Yazoo songs (bizarre, considering that Bell co-wrote most of them), which is a mixed sin. On one hand, it's disconcerting, on the other, Yazoo was a fine band, and Clarke's more than welcome to keep up the good work, regardless of who with. The best tracks ("Heavenly Action" and "Oh l'Amour") are instantly memorable pop confections. [iar]

ROKY ERICKSON AND THE ALIENS

Roky Erickson and the Aliens (CBS/nr) 1980
The Evil One (nr/415) 1981

ROKY ERICKSON

Clear Night for Love EP (Fr. New Rose) 1985
Don't Slander Me (nr/Pink Dust) 1986

Roky Erickson established his reputation as a raving looney over a decade ago as lead singer of Texas' infamous psychedelic 13th Floor Elevators. On his 1980 UK LP, he plays that role to the hilt, singing such offbeat gems as "I Walked with a Zombie" and "Creature with the Atom Brain" in a tremulous voice that insists he's telling the truth—or at least believes he is. Former Creedence Clearwater bassist Stu Cook turned in an excellent production job, bringing the hard electric guitars into a sharp focus that underscores Roky's excitable state. Erickson and band seem less unstable than the drug-crazed Elevators (best remembered for their "You're Gonna Miss Me"), but just barely.

Ditto for **The Evil One**, which takes five tracks from the UK release and adds five more, including the ghastly "Bloody Hammer." Which LP is better? They're both wonderfully ominous and frightening—splatter-film soundtracks done with real rock'n'roll conviction.

The five songs on **Clear Night**, recorded in Texas with a rudimentary quartet, begin on a note of relative restraint. "You Don't Love Me Yet" is acoustic folk; the title track, which follows, recalls Creedence's rag-tag balladry. Side Two is a bit wilder, culminating in "Don't Slander Me," an angrily defensive accusatory diatribe. (It does, however, contain "Starry Eyes," which can only be described as Roky's Buddy Holly tribute.)

Erickson re-recorded (maybe not, in one instance) three songs from **Clear Night** for his subsequent full-length LP, cut with a five-man band that includes ex-Jefferson Airplane/Hot Tuna bassist Jack Casady **and** an electric autoharp player. Even without intentionally grisly put-ons, **Don't Slander Me** is typically gripping, although the inclusion of two Holly-inspired pop-tunes makes for a bizarre contrast to "Burn the Flames," a tune originally done for the **Return of the Living Dead** soundtrack. [jy/iar]

ESG

ESG EP (nr/99) 1981
ESG Says Dance to the Beat of Moody EP (nr/99) 1982
Come Away with ESG (nr/99) 1983

Who would have imagined that four sisters and a pal from the South Bronx would emerge as one of the most dynamic bands that New York could offer at the top of the '80s? Mixing a solid combination of dub, chant and beat, ESG—simply drums, bass and vocals—virtually stole the cosmic show with their first release, a six-song EP with a live side and a phenomenal studio side recorded under the hand of producer Martin Hannett.

Their second EP, produced by 99 Records head Ed Bahlman, is not quite as crisp as the debut, but no less enjoyable. ESG is a brilliant synthesis of rhythm and restraint. To say the following album stayed in a similar vein and improved little over live shows of the same material would be to damn a fine record with faint praise. ESG remains one of the few bands to emerge in and around the new new wave who offer bouncy funk instead of funk pretensions and elegant simplicity in place of mere primitivism. [jw/mf]

ESSENTIAL LOGIC

Essential Logic EP (Virgin/nr) 1979
Beat Rhythm News (Rough Trade/nr) 1979

LORA LOGIC

Pedigree Charm (Rough Trade/nr) 1982

Essential Logic quickly outlived its usefulness as a vehicle for Lora Logic, once a member of X-Ray Spex and a most distinctive talent. The original lineup—featured on the band's self-titled debut EP—includes two guitars, two saxes (including Logic herself) and a clunky rhythm section; a loose but comfortable ensemble. Logic's songwriting had yet to bloom, though her vocal style was already developing.

She was still loopy but lovable on **Beat Rhythm News**, but her singing had become highly stylized with a distinct edge. A tighter rhythm guitarist replaced the uninspired duo of the EP, and Essential Logic soared. The music's vivacity is occasionally undercut by tinny production and a tendency to ramble, and Lora's growth as a writer and performer warranted more versatile backing. The next Logical step: a solo career.

Logic continued to evolve on her first solo outing. Her voice—much better produced—had a slightly softer, jazzy inflection, and her eclectic writing assumed a poppy sheen. Even hitherto impenetrable lyrics revealed a translucent clarity in spots. Businesslike dance rhythms and fewer straying sax excursions took additional steps toward accessibility. **Pedigree Charm** is a delight.

Abandoning rock'n'roll, Logic—along with former bandmate Poly Styrene—wound up becoming a Hare Krishna devotee and playing in a (religious) cult band. [mf]

ETRON FOU LELOUBLAN

Batelages (Fr. Vergriffen) 1976
Les Trois Fou's (Fr. Vergriffen) 1978
Live in New York (Fr. Vergriffen) 1979
Les Poumons Gonflés (Sw. Turbo Music) 1981
Les Sillons de la Terre (Sw. Turbo Music) 1983
Face aux Elements Dechaines (Sw. Rec-Rec) 1985

FERDINAND

En Avant (Sw. Rec-Rec) 1984

An eclectic French avant-garde ensemble that's been going strong since the early '70s, Etron Fou Leloublan juxtaposes funk bass, jazz horns, prose vocals and free rhythms to create an ever-shifting hodgepodge that's difficult to follow—given the band's commitment to utter unpredictability—but worth investing some effort. Despite a clear refusal to honor traditional musical criteria, there's little on **Les Sillons de la Terre** that's unlistenably radical; obscurity is tempered with an overall good humour and lightness of sound and spirit. Challenging but alluring.

En Avant, the second solo album by bassist/vocalist Ferdinand Richard, is subtitled "Eight songs in eight tongues," and that's just what it is. Accompanied by a cellist, another bassist, a drummer and a singer, Richard presents each of his octet of creations in a different language, including Polish, English, French, Arabic, Vietnamese, German, Spanish and Dioula. (An insert provides additional translations to peruse while listening.) The lyrics are essential blank poetry; the music an experimental, free-form rock-jazz hybrid that's more pleasant than startling. Fascinating and educational. [iar]

EURYTHMICS

In the Garden (RCA/nr) 1981
Sweet Dreams (Are Made of This) (RCA) 1983
Touch (RCA) 1983
Touch Dance (RCA) 1984
1984 (For the Love of Big Brother) (Virgin/RCA) 1984
Be Yourself Tonight (RCA) 1985

Fresh from the unlamented ruins of the Tourists, Annie Lennox and Dave Stewart formed Eurythmics, at first to pursue their love affair with Germanic experimental/electronic music and attempt a translation into a peculiarly English form. Their first album features a wide variety of musicians—Blondie drummer Clem Burke, Can's Holger Czukay and Jaki Liebezeit, composer Karlheinz Stockhausen's son Marcus—and is filled with lyrical love songs and gently strident social anthems ("Your Time Will Come," "All the Young People of Today"). Empowering it all are Lennox's captivating, flexible but strong vocals and a commitment and humor that turn potentially pretentious material into unaffected, poetic work.

From such humble, non-mainstream beginnings was a new chart-topping, trend-setting group created. **Sweet Dreams (Are Made of This)**—thanks mostly to the horrible, monotonic dirge-song of the same name—took off, and lofted the pair into world prominence, a success they maintained on **Touch** by proving themselves capable of enormous stylistic and instrumental variety as well as exceptional songwriting. From lovely ("Here Comes the Rain Again") to jaunty ("Right by Your Side") to dramatic ("Who's That Girl?") and driving ("The First Cut"), **Touch** is an excellent record filled with invention and chicly styled nouveau pop. Who'd have thunk this pair was so talented? To take advantage of sudden global stardom, an album of remixes (four songs with vocals, three of them also presented as instrumentals) by "Jellybean" Benitez and Francois Kevorkian was issued as **Touch Dance**.

The **1984** album—as the result of a contretemps with the film's director, not exactly the soundtrack but "music derived from Eurythmics' original score"—finds the pair moving further into rhythmic experimentation, as on the crazed cut-up stylings of "Sexcrime" and "Doubleplusgood." A strange but affecting record, although clearly not one intended to be taken as a normal chapter in the group's development.

The hard-edged, relatively low-tech **Be Yourself Tonight** marks a real change in the duo's thinking. Exciting, catchy soul-rock ("Would I Lie to You"), insipid, aggravating soul-rock ("I Love You Like a Ball and Chain"), two swell duets ("Adrian," with Elvis Costello, and "Sisters Are Doin' It for Themselves," with Aretha Franklin), plus five more tracks all have an underlying stylistic consistency. That's a new twist for Eurythmics, but one they seem capable of handling. Turning into an '80s Motown factory might seem a little self-conscious, but they carry it off with aplomb and even a bit of heart. [sg/iar]

See also *Robert Görl, Ramones, Feargal Sharkey.*

EVERYTHING BUT THE GIRL

Eden (Blanco y Negro/Sire) 1984
Love Not Money (Blanco y Negro/Sire) 1985

TRACEY THORN

A Distant Shore (Cherry Red/nr) 1982 & 1985

BEN WATT

North Marine Drive (Cherry Red/nr) 1983

Ben Watt (guitar/keyboards/vocals/songs) and Tracey Thorn (vocals/guitar/songs) have been (individually) and presently are (collectively as Everything but the Girl)—in the vanguard of England's back-to-jazz minimalist pop movement. The current popularity of artists like Sade is due in large part to the pair's counter-current pioneering efforts, helping to lay the critical groundwork for acceptance of this decidedly non-rock style.

While also a member of an all-female trio, the Marine Girls, Thorn cut **A Distant Shore**, a brief album of nostalgic singer/songwriter modernism with little more than an acoustic guitar for accompaniment. Her somewhat monotonous delivery hampers the effort, but including the Velvet Underground's utterly appropriate "Femme Fatale" helps considerably.

Watt has recorded on his own as well as in conjunction with Robert Wyatt; **North Marine Drive** is alluring and airy—light, melodic songs given syncopated, quasi-Latin rhythms, played simply and sung sweetly and beguilingly.

Everything but the Girl's debut album, **Eden**, released later the same year in the US as **Everything but the Girl**, is a charming, fragile record delicately filled with winsome songs that drift in and out of neo-jazz-pop stylings but are never less than appealing and attractive. Showing enormous growth as a vocalist, Thorn makes the songs memorable even when the music is too low-key to stand out on its own. With harmonies that recall such wonders of the '60s as the Association, superbly understated pop creations prove EbtG to be an exceptional, unconventional band.

Love Not Money carries the pair away from jazz and into a pure pop approach that is far more accessible and immediately appealing. The album leads off with the band's most alluring song yet, "When All's Well," and continues with further literate considerations of growing up and getting along, including "Ugly Little Dreams," dedicated to doomed actress Frances Farmer. The US edition adds "Heaven Help Me" and a version of Chrissie Hynde's "Kid." [iar]

See also *Grab Grab the Haddock*.

EXPLOITED

Punks Not Dead (Secret/nr) 1981
On Stage (Superville/nr) 1981
Troops of Tomorrow (Secret/nr) 1982
Let's Start a War (Said Maggie One Day) (Pax/nr) 1983
Totally (Blashadabee/nr) 1984
Horror Epics (Konnexion/nr) 1985
Live at the White House (Saderal/Combat Core) 1985

Wattie and his band, the Exploited, are leaders in the newer breed of punkdom, musically harsher, darker, cruder and angrier than their '77 forefathers. If the Pistols had a slim chance of cracking the mainstream charts, bands such as the Exploited have no chance at all; thanks to a huge independent scene, however, they really don't care.

Punks Not Dead is full of angry, gritty anthems of pain and frustration. **On Stage** is strictly for fans, as the sound quality is bootleg-level poor. **Troops of Tomorrow** has a cleaner guitar sound, and the lyrics are a bit easier to understand—but the improved production doesn't mean they're getting slick; it's still rough as can be. **Live at the White House** was recorded in Washington D.C. and features many of their most popular tunes. All of the Exploited's albums express a great deal of anger, use a lot of four-letter words and rock from start to finish. [cpl]

EXPLORERS

The Explorers (Virgin/nr) 1985

On their own, post-Roxy Musicians Phil Manzanera and Andy Mackay—joined by singer James Wraith and a collection of familiar session cohorts—make polite, sophisticated pop music with no edge. Superficially not too different from the music Roxy was making towards the end, the LP is pretty undistinguished, lacking memorable songs and Ferry's unique touch. (Wraith's obvious attempt at imitation on "Venus De Milo" is in questionable taste.) Not bad, just not what you'd hope for from people this talented. [iar]

EXPO

Not-A-Talk-A (Hol. Epic) 1978

Switzerland strikes, with a quintet begging you to tell them how clever and cute they are. Producer Dave Goodman (Sex Pistols, etc.) took 'em to Rockfield Studios in Wales and made sure all that came across. Boy, what a tight, punchy little combo! (Too bad Goodman didn't rewrite a few of their trite tunes.) Snore. [jg]

EXPOSURE

Wild! (Statik/nr) 1984

Heavy, tightly-packed modern rock from an interracial English quintet who resemble a high-density version of U2. Differently put, if the Animals had changed with the times, they might sound like this: passionate, gruff vocals (with leavening harmonies); muscular rhythms with lots of power; multi-layered, danceable guitar-based music and nebulous positive protest lyrics about the state of the world. **Wild!** is an invigorating record—urgent and exciting—that, excepting a few romantic ballads, never lets up the pressure. If you're not out of breath after two sides, you'd better get a checkup. [iar]

EXPRESSION

The Expression (Oz-A&M) 1984

This Australian synth'n'guitar quintet is an MTV-generation hybird that bears a passing resemblance to several bands— Men Without Hats, Talk Talk, Psychedelic Furs (largely because of vocal stylings). The lyrics are clumsy and in spots pretentious, but the music has a variety of modes (maybe too many) and is well-played. Nothing worth recommending here at this point, but nothing horrible either. [iar]

EXPRESSOS

Promises and Ties ... (WEA/nr) 1981

Proving that Los Angeles isn't the only town that grows '60s-styled female pop singers these days, England's Expressos offer a dozen sparkling tunes full of jangly guitars and heartfelt crooning in a nearly forgotten mold. (Nancy Sinatra and Stone Ponys-era Linda Ronstadt provide reasonable comparisons.) The Expressos—one woman and three men—have the advantage of great songwriting ability, making each wonderful track count. [iar]

EXTRABALLE

Extraballe EP (Fr. Carrere) 1979
Sales Romances (Fr. CBS) 1980
Extraballe (Fr. CBS) 1981

On their self-titled EP, Extraballe—whose drummer at the time was Michel Peyronel, brother of Heavy Metal Kids/UFO keyboardist Danny—offered high-speed refried punk-a-boogie with hot axework and little else. Thereafter, the band became nothing more than a name owned by vocalist John Ickx, who wrote the songs anyway. Just about on key, Ickx's French speak/singing covers most typical punk subjects (sex, violence, power, movies) plus a couple of less likely topics for a young Frenchman. There's potent high-energy accompaniment with lots of organ and guitar vying for domination of the serviceable tunes. (The temporary band for **Sales Romances** included one-time Be-Bop Deluxe *batteur* Simon Fox; Blockhead Davey Payne blew some sax.) Ickx formed a different band for the **Extraballe** album; a pity he couldn't update the sound more. [jg]

EYELESS IN GAZA

Photographs as Memories (Cherry Red/nr) 1981
Caught in Flux (Cherry Red/nr) 1981
Pale Hands I Loved So Well (Nor. Uniton) 1982
Drumming the Beating Heart (Cherry Red/nr) 1982
Rust Red September (Cherry Red/nr) 1983

Named for Aldous Huxley's ode to pacifist integrity, Eyeless in Gaza consists of Martyn Bates and Peter Becker, both credited with voice and instrumentation on the first album, a better-than-decent stab at hook-filled spareness. The tasteful music is marred only occasionally by overly anguished vocals. **Caught in Flux** has a more delicate flavor at first, then rapidly devolves into humpbacked squalor. This one-and-a-half-disc (LP/EP) set shows a hint of progress, with the vocals held in tighter rein. Caught in flux, indeed.

Drumming the Beating Heart has the duo streamlining their sound to good effect, relying on church organ leads and spontaneous rhythm approaches. If the vocals could be relieved of their melodrama, these boys might have something here. **Pale Hands**, released only in Norway, is fairly dissolute—a meandering, largely-improvisational attempt to make music out of aimless doodles.

[jw/iar]

FACE TO FACE

Face to Face (Epic) 1984
Confrontation (Epic) 1985

Depending on where you put your needle down on their first record, this Boston quintet is either a fascinating blend of hip-hop and rock'n'roll or a noxious pre-fab MTV creation. Four producers—including Arthur Baker and Jimmy Iovine—worked on the album, yielding both the annoying hit single "10-9-8" and a gripping piece of political consciousness, "Under the Gun," on which Baker (who produced both tracks!) drum-programs and scratch-mixes the band into a new realm that is both exciting and original. (A subsequent 12-inch further elaborates on "Under the Gun"—fifteen minutes' worth—with two remixes.)

Confrontation was mostly co-produced by Baker and Ed Stasium. Except for the increasing number of ballads, the band rocks enthusiastically, leaning into the rhythmic material. Singer Laurie Sargent remains a strong presence, but the overall routine presentation and sound make this **Confrontation** too radio-ready to really matter.

[iar]

FAD GADGET

Favourites (Mute/nr) 1980
Incontinent (Mute/nr) 1981
Under the Flag (Mute/nr) 1982
Gag (Mute/nr) 1984

FRANK TOVEY AND
BOYD RICE

Easy Listening for the Hard of Hearing (Mute/nr) 1984

FRANK TOVEY

Snakes and Ladders (Mute/Sire) 1986

The enigmatic Mr. Gadget (plain old Frank Tovey to his family) is a creative and unpredictable writer, singer and performer whose records differ considerably from each other; he's an acquired taste with little consistency.

After an eerie 45 ("Ricky's Hand," which features Mute head Daniel Miller on synthesizer and Fad playing a "Black and Decker V8 double speed electric drill"—hey ma, can I get one of those, please, huh?), his first album sounds awfully like pre-fame Human League. Except for the title track, which bounces along cheerfully, his basic approach is a mix of dour vocals, heavy, repetitive bass lines, solid drums and odd noises. Tacky tunes like "Coitus Interruptus" only cheapen the proceedings.

Incontinent pursues the grubby side of life, employing more instrumental variety and better production. Forgetting tripe like "Swallow It" and the title tune, there's some interesting stuff here, but nothing to really involve the listener—the album is self-indulgent and rambling.

Showing a quantum leap in maturity (lyrically and musically), **Under the Flag** joins pristine production quality with a no-nonsense synth drive that could pass for dance music, and shows absorption of a mild soul influence. (Then-labelmate Alison Moyet sings on a few tracks and even adds saxophone to one.) The funky approach gives Fad his most direct and

accessible sound to date, but that's not necessarily an accomplishment—it's hard to avoid the feeling that he's slumming in such relatively commercial seas.

[iar]

JAD FAIR

See *1/2 Japanese*.

MARIANNE FAITHFULL

Broken English (Island) 1979
Dangerous Acquaintances (Island) 1981
A Childs Adventure (Island) 1983

Resuming her lengthy recording career after a gap of several years, Marianne Faithfull presents a whole new persona on these intensely individual and powerful albums. Armed with a life-roughened voice filled with suffering and rage, and backed by brilliantly original electro-rock, she grapples with mostly political subjects on **Broken English** and even includes a fascinating interpretation of John Lennon's "Working Class Hero." For **Dangerous Acquaintances**, Faithfull takes a more resigned outlook, and sings of relationships and the passage of time with strength and depth. Although the music on it is less exemplary, **A Childs Adventure** continues her harrowing voyage. Other than the political commentary of "Ireland," the songs concentrate on personal struggles, with only a glimmer of hope ("Ashes in My Hand") emerging from the otherwise bleak appraisal. A unique chapter in a bizarre musical career.

The latest music from Faithfull is on the soundtrack LP, **Trouble in Mind**, where she sings songs written by Mark Isham and Kris Kristofferson.

[iar]

FAITH GLOBAL

The Same Mistakes (Survival/nr) 1983

Although Faith Global features original Ultravox guitarist Stevie Shears, he shares control with singer/co-writer Jason Guy, a bored-sounding Ferry/Bowie dud. The music hasn't got much character either, relying on Shears' guitar, piano and synthesizer work to color the plodding creations. He shows signs of incipient creativity amidst the tedium (and the faster the tune, the less deadly the effect), but never quite enough to focus the songs or relieve the pervasive monotony.

[iar]

FALCO

Einzelhaft (A&M) 1982
Junge Roemer (A&M) 1984
3 (A&M) 1986

Falco (Johann Hoelcel) is something of a hero in his native Austria; although he sings (in a random mix of accented English and German) like an arch, Continental smoothie, his shtick is slick but thematically simpleminded chart fare, fashionably automated (lots of synth, computerized drums with roto-tom and cymbal overdubs) and syncopated. The best parts of **Einzelhaft** (co-produced with his songwriting partner, keyboardist Robert Ponger) are tedious rock; the tracks that have earned him international visibility ("Der Kommissar," a US hit when badly covered in English by After the Fire; "Maschine Brennt") are repulsive pseudo-funk with obnoxiously patronizing attempts at

urban Afro-American lingo, accents and music, sung in a constipated gurgle that sounds as appealing as someone vomiting in an alley.

On **Junge Roemer**, Ponger's generally lighter touch—leaning towards Philly soul in tone if not content—cuts a lot of the crap to expose a boring collection of tepidly delivered songs that drift dully from the speakers into the ozone without leaving a trace.

Lest anyone be lulled into imagining Falco on his way to Eurovision politesse, his third LP is one of the most grotesque musical monstrosities ever produced. With two new collaborators replacing Ponger, he essays a cultural outreach program with such garishly overproduced, overlong thumpers as "Vienna Calling" (7:40) and "Rock Me Amadeus" (8:20). Each repeats a cloying riff or chorus endlessly while all manner of gimmicky mix tricks (spoken word, scratching, dub echo, sound effects, etc.) attempt to obscure Falco's regurgo blather. Think of an endless loop of Queen's "We Will Rock You" with less melody and you'll get an idea of what a nightmare this is. To cap things off in maximally tasteless fashion, Fal' debases Dylan's "It's All Over Now, Baby Blue" as a sneery lounge singer, complete with spoken asides. What a jerk! (For masochists, **3**—brilliantly mastered, incidentally—runs over 50 minutes.)

[jg/iar]

TAV FALCO'S PANTHER BURNS

See *Panther Burns*.

FALL

Live at the Witch Trials (Step Forward/Step Forward-IRS) 1979
Dragnet (Step Forward/nr) 1979
Live Totale's Turns (It's Now or Never) (Rough Trade/nr) 1980
Grotesque (After the Gramme) (Rough Trade) 1980
Early Years 77-79 (Step Forward/ Faulty Products) 1981
Slates EP (Rough Trade) 1981
Live in London, 1980 [tape] (Chaos/nr) 1982
Hex Enduction Hour (Kamera/nr) 1982
Room to Live (Kamera/nr) 1982
A Part of America Therein, 1981 (nr/Cottage) 1982
Fall in a Hole (NZ Flying Nun) 1983
Perverted by Language (Rough Trade/nr) 1983
Wonderful and Frightening World of the Fall (Beggars Banquet/ Beggars Banquet-PVC) 1984
Call for Escape Route EP (Beggars Banquet/nr) 1984
Hip Priest and Kamerads (Situation 2/nr) 1985
This Nation's Saving Grace (Beggars Banquet/Beggars Banquet-PVC) 1985
The Fall EP (nr/Beggars Banquet-PVC) 1986

The Fall formed in 1977 in Manchester and has been a major cult favorite in numerous corners of the globe ever since, despite few commercial efforts and uncompromising artistic integrity. Their fans are rabid, and their influence on like-minded conceptual noisemakers—in England, the US, Iceland, New Zealand and elsewhere—can't be overstated. Led by acid-tongued poet Mark E.

Smith, whose lyrics and vocals provide the Fall's most distinguishing features, the band has created a huge body of unpleasant, challenging, inaccessible anti-rock that occasionally proves to be very moving. From humble experimental beginnings, the Fall have continued to explore and grow stronger over the course of eight prolific years, earning a place of real respect in left-wing musical circles. Whether you enjoy the sounds or not, the Fall have made a difference in the sound of modern music, and that counts.

After releasing some singles and contributing two tracks to the watershed Manchester compilation, **Short Circuit/Live at the Electric Circus**, the Fall recorded and mixed their debut LP, **Live at the Witch Trials** in an economical two-day studio session with producer Bob Sargeant, who did nothing (audible) to soften their dissonant but well-organized rock noise. At once leaning toward punk's directness and charging headlong into poetic pretension, Smith and company (bass, drums, electric piano, guitar) drip sincerity on tracks like "Rebellious Jukebox" and "Crap Rap 2/Like to Blow," occasionally sounding "normal" amidst the tempest. **Dragnet** followed with a rougher-edged sound as well as a new lineup. (The Fall are a biographical nightmare.) The first album to feature Craig Scanlon's trademark scratchy, dissonant guitar (which has played a major role in the band's noise ever since), **Dragnet** is not one of the Fall's best efforts, but contains at least two of their classic numbers, "Spectre vs. Rector" and "A Figure Walks."

By the time of the Fall's first live album, **Totale's Turns**—recorded in late '79 and early '80—the band had consolidated a more commanding style, although it's no easier on the aurals. Jagged, largely recitative and nearly oblivious to musical convention, Smith's witty repartee carries the show—he sounds a bit like the Stranglers' Hugh Cornwell, only *less* melodious. The band lurches and grunts along noisily; 43 minutes of this is a bit much for non-fanatics.

Grotesque removes the Fall even further from the world of easy listening. The songs are mostly one-or-two-chord jams played too slowly to be hardcore, but structured similarly. Smith grafts on sociopolitical lyrics that would be more interesting on paper than accompanied by this strictly one-take-live-in-the-studio atonality.

All of the Fall's pre-LP singles (featuring a lineup with keyboardist Una Baines and guitarist Martin Bramah, who went on together to form the Blue Orchids) are on one side of **Early Years**; the other collects later 7-inch efforts. One imagines that Public Image listened to the 1977 vintage "Repetition" a couple of times before mapping out their first LP.

The 10-inch **Slates** has six tracks with substantially better production than the Fall's preceding ventures; evidence of much greater studio effort abounds. While still not quite Abba-smooth, several numbers, especially "Fit and Working Again" and "Leave the Capitol," are as close to enjoyable, routine (ahem) rock as the Fall have come. A solid record of greater potential appeal than just to cultists.

Part of **Hex Enduction Hour** was

recorded in Iceland, a nation where the Fall's music is widely influential. An expanded lineup with two drummers greatly affects the sound, making it large and more rhythm-conscious. Despite a tendency to lumber along at a slow, methodical pace (a common hazard with multiple drummers), some of the tracks are an interesting departure. **Room to Live** features a sparser, less rhythmic sound than **Hex Enduction Hour**, occasionally returning to **Grotesque**'s flirtation with raw rockabilly. Smith is in top lyrical form, with pungent, satirical views of British life: "Marquis Cha Cha" offers biting commentary on the Falklands War.

Around this time, two live Fall discs emerged. **A Part of America Therein** was taped at a half-dozen gigs along a US tour. The sound quality varies considerably from track to track, but the performances are uniformly strong, particularly the epic "N.W.R.A." Even better, though, is **Fall in a Hole**, a two-disc authorized bootleg released only in New Zealand. Recording quality, execution and song selection (mostly from **Hex** and **Room to Live**) are superb, but suffice to say, it's not a common sight in record stores.

The **Live in London, 1980** cassette was recorded in front of a none-too-enthusiastic audience at Acklam Hall; it's of dubious legal origin, listing neither songwriting nor publishing credits. Drawing mostly from **Grotesque** and **Slates**, it warrants mention due to sharp performances (except for "Prole Art Threat," which falls apart) and very good sound quality.

Their next studio LP, **Perverted by Language**, marked a brief return to Rough Trade. On the first Fall record with Smith's American wife Brix as co-guitarist, they chug away with more conviction than ever, particularly on the relentless "Smile" and "Eat Y'self Fitter." Hindsight now shows it to be priming the audience for what was to follow: **The Wonderful and Frightening World of the Fall**, perhaps their finest work to date, produced by John Leckie. Strengthened by Brix's songwriting and gutsy guitar, the Fall are able to beckon a variety of styles with panache. All nine tracks (eleven on the American release, which adds "C.R.E.E.P." and "No Bulbs," the latter from the subsequent EP, **Call for Escape Route**) jump out, highlighted by the fierce "Lay of the Land," "Elves" and the almost Syd Barrett-like "Disney's Dream Debased."

Hip Priest and Kamerads is a compilation of the band's releases on the Kamera label. Except for a live version of "Mere Pseud Mag Ed.," there's nothing otherwise unavailable, but it does offer a good introduction for the uninitiated. The tape has extra tracks.

With what at this point seems like an embarrassment of riches, the Fall unleashed **This Nation's Saving Grace**. Tracks like the (gasp!) synthesized and danceable "L.A." and the contemporaneous 45, "Cruiser's Creek," show that the Fall is not completely averse to commercial potential, but it's really just another new type of ammunition added to the arsenal. "Bombast" builds a guitar din that would make Sonic Youth jealous, while "Paintwork" and "I Am Damo Suzuki" (a song about Can's one-time lead singer) are two of the strangest

things they've ever done. The tape adds tracks, and the US release substitutes "Cruiser's Creek" for "Barmy," which subsequently turned up on the eponymous American EP, alongside other 45 cuts like their unlikely cover of Gene Vincent's "Rollin' Dany."

The Fall is requisite listening for anyone interested in a challenging, uncompromising band that refuses to stand still or follow any trends not of its own creation.   [iar/dgs]

See also *Blue Orchids, Marc Riley with the Creepers.*

FAMILY FODDER

Monkey Banana Kitchen (Fresh/nr) 1980
All Styles 2 x 33 (Jungle/nr) 1983

These records are bizarre works of multifaceted genius from a strange musical collective. Let me try and elaborate: **Monkey Banana Kitchen**, listing fifteen first-name-only musicians and produced by "The People in Control," begins with a choral piece and then slowly drifts into a lengthy dub workout; when that ends, a female voice sings a chipper pop song with weedy organ and a verse in French. After that, things begin to get odd . . . Every track on **Monkey Banana Kitchen** is an adventure—there is absolutely no consistency. Often dada, the results run from likable to heinous. Remarkable and great fun, it's a record that will keep you on the edge of your seat.

All Styles, its cover adorned simply by a peace sign, is hypothetically just what the title suggests: two discs (fifteen discrete songs in all) that give new meaning to the word "variety." Pre-pigeonholed for ease of reviewing, Family Fodder (here a quartet) ostensibly essay folk, classical, soul, punk, easy listening, Euro-pop, opera, jazz, country- western and more, adapting existing material as well as writing their own. In point of fact, these styles, charming and rewarding as they may be, are not very disparate at all, undoubtedly due to self-definition/delusion and the limitations of 4-track at-home recordings. They are, however, consistently enjoyable and infused with invention, cleverness, talent and a totally open outlook that discards nothing without first having an enthusiastic go at it.   [iar]

FANATICS

Fanatics (Fr. Epic) 1981

Zut alors! These French kids rock like the essence of punchy London punk circa 1977-78, only in a different language. Not brilliant, but solid. Produced by Hugh Jones.   [jg]

FARMER'S BOYS

Get Out and Walk (EMI/nr) 1983
With These Hands (EMI/nr) 1985

If you'd heard their early singles without paying much attention, you might have thought this quartet to be just another Anglo-dance-rock group: the usual rhythms (drum machine), the usual keyboards, the usual sort of a vocalist. One of the 45s (quite good, actually) even sounds like a cross between ABC and Dexys. But what's different? There's no overwrought melodrama, *that's* what—no posing. Stylistically, the sound just provides a jumping-off point for their catchy,

distinctive songs; cleverly arranged, succinctly produced. They don't overdo a thing, so you can really relate to their tales of botched romance, self-doubt, even drinking too much after a long day's work. The Farmer's Boys get the points across engagingly, with feeling but without taking themselves too seriously. The second album is more stylistically diverse than the first—leading off with a Shadows (!) tune about going out in the country-side (!!), done up in a marginally retooled version of '60s pop-rock somewhere between Spanky and Our Gang, the Turtles and the Grass Roots! (That track is one of four produced by Bruce Woolley; horns grace several others.)

The Farmer's Boys are a gas: four normal-looking guys from Norwich making consistently good, durable music. No brilliance here—they haven't got the killer instinct—but these two albums provide solace for sore (or cynical but open-minded) ears with cut after cut of enjoyable tunes. Suggestion for trendies and art-lovers: get out and walk.   [jg]

MICK FARREN

Vampires Stole My Lunch Money (Logo/nr) 1978

Mick Farren—journalist, novelist, vocalist, founding member of the Pink Fairies, Motorhead song collaborator/contributor, etc., etc.—ventured into solo recording work several times in the '70s; this album is his most recent. With musical assistance from Wilko Johnson, Chrissie Hynde, Larry Wallis and others, Farren dishes out a harrowingly honest collection of songs about drinking, dissolution, depression, self-destruction and desperation. About as powerful as rock gets, this LP is most definitely not recommended to sissies, born-again Christians or prohibitionists.   [iar]

FASHION

Product Perfect (Illegal/IRS) 1979
Fabrique (Arista) 1982
Twilight of Idols (Epic) 1984

Fashion emerged from Manchester during that city's great rock explosion of 1978/9 with a facility for clever pop that cannibalized aspects of reggae, punk and electro-pop and converted them into a mode that scarcely resembled the parent forms. **Product Perfect** verges on being cheerless, but Fashion infuses it with such good humor and imaginative effects that it seems a wry parody of everything from Madness to Joy Division. Lyrics and tunes are at first unmemorable, but subtle hooks become apparent after several listenings.

Fabrique finds the group, expanded from a trio to a quartet, in a more serious mood, exchanging jokey pop for fierce, funky dance music, including the striking "Move On." Curiously, the songs have immediate impact (in comparison to those on the first LP) but lack the staying power of their earlier work. Nevertheless, the playing is precise and energetic, with more distinct lyrics sung better than ever.

Despite a third label and another personnel change, the same musical style prevails on much of **Twilight of Idols**: muscular dance-rock with the emphasis on solid rhythms and rich vocals rather

than gimmicky effects or stylish textures. The exceptional tunes (like the delicate instrumental title track) hold down the energy and get sensitive, at times nearing a Pink Floyd (!) sound. On the hotter numbers, wild guitar (Alan Darby, also the writer of nearly all the material) and slick production gambits (by Zeus B. Held) provide the character the songs themselves lack.   [sg/iar]

FAT BOYS

Fat Boys (Sutra-WEA/Sutra) 1984
The Fat Boys Are Back (Sutra-WEA/Sutra) 1985
Big & Beautiful (Sutra) 1986

In a medium like rap, it helps to have a gimmick, and the former Disco 3 have several. While most rappers brag about what great lovers they are, the plump MC's brag about what great eaters they are. In this, their claim to originality is undisputed. Gimmick number two is the Human Beat Box (not to be confused with Doug E. Fresh, the self-proclaimed "Original Human Beat Box"), who uses lips, cheeks and tongue to create a surprisingly varied array of rhythmic beat box noises. The raps themselves are also gimmicky. If the Fat Boys aren't the most talented crew in the business, they're at least consistently good fun. (See for yourself in **Krush Groove**, which recounts their legend.)   [jl]

See also *Force M.D.'s.*

FEAR

The Record (nr/Slash) 1982
More Beer (nr/Restless) 1985

Fear was an early standout on the Los Angeles hardcore scene; at this stage, though, they bear only marginal resemblance to the thrash compactors who now abound. Skilled, varied, instrumentally confident and inventive, Fear invests **The Record** with searing rock'n'roll and a wild-eyed sense of humor that seems somehow wholesomely good-natured. Lee Ving (who has also pursued a reasonably successful acting career) sings like a drunk baseball fan bellowing in the bleachers, roaring like a lout, but completely intelligible, which allows funny—if disturbingly nasty with regard to women and homosexuals—lyrics to rise above the well-ordered din. Guitarist Philo Cramer tosses instrumental cleverness into the material, making Fear something of a cross between the Dictators and Dickies. **More Beer** seems unnecessary, but is as loud, fast and viciously sarcastic as ever. The sporadic inter-song patter is more amusing than the actual tunes themselves, which are in fact pretty stupid, but there's something pathetically wonderful about Fear, like a dog that you don't really like but keep around anyway because he's so faithful and predictable. (The best Fear on record remains **The Decline of Western Civilization** soundtrack, where Ving raises audience baiting to a sidesplitting art and another bandmember coins a new usage for a traditional colloquialism.)   [iar]

FEELIES

Crazy Rhythms (Stiff) 1980
The Good Earth (nr/Coyote) 1986

These four New Jerseyites are the stuff of legend and cults. Led by guitarists Glenn Mercer and Bill Million (and originally featuring a future avant-star, drummer Anton Fier), the Feelies dressed like nerdy preppies and paid only passing attention to the conventional demands of rock'n'roll. Even during the band's period of highest visibility, for example, live dates in New York tended to be infrequent and often fell on holidays.

Crazy Rhythms is far more unequivocal than the group's performances. Mercer and Million draw inspiration from the Byrds, Television and Velvet Underground, emphasizing the interplay of their electric guitars above all else. The rigid vocals and lyrics take a back seat to the pure textures of the driving rockers and more avant-garde drones. Despite its distinct bloodlessness, **Crazy Rhythms** exudes a principled charm.

In the years that followed, the Feelies laid low, but never really disbanded, continuing on in various permutations and guises around the New York/New Jersey area. In 1986, following their reappearance on the circuit as the Feelies, they released an all-new LP, **The Good Earth**. [jy]

See also *Lounge Lizards, Trypes.*

FELT

Crumbling the Antiseptic Beauty (Cherry Red/nr) 1982
The Splendour of Fear (Cherry Red/nr) 1984
The Strange Idols Pattern and Other Short Stories (Cherry Red/nr) 1984
Ignite the Seven Cannons (Cherry Red/nr) 1985

This young trio (two guitarists and a drummer plus a guest bassist) patterned their passionate debut LP on the kind of guitar interplay pioneered by Television. The instrumental passages are the true high points here, as the guitarists are both melodic and sympathetic to each other. The vocals have an eerie quality without being self-conscious. An odd but exciting band. [cpl]

FERDINAND

See *Etron Fou Leloublan.*

BRYAN FERRY

These Foolish Things (Island/Atlantic) 1973 (Polydor/nr) 1977
Another Time, Another Place (Island/Atlantic) 1974 (Polydor/nr) 1977
Let's Stick Together (Island/Atlantic) 1976 (Polydor/nr) 1977
In Your Mind (Polydor/Atlantic) 1977
The Bride Stripped Bare (Polydor/Atlantic) 1978
Boys and Girls (EG-Polydor/Warner Bros.) 1985
Windswept EP (EG-Polydor/nr) 1985

BRYAN FERRY/ROXY MUSIC

Street Life (EG/nr) 1986

Braving waves of contemptuous reviews, the voice of Roxy Music (until 1983 or so) has sortied out irregularly to advance his solo career; while the results have been inconsistent, his far-reaching stylistic influence can be felt throughout the new music world. Despite their claims of total self-invention, many nouveau poseurs have let Ferry's solo work point the way for them to be themselves.

The shocking **These Foolish Things** quickly established the

difference between Roxy Music's intensely original creations and Ferry's suave solo interpretations. (For a number of obvious reasons this gap closed over the years to the point of near-unseparability.) With a backing group that included then-Roxy drummer Paul Thompson as well as future Roxyite Eddie Jobson, Ferry croons his way through such surprising '60s selections as Bob Dylan's "A Hard Rain's A-Gonna Fall," the Beatles' "You Won't See Me" and the Stones' "Sympathy for the Devil." Even a dozen years later, this warped '70s jukebox sounds weird but wonderful. **Another Time, Another Place** reprised the exercise, choosing songs from various epochs like "The 'In' Crowd," "You Are My Sunshine," "It Ain't Me Babe" and "Smoke Gets in Your Eyes." Only the title song is a Ferry original.

For **Let's Stick Together**, Ferry reached into the vaults for five Roxy Music songs (four from the first LP) and did something with them—either recut the vocals, turned up alternate versions or simply re-edited/re-mixed the tracks. Some of these sound fine, but a funked-up "Re-Make/ Re-Model" is vile and too revisionist for words. The record is fleshed out with another brace of neat covers, including the wonderful title track, "Shame Shame Shame" and the Everly Brothers' "Price of Love." It's a strange assemblage with some jarring contrasts; still, **Let's Stick Together** has more great tracks than any of Ferry's other solo records.

In Your Mind, produced during a period of Roxy inactivity, tries to be a normal solo album—all of the material is Ferry's and new—but, bereft of a gimmick and lacking the involvement of his usual collaborators, falls short of Ferry's best work. Despite some good tunes ("This Is Tomorrow," "Tokyo Joe"), the bland sound allows little of Ferry's brilliance to shine through, and the writing could have been a lot better. Easily ignored.

Inspired by his broken romance with the future mother of Mick Jagger's children, Jerry Hall, who had modeled for some of Roxy's LP covers, **The Bride Stripped Bare** (loosely named after a surrealist work by Marcel Duchamp) is Ferry's most translucently revealing album. The hybrid approach— half new originals, half appropriate revivals—and a new coterie of session-pros (including Waddy Wachtel, Neil Hubbard and Alan Spenner) as backing musicians make it radically different in both construction and sound. Some of the tracks are intensely gripping ("Sign of the Times," Lou Reed's "What Goes On"); others are subtler and less rewarding. Mixed, but the good spots are great.

Since it became clear that Roxy Music is no longer a revivable proposition, Ferry's solo career has taken on a new significance. Unfortunately, it's also inherited the torpid nature of end-time Roxy Music: perfectionist studio technique and seamless production of songs that are, at best bland and more often lifeless. Despite its extraordinarily sleek veneer, **Boys and Girls** (dedicated to Ferry's late father) is so short on tunes that several of the numbers rely on fatiguing one-note vamps to carry them along. If the lyrics were exceptional, one might overlook such inadequacy, but

there's nothing much happening on that front either. I find it impossible to dislike this album with any enthusiasm: considerable care, thought and effort obviously went into its creation. Still, the lack of even a trace of extremism or subversion, no matter how subtle, is unforgivable.

Street Life is a two-record career retrospective: 20 songs drawn from Roxy Music as well as Ferry solo releases, stretching from "Virginia Plain" to "Slave to Love." [iar]

FETALMANIA

Fetus Productions EP (NZ Flying Nun) 1982

A weird blend of scratchy guitar, prominent percussion, disquieting noises and disembodied vocals— the Residents go to a disco, or Tuxedomoon takes a trip Down Under. There's enough melody and structure to make up for the obnoxious imagery and self-conscious strangeness, and the songs gallop along nicely. Very obscure. [iar]

FETCHIN BONES

Cabin Flounder (DB-Stiff/DB) 1985

Like the sublimely seedy roadside joints of America's rural south—where you can shoot pool, buy fishing worms and have your lawn mower repaired all in the same room—Fetchin Bones are dedicated to the sort of unexpected variety that somehow seems to work. On their debut album, the North Carolina quintet peddles an exciting mix of revved-up rock, country twang, folk, blues and swing, driving it all home with hardcore energy and unpolished charm. The crazed quaver in singer Hope Nicholls' voice (a rougher, more manic version of Lone Justice's Maria McKee) provides the heart of the Bones' sound; three (of eleven) songs without her lead vocals are the album's weakest cuts. Producer Don Dixon admirably translates the group's wild-eyed persona to vinyl, but this is a band that must be seen live to fully grasp the eclectic frenzy. Delightfully different graduates of the R.E.M.-inspired school of Southern pop. [kh]

FINE YOUNG CANNIBALS

Fine Young Cannibals (London/IRS) 1985

Factionalism led to the disbandment of the Beat; when the two mainmen formed General Public, the others looked set to fade from sight. But the group formed by guitarist Andy Cox and bassist David Steele, joined by fine young vocalist Roland Gift, has proven a most worthwhile venture. **Fine Young Cannibals** approaches modern R&B and soul from a number of fresh rock perspectives, but it's really Gift's classically Motownish, richly emotional vocals that ignite originals like "Johnny Come Back" and "Don't Ask Me to Choose" as well as a rousing cover of Elvis Presley's "Suspicious Minds." [iar]

FINGERPRINTZ

The Very Dab (Virgin/Virgin International) 1979
Distinguishing Marks (Virgin) 1980
Beat Noir (Virgin/Stiff) 1981

It's difficult to categorize Fingerprintz, which may explain why this now-defunct group never garnered a large following. The primitively-recorded first album occupies a dark, throbbing zone of bobbing pop and wry-to-bizarre lyrics ("Punchy Judy," "Beam Me Up Scotty"). Leader/guitarist Jimme O'Neill's Scottish accent and offbeat songwriting combine to chilling effect on the crime-obsessed narratives "Fingerprince" and "Wet Job"; the former's music also suggests a valid response to reggae/dub influence.

The considerably slicker **Distinguishing Marks**, in contrast, is pure pop in extremis—musically, anyway. The songs hum like a finely-tuned motor, with producer Nick Garvey removing any rough sonic edges. Only the relentlessly perverse lyrics betray a refusal to play by the book; O'Neill's disjointed visions are inspired by pulp fiction, police blotters and hospital charts. A catchy collection that all sounds like hit single material.

Beat Noir took yet another 180-degree turn, away from pop and toward a rock/funk fusion. Finally in synch with the times, Fingerprintz delivered a stunning, idiosyncratic package of heavy bass lines, winsome melodies and O'Neill's thematic fetishes (paranoia, frustration). The album was kinky enough to catch on in rock clubs, but too peculiar to reach a broader audience. (The US version deletes two songs.) Drenched in atmosphere, it remains a compelling work.

O'Neill subsequently co-wrote, co-produced and played on an excellent album (**Sob Stories**) by singer Jacqui Brookes. Drummer Bogdan Wiczling worked on that record as well, and later toured and recorded with Adam Ant. [si]

TIM FINN

Escapade (Oz-A&M) 1983
Big Canoe (Virgin/nr) 1986

Split Enz's singer successfully carved out an identity distinct from his now-defunct band with **Escapade**, Finn's first solo album. On his own, he's milder, sweeter and more conventional (though still worth the time). The precedent for **Escapade** can be found in the romantic grandeur of **True Colours**' "I Hope I Never." One track here, the moving "Not for Nothing," is a bona fide lump-in-the-throat masterpiece. [jy]

FIRE ENGINES

Lubricate Your Living Room (Pop: Aural/nr) 1980
Aufgeladen und Bereit fur Action und Spass (nr/Fast America) 1981

Fire Engines were the most manic of the new Scottish pop crop that surfaced around 1979: primal rock'n'roll drawing more on raw passion (via guitar din and repetitive noise) than melody or captivating structures. The quartet offers no traditional hooks, just six-string fire and aggressively unpleasant vocals. The two enigmatic albums have a lot of overlap: the American release with the German title adds two of the band's catchier numbers, the punk-country-flavored "Candyskin" (with ridiculously anomalous strings) and "Everythings Roses." It also replaces the tedious "Lubricate Your Living Room Pt. 2" with the more exciting "Meat Whiplash."

Using electric guitars without regard to typical pop traditions, the abrasive but ruggedly handsome Fire Engines—kind of a blend of the Contortions and early Television—will poke and scratch their way into your heart if you let them. [gf/iar]

FIRMAMENT AND THE ELEMENTS

See *Bruce Woolley.*

WILD MAN FISCHER

An Evening with Wild Man Fischer (nr/Bizarre) 1969
Wildmania (nr/Rhino) 1977
Pronounced Normal (nr/Rhino) 1981
Nothing Scary (nr/Rhino) 1984

One of the true wackos of our time, Los Angeles crypto-singer Wild Man (Larry) Fischer has been around forever. Originally discovered, signed and produced by Frank Zappa in the late '60s, he resurfaces periodically through the auspices of Dr. Demento and Rhino Records, for whom he first began recording in 1975, with a blatantly commercial single, "Go to Rhino Records." Utterly uninhibited and basically incapable of carrying a tune, Fischer recorded some of **Wildmania** in the left field (ahem) stands of Dodger Stadium; largely unaccompanied, he moans such dadaist attempts at musical expression as "My Name Is Larry" (twice) and generally performs in truly sad fashion. **Pronounced Normal** is much better, an entertaining and funny program of music and "skits" that ranges from a lovely (if atonal) guitar-assisted version of Brian Wilson's "In My Room" to a solo vocal rendition of "Fish Heads," composed (as is much of the material) by Barnes & Barnes, the disciples who also produced it.

They did the same (and more) for **Nothing Scary**, an assemblage of three years' worth of odds and ends. The LP contains 34 separate items (e.g., "Outside the Hospital," "Larry in Las Vegas," "Oh God, Please Send Me a Kid"), with Fischer's vocals recorded, besides in a studio, "on location in a park, in a tunnel, and over the telephone." The living art project continues . . . [iar]

FISCHER-Z

Word Salad (UA) 1979
Going Deaf for a Living (Liberty-UA/UA) 1980
Red Skies over Paradise (Liberty/nr) 1981

JOHN WATTS

One More Twist (EMI/nr) 1982
The Iceberg Model (EMI/nr) 1983

An often excellent but widely ignored outfit, Fischer-Z was primarily a vehicle for John Watts, a singer/guitarist/songwriter whose intense vocals and semi-neurotic outlook provided its character. A flair for intricate but accessible arrangements and novel subject matter made Fischer-Z both easy to like and hard to dismiss.

Word Salad, produced by Mike Howlett and recorded as a quartet, displays Watts in the process of searching out an ego, still sharing songwriting credits and vocal chores with the others. It's an impressive debut album, full of great songs, fine musicianship and

stylistic variety, all colored by Watts' reedy voice.

With the same personnel and producer, **Going Deaf for a Living** went for a sparer sound, downplaying the keyboards in favor of Cars-like simplicity, best exemplified on "So Long." An odd direction for a second record, but the band's attributes remained unchanged, and it's as good as the first.

Red Skies over Paradise is a solo album waiting for someone to inform the other members of the group. Watts co-produced, played the keyboards and allowed his songwriting to become entirely self-indulgent. With a serious baritone replacing the plaintive tenor (it's always a bad sign when singers change their voices) and no-nonsense message lyrics, there's a lot wrong with this disappointing album, despite four or five good numbers.

As a predictable next move, Watts went solo. The material on **One More Twist** is a bit forced and clearly less interesting than his earlier songwriting, with only the Tom Robinson-sounding single, "One Voice," showing any real signs of life. [iar]

FISHBONE

Fishbone EP (CBS/Columbia) 1985

One of America's brightest young hopes, this rowdy six-piece from LA specializes in ska with overtones of go go, funk and rock. (Imagine George Clinton producing the first Beat LP.) Their sense of humor is surpassed only by the six tracks' non-stop hyperkinetic energy. Whether the lyrics are socially relevant ("Party at Ground Zero," "Another Generation") or just plain silly ("Ugly"), the vim and vigor level is maintained. If you can sit still throughout this, you're probably dead. Let's hear some more! [dgs]

PATRIK FITZGERALD

Grubby Stories (Small Wonder-Polydor/nr) 1979
Gifts and Telegrams (Red Flame/nr) 1982
Drifting Towards Violence (Red Flame/nr) 1983

London punk folk singer Fitzgerald first attracted attention with his 1977 single, "Safety Pin Stuck in My Heart." After a few years and a few more 45s, he delivered the aptly titled **Grubby Stories** LP. Some tracks use just acoustic guitar and vocals, while others employ a full backing band that features the bassist from Penetration, the Buzzcocks' drummer and producer Peter Wilson on guitar and keyboards. The music is pretty mundane—Fitzgerald's strength is his angry/sad/pathetic/strange lyrics, not lasting melodies—but the singing and unique attitude expressed make **Grubby Stories** a slight treasure for occasional enjoyment. The similarity to pre-rock Bowie is striking, although probably unintentional. [iar]

FIXX

Shuttered Room (MCA) 1982
Reach the Beach (MCA) 1983
Phantoms (MCA) 1984
Walkabout (MCA) 1986

Although they sound like a dozen other pretentious synth-heavy atmospheric English dance

bands, the vile Fixx, aided immeasurably by producer Rupert Hine's sculpting their mundane songs to uncover marginal tense appeal, have managed to become enormously successful, drawing a couple of hits from each album so far. **Shuttered Room** offers "Red Skies" and "Stand or Fall"; **Reach the Beach** contains "One Thing Leads to Another" and "Saved by Zero"; **Phantoms** has "Are We Ourselves." All four records are quite forgettable. [iar]

FLAG OF CONVENIENCE

Life on the Telephone EP (Sire/PVC) 1982

Flag of Convenience may contain half of the Buzzcocks (guitarist Steve Diggle and drummer John Maher), but shows none of that late, lamented band's old fire. **Life on the Telephone** is nonetheless immediately agreeable, and the clever parts come into focus after a while. Diggle plays mean guitar, but this evidence suggests that those distinctive guitarisms on the Buzzcocks' records were all Pete Shelley's doing. (The UK release has one less track.)

After a lengthy silence, FoC returned to action with a 1986 single. [jg]

FLAMIN' GROOVIES

Sneakers EP (nr/Snazz) 1968
Supersnazz (nr/Epic) 1969 (Edsel/nr) 1986
Flamingo (nr/Kama Sutra) 1970
Teenage Head (Kama Sutra) 1971
Flamingo/Teenage Head (Kama Sutra/nr) 1976
Shake Some Action (Sire) 1976
Still Shakin' (nr/Buddah) 1977
Now (Sire) 1978
Jumpin' in the Night (Sire) 1979
Flamin' Groovies '68 (Fr. Eva) 1983
Flamin' Groovies '70 (Fr. Eva) 1983
Bucketful of Brains (nr/Voxx) 1983
Slow Death, Live! (Fr. Lolita) 1983
The Gold Star Tapes (Fr. Skydog) 1984
Live at the Whisky A Go-Go '79 (Fr. Lolita) 1985
Roadhouse (Edsel/nr) 1986

Starting out in San Francisco as early as 1965 (predating the Grateful Dead), the Flamin' Groovies have always been out of step with the rock world. Ten years before anyone knew about bands releasing their own independent records, the Groovies issued a 10-inch mini-album, **Sneakers**; in the '70s, when that same do-it-yourself spirit was inspiring countless innovative bands to try and challenge the old boundaries, the Groovies retreated to make albums of beat group nostalgia, wearing period clothes and refusing to acknowledge that times had indeed changed.

Always more cult-popular and influential than commercially successful, the Groovies—led by irascible but talented guitarist/singer Cyril Jordan and (until 1972) singer/guitarist Roy A. Loney—have always embodied the rebellious, youthful spirit that fueled punk, but have held tenuously to their musical roots—'50s American rock'n'roll and '60s British pop. In effect, they have provided inspiration for everyone from Dr. Feelgood to the Romantics, and are legendary for good reason.

The Groovies' recording career, generally more exciting on hit-and-run singles than in a sustained

album situation, began with the competent amateurism of **Sneakers**—Loney originals played with great energy and a slight psychedelic undercurrent—and continued on their major-label debut, **Supersnazz**, which encompasses a variety of disparate styles and is more ambitious than impressive. **Flamingo** and **Teenage Head** (repackaged together and issued years later in the UK) are the band's strongest pre-nostalgia efforts, taking advantage of improved skills and equipment to make loud, brash records in sharp contrast to the era's prevailing bland music. After moving to England and hooking up with Dave Edmunds (as producer), the reconstituted Groovies cut **Shake Some Action**, which features their finest pop creation, the title track, an apocalyptic Byrds-like classic. **Still Shakin'** was issued by their old label (Buddah and Kama Sutra being related) as a last-chance cash-in, pairing tracks from **Flamingo** and **Teenage Head** with a live side. **Now** and **Jumpin' in the Night** further explore Jordan's fixation with the past, mixing '60s standards with new soundalike originals. While this Groovies era is flawed and not above being awful at times, each of the three Sire albums does contain catchy, melodic pop tunes given careful, faithful and enthusiastic treatment.

With no new recordings since 1979, the band has apparently been dormant (or defunct) for several years now. Ongoing French interest has nonetheless led to the release of various albums—reissues, compilations, vault stuff and old concert material. **Slow Death, Live!** and its equivalent American release, **Bucketful of Brains**, date from a 1971 Fillmore West show. The most recent item in the discography is **Roadhouse**, a British release combining tracks from the two Kama Sutra albums. [iar]

See also *Kingsnakes, Roy Loney and the Phantom Movers.*

FLESH EATERS

No Questions Asked (nr/Upsetter) 1980
A Minute to Pray, a Second to Die (Initial/Ruby) 1981
Forever Came Today (nr/Ruby) 1982
A Hard Road to Follow (nr/Upsetter) 1983

CHRIS D./DIVINE HORSEMEN

Time Stands Still (nr/Enigma) 1984

Young poets on the East Coast were originally attracted to punk by its simplicity, directness and malleability. Most prominently, Patti Smith and Richard Hell found that crudely executed rock'n'roll provided the perfect backdrop for their verbal barrages. Though less celebrated, California's Chris Desjardins has made equally ambitious records backed by constantly changing musicians. Singing in a style akin to Hell's delirious hysterics, Chris D. (as he calls himself) has made morbid, sensational subjects like murder, vampirism and necrophilia into diverting entertainment through relentlessly intense lyrics. And though their demented tone will drive off most listeners, his albums bear hearing.

Cramming fourteen tracks into twenty-five minutes, **No Questions**

F

58

Asked uses the simplest punk structures to illustrate such overbearing tales as "Cry Baby Killer" (the name comes from an early Jack Nicholson film), "Suicide Saddle" and "Dynamite Hemorrhage." A formative effort.

By comparison, **A Minute to Pray** is like seeing Technicolor after a grimy home movie. Partial credit goes to a stellar band that includes the Blasters' Dave Alvin and X's John Doe and D.J. Bonebrake, but primarily it's due to Chris D.'s increased flamboyance. He roars instead of snarling, and his tunes are lively and varied horror-movie stuff. Highlights: "Digging My Grave," "See You in the Boneyard" and "Divine Horseman." For fans of carnival funhouses.

Forever Came Today reverts to a spot about midway between the first two LPs, but it's still riveting. The rudimentary quality of the band matters little when Chris tears into epics of sweaty desperation like "The Wedding Dice" and "Drag My Name in the Mud."

A Hard Road to Follow features a revamped lineup and the closest Chris D. has come to a conventional attack. With the group offering its own warped approximation of hard-rock, he chews through a fetid batch of tunes that includes "Life's a Dirty Rat" and the Sam and Dave classic, "I Take What I Want."

On the mostly-acoustic **Time Stands Still**, without an electric band churning away steadily behind him, Chris D.'s more appallingly effective than ever. The attractive, understated music belies such sentiments as "Past All Dishonor" and "Hell's Belle"; the all-star supporting cast includes Blasters, Gun Clubbers, an X and Texacala Jones from Tex and the Horseheads.

If this isn't a joke, he's a sick kid.
[jy]

FLESH FOR LULU

Flesh for Lulu (Polydor/nr) 1984
Blue Sisters Swing EP (Hybrid-Statik/nr) 1985
Big Fun City (Statik/Caroline) 1985

The ready adaptability of this Brixton quartet enabled them to rise from the ashes of London's ill-fated Batcave scene—a curious association to begin with, since these mascaraed, leather-clad poseurs are more akin to old-fashioned rock than gothic grave-robbing. With undisguised superstar aspirations, they signed to Polydor and released two excellent singles ("Restless" and "Subterraneans"). The self-titled album that followed, despite the inclusion of both songs, sinks into the mire, an overlong, overproduced '80s punk take on the Rolling Stones (check the cover of "Jigsaw Puzzle")—not exactly a commodity in great current demand.

Retreating to the world of independent labels, Flesh for Lulu released the controversial (some deemed the cover art sacrilegious) **Blue Sisters Swing** EP. An unexpected and most impressive change of course, the five tracks rock with verve and abandon and sometimes approach heavy metal. Best song title: "I May Have Said You're Beautiful, but You Know I'm Just a Liar."

Big Fun City marks yet another transformation. Though sticking to rock, traces of other musical styles enter the mix: funk, country-western, punk-pop. Still a bunch of

vain poseurs, their musical changes don't follow any fashion trends. Flesh for Lulu may have said they want to be rock stars, but you know they're just liars. [ag]

FLESHTONES

Up-Front EP (nr/IRS) 1980
Roman Gods (IRS) 1981
Blast Off [tape] (nr/ROIR) 1982
Hexbreaker! (IRS) 1983
Speed Connection (Fr. IRS) 1985
Speed Connection II (IRS) 1985

FULL TIME MEN

Full Time Men EP (nr/Coyote) 1985

New York's Fleshtones are caught in the common contradiction of self-consciously seeking to re-create the unselfconsciousness of '60s rock'n'roll, pre-*Sgt. Pepper* and pre-psychedelia. In other words, they've put a lot of thought and effort into becoming a mindless party band. Although the Fleshtones only occasionally fully capture their high spirits in the studio, the payoff is swell when they do.

Up-Front's five-song menu includes a fake surf instrumental and a jumped-up account of the Stones' "Play with Fire." Frontman Peter Zaremba's humorously tough approach comes through loud and clear, but the recording's cleanness borders on aridity.

On **Roman Gods** the Fleshtones take a big leap forward by adding new personality and passion to the beat, as witnessed by "I've Gotta Change My Life" and "Let's See the Sun." However, the album's standout underlines the progress remaining to be made elsewhere: "The World Has Changed" crackles like vintage Yardbirds, making ill-advised ventures such as the cover of Lee Dorsey's "Ride Your Pony" seem all the more unfortunate.

Blast Off dates from the Fleshtones' abortive 1978 sessions for Red Star Records and succeeds beautifully on its own limited terms. It's raw, noisy and incomplete-sounding—just right for keeping debauchery ongoing, though unsuitable for careful listening.

Hexbreaker! is the Fleshtones' finest record so far, an exuberant collection of memorable numbers made even better by brilliant playing and spot-on production by Richard Mazda. "Right Side of a Good Thing," with its hysterical falsetto chorus, "New Scene," a pulsing fuzz-guitar punk rave-up, and the shingaling title tune all roll with soul and frolic in the sounds of the '60s without ever losing their grip on the band's own identity. An ultimate '80s garage-rock classic.

The only way to live up to that achievement was to do it live, smearing as much sweat and personality on the vinyl as possible. It took two attempts: the first **Speed Connection** was issued in France but deemed inferior to the second, which was recorded at a different 1985 Paris show and released in the US and UK. Although technically casual, **Speed Connection II** is a stupendous, old-fashioned warts'n'all concert record, with all the chaos and frantic rock panache the Fleshtones possess. Especially potent is their brilliantly-titled "Kingsmen Like Medley," as well as "Return to the Haunted House" and "Wind Out," the latter featuring guest guitarist Pete Buck of R.E.M.

Buck also collaborated on Fleshtone Keith Streng's Full Time Men record, a pleasant but unchallenging trio of slightly retro-minded countryish pop tunes that would have benefited from a more confident vocalist than Streng. [jy/iar]

FLIPPER

Generic Album (nr/Subterranean) 1982
Blow'n Chunks [tape] (nr/ROIR) 1984
Gone Fishin' (nr/Subterranean) 1984

Like a 45 slowed down to sub-LP pace, San Francisco's Flipper delivers a flawless impression of a downed-out hardcore band. The harsh music lumbers and creaks, oozing feedback all the way, while the singer (variously bassist Will Shatter and bassist—yes, that's right—Bruce Lose) moans and shouts painfully. Flipper could be your car on the verge of a total breakdown or your worst hangover nightmare amped up to brain-splitting volume. And yet, for all the intentional sloppiness and gratuitous noise, not to mention the superficial shock of tunes like "Life Is Cheap" and "Shed No Tears," Flipper can be uplifting. Underneath the tumult you'll find compassion, idealism and hope, best represented by "Life" ("the only thing worth living for"). That kind of moral statement takes courage.

The aptly-titled **Blow'n Chunks** is a primo live tape of the band onstage in New York, November 1983. Playing all the hits that made them a legend—like "Love Canal" and "Ha Ha Ha"—as well as previewing some songs that made it onto the next LP, the quartet drones along like a factory shutting down for the weekend, a stunning roar of guitar noise and bass pounding that is simply the ultimate rock'n'roll imaginable. A real classic album, and the ideal floor-clearer for any club.

Flipper's second studio album, **Gone Fishin'**, makes an ambitious effort to add unexpected sonic components to the din. With vocals taking a clearly predominant role, oddities like clavinet, sax and piano (and even open spaces) lurk around, while newly sophisticated rhythms (as on the consti/syncopated "First the Heart") and the relatively restrained mix make Flipper resemble a "normal" band at times. If all you want from Flipper is a visceral thrill, try the live tape; if you want to understand their creative mind, **Gone Fishin'** is the ideal synthesis of sickness and health.
[jy/iar]

FLOAT UP CP

Kill Me in the Morning Rough Trade/Upside) 1985

Float Up CP's album lacks the diversity of the band's predecessor, Rip Rig & Panic. The material is straightforward funk/soul/jazz, with the rough edges left intact in just the right places. The real star is Neneh Cherry (daughter of avant-jazz trumpeter Don Cherry) who sings up a storm, even when the sexual metaphors ("Chemically Wet," "Joy's Address") get a bit trite. The band chugs along behind her with energy and panache, but there's nothing unique or catchy enough on **Kill Me in the Morning** to make a lasting impression. [dgs]

FLOWERS

See *Icehouse*.

FLOY JOY

Into the Hot (Virgin/nr) 1984

Following his straight dance-music muse, Don Was produced this English trio's debut LP, giving it a full-blown wash of horns, synthesized strings and other high-tech keys to commercial success. Carroll Thompson has a swell, big voice; her two compatriots, the brothers Ward (with assistance from illustrious guests, including Yogi Horton and Monsieur Was), churn out the music they wrote with ease and style. On a contextual note, however, the band's kicky name and the kitsch artwork aside, it's hard to discern how this differs from a hundred other mainstream/radio-minded records by talented black singers. [iar]

FLUX OF PINK INDIANS

Strive to Survive Causing Least Suffering Possible (Spiderleg/nr) 1982
The Fucking Cunts Treat Us Like Pricks (Spiderleg/nr) 1984

Instead of the near-illiterate (and proud of it) hedonistic rough-neckism of some hardcore outfits, this quartet (on a Crass-affiliated label) is one of the semi-intellectual, fiercely political bands who use punk-style rock as a medium for their strong leftist and/or anarchist views. Also similarly, Flux's packaging standards are impressive—the first LP boasts a twelve-page graphics-packed booklet enclosed in a dignified gatefold jacket. The band has a good deal of punchy precision to its crisp drumming and distorto-chord guitar. The catch is that it's all sort of military, as in the way the tuneless vocals resemble the bark of a drill instructor. Like the graphics, these "melodies" and lyrics (not to mention the politics) are all black and white, and aside from the sterility inherent in preaching to the converted, Flux's monochromatic asceticism is ultimately quite numbing. [jg]

FLYING LIZARDS

The Flying Lizards (Virgin) 1979
Fourth Wall (Virgin/nr) 1981
Top Ten (Statik/nr) 1984

DAVID CUNNINGHAM

Grey Scale (Piano/nr) 1980

Led by pianist David Cunningham, the Flying Lizards started as (and largely continues to be) a novelty group that took classic rock songs and reduced them to parody with neo-Kraftwerk synthesizer minimalism and robotic deadpan vocal readings (as epitomized on the eponymous debut album by "Summertime Blues" and "Money"). The serious work shows Cunningham leaning toward the arty high-tech drone of Tangerine Dream, though, and that suffers from comparison with the inspired lunacy of the comedy turns.

Fourth Wall attempts to evolve a happy medium, with helpers including New Yorkers Pat Palladin and Peter Gordon and new-jazz artist Steve Beresford. Cunningham moves uneasily between electro-pop and trance music (as in Steve

Reich and Philip Glass). Well-produced and interesting as individual songs, but it fails to jell as an album.

Cunningham attempts strictly serious music on **Grey Scale**, improvising on the piano by allowing the course of the music to be altered by random outside events. Though the technique derives from John Cage, the result falls closer to Reich and Terry Riley.

Following a long layoff, the Lizards returned in 1984 with **Top Ten**, another wacky album of demented rock'n'roll revisionism, this time assaulting the songwriting of Little Richard, Jimi Hendrix, James Brown, Leonard Cohen, Larry Williams and others. Purists and musical conservatives will find this impossible; keep an open mind and forget about the originals, and you'll be amazed at Cunningham's arcane wit and inventive dissection/reconstruction skill. Play this loud at your next party and watch the fun start!

[sg/iar]

FLYIN' SPIDERZ

The Flyin' Spiderz (Hol. EMI) 1977
Let It Crawl (Hol. Bovema Negram) 1978

These four erratic Dutchmen, led by rhythm guitarist/singer/songwriter Guus Boers, put forth solid, Stonesy punk just a hair better than a hundred others of like mind, threatening to turn derivation to their advantage but never quite succeeding. Neither album shows more than fleeting signs of excitement, and neither has better than perfunctory production.

Boers' declamatory vocals are often let down by his banal lyrics (the best are complaints about cramped housing and nosy groupies), but how frustrating it all is when out of the blue they turn around and serve up a track like **Let It Crawl**'s "Paper Girl," which sounds for all the world like an out-take from **Between the Buttons** or **Flowers**. Sigh. [jg]

FLYS

Waikiki Beach Refugees (EMI/nr) 1978
Own (EMI/nr) 1979

Although they neither dressed the part nor were tied down by its musical clichés, Coventry's Flys used the feel of mod-era bands like the Who and Creation as a jumping-off point for the highly individual songs of guitarist/singer Neil O'Connor. **Waikiki Beach Refugees** is one of those minor masterpieces that passed unnoticed, probably because it preceded the full-scale mod revival (by months). Nevertheless, the songs are beautifully contructed, O'Connor's jangling 12-string meshing with Rob Freeman's power chords to create a brilliant metallic sound. The best songs—"We Don't Mind the Rave," "Don't Moonlight on Me" and "I Don't Know"— express both the bravado and confusion of adolescence with a rare eye for detail.

Own is, by contrast, rather bland. The songs, co-written by O'Connor and Freeman, lack the urgency of those on the first album. Not bad, mind you, but a letdown from the expectations the previous outing engendered. [ds]

FOETUS OVER FRISCO

See *Scraping Foetus Off the Wheel.*

ELLEN FOLEY

Spirit of St. Louis (Epic/Cleveland International) 1981

Ellen Foley made other solo albums after gaining fame in the performing company of Meat Loaf, but this one is very different. It was produced by "my boyfriend"—in this case and at this point Mick Jones of the Clash—and features his band in toto plus its musical associates (Tymon Dogg, Mickey Gallagher, etc.) as her accompaniment. Additionally, half the songs are new (and otherwise unissued) Strummer/Jones compositions; three others are Dogg's. Coming right after the loose, throwaway feel of **Sandinista!**, Jones did an about face and created precious arty backing that strains Foley's vocal talent beyond endurance. Foley's interpretive abilities disappear under the weight of such screamingly pretentious tripe as "The Death of the Psychoanalyst of Salvador Dali." (*What* books were those boys reading?) Still, an important if not entertaining chapter for Clash fans to consider. [wk/iar]

FONTANA MIX

The Noise Spiral (Compact Organization/nr) 1984

An eccentric but musically responsible duo (mainly Michael Atavar) who blend the sensibility of Eno's early work (among many other stylistic avenues) with bizarre near-dada subjects/lyrics. Fontana Mix use synths and guitars to produce oddly embroidered songs that are neither too weird for normals nor overly mundane for those who demand fringiness. (The band bills the LP as "nine chill splinters of unreality.") Mostly whimsical, occasionally serious, **The Noise Spiral** offers charming moments, witty turns and amazing treats. Fascinating and entertaining. [iar]

FORCE M.D.'S

Love Letters (Tommy Boy) 1984
Chillin' (Tommy Boy-Warner Bros.) 1985

This clean-cut and stylish quintet from Staten Island, New York sets classic black vocal group harmonies to a streetwise hip-hop beat. They rap occasionally, but even with the old Sugar Hill rhythm section backing them on **Love Letters**, they're too sugary to throw down with much authority; their strength is an ability to wrap five fresh voices around a romantic ballad. On tracks like "Tears," "Let Me Love You" and "Forgive Me Girl," the infectious hooks and falsetto crooning defeat all critical cynicism. Elsewhere, the battle isn't so one-sided. Less cloying but also a little less talented than New Edition, the Force M.D.'s have tamed the beat-box without yet establishing an entirely credible identity or a consistent sound.

Chillin', the first record to be distributed by Warners under a deal with Tommy Boy, made the Force M.D.'s a major band in the US, and with good reason. From the ridiculous rap of "Force M.D.'s Meet the Fat Boys" (partially sung to the melody of "Gilligan's Island" and guest-starring the tubby three) to

the catchy, falsetto-over-scratch-beats title track, the versatile M.D.'s mix credible urban savvy with enough smooth showbiz to please hard beatboys and mature soul fans alike. "Tender Love," a hit single from the Jimmy Jam/Terry Lewis hit factory is spectacularly heart-rending; "One Plus One" and "Uh Oh!" are perfectly charming New Edition-styled pop with a bigger drum sound; "Walking on Air" might be mistaken for an old O'Jays standard. (Anti-sexism footnote: the album was produced, arranged and mixed by a woman, the talented Robin Halpin.) [jl/iar]

FORGOTTEN REBELS

This Ain't Hollywood . . . (Can. Star) 1983
In Love with the System (Can. Star) 1984

Ridiculous but fun, these Ontario glam dandies lead off their first LP with a buzz-saw version of Gary Glitter's "Hello Hello" and then blast a perfect Merseybeat melody into the Ramonized present. Elsewhere, they cover "Eve of Destruction," go "Surfin' on Heroin" and vent their frustration about the balance of rock trade in "England Keep Yer Stars." Throughout, singer Mickey De Sadist fights off an overactive echo chamber and the other three Rebels pound out efficient wall-of-guitar punk.

The second LP finds the Rebels in a much more aggressive mood, cursing a lot and resembling Sham 69 on shoutalong choruses like "Bomb the Boats and Feed the Fish" and the title track. In spots, De Sadist affects an outdated Johnny Rotten voice; the subject matter is similarly well-trod: "Rich and Bored," "Elvis Is Dead," "The Punks Are Alright" (rewriting the Who's "Kids Are Alright"). Also, the playing is fancier, with dynamics and arrangements that often resemble early Clash. It's a weird mixture: punk pop and straight punk. Not very inventive, but a highly enjoyable throwback. [iar]

45 GRAVE

Phantoms EP (nr/Enigma) 1983
Sleep in Safety (nr/Enigma) 1983

Acknowledged kings of the California ghoul-rock school, 45 Grave take a gloomy approach far less interesting than the flip swamp stylings of East Coast creatures like the Cramps. Playing with punky venom and a slick metallic sound, the fearsome fivesome is led by guitarist Paul Cutler, who has become quite an important figure working as a producer for various bands. The songs on **Sleep in Safety** have titles like "Evil" and "Violent Love" and sound like junior Black Sabbath/Kiss with a female singer and no mindless devotion to guitar solos. Why this is appealing to young people I do not know. In 1986, Paul Cutler joined the Dream Syndicate. [iar]

4-SKINS

The Good, the Bad & the 4-Skins (Secret/nr) 1982
A Fistful of 4-Skins (Syndicate/nr) 1983
From Chaos to 1984 (Syndicate/nr) 1984

There hasn't been a recorded concert as powerful as Side Two of **The Good, the Bad & the 4-Skins**

since the MC5's immortal **Kick Out the Jams**. This smokes! One of the leading Oi!/hardcore bands, the 4-Skins play with impressive force and anger. The studio side is more structured and therefore less intense, but it's still several notches above most of the Skins' contemporaries. [cpl]

KIM FOWLEY

Sunset Boulevard (Illegal/PVC) 1978
Snake Document Masquerade (1980—1989) (Island/Antilles) 1979

Kim Fowley is less important for what he's done than what he gets away with. Once described as "the king of rock'n'roll pimps," Fowley is a master manipulator of artists and creator—as writer/producer/entrepreneur—of hit records that are both crassly commercial and smugly subversive. Fowley first scored big in 1960 with the million-selling "Alley Oop," by the Hollywood Argyles. His career in the '70s involved orchestrating the careers of the Runaways, Quick, Orchids and Venus and the Razorblades; in more recent years he has successfully infiltrated the MOR world, working with Helen Reddy and Steel Breeze. In Fowley's defense, he was the first person to record Jonathan Richman and the Modern Lovers.

Fowley periodically used to convince record companies to issue his own solo records. Over a dozen albums—ranging from psychedelic organ instrumentals to passable glitter pop—have been released since 1967, although he has refrained from making a new one for some time. **Sunset Boulevard**, like many of his records, is consumed with Hollywood pop decadence. Fowley's minimal singing talent—more like dry sing-speak dripping with cynicism—doesn't stop him from essaying a long Springsteenish piano ballad called "Black Camels of Lavender Hill" or copying the Music Explosion in his own song "Control."

Snake Document Masquerade (does that sound like a Captain Beefheart title or what?) is his twisted idea of a new wave concept album, a vision of '80s pop apocalypse that gets by on sheer audacity. Musically, it's a limp melange of disco, reggae, punk-funk and electronic meditations distinguished by the spacey rap "1985: Physical Lies" (modeled on his own 1966 acid-rap hit, "The Trip") and robot sex fantasy "1988: Searchin' for a Human in Tight Blue Jeans."

There's plenty more where that came from: the paisley gimmickry of his 1967 LP debut, **Love Is Alive and Well, Outrageous** (1967; cheap Steppenwolf imitations) and the punkier **Animal God of the Streets** (1979). His **International Heroes** (1973) features the near-hit single of the same title, a clever variation on "All the Young Dudes." [df]

See also *Quick, Runaways, Venus and the Razorblades.*

BRUCE FOXTON

Touch Sensitive (Arista) 1984

Although he was one-third of an ultra-successful band, bassist Foxton had to relaunch his career virtually from ground zero after Paul Weller bagged the Jam in 1982. Surprisingly, his first solo album is quite good, and happily free of any attempt to recapture the sound which made him a star. With a four-man band and a bunch of guests, Foxton sings and plays his way through ten original tunes in a number of styles, from busy dance-rock to wistful big-production pop. Throughout, he adapts his bluff voice as best he can; ingenuous earnestness is a strong suit. The lyrics regularly mention loss, individual responsibility and uncertainty—it's obvious the Jam's end was a traumatic experience—but **Touch Sensitive** is a very promising new beginning for a sincere, talented performer. [iar]

JOHN FOXX

Metamatic (Metal Beat-Virgin/nr) 1980
John Foxx (Can. Virgin) 1981
The Garden (Metal Beat-Virgin/nr) 1981
The Golden Section (Metal Beat-Virgin/nr) 1983
In Mysterious Ways (Metal Beat-Virgin/nr) 1985

After three albums as lead vocalist, John Foxx left Ultravox to pursue a solo career. A prime factor in the group's sound, Foxx was, by extension, a major influence on the new romantic movement that followed in its wake. Fortunately, both Ultravox and Foxx solo have continued to make music of quality and distinction.

Metamatic is Foxx's first venture alone into the world of synthesizers, Ultravox's subsequent instrument of choice. In emulation of his own work and Conny Plank's production on Ultravox's **Systems of Romance**, Foxx finds the perfect counterpart for his themes of alienation and dislocation in sterile, minimalist electronic sounds. His vocals are oddly distant, like echoes, but the record has an honesty and directness that are quite affecting. (**John Foxx** is a Canadian compilation that rearranges a number of songs from **Metamatic**.)

The Garden is a lush, thick paean to Foxx's Catholicism and the mysticism that has always lurked beneath his austere urbanity. Pastoral in tone, the album explodes under a denser sound, replete with acoustic instruments that offset the onslaught of synthesizers. Foxx's themes remain the same, which is good, and his songwriting and flair for imagery reach new peaks on masterpieces like "Europe After the Rain" and "Walk Away," which provide melancholy views of familiar, mysterious worlds.

Co-produced by Foxx and the ubiquitous Zeus B. Held, **The Golden Section** has a bizarrely Beatlesque sound on several tracks, mildly resembling the Fab Four's later takes on psychedelia. Foxx is his usual enigmatic, inventive self, spinning moody creations that neatly sidestep synthesizer clichés; the only flaw is in his dramatic vocals. Previously released as a single, "Endlessly" is the album's clear standout, a magnificent multi-level pop creation that parallels Foxx's former group's development while clearly displaying a character all his own. The cassette version has six extra tracks. [sg/iar]

FRANK CHICKENS

We Are Frank Chickens (Kaz/nr) 1984

Frank Chickens are a pair of Japanese women (Kazuko Hohki, Kazumi Taguchi) who are both proud of and amused by their country's diverse cultural contributions to the world. On one hand, they pay tribute to Ninja warriors and emotional Enka ballads, but sing with mock reverence on "Mothra," named for a classic low-budget monster movie. Lyrics and liner notes are both hilarious and/or absurd (see "Shellfish Bamboo"). Musically mixing synth-pop with funk and jazz, the Chickens also incorporate Japanese musical traditions along the way. Guest musicians include Annie Whitehead and Lol Coxhill. Very entertaining. [dgs]

FRANKIE GOES TO HOLLYWOOD

Welcome to the Pleasuredome (ZTT-Island) 1984

In one of the most spectacular hype jobs in rock history, Frankie Goes to Hollywood—a minor outfit with its origins in the watershed '70s Liverpool scene—became a highly controversial and enormously successful band in 1984, thanks to the combined talents of producer Trevor Horn and propagandist Paul Morley, via their ZTT label. The homo-erotica of "Relax" got Frankie banned on English radio while the leather-bar setting of its accompanying video earned them similar turndowns on television. "Two Tribes" continued the band's phenomenal rise, inchoately damning both superpowers for the nuclear threat, accompanied by a thundering dancebeat. Having risen to dizzying heights thanks to what seemed like dozens of remixes of the two songs, all that remained for Frankie—by now also the stars of a million T-shirts—was to record an album. And make one (or, more precisely, two) they did. **Welcome to the Pleasuredome** has four sides of Frankie in all their artificial/superficial glory. From the hits (the two pre-LP singles plus "War" and "Welcome to the Pleasuredome") to the pits ("Ferry Cross the Mersey" "Do You Know the Way to San Jose," "The Power of Love"), Frankie say, "We may not be able to do it ourselves, but when you care enough you get the very best to cover for us." A brilliant load of bullshit, served with as much panache—marketing and musical—as the 1980s can muster. [iar]

FREUR

Doot—Doot (CBS/Epic) 1983
Get Us Out of Here (CBS/nr) 1985

This insular British art band was originally identified only by an unpronounceable squiggle in lieu of a name; later they relented and allowed that they would answer to "Freur" as well. Despite the gimmicky hubbub, however, the only truly memorable track on their first LP is the title song, four magnificent minutes of lilting, haunting synthesizer ambience with quirky vocals and choral backing—a real masterpiece. [iar]

ROBERT FRIPP

Exposure (EG-Polydor/Polydor) 1979 (EG) 1985
God Save the Queen/Under Heavy Manners (EG/Polydor) 1980
Let the Power Fall (EG) 1981

The League of Gentlemen (Polydor/EG) 1981 (EG) 1981 & 1985
Network EP (EG/nr) 1985

ROBERT FRIPP/THE LEAGUE OF GENTLEMEN

God Save the King (EG) 1985

In the last half of a seven-year hiatus between King Crimsons, Robert Fripp—self-styled thinking-man's musician and guitarist's guitarist—played axeman/producer to the stars (David Bowie, Peter Gabriel, Blondie, Talking Heads, Brian Eno, Hall and Oates, the Roches) and contemporaneously cut a series of solo LPs reflecting his then-current obsessions.

The loosely autobiographical **Exposure** is the closest Fripp has come to a pop effort, with guest vocals by Gabriel, Daryl Hall, Peter Hammill and Terre Roche. Interlarded with tape-loop guitar episodes and enigmatic spoken-word communiques from several sources, the record manages to overcome the self-referential preciousness inherent in such an enterprise—but just barely.

God Save the Queen/Under Heavy Manners offers two concepts for the price of one; both, unfortunately, are flops. The first half gets "Frippertronics" off to a bad start with a suite of samey, lackluster performances. It was Eno who showed Fripp this two-tape-recorder strategy that allows accumulation of rich textures. In performance, Fripp would build towering edifices of looped guitar sound and then spin stunning lead solos over them. The loops remained on tape; the solos didn't, thus the best parts of the concerts that produced **God Save the Queen** never made it onto the record. **Under Heavy Manners**, Fripp's first stab at "discotronics" (his version of dance-oriented rock) sounds less austere than impoverished, despite a memorable David Byrne vocal.

The next pair of LPs, continuing Fripp's self-appointed "Drive to 1981," gamely picked up the pieces. **Let the Power Fall** continues the Frippertronics methodology of **God Save the Queen**; although both were recorded during the same 1979 tour, this album's loops provide a far greater wealth of sounds, moods and ideas—Fripp's editing skills evidently having improved with time. However, several bootlegs documenting Frippertronics with the leads intact remain definitive, as much as Fripp may detest them.

Harnessing himself and keyboardist Barry Andrews (ex-XTC) to an okay rhythm section (that included future Gang of Four bassist Sara Lee), the one-shot League of Gentlemen band/tour/LP firmly established Fripp's dance-rock territory. A typical League cut took a simple medium-to-fast backbeat over which Fripp and Andrews locked horns, with melodic development emerging slowly, surely, subtly. On the tour, Fripp played marvelous leads; on the LP, they are replaced by spoken-word in-jokes. The album is still good, but the bootlegs are better.

God Save the King is a revised, remixed, remastered single-disc distillation of **Under Heavy Manners/God Save the Queen** and **The League of Gentlemen** albums. [mf] See also *Shriekback*.

FRIPP & ENO

(No Pussyfooting) (Island/Antilles) 1973 (EG) 1981
Evening Star (Island/Antilles) 1975 (EG) 1981

These two collaborations between Fripp and former Roxy Music muckraker Brian Eno are excursions into effete electronics, with Fripp simply playing his guitar through Eno's synthesizers/tape recorders. The resulting montage of loosely structured sound on the first album is pleasant and recalls the work of Terry Riley. **Evening Star** breaks no new ground; it is more a re-exploration of similar terrain. [jw]

FRIPP & SUMMERS

I Advance Masked (A&M) 1982
Bewitched (A&M) 1984

What did Fripp and Policeman Andy Summers do on their summer vacations? Using a wide harmonic palette, they recorded **I Advance Masked**, a duet LP whose primary mood is tranquility, although Fripp the soloist ultimately reveals himself in ecstatic flights of fancy.

As the sequel proved, however, Andy Summers is no Brian Eno. Given another brief reprieve from producing those lighter-than-air guitar textures for the Police, he thickens the mix with electronic muck, leaving little solo space for himself or Fripp, who co-wrote only half the material on **Bewitched**; the rest is Summers' alone. Maybe they were too busy toying with the synth-pop trappings that dominate the record to bother playing much guitar. [mf]

FRED FRITH

Gravity (nr/Ralph) 1980
Speechless (nr/Ralph) 1981
Live in Japan (Jap. Recommended) 1982
Cheap at Half the Price (nr/Ralph) 1983

If Fred Frith were remembered only for being the guitarist in Henry Cow he would be just another shadowy figure in the history of art rock. Instead he has pursued a unique and influential solo career in the '80s that has made its mark on leading avant-gardists worldwide. Frith's sessioneering and collaborative work has figured prominently on records by Material, the Golden Palominos, Brian Eno, John Zorn and others. Massacre, his trio with the Material rhythm section, produced an unforgettably powerful record. His duo, Skeleton Crew, beguiled audiences all over the world. He has played and recorded effectively with Voice of America, compiled three early records of avant-guitar playing (**Guitar Solos 1, 2 and 3**) and recorded duet LPs of varying quality with Cow drummer Chris Cutler, saxophonist Lol Coxhill and Henry Kaiser.

But Frith's most engaging work has been for Ralph, the Residents' label. Structurally the records resemble Henry Cow's early album in that they, like Frith himself, tend not to stay in one place long enough to try the attention span of neophytes. As such they are perfect vehicles for corrupting straitlaced rock'n'rollers into this world of joyful noise, which can include anything from polytonal polyrhytherama to Eastern European folk tunes to a taped snippet by New York's 13th Street Puerto Rico Summertime Band.

Gravity was recorded with members of several bands, the most substantial contributions coming from Sweden's Zamla and the Maryland-based Muffins (not Martha's). Frith's bass, guitar and violin are prominent, yet merged into a whole that is stronger than its dovetailed parts, all held together by ingenuity and force of will. Yes, "Dancing in the Streets" is a cover of you-know-what.

Speechless continues the process with a greater emphasis on reeds that should give Henry Cow fans a strong sense of deja vu—yet Cow never did anything this strong. Many of Frith's melodies are influenced by the same strain of European folk music that inspired Bela Bartok. Helping out are Etron Fou Leloublan on one side and Massacre on the other. (Some of the latter's material has turned up, rearranged, on Massacre's album and during Skeleton Crew gigs.) Endlessly fascinating, this is Frith's best solo record.

Cheap at Half the Price marks not one departure but several. For the first time on a solo album, Frith sings. The songs are edgy whimsy squeezed out in a weird high-pitched tone, except "Same Old Me," whose rough lyrics emerge in a tape-slowed drawl over angry riffing. Much of the record, especially instrumental tracks, suffers from an experiment in recording "at home on a 4-track."

For those ready to graduate from the prog-rock safety of the Ralph platters to something harder and weirder, there's **Live in Japan**, which captures Frith's "guitars on the table" approach, concentrating not on standard instruments but on homemade ones that are plucked, raked, abraded and assaulted with a variety of objects. The two discs can be bought separately or together in a black corrugated box containing booklets in English and Japanese. A must for noise fans.

[mf]

See also *Golden Palominos, Massacre, Material, Skeleton Crew.*

FULL FORCE

Full Force (CBS/Columbia) 1985

LISA LISA & CULT JAM WITH FULL FORCE

Lisa Lisa & Cult Jam with Full Force (CBS/Columbia) 1985

New York's Full Force are six guys—three brothers and three others—who write, play, sing and produce themselves, as well as other artists. Cult Jam are two guys who play and sing. Lisa Lisa is a girl who sings. The story begins when Full Force wrote, produced and performed the music for U.T.F.O.'s "Roxanne, Roxanne" rap smash. Then they did the same for Lisa Lisa and Cult Jam, yielding a huge hit in "I Wonder If I Take You Home." Their own album ties things up in a neat package, with "United," a track that features U.T.F.O., Lisa Lisa with Cult Jam and the Real

Roxanne with Howie Tee. It also includes an answer to their own (rhetorical) song, "Girl If You Take Me Home." Both of these full-length albums contins nothing but genuine 1985 urban contemporary music, a vibrant mix of rap, rhythm, soul and rock. [tr]

FULL TIME MEN

See *Fleshtones.*

FUN BOY THREE

The Fun Boy Three (Chrysalis) 1982
Waiting (Chrysalis) 1983
The Best of Fun Boy Three (Chrysalis/nr) 1985

It came as quite a surprise when, at the height of the Specials' popularity, the group's vocalists (Terry Hall and Neville Staples) and rhythm guitarist (Lynval Golding) broke away to form their own self-contained group, making an offbeat LP that spawned two UK hit singles and took a large step toward injecting African influences into the new pop music vocabulary. On that first album, the Fun Boys' imaginative use of various conventional and exotic instruments—though the emphasis is on vocals and percussion—is countered by a pervasively dark, pessimistic feel, more so on the US edition, which places most of the brooding stuff on Side Two. Dick Cuthell (horns) and vocal trio Bananarama, whom the Fun Boys backed in return, occasionally brighten the proceedings.

Waiting, produced by David Byrne, follows that somber avenue much further, using assorted jazzy styles in minor keys to express cynicism in "The More I See (the Less I Believe)," tell a harrowing tale of molestation on "Well Fancy That!" and explode the mythical side of young romance on "The Tunnel of Love." The centerpiece of the album, however, is "Our Lips Are Sealed"—the Go-Go's' hit co-written by Hall and Jane Wiedlin—given a dramatically different reading here, slowed to dirge speed and laden with heavy atmosphere and a resigned feel, yet somehow played with a preternatural lightness. A remarkable track on a phenomenally powerful album.

The ever-restless and unsatisfied Hall subsequently left the band to form another trio, the Colour Field; Chrysalis issued a compilation. [jg/iar]

See also *Colour Field.*

FUNKAPOLITAN

Funkapolitan (London/Pavillion) 1982

The name says it all: These eight multi-ethnic Britons play modern rhythmic dance music that doesn't skimp on melody, lyrics or invention. Produced by August (Kid Creole) Darnell, the eight long cuts bear some resemblance to other like-minded neo-soul/funk machines like ABC. Funkapolitan's unique listenability stems from myriad percussion instruments and no horns—synthesizers and varied vocals add subtle shading to otherwise straight thump-thump-thump numbers. [iar]

FUZZTONES

Leave Your Mind at Home (nr/Midnight) 1984
Lysergic Emanations (ABC/Pink Dust) 1985

SCREAMIN' JAY HAWKINS AND THE FUZZTONES

Live EP (nr/Midnight) 1985

New York's garage-rocking Fuzztones—Rudi Protrudi, Deb O'Nair and three lesser-named cohorts—do their wild Crampabilly thing on **Leave Your Mind**'s seven numbers, recorded live. The sound approaches near-bootleg quality, but that hardly matters—the shrieks and demented guitar solos here don't exactly call out for laser disc fidelity. Rave-up enthusiasm is all that counts, and that's exactly what the record delivers.

Lysergic Emanations is a fabulous studio LP, released originally in the UK and then, a year later, with new graveyard cover art (by Protrudi) and two different tracks, in the band's own homeland. The sound is pure '60s garage punk—the Seeds, Chocolate Watch Band, Yardbirds, Animals, ?, Standells, Shadows of Knight— produced clearly but without any excessive slickness. Absolutely first-rate—as good as the Lyres.

In fine early '60s rock'n'blues tradition, the live EP consists of the Fuzztones backing up grandmaster Screamin' Jay Hawkins on four of his classic songs, including "I Put a Spell on You" and "Constipation Blues." [iar]

PETER GABRIEL

Peter Gabriel (Charisma/Atco) 1977
Peter Gabriel (Charisma/Atlantic) 1978
Peter Gabriel (Charisma/Mercury) 1980
Peter Gabriel (Charisma/Geffen) 1982
Plays Live (Charisma/Geffen) 1983
Music from the Film *Birdy* (Charisma/Geffen) 1985
So (Charisma/Geffen) 1986

As longtime Genesis lead vocalist, Peter Gabriel was the grand old man of the theatrical art-rock movement, but abandoned that road in 1975 for a solo career, and has successfully positioned himself as the prototypically individualistic musician. His work is marked by dark humor, strong compositional skill and excellent, often innovative use of rhythm and electronics. Like issues of a magazine, his first four albums are titled only with his name. (The fourth **Peter Gabriel** was issued as **Security** by his American label, a move he did not endorse.)

The symphonic pretensions of the first **Peter Gabriel** power a dramatic perception of personal and global apocalypse. Produced by Bob Ezrin, and featuring the playing of Robert Fripp, Tony Levin, Steve Hunter and the London Symphony Orchestra, the album's dark rock songs ("Solsbury Hill," "Modern Love,") on Side A are paired with disturbing visions of armageddon ("Slowburn," "Here Comes the Flood") on Side B, delivered in a wall of sound that fills in every musical niche. Recommended.

In contrast, the second **Peter Gabriel**, produced by Fripp, employs the spare and uncluttered sound popularized by the punk movement (though you would hardly mistake this for a punk album). The new method showed Gabriel condensing his songs into tight units linked by themes of paranoia. Freed from the onus of art-rock, Gabriel presents his most obsessive and personal compositions, packets of insight that are misleadingly restrained.

Gabriel returned to a fuller sound on his third album, emphasizing striking electronics developed over unusual rhythms and delivered with seeming desperation. The ballads of social violence and urban fear—including "Games Without Frontiers" and "I Don't Remember"—feature lyrics and intricate music finally blended (under producer Steve Lillywhite's direction) into perfectly integrated high pop. Recommended.

The fourth **Peter Gabriel** refines this, drawing further on exotic rhythms (from Africa, the Orient and native Americans) with a musique concrète technique made possible by the Fairlight synthesizer (which allows unlimited manipulation of recorded sounds). Gabriel delivers his examinations of fear and disaster with an oddly paradoxical new emphasis on hope and restraint, displaying his usual fine craft and quality.

Peter Gabriel numbers three and four were also issued in Germany (the third in Canada as well) as **Ein Deutsches Album** with Gabriel singing all the lyrics in German.

Three live tracks, recorded in 1979 and 1980, appear on the second edition of the **Bristol Recorder**, a combination album/magazine

issued by a small English label in 1981, a forerunner of Gabriel's full-length live album. The two-disc **Plays Live** was recorded in America in 1982 (although some acknowledged "cheating" was later done) and features a good cross-section of his solo work, relying most heavily on the previous two records. The four-piece band includes Tony Levin and Larry Fast.

Gabriel's recent career, like that of former bandmate Phil Collins, has involved a lot of appearances on film soundtracks. For the movie *Birdy*, however, he singlehandedly created the entire score, writing new material as well as adapting instrumental tracks from previous recordings. (And carefully explaining that on the back cover, lest there be any misapprehension.) Although it's uncommon to hear sustained instrumental work from someone so known for vocal music, the score is audibly identifiable, and provides a fascinating glimpse into his adaptational thinking. A strongly affecting work, and a major challenge vanquished admirably with style and character.

With the announcement that Gabriel would end a four-year gap in new studio albums, curiosity about **So** ran understandably high. No need to worry: the ever-deft artist made another adventurous, varied and striking record, with atypically self-reflective lyrics, some of them clearly demarcating a past-present-future boundary. (The cover portrait also suggests an attitudinal change of some sort.) Gabriel's characteristically sophisticated music touches on funk ("Sledgehammer"), lightly gospel-inflected balladry ("Don't Give Up," with prominent vocals by Kate Bush), folk ("In Your Eyes," with vocal backing by Jim Kerr and others) and catchy dance-rock ("Big Time," featuring Stewart Copeland on drums).

[sg/iar]

GANG OF FOUR

Entertainment! (EMI/Warner Bros.) 1979
Gang of Four EP (nr/Warner Bros.) 1980
Solid Gold (EMI/Warner Bros.) 1981
Another Day/Another Dollar EP (nr/Warner Bros.) 1982
Songs of the Free (EMI/Warner Bros.) 1982
Hard (EMI/Warner Bros.) 1983
At the Palace (Phonogram/nr) 1984

If the Clash were the urban guerillas of rock'n'roll, the Gang of Four were its revolutionary theoreticians. The band's funk-rock took its edge from lyrics that dissect capitalist society with the cool precision of a surgeon's scalpel. The Gang saw interpersonal relationships—"romance," if you must—as politics in microcosm, a view that gives **Entertainment!** its distinctive tartness. Jon King declaims brittle sentiments with the self-righteous air of someone who couldn't get to first base with his girlfriend the previous evening. The basic backing trio churns up a brutal, nearly unembellished accompaniment. A challenging debut.

Solid Gold delves further into a quicksand of discontent. More choppy rhythms and pared-down arrangements drive home cries of despair like "Paralysed," "Cheeseburger" and "What We All Want." Not the sort of thing to pack discos,

but as compelling as a steamroller.

Songs of the Free is a more upbeat dance of death. New bassist Sara Lee (fresh out of Fripp's League of Gentlemen) and Joy Yates' backing vocals relieve the gloom of "We Live as We Dream, Alone" and (with typical irony) contribute to the dance-floor success of the anti-militaristic "I Love a Man in Uniform." King's characteristic delivery, the songs' on-target attacks on society's ills and the band's musical wallop make **Songs of the Free** one of the most stirring, innovative "rock" albums you can find.

Unfortunately, the Gang's next outing exposed an aesthetic about-face of Stalinesque proportions. Inappropriately co-produced by Ron and Howard Albert, **Hard** shifts from a political to a personal frame of reference; King drones lyrics against dirge-like music. It might be symbolic of disillusionment. It's certainly a sorry end to the group's career.

And it *was* the end: drummer Hugo Burnham left months prior to **Hard**'s release. (There is no drummer credited on the LP.) **At the Palace** (Hollywood's, that is) is a post-mortem souvenir of the Gang's final tour. With Steve Goulding replacing Burnham (who briefly sat in with ABC before joining Illustrated Man, later becoming Shriekback's manager), the album listlessly rehashes better days. Farewell, comrades!

To relieve between-album tension, the band's US label twice released 12-inch EPs consolidating British singles. **Gang of Four** contains one cut from their 1978 debut EP, a non-LP flipside and both sides of the then-current "Outside the Trains Don't Run on Time" 45 (both later re-recorded for **Solid Gold**). **Another Day/Another Dollar** has both sides of the "To Hell with Poverty" single, another non-LP flip, "History's Bunk!"—all required listening for fans—and two live versions of **Solid Gold** songs showing Gang of Four's prime-time concert intensity. [si]

See also *Illustrated Man, Shriekback*.

NICK GARVEY

Blue Skies (Virgin/nr) 1982

This ex-Motors/Ducks Deluxe guitarist/bassist/producer has a versatile voice (clear tenor, hoarse baritone, agile falsetto), but is even more adroit at the mixing console, able to whip up tuneful, ringing Spector/Springsteen pop melodrama—even make lush, spacious pop-rock out of the riff from "Willie and the Hand Jive." He also throws a curve or two, like the clever, 10cc-ish "(Think) Tough" or the semi-parodic Squeeze-cum- Bowie of "Skin." But even the support by members of the Motors/ Tyla/Bram Tchaikovsky axis and his own genuine likability can't save this record when Garvey descends into schlocky, banal romanticism. [jg]

GAS

Emotional Warfare (Polydor/nr) 1982

While a band whose drummer was once in megahype flop Stray Dog would seem unlikely to harbor any sympathies for modern music, this trio cribbed all their styles from the Clash, Graham Parker and Elvis Costello. Granted, they play loud and sharp with not inconsiderable

skill, but there's a sense of fraudulence and unoriginality that diminishes this record's impact to nearly zip. [iar]

GEILE TIERE

Geile Tiere (Ger. GeeBeeDee) 1981

To underline the meaning of their name ("wild animals"), this self-billed "electronic sex band" put a photo of one horse mounting another on the cover. That aside, there's nothing erotic or even vulgar (in a sexual sense) about this German duo's music or bilingual lyrics. The vocals are heavily emphasized, processed through a harmonizer, adding or subtracting Mickey Mouse and/or Darth Vader vocal timbres, and other electronic devices, but Geile Tiere's staple tactic of repetition removes meaning from words like "sex" and "love." Luciano Castelli and ex-Nina Hagenite Salome (an androgynous male) fill the rest of their soundscapes with scratchy guitar and bleepy synth in terse phrases with the beat supplied by a rhythm box. Not only is it unencouraging as dance music, Geile Tiere goes nowhere with no flair. [jg]

GENE LOVES JEZEBEL

Promise (Situation 2/nr) 1983
Bruises EP (Can. Beggars Banquet-Vertigo) 1983
Immigrant (Situation Two/ Relativity) 1985
Desire EP (Situation Two/ Relativity) 1985

On most of **Promise**, Jay and Michael Aston—two Welsh brothers—generate a powerful, dense sound that falls somewhere between U2, Adam Ant and Public Image: thickly textured guitars coloring a driving beat under aggressively impassioned, tuneless (but surprisingly not so tuneless at times) vocals that occasionally lapse into Yoko Ono wailing. The songs have a decidedly sexual air, but it's the sheer din—roughly-produced but convincing—that makes **Promise** worth repeated listenings. The numbers that don't go for maximum impact peddle a sensitive, spacious attractiveness that suggests considerable range and skill. (**Bruises** selects six of the album's ten tracks.)

On the enjoyable, atmospheric **Immigrant**, intelligently produced by John Leckie, Gene Loves Jezebel (acknowledging a five-piece lineup) resembles a pop-sensitized version of Bauhaus, a gritty U2, or a smacked-out Duran Duran. "Always a Flame" is aggro-dance rock with a walloping beat and an attractive melody; "Shame" has similar attributes, but adds a catchy refrain. The US edition of the LP appends "Bruises," a solid number which brings all of GLJ's U2 tendencies to the fore. ("Worth Waiting For" is equally Bonoesque.) The **Desire** 12-inch combines two mixes of that song with three album tracks for a dose of GLJ's best. [iar]

GENERAL PUBLIC

... All the Rage (Virgin/IRS) 1984

After terminating the wonderful Beat, leader Dave Wakeling and color commentator Ranking Roger stuck together to form General Public, eventually involving several other 2-Tone veterans. The loss of the former band is a shame and it's hard to hear why the Beat had to die for General Public to live, but

63

evidently the pair felt they needed to leave the Beat's personnel and other career baggage behind. It may not be an equal trade, but General Public is certainly maintaining the commitment to excellence that hallmarked the Beat.

Ex-Clashman Mick Jones plays guest guitar on the LP (although just where on this democratic undertaking eludes my ears); other luminaries, such as Aswad's brass section and Gary Barnacle add bits as well. For their part, Wakeling and Roger craft passionate pop, packed with clever tempo shifts, in several styles: a happy Motown bounce ("Tenderness" and the romantic "Never You Done That"), textured drama ("General Public" and the political "Burning Bright"), a bluebeat kick ("Where's the Line"). On the negative side, GP engage in annoying verbal play on "Hot You're Cool" and "As a Matter of Fact"; additionally, some tracks go on too long and a few of the arrangements are overly busy. But those are small quibbles. **All the Rage** is a rich, mature album filled with intelligence and invention from a band bursting with talent.   [iar]

GENERATION X

Generation X (Chrysalis) 1978
Valley of the Dolls (Chrysalis) 1979
Kiss Me Deadly
   (Chrysalis/Chrysalis) 1981
Dancing with Myself EP
   (Chrysalis/ nr) 1981
The Best of Generation X
   (Chrysalis/nr) 1985

Appearing on the London punk scene shortly after the Sex Pistols, Generation X was an extraordinary but ill-fated outfit that issued five tremendous singles, one classic album and some real dross. It also launched the mega-career of Billy Idol, a development one has to weigh when considering the band's historical significance.

With Idol as the band's voice and image and guitarist Bob "Derwood" Andrews providing its rock power, Generation X broke a lot of punk conventions, and were ultimately ostracized by their peers for refusing to be (or even feign being, as many others did) anti-commercial. Their breakup can be viewed as a parallel to the dispersal of the original punk spirit, although Billy Idol's phoenixlike ascent to world chart domination is equally indicative of the subsequent saleability of that ethos.

Following a string of 45s ("Your Generation," "Wild Youth," "Ready Steady Go," all included on the US version of the first LP) that crossbred punk insolence with kitschy '60s pop culture to produce catchy, roaring anthems for disaffected youth, Generation X's self-titled debut album bore out their promise—not a bum track in the bunch. A commercial streak didn't preclude a punky outlook or closeness to their audience; while the songs don't threaten the established order, they do retain a cocky irreverence that made Generation X more than a latter-day Mott the Hoople. **Generation X**, regardless of the reputational damage Billy Idol may have subsequently caused, remains a classic record.

Valley of the Dolls, produced by Ian Hunter, pales in comparison. Two or three numbers recall the early singles, but the surrounding tracks

64

leave much to be desired. A typical sophomore-record material shortage.

Kiss Me Deadly, recorded after Idol and bassist Tony James (co-writer with Idol of the band's songs) had sacked Andrews and drummer Mark Laff, is a shoddy affair, containing only the wonderful "Dancing with Myself" (later recut by Idol) to recommend it. Their moniker truncated to Gen X, Idol and James employed once and future Clash drummer Terry Chimes and a trio of guitar stars—Steve Jones, John McGeoch and James Stevenson—but the spirit was gone from the music, and this sounds like a pale shadow of the band's early glories.
   [iar]

See Empire, Billy Idol, Sigue Sigue Sputnik.

GERMS

(GI) (nr/Slash) 1979
What We Do Is Secret (nr/Slash) 1981
Germicide-Live at the Whisky [tape] (nr/ROIR) 1982
Let the Circle Be Unbroken (nr/ Gasatanka) 1985

In retrospect, it's easy to dismiss the Germs as the epitome of LA's early identipunk scene. Singer Darby Crash (real name Paul Beahm) was a spikey-haired barking brat, an alarming combination of Johnny Rotten's snarling vocal ferocity and Sid Vicious' self-destructive cool. Three years after the band's first live performance at the Whisky in 1977, Crash died of a drug overdose, reportedly self-inflicted in morbid tribute to Vicious' own fatal OD in 1979.

Germicide, a cassette release of that first show (originally issued as a limited-edition bootleg LP), reinforces that notion. The tape is a raw documentary of spirited incompetence, with Crash ranting through "Sex Boy" and the rather prophetic "Suicide Madness" in a cynical bawl. Behind him, the band plods along with all the cheer of a migraine. A good third of the tape consists of Crash trading obscene insults with the crowd. Also of note: their disembowelment of the Archies' "Sugar Sugar."

After that, **(GI)** is a revelation, a kinetic outburst of brute punk force. Two years of tightening up and a new drummer turned the Germs into a manic punk locomotive, speeding along with Damned-like intensity in spite of tinny production by Joan Jett. Aside from the overlong live "Shut Down," the songs go by in a breathless rush fueled by Pat Smear's staccato fuzz guitar and Crash's sometimes confused but often potent punk protest imagery. **(GI)** is a key album in the development of American hardcore.

A posthumous bow to the late Crash, **What We Do Is Secret** packages what's left of the Germs' recorded legacy on a 12-inch mini-album. The material includes a 1977 stab at Chuck Berry's "Round and Round" with X drummer D.J. Bonebrake, an outtake from **(GI)** and live tracks recorded in late 1980, shortly before Crash's death. **Let the Circle Be Unbroken** is another document of the band's chaotic concert existence.   [df]

ALEX GIBSON

Passionnel EP (nr/Faulty Products) 1981
Suburbia (nr/Enigma) 1984

BPEOPLE

BPeople EP (nr/Faulty Products) 1981

PASSIONNEL

The Apostle EP (nr/Enigma) 1984
Our Promise (Stiff/Enigma) 1985

BPeople was a Los Angeles quartet led by Alex Gibson (vocals, guitar, composition of most of the songs). Their EP consists of dark, moody music somewhere between Joy Division and Soft Cell, neither as jarring or desperately distorted as the former, nor as pervasively pop as the latter. On the positive side, there's smart use of sax and organ, but at times the music seems to be pulling in different directions despite its tightness, and poetic license should not be granted for lyrics like "We, they, it, that" (an actual line!).

After BPeople collapsed, Gibson wrote, singlehandedly performed and produced **Passionnel**, an excellent four-song 12-inch of wide-screen rock, made grandiose with tympani and long strains of synthesizer that lurk prominently in the near-background. Very English in sound—like Simple Minds or Ultravox—but not particularly derivative, **Passionnel** is a remarkable achievement for an individual, and a frighteningly good piece of theatre in itself.

Not content with the confusion level his career had engendered up to that point, Gibson's next move was to create a band called Passionnel. **The Apostle** (including a surprisingly straight cover of the Beatles' "Glass Onion") offers rhythmic rock of varying intensity—from even-handed ("Make Like You Like It") to intense sheets of dense sound ("Everything Golden")—over which Gibson spills emotional, semi-tuneful vocals. Occasionally chaotic to the point of unpleasantness; elsewhere delicate and pretty, **The Apostle** is striking, but not always for the right reasons.

Gibson scored Penelope Spheeris' punk film, Suburbia, the results of which occupy one side of the soundtrack album. Performed with only Passionnel's drummer joining him, the music consists of brief, aggressive rock instrumentals that rely on drums for drive and sharp-edged guitar for flavor. Several pieces sound as if they might have been edited from a long jam session (hard to imagine given the size of the band); other portions create a somber, relaxed mood with synthesizer and piano.

Released under the Passionnel moniker, **Our Promise** pairs the contents of **The Apostle** on one side with five new tracks. Well-crafted, cleanly produced and varied (within Gibson's limited musical field), the songs make some impact but leave only a faint impression.
   [jg/iar]

BRUCE GILBERT

See Dome.

GINA X PERFORMANCE

Nice Mover (EMI/nr) 1979
X-traordinaire (EMI/nr) 1980

GINA X

Yinglish (Statik/nr) 1984

Gina X is Gina Kikoine, a beautiful Teutonic singer, with backing

from a German synths-and-drums trio (adding guitar for the second album) that plays technically impressive smooth-but-dull dance rock. On **Nice Mover** and **X-traordinaire**, Kikoine's expressionless voice isn't exactly pleasant; her lyrics are in English (and occasionally French), but that doesn't help the lifeless songs any. Boring!

Dropping the "Performance" in favor of solo billing, **Yinglish** continues Kikoine's association with producer/keyboard player/co-writer Zeus B. Held (Dead or Alive, Fashion) and guitarist Dierk Hill; otherwise the cast is new. She sings nonsensical poseur lyrics variously in English, French and German; a cover of the Beatles' "Drive My Car" leads off the LP, and she sings a Serge Gainsbourg song as well. The music displays an awareness of Yello and dance music developments like scratch mixing while expanding the palette to include subtler forms; still, Gina'n'Zeus reach for a fey artiness that isn't worth finding. Kikoine's vocal skills are improved, but sometimes misdirected; the album has its moments, but a lot of tedious patches as well.   [iar]

GIRLS AT OUR BEST!

Pleasure (Happy Birthday/nr) 1981

Judy Evans is the only female Girl at Our Best! but her untrained trilling is the band's most distinctive element. The male musicians play pep-charged tunes about narcissistic youth; unflagging chord changes and witty lyrics prevent portentousness. A good romp.   [si]

GIST

Embrace the Herd (Rough Trade/nr) 1983

This record marks the return of Stuart and Phil Moxham, the Welsh brothers who comprised two-thirds of the Young Marble Giants. (Actually, the gist of the Gist is Stuart, although he receives assistance here from Phil on three tracks and other friends on several more.) **Embrace the Herd** is an unassuming (early) Enoesque album of fragile pop songs and delicate-but-weird instrumentals; slight but special.   [iar]

PHILIP GLASS

Music in Twelve Parts Parts 1 & 2 (Caroline/nr) 1974
North Star (Virgin) 1977
Einstein on the Beach (nr/Tomato) 1979 (CBS/CBS Masterworks) 1982
Glassworks (CBS) 1982
Koyaanisqatsi (Island/Antilles) 1982
The Photographer (Epic/CBS) 1983
Mishima (Nonesuch) 1985
Satyagraha (CBS Masterworks) 1985
Songs from Liquid Days (Portrait/FM-CBS) 1986

Though primarily renowned as a composer of experimental music, onetime taxi driver and plumber Philip Glass entered the rock domain via his production work with Polyrock and others. His compositional ideas and methods have been adopted by various progressive-thinking groups, especially in New York.

Music in Twelve Parts (not his first record) exemplifies his basic style: near-mantric repetition of rhythms of different rates, looping and overlapping in ever-changing harmonic patterns. The minimalist method reduces musical composition to atomic components of rhythm and counterpoint. **North Star** polishes the technique, applying it to shorter pieces that sound uncannily like works of electronic music. **Einstein on the Beach**, an opera with libretto by Robert Wilson, was Glass' longest sustained example of minimalist technique to date. The work uses familiar music for its starting point, stripping it of its history and Glass-filtering it to give it new and unfamiliar meanings.

Glassworks is an attempt, following his work with Polyrock, to cross over into the pop market. Unlike most other Glass works, the source of rhythm is a steady beat (like dance music) and instruments—specifically horns and keyboards—are identifiable in themselves, whereas previously they would have been rendered anonymous.

Delving into a different aspect of the pop world, Glass wrote **The Photographer**, a music/theatre piece, chronicling the life of pioneering photographer Eadweard Muybridge, which was staged in Europe. Glass co-produced the record and contributes organ; an orchestra and chorus plays the three-act piece which, in performance, includes dance and projections.

The first of Glass' film music albums, **Koyaanisqatsi** is an hypnotic score for a bizarre dialogueless travelogue/documentary. In addition to his normal reliance on woodwinds and keyboards, Glass uses a large brass section and massed vocals to evoke a mood that is unusually dark and somber; parts could be a *Star Trek* soundtrack. **Mishima** accompanies a Paul Schrader film biography of the noted Japanese author.

One of the most ambitious efforts in a generally ambitious career, **Satyagraha** is a three-disc boxed set (with complete libretto and background notes) recording of an opera about Gandhi commissioned by the city of Rotterdam. First performed in 1980, the album was digitally recorded—with overdubbing, an uncommon gambit for an orchestral/choral piece—in a New York studio.

Songs from Liquid Days, ostensibly an experimental effort in the pop song form, consists of six lengthy tracks, co-written with Paul Simon, Suzanne Vega, Laurie Anderson or David Byrne and sung by a guest vocalist (Linda Ronstadt, the Roches, Bernard Fowler, etc.). Most of the music is very much in Glass' recent mode (rolling, keyboard-driven mood pieces, like burbling streams) over which pretentious "art" lyrics sound quite ludicrous. "Open the Kingdom," on the other hand, takes the same compositional direction, but builds it up to awesome proportions with a large brass section and Douglas Perry's operatic vocals; "Forgetting" resembles (is?) a tiresome piece of draggy musical theatre. The nicest track is "Freezing," which uses the Roche sisters' unique harmonies to fine effect. [sg/iar]

See also *Polyrock*.

GLAXO BABIES

Nine Minutes to the Disco (Heartbeat/nr) 1980
Put Me on the Guest List (Heartbeat/nr) 1980

This Bristol quintet begs comparison to the Residents, as their first album uses all manner of noises to intrigue, confound, aggravate and entertain. Except for three song-like tracks that actually resemble rock music, **Nine Minutes to the Disco** consists mainly of formless sonic experiments, piling up seemingly unrelated sounds into an electronic jungle full of disjointed voices. Somehow, though, there's a pleasing quality to these random adventures; low-budget ambient insanity.

The second album actually consists of earlier recordings—essentially a compilation of previously unreleased studio efforts dating from 1978-9. There is a lot of variety, from disarmingly fragile pop to lightweight Public Image maunderings, with glimpses of Pere Ubu, Modern Lovers, Television and even the Cramps filling the spaces in between. As musical sketches for a group in progress, the tracks offer an interesting pastiche; taken as a proper album, what it lacks in consistency it makes up in unpredictability. [iar]

See also *Transmitters*.

GLOVE

Blue Sunshine (Wonderland-Polydor/nr) 1983

The band is named after the villain in *Yellow Submarine*, the re-cord after a variety of LSD. The cover is filled with photos of '60s memorabilia. This one-off project by Banshee bassist Steve Severin and Cure/then-Banshee guitarist Robert Smith sounds much like their own bands crossed with the Beatles, ca. 1967. The ten pseudo-psychedelic ditties show neither participant in top form, although the single "Like an Animal" (with Siouxsie-like guest vocalist Landray) and "Mr. Alphabet Says" do stand out. Not a band to make a career of, but good harmless fun nonetheless. [dgs]

GO-BETWEENS

Send Me a Lullaby (Rough Trade/nr) 1981
Very Quick on the Eye—Brisbane, 1981 (Aus. Man Made) 1982
Before Hollywood (Rough Trade/nr) 1983
Springhill Fair (Sire/nr) 1984
Metals and Shells (nr/PVC) 1985
Liberty Belle and the Black Diamond Express (Beggars Banquet/nr) 1986

One of the most critically respected and cultily adored neo-pop bands to emerge from Australia, the Go-Betweens began as a Dylan-inflected duo but had expanded to a more original-sounding trio by the time **Send Me a Lullaby** was recorded. Cool but not chilly, the LP offers a charming view that isn't overly pop—no slick gimmickry here—and songs that are more fascinating lyrically than melodically. The band's jagged, slightly coarse guitar sound has little trouble accommodating occasional intrusive blurts of blank sax noise. Shades of Television and the Cure. **Very Quick on the Eye** is a collection of outtakes and demos, some of which made it on to **Lullaby**.

Before Hollywood is a major improvement—more tunefulness, stronger harmonies, less stridency—suggesting such stars of nouveau pop as R.E.M. and Aztec Camera. The Go-Betweens, however, are clearly not just like anybody. Stand-out tracks: "Two Steps Step Out," "Dusty in Here" and the utterly wonderful, airy "Cattle and Cane." A marvelous, invigorating record.

Signed to a (relatively) major label, a four-person Go-Betweens recorded the more mellifluous **Springhill Fair** in France, making it so smooth and well-ordered that it verges on commercialism. They still make genteel pop music, but color it with guest keyboards, strings, horns and even (gasp!) synthesizer. Fortunately, the Go-Betweens write such musically pleasant and lyrically fascinating, intelligent songs that even creeping complexity and slickness can't seriously damage their appeal.

Liberty Belle marked a prompt return to indie land, this time on Beggars Banquet. Leaving a few more rough edges intact than its predecessor, **Liberty Belle**'s songwriting is again sharp and the sound nicely augmented with light touches of strings, vibes, bassoon, accordion and Tracey Thorn's backing vocals—all without even approaching over-production.

Metals and Shells is a get-acquainted compilation for America, where the band has yet to break much ground. Crafty and astute without ever condescending, we could use a few more pop bands like the Go-Betweens. [iar/dgs]

VIC GODARD & THE SUBWAY SECT

What's the Matter Boy? (Oddball-MCA/nr) 1980 & 1982
Songs for Sale (London/nr) 1982
A Retrospective 1977-1981 (Rough Trade/nr) 1985
T.R.O.U.B.L.E. (Rough Trade/Upside) 1986

Although the Subway Sect shared stages with the Clash, Sex Pistols and Buzzcocks as far back as 1976, the group's debut vinyl was a 1978 single; their first longplayer followed two years after that. By 1980, Bernard Rhodes (between careers with the Clash) had become manager and producer of the Sect, which had been totally revamped and was serving merely as a backing band for singer/songwriter Vic Godard. Over the course of four years, Godard had developed from an offbeat young punk shouter into a skillful vocalist with an predilection for sophisticated low-key, non-aggressive—hell, non-rock!—music. Considering the band's background, **What's the Matter Boy?** is a surprising belated debut.

Songs for Sale is largely a solo endeavor, consisting of (mostly) self-penned homages to his idol, Cole Porter. Despite its total abandonment of rock'n'roll, **Songs for Sale** is a wonderful record filled with excellent pop melodies sung by Godard in a cool, suave voice. He manages to update 1930s/40s Tin Pan Alley traditions without resorting to mimickry or falling prey to self-consciousness. The tunes sound of the period without being corny. Sure it's a pose, but Godard seems sincere in his nostalgic affection, and he makes the music his

own with real panache, so what's the matter? Members of the Sect subsequently became the JoBoxers. [iar]

See also *JoBoxers*.

PETER GODWIN

Images of Heaven EP (nr/Polydor) 1982
Correspondence (Polydor) 1983

Once a member of the group Metro, Godwin turned into a synth-rocker and cut some pleasant tracks as a solo artist. Three of the EP tracks (singles in the UK) were produced by budding techno-sound designer Georg Kajanus (once of Sailor); the remaining entry by Midge Ure (still of Ultravox), whose bandmate, drummer Warren Cann, helps out here. The one outstanding track is the title tune, which resembles Ultravox or Simple Minds. **Correspondence** continues Godwin's association with Kajanus and imports a batch of keyboard players and guitarists for more well-crafted, occasionally memorable adult synth-rock. [iar]

GO-GO'S

Beauty and the Beat (IRS) 1981
Vacation (IRS) 1982
Talk Show (IRS) 1984

The enormous commercial success of **Beauty and the Beat** in America was not only a welcome breakthrough for new music, but proof that an all-female band could make it big without a man pulling the strings and without resorting to an image grounded in male fantasy, be it sex kitten or tough leatherette. The album mixes honest pop with healthy infusions of rock'n'roll and, besides containing two bona fide hit singles ("We Got the Beat" and "Our Lips Are Sealed"), provides a refreshingly different point of view on some familiar themes ("Lust to Love," "Skidmarks on My Heart").

Vacation, though not as exuberant or confident as its predecessor, is more ambitious. The band sounds more distinctive and skillful, but the songs generally fall short of the standards set by **Beauty and the Beat**, a not-uncommon sophomore album hazard. The exceptions, however, are delightful: "I Think It's Me," the bubbly, modernized girl-group sound of "This Old Feeling" and the crisp, wistful title track.

Following a horrible series of unforseen maladies and delays, the Go-Go's finally released their third album, exchanging the wise punk-pop production hand of Richard Gottehrer for a more challenging experience with Martin Rushent. **Talk Show** attempted a major revamp, turning up the rock energy on all fronts: Gina Schock's drumming received new prominence in the mix while guitars blazed with added bite. As on the preceding two LPs, the material includes a few great single sides ("Turn to You," "Head Over Heels" and "Yes or No," the last co-written by guitarist Jane Wiedlin with Ron and Russell Mael), plus a lot of forgettable filler. **Beauty and the Beat** remains the most impressive of the three albums.

Jane Wiedlin dropped out of the band after **Talk Show** in 1984 to pursue a solo career; the Go-Go's subsequently broke up. Belinda Carlisle, joined by Charlotte Caffey, made her own album in 1986. [ks/iar]

See also *Belinda Carlisle, Jane Wiedlin*.

GOLDEN PALOMINOS

The Golden Palominos (Rough Trade/OAO-Celluloid) 1983
Visions of Excess (Celluloid) 1985

The Golden Palominos—an above-average avant-funk album—would have been a milestone if it had sounded anything like the Palominos' New York gigs. At one memorable show, the lineup included bandleader Anton Fier (drums), David Moss (drums/noise), Arto Lindsay (guitar/vocals), John Zorn (reeds), Bill Laswell (bass) and Jamaaladeen Tacuma (bass). The double rhythm section packed a wallop in unison, but more often the players broke off into intense and fascinating duets and trios.

On the first record, the Palominos add (Mark Miller, Fred Frith, Nicky Skopelitis) and subtract (most often Tacuma and Moss) players while preserving the basic material, tossing in a couple of new things ("Hot Seat," a song mostly by Miller, and "Cookout," a Fier percussion piece). Those who knew the magic of the Palominos' noise/funk synthesis firsthand will regret Fier's decision to go for the trendier Material sound in his co-production with Laswell. Still, when Lindsay rakes his untuned guitar and lets out a trademark yelp, or Zorn lowers some fragment of a clarinet underwater and gurgles with weird ferocity, you know you're hearing a trace—just a trace—of the real thing.

Visions of Excess is a totally different kettle of worms—a brilliant neo-pop album of tuneful, lyrical songs featuring such luminaries as Michael Stipe, John Lydon, Richard Thompson, Jack Bruce, Chris Stamey and Jody Harris. As producer, drummer and co-writer of the songs, Fier is on stylistically unprecedented ground careerwise, but his control and taste are impeccable. A version of Moby Grape's "Omaha" sung by Stipe is a truly incisive piece of '80s psychedelia (with a crazed Stamey breakdown solo) that sounds like a pop hit; "(Kind of) True" and "Buenos Aires," both starring talented Hoboken singer Syd Straw, are equally memorable. Lydon's "The Animal Speaks" is, well, what you might expect from him. The LP closes with an Arto Lindsay extravaganza, "Only One Party," just so no one should forget where this project is coming from. Essentially a recap of 1985's semi-underground stars and sounds, **Visions of Excess** is one disc everyone should own. [mf/iar]

GONE

See *Black Flag.*

GOOD MISSIONARIES

See *Mark Perry.*

PETER GORDON

Innocent (FM-CBS) 1986

New York downtown hornman/synthesist/composer Gordon—erstwhile leader of the pioneering Love of Life Orchestra— made his solo debut with the help of various East Coast art-music luminaries. Except for an old LOLO recording, "Diamond Lane," **Innocent**'s tracks

are all new, demonstrating Gordon's grasp of both the mainstream and the fringe in (mostly instrumental) music. The tracks are carefully structured, and seem to allow the sensual, rhythmically rich sounds to be an audio end in themselves. Esoteric, but easy to enjoy.   [tr]

ROBERT GORDON

Robert Gordon with Link Wray (Private Stock) 1977
Fresh Fish Special (Private Stock) 1978
Rock Billy Boogie (RCA) 1979
Bad Boy (RCA) 1980
Are You Gonna Be the One (RCA) 1981
Too Fast to Live, Too Young to Die (nr/RCA) 1982

Singer Robert Gordon made one of the sharpest *volte-faces* in musical memory when he left New York pseudo-punkers Tuff Darts to reappear as a freeze-dried '50s rocker, complete with sideburns, pompadour, a songbook of Sun Records oldies and authentic guitar icon Link Wray in tow.

Superficial trappings aside, Gordon's strongest asset is his magnificent voice—a clear, clean baritone rarely heard in pop music of any stripe. His debut album, **Robert Gordon with Link Wray**, is suffused with rockabilly material (songs from Carl Perkins, Gene Vincent, Billy Lee Riley and Eddie Cochran), but the accompaniment by the Wildcats is more contemporary, with Wray contributing sizzling guitar licks.

Fresh Fish Special (named after Elvis Presley's haircut in *Jailhouse Rock*—typical homage) is more of the same, with barely more sophisticated tunes. The odd track here is Bruce Springsteen's "Fire," which was a hit for the Pointer Sisters. Nevertheless, its inclusion proved Gordon didn't need to rely exclusively on nostalgia.

Besides the addition of echo, **Rock Billy Boogie**'s distinction is the replacement of Wray with nimble guitarist Chris Spedding. On **Bad Boy**, Gordon seems to be evolving from the '50s into the '60s via schlockier songs (Roy Orbison's "Uptown," Kris Jensen's "Torture"). Gordon's time-traveling into the present continues on **Are You Gonna Be the One**, his most accessible album for those who don't worship at the House of Butchwax. Despite his '50s fixation, Gordon best puts across those songs without a 25-year-old aroma.

Too Fast to Live, Too Young to Die is a compilation of tracks from all the preceding albums except **Bad Boy**, plus a live version of "Black Slacks" and previously unreleased recordings of two Marshall Crenshaw songs.   [si]

GORILLAS

Message to the World (Raw/nr) 1978

In the beginning, it seemed as if the only new wave/punk bands to get noticed were politically minded, like the Pistols or Clash, which was tough luck for the (Hammersmith) Gorillas, an underrated London trio. Their first few singles—especially "Gatecrasher" and "She's My Girl"—were tight, mod-inspired rockers. Jesse Hector's strained vocals recalled the best of Steve Marriott, and the rhythm section rocked with the fire of the Who.

Their lone album isn't as strong as prior 45s suggested, and a few of the tracks (such as an ill-advised version of Hendrix's "Foxy Lady") are dismal, but **Message**, for the most part, is upbeat and enjoyable.   [cpl]

ROBERT GÖRL

Night Full of Tension (Mute/Elektra) 1984

It helps to note that Görl was the *instrumental* half of German synth duo D.A.F.; his flat singing (mostly in English) on this solo debut leaves a lot to be desired. That he also wrote all of D.A.F.'s music, however, doesn't appreciably aid these dull lumps of spare, rhythmic, go-nowhere electronics. The LP's only notable success is "Darling Don't Leave Me," an angst-ridden duet with Annie Lennox (who appears on several other tracks as well) that has an unpleasant air of sado-masochism.   [iar]

ERIC GOULDEN

See *Wreckless Eric.*

HUW GOWER

Guitarophilia EP (nr/X-Disque) 1984

Gower was a guitarist—not a major songwriter—in the pure-pop Records; he later played with David Johansen. This solo EP is pretty much in the vein of the former: well-crafted, unprepossessing rock-pop, but without the Records' often-cloying preciousness. An earnest enough performer, Gower is a limited songwriter and not much of a singer; the best track here is a fascinating cover of Graeme Douglas' brilliant "Do Anything You Wanna Do," recorded originally by Eddie and the Hot Rods.   [iar]

GRAB GRAB THE HADDOCK

Three Songs by Grab Grab the Haddock EP (Cherry Red/nr) 1984
Four More Songs by Grab Grab the Haddock EP (Cherry Red/nr) 1985

A daft name if ever there was one, this terminally cute quartet London quartet is a spinoff from the defunct Marine Girls. Unlike former bandmate Tracey Thorn (now in Everything but the Girl), Alice Fox and her crew still hawk the chaotic tunelessness that made the Marine Girls so insufferable.

The first EP has a sparse, almost minimalist feel; even the use of atypical pop instrumentation (maracas, conga drum, cello) does little to alleviate the disjointed clatter. Fox's childlike caterwauling further adds to the annoyance. **Four More** is a slight improvement—clear melodies and an organization level that approaches the logical enhance the tracks. Guitarist/songwriter Lester Noel takes over vocal chores on "Last Fond Goodbye," a bright pop song that provides the 12-inch's only worthwhile interlude.   [ag]

GRANDMASTER FLASH AND THE FURIOUS FIVE

Greatest Messages (Sugar Hill) 1983

GRANDMASTER FLASH

They Said It Couldn't Be Done (Elektra) 1985
The Source (Elektra) 1986

GRANDMASTER MELLE MEL AND THE FURIOUS FIVE

Work Party (Sugar Hill) 1984
Stepping Off (Sugar Hill) 1985

Although they were hardly the first rap stars, it was Grandmaster Flash's galvanizing 1982 hit, "The Message," that demonstrated the form's potential for socio-political commentary and, preceding Run—D.M.C., initially served to convey rap's urban excitement to a non-black audience. Unfortunately, most of the crew's numbers are of the let's-party-and-tell-our-zodiac-signs variety with absolutely no consciousness, political or otherwise—good for dancing, but not very stimulating. (Despite his star billing, dj Flash is not the rapper; lead vocals are by Melle Mel and others. Adding to the credit-where-due confusion, the band itself wasn't really responsible for either writing or performing the music at the start.) **Greatest Messages** is, as a result, a two-side split between hard-edged social realism and mindless partytime, from "Freedom" (their first hit) and "Flash to the Beat" to "Survival (Message II)" and "New York, New York," which actually was the follow-up to "The Message." What the LP doesn't include is the brilliant 1983 Flash/Mel anti-cocaine song, "White Lines (Don't Do It)," the music of which, incidentally, comes from a prior Liquid Liquid instrumental. (The **Greatest Messages** cassette has two bonus tracks.)

Following a bitter legal dispute over contracts and ownership of the name, the band split in two: most of the members remained with Grandmaster Flash, dropped the "Furious Five" appelation and signed to Elektra; Melle Mel, who also got to wear the Grandmaster crown, recruited a mostly-new Furious Five and stuck with Sugar Hill. The former's **They Said It Couldn't Be Done** is a strained effort to diversify and make up for lost time and momentum. There's a rapped-up version of Fats Waller's "The Joint Is Jumpin'," a Run—D.M.C. imitation called "Rock the House" and two soulful all-singing tunes. Only "Sign of the Times" dips into topicality, employing a sound reminiscent of "White Lines."   [iar]

EDDY GRANT

Message Man (Ice/nr) 1977
Walking on Sunshine (Ice/Epic) 1979
Love in Exile (Ice/nr) 1980
My Turn to Love You (nr/Epic) 1980
Live at Notting Hill (Ice/nr) 1981 & 1984
Can't Get Enough (Ice/nr) 1981 & 1983
Killer on the Rampage (Ice/Ice-Portrait) 1982
Going for Broke (Ice/Ice-Portrait) 1984
All the Hits (K-Tel/nr) 1984

Three expatriate Caribbeans plus two Englishmen equalled the Equals, whose blend of pop-rock, psychedelia, blues, R&B and, of course, slight Carib accent yielded a wildly diverse and uneven batch of singles and albums in the late

'60s. Despite their problems, they amassed a few Top 10 hits, including the oft-revived (most recently by Grant himself) "Baby Come Back," a major hit on both sides of the Atlantic in 1968. Several of their other hits now sound like utter tripe, but "Black Skin Blue Eyed Boys" and the LP track "Police on My Back" (covered by the Clash) show just how talented they could be.

The group provided a musical (and music-business) education for its guitarist/chief songwriter/leader (but not lead singer) Eddy Grant, who eventually left to go solo and set up his own record company, Ice. He plays almost everything on his studio albums, except sometimes bass and/or drums, plus horns (when he doesn't use synthesizer instead).

Message Man was a dodgy start, yet he immediately began forging his own reggae style ("Jamaican Child") and continued the interracial/cultural theme begun with the Equals ("Cockney Black").

Walking on Sunshine shows the full flowering of his potential: "Living on the Frontline" was a superb electronic-reggae single, and its remarkable extension into "The Frontline Symphony" on the LP is a lengthy tour de force that features a mock-classical vocal section. The title track and "Say I Love You" (a monster hit in Nigeria) add extra value to an LP already well worth owning.

Love in Exile showcases Grant working in various soul styles (like the Teddy Pendergrassish semi-funk of the title track), albeit with his own oddly-inflected vocals. "Preaching Genocide" is the one exception, a long mutant calypsoid political chant, but all in all it's only musical water-treading, and inferior. **My Turn to Love You** is the same record with an alternate title and graphics.

The live album is an excellent display of both Grant's talent as a performer and his best solo songs up to that point. It also makes available about half the otherwise rare songs from **Message Man**. Despite the usual live record drawbacks—maybe it needn't have been a double—its best is mighty good.

Can't Get Enough is Grant's "I'm a love man" album, but it's great for what it is, the catchy numbers taking full advantage of Grant's genre-bending and blending. (The reissue adds a nifty instrumental, "Time Warp," that was available as the B-side of "Electric Avenue.")

The rock-oriented **Killer on the Rampage** is Grant's most consistent album to date, as well as his biggest commercial success in the US. "Electric Avenue" (the most rock-based track, save for some muscular guitar playing here and there) may prove to be an anthem of classic stature, and cuts like the title track and "I Don't Wanna Dance" demonstrate how Grant's songwriting has matured. The proof that it was no fluke is that **Going for Broke**, though lacking an equal to "Electric Avenue," is otherwise very nearly as good (and includes "Romancing the Stone"). [jg]

JOHN GREAVES
Accident (Europa) 1982

JOHN GREAVES & PETER BLEGVAD

Kew Rhone (Virgin/nr) 1977

Greaves—who has played bass with such progressives as Henry Cow, National Health and Robert Wyatt—encompasses a wide variety of sounds and moods on his first solo venture. Some of the instrumentation recalls Henry Cow, and Greaves employs the Cow principle: if a particular sound doesn't pull you in, the one on the next cut might, and all the songs are distinct unto themselves, even on first listening. Greaves' singing, however, is too flat and unemotive to sustain interest.

Greaves (music, keyboards) and ex-Slapp Happy member Peter Blegvad (lyrics, guitars) essay a jazzy theatricalilty on **Kew Rhone**, a stunning joint endeavor with singer Lisa Herman. Featuring a large cast of new music sidepeople, including Carla Bley and Michael Mantler, the album is consistently lyrical and lovely, incredibly precise and enduringly intelligent. [mf/iar]

D. GREENFIELD/ J.J. BURNEL
See *Stranglers.*

GREEN ON RED
Green on Red (nr/Down There) 1982 (Zippo/Enigma) 1984
Gravity Talks (nr/Slash) 1983
Gas Food Lodging (Zippo/Enigma) 1985
No Free Lunch (Mercury) 1985

While many of California's psychedelic revival bands draw on spacey/chaotic sources like the Velvet Underground, Pink Floyd or classic trance-inducers like the Serpent Power, Green on Red's early records alternately recall the fuzzified raunch of the Electric Prunes and Seeds, and the merry flower power of the Strawberry Alarm Clock. Filling the tracks of its eponymous seven-song debut with buzzing guitars, droning organ and pretty melodies, the quartet delivers transcendental lyrics in a monotonic stupor that precisely suggests total pharmaceutical oblivion. Good studio sound helps convey the sincere nostalgia.

Gravity Talks, produced by head Flesh Eater Chris D., has a simplified, in one spot Dylanized, feel. (The title track uses chipper organ and reeling vocals to evoke "Most Likely You Go Your Way and I'll Go Mine.") Elsewhere, the band largely abandons its previous style in favor of unembellished rock and folk-rock. At the LP's relative weirdest, Chris Cacavas' organ-playing sounds like several genres from the '60s, but only mildly; **Gravity Talks** never gets as intentionally mannered as **Green on Red**. Unfortunately, Dan Stuart's not much of a singer and his songwriting could likewise be stronger.

Gas Food Lodging introduces guitarist Chuck Prophet IV to the lineup and adopts a full-scale countryfied sound, a mangy cowpoke hybrid somewhere between **Pat Garrett**-era Dylan and old Neil Young. Stuart's singing suits the sloppy playing and demi-melodies; the band's comfy enthusiasm covers a lot of the record's flaws. (Original US copies were pressed on green vinyl.)

On the strength of their 100 percent country-rock major-label unveiling, it's difficult to imagine

that Green on Red was ever remotely connected to psychedelia. At its most believable, **No Free Lunch** includes a cover of Willie Nelson's "Funny How Time Slips Away." Otherwise, the band makes way too much of an effort to be perceived as hard-drinkin', populist-minded Amuhricuhns for the contents to be taken seriously. The music is adequate (for a drunk, amateurish C&W bar band), but the fake accents and predictable lyrical imagery make this sincere mini-album a pretentious muddle. [iar]
See also *Danny & Dusty.*

CLIVE GREGSON
See *Any Trouble.*

GROUP
I Hear I See I Learn (Jive) 1984

Articulate lyrics and strong mainstream rock make this English trio's album a big improvement over their Thomas Dolby-produced introductory 12-inch, which consisted of three versions—25 minutes' worth!—of one terrible song, thankfully not reprised here. **I Hear I See I Learn** is a little short on personality—despite slick production, the songs are essentially banged out with little fanfare—but has a good overall sound and singer/guitarist Ian Martin's provocative lyrics to recommend it. [iar]

GRUPPO SPORTIVO
10 Mistakes (Epic/nr) 1978
Back to '78 (Epic/nr) 1978
Mistakes (nr/Sire) 1979
Copy Copy (Can. Attic) 1980
Pop! Goes the Brain (Can. Attic) 1981

Holland's Gruppo Sportivo specialized in combining familiar rock riffs with outrageous humour, a group to be laughed with more than a band to be heard.

Mistakes is an American compilation, including a bonus six-song EP, of the band's first two albums. Cannibalizing the pop music world (in both form and lyric) for laughs, this gruppo romps blissfully across the prostrate forms of Eric Clapton, the Shangri-Las, Beatles and Wings (among others), elevating mere parody to the level of satire. They have the musical ability to pull it off, and wind up somewhere between Abba and early Squeeze.

Copy Copy falters as the lyrics take precedence over the music, despite an emphasis on dance beats and good vocal support from Bette Bright. Fortunately, their satire strikes firmly—at radio, the Westernization of Japan, airport dogs, etc.—and the words' savage precision somewhat compensates for the meandering, frequently nonexistent tunes.

Pop! Goes the Brain rediscovers melody, and leader Hans Vandenburg drops his Dutch accent for a pseudo-English voice that sounds disturbingly like Nick Lowe. A greater role for synthesizer and its attendant rhythmic noises corresponds to lighter satire, and an incursion of serious numbers. [sg]

GUADALCANAL DIARY
Walking in the Shadow of the Big Man (Hybrid-Statik/DB) 1984 (nr/Elektra) 1985
Jamboree (WEA/Elektra) 1986

A divergent debut album by a talented Georgia quartet, produced by Don Dixon, **Walking in the Shadow of the Big Man** offers attractive, harmony-laden folk-rock on some tracks, but then there's wiseacre music, energetic Bongosish music and surf guitar on "Watusi Rodeo"; a country punk number, "Ghosts on the Road"; and the Everlys/Edmunds-styled "Pillow Talk." The band write great songs; their delivery in spots resembles R.E.M. without that group's unique vocal style. Elsewhere, they get heavier, letting drummer John Poe dominate the sound with a ferocious attack, considerably firing up the band. Although each track is excellent, the stylistic inconsistency is disconcerting. It would help Guadalcanal Diary to find an accommodation that preserves their multifariousness while reducing the schizophrenia. [iar]

GUN CLUB
Fire of Love (Beggars Banquet/Ruby) 1981
Miami (Animal) 1982
Sex Beat 81 (Fr. Lolita) 1983
Death Party EP (Animal/nr) 1983
The Birth the Death the Ghost (ABC/nr) 1984
The Las Vegas Story (Animal) 1984
Two Sides of the Beast (Dojo/nr) 1985
Dance Kalinda Ballroom: Live in Pandora's Box (Dojo/nr) 1986

JEFFREY LEE PIERCE
Wildweed (Statik/nr) 1985

Transplanted Texan Jeffrey Lee Pierce pulled together a band in LA around his obsession with the blues. But being unseasoned, young, middle-class, white and barely able to play guitar didn't mean he had to be to the blues what the Cramps are to rockabilly. For Pierce, the blues is a highly personal medium through which he can (and does) broadcast/exorcise inner demons.

Fire of Love is bona fide mutant blues, with Pierce using the musical structures and lyrical imagery for his own ends. Exciting, intense—even cathartic—and badly (if appropriately) recorded, with a dash of punk leavening, this also has homey and effective touches like bits of violin and slide guitar. **Miami** expands to include a little folk, country and pop-rock without diluting the strength one whit, not even via harmony vocalizing (by a pseudonymous Debbie Harry, for one). Producer and Animal label magnate Chris Stein does procure a clearer sound, although bringing Pierce's generally strong Jim Morrison-styled vocals to the front of the mix does focus attention on his disconcerting tendency to hit notes sharp.

The next couple of turbulent years yielded little of value. The lineup of the first two albums is documented live on the poorly recorded, indifferently performed **Sex Beat 81** LP; the somewhat better live album on ABC features a later lineup, with pre-**Fire of Love** guitarist Kid Congo Powers back in the Club following his stint with the Cramps. There's an overlap of five songs; **The Birth** also has several otherwise unreleased numbers. **Death Party** dates from Pierce's sojourn in New York with a pick-up edition of Gun Club that includes a Bush Tetra and a member of Panther

Burns; it's a lackluster episode that can be forgotten at no great loss.

By **The Las Vegas Story**, the band was properly reconstituted (notwithstanding a switch of bassists). Even with the sound realigned (and some guest guitar from Blaster Dave Alvin), it's an uneven album. Evidently intended as a snapshot-mosaic portrait of America, with Pierce attempting to carve himself a Morrison/John Fogerty niche, it simply doesn't wash. That's not to say it's bad—just too unfocused and ineffectual for its ambitious goal. (The issue is further confused by opening Side Two with Pharoah Sanders' "Master Plan" and following it with "My Man Is Gone Now" from **Porgy and Bess**.) Finally, it's instrumentally too sloppy/punky for the Middle America saga it aspires to be.

Wildweed is another matter altogether. Although typically erratic and idiosyncratic, it's also Pierce's best, most fully-formed work since **Fire of Love**. Produced by Craig Leon in London, it's crisply played by a good little band, and Pierce helps himself surprisingly well on lead guitar. All nine songs are strong; if at times the lyrics seem offhand, the music backs it up. He has apparently become a consistently worthwhile songwriter; one can only hope that he gets a chance to develop even further. (There's also a bonus 45 which features silliness like a drunken Pierce reciting a strange poem as if he plans to become William S. Burroughs.) [jg]

NINA HAGEN

Nina Hagen Band (CBS/nr) 1979
Unbehagen (CBS/nr) 1980
Nina Hagen Band EP (nr/ Columbia) 1980
Nunsexmonkrock (CBS/Columbia) 1982
Fearless (CBS/Columbia) 1983
Nina Hagen in Ekstasy (CBS/ Columbia) 1985

Although born in East Berlin, one-of-a-kind singer/songwriter Nina Hagen is restricted by no national boundaries, working and living in Germany, England and America. Her approach to singing is consistently bizarre—on her albums she runs the gamut from quirky sing-song (a la Lene Lovich, whose "Lucky Number" gets a translation/transmutation on **Unbehagen**) to an anguished howl (much of **Nunsexmonkrock**) that sounds like Marianne Faithfull's contemporary work. Throughout, Hagen projects amazing intensity and a total lack of self-consciousness in both delivery and subject matter. Whether despised (by the unimaginative) or hailed as a genius, Nina Hagen is a truly radical talent.

Nina Hagen Band, her first LP, is relatively restrained; all-German vocals mask the subject matter for non-linguists. (Although "TV Glotzer" is an adaptation of the Tubes' "White Punks on Dope.") A serviceable rock trio provides generic rock'n'roll backing which she easily upstages, even without dipping far into her seemingly bottomless bag of vocal tricks.

Unbehagen is light years better. The band (expanded to a much-improved quartet who later recorded on their own as Spliff) offers convincing, precise modern rock with neat keyboard work, while Hagen's out-of-control persona takes center stage to sing, scream, growl, whisper and wail her way through nine gripping tales of decadence. Listening to **Unbehagen** is like stumbling into a monster's lair—feelings of revulsion and transfixion mingle to make this true rock-at-the-edge art.

The American EP is a 10-inch with a pair of songs from each of the first two albums, including the aforementioned cover versions.

Hagen recorded **Nunsexmonkrock** in New York with a band that includes Chris Spedding. To describe it as wild hardly suffices—the drugs-sex- religion-politics-mystical imagery that spills out is nearly incomprehensible in its bag-lady introspection, but the music and singing combine into an aural bed of nails that carries stunning impact. It almost doesn't matter that Hagen sings in English; what counts is the phenomenal vocal drama. Her range seems limitless, and the countless characters she plays make this fascinating.

Conceptually outdoing herself again, Hagen enlisted Giorgio Moroder and Keith Forsey to produce **Fearless** in California; unlike most of their projects, however, she emerges the dominant force. The album finds her in a dance frame of mind, singing about club life ("New York New York"), enlisting the Red Hot Chili Peppers for a rap number ("What It Is"), doing the funky Hare Krishna ("I Love Paul") and generally acting the warped disco queen while her Felix the Cat bag of voices stretches from operatic to munchkin, Grace Jones to Mr T. It's not clear whether this alliance with naked commercialism was expected to deliver a hit record; fans know that Hagen's rampant individuality almost precludes mass comprehension, let alone full-scale popularity. Nonetheless, **Fearless** —which bears out its title— is hypnotic and hilarious. One of her best records.

Reflecting Hagen's continuing fascination with Los Angeles, **Ekstasy** pursues a similar set of mental and musical notions. "Universal Radio" and "Gods of Aquarius" are straightforward (well . . .) catchy dance rock with metaphysical lyrics. "Russian Reggae" and "1985 Ekstasy Drive" are Hagenized metal; her "Lord's Prayer" adds new meaning to the word sacrilegious. But then, for different reasons, so do her versions of the Sex Pistols' "My Way" (take that, Sid Vicious!) and Norman Greenbaum's god-junk classic, "Spirit in the Sky." More joy from the planet Nina! [iar]

PAUL HAIG

Rhythm of Life (Crepuscule-Island/nr) 1983
Paul Haig EP (nr/Crepuscule-Island) 1984
Swing in '82 (Crepuscule-Island/nr) 1985
The Warp of Pure Fun (Crepuscule-Island/nr) 1985

For his first album following the dissolution of Scotland's Josef K, singer-guitarist-keyboardist Paul Haig enlisted some posh sidemen, including Anton Fier, Tom Bailey and Bernie Worrell, and got Alex Sadkin to produce. A mostly pleasant but unexceptional and uneven record, the synth-driven tracks variously resemble lighter-hearted versions of New Order, Ministry and the Human League. Haig demonstrates a danceable solution that doesn't bang on your head; some of the numbers, however, drag along tunelessly, replacing invention with mere repetition and nuance with clumsiness. The subsequent American EP offers five-ninths of the album (a wise condensation) as remixed by an obscure New York club dj. By leaving off a couple of dogs, it's a better way to meet Mr Haig (musically speaking).

The Warp of Pure Fun teams Haig with ex-Associate Alan Rankine for a slicker, more adventurous and entertaining excursion. He's not much of a singer—a little dramatic and gruff for the dance-poppish material—but the nimble arrangements and some resilient melodies cover such deficiencies. "The Only Truth" crosses New Order with the Thompson Twins and, like "Love & War," features Bernard Sumner on guitar; "Heaven Help You Now" injects a bit of folk into synth-rock. A triumph of style over substance, but a likable record with some fine moments. [iar]

HAIRCUT ONE HUNDRED

Pelican West (Arista) 1982 (Fame/nr) 1984
Paint and Paint (Polydor/nr) 1983

One of 1982's brightest new modern chart groups, these six energetic young Londoners created a crisp mixture of melodic pop and Afro-American and Latin rhythms, seasoned with horns and an occasional dash of jazz. Haircut's funk-oriented songs tend to be a bit samey (and placing three of them—

"Favourite Shirts," "Lemon Firebrigade" and "Marine Boy"—together on the American version of **Pelican West** doesn't help); their pop songs are arguably more successful. "Love Plus One" and "Fantastic Day" are delightful, near-perfect pop tunes with hooks that even the tone deaf can catch, and "Snow Girl" and "Surprise Me Again" run a close second. Following the departure of leader/singer Nick Heyward, Haircut proved their resourcefulness by returning with a credible second album, **Paint and Paint**. [ks/iar]

See also *Nick Heyward*.

1/2 JAPANESE

1/2 Gentlemen/Not Beasts
   (Armageddon/nr) 1980
Loud (Armageddon/nr) 1981
Horrible EP (nr/Press) 1983
Our Solar System (nr/Iridescence) 1984
Sing no Evil (nr/Iridescence) 1984

JAD FAIR

The Zombies of Mora Tau EP
   (nr/Press) 1983
Everyone Knew . . . but Me
   (nr/Press) 1983 & 1985
Monarchs (nr/Iridescence) 1984

Noise rock from the Washington, DC area. Brothers Jad and David Fair are idiot savants of rock music, playing untuned guitar with a variable backup band providing minimalist settings from art rock to pre-punk.

Heavy on the percussion and making no claims to melody, **1/2 Gentlemen/Not Beasts** is a three-record set that combines elementary musicianship and electronics with tuneless vocals bursting with angst and ennui. Nods to Devo, the Ramones and Iggy Pop (whose "Fun Time" they crush) indicate that the atonal, jagged results are no accident. Many favorite punk tunes are "covered" with surprising results.

Loud expands the music's range, with help from six-part accompaniment, including horns, more guitar, and almost-avant-garde drumming. The tendency toward jazz doesn't strip 1/2 Japanese of their primitive charm, with all its chaotic raucousness. **Loud** includes a dirgelike rendition of Jim Morrison's "The Spy."

Horrible, the pair's first release after a long vinyl silence, is a five-song 12-inch obsessed with ghouls and horror movies. "Thing with a Hook" matches the tale of a one-handed insane man-beast "pulling heads off boy/girlfriends down in lover's lane" with truly distressing music; other tracks are about "Vampire" and "Rosemary's Baby." Where the Cramps do this type of cinematic craziness for fun, 1/2 Japanese sound genuinely tormented.

Jad's solo records are even weirder than the duo's, but it's impossible to compare them with any critical surety. **Everyone Knew . . . but Me** contains 29 cuts (most of them originals about girls, but two James Brown covers as well) of him whining and vocalizing (singing isn't exactly the word for it), accompanying himself on what sounds like pots, pans and guitar. Emerging amidst all the painful primitivism, however, is touching naivete and defenselessness, a pitiful lack of social abilities/success that makes Fair seem something of a tortured, not torturing, artist. [sg/iar]

HALF MAN HALF BISCUIT

Back in the D.H.S.S. (Probe Plus/nr) 1985
The Trumpton Riots EP (Probe Plus/nr) 1986

This entertaining Liverpool quintet emerged from total obscurity to become a dominant indie chart regular in the first half of 1986. Playing low-key garage-punk singalong ditties (imagine a cross between Mark Riley and Jonathan Richman), the Biscuits like to name names—titles on **Back in the D.H.S.S.** include "Fuckin' 'ell, It's Fred Titmus," "The Len Ganley Stance" and "99% of Gargoyles Look Like Bob Todd." Throughout, they remain completely unassuming, and exhibit a dry, sarcastic wit. (As if a band with such a name would likely be dead serious.) One of the best debuts in recent years.

The Trumpton Riots EP is a little heavier—with raw drive and distorted synths, the snarling title cut and "Architecture, Morality, Ted and Alice" are both reminiscent of the early Stranglers. Side Two lightens up with the more hilarious "1966 and All That." Fans should look for the edition which adds a fifth track, "All I Want for Christmas Is a Dukla Prague Away Kit," the best football song since the Fall's "Kicker Conspiracy." [dgs]

HAMBI AND THE DANCE

Heartache (Virgin/nr) 1982

Liverpool's Hambi and the Dance attempt an interesting combination of synthesized art rock and traditional rock'n'roll, with mixed results. When singer/songwriter Hambi Harambolous draws on influences ranging from Phil Spector and the Searchers to the Roxy/Bowie/Ultravox school, the record can be very impressive ("Living in a Heartache," "Madelaine"). He is less successful when trying arty synthesized rock that sounds at best like Ultravox outtakes. [ks]

HAPPY FAMILY

The Man on Your Street (4AD/nr) 1982

A true cipher. Subtitled "Songs from the Career of Dictator Hall," this album tells a story not unlike the Kinks' **Preservation Act II** with none of that admittedly flawed work's virtues. It *is* lyrically less aphoristic, but Family head Nicholas Currie lacks anything approaching the charisma and style of Ray Davies and the songs are completely unmemorable. That goes for the music as well; as tuneless and colorless as much of it seems, whenever a melody looks to rise above it, the presentation stifles it. [jg]

PEARL HARBOR AND THE EXPLOSIONS

Pearl Harbor and the Explosions (Warner Bros.) 1980

PEARL HARBOUR

Don't Follow Me, I'm Lost Too (Warner Bros.) 1981
Pearls Galore (Island) 1984

Pearl Harbor and the Explosions came out of San Francisco's new wave scene, but their album consisted of bouncy little pop tunes

suitable for FM radio with watered-down soul and funk overtones, topped off by Pearl E. Gates' theatrical vocal posturings. Danceably forgettable.

Harbour (dropping Gates and adopting the British spelling) hit her stride as a solo artist on **Don't Follow Me, I'm Lost Too**, a headlong plunge into rockabilly and similarly ancient styles. Smothered by producer Mickey Gallagher in waves of flutter echo, Pearl wails like a demon, obviously happy to have a sympathetic setting. "Fujiyama Mama" and "At the Dentist" rock wildly with old-fashioned panache; "Heaven Is Gonna Be Empty" takes a more countryfied, though equally quaint, approach. This one's a memorable instant party.

A belated follow-up produced by Richard Gottehrer employs 20 musicians—from Ellie Greenwich to Chris Spedding to Masa Hiro Kajiura—for more fun in the old world. Harbour starts off by covering a chestnut, "Killer Joe," and then launches into a program of girl-group soundalikes that quiver with melodic conviction and shake with appropriate, cliché-free backing. Sounding uncannily like Kirsty MacColl in spots, **Pearls Galore** is a winning collection of tunes by a talented, adaptable vocalist who should be far better known than she is. [jy/iar]

CHARLIE HARPER

See *U.K. Subs, Urban Dogs.*

JODY HARRIS

It Happened One Night
   (Compendium-Rough Trade/Press) 1982

JODY HARRIS AND ROBERT QUINE

Escape (nr/Lust/Unlust) 1981

Jody Harris has worked with such New York luminaries as the Raybeats and James White and the Blacks, but remains one of the most underrated guitarists on the scene. His schizophrenic solo album proves him to be an accomplished composer as well, turning his talents toward straight pop ("It Happened One Night"), rockabilly ("I'm After Hours Again"), blues ("You Better Read This Before You Sign") and various forms of jazz, from be-bop to Stephane Grappelli. Harris is aided here by the likes of David Hofstra and Don Christensen, and amply proves that old forms can be given new life, especially with his exquisite, modernistic guitar work.

Along with Robert Quine from Richard Hell's Voidoids, Harris made the beautiful **Escape**, which drifts through a plethora of styles—Frippist dronetunes, jazz, country swing—and proves that these two consistently surprising guitarists are even more surprising than suspected. Though hardly rock, **Escape** has a vitality and joy missing in most records today, and so much fun it's sexy. Highly recommended. [sg]

JERRY HARRISON

See *Talking Heads.*

DEBBIE HARRY

See *Blondie.*

JON HASSELL/BRIAN ENO

Fourth World Vol. 1: Possible Musics (EG) 1980

JON HASSELL

Fourth World Vol. 2: Dream Theory in Malaya (EG) 1981
Aka/Darbari/Java: Magic Realism (EG) 1983

Canadian trumpeter Hassell proposes, in his own words, "a coffee-colored classical music of the future" in which Third World traditions from all over the globe mingle with Western technology. This is hardly a novel notion for new music, but Hassell's brief association with Brian Eno has brought him closer to the rock audience than most of his peers have come. Add his heavily processed trumpeting, which sounds most often like a breathy chorus of flutes, and the result can be diffuse but very pleasurable. As a balm for jangled urban nerves, Hassell can be more medicinal than Mozart.

Hassell co-composed with Eno on **Possible Musics**; those who enjoyed the ethno-musical mucking about of **My Life in the Bush of Ghosts** will find this similar, but on a more discreet level. The record is an ideal introduction to Hassell: alluring and evanescent.

Given Hassell's limits as a player, settings become more important than performances on his records. His next LP, **Dream Theory in Malaya**, stands out for its deliberate effort to abruptly change pace from cut to cut. One all-too-brief piece, "Chor Moire," is startling as he temporarily abandons his usual long phrases in favor of staccato bursts that sound like rushing masses of maddened birds. **Magic Realism** goes in the other direction and is almost soporifically subdued on two side-long multi-section compositions. [mf]

DIE HAUT

Schnelles Leben (Ger. Monogam) 1982

DIE HAUT WITH NICK CAVE

Burnin' the Ice (Illuminated/nr) 1983

Rising out of Berlin's post-punk bleakness, die Haut ("the skin") is a largely instrumental quartet with Beefheartian and psychedelic overtones but possessing a disciplined ferocity that gives them a strikingly Germanic sound. **Schnelles Leben** is a seven-song, eighteen-minute disc which utilizes terse bass and drum rhythms topped with scratchy guitar work, rarely settling into a tonal center. Five of the tracks are vocal-less and tend to lack development and textural variety. Not so much produced as simply recorded, in many places vocals are conspicuous by their absence.

Die Haut enlisted the services of Birthday Party singer Nick Cave for **Burnin' the Ice** and even gave him co-billing. Cave supplies all vocals and lyrics (for four of the seven cuts), generating an effect of leader and backing band. Much of the manic double-digit work on **Schnelles Leben** turns into psychedelic droning behind Cave's bellowing, but at least the songwriting and production show improvement. Die

Haut is a promising band that needs to locate a personality of its own. [dgs]

See also *Lydia Lunch*.

GREG HAWKES

See *Cars*.

HAYSI FANTAYZEE

Battle Hymns for Children Singing (Regard/RCA) 1983

One of the most intentionally annoying records of all time. This now-defunct London trio—singing characters Jeremiah Healy and Kate Garner plus string-puller Paul Caplin—spewed out juvenile nonsense lyrics attached to bouncy rock, gussied up with gimmicky production to make it reach maximum quirky obnoxiousness. A few tracks (like the McLarenesque square-dance rocker, "Shiny Shiny," and the Bow Wow Wow-like "More Money") are fine for *very* occasional listening, but enduring this entire album in one sitting is like having painful dentistry performed by an overbearing three-year-old. Garner has since made solo records. [iar]

ROBERT HAZARD

Robert Hazard EP (nr/RCA) 1982
Wing of Fire (RCA) 1984

A popular figure on the Philadelphia scene before signing a big record contract, Hazard's debut EP delivers one great wriggly-rock track ("Escalator of Life"), three so-so numbers and a powerful (but irrelevant) update of Bob Dylan's "Blowin' in the Wind." Although talented, Hazard hasn't got much individual character—traces of Bowie, Cars, Petty, Springsteen et al. abound.

Cyndi Lauper assured Hazard of a comfortable retirement by recording "Girls Just Want to Have Fun," which he wrote in 1979. Although that high-water mark achievement makes the relative failure of **Wing of Fire** largely academic, it is an okay album, kind of Tom Petty-meets-Willy DeVille (horns, modern outlook, drama, melody). The songs go on too long—or at least seem to—and David Kershenbaum's production could be a lot more exciting but, all in all, a solid effort from a reasonably talented guy. [iar]

TOPPER HEADON

See *Clash*.

HEARTBREAKERS

L.A.M.F. (Track/nr) 1977
Live at Max's Kansas City (Beggars Banquet/Max's Kansas City) 1979
D.T.K.—Live at the Speakeasy (Jungle/nr) 1982

JOHNNY THUNDERS & THE HEARTBREAKERS

L.A.M.F. Revisited (Jungle/nr) 1984
D.T.K L.A.M.F. Revisited [tape] (Jungle/nr) 1984
Live at the Lyceum Ballroom 1984 (ABC/nr) 1984

The New York club circuit's first supergroup, the early Heartbreakers (circa '75) consisted of ex-NY Dolls Johnny Thunders and Jerry Nolan, ex-Television bassist Richard Hell and newcomer Walter Lure. After Hell went solo, to be

replaced by Billy Rath, the band moved to England and recorded a technically disappointing debut LP, **L.A.M.F.**, for Track Records. The irony of that label's name was not lost on Heartbreakers fans, who suspected that the group's move to Britain was motivated primarily by the UK's heroin- maintenance program. So feeble was the mix on **L.A.M.F.** that drummer Jerry Nolan actually quit over it, though the material itself shows the band to be masters of the stripped-down, souped-up arrangement later copied by many punk groups.

The Heartbreakers subsequently returned to New York, where they performed an endless succession of "farewell" gigs with pickup drummers, usually Ty Styx. One of these shows was recorded for the **Live at Max's** LP, an ultimate party record—loud and sloppy with lots of dirty talk—and probably the best official document of any local band of the era.

In 1982, Jungle rescued a 1977 performance from the vaults and released it as **D.T.K.—Live at the Speakeasy.** Recorded with Nolan, it presents the darker side of the ambience that pervades the **Live at Max's** set if only because the band has a more secure drummer. Clearly the Johnny Thunders show, it exposes some incredibly sloppy playing, self-righteous audience baiting and a few devolved lyrics (like reworking "Can't Keep My Eyes on You" into "Can't keep you cock in you.")

Another live release—this one from a March '84 show at London's Lyceum—turned up a few years later, showing how far the Heartbreakers had come and how little they had changed. The program is a full-fledged Thunders retrospective: the Dolls' "Personality Crisis," the Heartbreakers' "Born To(o) L(o)ose," "So Alone" from his solo career and a couple of classics (like "Pipeline" and "Do You Love Me?") from his youth. And there's more! The show is hot and reasonably coherent, with fine singing by JT and Walter Lure; clear production (Thunders, assisted by Tony James) helps immeasurably.

Remixed to fix the miserable original sound, **L.A.M.F.** got a much-improved second life when it was reissued as **L.A.M.F. Revisited.** Jungle also issued a double-play cassette under the name **D.T.K L.A.M.F.**, slapping the '77 live LP on the flip side for maximum punk pleasure. [jw/iar]

See also *Richard Hell, Johnny Thunders, Sid Vicious*.

HEAVEN 17

Penthouse and Pavement (B.E.F.-Virgin/nr) 1981
Heaven 17 (nr/Arista) 1982
The Luxury Gap (B.E.F.-Virgin/Virgin-Arista) 1983
How Men Are (B.E.F.-Virgin/Virgin-Arista) 1984

After disproving all accusations of synthesizers as limited vehicles of expression, the British Electric Foundation retreated to produce an LP with dance-troupe-turned-recording-group Hot Gossip and let themselves in—in their alter-ego as the trio Heaven 17—get on with **Penthouse and Pavement.** Lyrically, the album ranges from silly to exciting; musically, it's an almost

flawless blend of funk and electronics. (The American **Heaven 17** release combines six cuts from **Penthouse and Pavement** with three new tracks.)

Two of those—the top-notch pop soul of "Let Me Go" and "Who Will Stop the Rain"—surfaced on **The Luxury Gap**, although they were replaced by a new pair on the American LP. Common to both, "Crushed by the Wheels of Industry," "Temptation" and "We Live So Fast" (even if the last song's refrain of "motion" sounds *exactly* like "bullshit") are stellar examples of Heaven 17's chartbound craftsmanship: catchy, toe-tapping dance-pop with horns, guitars and an orchestra providing musical depth behind Ian Craig Marsh and Martyn Ware's synthesizers. Glenn Gregory's gruff vocals don't immediately sound mellifluous, but suit the material and ambience perfectly.

With B.E.F. (the Concept) receding into the background for want of activity, Heaven 17 made their third album, graced with another awful cover painting. **How Men Are** features an expanding cast of musicians and concomitant sprawl—"And That's No Lie" runs over ten tedious minutes! The LP has a few lively cuts—"This Is Mine" and "Sunset Now" in particular—but is otherwise overblown, indulgent and excessive. [sg/iar]

See also *British Electric Foundation*.

RICHARD HELL AND THE VOIDOIDS

Richard Hell EP (Stiff/Ork) 1976
Blank Generation (Sire) 1977
Richard Hell/Neon Boys EP (nr/Shake) 1980
Destiny Street (ID/Red Star) 1982

RICHARD HELL

R.I.P. [tape] (nr/ROIR) 1984

Richard Hell embodied punk with his fierce poetic nihilism. He founded the prehistoric Neon Boys with Tom Verlaine in 1971; several years later, they changed its name to Television. Malcolm McLaren used Hell's mode of dress as the prototype for punk style.

Employing the double guitar threat of Ivan Julian and Robert Quine (later a Lou Reed sideman) and drummer Marc Bell (who departed to become Marky Ramone for several years), Hell formed the Voidoids, whose unwavering individualism kept the group out of the big time while producing a demanding and impressive corpus of work. "I was saying let me out of here before I was even born," opens Hell's masterpiece, "(I Belong to the) Blank Generation," on the 7-inch **Richard Hell EP**, which also included "Another World" and "You Gotta Lose." The line sums up Hell's attitude, expanded and perfected on **Blank Generation.** It combines manic William Burroughs-influenced poetry and raw-edged music for the best rock presentation of nihilism and existential angst ever. Hell's voice, fluctuating from groan to shriek, is more impassioned and expressive than a legion of Top 40 singers.

After a gap of three years (issuing a single produced by Nick Lowe during brief management by Jake Riviera), the 7-inch **Richard Hell/Neon Boys** was released, featuring grimly touching songs by the

modern Voidoids on one side and old demos by the Neon Boys on the other.

Destiny Street shows a more contemplative Hell, with even sharper imagery and guitar work (again courtesy of the stunning and underrated Robert Quine) and expressively painted poetry. Ruthless yet touchingly romantic, Richard Hell may be rock's last real visionary.

R.I.P. is a resume of Hell's post-Television decade, from his 1975 days with the Heartbreakers through 1984 sessions in New Orleans. It is inevitably his least polished and most inconsistent work, which may be why it sums up his style so well. Neither as mannered as his first LP nor as professional as his second, this collection showcases his most uninhibited singing on retreads, live takes and previously unissued material alike. Although the liner notes (signed with the artist's real name—Lester Meyers) describe the tape as the Richard Hell's swansong, he nonetheless pressed on, unveiling a new band in New York a few months after its release. [sg/mf]

See also *Heartbreakers, Robert Quine, Ramones*.

NONA HENDRYX

Nona (RCA) 1983
The Art of Defense (RCA) 1984
The Heat (RCA) 1985

Following a hard-rock solo album in the '70s, longtime Labelle member Nona Hendryx has upped her hipness quotient considerably this decade. **Nona** was co-produced by Material (Bill Laswell and Michael Beinhorn) and features an all-star cast, incorporating members of Talking Heads, the Go-Go's and Rough Trade, as well as Nile Rodgers, Laurie Anderson, Jamaaladeen Tacuma and Sly Dunbar. The music is straight dance-funk that's more stimulating on paper than disc; Hendryx is a powerful singer and there are some slick production moves, but the tunes (except for the memorable "Keep It Confidential") are too shapeless to be gripping.

On **The Art of Defense**, again teamed with Material (as well as much of the preceding LP's cast plus Afrika Bambaataa and Eddie Martinez), Hendryx sings seven long songs about passion with passion, obliterating any possible emotional impact with numbing one-note, one-beat repetition. Technically excellent and funky as hell, but boring beyond words.

Produced in large part by Bernard Edwards and Arthur Baker, **The Heat** is a lot better. The songs—more melody, less bombast—take maximum advantage of the musical interplay possible with electronic percussion and studio wizardry. She evidently still believes that any line worth singing is worth singing half a dozen times, but the well-arranged, muscular backing tracks keep moving, so things don't wind down even when Hendryx drills a lyric ad nauseum into the ground. "If Looks Could Kill (D.O.A.)" returns Hendryx to her soul roots, and sounds like a huge hit single. Keith Richards guests on "Rock This House," providing trademark rhythm riffing that fits just so. [iar]

HENRY COW

The Henry Cow Legend (Virgin)

70

1973 (nr/Red) 1979
Unrest (Virgin/Red) 1974
Concerts (Caroline/nr) 1976
Western Culture (Interzone/nr) 1978

HENRY COW/SLAPP HAPPY

Desperate Straights (Virgin/Red) 1975
In Praise of Learning (Virgin/Red) 1975

ART BEARS

Hopes and Fears (Re/Random Radar) 1978
Winter Songs (Re/Ralph) 1979
The World As It Is Today (Re/nr) 1981

With its rock-and-reeds lineup and audible debt to both European and American classical music, Henry Cow ostensibly took its original cues from the first few lineups of King Crimson. But whereas Crimso's borrowings from jazz were shallow at best and its symphonic aspirations safely melodic, Henry Cow—trailblazers of British progressive rock—dug deeper. A lot of their unison melodies qualify as solid modern-jazz composition, and their tunes range from heavily chromatic to atonal. The band is also remembered for spawning Fred Frith, one of the few leading musicians of that era to emerge with his integrity and enthusiasm intact.

The Henry Cow Legend (just **Henry Cow** when released in the US), remains their best album, mostly because it avoids the problems that marred later records. Reedmen Geoff Leigh (later replaced by Lindsay Cooper) and Tim Hodgkinson mesh with Frith's guitar to produce rich, carefully ordered textures using material written mainly by Frith and Hodgkinson. Meanwhile, drummer Chris Cutler pioneers a unique style, a light jazz-derived sound that seems offhandedly diffident most of the time but is capable of heating up with the music. Except for three pieces by Frith and one by bassist John Greaves, **Unrest** concentrates on group improvisation. The idea of having this ensemble thrash to its heart's content may have seemed tempting at the time (remember the time), but the results are less impressive than the band's more ordered music.

Henry Cow then melded with likeminded labelmates Slapp Happy for two joint albums. **In Praise of Learning** comes up with a sound only hinted at on **Legend:** Henry Cow with lyrics. With the now-familiar front cover sock turned flaming red, the record's political orientation is unambiguously leftist. The sound, mainly composed and fronted by Slapp Happyite Dagmar Krause's Teutonic-accented pipes, leaves this proggie feeling antsy, over-lectured and not at all amused. **Henry Cow Concerts** contracts the lineup back to **Unrest**-plus-Krause; its two records sport heavy doses of free-form improvs (phooey) along with composed numbers (including a tune by Robert Wyatt on which he duets with Krause). Despite uneven recording, **Concerts** has some zesty moments here and there.

Cow retrenched for **Western Culture:** no vocals, no improvisation. Hodgkinson wrote one side and Cooper (composing for the first

time) the other. This is classic Cow, but updated with a highly aggressive edge and a renewed appreciation for the delicate textural balances that made the first two albums so tastefully evocative. Oddly but fittingly, **Western Culture** finishes what the first two albums began, and Henry Cow's last album is the only one to clearly rank with its first.

What started out to be another Henry Cow album got sidetracked when the band broke up; as the Art Bears, however, Cutler, Frith and Krause released the outcome as **Hopes and Fears**, staying together to make two more albums. Frith subsequently went on to become an elder statesman of the rock avant-garde. He and Cutler made the badly recorded **Live in Prague and Washington** improvisations; Cutler also founded London's Recommended Records, which has been instrumental in the recording, release and distribution of a wide range of modern music from many countries. Cooper and Hodgkinson have each made solo records as well and continue to do so. Cooper's most recent projects were a tape-only release, **The Small Screen: Music for Television,** and an LP, **Music for Other Occasions.**   [mf]

See also *Fred Frith, John Greaves, Massacre, Anthony More, Skeleton Crew, David Thomas.*

HEROES

Border Rangers (Polydor) 1980

Led by singer Chris Bradford, this English quintet is yet another bland, well-scrubbed pop band given a brief airing in the wake of the Jam and Knack. They didn't become heroes to enough young listeners to stick around.   [jy]

HEY! ELASTICA

In On the Off Beat (Virgin/nr) 1984

Bright, eclectic dance pop produced (mostly) by Martin Rushent. The London band embraces '40s big-band harmony styles as well as '80s synth moves; throughout, a happy beat and inventive arrangements keep things hopping at a joyous, near-frantic pace. Swell fun!   [iar]

NICK HEYWARD

North of a Miracle (Arista) 1983

As leader of wimp-poppers Haircut One Hundred, twee Mr. Heyward was a spiffy talent of minor significance; on his own, he continues the band's lightweight, ultra-commercial pop style, with a few even-milder digressions. ("Whistle Down the Wind" sounds remarkably like the Association.) The pristinely-produced **North of a Miracle** is filled with layered vocals and peppy music played by a large collection of studio hands (including Steve Nieve!), given a slick veneer by co-producer Geoff Emerick. Obnoxiously, awesomely pleasant, it's everything a disposable pop record should be.   [iar]

JOHN HIATT

Slug Line (MCA) 1979
Two Bit Monsters (MCA) 1980
All of a Sudden (Geffen) 1982
Riding with the King (Geffen) 1983
Warming Up to the Ice Age (Geffen) 1985

After two mild singer/songwriter records for Epic, John Hiatt

exploded on the scene in 1979, a fiercely original soul-inflected rock character likened to Elvis Costello, Graham Parker and Joe Jackson but wholly his own man. These five albums are testimony to an exceptional, but largely overlooked, talent—both as a much-covered songwriter and as an emotional, intense performer.

Slug Line is the rawest and most powerful, with appropriately rudimentary production highlighting dynamic playing on a full set of Hiatt's angriest songs. Drawing with genuine conviction on both reggae and fiery R&B styles, Hiatt invests "Madonna Road," "You're My Love Interest," "The Negroes Were Dancing" and other tracks with bitterness, insightful intelligence and occasional tenderness, making it a stunning work by an exciting artist.

Two Bit Monsters essentially repeats **Slug Line**'s style, but with less bite. Several of the tunes are comparably impressive ("Back to Normal," "Good Girl, Bad World," "String Pull Job"), but the album is less focused and nearly haphazard. Hiatt's venom sears through, but it's not his best work.

Tony Visconti produced **All of a Sudden**, sympathetically if incongruously displaying the songs in a complex, highly arranged setting that works to good advantage most of the time. With a nod to rockabilly ("Doll Hospital") and a dose of Motown soul ("Getting Excited"), other excellent songs like "Something Happens" and "I Look for Love" get filtered through Hiatt's expanding musical sensibilities plus Visconti's synth-rocking Bowieness, making it a strange collision of differing modern rock sensibilities.

Hiatt's bumpy career subsequently brought him into contact with Nick Lowe and his manager, Jake Riviera. The former produced and led the backing band on one side of **Riding with the King**, while the latter loaned an eye-popping motorcycle for the front cover photo. The record's other side was produced by Scott Matthews and Ron Nagle; Matthews and Hiatt are the only musicians on those tracks. Although it may be down to the allotment of material, Lowe comes up the loser; on his side, Hiatt affects a languid swamp sound that doesn't convey much excitement. He comes alive only for Matthews/Nagle-produced tracks like "Death by Misadventure," "Say It with Flowers" and "I Don't Even Try," prime songs given modest but appealing treatment.

Veteran mush-rock producer Norbert Putnam got the nod for **Warming Up to the Ice Age**. On the first track, "The Usual," we find Hiatt in raucous heavy metal guitars and arena-sized drums; fortunately, that's not the only sound on this weird record, which also contains a great soul duet with Elvis Costello ("Living a Little, Laughing a Little"), an emotion-laden ballad ("When We Ran") and other typically on-the-mark slices of Hiatt's cynical viewpoint ("She Said the Same Things to Me," "Number One Honest Game"). The mix is consistently too rock-oriented—these aren't dance tracks, for crying out loud!—but Hiatt's subtle vocals keep things balanced.

Although quiet on the recording

front of late, Hiatt has been performing regularly as a solo artist. [iar]

HILARY

Kinetic EP (nr/Backstreet-MCA) 1983

Dunno who Hilary is but, in partnership with producer Stephen Hague, she came up with one wacky disc here. "Kinetic" takes a strong, happy synth-dance beat and then layers on a repetitive riff that's exactly one note too short, making the entire five-minute escapade as distracting as a leaky faucet. Taking a different approach, "Drop Your Pants" is musically saner and equally catchy, but the lyrics offer virtually every coy (and not-so-coy) sexual metaphor possible in a (hopefully) tongue-in-cheek bit of libidinous silliness. The other side is less notable, but this 12-inch remains a bizarre and memorable one-off from a singular talent.   [iar]

HOLGER HILLER

A Bunch of Foulness in the Pit (Cherry Red/nr) 1984

Virtually the only English on this album (originally released by German Ata Tak) is the translated title; otherwise, you're on your own linguistic own. Hardly the horrorshow the billing might have you imagine, Hiller—formerly in Palais Schaumburg—conveys bemusement and tension rather than misery or desperation, using overlaid and not always musically related instrumental lines (mostly keyboards and—if my dictionary guessed correctly—percussion), detached vocals, plus found sounds and assorted blips and squeaks. While the effect is not exactly pleasant (although a few songs, notably "Jonny (du Lump)," are), it is riveting, and Hiller is a master at aurally painting a scene in living color.   [iar]

RUPERT HINE

Immunity (A&M) 1981
Waving Not Drowning (A&M) 1982
The Wildest Wish to Fly (Island) 1984

Hine, best known for his successful work producing the Fixx, Howard Jones and Tina Turner, has recorded five albums under his own name. (The first two were done in the '70s.) It says something about the nature of pop stardom that he's virtually as capable of writing and performing credible if vapid electro-rock-pop as his charges, but without any concomitant chance of matching their commercial achievements.   [iar]

HIPSWAY

Hipsway (Mercury/nr) 1986

This stylish but boring Scottish soul-funk quartet includes ex-Altered Images bassist John McElhone. (His brother, another former Image, manages the band.) Not unlike several other current Scottish bands, Hipsway takes its cues from various black American artists, mixing dance rhythms, percussive guitar and smooth vocals, but winds up mostly sounding like Inxs. "The Broken Years" is annoyingly herky-jerky; "The Honeythief" is nearly as distracting for the same reasons. Grahame Skinner has an appropriately husky voice, but is not an especially interesting singer;

the backing is clever and varied, but never captivating. [tr]

ROBYN HITCHCOCK

Black Snake Diamond Role (Armageddon/nr) 1981 (Aftermath/nr) 1986
Groovy Decay (Albion/nr) 1982
I Often Dream of Trains (Midnight Music/nr) 1984

ROBYN HITCHCOCK AND THE EGYPTIANS

Fegmania! (Midnight Music/Slash) 1985
Gotta Let This Hen Out! (Midnight Music/Relativity) 1985
Exploding in Silence EP (nr/Relativity) 1986

Robyn Hitchcock's entire body of work—both as leader of the Soft Boys and as a solo performer—remains one of the great undiscovered treasures of modern pop music. His melodic, emotional compositions place him in a songwriting peerage that includes Elvis Costello, XTC's Andy Partridge and very few others. Psychedelic pop of the '60s provides the touchstone for his sound, but Hitchcock blends his own ideas with those of John Lennon, Syd Barrett, the Doors and Byrds to create music that advances the tradition rather than merely recapitulating it.

Black Snake Diamond Role, his first solo salvo, opens with two jaunty music hall ditties but quickly descends to Hitchcock's typical deranged concerns: a sardonic knock at authority in "Do Policemen Sing?" (which features a chorus like a frenzied hail of blows); a melodic, cracked-crystal ballad, "Acid Bird," whose mood and production could stand proud next to "Eight Miles High"; and alternate takes on emotion, "Meat" (all brash) and "Love" (all heart) to finish off each side.

Groovy Decay, produced by Steve Hillage, has a smoother sound that somewhat undermines the dark emotion and irony that are Hitchcock's greatest strengths. Still, great songs gleam through the mix. "52 Stations" stunningly captures the alternation of rage, resignation and hope that follows the failure of love; "St. Petersburg" views only the black side. "Groovin' on an Inner Plane" blends an arch rap-styled vocal into a fluid groove with stirring results.

After nearly two years of self-imposed retirement, Hitchcock returned in 1984 with a surprising, mostly acoustic album, **I Often Dream of Trains**. Performing all instruments and vocals himself, he echoed the solo work of his models—Barrett in the amiably slapdash production and Lennon on an aching ballad, "Flavour of Night." The album features Hitchcock's usual balance of bitterness and weirdness in unusual settings, rounded off with piano nocturnes at the start and finish. Two bizarre *a cappella* close-harmony essays—"Uncorrected Personality Traits" (about difficult children when they grow up) and "Furry Green Atom Bowl" (about life on earth)—make this one of the stranger outings in a career dedicated to strangeness.

Fegmania!, which features several erstwhile Soft Boy cronies in a new band, the Egyptians, shows Hitchcock polishing the best aspects of his craft to a new sheen, achieving a mature merger of lyric with melody (particularly on the morbidly catchy "My Wife and My Dead Wife" and the beautiful emotional study, "Glass") that sacrifices none of the urgency that brings his best songs to life. He has also continued to hone his sound, adding instruments to create a rich, ringing production that highlights his superb guitar textures and Andy Metcalfe's moody bass lines amid a variety of settings.

Gotta Let This Hen Out! is an essential live album recorded April '85 at the Marquee. Sampling all of his albums for items like "Brenda's Iron Sledge," "Heaven," "My Wife and My Dead Wife," and tossing in the acerbic "Listening to the Higsons" (a non-LP 45), Hitchcock and the three Egyptians do a fine job of putting the songs across in crisp, energetic fashion. A great introduction for neophytes, a treat for fans. (**Exploding in Silence** is a live picture disc with some of the same cuts.)

Hitchcock isn't for everyone. His songs can be repetitious and lean heavily toward darkness. But the intelligence and emotion of his work, together with his devotion to electric guitar as the heart of his music, make him one of the most rewarding performers around.

[mp/iar]

HITMEN

Aim for the Feet (Urgent-CBS/Columbia) 1980
Torn Together (CBS/Columbia) 1981

The Hitmen's d.i.y. debut single, "She's All Mine" b/w "Slay Me with Your 45," was razor-sharp rhythm'n'pop, meshing terse but tasty guitar and keyboards over snappy bass and drums, topped by Ben Watkins' Graham Parker-cum-David Bowie vocals. Yet on **Aim for the Feet**, re-recorded versions of those songs fall flat; it takes repeated listenings to discover that they— along with a passel of other tunes as good and better—have fallen victim to colorless, punchless production.

With producer Rhett Davies at the helm on **Torn Together**, the London-based quintet fares far better, crafting a succession of cleverly arranged and smartly played hooks that grow more impressive (not to mention catchier) with each hearing. The format incorporates more modern, Ultravoxian elements while avoiding the inherent pitfalls—until Side Two, that is, which is alternately arty and bathetic instead of hewing to the earlier, earthier approach. (The Hit-or-Missmen?)

[jg]

See also *New Asia, Youth and Ben Watkins.*

JOOLS HOLLAND

Jools Holland and his Millionaires (A&M/IRS) 1981
Jools Holland Meets Rock'a'Boogie Billy (IRS) 1984

This flamboyant pianist and Tube presenter provided a lot of the zest on Squeeze's first three albums; he's a cigar-chomping hustler able to energize even the most blase audience. For his solo debut, Jools adopted a less-contemporary stance, playing old-fashioned barroom romps with energy and panache. The record, produced by Glyn Johns, contains one classic oldie ("Bumble Boogie") amid rollicking originals, some co-written with Squeezeman Chris Difford.

Leaving his Millionaires behind, **Rock'a'Boogie Billy** reunites Holland with once-and-future Squeeze drummer Gilson Lavis; otherwise, the self-produced album was recorded solo "at the back room of Holland's home (which accounts for the authentic sound)." The eight tracks, including four Difford collaborations and the old "Flip, Flop & Fly," offer more rustic uptempo friskiness soaked with American barrelhouse and ragtime atmosphere—imagine a young Jerry Lee Lewis in prime condition with no religious hangups. Turn it up and hoist a few!

In 1985, Squeeze reformed with Holland again in the piano seat.

[iar]

HOLLY AND THE ITALIANS

The Right to Be Italian (Virgin/Virgin-Epic) 1981

HOLLY BETH VINCENT

Holly and the Italians (Virgin/Virgin-Epic) 1982

Singer/guitarist Holly B. Vincent formed her band in Los Angeles, but it took a move to England to secure a recording deal. That led to a single ("Tell That Girl to Shut Up") which established her tough pop-rock style and captured the attention, albeit briefly, of the British press and public alike. The band's first/last album was hindered by numerous problems (like firing the producer halfway through and starting from scratch with another, losing the drummer in midstream and having to find a replacement) and wasn't finished until over a year later, but it was well worth the wait. Richard Gottehrer's production fits the melodic rock songs perfectly, melding the hybrid LA/London sound—with glimpses of the Ramones, Blondie and Cheap Trick—into a powerful and original creation. The songs (mostly Vincent's) concern troubled romance, successful romance, teenage rebellion and kitsch culture; Holly's convincing delivery gives them import, and the catchy phrases and solid rock foundation make it a masterful record by an important young talent.

But **The Right to Be Italian** wasn't a commercial success, and Holly broke up the band, opting instead for a solo career. The stunning resultant LP, produced by Mike Thorne, has a misleading title and bears little resemblance to its predecessor. **Holly and the Italians** plays up her voice and songs, providing ample room for far-reaching emotional expression; the striking, atmospheric music is based on violin and keyboards as much as guitar. (The American release has one different cut and a vastly improved track sequence.) Although Vincent took some flak for recording a totally overhauled version of the Buffalo Springfield's "For What It's Worth," she does manage to make something new and different out of it. Elsewhere, sensitive, moody originals like "Samurai and Courtesan" and "Uptown" contrast with upbeat rockers like "We Danced" and "Honalu," all displaying a unique viewpoint in subtly evocative lyrics. Even more than its predecessor, this is an incredible

album by an enormously gifted singer, writer and performer.

Despite her considerable talent, Vincent has not made an album since, although she did duet with Joey Ramone on a 45 of "I Got You Babe" and served a brief, unrecorded stint in the Waitresses. [iar]

HOMOSEXUALS

The Homosexuals' Record (Recommended/nr) 1984

A posthumous labor-of-love compilation of late '70s singles and rough mixes, this sixteen-song 45-rpm album has technical shortcomings but lots of justifying character and rock energy. While the vocalist displays incipient David Thomas screech potential, the almost-catchy songs are well-constructed Brit-punk—early Buzzcocks-meets-Vibrators—with more intelligence and sense than blind aggression; unexpected production fillips add to the fun. [iar]

HOODOO GURUS

Stoneage Romeos (Demon/A&M) 1984
Mars Needs Guitars! (Big Time-Chrysalis/Big Time-Elektra) 1985

Australia has produced few bands as crazily entertaining as Sydney's Hoodoo Gurus. Who else would dedicate their debut album to, among other pop culture giants, television actor Larry Storch and Arnold [the pig] Ziffel? That their music is an invigorating combination of cow- punk, garage-rock and demi-psychedelia only makes it more fun. "(Let's All) Turn On" is as good as any Lyres song; "In the Echo Chamber" has the mad abandon of prime Cramps; "I Want You Back" is winsome teen-angst power pop; "I Was a Kamikaze Pilot" resembles the Fleshtones and displays a brilliant sense of absurd humor. (Think about that title again for a second if you didn't get it.) **Stoneage Romeos** is a great record that out-ethnics a lot of back-to-the-roots American bands.

Mars Needs Guitars! boasts a great title, spiffy cover art, characteristically kitschy thank-you's and a top-notch opening tune in "Bittersweet." Otherwise, while the band's spirit is as willing as ever, an ill-considered mix and several clumsy arrangements hamper the rough'n'ready delivery, letting melodies founder amidst impressive rave-up playing. Other disappointments: promising numbers like the countryfied "Hayride to Hell" aren't parodic enough; "Like Wow—Wipeout" neglects to quote the classic instrumental; the title track has clever lyrics but no tune or direction. The Gurus are great, but they can make better albums than this. [iar]

HOOTERS

Amore (nr/Antenna) 1983
Nervous Night (CBS/Columbia) 1985

Proving that you can't judge a band by its extracurricular activities, Philadelphia's Hooters—led by the two main musicians on Cyndi Lauper's first solo album—skillfully and wholeheartedly play mundane, prosaic quasi-intelligent would-be arena rock on **Amore**, evidencing no wit and little creativity. And their idea of ska is sad. Except for one poorly sung but excellent tune ("Blood from a Stone," later covered brilliantly by Red Rockers), this is really bad.

Some of **Amore**'s songs were re-cut for **Nervous Night**, an appallingly successful record produced by Rick Chertoff, who also did Lauper's multi-platinum record. The moronic "All You Zombies" is as clumsy as it gets; most of the other tunes sound the same, employing mandolin and a melodica. A version of Love's "She Comes in Colors" is welcome but hardly excuses the slickly soulless radio fare that surrounds it.　　　　　　　　　　[iar]

HORIZONTAL BRIAN

Vertical (Gold Mountain) 1983

This wonderful British quartet plays lyrically observant melodic rock, much in the same vein as Stackridge did in oldentide. Bassist Tony Phillips sings his own songs in an engaging, unprepossessing voice, humorously satirizing the shortcomings of parenthood ("Playing with the Babies"), obsession with the colonies ("Everybody Wants to Be an American"), death ("Buried in Your Best Suit") and more. Although not as sharp as the words, the music is dandy as well.　　　　　　　　　　　　　　[iar]

HOT TIP

See *Numbers*.

HOUSEMARTINS

Flag Day EP (Go! Discs/nr) 1985
Sheep EP (Go! Discs/nr) 1986

As the cover of their first EP boasts, this quartet from Hull are quite quick, creating distinctive, finely-crafted pop songs. **Flag Day** is an outstanding debut, four polished tunes that are memorable and intelligent. No fey pop wimps here. The melancholy title track laments the economic deterioration of Great Britain; the punchy and percussive "Stand at Ease" offers an unusual view of militarism. "You" is bright, bouncy pop with spectacular harmonies; "Coal Train to Hatfield Main" is a country stomp. Paul Heaton's vocals shine throughout, providing an integral part of the Housemartins' overall charm.

They followed with **Sheep**: three fine pop songs plus an extraordinary *a cappella* cover of Curtis Mayfield's "People Get Ready" and an uplifting gospel song (with choir). As the sleeve states, "The Housemartins are my bestest band." If they continue to make records like these, that sentiment may become universal.　　　　　　　　　[ag]

HUANG CHUNG

See *Wang Chung*.

HUMAN LEAGUE

Dignity of Labour Pts. 1—4 EP (Fast Product/nr) 1979
Reproduction (Virgin/nr) 1979
Travelogue (Virgin/Virgin Int'l) 1980
Dare (Virgin/A&M) 1981
Fascination! EP (Virgin/A&M) 1983
Hysteria (Virgin/A&M) 1984

LEAGUE UNLIMITED ORCHESTRA

Love and Dancing (Virgin/A&M) 1982

PHILIP OAKEY & GIORGIO MORODER

Philip Oakey & Giorgio Moroder (Virgin/Virgin-A&M) 1985

It took a near-fatal lineup overhaul, two developmental albums and a fortuitous partnership with the right producer to put the Human League in a position to make the record that would crown them unchallenged world champs of synthesizer pop. Although the time span is brief, the group that topped the charts in 1982 with "Don't You Want Me" bears almost no resemblance to the dour trio that recorded "Being Boiled" for Fast Product in 1978.

The first two albums were the work of Sheffield's Phil Oakey, Ian Craig Marsh, Martyn Ware (all synth/vocals) and Philip Adrian Wright, who handled visual chores. **Reproduction** suffers from a cold, simplistic approach—high-tech primitivism—given added monotony by deadpan vocals. Amid all the glum sonic novelties was one track, "Empire State Human," that indicated incipient pop sense and brought the League some success on the British charts.

Travelogue is much better, broadening the palette to include a wide variety of subtle synthesizer shadings, from the arcane to the sublime, and introducing vastly improved material. Lyrical subjects concern science fiction and kitsch culture, two facets of the League's personality illustrated in concert through Wright's slide projections. Although still an emotionally ambivalent record, **Travelogue** is warmer and more fun than its predecessor, and suggests a possible rewarding direction for the band to pursue.

And pursue they did. After a schism left Oakey and Wright in the Human League and Marsh and Ware as the British Electric Foundation, the band was revamped to include four new faces and a commitment to danceable pop music. That intent, along with producer Martin Rushent—whose skills dovetailed with almost all of the band's shortcomings (there's no cure for Oakey's basically amelodic crooning)—ultimately led to such interplanetary hits as "Don't You Want Me" and "Love Action (I Believe in Love)." The irresistible mix of state-of-the-art technology and old-fashioned pop single formulae set millions of toes tapping, although the **Dare** LP indeed contains much headier and heavier stuff as well. With incredible ambience and subtle tension, "Seconds"—about the Kennedy assassination—is, in fact, the LP's unheralded best track. A great record, but not just for its popular songs.

Love and Dancing (released under a pseudonym that pays homage of sorts to Barry White) is a Rushent remix of seven **Dare** cuts plus one extra tune, all of which makes great dance fodder. Some of the record bears listening to; other parts, however, are either repetitively dull or noisily annoying.

Subsequently proven incapable of delivering a timely follow-up to sustain their newfound mega-stardom, the Human League had to make do with sporadic stop-gap singles, two of which were compiled for the **Fascination!** EP. "Mirror Man" is pedestrian but catchy; "(Keep Feeling) Fascination"

(which appears here in its original form and an extended remix), however, is ruined by the awful sick-cow vibrato on the synthetic horns.

Three years after **Dare**, following a pitched battle with their commercial insecurities, the League finally came up with **Hysteria**. Having split with Rushent, the album was produced by the band with Chris Thomas and Hugh Padgham, and wisely omits the prior 45s in favor of new songs, some of which are quite good. Stretching their style to encompass a subtler, tender side, the ballads ("Louise," "Life on Your Own") provide the record's most engaging moments. (Never mind that the quieter, slower material exacerbates Oakey's vocal problems.) Taking a political stand, "The Lebanon" offers simpleminded drama with a pop hook; "Don't You Know I Want You" is an almost-clever attempt to acknowledge and recycle the sound (and title) of their biggest hit.

During another patch of Human League hibernation, Oakey collaborated with Giorgio Moroder, first on the entertaining **Electric Dreams** film soundtrack, then on a joint album. Giorgio wrote the music and produced; Phil added lyrics and sang; Arthur Barrow and Richie Zito provided the backing tracks on, respectively, synth and guitar. With a bouncy, upbeat sound, it's an unchallenging bit of fun that could easily be mistaken for a jollified League record but for Moroder's lighthanded, deft arrangements and percolating tunes. "Good-bye Bad Times" and a reprise of "Together in Electric Dreams" stand out, but the rest is almost as immediately enjoyable.

A troubled band with lots of problems—structural and musical—the Human League has nonetheless played a critical role in pioneering synthesizer rock, and made some tremendous records along the way.　　　　　　　　[iar]

See also *British Electric Foundation, Heaven 17, Shake*.

HUMAN SEXUAL RESPONSE

Figure 14 (Don't Fall Off the Mountain/Eat-Passport) 1980
In a Roman Mood (Don't Fall Off the Mountain/Passport) 1981

A most promising (but ultimately unsuccessful) band from Boston, the seven-person HSR (including four vocalists!) explored sexual identities, both physical and mental, on **Figure 14**, as on the wonderful "What Does Sex Mean to Me?" Elsewhere, there's a healthy irreverence towards the famous and the neurotic, with sex never quite out of the picture. Leanings in the direction of art rock, led by singer Larry Bangor's Tom Verlaine-style vocals, occasionally get HSR in trouble, coming off too cute.

In a Roman Mood is darker and more oblique than **Figure 14**, showcasing the band's growing lyrical complexity regarding human beings and what they expect from each other. Again their nervous rhythms—over an entire LP—don't produce anything outstanding. Human Sexual Response makes background music for difficult relationships.

The band broke up in 1982, but has spawned several offshoots (Wild Kingdom, the Zulus, etc.) who have continued to be active on the

Boston scene. HSR got back together for a reunion show on Halloween 1984.　　　　　　[gf]

HUMPE-HUMPE

See *Ideal*.

IAN HUNTER

Short Back n' Sides (Chrysalis) 1981

Ian Hunter emerged as an early patron saint of punk, quite a feat considering that the movement was allegedly based on the rejection of old wave musicians just like him. Hunter's popularity with the young rebels stemmed primarily from his salad years as leader of Mott the Hoople and was based on attitude as much as music. In the late '60s and early '70s Hunter and band were down-to-earth, streetwise blokes who voiced a sense of disillusionment and failure instead of indulging in the fantasy and self-aggrandizement typical of so many big-league rockers. Punks of the later '70s saw themselves as fighting against the same climate of unreality and vanity. Specifics: Beginning with Mott's debut, **Mott the Hoople**, you can hear the tight, driving guitar of Mick Ralphs, later appropriated in whole by the Clash, Pistols and Generation X. **Mott**'s "Violence" and **The Hoople**'s "Crash Street Kids" both forecast with uncanny accuracy the emergence of a new generation of disaffected, angry kids.

Hunter produced Generation X's second LP, **Valley of the Dolls**. The late Guy Stevens, who assembled Mott and produced their first four LPs, also produced what many consider the Clash's finest album, **London Calling**.

Mick Jones joined with longtime Hunter-mate Mick Ronson to produce Ian's sixth solo effort, **Short Back n' Sides**, an ambitious, unfocused LP that covers more styles than a single record should. Still, Hunter continues to be the straight-shooter that originally endeared him to his "kids."　　　　　　[jy]

HUNTERS AND COLLECTORS

Hunters and Collectors (Aus. White Label) 1982
Hunters and Collectors (Virgin/Oz-A&M) 1983
The Fireman's Curse (Virgin/nr) 1983
The Jaws of Life (Epic/Slash) 1984

Melbourne's Hunters and Collectors offer one of Australia's answers to the Fall, an unremitting, bleak and powerful ensemble capable of horrendous noise, gripping drama and slithery funk. They do all three on both eponymous albums, which are almost entirely different records. The Australian is a self-produced double 12-inch with only three tracks common to the UK/US single disc of the same name, which Mike Howlett produced. (And remixed "Talking to a Stranger.") Utterly oblique lyrics (and a credit to the band as a whole for "lyrics, music, artwork, management") typify this enigmatic album. Fans of challenging, noisy rock and rhythm should enjoy, if not understand; real enthusiasts would do well to seek out both versions.

It took a while to locate another American label courageous enough

73

to take the band on, but eventually Slash saw their way clear to releasing **The Jaws of Life**, recorded in Germany with Conny Plank. Thanks to normal cover info, it becomes possible to compliment bassist John Archer and drummer Doug Falconer for their dominant rhythm work, suggest that guitarist Mark Seymour let someone attempt to sing next time and praise keyboard player Geoff Crosby for the nifty cover assemblage.   [iar/dgs]

HÜSKER DÜ

Land Speed Record (Alternative Tentacles/New Alliance) 1981
Everything Falls Apart (nr/Reflex) 1982
Metal Circus EP (SST) 1983
Zen Arcade (SST) 1984
New Day Rising (SST) 1985
Flip Your Wig (SST) 1985
Candy Apple Grey (WEA/Warner Bros.) 1986

Hüsker Dü is presently the unchallenged premier American punk rock band. Often erroneously lumped with hardcore, the Minneapolis trio makes bracing, exhilarating loud music with songs R.E.M. would die for. Although vast improvements in their songwriting over the years have changed the shape of their music, they've stuck with their basic sound: Bob Mould's impassioned screaming and buzzsaw guitar overlayed with feedback and amplifier distortion, Greg Norton's straight-ahead driving bass and Grant Hart's only slightly less demented singing and excessive drumming. The Hüskers overload the hooks in their songs to the point of explosion, creating a startling rush of momentum. These fashionless guys from the Midwest (where the best new punk comes from nowadays) are capable of putting on the planet's most exciting live shows.

The live **Land Speed Record**, however, isn't one of them. Basically a tour document from a year in which they covered a lot of land and took a lot of speed, it's a cheap recording that only hints at any juice there may have been in the performance. The group is by nature sloppy, and this disc captures the mess but not the overkill power.

Everything Falls Apart, in fact, puts everything back together. While the band hadn't totally mastered the studio, this is a great improvement over the live record. And it offers the first taste of pop-oriented things to come: a cover of Donovan's "Sunshine Superman."

Metal Circus marks a giant leap forward. With this disc, the band began to reach a broader audience. Although often misconstrued, the title refers not to heavy metal (an area of exploration for many hardcore bands), but to the flat gray solidity of alloys, which fairly describes the record. **Metal Circus** is a collection of anthems, slow and fast, with twisted, abrasive guitar licks and twisted lyrics. The rousing Mission of Burma-ish "It's Not Funny Anymore" is the most potent track, but "Diane" is the most haunting, a Hart-penned power dirge about rape and murder. When he screams the title over and over, it sounds like "dying." A monster song from a heavy record.

After **Metal Circus**, Hüsker Dü released a 7-inch statement of purpose, the totally gonzoid cover of "Eight Miles High." The single brings together Mould's love of jangly '60s pop with the band's adrenaline charge. Unlike most punk covers of '60s songs, which generally devolve into camp, this retains the flavor of the original without compromising the punkers' sonic blitz.

Zen Arcade, an ambitious double-record concept album about the strange adventures of a kid leaving home, covers more ground than Greyhound and is successful a surprisingly high percentage of the time. The band plays acoustic, psychedelic and unabashedly poppy songs. When it's good, the material is among their best. A straight rocker, "Turn On the News," deserves to be a classic. Unfortunately, there's also some over-reaching and self-indulgent dross. As on **Sandinista!**, it isn't really filler because too much work obviously went in; still, backwards tape loops and extended drones dilute the album's effect.

By contrast, **New Day Rising** is as tight as a duck's behind, and that's waterproof. The band flails the hell out of the kind of loping melodies currently ringing out of the New South. The album is LOUD, intense, funny, accessible and downright catchy. From the opening cut, in which Mould just screams "new day rising" over and over above a rising tide of triumphant sound, to the elliptical closer, "Plans I Make," they do the Dü with nary a false step. Seldom have hooks been this powerful and exhilarating, nor full-throttle punk this melodic.

The Hüskers' final independent label release, **Flip Your Wig** is positively brilliant—fourteen unforgettable pop tunes played like armageddon were nigh. The production is taut and claustrophobic, pushing the echoless drums right into your head, competing with Mould's precise stun-assault guitar wash and vocals. Besides the compressed, efficient Top 40 sound of "Makes No Sense at All" (one of 1985's best 45s), the LP boasts such classic fare as the loving, fragile "Green Eyes," the boppy, bubblegummy "Hate Paper Doll," and the somberly psychedelic (complete with backwards guitar) of "Don't Know Yet," which closes things out in appropriately enigmatic fashion.

Following the Replacements to Warner Bros., Hüsker Dü self-produced **Candy Apple Grey** with an equally unselfconscious lack of commercial consideration, sacrificing nary a dB of energy nor an ounce of spirit. (They did, however, cut back to ten songs.) Starting off too many cuts with a brief Hart-beat adds an unneeded sense of similarity, but charged, varied music and never-better reflective, adult lyrics on Mould's six compositions provide a seductive wallop. "Sorry Somehow" (with surprising Deep Purple organ), "Don't Want to Know If You Are Lonely" and "Dead Set on Destruction" are typically staggering rock; "I Don't Know for Sure" sounds good but resembles "Makes No Sense at All" a tad too much. Two all-acoustic numbers ("Too Far Down" and "Hardly Getting Over It") demonstrate the band's flexibility and a take-it-or-leave-it attitude towards electric punk conventions. Ultimately, while more diverse, **Candy Apple Grey** falls a bit short of **Flip Your Wig** in intensity and impact.   [jl/iar]

HYBRID KIDS

Hybrid Kids (Cherry Red/nr) 1979
Claws (Cherry Red/nr) 1980

What happens when Jah Wobble meets country clods the Wurzels for a rave-up on Kate Bush's greatest hit? You get Jah Wurzel's version of "Wuthering Heights," zonked out reggae with quizzical vocals in a back-country accent, that's what. Actually, this is Morgan Fisher, ex-Mott the Hoople keyboardist, pretending (with a dab of help from uncredited friends—he himself is billed as "producer/director") to be a baker's dozen different acts having a go at their fave tunes. What purports to be British Standard Unit takes a pretty amusing off-the-wall industrial-synth whack at "D'Ya Think I'm Sexy," but most of the rest of **Hybrid Kids** tends to be gratuitously high in the ozone, or tediously puerile (or both). Nice version of Sun Ra's "Enlightment" (sic), allegedly by Combo Satori, all the same.   [jg]

PAUL HYDE AND THE PAYOLAS

See *Payolas*.

ICEHOUSE

Icehouse (Chrysalis) 1981
Primitive Man (Chrysalis) 1982
Fresco EP (nr/Chrysalis) 1983
Sidewalk (Chrysalis) 1984
Measure for Measure (Chrysalis) 1986

FLOWERS

Icehouse (Aus. Regular) 1980

For the record: Australian band Icehouse began as Flowers. For their first US/UK release, the band renamed itself after the title of the Flowers LP, subtracted one cut, resequenced and remixed it.

The first Icehouse LP effectively mates emotional tension with the streamlined efficiency of modern synthesizer bands. "Icehouse" and "Can't Help Myself," in particular, exploit the contrast between smooth surfaces and frontman Iva Davies' anxious singing. Despite inconsistent material, this is a promising start.

Unfortunately, he let it all go to his head on **Primitive Man**, hiding the underrated band and declaring allegiance to empty stylishness. By emphasizing the elegance in his artful compositions and restricting his passions to poses, Davies ends up with a slick, pretty product that demands no involvement from the listener. (The LP does, however, contain the global hit single, "Hey Little Girl," a remarkably lifelike Roxy Music simulation.)

That song, two others from **Primitive Man**, plus two new tracks of forgettable roaring rock comprise the **Fresco EP**, evidently issued to capitalize on the band's sudden commercial emergence. **Sidewalk** is a tedious two-voiced exercise: fake Bryan Ferry (hey—doing it once may be cute, but two albums in a row is lame!) and histrionic guitar rock; occasionally the two are blended together in a misbegotten vision of Roxy Metal. Melt this sucker down.

While retaining the mannered Ferry imitation in spots, **Measure for Measure** adds an equally artificial version of David Bowie (ca. **Lodger**) and drops **Sidewalk**'s over-energized sand-trap. "No Promises" is the atmospheric pop hit (one of three cuts on which ex-Japan drummer Steve Jansen plays; Eno receives an all-LP credit for backing vocals, treated piano and keyboards), but other songs are more memorable. (Most are less.) Smooth, crafty, pointless.　[jy/iar]

ICICLE WORKS

The Icicle Works (Beggars Banquet/Arista) 1984
The Small Price of a Bicycle (Beggars Banquet/Chrysalis) 1985
Seven Singles Deep (Beggars Banquet/nr) 1986

"Whisper to a Scream (Birds Fly)," which leads off this Liverpool trio's debut album, is a brilliant pop single filled with jangly guitars, a hook-laden chorus and Chris Sharrock's surprisingly powerful, creative drumming. Unfortunately, the LP (and Icicle Works' career) runs downhill from there, with only brief interludes of nearly similar inspired creativity. The second album appeared and disappeared without fanfare. **Seven Singles Deep** is a compilation, the tape of which adds seven extra tracks.　[iar]

ICONS OF FILTH

Onward Christian Soldiers (Mortarhate/nr) 1984

Shouted vocals and medium speed raw guitar punk provide London's Icons of Filth with their musical formula; generally well-put, lengthy political lyrics make the band's activist statements on such typical topics as class society, vivisection and nuclear war. ("You're better active today than radioactive tomorrow" may not be catchy, but it is sane.) A far cry from Woody Guthrie perhaps, and not exactly high on the light entertainment scale, but a positive effort to reclaim some of rock's once-lofty ideals.　[iar]

IDEAL

Ideal (Ger. Innovative Communications) 1980
Der Ernst des Lebens (Ger. Eitel Optimal) 1981
Bi Nuu (Ger. Eitel Optimal) 1983

HUMPE-HUMPE

Humpe-Humpe (WEA/Warner Bros.) 1985

Odd pop from an innovative and intelligent German quartet. Ideal plays kinetic, herky-jerky guitar-based rock sung in her native tongue by Anete Humpe, a rough but convincing vocalist. Given the Teutonic predilection for electronics and progressive music, Ideal's Anglo-American-styled approach—on Tangerine Dreamer Klaus Schulze's label no less—is quite unexpected. Although not too structurally bizarre on the almost-rudimentary first LP, the band displays incipient invention with all sorts of delightful bits thrown in to keep things hopping.

On the Conny Plank-produced **Der Ernst des Lebens** ("The Seriousness of Life"), however, the polished sound makes the record seem superficially less idiosyncratic, although drippy organ and surprises like cello and extraneous audio effects provide considerable evidence to the contrary. The songs concern some pretty interesting subjects as well—e.g., "Sex in the Desert," "Tension" and "Shoot." With Humpe letting one of her male bandmates sing a good portion of the tunes, they subtly absorb rockabilly, reggae and other influences into the stew.

Bi Nuu exposes Ideal's singing and songwriting shortcomings and is inferior to the prior LPs. In an attempt to keep things happening, the band incorporates more Carib-beats and even jazzy stylings, as well as studio gimmickry, but all for nought—this brief album has precious little life in it.

Following the end of Ideal, Anete and her younger sister, Inga, formed a band which, with producer Roma Baran (a Laurie Anderson associate) as catalyst, transmuted into Humpe-Humpe. Baran wound up splitting the studio chores on **Humpe-Humpe** with Plank, Gareth Jones and the Humpes; somehow, they collectively came up with something like a modern-age electronic Eurovision record. The sisters sing their compositions in English and German with agreeable harmonic skill if not much raw vocal talent. The album neglects to include any musician

credits, but it sounds like synthesizers are doing it all. Anderson's ghost is audibly present in the gimmicky effects and self-amused tone, but the commercial pop basis puts an utterly different bias on the proceedings. A neat, offbeat pop record.　[iar]

BILLY IDOL

Don't Stop EP (Chrysalis) 1981
Billy Idol (Chrysalis) 1982
Rebel Yell (Chrysalis) 1983
Vital Idol (Chrysalis/nr) 1985

After Generation X's demise, Idol packed his bags and moved to New York, got himself managed by former Kiss svengali Bill Aucoin, and began recording with local players and producer/drummer Keith Forsey, a protege of Giorgio Moroder. The first result—a four-song EP—had only an awkward but entertaining cover of "Mony Mony" and a phenomenal five-minute remake of Gen X's "Dancing with Myself" to recommend it.

Billy Idol (and a series of generally noxious videos) made Billy Idol a huge star while providing erstwhile fans of his original band with an ideological dilemma: was he the ultimate Frankenstein mutation of new wave or an arena-metal fraud masquerading as a punk? In any case, the record—marrying Moroder's trademark *Midnight Express* sequencer sound to a throbbing rock beat—proved to be a lode of memorable hits ("White Wedding," "Hot in the City," "Love Calling"). Idol's macho postures and sneering vocals are noisily matched by Steve Stevens' caricatured Ronson/Thunders guitar wildness and a powerfully-built modern rock band with subtlety *and* near-metal strength. An album to despise while you hum along.

With only writing partner Stevens held over from the previous band, Idol kept the same producer and formula on **Rebel Yell**, another collection of hits that run hot ("Rebel Yell," "Blue Highway," "Flesh for Fantasy") and cool ("Eyes Without a Face," "Catch My Fall"). Refined and carefully groomed for platinum success, it's an undeniably good rock'n'roll record that is also reprehensible for its phoniness and calculation.

Vital Idol is a remix LP which presents extended versions of such Idolisms as "White Wedding," "Catch My Fall," "Dancing with Myself" and "Flesh for Fantasy."　[iar]

IGGY AND THE STOOGES

See *Iggy Pop*.

IKE YARD

Night After Night EP (Bel. Crepuscule) 1981
A Fact a Second (nr/Factory America) 1982

Ike Yard—not a person, but a New York-based quartet—mixes vocals not unlike the zombie mutterings of a bum in the tube (and barely more intelligible) with spurts of electronic noise to create minimalist "music" with a funny sort of force. The emphasis is on percussion and rhythm, although there are traces of distinct pitch, courtesy assorted drones and grunts. By and large, the sounds resemble audio verite—street noises, howling winds, guns, clanging doors—more so on **A Fact**

a Second, the EP being more musical.

Ike Yard's Stuart Arbright subsequently went on to more commercial endeavors, such as Dominatrix.　[jg]

See also *Dominatrix*.

LOS ILLEGALS

Internal Exile (A&M) 1983

On paper, this looked great—an East Los Angeles Mexican-American rock quintet with a strong political consciousness and tremendous local following getting a major label deal. On vinyl, however, what comes across is characterless (except for a bit of Latin percussion) rock'n'roll with clumsy but righteous lyrics, some in Spanish. Los Illegals don't give away anything in terms of skill, energy or integrity, but it's hard to get excited about their anyband guitar-laden rock and torpid songwriting. Mick Ronson co-produced.　[iar]

ILLUSTRATED MAN

Illustrated Man EP (EMI/Capitol) 1984

I'm not sure if I-Man's brief and miserable existence quite qualified it as a supergroup: Hugo Burnham (ex-Gang of Four), Roger Mason (a Gary Numan sideman), Robert Dean (ex-Japan) and singer/bassist Philip Foxman, an Australian with no familiar credits. I hope not, because their overbearing, overproduced, soul-free dance-funk hardly reflects well on any of the participants. Actually, if they had lost Foxman—his voice was the band's worst feature—Illustrated Man might have had a future. Instead, this is just corporate bandwagon-jumping of no merit.　[iar]

75

I'M SO HOLLOW

Emotion/Sound/Motion (Illuminated/nr) 1981

A moderately unpleasant new-dance quartet from Sheffield, I'm So Hollow has two awful singers (Jane Wilson and Rod Leigh), a solid drummer and a tendency to toss in odd noises and "treatments" when the songs bog down. The music's competently dull—Wilson's not a bad synth-player—but it never rises above passable and, when the vocals are prominent, often falls well below.　[iar]

INCA BABIES

Jugular EP (Black Lagoon/nr) 1984
Rumble (Black Lagoon/nr) 1985
Surfing in Locustland EP (Black Lagoon/nr) 1985

There's not much to say about this quartet beyond noting that they make every conceivable effort to be the Birthday Party. Each member emulates his BP counterpart, with a pounding rhythm section and apocalyptic guitar, but the Inca Babies lack the original's power and completely miss the dark humor. Even the song titles have a familiar ring: "16 Tons of Fink," "Cactus Mouth Informer," "Luecotomy Meat Boss." Put these guys on the tribute-band circuit.　[dgs]

INDOOR LIFE

Indoor Life (Fr. Celluloid) 1981
Indoor Life (nr/Relativity) 1983

Indoor Life formed in San Francisco but later emigrated to New

York City. On their first album, they fielded a five-piece lineup that included trombone, tapes and synthesizer. The music—while generally structured into song form—also contains heaps of silly noises and improvised bleeps and squawks. The lyrics (in English, French and German) are interesting, but not all supported by melodies. Overall, Indoor Life seemed to be an artful, pretentious collective of progressive intellectuals bent on making accessible cleverness for their own satisfaction. Maybe you'll like it, too.

Recorded as a trio, the second album is better organized but no less self-indulgent, drawing out simple song ideas into overly long, repetitive excursions. Jorge Socarras has a pleasant, flexible voice; his two cohorts (synths and guitars) evince much technical prowess, but these monotonous creations are only intermittently entertaining and rarely captivating.

In 1985, Indoor Life signed to a new label, J-Mark, and released a 12-inch single.   [iar]

INDUSTRIALS

Industrials (Epic/nr) 1980

There are very few worthy moments on this British synth-pop group's album, and those brief snatches are provided by the comic-book lyrics, not the music. Although the record is technically well-produced, its overall effect is so bland and cynical that it becomes nothing more than disposable background music. MOR for a new generation.   [cpl]

INMATES

First Offence (Radar/Polydor) 1979
Shot in the Dark (Radar/Polydor) 1980
True Live Stories (Fr. Lolita) 1983
Five (Fr. Lolita) 1985

This British band had a big American radio hit with a cover of the Standells' "Dirty Water"; overall, their records sound like a cross between early Stones and early Dave Edmunds. Drawing on realistic-sounding originals plus well-chosen oldies, the Inmates don't offer anything new, but make good, primal rock'n'roll. **First Offence** contains "Dirty Water" as well as Jimmy McCracklin's "The Walk" and Don Covay's "Three Time Loser," one of several tracks employing the Rumour brass section. Thanks, no doubt, to shared icons, there are audible similarities to everyone from Creedence Clearwater to Robert Gordon.

Shot in the Dark dredges up the old Jagger/Richards gem, "So Much in Love," the Music Machine's "Talk Talk," and some real obscurities to repeat the formula. Fun, but too faceless to make any difference.

Continuing on with a new lineup that features original Eddie and the Hot Rods vocalist Barrie Masters, the 1983 live album on Lolita reprises both the Inmates' best-known tracks ("Dirty Water," "The Walk") and the Hot Rods' "Get Out of Denver").   [iar]

INNER CITY UNIT

Pass Out (Riddle/nr) 1980
The Maximum Effect (Avatar/nr) 1981
Punkadelic (Flicknife/nr) 1982
New Anatomy (Demi Monde/nr) 1985

If you can accept the notion that Hawkwind was the original punk-psychedelic-heavy-metal-dada fusion band, then it makes sense that saxophonist Nik Turner should be behind this devolving London five-piece, so far over the edge that their music almost defies comprehension. Theoretically, taking mind-expanding drugs is essential to appreciation here, but the frantic rock-with-horns of numbers like "Watching the Grass Grow" and "Cars Eat with Autoface" (on **Pass Out**) update the Hawkwind legend with style and energy that anyone can enjoy.   [iar]

INSISTERS

Moderne Zeiten (Ger. CBS) 1981

The Aryan Go-Go's? This Berlin guitar/keys/bass/drums/vocals outfit certainly was slicker (the vocals more full-throated) and more reggae/R&B-oriented than their American counterparts, but with much the same cheerful, cutesy bounce. Good songs will out, regardless, as the Insisters' do, even if they *are* in German.   [jg]

INVADERS

Test Card (Polydor/nr) 1980

Take pomp-rock, shorten its sights (unpump the pomp a bit), inject a bit of youth, alternate male and female vocals, and what have you got? The Invaders (from West Yorkshire—not to be confused with two American bands of the same name), who still manage to have all the snap and appeal of week-old pastry. Too much of their "Rock Methodology" and not enough playfulness makes the Invaders a dull band.   [jg]

INXS

Inxs (Aus. Deluxe) 1980 (nr/Atco) 1984
Underneath the Colours (Aus. Deluxe) 1981 (RCA/Atco) 1984
Shabooh Shoobah (Mercury/Atco) 1982
Inxsive (Aus. Deluxe) 1982
Dekadance EP (nr/Atco) 1983
The Swing (Mercury/Atco) 1984
Listen Like Thieves (Mercury/Atlantic) 1985

It took these six Australians (three of them brothers) a long time to develop into something interesting; **Inxs** is dull rock that sounds like a less musical Joe Jackson or a no-soul Graham Parker. **Underneath the Colours** (like its predecessor, budget-line issued in the US only after the band became successful there) has much better audio quality (although they neglected to integrate the drums into the mix) and shifts the focus among keyboards, sax and guitar in a vain effort to vitalize the underwhelming songs.

Shabooh Shoobah, with good, loud production by Mark Opitz (and one Farriss brother mysteriously missing from the credits), was Inxs' first album to be released in the US and UK. Despite major strides in several areas, on the whole it's still not a happening record. A few outstanding numbers do display growth in personality and style: "The One Thing" sews a bunch of riffs together into an energetic, dense fabric; "Soul Mistake" generates a foreboding mood; "Don't Change" gets up a good head of textured rock steam.

Following an Australian label change, Inxs' former record company issued **Inxsive**, a compilation that includes outtakes and obscurities as well as hits.

Four songs from **Shabooh Shoobah** (three extended remixes plus a wholly new version of a fourth) comprise the club-oriented **Dekadance** EP. Not much of an adventure; six minutes of "The One Thing" is certainly longer if not specifically better.

The Swing proved to be the first Inxs LP of any real significance, moving the group clearly into the mainstream of modern dance-rock with the inclusion of the suavely insistent "Original Sin," produced by Nile Rodgers. (Otherwise, the record was done with Nick Launay.) "Burn for You" is another highlight, using a female backing chorus to affect an amusing resemblance to Roxy Music. On the other hand, "I Send a Message" finally reveals Inxs' enormous potential to annoy: a basically tuneless song synthfunked into repetitive and grating obnoxiousness. Elsewhere, **The Swing** offers strong beats, mannered vocals and a unified, au courant sound.

Listen Like Thieves, produced by Chris Thomas, is crisp, lively rock, with as little vocal posturing as Michael Hutchence seems capable of and substantial aggressive guitar work where required. The title tune, "What You Need" and "This Time" all have solid melodies, strong rhythms and decisive hooks. "Shine Like It Does" attempts to generate a folk-rock sensibility with moderate success; other tracks are, at worst, negligible.   [iar]

IPPU-DO

Normal (Jap. Epic-Sony) 1979
Real (Jap. Epic-Sony) 1980
Radio Fantasy (Epic/nr) 1981
Lunatic Menu (Epic/nr) 1982
Some-Times (Jap. Epic-Sony) 1982
Live and Zen (Jap. Epic-Sony) 1985

MASAMI TSUCHIYA

Rice Music (Epic/nr) 1982

Led by guitarist Masami Tsuchiya, an androgynous, Bowiesque character, this trio has stepped into the commercial void created by Yellow Magic Orchestra's increased inactivity as a group. It's hard to make out what the songs are really about since most are sung in Japanese with only a chorus or bridge in English, but they seem simple-minded enough lyrically—themes of romantic fantasy, travel and technology evidently dominate. Tsuchiya's voice is high but gutsy and always in control (even when yelling)—he's got his shtick down pat, and his guitar playing fits as well. Ippu-Do alternates between modernized arrangements of '50s and early-'60s vocal pop-rock melodies and steaming, heart-pounding rock'n'roll, sometimes in the same song. They also use reggae syncopation and synthesizers, so all bases are covered—except originality. (**Lunatic Menu** and **Some-Times** are anthologies of the other LPs.)

It sounds like these fellas, especially Tsuchiya, have got the ability to go further but just aren't sure how. Tsuchiya gives it a try on his solo LP with lots of help from YMO's Riuichi Sakamoto, though several tracks include members of Japan (the *English* band) and Bill Nelson on e-bow guitar. Most successful when he tries to mildly funkify Japanese music, with further cross fertilization, Tsuchiya could be a real innovator.

By 1985's live album, Ippu-Do was just a duo, aided by two former members of Japan (with whom Tsuchiya had toured and recorded) plus bass ace Percy Jones. Despite its recent vintage, the album portrays the band treading musical water with jagged, arty treatments of old material (the group's and Tsuchiya's), plus a version of "Time of the Season." Despite stylistic growth, Ippu-Do needs new—not old—content to make it meaningful.   [jg]

GREGORY ISAACS

In Person (Trojan/nr) 1975 & 1983
All I Have Is Love (Trojan/nr) 1976 & 1983
The Best of Gregory Isaacs Vol. 1 (Jam. GG) 1977
Cool Ruler (Front Line/nr) 1978
Soon Forward (Front Line/nr) 1979
Showcase EP (Taxi) 1980
The Lonely Lover (Pre/nr) 1980
Extra Classic (Micron/Shanachie) 1981
The Best of Gregory Isaacs Vol. 2 (Jam. GG) 1981
The Early Years (Trojan/nr) 1981
More Gregory (Pre/Mango) 1981
The Sensational Gregory Isaacs (Vista/nr) 1982
Lover's Rock (Pre/nr) 1982
Night Nurse (Island/Mango) 1982
Mr. Isaacs (Vista/Shanachie) 1982
Crucial Cuts (Virgin/nr) 1983
Out Deh! (Island/Mango) 1983
Reggae Greats (Live) (Mango/Island) 1984
Live at the Academy Brixton (Rough Trade/nr) 1984
Private Beach Party (nr/Ras) 1985

The Cool Ruler, Gregory Isaacs, is one of the best-loved and most durable reggae singers. Highly prolific (he writes nearly all his material) and business-savvy (he runs his own Jamaican label, African Museum), Isaacs' voice is still the key to his success. His delivery is marked by a combination of ice and fire rare even among soul singers—an urgent longing tempered with cool control. Comparable to Al Green or Marvin Gaye, Isaacs is nevertheless a completely unique stylist. His repertoire is equal parts lovers rock and Rasta protest; the link is his seductive delivery. Whether he's urging romance or reform, the call to action will give you goosebumps.

Like many popular reggae performers, however, Isaacs' recording career is a confusing configuration of producers and labels that proves difficult to untangle. For his early work, he relied on a number of producers. **Sensational**, for instance, has one side produced by Rupie Edwards and one by Ossie Hibbert, resulting in a mix of hits ("Black and White," "Mr. Know It All") and duds. **Extra Classic** compiles his work with Pete Weston and Lee Perry, as well as his first self-produced sessions. While also spotty, the record offers early proof of Isaacs' authority and strength as a songwriter.

Isaacs' career began to move under the guidance of producer Alvin Ranglin. Their collaboration is chronicled on the two excellent **Best Of** collections. Though available only as Jamaican imports, these consistently strong LPs are worth finding, and crucial for fans. Another Ranglin/Isaacs session, **In Person** (which includes the UK hit, "Love Is Overdue") is available on Trojan, along with an LP produced by Sidney Crooks, **All I Have Is Love**. Both are of mixed quality, but Trojan took the best from each and combined them with a third batch (produced by Winston "Niney" Holness) for **The Early Years**, good all the way through.

For his next career phase, Isaacs chose to produce himself. Despite weak covers of the Temptations' "Get Ready" and Billy & Vera's "Storybook Children," **Mr. Isaacs** has bold, assured singing, and at least one classic ("Slave Master").

Virgin's Front Line label then released two inconsistent albums, subsequently culling the best tracks for an edition of the **Crucial Cuts** series; still, it's pretty weak. The outstanding **Soon Forward**, however, launched his collaboration with Sly Dunbar and Robbie Shakespeare. The title song of that record also appears on the **Showcase** EP, released on Sly and Robbie's Taxi label, which adds a version of Marley's "Slave Driver." Tight and lively from start to finish, although Isaacs' personality is somewhat overshadowed by the duo's fine playing. Besides his work with Sly and Robbie, Isaacs began an association with Roots Radics, another fine Jamaican session band, that would last several LPs.

The Lonely Lover and **More Gregory** contain his finest middle-period work. Both feature excellent backing (divided between the Radics and Dunbar/Shakespeare) and a steady stream of high-quality material. Best of all, Isaacs is singing at the peak of his form. **More**, in particular, firmly establishes his loverboy persona in an easygoing groove that lasts for all ten cuts.

By contrast, Isaacs' work on Island is marred by inconsistency. Both **Night Nurse** and **Out Deh!** boast first-rate singing and playing, but the material is erratic, frequently weak—more a series of gestures than songs. To compensate, perhaps, two live albums were released around the same time. The song selection—an essential greatest hits—is similar on both, but the Brixton set has the edge, featuring a horn section and a more enthusiastic performance.

A short period of inactivity was broken in 1985 by the release of **Private Beach Party**. In a clear effort to lighten the load, Isaacs enlisted the help of an outside producer, Augustus Clarke, and several songwriters. The result is his best album in years, a fresh, diverse package that demonstrates rather nicely how Gregory Isaacs' professionalism and talent have survived the test of time.   [bk]

DEBORA IYALL

See *Romeo Void*.

JOE JACKSON

Look Sharp! (A&M) 1979
I'm the Man (A&M) 1979
Beat Crazy (A&M) 1980
Jumpin' Jive (A&M) 1981
Night and Day (A&M) 1982
Mike's Murder (A&M) 1983
Body and Soul (A&M) 1984
Big World (A&M) 1986

Joe Jackson's debut LP, **Look Sharp!**, was hot stuff indeed, spawning the wry hit "Is She Really Going Out with Him?" and making him the first member of England's young triumvirate (filled out by Graham Parker and Elvis Costello) to really sell records in America. Tough and wiry, Jackson's songs mixed an edgy sensibility with a self-deprecating wit that put him in a class apart from his more serious peers.

The follow-up, **I'm the Man**, was an extension of **Look Sharp!**. Material ranged from the banal vindictiveness of "On Your Radio" to the haunting approximation of genius, "It's Different for Girls." While much of the material dates from **Look Sharp!**, the production is less crisp and the record lacks its predecessor's impact.

Beat Crazy is Jackson's final LP with the tight-knit J.J. Band. A conscious reaction to the pop of his first two albums, **Beat Crazy** drifts with an eerie sense of objectivity. In the liner notes, Jackson puts it bluntly: "This album represents a desperate attempt to make some sense of Rock and Roll. Deep in our hearts, we knew it was doomed to failure. The question remains: Why did we try?"

The Joe Jackson Band dissolved, and Joe took a musical detour, recording **Jumpin' Jive**, an attack of cool jazz vocals over mock big-band swing. Obviously enjoying himself (for once), Jackson romps his way through "Is You Is or Is You Ain't My Baby" and suchlike. Jackson's production is warm and loving, and though **Jumpin' Jive** was a clear respite from the official progress of his music, the album is enormous fun and holds up.

Night and Day proved to be Jackson's most successful outing since **Look Sharp!**, although the urban/Latin flavor bears not the slightest resemblance to the white-hot sound of his early days. The Latin rhythms seem somehow less honest even than the buoyant bop of **Jumpin' Jive**, yet Jackson is obviously sincere.

Jackson's next departure proved to be a hypothetical film soundtrack. Months after the album, billed as the music from **Mike's Murder**, appeared, the movie still hadn't, and rumours began to circulate that various problems were causing the delay—among them, the decision not to use Jackson's songs in the film. **Mike's Murder** is a record adrift, created but not used for a specific purpose. In any case, it's a very weak showing—Jackson at his least confident—notable mostly for "Memphis," whose organ line and rhythm are lifted straight from Steve Winwood's "Gimme Some Loving."

Jackson survived that debacle to make **Body and Soul**, an ambitious attempt to simplify and repersonalize the recording process as much as possible. With a distant, light sound—quite in contrast to the stuffy closeness of most contemporary records—and '50s jazz stylings tinged by Jackson's ongoing affection for Latin music, the record has plenty of atmosphere, and contains some of his strongest, most mature songwriting. Unlike his previous time tunnel trip, **Body and Soul** eschews period re-creation (except on the cover) in favor of a wistful ambience indicative of Jackson's distaste for much modern music.

The three-sided **Big World** was recorded live with a small band directly to a digital stereo master at a special three-day New York concert engagement held for that purpose in January 1986. With no post-production tinkering of any sort, the fifteen new songs—some about current world political affairs, others about societal issues—are reproduced on two discs as accurately as possible. Stylistically, **Big World** is a return to the stripped-down lightly-seasoned jazzy rock of Jackson's early records. A little self-important (the rampantly multilingual booklet seems like unnecessary grandstanding) and creatively inconsistent, but an impressively ambitious effort.

[jw/iar]

JACOBITES

See *Swell Maps*.

JAGS

Evening Standards (Island) 1980
No Tie Like a Present (Island) 1981

These English one-hit-wonders' one hit, "Back of My Hand," sounded remarkably like Elvis Costello. (Once other bands repeated that feat, the Jags faded into obscurity.) Surprisingly, their first album, **Evening Standards**, contained other interesting examples of enthusiastic rock-pop, and indicated possible staying power. Despite a lineup change, new producer and an amusing title, their follow-up, **No Tie Like a Present**, failed to get the Jags back in the public's ear. Not a bad band by any means, but one that promised great things and delivered far less.   [iar]

JAM

In the City (Polydor) 1977
This Is the Modern World (Polydor) 1977
All Mod Cons (Polydor) 1978
Setting Sons (Polydor) 1979
Sound Affects (Polydor) 1980
The Jam EP (nr/Polydor) 1982
The Gift (Polydor) 1982
The Bitterest Pill EP (nr/Polydor) 1982
Beat Surrender EP (Polydor) 1982
Dig the New Breed (Polydor) 1982
Snap! (Polydor) 1983

How ironic that the band from the class of '77 that seemed to stand least for the tenets of punk at the outset should end up being the one that remained truest to them over the long haul. The Jam's refusal to compromise their ideals and integrity during a six-year career tends to polarize reactions to them. In the end, once-common complaints about unoriginality and Paul Weller's lack of vocal prowess are overshadowed by their accomplishments as songwriters, musicians and commentators, but mostly by the Jam's living example that a band's commercial success need not divorce it utterly from its fans or sense of purpose. The trio's parting at the end of 1982 is either symbolic of victory—a courageous decision not to become pointless superstar dinosaurs—or of their failure to find an alternative. Regardless, the Jam left behind a recorded legacy as important as any the new wave produced.

Black mohair suits, white shirts, skinny ties, stylish razor-cut hair, Rickenbacker guitars—on **In the City** the Jam were the "new mods," emerging from a sea of spiky-haired leather-and-chain-clad punks. They may have looked different, but their energy level gave no ground, with Weller's jagged, choppy double-tracked guitar leading the attack over Bruce Foxton's busy, melodic bass lines and Rick Buckler's stiff-backed drumming. The songs themselves are as taut and well-manicured as the group's photos, but match the explosiveness and attitude of the punks easily enough to establish an indisputable kinship to bands like the Sex Pistols and Clash. (It's not surprising that the Pistols swiped the riff for "Holidays in the Sun" from Weller's "In the City.")

If the songs and playing of **In the City** are derivative—especially of **The Who Sings My Generation** and Motown—there's no arguing that the Jam was speaking to another generation for whom it was all new. Also, the main points—youth regaining pop culture from the grasp of conservative people with old-fashioned ideas, the individual vs. the crowd—were well taken by the group's growing British following.

This Is the Modern World, recorded just months after **In the City** was released, is a cleaner-produced version of its predecessor, breaking little new ground. The songs themselves are hit-and-miss, with "This Is the Modern World," "Standards" and "All Around the World" (their brilliant second single, included only on the US version of the LP) the obvious standouts.

Since they had by then spawned dozens of neo-mod soundalikes, the Jam needed a change of direction, and on **All Mod Cons**, rose to the challenge. Prior inconsistency is replaced by an album that explores new avenues with almost complete success, while never straying too far from the band's roots. Weller's writing showed him to have blossomed into a major-league tunesmith, as well as a lyricist possessing a keen eye for detail and a refreshing sense of the vagaries of his own position. While keeping a great deal of the early Who influence, the Jam also began to incorporate other sources (especially Ray Davies, resulting not only in a hit version of the Kinks' "David Watts" but also in the biting social commentary of "Mr. Clean"). On "In the Crowd," Weller gets his chance to open up as a guitarist and proves that he's more than just a Townshend copyist. **All Mod Cons** is a brilliant record.

Setting Sons takes five songs from a scrapped concept album about three friends who meet after much of England has been destroyed by atomic war and combines them with four even bleaker tracks, then lightens up by ending the LP with a version of "Heatwave." The album is the Jam's most somber—not that any of their records are big on humor—but it is also their most effective. Weller's songs stick, and the beauty of his

melodies provides stark contrast to the blackness of his lyrical vision.

Perhaps as a conscious change from the heaviness of **Setting Sons**, **Sound Affects** is more danceable and, for the most part, less pointed, although songs like "That's Entertainment" are hardly cheerful. The rage is still there, but the group channels it more into fiery playing and singing, loosening up somewhat on the lyrics.

The Jam EP—five songs previously released on singles—served mostly as an interim measure between LPs, but includes essential Jam tracks like "Absolute Beginners" and "Funeral Pyre."

The Gift explores a lot of new territory on songs like "Trans-Global Express" and "Precious," where a strong funk/Latin rhythm fueled by loads of percusssion is heavily in evidence. The album takes a lot of chances and doesn't always succeed; some of the rhythmic experiments sound forced, others fall victim to overly dense, ponderous production. **The Gift** has its moments, notably "Happy Together," "Ghosts" and the Motownish single, "Town Called Malice." Still, it does offer some evidence as to why Weller may have felt the band had exhausted its possibilities together.

The Bitterest Pill (named for an emotional song with one of Weller's best vocals) shows the band forging still further into the realm of R&B. With five tracks in all (including the band's penultimate studio sessions), it's a cohesive piece of work, although not recorded as such.

Beat Surrender, containing the Jam's last studio visit together, was released as a British double-45 and an American 12-inch. The driving title track is absolutely smashing, and the four accompanying tracks are swell as well, including a lively rendition of Curtis Mayfield's "Move on Up." The record is additionally noteworthy for its audible indications of Weller's subsequent direction with the Style Council.

Dig the New Breed, issued after the band's split had been announced, is an honest, retrospective live album (complete with bum notes) recorded at gigs during various stages of the Jam's career. A powerful parting shot. **Snap!** is an awesome two-disc career retrospective. [ds/iar]

See also *Bruce Foxton, Style Council, Tracie*.

JAMES
Village Fire EP (Factory/nr) 1985

Winsome and demure, Manchester's James proffer a folksy, intricate version of pop with top-notch percussion and vocals that range from baritone to falsetto, often in the same verse. The EP collects the five tracks on James' first two singles, presenting a diverse range—folk enhanced with numerous layers of acoustic guitar to revved-up funk and keen-edged punk. James occasionally stray near the wimpy end of the spectrum, but usually have the good sense to fall back and regroup. [ag]

JAPAN
Adolescent Sex (Ariola/Ariola-Hansa) 1978 & 1982
Obscure Alternatives (Ariola/Ariola-Hansa) 1978 & 1982

Quiet Life (Ariola-Hansa/nr) 1979 (Fame/nr) 1982
Gentlemen Take Polaroids (Virgin/nr) 1980
Tin Drum (Virgin/nr) 1981
Assemblage (Hansa/nr) 1981 (Fame/nr) 1985
Japan (nr/Virgin-Epic) 1982
Oil on Canvas (Virgin/nr) 1983
Exorcising Ghosts (Virgin/nr) 1984

MICK KARN
Titles (Virgin/nr) 1982

In one of rock's most remarkable examples of bootstrapping, Japan pulled themselves up from lowly beginnings as a ludicrously over-dressed glam-punk-pose band, (badly) emulating the New York Dolls and Alice Cooper, to finish, five years later, as one of the most sophisticated art-rock-pose outfits, respected by other musicians and branching out into such fields as sculpture and photography. Amazing.

Adolescent Sex introduces the band in all its guitar-rock misery, playing such Bowie-influenced tripe as "Wish You Were Black" with less style than a sense of urgency. **Obscure Alternatives** introduces more keyboards but still relies on buzzing guitars and David Sylvian's sneery vocals for its sound. (Ill-advised digressions into reggae and funk are strictly dilettantism and sound like it.) The songs are fairly unmelodic, production nondescript. With a quick listen, you might mistake this for a junior-league Stones imitation.

Quiet Life marked Japan's entry into the modern world. The choice of John Punter as producer is significant, because the band's sights had shifted from gutter-glam to sophisticated decadence, and Punter had worked with Roxy Music. A cover of the Velvet Underground's "All Tomorrow's Parties" allows the group—and especially Sylvian, sporting a totally revised singing voice—to show off their new suave reserve, relying on sequencers, Mick Karn's proto-funk basswork and generally understated aplomb. Around this time, Japan also released a marvelous single of Smokey Robinson's "I Second That Emotion."

With the band's new direction clearly not requiring his presence, guitarist Rob Dean took a powder, and Japan recorded the excellent **Gentlemen Take Polaroids** as a quartet. Sylvian's debonair Ferryisms—more shyly quiet than dissipated—were met by Karn's astonishing fretless bass work, Richard Barbieri's wide-ranging keyboard work (incorporating Oriental and other traditions) and Steve Jansen's inventive drumming, creating a unique sound with lots of atmosphere but a very light touch. Technically exquisite, musically adventurous. Sylvian's songs are, however, very hard to grab ahold of, as many lack a backbone, seeming to ooze along with little structure.

Tin Drum presents Japan at the peak of its form, playing exquisite, subtle creations with intricate rhythms, tightly controlled dynamics and technical excellence. Spare but strong drumming (abetted by Karn's rubbery bass) provides needed propulsion, and the breadth of influences—from Middle Eastern to funk—color the music a number of fascinating shades. Having

almost totally escaped pop constraints, Japan's sound here—except for a few tunes (especially "Ghosts") that strongly resemble latter-day Roxy Music—is a willowy fabric of interwoven threads.

Assemblage, as the title might indicate, is a collection of songs, from the band's pre-Virgin period, including "Adolescent Sex," "Quiet Life," "I Second That Emotion" and "All Tomorrow's Parties." (The cassette version adds remixes, an extra studio track and three otherwise unreleased live recordings.) In a new effort to interest America, Epic issued **Japan** (**Tin Drum**, minus two tracks replaced by three from **Gentlemen Take Polaroids**).

Oil on Canvas is a crystalline live set featuring Ippu-Do guitarist Masami Tsuchiya as an adjunct fifth member. The two records offer a good cross-section of the band's repertoire, starting with "Quiet Life," and also introduces some new material that never made it onto any of the group's studio records. Following much speculation, Japan finally dissolved, and Virgin issued a two-record anthology, **Exorcising Ghosts**, of their later work.

Mick Karn's **Titles**, recorded while the band still appeared to be an ongoing proposition, is essentially a showcase for his proficient bass stylings and grasp of woodwinds and keyboards, all very impressive but rather vague and pointless. Karn's guests include Jansen and Barbieri, Ricky Wilde (!) and several others. He subsequently formed Dalis Car with Peter Murphy of Bauhaus.

See also *Dalis Car, Ippu-Do, Riuichi Sakamoto, David Sylvian*.

JASON AND THE SCORCHERS
Reckless Country Soul EP (nr/Praxis) 1982
Fervor EP (nr/Praxis) 1983 (EMI America) 1984
Lost & Found (EMI America) 1985

In 1981, as the legend goes, Jason Ringenberg left his daddy's Illinois hog farm for the bright lights of Nashville and promptly stumbled upon guitarist Warner Hodges and bassist Jeff Johnson in a gutter. With drummer Perry Baggs, they became Jason and the Nashville Scorchers, and recorded a bunch of tunes on a 4-track during a drunken night in the studio. The resulting **Reckless Country Soul** EP, a 7-inch released by a Nashville indie label, is rough-hewn and half-realized, but enough to help the band earn a rep as the best country-metal-thrash band in the state of Tennessee.

Rigorous touring and wild shows helped spread the Scorchers' noisy mutant gospel. On the 12-inch **Fervor**, the Scorchers play tighter and nastier, displaying Ringenberg's knack for clever songwriting. The band signed to a major label, dropped the Nashville from their name, and saw their second EP reissued with the addition of a smoking version of Bob Dylan's "Absolutely Sweet Marie."

Lost & Found puts the Scorchers in the forefront of an ever-growing country-punk genre, only they've got the roots others lack: Hodges' folks toured with Johnny Cash, Baggs' dad sang gospel and Johnson was reared in the Blue Ridge mountains. More than just a pedigree to brag about, the band's genuine hick beginnings make them a lot less inhibited, and more apt to cross from cool to corny, punk to heavy metal without fretting much about it. There's great tension between Ringenberg's two sides—bible-quoting, straitlaced country boy and yelping, flailing, demon-possessed madman—and the cigarette-chomping, white-noise-mongering Hodges. On **Lost & Found**, Jason and the Scorchers burn like nothing since General Sherman's troops marched through Georgia. [ep]

JAZZ BUTCHER

A Bath in Bacon (Glass/nr) 1982
A Scandal in Bohemia (Glass/nr) 1984
The Gift of Music (Glass/nr) 1984
Sex and Travel (Glass/nr) 1985
Bloody Nonsense (nr/Big Time) 1986

JAZZ BUTCHER AND HIS SIKKORSKIS FROM HELL

Hamburg (Ger. Rebel) 1985
Hard EP (Glass/nr) 1986

In four years, the Jazz Butcher has undergone more transformations than most bands do in a lifetime. Led by the Jazz Butcher (aka Butch) himself, it is, regardless of incarnation, his lyrical witticisms and humorous critiques around which the music revolves.

The debut LP, **A Bath in Bacon**, is for all intents and purposes a one-man show. Butch plays a startling array of instruments, from guitar to xylophone, and employs a legion of session musicians to help create an album that encompasses an awesome variety of styles. Good ideas abound in songs like "Love Zombie," "Sex Engine Thing" and "Gray Flannelette"; there's just some uncertainty as to where they're going.

The second album was recorded with a stable quartet that included ex-Bauhaus bassist David J. Almost exclusively in a folky pop-punk format, the songs are better developed and reach logical conclusions. Among the gems: "Southern Mark Smith" and the hysterical anti-macho anthem, "Real Men" ("Some things never change/Notice how they never sit together on buses?").

The Gift of Music is a collection of single sides, an excellent package that affirms the band's folky-punk commitment. Of special note: the initial up-tempo version of "Southern Mark Smith" and the pop gospel "Rain."

Sex and Travel is the Jazz Butcher's crowning achievement. The eight near-perfect tracks run the gamut from funk to folk to country-western and punk. Butch's lyrics aim at more far-reaching concerns; subject matter more than anything else determines the style of each song. "President Reagan's Birthday Present" addresses the problems of America, Russia and nuclear arms with a healthy chunk of dance funk. "Holiday" uses a typewriter backing track and cabaret stylings to make light of the staid British persona. And the frantic adrenalin punk of "Red Pets" tackles preconceptions about Russians: "Everyone says they lift weights/Except for me, I think they're great." All this plus two great pop tunes, "Big Saturday" and "Only a Rumour."

With a new bassist replacing David J (off to join Love and Rockets), the rechristened Jazz Butcher and His Sikkorskis from Hell issued the live **Hamburg** LP and an EP, **Hard**, which picks up where **Sex and Travel** left off, adding blues and merseybeat to the Jazz Butcher's seemingly bottomless bag of musical tricks.

Bloody Nonsense is an American collection that includes some of the above-mentioned tracks. [ag]

JAZZY JEFF

On Fire (Jive) 1985

Solid rap action with a strong, clear delivery, significantly cliché-reduced rhymes and a variety of interests. Jeff warns about "King Heroin (Don't Mess with Him)," asks that dj to "Mix So I Can Go Crazy" and "Rock It (Rock It Again)" and shows a real soft spot with "My Mother (Yes I Love Her)." Incorporation of electric guitar, inventive percussion and mix gimmickry give this a fairly familiar sound, but Jazzy Jeff is an above-average rapper. [tr]

JELLYBEAN

Wotupski!?! EP (EMI America) 1984

New York mixer/producer John "Jellybean" Benitez steps out under his own name on this five-song mini-album. The only problem is he doesn't play or sing on it and didn't write any of the material either. Benitez did, however, produce it, bringing together such stellar friends as Nile Rodgers, Madonna, John Robie and Dan Hartman to create a long instrumental and a batch of dance tunes. Best track: an otherwise unrecorded Madonna composition, "Sidewalk Talk." [iar]

JESUS AND MARY CHAIN

Psychocandy (Blanco y Negro/Reprise) 1985

By blithely combining power-pop melodies with industrial strength noise and lowbrow lyrical perversity, the Jesus and Mary Chain—Glasgow brothers Jim and William Reid, bassist Douglas Hart and rotating drummers—created a sound that can't quite be described as new, but does stand miles apart from anything that's been done before. **Psychocandy** generated a storm of discussion, with critics comparing them to everyone from the Velvet Underground and Chad & Jeremy to the Ramones and Sonic Youth. Awash in feedback and fuzz, tunes and drones, wit and vulgarity, **Psychocandy** is the perfect soundtrack to these high-pressure multiphasic times: music for rush hour trains. The band's three exceptional pre-LP singles ("Never Understand," "You Trip Me Up," "Just Like Honey") are only the most immediately striking of the fourteen cuts; such others as "Inside Me," "Cut Dead" and "Sowing Seeds" further illustrate the group's variety, imagination and ability to enthrall. An utterly classic record. [iar]

JETS

Jets (EMI/nr) 1981 (Fame/nr) 1982
100% Cotton (EMI/nr) 1982

The three Cotton boys (rockabilly Ramones?) are far from the worst English nouveau rockabilly band you're likely to encounter, although they don't go out of their way to leave a lasting impression.

The debut consists primarily of well-worn oldies like "My Baby Left Me" and "Honey Hush." **100% Cotton** constitutes a distinct improvement—sharper playing, more original material and a shiny, gritless sound courtesy of Shakin' Stevens producer, Stuart Coleman. The birds-of-a-feather rule applies here, at least. [jy]

JETSET

There Goes the Neighbourhood! (Dance Network/nr) 1985

Complete with matching mod uniforms, Jetset play ingenuous, ultra-polite '60s pop with strong ties to the Turtles, Beatles, Cowsills and other harmony-heavy melodic outfits. It's hard to remain patient with such preciousness over the course of a dozen featherweight numbers—after all, times *have* changed whether they like it or not—but it's equally impossible to dislike the naive charm of their facile fancifulness. [iar]

JFA

Blatant Localism EP (nr/Placebo) 1981
Valley of the Yakes (nr/Placebo) 1983
JFA (nr/Placebo) 1984
Mad Garden EP (nr/Placebo) 1984

These Phoenix, Arizona skate-punks—the initials stand for Jodie Foster's Army—are major figures on the Southwest hardcore scene. Besides touring extensively and releasing lots of records, their Placebo label is the most active outlet in the area, and has issued discs by a number of bands.

Blatant Localism is a 7-inch whose six songs race along cohesively at warp speed with vocals that mostly defy comprehension. There's an eponymous number explaining the group's name as well as a relatively prolix exposition on "Beach Blanket Bong-Out" and a four-second display of counting. (I used a stopwatch, that's how.) **Valley of the Yakes** stretches fifteen songs out to fill a 12-inch, slowing things down in spots, but not increasing vocal articulation much. Still, a crisp, well-played slice of hardcore with real drive and commitment, plus two great, normal-sounding, reverb-splattered surf-guitar instrumentals, "Walk Don't Run" and "Baja."

JFA exposes increased sophistication and wit, starting with a backwards snippet called "Deltitnu" and continuing by tempering the thrash with variety, understatement and other interesting digressions. In a fit of major cleverness, JFA crash the Ventures into the Dead Kennedys for "Pipetruck," and (allegedly) cover both David Bowie and George Clinton during the course of the album. (JFA's funky-butt turn on "Standin on the Verge" is nifty.) A bit unfocused, but much more than a mere hardcore record. Standout track: "The Day Walt Disney Died."

Mad Garden, a four-song 12-inch with a wrestling cover and a new bassist in the lineup, encompasses more-or-less straight speed-rock plus one milder (non-surf) instrumental with keyboards. [iar]

JILTED JOHN

True Love Stories (EMI International/nr) 1978

In between releasing early punk records by Slaughter and the Dogs, the Nosebleeds and Ed Banger, Manchester's Rabid label found time to have an enormous chart hit with the novelty shtick of Jilted John, sung in an acne-riddled wideboy voice by Graham Fellows. Gordon the Moron, Julie and other assorted fictitious characters all joined John in this semi-narrative tale of teen angst set to pop music dopier than anything Herman's Hermits ever imagined. More ridiculous: the unavoidable catchiness of the whole affair. An embarrassingly likable record. [iar]

JOBOXERS

Like Gangbusters (RCA) 1983

Instigators of a brief Dead End Kids clothes fad in Great Britain, the JoBoxers melded Dig Wayne, a black singer from New York, with the (non-Vic Godard) remnants of Subway Sect to play bouncy, catchy R&B tinged with big-band jazz. **Like Gangbusters** contains a couple of swell singles ("Boxerbeat," "Just Got Lucky") but is otherwise formulaic and uninspired. [iar]

DAVID JOHANSEN

David Johansen (Blue Sky) 1978
In Style (Blue Sky) 1979
Here Comes the Night (Blue Sky) 1981
Live It Up (nr/Blue Sky) 1982
Sweet Revenge (10-Virgin/Passport) 1984

Having escaped his sordid reputation as prime instigator of the New York Dolls, singer David Johansen has managed to earn himself a solid American following. While keeping a firm grip on the soul and rock'n'roll values that originally inspired the Dolls, Johansen has crafted a uniquely urban style that suits his rough-throated singing as well as his Lower East Side personality.

David Jo's debut contains the majority of his popular solo material—"Funky but Chic," "Donna," "Frenchette," "Cool Metro"—played in grand post-CBGB fashion by some of the Bowery's best vets. Better than bar-band but decidedly unslick, **David Johansen** perfectly transforms an insolent punk into a rock'n'roll adult. Without destroying his urban soul, **In Style** makes an effort to clean and dress up Johansen's sound. Adding synthesized strings and horns, attempting overambitious stylistic experiments and relying on decidedly second-album-shortage material, **In Style**'s two good tracks ("She" and "Melody") are lost in the morass.

The failure of **In Style** undoubtedly inspired the misdirected **Here Comes the Night**, an attempt to make Johansen simultaneously into a heavy metal shouter and a sensitive, poetic artist. A lot of very talented people had their hands in this project, but weak songs and the lack of cohesion make it a disaster.

Fortunately, **Live It Up** put Johansen's career right back on course. With his longstanding reputation as a great performer and empirical evidence of a well-received live promotional-only record made for radio in 1978, it was a judicious tactic to cut a live album for regular release. Benefiting from carefully chosen classic tunes and Johansen's extraordinary skill as a song interpreter, **Live It Up** is a great party record by a great singer. Johansen comes alive!

Relieved of his CBS-affiliated record contract, Johansen concentrated on performing (appearing regularly in New York as his alter-ego, Buster Poindexter) for over a year before returning to the vinyl jungle with **Sweet Revenge.** Sharing the bulk of the songwriting and production with keyboard player Joe Delia and joined in a half-dozen studios by a large collection of sidemen, Johansen disconnects from the R&B rootsiness that, to some extent at least, characterized all of his work to date, replacing it with strong, synth-heavy rock that would be regrettable were it not for distinctive vocals and witty songwriting. Some of the record flops, but "Heard the News," complete with ersatz Spanish newscaster, blends Latin American political commentary with one of the catchiest melodies of his career. "King of Babylon" is a clever novelty item with egocentric lyrics and ambitiously-realized music. [iar]

JOHNNY G

G Sharp/G Natural (Beggars Banquet/nr) 1979
G-Beat (Beggars Banquet/nr) 1980
Water into Wine (Beggars Banquet/nr) 1982

Erstwhile one-man band and pub-rocker Johnny G takes after Nick Lowe, with a similar sense of humor and absurdity, an alarming variety of musical idioms and a seemingly effortless ability to make sounds fit together in a consistently pleasant manner. But this eccentric's his own man, and his records, while jumping wildly from reggae to R&B, folk music to dub, country blues to cocktail-lounge mush, all have a unique trademark quality. With unerring wit and overall good humor (even on the gloomy songs) Johnny G is perpetually surprising, and never fails to be solidly entertaining.

His early recordings—sarcastic (and, as a result, largely misunderstood) singles like "Call Me Bwana!" and "Hippys Graveyard"—were followed by an EP and finally a first album, **G Sharp/G Natural**, which touches on (among other areas) maudlin pop and jovial jug-band skiffle. The album features such luminary sidemen as Steve Lillywhite (who plays bass and didn't produce), the entire cast of skiffle band Brett Marvin and the Thunderbolts and even Mark Hollis, brother of Ed Hollis (who did produce the LP) and now lead singer of Talk Talk. Enough history? This record, while fun, is not essential to the Johnny G story. Proceed directly to his superior second effort.

G-Beat, recorded with only two sidemen, has such charming tracks as "Rubber Lover," "Suzy (Was a Girl from Greenford)" and "Night After Night (The Last Drink)," all given varied and inventive treatments that hide the low-budget recording circumstances. Using only voice, guitar, minimal drums, keyboards and (mostly acoustic) bass, **G-Beat** accomplishes some great things that must be heard to be appreciated. The LP comes with a bonus: an entire second album, **G-Beat 2 (Leave Me Alone)**, consisting of singles, outtakes and alternate versions that provide a concise background listen for the converted.

After the underproduced (but effective) **G-Beat**, **Water into Wine**

sounds state-of-the-art, with a cast of ex-pub luminaries playing on it and Bob Andrews (formerly of the Rumour) producing. It's a much finer record, with sensitively arranged tracks like "Carving up the Concrete" and a totally bizarre slide-guitar blues version of King Crimson's "21st Century Schizoid Man." **Water into Wine** also includes a bonus LP—**Pure Beaujolais**—half live, half outtakes and unreleased singles. Both discs are great fun with something for everyone. I like the "Johnny G Fan Club Song," a totally over-the-top tribute sung by labelmate Ivor Biggun. [iar]

JESSE JOHNSON'S REVUE

Jesse Johnson's Revue (A&M) 1985

Former Time guitarist Johnson reckons himself another pretender to Prince's throne, and his album reeks of self-conscious imitation, from the chronic pink color scheme to the band's carefully shaped mustaches. The self-produced music likewise favors a mixture of his former band and Prince's **Purple Rain**; not unpleasant, occasionally catchy ("I Want My Girl"), but no threat to the reigning monarch. [iar]

LINTON KWESI JOHNSON

Forces of Victory (Island/Mango) 1979
Bass Culture (Island/Mango) 1980
LKJ in Dub (Island/nr) 1980
Reggae Greats (Island/Mango) 1984
Making History (Island/Mango) 1984
In Concert with the Dub Band (Rough Trade/Shanachie) 1985

POET AND THE ROOTS

Dread Beat an' Blood (Front Line/Heartbeat) 1978

More a poet and social critic (as the name Poet and the Roots suggests), Johnson bridged the gap between reggae and punk, infusing the music with powerful political content and an urge for freedom rooted in his experience as a black man living in Brixton.

Dread Beat an' Blood was a call to arms, a dark commemoration of police harassment and social repression of blacks told in a forceful but strangely spiteless manner. Speaking his poems over absolutely flawless, throbbing reggae, Johnson uses the patois of the streets to speak to his audience, calling for brotherhood and vigilance. The clean, supple, vibrant music and incisive, pointed words make it a powerful and memorable political statement. Highly recommended.

Forces of Victory continues Johnson's call to action. Again supported by feverish reggae, Johnson's voice gains greater range and expressiveness while his poetry speaks of dire truths, and sounds increasingly complex, compact and expert. Muscular, dramatic stuff.

Bass Culture expands Johnson's style, including more humor and even a shy, touching love song. The music is sparer and more coherent, and Dennis Bovell's co-production slickens the sound just enough to remove its rough edges. Johnson is no less determined on his political numbers, but it's nice to know there are other things on his mind as well.

LKJ in Dub is a tribute to Bovell's engineering talents; while it has little to do with the Linton Kwesi Johnson canon, it's an interesting and successful example of dub technique.

In the four-year sabbatical that followed, only **Reggae Greats**, a sturdy compilation, was released. Johnson and Bovell then reunited for **Making History**, a "comeback" album as vital as any they had made together. The two-disc **In Concert** documents Johnson's strength and onstage presence. Though hardly perfunctory (the performances are all first-rate), it's still a greatest-hits-live package, and shouldn't deter listeners from acquiring any or all of the studio LPs. [sg/bk]

MATT JOHNSON

See *the The*.

JOLT

The Jolt (Polydor/nr) 1978

Little wonder the Jolt were written off as a Scottish Jam clone. This trio had—what a coincidence!—the same label, producer, image, name (almost) and sound. The Jolt's album shows they could work up a good sweat, but the material is strictly two-dimensional, not a patch on even Weller's most derivative early stuff. [jg]

JON & THE NIGHTRIDERS

Surf Beat '80 (Charly/Voxx) 1980
Recorded Live at Hollywood's Famous Whisky a Go-Go (Charly/Voxx) 1981
Splashback! EP (Rockhouse/Invasion) 1982
Charge of the Nightriders (nr/Enigma) 1984

Although probably still in nursery school when guitar instrumentals filled the American record charts, John Blair and his three cohorts brilliantly re-create the innocence and excitement of that long-lost genre. With resplendent, ringing tones, vibrato and mountains of reverb, **Surf Beat '80** pays homage with fourteen numbers, including a few soundalike originals amid a selection of covers that prove the band's dedication to and familiarity with their forebears. All of the tracks sound the same, but that's the idea. Great!

The live LP reprises some of the studio record's items, but also incorporates new material and spot-on renditions of more familiar neo-classics like "Pipeline" and "Hawaii Five-0." **Splashback!**, produced by Shel Talmy (to no particular effect except perhaps spiritual), features a six-minute medley that touches on eleven instantly recognizable melodies in one seamless nostalgia romp. [iar]

GRACE JONES

Portfolio (Island) 1977
Fame (Island) 1978
Muse (Island) 1979
Warm Leatherette (Island) 1980
Nightclubbing (Island) 1981
Living My Life (Island) 1982
Island Life (Island) 1985
Slave to the Rhythm (ZTT/Manhattan Island) 1985

At the outset of her singing career, model Grace Jones was a musical product in the truest sense of the word, more or less invented by artist Jean-Paul Goude. When

new wave became the dance-club staple of the '80s, Grace—whose previous records were strictly disco—sailed into the genre on an airbrush jetstream, performing slickly produced covers of mainstream modern material on loan from Chrissie Hynde, Bryan Ferry, et al., while mixing in a safe dose of thumped-up funk. **Warm Leatherette** (named for the pioneering Normal/Daniel Miller electro single, which she courageously covers) was the first Jones disc to embrace this formula; **Nightclubbing** followed suit, utilizing songs by Iggy and Sting. The balance of this LP features a slightly more fluid vocal style than the monotone that rules the previous album. **Living My Life** shows Grace at her most mature, escaping the restrictive machinations that had controlled her. The material allows more personality to show through, and songs like "My Jamaican Guy" and "Nipple to the Bottle" show the Sly-and-Robbie reggae team to be more into the music at this point. **Island Life** recaps her entire career to date, compiling such tracks as "La Vie en Rose," "Pull Up to the Bumper" and "Love Is the Drug," adding in a new single, "Slave to the Rhythm," extracted from her next studio album, released almost simultaneously.

Some bizarre business dealings must have led to the one-off alliance of Island and Manhattan Records which issued **Slave to the Rhythm** Stateside. Trevor Horn produced this outrageous, astonishing, so-called biography, including inter-track recitations, recollections and interview bites, and creating theatrically massive orchestrations. The songs—written by a collective of Horn, Bruce Woolley and others—aren't intrinsically strong or interesting, but the ZTT Big Beat Colossus does such a job filling the grooves with beats, strings, horns, vocals, keyboards and god knows what else that the material counts for relatively little. But by the same token, Grace's vocal contribution to this audio love fest seems disconcertingly expendable compared to her spiritual presence. [jw/iar]

HOWARD JONES

Human's Lib (WEA/Elektra) 1984
The 12-Inch Album (WEA/nr) 1984
Dream into Action (WEA/Elektra) 1985
Action Replay EP (nr/Elektra) 1986

Howard Jones is the '80s answer to early Marc Bolan—a scruffy, self-possessed imp with all the best intentions and incredibly acute pop sensibilities. If he were emerging a decade ago, Jones would surely have been a free-festival hippie attraction; as it's 1985, the lad with the silly hair doesn't play acoustic guitar with a bongo drummer for accompaniment, he controls an array of electronic keyboards, singing earnest, reflective lyrics of personal awareness and individualist philosophy. **Human's Lib**, produced mainly by Rupert Hine, boasts a few standouts—"New Song," "Pearl in the Shell" and "What Is Love"—which stop just short of over-perkiness or saccharine platitudes.

Dream into Action involves more outside musicians (horns, vocalists, a cellist) to vary the sound more and offers another stack of engaging nouveau-pop creations

("Things Can Only Get Better," "Life in One Day," "Like to Get to Know You Well.") The album does, unfortunately, contain an extremely duff howler—"Bounce Right Back"—which I first mistook for one of Falco's onerous rants. **The 12-Inch Album** compiles six hits in their remixed forms.

Taking advantage of Jones' inordinate American popularity, Elektra issued **Action Replay**—a collection of five alternate versions and remixes of songs from **Dream into Action** and other sources, plus the previously unreleased "Always Asking Questions"—for his fans. [iar]

MARTI JONES

Unsophisticated Time (A&M) 1985

COLOR ME GONE

Color Me Gone EP (A&M) 1984

Color Me Gone has a nice reedy vocalist in guitarist Marti Jones; rich arrangements and clear production allow her to draw everything out of the six agreeable songs on the band's EP. Without really holding to any one style, the foursome flirts with radio rock, neo-ethnic Americana, country (in that mode, the downcast "Hurtin' You" is the best thing here) and '60sish folk-rock, winding up ultra-pleasant but unmemorable.

Jones' solo debut—brilliantly produced by Don Dixon, who also plays most of the instruments —is much more promising, drawing strength from a very astute selection of neo-pop tunes. Jones sympathetically covers the dB's, Bongos, Costello and Dixon, singing them all in a clear, pleasing voice. A delightfully unprepossessing album. [iar]

JOSEF K

The Only Fun in Town (Postcard/nr) 1981

A leading light in Scotland's neo-pop revival, Josef K attempted an uneasy marriage of pop form and psychedelic sensibilities on a string of melancholic singles, all contained on their LP. Singer Paul Haig is the only member identified by name, and his presence is certainly the strongest here. There is a fragility in Josef K's gentle but foreboding work, produced in darkest wall-of-molasses sound, that suggests an intensity of thought comparable to Joy Division's. (Some of Haig's subsequent solo work sounds not unlike New Order.) But the album never reaches the level of animation found in the singles, and it was neither surprising nor inappropriate when the group broke up shortly after its release. Dank but intriguing. [sg]
See also *Paul Haig*.

JOY DIVISION

An Ideal for Living EP (Enigma/nr) 1978 (Anonymous/nr) 1978
Unknown Pleasures (Factory) 1979
Closer (Factory) 1980
Still (Factory/nr) 1981

Coming from the industrial desolation of Manchester, Joy Division expressed, in uncompromising terms, the angst of the great wrong place in which we live, and their updating/refinement of heavy metal music combined with singer Ian Curtis' tormented lyrics and

Martin Hannett's crystalline production to make a quantum jump onto totally original ground. The band came to an end when Curtis hung himself hours before they were to do their first American tour, thus (though it may be cynical to say so) proving the strength of his convictions. The remaining members have continued, with far more commercial success, as New Order.

Unknown Pleasures contrasts the message of decay and bemused acceptance of life's paradoxes with the energy and excitment of a band set loose in a studio for the first time. Hannett glazes the chilling, despondent music with a Teutonic sheen, fusing medium and message into a dark, holistic brilliance. The grim songs are punctuated by the sounds of ambulance sirens and breaking glass, picturing a world speeding toward incomprehensible chaos. Very highly recommended.

Closer has a sound that is emptier and more distant, with emphasis on strangely distorted synthesizer and a dislocated Curtis, who meanders through a world that robs him of joy and hope. A refinement of the Joy Division ethos produces a purgatory of sound. A stunning, deeply personal album.

After Curtis' death, much of the extant Joy Division work not already included on an album was gathered for **Still**, a two-record set consisting of studio outtakes (including a version of the Velvet Underground's "Sister Ray") and a live disc. Being a compilation, **Still** lacks the coherent intensity of the other two albums, but features a good representation of the various facets of Joy Division's intimate, desperate music. [sg]
See also *New Order*.

PHIL JUDD

The Swinger EP (MCA) 1983

Following his stint leading the Swingers, ex-Split Enz guitarist Judd made this six-song EP (edited from a full-length Australian album, **Private Lives**) under the production guidance of Al Kooper. Dropping any vestigial audible connection (the cover is nicely surreal) to his once-eccentric outlook, Judd offers mild mainstream music that is, regrettably, quite forgettable. (And does the lack of musician credits mean Judd played this all by himself?) [iar]

JULUKA

Scatterlings (Safari/Warner Bros.) 1982
Stand Your Ground (Warner Bros.) 1985

In a grand gesture of political unity, Johnny Clegg joined forces with Sipho Mchunu, a black South African street musician, to form this band, whose name means "sweat." Unfortunately, the experiment of combining rock with the *mbaqanga* sound of South African townships and Zulu chants fails, resulting in a disappointing mush of sweet, laidback, California-style harmonies sung over a loping backbeat. [rg]

JUNE BRIDES

There Are Eight Million Stories... (Pink Label/nr) 1985

The London-based Brides play tuneful, madly strummed guitar-pop with trumpet, viola and occasionally striking lyrics. On their seven-song

mini-album, singer/guitarist Phil makes the best of a demi-musical voice, while the others race along in almost coherent, loose fashion. Minor but enjoyable. [tr]

JUNGLE À FERRAILLE

Jungle à Ferraille (Fr. CBS) 1980

Hailing from the improbable environs of the Jura Mountains region (between Lyon and Lake Geneva), this French foursome makes you sit up and take notice with tight, terse punk-rock, like a splash of pungent aftershave. Too bad they lack that extra bit of charisma that would make you remember what you heard. [jg]

HARRY KAKOULLI

Even When I'm Not (Oval/nr) 1981

Following his involuntary departure from Squeeze, bassist Harry Kakoulli recorded this like-minded set of dignified pop tunes. It's an adequate record, although his compositions lack the clarity and crackle that typifies the best work of head Squeezers Difford and Tilbrook. [jy]

KANE GANG

The Bad and Lowdown World of the Kane Gang (Kitchenware/London) 1985

Very interesting: two vocalists—but *not* a harmony duo—plus an instrumentalist who plays (or programs) most everything else. True, they've got some help on drums, horns and keyboards (notably by veteran Pete Wingfield, who produced a lot of the LP as well). But the record nearly realizes its potential in one fell swoop, and is terrific! The Gang—neither purists nor trendies—move comfortably through a variety of soul sub-styles, distinctly blue-eyed but needing no apology. (Aside, arguably, from their vocals on the one oldie, the Staple Singers' very dated "Respect Yourself," which features an assist from singer P.P. Arnold.) The Kanes even throw in a blues and a wistful pop ballad. Reservations: the songs aren't superb (just really, really, really good) and the musical identity needs a bit of fine tuning. (In the US, the title became simply **Lowdown**.) [jg]

BILLY KARLOFF & THE EXTREMES

Let Your Fingers Do the Talking (nr/Warner Bros.) 1981

In 1977, Billy Karloff & the Goats regularly gigged at the Roxy, London's fabled punk venue of the time, and made an obscure album called **The Maniac**. Having been enjoined from using the name Billy Karloff & the Supremes, a later incarnation (including ex-Tom Robinson Band drummer Dolph Taylor) ultimately became the Extremes. For reasons unknown, this unreconstructed Sham 69-like punk band wound up with an American label deal and recorded a glossily-produced batch of sarcastic shouters. No big deal. [iar]

MICK KARN

See *Dalis Car, Japan*.

KAS PRODUCT

Try Out (Fr. RCA) 1982
By Pass (Fr. RCA) 1983

Kas Product was a French synth/vocal duo in the Suicide/Soft Cell mode, although that comparison is a bit generous. Singing in a frigid, aloof voice, Mona Sayol sounds very impressed with herself; the effect is overwrought, precious and pretentious. "Loony-Bin" (from **By Pass**) is one of the few numbers that stick, but the exaggerated vocals ruin it after awhile. Former Birthday Party guitarist Rowland S. Howard played with this crew on a semi-regular basis, but it's not easy to envision how he would have fit in. [dgs]

KATRINA AND THE WAVES

Walking on Sunshine (Can. Attic) 1983
Katrina and the Waves 2 (Can. Attic) 1984
Katrina and the Waves (Capitol) 1985
Waves (Capitol) 1985

WAVES

Shock Horror! (Aftermath/nr) 1983

Further extending the influence and legend of the Soft Boys, guitarist Kimberley Rew found a wonderfully sympathetic outlet for his ace songwriting in this Anglo-American quartet whose other major asset is singer/guitarist Katrina Leskanich, a Kansas native with a great, flexible, strong voice equally suited for full-tilt pop harmonies and belt-it-out rock'n'roll. The band melds a remarkable hybrid of styles, personalities and ethnic backgrounds and seems capable of enormous variety.

Walking on Sunshine contains such absolutely brilliant songs as "Going Down to Liverpool" (cleverly covered by the Bangles, who can spot a tune worth singing) and the infectious title track. Guarantee: hear this record once and you'll find yourself humming at least one track from it a week later. It flows magnificently from start to end, and subsumes individual accomplishments into a truly group effort. A greatest hits album the first time out. (Actually, the second—Rew included two tracks with the Waves on his 1982 LP, **The Bible of Bop**.)

KATW 2 takes a harder-rocking bent, downplaying the tunefulness slightly to highlight jumping numbers like "She Likes to Groove," the nutty "Maniac House" and a powerful, Janis Joplin-like blues, "Cry for Me." Pointing up the band's only weakness, the lyrics to "Mexico" (written by bassist Vince de la Cruz) don't achieve much in the way of profundity; the soaring vocals and ethnic-flavored Cars-like simplicity, however, make that a strictly academic problem. Other great tracks: "Red Wine and Whisky" and "The Game of Love." Not as glorious as the debut, but a boss record nonetheless.

Katrina and the Waves consists entirely of songs from the first two albums, but they've all been re-recorded or remixed. In most cases, it's an improvement, exposing untapped realms of both pop and power, but the second "Going Down to Liverpool" is a cock-up, obliterating the atmosphere and the hooky melody of the original in an ungodly overheated arrangement. With that one caveat, **Katrina and the Waves** is a rare and delightful triumph.

Evidencing mild signs of commercial self-consciousness, **Waves**, their follow-up, isn't as charming, although several of the tunes have the attributes that make the band so appealing. Foamy Hammond organ, prominent in spots, matches Leskanich's newly soulized singing to push the group towards a Stax sound. The songs aren't as memorable, but are solid enough to make this a reasonably pleasing, albeit not strikingly great, record.

Shock Horror! is a low-budget 1983 release that contains early versions of eight songs, only two of which have since surfaced on the band's albums. "Strolling on Air,"

cut with a former bassist, is an especially rich find; the other tunes (except for an MC5-ish raver, "Atomic Rock'n'Roll") are typically engaging but not particularly well-recorded. Interesting and certainly no embarrassment. [iar]

See also *Kimberley Rew*.

LENNY KAYE CONNECTION

I've Got a Right (nr/Giorno Poetry Systems) 1984

Rock critic, historian, guitarist, Patti Smith musical cohort, New York scene veteran, **Nuggets** albums compiler, Jim Carroll sideman—Lenny Kaye has done a bit of everything, distinguishing himself in most areas. He also leads a band under his own name and released this solo album. Kaye may fumble a few lyrics in an attempt to express schmaltzy emotions, but his obvious sincerity makes up for the occasional prosaic excess. The title track is brilliant pop with an infectious hook and anthemic sound; "Luke the Drifter" is a memorable old-fashioned cowboy ballad updated with a pumping rock beat. A swell record from a swell guy. [iar]

TOMMY KEENE

Strange Alliance (nr/Avenue) 1982
Back Again (Try . . .) EP (nr/Dolphin) 1984
Places That Are Gone EP (nr/Dolphin) 1984
Songs from the Film (Geffen) 1986

The jacket blurb on **Strange Alliance** likened Keene's music to the Only Ones and U2, a superficially accurate but dangerous comparison. In all fairness, he did almost all of it himself (literally, on one tune; with former Washington, DC bandmates from the Razz on bass and drums on the rest of the tracks). The album contains immediately likable, if somewhat melancholy, tunes (with no small debt to the Beatles, as long as we're dealing in comparisons), every one a winner. A later pressing tacks a subsequent single onto the eight original tracks. Lightweight, but Keene's reedy-voiced chiming, arpeggio guitar chords and a piano occasionally icing the cake all suggest he could be a contender.

Back Again (Try . . .) offers a pair of cool covers, recorded live at Boston's Rat plus two of Keene's own tunes. Roxy Music's "All I Want Is You" (why didn't anyone think of doing that sooner?) and the Stones' "When the Whip Comes Down" show Keene's rock'n'roll abilities, while the title track and "Safe in the Light" are in more of a Tom Petty power pop vein, and quite striking at that. **Places That Are Gone** mixes five originals with an Alex Chilton song, all riddled with strong harmony vocals, memorable melodies and a gutsy, even abrasive edge to the guitar-based pop music.

Finally signed to a major label, Keene hooked up with producer Geoff Emerick to make **Songs from the Film**, a confident-sounding album with guts, melodies and occasionally substantial lyrics. A new version of "Places That Are Gone" is the standout, but equally sturdy new songs indicate the depth of Keene's creative resources. Besides a cover of Lou Reed's "Kill Your Sons," the best title here is "My Mother Looked Like Marilyn

KLARK KENT

Music Madness from the Kinetic Kid (A&M/IRS) 1980

Though possessing competence on all the necessary instruments, not to mention a homely yet winningly boy-next-doorish voice, Police drummer Stewart Copeland—here in the guise of Welsh looney Kent—turns in less a do-it-yourself showcase than a mildly amusing show of self-indulgence, pressed on ten inches of green vinyl in a K-shaped jacket, no less! There are plums to be found in the tongue-in-cheek pop-punk of "Don't Care" and the clever Zappaesque instrumental, "Kinetic Ritual," but the other six tracks are merely variations on these two styles.   [jg]

NIK KERSHAW

Human Racing (MCA) 1983
The Riddle (MCA) 1984

On his first album, Nik Kershaw seemed to be a pre-fab pop star with one great song ("Wouldn't It Be Good") and a predilection (not to mention surprising facility) for vocally imitating Stevie Wonder (try "Faces" if you don't believe it) while producing bland and pale electro-dance funk. **Human Racing** was just a hint, however, of Kershaw's sizable talent, much more of which surfaces on **The Riddle**. The title track and the mildly self-critical "Wide Boy" at least double his batting percentage, and the inclusion (again) of "Wouldn't It Be Good" on the US edition makes it even stronger. Kershaw still spends most of his time making wanky dance music, but now seems destined to turn into a junior league Elton John.   [tr]

KEYS

The Keys Album (A&M/nr) 1981

This overlooked gem of a pop album was criminally ignored in England and never released in the States. The four Keys may wear their influences (mainly the Beatles and their producer, Joe Jackson) a bit too much on their sleeves—several of the songs sound unfortunately like outtakes from Joe's **Look Sharp!**—but their knack for pretty melodies, close harmonies and intelligent lyrics make the overall sound original and fresh. And any band that can write such sparklers as "If It's Not Too Much" and "I Don't Wanna Cry" can be forgiven a few minor flaws.   [ks]

CHAKA KHAN

I Feel for You (Warner Bros.) 1984

Soul belter Khan made quite a few albums after quitting Rufus to go solo in 1973, but this one, her most recent, is a real standout, a compelling absorption of beat box percussion, rap and scratch-mix production. A veritable menagerie of producers (9, including Arif Mardin, John Robie, David Foster and Russ Titelman), writers (21, including Prince, Mic Murphy & David Frank and Gary Wright), studios, players and engineers contributed to this amazingly varied sonic menu. The two most notable tracks are "My Love Is Alive," a dynamic assemblage of John Robie synths and cut-up edits, and Prince's "I

Feel for You," a horny love song with guest rapper Grandmaster Melle Mel and harmonicat Stevie Wonder.   [iar]

KID CREOLE AND THE COCONUTS

Off the Coast of Me (ZE-Island/ZE) 1980
Fresh Fruit in Foreign Places (ZE-Island/ZE-Sire) 1981
Tropical Gangsters (ZE-Island/nr) 1982
Wise Guy (nr/ZE-Sire) 1982
Doppelganger (ZE-Island/ZE-Sire) 1983
Cre-Ole: The Best of Kid Creole and the Coconuts (ZE-Island/ZE-Sire) 1984
In Praise of Older Women and Other Crimes (Sire) 1985

COCONUTS

Don't Take My Coconuts (EMI America) 1983

In an interview, black Bronxite August "Kid Creole" Darnell—writer, singer, producer—once alluded to not being able to play reggae as well as Bob Marley or salsa as well as Tito Puente, but possibly being able to combine the two styles better than anyone else. Darnell's internationalist fusion may indeed be one of the freshest new sounds of the '80s, drawing together strains of Latin, reggae, calypso, disco, rap and rock into a unique sound. Add to his vision and smarts an amiable partner in "Sugar Coated" Andy Hernandez (aka Coati Mundi, a solo artist in his own right), the singing, dancing Coconuts and a medley of talented sidepeople of every race and sex, and you have one of the most unusual, influential and formidable bands around.

Thus far, however, he/they have been inconsistent on record: a tentative debut album, a brilliant conceptual follow-up and a less exceptional but more commercially viable third album. On **Off the Coast of Me**, Darnell and company introduce their unusual sound (more Latin-tinged here than on any subsequent LP). Although the material isn't strong enough to make this more than okay, its uniqueness and danceability, along with the Kid's occasionally risqué wordplay, are enough to suggest the band's potential. If Darnell's mindset isn't apparent from the music, the lyrics to "Darrio . . ." make clear the course he intends to follow, abandoning Studio 54 to "check out Mr. James White!"

Launching a conceptual album trilogy, **Fresh Fruit in Foreign Places** stands as Kid Creole's tour de force, a musical odyssey in which the Kid and the Coconuts set off from New York in search of the elusive Mimi. The flavor of the music changes with each stop on the journey, providing a perfect setting for the band to display its mastery of intercontinental bop. Each cut is an adventure, and the album works as well as any rock concept LP ever has. A major achievement.

After the perfect realization of **Fresh Fruit**, nearly anything would have seemed like a bit of letdown. **Tropical Gangsters** (entitled **Wise Guy** in the US) continues its predecessor's concept, but much more loosely. The material is far less adventurous, with the wonderful diversity of the former toned down

in favor of the latter's straighter dance music approach. As a commercial move it worked, at least in Europe, where two tracks ("Stool Pigeon" and "I'm a Wonderful Thing, Baby") became hit singles and raised Darnell to stardom.

Doppelganger is posited as the continuation of "the saga": in this installment, the Kid is cloned by King Nignat's evil scientist. The songs don't all move the story along in narrative fashion—they sound more like the disjunct score of a Broadway musical—but that's fine, since each stands as a marvelous example of Darnell's multifarious brilliance. Mixing '40s be-bop with Carib-beat, reggae, country, funk, salsa and something like highlife, the record sparkles with a cover of "If You Wanna Be Happy" (a 1966 American hit for the Jimmy Castor bunch as "Hey Leroy") as well as such original frolics as "The Lifeboat Party" and "Bongo Eddie's Lament." "Survivors" laments the death of rockers from Frankie Lymon to Sid Vicious, partially in Spanish.

Although less spectacular, **In Praise of Older Women** is another (ca)rousing success, a collection of wittily written, sublimely arranged, energetically performed songs—"Endicott" (cleverly verbose), "Caroline Was a Drop-Out" (a nasty character study), "Particul'y Int'rested" (exaggerated, showy torch song), to name but three—all reflecting the Kid's wonderful attitude and outlook. With Coati Mundi and the Coconuts, plus a stageful of sidemen, King ("self-appointed in Feb. this year") Creole demonstrates his stylistic transcendence by making every track sound different but identifiable; no longer a mere genre dabbler, he's developed the Kid Creole format.

The Coconuts' solo album, produced by Darnell to resemble a stage revue (complete with crowd sounds and stage introductions), is rife with innuendo and internecine squabbling. Darnell sings the introductory title track without the three ladies; the inclusion of "If I Only Had a Brain" (from *Wizard of Oz*), might be someone's idea of an editorial comment. Otherwise, it's a typically rich, clever Darnell dance-funk-Carib-salsa-tango stew, and the Coconuts' smooth harmony vocals are as appealing as ever.   [ds/iar]

See also *Coati Mundi*.

KILBURN AND THE HIGH ROADS

Handsome (Dawn/nr) 1975 (Pye/nr) 1977
Wotabunch! (Warner Bros./nr) 1978
Upminster Kids (PRT/nr) 1983

Although it was still two years before new wave, the London music scene of 1975 wasn't all Queen and the Rolling Stones; pub-rock bands were making fresh and exciting music, laying the groundwork for more radical outfits to follow. Some included musicians whose skills came in very handy when the dam broke in 1977; Kilburn and the High Roads (named after a highway sign), for example, included Ian Dury, saxman Davey Payne (a future Blockhead) and Keith Lucas, who changed his name and helped found the group 999. During a commercially frustrating career that lasted from 1970 to 1976, the Kilburns were cult-popular and influential. Their records serve as neat reminders of a wonderful band.

An album cut in 1974 was shelved due to record company politics; the band's debut was in fact their second recording. (That first LP, **Wotabunch!**, was dredged up and finally released once Dury's solo career took off.) The subsequently-recorded **Handsome** contains much of the same material (co-written by Dury and pianist Russell Hardy) that the group had used the first time. Got that?

Handsome is musically low-key, featuring Dury's clever cockney wordplay and a bit of high-powered blowing from Payne, but it leans overly toward understatement, touching on rockin' '50s styles and dapper '40s lounge subtlety to make it a generally debonair record not above some raving. **Upminster Kids** is a reissue of **Handsome** with several tracks deleted.   [iar]

See also *Ian Dury*.

KILLING JOKE

Almost Red EP (Malicious Damage/nr) 1979 (Island/nr) 1981
Killing Joke (Malicious Damage-Polydor/EG) 1980
what's THIS for . . . ! (Malicious Damage-Polydor/EG) 1981
Revelations (Malicious Damage-EG) 1982
Birds of a Feather EP (Malicious Damage-EG) 1982
"Ha" EP (Malicious Damage-EG) 1982
Fire Dances (EG) 1983
Night Time (EG) 1985

Killing Joke are practitioners of intellectual dance-thrash-rock with a penchant for apocalypse. Something like Birthday Party but more restrained and rhythmic, they have made quite a few intense, angry records of striking strength and fringe weirdness.

Killing Joke is an interface between heavy metal and new wave. With a few synthesizer incursions, the music fields a basic guitar/bass/drums attack, filtered through distortion and tone modulation. Pounding and pulsating at breakneck speed with occasional funk or reggae overtones, the songs ("Wardance," "Tomorrow's World," "Bloodsport") are cold but compelling doomsday anthems.

what's THIS for . . . ! brings funk to ambient music, implying feeling sublimated in a chaotic world. The retreat from empathy and communication doesn't prevent inventive guitar work that hides steady, rhythmic alterations against repetitious, thumping drums—the post-modern dance.

Revelations returns to the brutal stride of **Killing Joke**, racing atonally toward total collapse, social and otherwise. Conny Plank's production hinders the sound, trying to normalize the enchanting wrongness of the group. Perhaps expecting the end of the world, two Jokesters vanished to Iceland before this album was released and worked with bands there, notably Theyr. Far from being pop stars, the quixotic Killing Joke make a habit of putting their money where their mouths are.

The first release after the band's traumatic reorganization, **Birds of a Feather** showcases a more accessible Killing Joke, less shrill and more tuneful, yet retaining all of the manic depression. The 10-inch **"Ha"** was recorded live in Toronto, proving that this is a trend,

83

not a fluke. Both boast excellent production by the band and Conny Plank.

Fire Dances continues in this manner, but with further sonic refinement. "Rejuvenation," "Frenzy" and "Feast of Blaze" all rank among Killing Joke's very best; **Fire Dances** is a frighteningly solid album. After a sabbatical of nearly two years, **Night Time** was released in 1985. Still concentrating on sharpening their overbearing presence by incorporating some space amidst the fury, it contains "Love Like Blood," their catchiest number yet, and a successful single.

The band has never strayed far from the general formula of scorching guitar blur, pounding rhythms and apocalyptic lyrics. However, operating within this framework, they've been able to hone their music to combine the early noise assault with a maturing melodic sense, for a marriage of beauty and the beast few can successfully imitate.   [sg/dgs]

See also *Youth*.

KING

Steps in Time (CBS/Epic) 1984
Bitter Sweet (CBS/Epic) 1985

From the ashes of promising rock-ska band the Reluctant Stereotypes, Coventry "singer" Paul King decided to go for the gold ring with a crass chart-geared quartet he thoughtfully named after himself. Launched in 1983, King perfected a noxious, unmelodic pseudo-funk concoction, dressed themselves in colorful uniforms, and unleashed **Steps in Time** to an inexplicably favorable response. Produced (and drummed on) by Richard James Burgess, who seems to have a facility for such affairs, the album is filled with alarmingly stupid lyrics, fickle stylistic dabbling, arena-rock attributes and art-school pretensions. Awful. "Love and Pride" and "Won't You Hold My Hand Now" became hits.

Bitter Sweet is precisely more of the same. (In fact, the American edition includes "Won't You Hold My Hand Now" for the second time!) Ex-Member Adrian Lillywhite played the drums, resulting in some improvement in that area, but P. King's overbearing, tuneless vocals continue to dominate the band's unpleasant sound. The best thing about this LP is its lyric sheet, which offers no end of giggles.   [iar]

KINGBEES

The Kingbees (Bronze/RSO) 1980
The Big Rock (nr/RSO) 1981

Prefiguring the Stray Cats, the Kingbees were one of the first neo-rockabilly bands to augment nostalgia with an original approach. The West Coast trio's sound on these two albums is sinewy and unpretentious, thanks primarily to frontman Jamie James' economical guitar and no-nonsense vocals. What's more, the material is a first-rate blend of his originals and well-chosen songs by Charlie Rich, Buddy Holly, Carl Perkins, et al. So how come the Kingbees aren't stars?   [jy]

KING CRIMSON

Discipline (EG-Polydor/Warner Bros.) 1981
Beat (EG-Polydor/Warner Bros.) 1982
Three of a Perfect Pair (EG-Polydor/Warner Bros.) 1984

King Crimson, always centered around guitarist extraordinaire Robert Fripp, is a seminal band of our time. Formed originally in 1969, King Crimson from the outset had pivotal influence on both heavy metal and art rock. The ever-principled Fripp, refusing to let Crimson become a dinosaur, broke up the band in 1974, retreating from the tour-album-tour grind to do solo and session work as a self-styled "mobile compact unit." One of his endeavors, the dance-rock oriented League of Gentlemen, spurred Fripp to organize a new King Crimson at the start of the '80s.

Consisting of guitarist/vocalist Adrian Belew, Chapman Stick/bassist Tony Levin and drummer Bill Bruford (the only pre-split vet other than Fripp involved), the current Crimson is a patchwork of modern influences: dance music, art rock, mysticism, minimalism.

Discipline introduces the new cast of characters and displays their attempt at cerebral dance rock; here Fripp is at least as interested in touching the mind as the heart. Not really songs, these pieces are unfolding musical sculptures, played with precision and rare imagination, a mostly-successful synthesis of art rock ambition, new wave simplicity and Kraftwerkian clarity, made with dance clubs in mind.

Beat achieves Fripp's long-sought union of mind, soul and body, centering around the anniversary of Jack Kerouac's *On the Road*. An ode to the beat generation, the album elucidates Crimson's past and purpose, melding Frippertronic tape techniques in equal partnership with Belew's manic physicality. Picking up foreign rhythms and electronic overdubs, the players push their instruments into a new form, akin to fusion and art rock, but miles beyond either, and beyond description as well.

Three of a Perfect Pair is the most disjunct album in recent memory, even from a band that has prided itself on carefully matched contradictions. Side One sports four of Adrian Belew's poorer songs and a self-derivative instrumental; Side Two is nearly all-instrumental, nearly free-form, nearly brilliant. As a bonus, the LP ends with "Larks' Tongues in Aspic Part III," the latest and possibly last in a distinguished series of rhythmically skewed tours de force. Apparently the Frippressive "discipline" that forged the critically acclaimed pop/art synthesis of the first two latter-day Crimson albums is not a permanent condition.   [sg/mf]

See also *Adrian Belew, Robert Fripp, Fripp & Eno, Fripp & Summers*.

KING KURT

Ooh Wallah Wallah (Stiff/nr) 1983
Road to Rack & Ruin (nr/Ralph) 1985
Second Album (Stiff/nr) 1986

This bunch of goofballs picks up exactly where "Stranded in the Jungle" and "Alley Oop" left off—mixing big-band rockabilly with a crazed, comic book mentality and lots of drums. Dave Edmunds produced their first boisterous LP, which raucously proffers such non-classics as "Bo Diddley Goes East" and "Destination Zulu Land." A bit too formulaic for mega-fun, but a good smirky laugh nonetheless.

KK's **Second Album**, known semi-offically as **Big Cock** thanks to a surly looking rooster on the cover, is great, a wildly out-of-control ride through a half-dozen areas of lighthearted rock'n'roll fun, kicking off with an energetic, distinguished version of "Nervous Breakdown." Side One ends with an uncredited voice that sounds suspiciously like Nigel Planer lost in a jazzy novelty number called "Billy." "Horatio" recalls the much-missed Tenpole Tudor; "Pumpin' Pistons" leers like a drunk in a strip joint; the horrific thought of there being a "Momma Kurt" is enough to power this greasy R&B number along. Keep up the bad work, lads. (The disc is available in either black or red vinyl; the tape has two extra tunes.)

Road to Rack & Ruin is an American mini-album culled from tracks on the first LP plus a couple that wound up on the second.   [iar]

KINGSNAKES

How Tuff (Fr. New Rose) 1983
Kingsnakes (nr/Midnight) 1986

Ex-Flamin' Groovies drummer Danny Mihm's band, which otherwise includes Swiss (or French) members, plays in a universal language: smoking, uncomplicated barrelhouse rock'n'roll. The uncredited original songs aren't exactly precedent- setters, but the hard-rocking piano and guitar energy here tells you everything you might need to know, and then some. If there had been more bands like this back in 1976, punk might never have happened.   [iar]

RICHARD H. KIRK

See *Cabaret Voltaire*.

KNITTERS

See *X*.

KNOX

See *Urban Dogs, Vibrators*.

KONK

Konk Party EP (Rough Trade/nr) 1982
Yo (Crépuscule-Island/nr) 1983

Slick and supple New York big-band funk: Konk's seven-piece lineup includes three horn players and a vocalist who also plays conga drum. The sound leans toward Latin, with scads of percussion and sharp arrangements, plus some subtle dub effects thrown in for good measure. Clocking in at over 23 minutes, the four songs on the EP are indeed best for partying, and probably best heard on a mammoth boom box.   [iar]

KRAFTWERK

Kraftwerk 1 (Ger. Philips) 1971
Kraftwerk 2 (Ger. Philips) 1972
Kraftwerk (Vertigo/nr) 1973
Ralf and Florian (Vertigo) 1974
Autobahn (Vertigo) 1974 (EMI/nr) 1982 & 1985
Exceller 8 (Vertigo) 1975
Radio Activity (Capitol) 1975
Trans-Europe Express (Capitol) 1977
The Man Machine (EMI/Capitol) 1978 (Music for Pleasure/nr) 1985
Elektro Kinetik (Vertigo/nr) 1981
Computer World (EMI/Warner Bros.) 1981

Kraftwerk (German for "power station") began in the electronic-heavy metal trend that erupted in Germany in the early 1970s. The four-piece synthesizer group has shown amazing resiliency since, tightening its electro-pop formula to fit smoothly into art rock, then disco and, ultimately, creating the sonic blueprint from which the British new romantic and techno-pop movements arose.

Autobahn is built around an epic version of the title track, a bizarre hit single that broke the band in numerous countries. Enchanting in its simplicity, hypnotic in its construction, the song introduces the repetitiousness that earmarks Kraftwerk's music, but the record's other pieces are less-inspired synthesizer noodling.

Radio Activity coincided with a change of image that sliced away beards and hair and converted Kraftwerk from old hippies into ultramodern sonic engineers; greater use of repetition and purposeful self-limitation is evident, though there is no breakthrough.

Trans-Europe Express introduced Kraftwerk's robotic mask and placed mechanistic aspects of the music up front, in a brilliant epiphany of style. Rhythms and themes recur throughout, with little emotion expressed in the vocals; lyrics emphasize the dehumanization suggested by the production and delivery. Recommended.

The Man Machine further builds on the developments of **Trans-Europe Express**, with the one humanizing effect, background music, giving way to *Star Wars* noises. More work with manipulated vocals—especially on the title track and "We Are the Robots"—takes the automaton stance to the limit. Despite the science fiction themes and heavy musical repetition, the album has inventive, catchy compositions and an eerie warmth. Highly recommended.

Computer World broke years of silence, bringing Kraftwerk into a world that had largely embraced and vindicated their social and musical visions. Improved machinery made for sharper, brighter music, but otherwise Kraftwerk didn't tamper with their style, except that their thematic content shifted from science fiction to industrial documentary. Excellent synthesizer pop.

There are German-language versions of many, if not all, of Kraftwerk's albums. There have also been several compilations released in the UK.   [sg]

ED KUEPPER

See *Laughing Clowns*.

KURSAAL FLYERS

Chocs Away (UK/nr) 1975
The Great Artiste (UK/nr) 1975
Golden Mile (CBS/nr) 1976
Five Live Kursaals (CBS) 1977
In for a Spin: The Best of the Kursaal Flyers (Edsel/nr) 1985

Another seminal pub-rock outfit, the Kursaals are of more interest for what the individuals did after the group split than for their recordings while together. Drummer Will Birch went on to found the Records with guitarist John Wicks (who was a Kursaal Flyer briefly at the end of the band's existence) and has produced a lot of records for various people. Graeme Douglas, whom Wicks replaced, joined Eddie and the Hot Rods, and wrote many of their best songs.

The Kursaals' first two LPs are thinly-produced countryish rock'n'roll, bolstered considerably by Birch's witty lyrics. **The Great Artiste** does contain what may be the earliest recorded cover of a Nick Lowe composition, "Television," later done to better effect by Dave Edmunds.

With Mike Batt producing, the group tried something completely different on **Golden Mile**, an eclectic musical travelogue through rock'n'roll's root styles from swing to Spector to ska to '60s pop-rock. The album is a little-known treasure, similar in concept to the Turtles' equally ignored and enjoyable **Battle of the Bands**.

By the time of **Five Live**, the Kursaals had almost totally weeded out their country strain and, showing the influence of the punk revolution going on around them, got into music with a more driving beat. The band's last hurrah, the "Television Generation" single, is great, proof positive that the band had seen the new light. What else could they do but break up? [ds]

See also *Eddie and the Hot Rods, Records*.

FELA ANIKULAPO KUTI

Fela's London Scene (EMI/nr) 1970
Fela Ransome-Kuti and Africa '70 with Ginger Baker: Live! (Regal Zonophone/Signpost) 1972
Zombie (Creole/Mercury) 1977 (Celluloid) 1985
Gentlemen (Creole/nr) 1979
Everything Scatter (Creole/nr) 1979
Black-President (Arista/Capitol) 1981
Original Sufferhead (Arista/Capitol) 1982
Live in Amsterdam (Arista/Capitol) 1984
Army Arrangement (Celluloid) 1985
Shuffering and Shmiling (Celluloid) 1985
No Agreement (Celluloid) 1985
Upside Down (Celluloid) 1986
2,000 Black (Celluloid) 1986
Mr. Follow Follow (Celluloid) 1986

One of the world's true musical revolutionaries, Fela Kuti's life and work embody most of the contradictions inherent in any major collusion of Western and African styles of thought and art. Born in Nigeria to an affluent Christian family and educated in London, Fela was just another minor highlife bandleader until he received funk's call through Sierra Leonese James Brown-imitator Geraldo Pino in 1966. By weaving funk rhythms into highlife, Fela developed Afro-beat, a mesmerizingly potent style he has refined over the years. Most of his recorded pieces run between seven and seventeen minutes long, beginning rather slowly, with a lengthy piano and/or saxophone introduction (Fela plays both instruments), before breaking into exuberant horn fanfares followed by his call-and-response vocals with a chorus and interlocking polyrhythmic patterns.

In the late '60s, during a stint in Los Angeles, Fela was introduced to black radical politics. Shortly thereafter, EMI released **Fela's London Scene**, which made him

considerably more popular and led to a friendship and collaboration with drummer Ginger Baker. (Their **Live!** album provides a fairly tame example.) But the road of a True Musical Revolutionary is lined with reactionary bushwackers, and the Nigerian government began persecuting him upon his triumphant return from London in the early '70s. As Fela's fame grew, so did his influence. Castigatory songs about government corruption (**Black-President**'s "I.T.T. (International Thief Thief)," for instance), military fascism ("Zombie") and national apathy ("Army Arrangement"), sung by a rich marijuana smoker with a couple of dozen wives who isolated himself in a concrete fortress called the Shrine, challenged the local authorities in a manner they couldn't ignore.

Since 1974, Fela has been arrested several times for various crimes; during a particularly vigorous 1981 crackdown a beating by soliders left him incapable of playing saxophone. His most recent incarceration came in 1984, when he was arrested on money-smuggling charges on the eve of his first major American tour. He was released in April 1986, ending a five-year sentence early.

Celluloid re-released several of Fela's many records in 1985. The most controversial of these was Bill Laswell's remix of **Army Arrangement**, to which he added tracks—by keyboardist Bernie Worrell, drummer Sly Dunbar and talking drummer Aiyb Deng—which reportedly displeased Fela greatly. **Black-President** and **Zombie** are the classics of the batch. [rg]

LADYSMITH BLACK MAMBAZO

Induku Zethlu (Earthworks/Shanachie) 1984
Ulwandle Oluncgwele (Earthworks/Shanachie) 1985

For sheer vocal ecstasy, few groups can match the lush, comforting and sophisticated choral harmonies of the most popular *mbube* group in the South African townships. Using from seven to twelve singers, *mbube* is characterized by uniform *a cappella* harmonies of short phrases sung either in unison or against an overlapping call-and-response pattern. Reflecting on matters both familial and spiritual, and closely tied to their Zulu culture, Ladysmith Black Mambazo's songs (in Zulu) are either hymns or proverbial tales. Rarely has the naked human voice sounded so heavenly. What these two records lack in variety (each contains a dozen or so songs, most of which end on a revelatory "Amen"), they make up for in joyous emotional consistency. [rg]

LAMBRETTAS

Beat Boys in the Jet Age (Rocket/MCA) 1980
Ambience (Rocket/nr) 1981

Sad. This Sussex foursome had most of the pop smarts of fellow neo-mods Secret Affair and none of their arrogance, but evidently believed too strongly in the up-the-movement sentiments of **Beat Boys'** title song ("so sure in what we do") not to be blown away when the fad faded. The first LP is mostly pretense-free, with some great hooks in among a batch of good songs (including two hit singles, "Da-a-a-ance" and a cover of "Poison Ivy.") They even have a sense of humor.

Ambience, however, shows the Lambrettas to be utterly lost. The tunes aren't nearly as catchy and there's obvious confusion as to which stylistic fork in the road to follow, despite uncredited synth dribbles and sax courtesy of Wesley Magoogan, subsequently a member of the Beat. The lyrics, while reasonably intelligent, just aren't smart enough to get serious and still be taken seriously. [jg]

LANDSCAPE

Landscape (RCA/nr) 1980
From the Tea-rooms of Mars . . . to the Hell-holes of Uranus (RCA) 1981
Manhattan Boogie-Woogie (RCA) 1982

RICHARD JAMES BURGESS

Richard James Burgess EP (EMI/Capitol) 1984

A high-tech synthesizer group led by Richard Burgess, producer of Visage, King and Spandau Ballet and one-time soft-rocker (as a member of Easy Street). In Landscape, Burgess sang and handled synthetic and acoustic drums, while his four collaborators played bass, keyboards, trombone and woodwinds, all employing both electronic and traditional instruments. Their work is slick and polished, perfect for sophisticated dance parties, but the songs retain a lyrical cleverness that prevents total bland-out. Not

K L

85

quite an '80s version of 10cc, Land-scape played rhythmic rock, but with a heavy dose of jazzy fusion.

From the Tea-Rooms of Mars has a witty paean to Japanese indus-try ("Shake the West Awake") and a tongue-in-cheek tribute to the film Psycho ("Norman Bates"). Manhat-tan Boogie-Woogie is more directly disco-oriented, with a driving beat and popping bass, but also man-ages clever bits like "It's Not My Real Name" ("I got it from a book . . . ") There was always some-thing detached and artificial about Landscape—as though they were slumming in contemporary music and would rather be doing some-thing more artistic—but they did make enjoyable records that work on a number of different levels.

Burgess' self-produced solo record—six long numbers with a large collection of sidemen (one Landscape bandmate) adding syn-thesizer and guitars—is sophisti-cated and tedious commercial dance music of little interest. (Unless anyone's feminist hackles are piqued by a noxious song called "Thank You Ladies.") [iar]

CLIVE LANGER AND THE BOXES

I Want the Whole World EP (Radar/nr) 1979
Splash (F-Beat/nr) 1980

The big disappointment of Clive Langer's solo career is that he doesn't give it top priority. Presum-ably freed from financial pressures by co-producing numerous hit records for Madness and others, the talented singer/guitarist—judging by his lack of "product"—seems to take only passing interest in making records of his own.

As chief songwriter for the late Deaf School, Langer successfully mated the music hall tradition with highly melodic rock'n'roll, topped off with anxious lyrics about modern day pressures—i.e., a cross between the Kinks and Roxy Music. His solo works are more personal, and lean decidedly to the Ray Dav-ies school, partly because Langer's weary singing has a similar charm.

The five tunes on **I Want the Whole World** are nearly perfect vignettes of anger, tenderness and regret, performed with casual unpretentiousness. Though less effective, **Splash** has its moments, including the charming "Had a Nice Night" and the embarrassingly abject "Splash (a Tear Goes Rolling Down)." Elvis Costello produced two of the tracks.

Clive Langer seems like a guy you wouldn't mind inviting to your house for dinner. [jy]

LAST

L.A. Explosion (Bomp-London/ Bomp) 1979
Fade to Black EP (nr/Bomp) 1982
Painting Smiles on a Dead Man (Fr. Lolita) 1983

The Last, an LA band heavily indebted to the sounds of the '60s—they touch freely on surf-rock, psy-chedelia, folk-rock, etc.—play with modern-day punk intensity. **L.A. Explosion** is a near-perfect debut, marred only by flat production. The performances are stunning, with authentic Vox/Farfisa organ riffs adding color to the melodic guitar leads and Joe Nolte's distinctive vocals. Every track holds up, especially the hypnotic rocker "She

Don't Know Why I'm Here" and the surf-inspired ode to lost youth, "Every Summer Day."

Fade to Black, a 12-inch EP, shows that the Last are indeed a group worth taking seriously. The four tracks are darker and moodier, yet the melodies are so enticing it's a crime this stuff can't find a com-mercial opening.

The Last's second album is another winner, moving the organ up front and showcasing vocals that are at once more confident and demanding. The Last are, without question, one of Los Angeles' most gifted groups. [cpl]

BILL LASWELL

Baselines (Rough Trade/Celluloid-Elektra-Musician) 1983

Material mainman Laswell released his only solo album right around the time people began to realize that his talents extend beyond excellent bass playing into the conceptual stratosphere. **Base-lines'** gutbucket funk foundation and experienced experimentalism provides a convincing resume for his subsequent work as producer to the stars (Mick Jagger, Yellowman, Herbie Hancock, Afrika Bambaataa, etc.). Guests here include fellow/-former Materialists Michael Bein-horn (a frequent co-writer on the LP) and Martin Bisi, percussionist Ronald Shannon Jackson, the ubiquitous Fred Frith and avant-noisemaster extraordinaire David Moss. [mf]

See also *Golden Palominos, Massacre, Material.*

LAUGHING CLOWNS

Laughing Clowns EP (Aus. Missing Link) 1979
Sometimes . . . the Fire Dance EP (Aus. Prince Melon) 1980
3 EP (Aus. Prince Melon) 1981
Mr. Uddich Schmuddich Goes to Town (Aus. Prince Melon) 1982
Laughing Clowns (Red Flame/nr) 1982
Laughter Around the Table (Red Flame/nr) 1983
Law of Nature (Aus. Hot) 1984
Ghosts of an Ideal Wife (Aus. Hot) 1985

ED KUEPPER

Electric Storm (Aus. Hot) 1986

After the Saints broke up in 1978 (and before Chris Bailey reformed it with new personnel), guitarist/ songwriter Ed Kuepper returned to Sydney to form a band with a couple of early Saints' alumnae. The result-ant quintet, dubbed Laughing Clowns, included sax and acoustic piano and cut a strange but remark-ably bracing EP in 1979. The piano both meshes its timbral resonance with Kuepper's guitar chording and co-states melodies with the sax, as well as—at one point—providing an unnervingly calm chordal anchor while the drums run wild. Consider-ing the source, it's a somewhat astonishing, eloquently intense statement of disillusionment and frustration, the romantic and musi-cal clichés of supper club/movie jazz gone berserk.

Oddly enough, the manic energy and tunefulness seemed to dissipate—over the course of two additional EPs—in favor of despair, ennui, cynicism (or just sarcasm?) and decidedly less lustrous music,

in both text and texture. The addition of a trumpeter on 3 does provide a spark, only to be neutral-ized by satirically discordant riffing. By this point, the moments of musi-cal anarchy seem less passionate than perverse.

On **Mr. Uddich Schmuddich Goes to Town**, a shift in the lineup brought in a new saxman and bass-ist (playing acoustic stand-up) and dropped the pianist. The tracks are more succinct, and the overall impression is that of consolidation and retrenchment.

The Red Flame **Laughing Clowns** is a compilation that includes both Prince Melon EPs plus three tracks from the album.

By **Laughter Around the Table**, the Clowns' sound had coalesced into something resembling the Cure gone avant-jazz. The sax playing states the melody lines and pro-vides some credible solos, but the overall effect—while suggesting promising possibilities—is, with one exception, too willfully abrasive and reaches beyond its musical grasp, especially the drumming. [jg]

CYNDI LAUPER

She's So Unusual (Portrait) 1983

This certainly didn't sound like a multi-platinum piece of music or first (or even third) listen, but that just shows to go you. Recognized as the only memorable member of the unlamented Blue Angel, Lauper's big voice grew to scarifying pro-portions here under the sympath-etic production of Rick Chertoff, supported by the able playing of Eric Bazilian and Rob Hyman, lead-ers of Philadelphia's then-obscure Hooters. Since Lauper's songwrit-ing was just getting started, the album depended on a selection of outside material—a potentially dis-astrous minefield—which proved superb, from the Brains' "Money Changes Everything" (much better in Lauper's live 45 version than on the album's somewhat turgid ren-dition) to Prince's unforgettable "When You Were Mine" and, of course, Robert Hazard's "Girls Just Want to Have Fun." It's hard to criti-cize such a popular record contain-ing four huge, diverse hits, but there's really no need to. The big-gest issue as regards the diminutive dynamo is what (and when) she will do for an encore. [iar]
See also *Blue Angel, Hooters.*

LEAGUE UNLIMITED ORCHESTRA

See *Human League.*

THOMAS LEER AND ROBERT RENTAL

The Bridge (Industrial/nr) 1979

THOMAS LEER

4 Movements EP (Cherry Red/nr) 1981
Contradictions (Cherry Red/nr) 1982
Letter from America (nr/Cachalot) 1982
Scale of Ten (Arista/nr) 1985

Thomas Leer's method of recording is as unique as his work: He locks himself in his home studio alone with his synthesizers and tape machines and emerges months later with a record. Apart from pop trends, Leer turns out some of the

most creative and human synthe-sizer work on vinyl.

The Bridge, done in tandem with Robert Rental, is Leer's foray into Germanic technique, consisting of dark electro-pop songs under-lined by repetitious sound patterns and punctuated by appliance noises. Despite the music's hard edge, some tunes—notably "Mono-chrome Day's"—are masterpieces of the form. Uneven but entertain-ing.

With **4 Movements** and **Contra-dictions**, Leer maps out his own special turf: credible white electro-soul. The unselfconscious work bears signs of natural progression rather than conspicuous affectation. The four songs on **4 Movements** and seven numbers on the two 12-inch 45s of **Contradictions** prove beyond doubt that synthesizer music can have energy and warmth, especially on **4 Movements'** stun-ners, "Don't" and "Letter from America."

Letter from America compiles the contents of **Contradictions** and **4 Movements** in toto as a two-record set. [sg]

LEROI BROTHERS

Check This Action (Demon/ Amazing) 1982
Forget About the Danger Think of the Fun EP (Demon/Columbia) 1984
Lucky Lucky Me (nr/Profile) 1985
Protection from Enemies (Demon/nr) 1986

It goes without saying that the five members of Austin, Texas' rhythm'n'rockin' Leroi Brothers are neither related nor named Leroi. The six greasy slices of exuberant, unreconstructed rock'n'roll songs on the Columbia EP also need little explanation—they burn with the spirit of Jerry Lee Lewis pumping in their veins. "Treat Her Right," "Ain't I'm a Dog" and "D.W.I." state the Brothers' case with conviction and excitement. **Lucky Lucky Me** is even better—a full menu of high-energy rock'n'roll tunes played for keeps. "Fight Fire with Fire," the zydeco-tinged "The Back Door" and a quick history lesson, "Elvis in the Army" are among the best cuts. (The first LP, a US indie licensed for UK release, is also well worth hearing.) [iar]

LET'S ACTIVE

Afoot EP (IRS) 1983
Cypress (IRS) 1984
Big Plans for Everybody (IRS) 1986

Cursed by chronic cuteness, North Carolina's Let's Active is probably the most misunderstood of the South's new pop bands. Though dogged by a rosy-cheeked nicest-guys-of-wimp-pop image, they can be downright moody. Led by wunderkind producer/ multi-instrumentalist Mitch Easter, the trio began in 1981, but emerged nationally in the wake of R.E.M., whose first two discs Easter co-pro-duced in his now-fabled Drive-In garage studio. Joining that band's label, Let's Active released a six-song EP, **Afoot**, bringing new mean-ing to such overused pop adjectives as crisp, bright and ringing. All the songs, even those with melancholy lyrics, emerged hook-filled, boppy and ultra-hummable.

But things were not as they seemed. Although perceived as the engineer of the now-sound-of-today in American guitar pop, Easter's own tastes run towards the electronic gadgetry of techno-rock. Also, his two original partners—bassist Faye Hunter and drummer Sara Romweber—were viewed as sidepeople, notwithstanding Easter's egalitarian efforts to counter that impression. In real life, the trio were not just simple, cheerful popsters. Both Easter's love of "sounds" and the band's inner conflicts were explored on **Cypress**, making it deeper and more enduring, though not as immediately winning as **Afoot**. Denser, rambling textural pieces—some wistful, even angry—replaced the pure pop tunes. Few records sound so multidimensional, and Let's Active has, for that reason, been tagged psychedelic—they make sounds you can almost touch.

Both Romweber and Hunter subsequently left the band. Easter did shows with other players (including Windbreaker Tim Lee and Minneapolis' Jay Peck), recording **Big Plans for Everybody** piecemeal with four people, including Hunter and two seemingly permanent sidepeople, Angie Carlson (guitar, keyboards) and Eric Marshall (drums). Far less twinky and hardly cute, **Big Plans** is disturbingly downcast, a melancholy version of pop music that isn't about sad things, but leaves you feeling that way nonetheless. The album connects emotionally, with offbeat songs that really make an impression. [ep/iar]

LEVI AND THE ROCKATS
See *Rockats*.

GRAHAM LEWIS
See *Dome*.

LEW LEWIS REFORMER
Save the Wail (Stiff/nr) 1979

With a dab more arrogance and perhaps a touch more vocal assertiveness on Lewis' part, there'd be no disputing this LP's place on the shelf next to Dr. Feelgood and the first J. Geils Band LP. Lewis (who worked with the Feelgoods very early on and joined up with guitarist Wilko Johnson after this solo excursion) lacks no authority on blues harp, handily living up to the aspiration announced in the title (as does Rick Taylor's guitar). Gavin Povey (of the Edge and other groups) adds pianistic lubrication to a program that includes astute covers (especially James Brown and—yes!—Status Quo) as well as sharp originals. [jg]

LIJADU SISTERS
Horizons Unlimited (Afrodisia/nr) 1983
Double Trouble (Serenghetti/Shanachie) 1984

True eccentrics, the Lijadu twins were among the great unexpected pleasures to arrive via the West's mid-'80s affair with African music. Influenced equally by Fela Anikulapo Kuti's funk-mutated Afro-beat and juju, the Lijadu lay down their sweetly-sung unison vocals over drums that do the talking, and guitars and pianos that provide rhythmic bedrock. Unlike Fela, however, the Lijadus leave politics to politicians, and confine their Yoruban lyrics to such subjects as heart and home, kin and country. [rg]

LILIPUT
Liliput (Rough Trade/nr) 1982
Some Songs (Rough Trade/nr) 1983

Formerly known as Kleenex, with a batch of 45s under that name, the three Swiss women in Liliput play a now-popular form of anti-rock characterized by choppy rhythms, harsh melodies and atonal vocals. Amazingly, they exhibit such upbeat enthusiasm in their attack that the music acquires a prickly charm. Hard on the ears, though. [jy]

ARTO LINDSAY/ AMBITIOUS LOVERS
Envy (EG) 1985

Lindsay, an American who grew up in Brazil, came to New York in the mid-'70s intent on becoming an artist. Only later did he adopt music as his medium and develop a unique percussive style of singing and playing guitar—generally around the beat, seldom on it—and no melodies, thank you. His guitar is untuned; his voice strains to deliver its quota of sounds. (Lindsay's two main vocal influences are James Brown and the sound of people screwing.) In assembling the Ambitious Lovers, Lindsay balances the electronic expertise of Peter Scherer with Brazilian percussionists and injects himself as the catalyst, with help from chum Mark Miller of the Toy Killers.

On their debut outing, Lindsay and the Lovers recapitulate his career—the tight, anti-melodic structures of DNA, the charging funk-noise of the Golden Palominos—yet deliver something new as well. "Let's Be Adult" is an unabashed dance-floor move and, on "Dora," Lindsay turns crooner, caressing a soulful melody anyone could hum. The catch is that it's in Portuguese—oh, that Arto! Lindsay's words are tantalizingly oblique, but there's nothing oblique about his record's lusty cry for recognition. [mf]

See also *DNA, Golden Palominos, Lounge Lizards, Love of Life Orchestra.*

VIRNA LINDT
Shiver (Compact Organization/nr) 1984
Play/Record (Compact Organization/nr) 1985

This Swedish singer, co-writing her material with Compact's resident genius, Tot Taylor, mixes genres of alarming variety into one unpredictable mutation of '60s film themes, chilly electronic pop, barrelhouse ballads, Eastern European intrigue and dramatic tape effects, etc. Walking a centerpoint between flaky/fascinating and flaky/boring, **Shiver** is more an album to possess than play. [iar]

LINES
Therapy (Red-Fresh/nr) 1981
Ultramarine (Red/nr) 1983

A quest for creativity or self-indulgence of the highest order? Four Londoners construct rudimentary songs (actually just riffs, they're so skeletal) over repetitive drum rhythms with spare bass, guitar, vocal and trumpet accompaniment. Some are outré adventures (like a ragaesque track that sounds as though it were performed by bees),

others more conventional, though the fragile vocals are mostly blurred by echo. "Searching . . . for some jewel of the mind we hope that we'll never find." *Please,* look elsewhere. [jg]

JAH LION
See *Lee Perry*.

LIQUID LIQUID
Liquid Liquid EP (nr/99) 1981
Successive Reflexes EP (nr/99) 1981
Optimo EP (nr/99) 1983

Along with labelmates ESG, Liquid Liquid exemplified the minimalist funk movement that swept New York's music underground in 1981. The band's impressive five-song debut (one side recorded live) fused metalphones with congas, marimba and other percussive gadgetry to create hypnotic urban-tribal funk. Except for the vocals, that goal is realized. **Successive Reflexes** works also, although full-scale production values alter the previously skeletal sound.

Optimo—four more songs on another 12-inch—continues the rhythmic intensity, and is specially notable for "Cavern," a lengthy bass/drums groove that provided the musical basis for Grandmaster Flash & Melle Mel's "White Lines (Don't Do It)." [gf/iar]

LISA LISA & CULT JAM
See *Full Force*.

LITTLE BO BITCH/ LONELY BOYS
Little Bo Bitch (Cobra/nr) 1979
The Lonely Boys (nr/Harvest) 1979

A rare instance of an American improvement on a British album. Although this fresh-faced band's name and LP title was originally Little Bo Bitch, their US label wisely insisted on changing both. Overlooked in the imbroglio, unfortunately, was the record itself: competent non-wussy power pop with some amusing and memorable tunes, among them "Annoying All the Neighbours" which happily recalls the Members' early rabble-rousing. Andy Arthurs' production makes it all sound good. An album worth picking up in a bargain bin. [iar]

LITTLE BOB STORY
High Time (Fr. Crypto) 1976
Off the Rails (Chiswick/nr) 1977
Little Bob Story (Fr. Crypto) 1978
Come On See Me (Fr. RCA) 1978
Light of My Town (RCA/nr) 1981
Live (Fr. Seaside) 1985

Like a French version of Dr. Feelgood or early Eddie and the Hot Rods, Little Bob Story played a hot'n'sweaty blend of R&B, rock'n' roll and blues, alternating between well-chosen covers and credible originals. They got mixed up in the London punk scene just as it was getting underway in 1976, cutting some singles and a 1977 album for Chiswick, the first indie label there.

High Time, recorded as a quartet, features versions of "Lucille" (Chuck Berry), "I'm Crying" (the Animals), "It's All Over Now Baby Blue" (Bob Dylan) and "You'll Be Mine" (Willie Dixon) as well as five original songs written by singer Bob Piazza.

Off the Rails, produced in England by Sean Tyla, adds another guitarist to the lineup, and consists almost entirely of original material. **Little Bob Story** is a collection of singles, including "Don't Let Me Be Misunderstood" and "Tobacco Road," both of which predate the debut LP. [iar]

LIVE SKULL
Live Skull EP (nr/Massive) 1984
Bringing Home the Bait (Homestead) 1985

One of New York's currently (and deservedly) hip downtown bands, Live Skull is a guitars-bass-drums quartet who play slow, grinding hypno-rock that is occasionally strident but more often dense and ominous. There *are* vocals buried in the mix, but you won't notice them much—the relentless wash of semi-organized guitar noise is clearly the band's focal point. Not exactly memorable, but not easily forgettable, either.

Their first long-player features more prominent vocals as well as livelier tempos; some tracks move along at a hardcore tear. Guitar textures vary from an atonal din to Killing Joke-style ringing quasimetal, and parts of "Skin Job" sound exactly like Hüsker Dü. Vocals, whether by bassist Marnie Greenholz or guitarists Mark C. and Tom Paine, are all appropriately snarly. Most of the LP parallels the work of fellow New York avant-droners Sonic Youth, Lydia Lunch and Swans. Live Skull may be an LP away from forging their own sound, but **Bringing Home the Bait** shows much promise. [iar/dgs]

L

87

LIZARD
Lizard (Jap. King) 1979

Strangler Jean-Jacques Burnel produced this Japanese band's first LP in London, and gave it a not-surprisingly bass-heavy sound. But the comparisons don't end there: Lizard plays synth-laced dance music with simple rhythms and weird vocals (in Japanese). Politically aware, playful, squiggly and dense, Lizard's complex hybrid typifies the fascinating Japanese response to Anglo-American new wave. [iar]

L.L. COOL J
Radio (Def Jam-CBS) 1985

Fresh from his electrifying appearance in *Krush Groove* (a film whose plot is essentially the story of the Def Jam label), young rapper L(adies) L(ove) Cool J(ames) released **Radio**, a great full-length album—"reduced by Rick Rubin" —to enormous Stateside success. (It went gold.) From the monster box that gleams on the cover to grooves like "I Can't Live Without My Radio" and "You Can't Dance," J touches all the right cultural totems, delivering his sharp-tongued raps with adolescent urgency and a deliciously snotty attitude. The rhythm tracks are typically stripped-down and aggressive; raps on familiar subjects offer clever rhymes that bear repeated listening. [iar]

RICHARD LLOYD
Alchemy (Elektra) 1979
Field of Fire (Mistlur/Celluloid) 1985

The former Television guitarist's first solo album is a gem. Assisted by other New York scene veterans, Lloyd spins a beautiful, understated web that proves him to be a successful songwriter, a limited but engaging vocalist and a relaxed team player who never hogs the spotlight. The material (especially the wonderful title track) pursues the melodic, sensitive side of late-period Television, leaving all the rough edges and manic intensity to Tom Verlaine.

Six years and several lifetimes later, Lloyd returned from oblivion with an all-new album, recorded in Stockholm with local musicians and released in England (later America) via a Sweden-based label. Amazingly, it's another doozy, a loud, energetic rock record with sturdy melodies, intelligent lyrics and confident playing. Lloyd's singing in spots is too raw-throated to be pleasant, but the material holds up regardless, and fine guitar work is a fair trade-off. **Field of Fire** bears no resemblance whatsoever to **Alchemy**, but is just as relevant, enjoyable and welcome. [iar]

LOS LOBOS

...and a Time to Dance (Rough Trade/Slash) 1983
How Will the Wolf Survive? (Slash-London/Slash-Warner Bros.) 1984

Lacking serious competition, Los Lobos are the leading Mexican-American rock band of the '80s; it wouldn't matter if there were contenders for that honor, however—these four East Los Angelenos (plus ex-Blaster saxman Steve Berlin, who joined in time for the second record) are peerless masters of their music. Smoothly incorporating vastly divergent influences—early rock'n'roll, jazz, rockabilly, *norteño*, Tex-Mex folk music—into a multi-colored patchwork of joyous noise beautifully displayed on the seven-song **Time to Dance**. From a cover of Ritchie Valens' "Come on Let's Go" to the infectious, accordion-driven "Let's Say Goodnight," singer/guitarist David Hidalgo leads his merry men on a spicy romp (in two languages) back and forth across musical borders few can traverse with such easy dexterity.

How Will the Wolf Survive? is an occasionally more serious venture, delving into heavy blues ("Don't Worry Baby") and tender social commentary ("Will the Wolf Survive?," subsequently a big country hit for Waylon Jennings) as well as finding time for a jolly square dance ("Corrida £1") and an airy instrumental ("Lil' King of Everything"). Hidalgo's reedy tenor and the band's subtlety and skill make the album immediately likable; depth and variety ensure its enduring pleasure. [iar]

LOCAL HEROES SW9

Drip Dry Zone (Oval/nr) 1980
New Opium/How the West Was Won (Oval/nr) 1981

Unlike the Gang of Four, this London trio offered radical political perspectives that are neither simplistically axiomatic not delivered amid musical fireworks; the Heroes' brand of dialectical materialism largely avoids slogans and, while its more fluid rhythm'n'pop derives from a similar basis, odd bits of pop

and tricky turns here and there replace the Gang's jagged-edge approach.

The first album, **Drip Dry Zone**, is more accessible if less ambitious than the second, which is actually half the Heroes and half a solo outing by guitarist Kevin Armstrong. His side is less precise, more indulgent and meandering, but once acclimated to his tracks' reggaefied lope, you may well find that he's not as spaced out as he seems, but is as engrossing as his group. (Armstrong went on to work closely with Thomas Dolby.) [jg]

KEN LOCKIE

The Impossible (Virgin/nr) 1981

COWBOYS INTERNATIONAL

The Original Sin (Virgin) 1979

Ken Lockie, an early cog in the vague Clash/Pistols axis that revolved around guitarist Keith Levene and eventually led to the creation of Public Image Ltd., *was* for a time Cowboys International, specializing in deceptively chipper numbers about fear and loathing and love betrayed. **The Original Sin** is a cornucopia of clever and well-tooled high-tech pop songs, every one of them a should-have-been hit. Lockie's vocals provide a human counterpoint to the crisp metallic happenings in the instrumental work, aided by a musical team that includes drummer Terry Chimes as well as a guest turn by Levene.

The Impossible is less successful, due mostly to stiff production by Steve Hillage. Lockie's accompaniment is once again impressive—Magazine's John Doyle and John McGeoch, Nash the Slash, Steve Shears (then of Ultravox), among others—and his songs still have a guileless punch when they aren't buried under the slick production. The whole thing never quite meshes, but all the parts are there to be enjoyed if you have the patience.

Lockie, like Levene, subsequently relocated to New York, where he participated in numerous other musical projects. [sg]
See also *Dominatrix*.

LORA LOGIC

See *Essential Logic*.

LONDON

Animal Games (MCA/nr) 1978

Signed to an unhip label, London cut one lone LP without a proper producer, yet still earned posthumous notoriety when drummer Jon Moss, following stints in the Damned and other bands, surfaced in Culture Club. For London's part, maybe a producer could have sorted out the confusion that dominates **Animal Games**—an angry Pistols/Who wallop on one hand and a strong pop sensibility on the other, plus a vocalist who makes Hugh Cornwell sound like Paul McCartney. Still, two slashing yet tuneful tracks suggest the exciting sound that might have been. [jg]

LONE JUSTICE

Lone Justice (Geffen) 1985

It isn't that Lone Justice's album is bad—it's not—but all the build-up

that preceded the release of this LA quartet's record raised expectations that these frisky countryfied rock tunes—Linda Ronstadt on speed, perhaps, or Dolly Parton backed by the Blasters—couldn't possibly satisfy. Maria McKee is a fairly impressive singer, an energetic, melodic powerhouse with a Southern twang and a slight Patsy Cline catch, and the band's solid enough, but it still doesn't amount to anything out of the ordinary. McKee's "A Good Heart," ridden to the top of the charts by Feargal Sharkey, is far more memorable than anything here. [iar]

LONELY BOYS

See *Little Bo Bitch*.

ROY LONEY AND THE PHANTOM MOVERS

Out After Dark (nr/Solid Smoke) 1979
Phantom Tracks (nr/Solid Smoke) 1980
Contents Under Pressure (nr/War Bride) 1981
Having a Rock'n'Roll Party (Rockhouse/War Bride) 1982
Fast & Loose (nr/Double Dare) 1983

Singer/guitarist Roy Loney assembled the Phantom Movers after a four-year retirement from performing that followed his split from the Flamin' Groovies in 1975. While the Groovies without Loney turned to Merseybeat, Byrds covers and other '60s soundalikes, **Out After Dark** finds him rekindling the pure American rock'n'roll spirit that originally inspired them. Abetted by two ex-Groovies (drummer Danny Mihm and guitarist James Ferrell), Loney's band excels at straightforward, unsophisticated party music made strictly for fun. Loney's return is made more impressive by his singing, which lost nothing during his layoff.

Phantom Tracks consists of smokin' live tracks and new studio cuts that aren't terribly different from the material on **Out After Dark**. The only change worth noting is that about half of the **Phantom Tracks** are out-and-out rockabilly; **Out After Dark**, while rooted in rockabilly, is contemporary-sounding rock'n'roll.

Contents Under Pressure, recorded after both Mihm and Ferrell had been replaced, goes off in a number of directions: Yardbirds-type rave-ups, rockabilly, ska, heavy metal and even corporate mush. A total failure.

As the name implies, **Having a Rock'n'Roll Party** is a return to what Loney does best, and the results are accordingly a big improvement over the previous outing. The band even dips into the Groovies' catalogue for "Gonna Rock Tonight" and "Dr. Boogie." Also released in France, **Fast & Loose** features various lineups and includes a version of the Groovies' "Teenage Head."

He may not be an original, but as someone who sees a return to the carefree stance and simplicity of pre-progressive rock as a revitalizing force for today's music, Loney generally pulls it off with a lot more panache than most. [ds]

LONG RYDERS

10-5-60 EP (nr/PVC) 1983
Native Sons (Zippo/Frontier) 1984
State of Our Union (Island) 1985

TOM STEVENS

Points of View EP (nr/Pulse) 1982

With roots in the South but formed in California, the Long Ryders color mild '60s revivalism with country stylings (steel guitar, autoharp, mandolin, etc.) on the five-song **10-5-60 EP**, produced by Earle Mankey. Pleasant but too easygoing to be earthshaking, the foursome took care of that business on **Native Sons**, a stirring dose of memorable and unpretentious rock-country-rock that incorporates **Highway 61** Dylan, paisley pop, Kingston Trio balladry and wild rock'n'roll. All this and a guest vocal appearance by Gene Clark to legitimize the Long Ryders' update of the Byrds' pioneering hybrid. Great! **State of Our Union**, however, is a disappointing major-league debut, a sometimes corny collection of weak melodies, inane lyrics and misguided performances. The Ryders seem to have been fooled by their own image. "Looking for Lewis and Clark" is a pathetically bad monotone; other songs on which they align themselves with American populist sentiment are only slightly better. As produced by ex-Record Will Birch, it sounds good in spots, but heavyhandedness is clearly no asset.

On his early solo EP, bassist Tom Stevens (joined by two sidemen) plays guitar and sings half a dozen original melodic pop songs that wouldn't fit the band's cowpoke country format but are quite appealing on their own. [iar]
See also *Danny & Dusty*.

LORDS OF THE NEW CHURCH

Lords of the New Church (Illegal/IRS) 1982
Is Nothing Sacred? (A&M/IRS) 1983
The Method to Our Madness (IRS) 1984
Killer Lords (Illegal/IRS) 1985

Formed by ex-Dead Boy Stiv Bator (following a solo turn and the developmental Wanderers, during which time he misplaced the "s" from his surname) with ex-Damned guitarist Brian James, ex-Sham 69/Wanderers bassist Dave Tregunna and ex-Barracudas drummer Nicky Turner—what a pedigree!—the Lords emerged with a fully realized debut album that draws on their individual and collective strengths. Dense and powerful, with Bator's sneering whine setting the tone and attitude, the Lords combine '60s punk with '80s apocalyptics to create an original sound that updates the Stooges into the present post-punk world without taming their outrage. Only a few awful, indulgent lyrics (one song attempts a tribute to the New York Dolls by merely stringing song titles together) detract from the record's dark power.

Many took exception to the first LP's claustrophobic, murky production; **Is Nothing Sacred?** substitutes a livelier, crisper sound, with keyboards and horns contrasting the band's throaty roar. Thus armed, the Lords unfortunately ran out of material after the first song. Following the excellent "Dance with Me" (take that, Bauhaus!), it's straight down the songwriting slope, stopping off only briefly to ram through the Grass Roots' venerable "Live for Today" for no audible purpose. As a soundtrack for a gothic punk horror movie, the Lords' second album gets the ambience right, but that's all.

The third LotNC album hits a fair compromise, modulating both the volume and the velocity to lighten the mood and cut the stylishness. As a result, **The Method to Our Madness** resembles a cross between **Raw Power** and **Rebel Yell**. It's the band's least distinctive but most popular-sounding record, with "Murder Style," "Method to My Madness" (featuring a funny spoken interjection by IRS owner Miles Copeland) and a pretty ballad, "When Blood Runs Cold," to recommend it. By sacrificing their mystery and danger, the Lords of the New Church are revealed as nice guys after all.

The **Killer Lords** compilation includes not only remixes of essential album tracks but a hysterically nasty mugging of Madonna's "Like a Virgin," a solid and straight reading of John Fogerty's "Hey Tonight," and ex-Advert Tim Smith's duff but amusing "Lord's Prayer." [iar]

LOUNGE LIZARDS

The Lounge Lizards (Editions EG) 1981
Live from the Drunken Boat (Europa) 1983
Live 79/81 [tape] (nr/ROIR) 1985

TEO MACERO/LONDON PHILHARMONIC ORCHESTRA/LOUNGE LIZARDS

Fusion (Europa) 1984

EVAN LURIE

Happy? Here? Now? (Bel. Crepuscule) 1985

JOHN LURIE

Stranger Than Paradise (Crammed/Enigma) 1986

Despite some interesting personnel in their initial lineup and a memorable debut album, New York's Lounge Lizards will never be remembered as anything more than an interesting footnote in rock's history. This has less to do with the "fake jazz" label they took for themselves than with the purely social nature of their rock connection: they played jazz-as-exotica to a downtown new wave audience.

Nonetheless, **The Lounge Lizards** remains a minor masterpiece for the way it remains true to its Monk-derived jazz (including two covers of Thelonius Sphere himself) by subverting it still further with Arto Lindsay's atonal guitar playing. Whatever Lindsay may lack as a conventional guitarist, he makes up with an innate rhythmic savvy that never fails to entertain and engage. Drummer Anton Fier, as a rock player learning the jazz ropes, approaches his kit a bit cerebrally, but ironic detachment was never far from the Lizards' agenda. Saxman John Lurie's compositions here turn out to have been his best, alternating a loving, melodic lilt with film noir-ish exhilaration.

By the time of **Live from the Drunken Boat**, the Lurie brothers (John and pianist Evan) were playing with a different and less interesting band; the results are slight and forgettable. The Lizards joined

their producer, Teo Macero (veteran producer/arranger of many a distinguished jazz record) as he indulged his post-romantic orchestral fantasies with the London Philharmonic on **Fusion**, an uninteresting '50s "third stream" symphonic jazz composition.

The **Live 79/81** cassette features sharp performances from New York (including their first gig), Cleveland, London and Berlin. The core of the debut lineup (the Luries, Fier and bassist Steve Piccolo) remains intact, but two other guitarists besides Lindsay divvy up the tracks. Nine originals, plus covers of Thelonius Monk's "Epistrophy" and Earle Hagen's classic "Harlem Nocturne."

John Lurie went on to star in and score the film *Stranger Than Paradise*. Evan recorded a solo piano record. Lindsay and Fier, who left the Lizards after the first album, formed the Golden Palominos and have done many other interesting projects as well. In mid-'86, the Lounge Lizards (i.e., John Lurie) were signed to Island. [mf/dgs]

See also *Golden Palominos, Arto Lindsay*.

LOVE AND ROCKETS

Seventh Dream of Teenage Heaven (Beggars Banquet) 1985

The group that refused to die! Love and Rockets reunites three-fourths of Bauhaus, which was supposed to have broken up in 1983. Daniel Ash and Kevin Haskins formed Tones on Tail; bassist David J., following his stint with the Jazz Butcher, joined them, whereupon they ditched the only non-Bauhaus alumnus and transmuted into Love and Rockets. **Seventh Dream of Teenage Heaven** is an odd, unnervingly varied album. The absence of doom crooner Peter Murphy allows his three former bandmates to utterly avoid any trace of his poseur pretensions. There's folk-rock, funk, ominous rock and a number that resembles the Moody Blues crossed with Bow Wow Wow—a huge, boomy drum sound smothered with what sounds like a mellotron and close harmony vocals. "Saudade," a similar (albeit instrumental) piece, blends aspects of New Order and the Dream Academy. The faintly Beatlesque, pretty "Haunted When the Minutes Drag" suggests an '80s take on Donovan in a droney acoustic mode. Further blurring the stylistic concept, a version of the Temptations' "Ball of Confusion" is reasonably faithful to the original. Neat record. Wonder what it all means. (The British CD adds three tracks.) [iar]

LOVE OF LIFE ORCHESTRA

Extended Niceties EP (nr/Infidelity) 1980
Geneva (nr/Infidelity) 1980

Love of Life Orchestra was created by Peter Gordon (sax, keyboards, composition) and David Van Tieghem, a talented, smart-aleck avant-garde percussionist with ties to new music composer Steve Reich. Both have gone on to greater fame as elder statesmen of the downtown music scene in New York, but these early works stand as an important developmental chapter.

Extended Niceties debuted LOLO's avant-disco in fine form.

"Beginning of the Heartbreak"/"Don't, Don't" is quite powerful, pushed along by a vividly colored piano and the distinctive, kinetic rhythm guitars of guests Arto Lindsay and David Byrne. **Geneva** succumbs to blandness as Lindsay and Byrne are supplanted by less-inspired full-timers and Gordon attempts to spread his clichéd writing over a longplayer. Exceptions: "Revolution Is Personal" and "Lament," which offers the rarity of a truly interesting drum solo. [mf]

See also *Peter Gordon, David Van Tieghem*.

LOVE TRACTOR

Love Tractor (nr/DB) 1982
Around the Bend (nr/DB) 1983
'Til the Cows Come Home EP (nr/DB-Landslide) 1984
Wheel of Pleasure (Compendium-Rough Trade/DB) 1985

Like the Raybeats and others, Georgia's Love Tractor sticks (not quite exclusively) to instrumental rock'n'roll, with reference points in the non-vocal golden rock era of two decades ago. Unlike the Raybeats, they're not so style-conscious, so you get far fewer sly references to the Ventures and other camp heroes, and more outright flirtation with fusion and cocktail lounge muzaks. Though the material is inconsistent, **Love Tractor** never lacks poise.

Love Tractor exhibits new polish on **Around the Bend**, seeking to avoid stagnation by adding vocals on a few tracks. Not very memorable ones, though. The diverting **'Til the Cows Come Home** EP fails to answer questions about Tractor's future path, since it's a compilation of odds and ends. [jy]

See also *Method Actors*.

LENE LOVICH

Stateless (Stiff/Stiff-Epic) 1979
Flex (Stiff/Stiff-Epic) 1980
New Toy EP (Stiff/Stiff-Epic) 1981
No-Man's-Land (Stiff/Stiff-Epic) 1982

Lene Lovich helped pave the way for female vocalists to use as many vocal eccentricities as their male counterparts, to be unafraid to play a solo instrument (Lovich's is sax), and—as important as anything else—to feel free to adopt and project personae that are obviously feminine yet neither super vampish nor mellow/submissive.

During her erratic and sporadic career, Lovich has made a batch of good tracks, but has yet to deliver a whole satisfying LP. This seems to stem from the fact that she and husband/guitarist/songwriting partner Les Chappell are not exactly prolific; even with choice selection of other people's material (including songs given her expressly by Fingerprintz's Jimme O'Neill and Thomas Dolby) she has released only three full albums since 1979.

Her debut LP, **Stateless**, sports a pair of great singles: "Lucky Number" and "Say When." But despite her distinctive chirp'n'yodel vocals, the keyboard-dominated arrangements and the blend of great old American pop-rock with spooky occult and Balkan overtones, she needed more consistent material. Better production also might have helped; the US version has a reshuffled song order and a much-needed remix.

Flex has a more modern studio sound and uses synthesizers, adding more varied vocal colors (and emphasizing the distinctive deep male backing voices). The songs are more consistent, yet even the standouts, original and otherwise, don't match those on **Stateless**. The expansion of Lovich's religio-mystical worldview only partially compensates.

New Toy, a foretaste of **No-Man's-Land**, is a single expanded to EP length; only the title track is truly worthy of any attention. Surprisingly, although two of the songs appear in slightly altered versions on the subsequent LP, "New Toy" itself doesn't. Lacking it, **No-Man's-Land** is another half-good LP, with Lovich's appropriation of "It's You, Only You" (from Holland's Meteors) again demonstrating her ability to bring out melody and create her own airy, eerie atmosphere. Lovich has not released an album since then. [jg]

See also *Sinceros*.

NICK LOWE

Jesus of Cool (Radar/nr) 1978
Pure Pop for Now People (nr/Columbia) 1978
Labour of Lust (Radar/Columbia) 1979
Nick the Knife (F-Beat/Columbia) 1982
The Abominable Showman (F-Beat/Columbia) 1983
16 All-Time Lowes (Demon/nr) 1984
Nicks Knack (Demon/nr) 1986

NICK LOWE AND HIS COWBOY OUTFIT

Nick Lowe and His Cowboy Outfit (F-Beat/Columbia) 1984
The Rose of England (F-Beat/Columbia) 1985

Once a teen dream with pop group Kippington Lodge, then a pub-rocker with Brinsley Schwarz, Nick Lowe burst into new wave as a pop mastermind who could give you anything you wanted, and the heck with social significance. The cover of his first solo album graphically displays his kaleidoscopic versatility in six different poses/personae, all fairly sleazy. Lowe's tunes, though, are invariably well-crafted, charming (within a '60s pop context) and offbeat enough to hold attention.

For its US release, the wildly diverse **Jesus of Cool** was retitled **Pure Pop for Now People** by corporate wimps. Besides a well-scrambled track order, **Pure Pop** substitutes the smooth "They Called It Rock" for **Jesus'** stompy "Shake and Pop" (in fact, the same song with a different arrangement) and adds "Rollers Show," a parodic tribute to the Bay City Rollers. The US album also inserts Lowe's studio recording of "Heart of the City" in place of the searing live version on the British record. (The same live recording, but with a Dave Edmunds vocal replacing Lowe's, appears on Edmunds' **Tracks on Wax 4**.)

Labour of Lust is a calmer collection, sticking mostly to medium-tempo rockers played by the dependable Rockpile (Lowe, Edmunds, drummer Terry Williams and guitarist Billy Bremner). Instead of stylistic variety, Lowe concentrates on love songs, both silly ("Switch Board Susan," "American Squirm") and sincere ("Without Love," "You Make Me"). The album also contains his sole US hit single, "Cruel to Be Kind."

Following **Labour of Lust**, Lowe put his solo career on hold to assist Edmunds and play in Rockpile. He resumed with **Nick the Knife**, not surprisingly filled with more foot-tapping love songs. His emotional palette had broadened to include unhappy ("My Heart Hurts," "Too Many Teardrops," "Raining Raining") as well as happy ("Queen of Sheba," "Couldn't Love You Any More Than I Do") subject matter. And of course there are the obvious musical/lyrical borrowings Lowe-watchers enjoy getting incensed about.

The Abominable Showman is fast out of the starting gate with "We Want Action" and "Raging Eyes." After that, Lowe turns surprisingly serious on tracks like "Time Wounds All Heels" and "Wish You Were Here." The album closes on a curious (for Lowe) note: "How Do You Talk to an Angel" even has strings.

He returned to form on **Nick Lowe and His Cowboy Outfit** (which actually features almost the same band as on the preceding album). Once again, Nick essays a variety of pop styles, from Tex-Mex ("Half a Boy and Half a Man") to '50s instrumental ("Awesome"). Don't take the LP title too seriously; on a good day, Lowe takes nothing seriously.

Maintaining the same lineup but cobbling together a far better set of tunes, Lowe made **The Rose of England** with a lot more evident effort. While the stylistic variety is impressive, the lack of consistent quality mainly comes down to specific songs. Winners: Costello's "Indoor Fireworks" (predating its appearance on **King of America**), John Hiatt's "She Don't Love Nobody" and Lowe's own "Lucky Dog," "The Rose of England" and "(Hope to God) I'm Right." A new treatment of "I Knew the Bride," produced and performed by Huey Lewis and band, is unsettlingly anxious but reasonably entertaining; a few other items are throwaways or sappy ballads. **The Rose of England** offers some of the deepest, most reassuring music Lowe's done in ages.

16 All-Time Lowes is an aptly titled compilation of his early solo work, from "So It Goes" and "Heart of the City" through "When I Write the Book." Of special interest: precise musician credits for each track. Statisticians (and those who feel Lowe's quality level has been steadily waning) should note that almost half of these songs appeared on his first album. **Nicks Knack** is a complementary collection of another sixteen tracks, including Rockpile's "Now and Always," a rare B-side ("Basing Street") and a balanced selection of mostly second-string material from all of Lowe's pre-Cowboy Outfit albums.   [si/iar]

LUCY SHOW

The Lucy Show EP (Piggy Bank/nr) 1984
...undone (A&M) 1985

This quartet plays rich, mellifluous songs which owe more than a little to the Comsat Angels and early

Cure. On **...undone**, which is quite good for a debut LP, they weave nice webs of layered guitar, subtly accentuated with piano and occasional synth, but the dynamics and textures range from A to B. Despite several memorable songs—especially the opening "Ephemeral (This Is No Heaven)"—the Lucy Show don't give the impression their hearts are in it.
          [dgs]

LUNA TWIST

Luna Twist (Statik/nr) 1983

This commercial modern rock band from Belgium is basically interchangeable with Wang Chung, the Fixx and a hundred others. The only notable break in Luna Twist's routine comes from extraneous sounds, including free-form sax riffs, sequencer bursts, jet noises and vocal shrieks, which serve as distractions but nothing more. Like their equally indistinguishable competition, Luna Twist's songs are fine, their musicianship faultless and the whole exercise thoroughly redundant.   [iar]

LYDIA LUNCH

Queen of Siam (nr/ZE) 1980
   (Widowspeak/nr) 1985
13.13. (Situation 2/Ruby) 1982
The Agony Is the Ecstacy EP (4AD/nr) 1982
In Limbo EP (Doublevision/nr) 1984
The Drowning of Lucy Hamilton (Widowspeak/nr) 1985
The Uncensored Lydia Lunch [tape] (Rough Trade/nr) 1985
Hysterie (Widowspeak/CD Presents) 1986

Lydia Lunch's career since deep-sixing Teenage Jesus and the Jerks has been an unpredictable path governed by boredom, sarcasm, romance, perversity and whatever musicians or collaborators are convenient at the time. **Queen of Siam** proves, at the very least, that she can do more than just scream (although her version of the Classics IV hit, "Spooky," shows that she ain't exactly Beverly Sills, either). Half the album consists of muted, somber variations on her Teenage Jesus fear-and-suffering dirges, but the real surprises are songs like "Lady Scarface," in which the big band arrangements (by *Flintstones*- theme composer Billy Ver Planck) turn Lunch's wry asides into a Billie Holliday nightmare.

On the heels of **Queen of Siam**'s release, Lunch and the LP's co-conspirator, Pat Irwin, formed 8-Eyed Spy, the lifespan of which set the pattern for many of Lydia's later ventures: assemble a band, work with it for a while, disband it when she got "bored"; six months later some vinyl would appear. (One conglomeration, an alleged blues abortion called the Devil Dogs, didn't last long enough to be documented.)

13.13., concocted with a trio of ex-Weirdos, was hypothetically an attempt at new psychedelia; actually it revived the grind-and-caterwaul of Teenage Jesus as filtered through **Metal Box**-era PiL, all deviant guitar and rolling rhythms. Like her previous stuff, it manages to be simultaneously fascinating and annoying.

Lunch hung out in Europe for a

while with Nick Cave and the Birthday Party, a sympathetic association reflected in some recordings. **The Agony Is the Ecstacy** (a record on which she splits sides with the Party) captures an impromptu London gig featuring Banshees bassist Steve Severin on feedback guitar and is easily one of the most extreme Lunches to date. On the other hand, a 12-inch single done with Party guitarist Rowland Howard of "Some Velvet Morning" (an old Lee Hazelwood song—Nancy Sinatra has been a longtime touchstone for Lydia) recalls the softer moments of **Queen of Siam**.

In Limbo is a six-track disc with a supporting crew that includes Thurston Moore of Sonic Youth and former Contortion/Bush Tetra Pat Place. With snail's-pace tempos, Moore's shards of acrid, harsh guitar, and Lunch's trademark ululations, it's typically rough going, but recommended for anyone who has trouble contending with an entire album's worth of her clamor. **The Drowning of Lucy Hamilton** is the soundtrack to a film (*The Right Side of My Brain*) starring Jim Foetus and Henry Rollins. Lucy Hamilton herself is actually Lydia's collaborator on the record, which is all eerie instrumentals orchestrated with piano, honking bass clarinet and guitars that sound like they're being played with ice picks and hedge clippers. Something rather different for Lunch, and less like background music than most soundtracks. **The Uncensored** tape is all spoken-word; **Hysterie** is an ambitious two-disc career- spanning compilation, going all the way back to her TJ/Jerks days and winding up with some of her recent collaborative projects (Sonic Youth, die Haut, Einstürzende Neubauten and others).

Besides her recording career, Lunch has appeared in several underground films and collaborated with Exene Cervenka (of X) on a book of poetry. Throughout, she continues to project the most negative charisma since Johnny Rotten.
          [rnp/dgs]

JOHN LURIE

See *Lounge Lizards*.

LURKERS

Fulham Fallout (Beggars Banquet/nr) 1978
God's Lonely Men (Beggars Banquet/nr) 1979
Greatest Hit (Beggars Banquet/nr) 1980
Final Vinyl EP (Clay/nr) 1984

PETE STRIDE AND JOHN PLAIN

New Guitars in Town (Beggars Banquet/nr) 1980

Despite the occasional glimmer of greatness, the Lurkers were never much more than a lightweight, second-string punk band, playing simple numbers in a plodding manner over repetitive drum figures. The tantalizing bits suggested a much better band lurking (sorry) inside; the post-split record by southpaw guitarist Pete Stride and part-time Lurker Honest John Plain (otherwise in the Boys) proves that the group was not without talent, but simply lacked the ability to express itself successfully.

Fulham Fallout has the advantage of crystal-clear sound (thanks to producer Mick Glossop) and a few impressive songs ("Ain't Got a Clue," "Shadow") but suffers from tedium and general punky cloddishness. **God's Lonely Men** seems to employ only one beat; the overbearing rhythm section's dense, muffled pounding gives the record an air of mock metal. Two poppier tracks hint at better things ahead musically, but time had run out for the Lurkers. **Greatest Hit**, subtitled **Last Will and Testament...**, gathers up twelve numbers from the two LPs and adds a half-dozen single sides. Surprisingly enough, it's much better than either of the preceding albums, and has enough fun times to make it a worthwhile investment in low-brow punk. Not essential, but good enough.

The relationship between the Boys and the Lurkers began sometime before the latter broke up—guitarist John Plain appears on two of the **Greatest Hit** tracks, including one called "New Guitar in Town"—so it took only a melding of the two bands to provide backing for the collaborative effort by Stride and Plain. **New Guitars in Town** starts off with a Spectoresque version of Sonny Bono's "Laugh at Me" and gets better from there. Rather than a flashy collection of solos as the title suggests, the two stringleaders show off their singing and songwriting more than guitar pyrotechnics, which remain decidedly in the background. All in all, a delicious collection of rollicking pop-rock, played with spit and spirit.   [iar]

LYRES

The Lyres EP (nr/Ace of Hearts) 1981
On Fyre (nr/Ace of Hearts) 1984
The Box Set (Fr. New Rose) 1986

After the demise of DMZ—one of Boston's most exciting bands—singer/organist Jeff "Mono Mann" Conolly put together the Lyres to play authentic '60s garage-rock in the '80s. Once an imitator of his heroes, Conolly has become their equal, and the band's debut 12-inch EP showcases a tough, spirited brand of rock'n'roll that sets the standard other neo-garage rockers must aspire to.

On Fyre is simply the apex of modern garage rock, an articulate explosion of colorful organ, surging guitars and precisely inexact singing. Drawing on just the right selection of songwriters (Ray and Dave Davies each get tapped once; another esoteric cover revives a song originally recorded by ex-Beatle drummer Pete Best), and adding his own brilliant creations (especially the urgent "Help You Ann," powered by phenomenal guitar tremelo), Conolly leads the Lyres on a nostalgic trip that is utterly relevant to the here and now. [cpl/iar]

M

New York*London*Paris*Munich
(MCA/Sire) 1979
The Official Secrets Act (MCA/
Sire) 1980
Famous Last Words (nr/Sire) 1982
High Life Music EP (Swahili-
Albion/nr) 1983

Better known as Robin Scott, M
looks set to go down in Top 40 history as a glorious one-hit wonder.
But oh, what a hit! Easily the highlight of his first LP, "Pop Muzik"
combines the moronic appeal of a
brilliant semi-electronic novelty
record with the sturdy danceability
of a hot disco mix. Give this man
credit for partially inventing hip-
hop and modern electro-pop in one
fell swoop. Other cuts on the LP,
such as "Cowboys and Indians" and
"That's the Way the Money Goes,"
are just as silly but less immediate,
leaving the listener free to observe
how much Scott can sing like Bowie.

He shifts gears on **The Official
Secrets Act**, playing superficial
foolishness against an underlying
current of fear; "Join the Party,"
"Working for the Corporation,"
"Your Country Needs You" and
"Official Secrets" conjure up murky
images of a threatening world. Scott
clearly derives pleasure from
inventing unexpected melodies and
bending his tunes with quirky production touches.

On **Famous Last Words** Scott
confirms his status as a doodler; no
two tunes are alike. Everything's a
little odd, but never unpleasant, so.
In short, this third LP possesses
only the limited value of cleverness
in a vacuum. One longs for less calculation, and references beyond the
studio.

In 1981, Scott collaborated on an
album with Yellow Magic Orchestra
keyboardist Riuichi Sakamoto. [jy]
See also *Riuichi Sakamoto*.

KIRSTY MACCOLL

Desperate Character (Polydor/nr)
1981

Daughter of folk-music giant
Ewan MacColl, singer/songwriter
Kirsty cut one great two-sided 45
for Stiff ("They Don't Know"—later
a hit when covered by Tracey
Ullman—b/w "Turn My Motor On")
that went nowhere, and then scored
a major hit with the twangy "There's
a Guy Works Down the Chip Shop
Swears He's Elvis" (included on
Desperate Character in two versions). For the album, ace sidemen
like Billy Bremner, Lew Lewis and
Gavin Povey helped her whip up a
lively rock/country/pop stew that
resembles a female-singer version
of Rockpile. With nary a bad track
in the bunch, **Desperate Character**
cries out for a follow-up.

The story picks up in 1984, when
Kirsty married producer Steve Lillywhite. The first musical fruits of
this union appeared in early '85—
she released a Stiff single of Billy
Bragg's "A New England," drastically overhauling the once-spare
tune into a pop extravaganza that
earned her another hit. Ullman,
meanwhile, included another Mac-
Coll tune on her second album.
[iar]

TEO MACERO

See *Lounge Lizards*.

MADNESS

One Step Beyond . . . (Stiff/Sire)
1979 (Virgin/nr) 1985

Work Rest & Play EP (Stiff/nr) 1980
Absolutely (Stiff/Sire) 1980
(Virgin/nr) 1985
7 (Stiff/nr) 1981 (Virgin/nr) 1985
Complete Madness (Stiff/nr) 1982
Madness Present the Rise and Fall
(Stiff/nr) 1982
Madness (nr/Geffen) 1983
Keep Moving (Stiff/Geffen) 1984
Mad Not Mad (Zarjazz-Virgin/
Geffen) 1985

The world needs more bands
like Madness. One of the original
London perpetrators of the ska
revival, they've grown from a silly
novelty group into full-scale international superstars, beloved by
seemingly everyone in Europe, from
tot to pensioner. Though diversity
in contemporary music is generally
laudable, the factionalism it sometimes engenders isn't; Madness'
ability to appeal to different audiences suggests that pop needn't
always polarize listeners into
incompatible camps.

Produced by Clive Langer and
Alan Winstanley, Madness records
tend to sound the same, which
testifies more to their light-hearted,
bubbly style of execution than any
actual uniformity of material. The
band's inspirations originally came
(less nowadays) primarily from ska
and the music hall—i.e., sing-along
music—though you're likely to find
classic rock'n'roll, Arabic overtones, utterly insipid jokes, easy-
listening pop, incisive observations
on society (not unlike Ray Davies)
and just about everything else.

Highlights of **One Step Beyond**
include "Night Boat to Cairo,"
Prince Buster's "Madness" and
"Chipmunks Are Go!" (The subsequent 7-inch EP has four cuts,
including "Night Boat.") **Absolutely**
features the giddy "Baggy Trousers" and "Return of the Los Palmas
7." **7** contains "Grey Day," an
uncharacteristically somber ballad,
and "The Opium Eaters," a tinkly
movie-music instrumental.

Complete Madness is highly
recommended because it collects
the band's many hits, but in reality
any Madness LP guarantees lively
and—dare it be said?—wholesome
fun.

Displaying added maturity and
creative breadth, **The Rise and Fall**
is another fine crowd-pleaser, with
such likable fare as "Tomorrow's
Just Another Day" and "Our House,"
a virtual sociology primer on
English family life.

The guys finally did themselves
a favor and signed in the US with
Geffen Records, who (in typically
golden-touch fashion) managed to
scare up a hit single for the band in
the form of the aforementioned "Our
House." That track is included on
Madness, a compilation of
previously-released UK tracks dating back to 1979. (**Madness** contains about half of **The Rise and
Fall** in addition to oldies like "Night
Boat to Cairo" and "It Must Be
Love.") Good stuff.

What followed was a period of
tumult: Madness left Stiff, keyboardist Mike Barson left Madness and
the band set up their own Zarjazz
label. **Keep Moving**, their final LP
as a septet, offers a full platter of
typically tuneful, thoughtful, lightweight pop songs covering familiar
ground, musically and lyrically.
"Wings of a Dove" incorporates a
gospel choir; "Michael Caine" uses
a cute pop-culture gimmick to sell
an otherwise weak number. The
growing vocal skills of Carl Smyth

and Graham McPherson have made
them the band's most recognizable
trait; the others' seemingly effortless playing is easy to take for
granted.

Although it has its moments,
Mad Not Mad is an uneasy, odd
record, sounding a bit like Bryan
Ferry in more than one spot
("Yesterday's Men," "Coldest Day"),
offering a quizzical look at America
("Uncle Sam") and covering Scritti
Politti's beautiful "Sweetest Girl"
with little élan. With Barson gone,
keyboards are played by Steve
Nieve and Roy Davies; a lot of guest
musicians add strings, horns, and
backing vocals. Not unpleasant, but
unsettlingly out of the Madness
mainstream.   [jy/iar]

MADONNA

Madonna (Sire) 1983
The First Album (Sire/nr) 1985
Like a Virgin (Sire) 1985
True Blue (Sire) 1986

Forget for a moment, if you can,
all the personality, press and image
that attends these albums and consider their contents. The first
(reissued in the UK with a different
cover as **The First Album**) consolidates simpleminded singles
("Lucky Star," "Borderline," "Holiday") and five other lengthy numbers for a bouncy program of dance
music that owes a lot to the remnants of disco. The album is a bit
slick; Madonna's lack of a discernable style keeps it from being a
creatively significant debut. Three
producers (Reggie Lucas, Jellybean
Benitez and Mark Kamins) make for
different sonic settings, but in every
case the beat and the voice—
alternately soulful and
coquettish—are the focal points.

Like a Virgin (reissued to add
the alluring "Into the Groove") is a
far more impressive affair, a full-
blown self-invention that covers all
the bases and made Maddy a global
star. Nile Rodgers' outrageous production packs every song with
hooks and gimmicks, finishing each
off with a fine sonic shine. "Material
Girl," "Like a Virgin," "Over and
Over," "Dress You Up" and others
(incidentally, Madonna the songwriter was involved in only one of
the tunes named) all serve to build
her character, fill dance floors and
remain in pop fans' memories
indefinitely. Love her or hate her,
Like a Virgin is a first-rate record.
[iar]

MAGAZINE

Real Life (Virgin) 1978
Secondhand Daylight (Virgin) 1979
The Correct Use of Soap (Virgin)
1980
Play (Virgin/IRS) 1980
Magic, Murder and the Weather
(Virgin/IRS) 1981
After the Fact (Virgin/IRS) 1982

Singer/writer Howard Devoto
left the Buzzcocks in an effort to
move beyond punk and power pop
and take rock music to new levels
of complexity and sophistication
without losing the recently
regained energy of the form. To this
end, he formed Magazine with
then-unknowns John McGeoch
(guitar/sax), Barry Adamson (bass),
Dave Formula (keyboards) and
drummer Martin Jackson (replaced
after just one LP). They advanced a
music of many styles and moods
with lyrics full of obfuscation and a
lush, many-faceted sound, still

maintaining the rudimentary passion au courant in the music of 1978. Devoto disbanded Magazine in 1981 to pursue a solo career.

Real Life sports an eerie Grand Guignol feeling throughout its nine punchy pop tunes, including the hit, "Shot by Both Sides." Adamson's driving bass and Formula's electronics dominate the sound, while Devoto paints a deranged world of betrayal and suspicion, mixing urban alienation with material like Tibetan mysticism and the Kennedy assassination. But beneath the dark veneer is humor and top-notch music.

Secondhand Daylight benefits from the change in drummers—John Doyle having a more fluid and less chunky style than his predecessor. Devoto's simplified lyrics focus on insurmountable emotional distances between people, aurally realized with dislocated, keyboard-heavy music.

The Correct Use of Soap is more upbeat, returning to **Real Life**'s popness less the manic depression, and shows Magazine to be a mature and cohesive band. The mix adds an element of funk, and Devoto shows a Costello-like flair for playful lyrics. The album includes some of Magazine's best songs, including "Sweetheart Contract," "Philadelphia" and "Song from Under the Floorboards." Highly recommended.

Play records an Australian concert, but a great performance is marred by production that distances Devoto's vocals from the music. Guitarist Robin Simon, John McGeoch's replacement, fails to integrate fully, but the band is relaxed and in control, and the album continues in **Soap**'s joyously sardonic vein. "Give Me Everything" and "Twenty Years Ago," both otherwise non-LP tunes, are included.

Magic, Murder and the Weather is controlled by Dave Formula's keyboards, with Devoto taking a turn for the grotesque, as on the casual ditty called "The Honeymoon Killers." The prevalent moods are sarcasm and resignation, making Devoto's decision to break up the band almost simultaneously to the record's release small surprise.

After the Fact collects Magazine's singles, including "Shot by Both Sides" and "Touch and Go," as well as a number of B-sides. The American version additionally contains "My Mind Ain't So Open," "Goldfinger" and "The Book," also originally issued as B-sides.   [sg]

See also *Armoury Show, Howard Devoto.*

FRED MAHER

See *Robert Quine.*

MALARIA!

White Water EP (Bel. Crépuscule) 1981
Emotion (Bel. Crépuscule) 1982
New York Passage EP (nr/Cachalot) 1982
...Revisited [tape] (nr/ROIR) 1983

Aggressively noisy and discordant, these five German women manage to make a surprisingly tedious, uninvolving racket—it's not even repulsive, just numbing. All in the name of art, mind you. And the problem on **White Water** isn't their German lyrics—they sound the same on the English side of **New York Passage**, recorded in NYC.

Emotion, the band's sole studio album, is far better organized and nearly acceptable, in a rugged, dissonant kind of way. The music is a varied mass of synthesizers, rhythms and sound effects; the German and English lyrics— blurted, chanted and yelled— take on such generalities as money, jealousy, power, death and passion. A virtual philosophy course on vinyl. Not easy listening, but powerful medicine with real impact.

Revisited—a live tape recorded in 1983 at two American club dates—suffers from mightily indistinct sound and an unnervingly loose sense of rhythm. (The vocals alternate languages, but that hardly matters.) Nonetheless, the relentless drive has an incantatory power, and other bands certainly have made far more horrific and less organized noise.   [jg/iar]

STEPHEN MALLINDER

See *Cabaret Voltaire.*

MANDINGO

Mandingo Griot Society (nr/Flying Fish) 1978
Watto Sitta (Celluloid) 1985

The Mandingo people of West Africa pass their folklore down through the griots, singers who tell stories and praise for pay, accompanied by the kora, a 21-string instrument that sounds like an oddly-tuned guitar. The group Mandingo (formerly the Mandingo Griot Society) fuses traditional kora plunking with jazz, blues and reggae tinges, supporting kora master Foday Musa Suso's tingly lines with Fender bass and a healthy percussion arsenal. Trumpeter Don Cherry is a featured soloist on the first LP; **Watto Sitta** is technically enhanced by ubiquitous producer Bill Laswell's electronic drums and guest musician Herbie Hancock. The group sounds like it's been put through a processor, emerging as Laswellian pitter-patter with a plain-wrap griot edge.   [rg]

ZEKE MANYIKA

See *Orange Juice.*

THOMAS MAPFUMO

Gwindingwi Rine Shumba (Earthworks/nr) 1980 & 1986
Ndangario (Earthworks/nr) 1983
Mabasa (Earthworks/nr) 1984
Mr. Music (Earthworks/nr) 1985
The Chimurenga Singles 1976— 1980 (Earthworks/Shanachie) 1985
Chimurenga for Justice (Rough Trade/Shanachie) 1986

From nightclub singer to political firebrand, Thomas Mapfumo's career has elevated him to near-sainthood in his native Zimbabwe. **The Chimurenga Singles**, recorded with the Acid (as in bitter) Band, carries an interesting disclaimer: "The quality of these tracks leaves much to be desired, but remember they were made under war conditions." Influenced by Voice of Zimbabwe radio broadcasts, Mapfumo participated in the country's liberation struggle, and was jailed for his troubles. The singles deal in political innuendo, are sung in the native Shona language. The sound is rushed, as if time were of the essence; as the cymbals hyperventilate and the guitars skitter along (in imitation of thumb piano), Mapfumo sings serious and subtle songs of revolution.

His later recordings, made with Blacks Unlimited, are more languid and even include some love songs. The grooves are lazier, but the guitar retains a rapid-fire hunt-and-peck quality.   [rg]

MARC AND THE MAMBAS

See *Marc Almond.*

MARCH VIOLETS

Natural History (Rebirth/nr) 1984
Electric Shades (nr/Relativity) 1985

Although they've been together five years, the March Violets have never actually recorded an album as such—both LPs are compilations of singles. They cite Beefheart as one of their main inspirations, but there's about as much audio evidence of that as there is of Bach. What is detectable is surging, guitar-based rock somewhere between U2 and the Cult. Generally running over five minutes each, most of the songs are longer than they need to be.

The Violets have had two different lead singers, and it makes a major difference in the quality of their sound. Original vocalist Simon D. (who left to form the Batfish Boys) sang with an unpleasant snarl; upon his departure, rhythm guitarist Cleo (no surnames in this band) took over, and her voice is truly lovely and tuneful, with a wide emotional range. Not only does she make the band sound warmer and more melodic, she's attractive enough to be an asset in the cruel commercial world. The Violets supported Siouxsie on a 1986 US tour, and may well be headed towards a major breakthrough.   [dgs]

MARTHA AND THE MUFFINS

Metro Music (DinDisc/Virgin International) 1979
Trance and Dance (DinDisc/nr) 1980
This Is the Ice Age (DinDisc/nr) 1981
Danseparc (RCA) 1982

M+M

Mystery Walk (RCA) 1984

Martha and the Muffins were originally just clever amateurs who had fun fooling around in Toronto. However, the subtly catchy "Echo Beach" made them chart stars in the UK, bringing their days of leisure to an abrupt halt. A minor miracle of this slick age, **Metro Music** captures a mild-mannered, unpretentious group at its most charming, before stress and self-consciousness took its toll. Vocalist Martha Johnson has a sometimes awkward but always personable style of singing on "Echo Beach," "Indecision" and "Paint by Number Heart"; it's as if she walked into a studio to tell what happened to her that day rather than to perform. Sax player Andy Haas adds jazzier, more exotic flavorings (à la Roxy Music's Andy Mackay), while a confident rhythm section preserves the hard foundation. Some might call **Metro Music** wimpy, but a more sensitive observer would judge it the result of introverts trying to rock, and—on their own terms— succeeding handily.

A more mature sounding effort, **Trance and Dance** treads admittedly less appealing waters. The title track and "Was Ezo" retain the haunting quality of "Echo Beach," but other songs seem a little glib and too willing to be cute. Martha and the Muffins sound like they're having less fun than before; second vocalist Martha Ladly (composer of "Was Ezo") left the group after this LP.

With **This Is the Ice Age**, the band painted itself into a corner. "Women Around the World at Work," a catchy stab at a mainstream single, lacks the innocence that was their strong point. Much of the LP suffers from arid artiness— they're too cool for pop but can't settle comfortably into another groove. Sax player Andy Haas left after this LP.

Thus reduced to a quartet, Martha and the Muffins ventured down funky Broadway on **Danseparc**, adding a throbbing beat to the blend. As a detour, the title track is fine, and the guest sax provides a bit of continuity, but in other spots, Johnson's self-important singing grates and Mark Gane's overdrive guitar isn't enough to cut through the repetitious, overbearing pounding. The tunes that have a jazzy pop sensibility are good, but the battle between humming and bumping is clearly lost to the forces of motion. On a positive note, the album ends with "Whatever Happened to Radio Valve Road?," a beautifully textured languid instrumental.

Mystery Walk presents the penultimately reductive group of Martha and Mark—billed as M+M— paradoxically playing prosaic social-conscience funk on "Black Stations/White Stations" and rediscovering delicate, attractive melodicism (best exemplified by "Cooling the Medium"). Throughout, the record mixes a less-aggressive intellectual dance-floor sound and enticingly atmospheric, jazz-tinged pop. An excellent return to form.   [jy/iar]

PATRICK D. MARTIN

Patrick D. Martin EP (nr/IRS) 1981

This American 12-inch was gathered from a batch of British singles; the mysterious Mr. Martin plays bright electro-pop that sounds like a simplified "Pop Muzik," but he sings in a heavy accent that eliminates any trace of mechanical coolness. "Computer Datin'" is the standout track.   [iar]

HUGH MASEKELA

Techno Bush (Jive Afrika) 1984
Waiting for the Rain (Jive Afrika) 1985

Trumpeter Masekela, in self-imposed exile from South Africa for more than two decades (he now lives and records in Goborone, Botswana) is a one-time jazz traditionalist who rediscovered his musical and political roots during the '70s, and the recorded evidence is on these two recent LPs. On **Techno Bush**, the *mbaqanga* rhythms support Masekela's trumpet percolating in staccato ecstasy. Like most secular South African township music, Masekela's songs combine the political with the pastoral. **Waiting for the Rain** is a more Westernized version, although it does

92

include a cover of Fela Kuti's first major hit, "Lady." His politics are still very evident, but he appears to be striving for an even wider audience. [rg]

MASSACRE

Killing Time (Celluloid/OAO-Celluloid) 1982

Punk-funkers Bill Laswell (bass) and Fred Maher (drums) of Material came together with avant-garde veteran Fred Frith (guitar) in this radical power trio. The distinctively skewed melodies of the album's composed half—mostly on the first side, a brilliant procession of techniques and ideas—bear the Frith hallmark. Propelled by the virtuoso Material rhythm section, Frith plays with unprecedented urgency—no cold cerebration here. The improvisations are tough and sinewy too, benefiting from Frith's experience in Henry Cow. Highlights: the bouncy title cut and "Corridor," a manic exercise in machine-gun feedback. [mf]

See also *Fred Frith, Bill Laswell, Fred Maher, Material, Skeleton Crew.*

JAMES MASTRO

See *Bongos.*

MATERIAL

Temporary Music 1 EP (Red) 1979
Temporary Music 2 EP (Red) 1981
Temporary Music (Fr. Celluloid) 1981
American Songs EP (Fr. Celluloid) 1981
Busting Out EP (ZE-Island) 1981
Memory Serves (Celluloid-Island/Celluloid-Elektra- Musician) 1981
One Down (Celluloid/Celluloid-Elektra) 1982

Originally formed to back Daevid Allen when the erstwhile Gong leader first toured the US, Material began as a small core of New York-based musicians around which an endless string of interesting one-shot gigging and recording bands have formed. Although bassist/producer Bill Laswell is the only remaining musician to carry the Material flag, the original triumvirate with Michael Beinhorn (synthesizer, tapes, vocals) and Fred Maher (drums) made a virtue of eclecticism, effectively blending funk, rock, experimentalism and jazz into a subtle, credible fusion music all their own.

Not that they managed it right away. **Temporary Music 1**, produced by Giorgio Gomelsky, shows a promising progressive-rock band toying with funk and quickly miring itself in extraneous noise. But the funk-rock fusion takes hold on the sequel, as Stockhausen (figuratively) meets Moroder, and that approach didn't let them down thereafter. The **Temporary Music** album reissues the two EPs on one disc.

American Songs, which features an intriguing appearance by guitarist Robert Quine on two new items, is just interesting enough not to be expendable.

Memory Serves is Material's most jazz-tinged album, with its complement of prominent jazz players on cut after relentless cut. Guitarist Fred Frith is also featured, starting an intermittently ongoing alliance. The procession of textures is dazzling, the funk cuts like a knife and the horn work is disciplined within tight structures. As "black" classical and dance music refined with a rock sensibility, **Memory Serves** is a highly original crossover.

One Down extends the experiment to urban pop music with almost equal success, aided by Nile Rodgers, Nona Hendryx, Frith, Oliver Lake and many others. However, it lacks the edge of **Memory Serves**, and Maher's departure is probably the reason. Saxophonist Archie Shepp, black power spokesman and angry young man of '60s jazz, puts in a politically interesting but musically low-key appearance on Hugh Hopper's "Memories."

Material's extraordinarily skillful rhythm section has been involved with many other projects. They formed Massacre as a trio with Frith; Maher has also worked with Richard Hell and Lou Reed, among many others. Laswell played with a lot of new musicians but has more recently become one of America's hottest producers, working with everyone from Yellowman to Mick Jagger. [mf]

See also *Afrika Bambaataa, Golden Palominos, Nona Hendryx, Bill Laswell, Massacre, Robert Quine.*

MAZARATI

Mazarati (Paisley Park) 1986

Another product of Prince's musical factory, Minneapolis' Mazarati have been favored with a record contract, the attentions of the Revolution's bassist as songwriter and producer, a paisley'n'jewelry fashion consult and one honest-to-god Prince song ("100 MPH"). Unfortunately, the band itself hasn't got an ounce of personality, and this album drifts along interminably through eight laborious, smooth rock-funk numbers. [iar]

RICHARD MAZDA

Hands of Fate (IRS) 1983

The producer of many cool people's records (e.g., the Fleshtones, Fall, Wall of Voodoo, Tom Robinson), Mazda's own music consists of slick soul-funk that bears more than a passing resemblance to ABC's first album. ("Big Sound" all but quotes the lyrics of "Look of Love.") Guest appearances by many of his studio charges get lost in the smooth, bass-popping sound; Mazda may be a multifarious musician (mostly keyboards and guitar) and an ace producer, but he's not much of a singer or songwriter. A flawless exercise in search of a talent to focus it on. [iar]

MC5

Kick Out the Jams (Elektra) 1969 & 1983
Back in the USA (Atlantic) 1970
High Time (Atlantic) 1971
Babes in Arms [tape] (nr/ROIR) 1983

The MC5's latter-day relevance lies less in their music—the in-concert **Kick Out the Jams** sounds closer to heavy metal than anything else—and more in the political attitudes behind that music; "Kick Out the Jams" and "Motor City Is Burning" are obvious harbingers of "Anarchy in the UK." Unfortunately for Detroit's 5, their utopian beliefs didn't translate to vinyl with the intensity of, say, the first Clash album. **Kick Out the Jams** has plenty of high energy rock, with science-fiction noise ("Rocket Reducer No. 62" and "Starship," co-credited to Sun Ra) thrown in for class. But will the revolution be recorded by Elektra Records?

Evidently not. The next MC5 album, produced by Jon Landau (before he met Springsteen), finds them downplaying the rabble-rousing in favor of under-three-minute odes to "High School," "Teenage Lust" and "Shakin' Street" ("where all the kids meet"). There are also performances of "Tutti Frutti" and the Chuck Berry title cut, with its refrain "I'm so glad I'm living in the USA." Sarcasm? A timely return to the roots? Probably both. At least the concise songs are easier to take than the first LP's hippie-era sprawl.

Having lost their audience between the first two albums, the MC5 felt free to put down the best playing of their recording career on the totally ignored **High Time**. Song lengths are back up, but the band stretches out comfortably on "Sister Anne," "Over and Over" and the jazzy "Skunk (Sonicly Speaking)."

The **Babes in Arms** tape is a belated appendix to the catalogue. It consists of early 45 sides done for indie labels, alternate takes and remixes (some scarcely different from the originals) from their albums, plus one otherwise unreleased cut.

Did the MC5's circular saga prove the invincibility of pure pop? In any case, their records and legend remain an oft-cited influence on the nose-thumbing irreverence and chaotic energy of punk groups. [si]

See also *New Order, Patti Smith.*

MALCOLM McLAREN

Duck Rock (Charisma/Island) 1983
D'ya Like Scratchin' EP (Charisma/Island) 1984
Fans (Charisma/Island) 1984
Swamp Thing (Charisma/Island) 1985

Besides being an imperialistic cultural plunderer (a non-judgmental designation), Malcolm McLaren is one of latter-day rock's true visionaries. His role in the formation and promotion of the Sex Pistols has been construed as everything from inspired instigator to Machiavellian manipulator, and his solo career has been as righteously criticized as it's been influential. The ever-provocative McLaren tends to bring out the moral indignation in people.

It's hard to say just what McLaren does. He's more an assembler than a creator, piecing together artifacts from various musical cultures in such a way that at the end of the day, his own input seems invisible. And yet his perspective, as hip outsider, has continued to provide a link between his Anglo-American audience and Third World forms. If McLaren's a musical tourist, these records are his home movies.

Duck Rock, produced by Trevor Horn and featuring the rapping Worlds Famous Supreme Team, is a vanguard album in the new music/rap crossover movement. It offers vignettes of hip-hop, Appalachian music (McLaren shows no real racial preference in his thievery), African music and **merengue**. Instead of assimilating the forms and reconstructing them, McLaren puts his actual source material on vinyl (and then his name to it). The most striking cut, "Buffalo Gals," sets a square dance call over a hip-hop scratch track. **D'ya Like Scratchin'** plucks three songs from the album and funks with the mix, adding two versions of a new tune as well.

Not one to stand still, McLaren succeeds against all odds in combining hip-hop with opera on **Fans**. The synthesis seems a highly unlikely one and it is, but McLaren mainly uses opera for its recitative form and story lines (namely *Carmen, Madam Butterfly* and *Turandot*). And damn it, the thing works more often than not.

The aptly named **Swamp Thing** is a murky and bizarre creature growing out of McLaren's 1982-4 scrap heap of various sessions. The title track perverts "Wild Thing" into a nightmarish but enjoyable mess. "Duck Rock Cheer" is so unlike the original that you'd never connect the two save for minor overlapping of mix components; "Duck Rockers/Promises" is only slightly more familiar. "Buffalo Love" has even less to do with "Buffalo Gals," offering instead a smooth disco creation breathily sung by an unidentified woman. "B.I. Bikki" combines McLarenize exercise exhortations with opera and all sorts of extraneous rubbish; "Eiffel Tower" turns the Bow Wow Wow song inside out to interesting effect. As aggravating as he often is, McLaren's work is invariably fascinating and provocative. [jl/iar]

See also *Bow Wow Wow, New York Dolls, Sex Pistols.*

MEATMEN

Crippled Children Suck (nr/Touch and Go) 1981
Blood Sausage EP (nr/Touch and Go) 1982
We're the Meatmen . . . and You Suck! (nr/Touch and Go) 1983
War of the Superbikes (Homestead) 1985

TESCO VEE

Dutch Hercules EP (nr/Touch and Go) 1984

Obnoxious, crude, offensive, blasphemous, tiresome and funny, Washington D.C.'s Meatmen are one band you'll never be able to explain to your parents (or even the vast majority of your peers). The rude punk parodists tramp their combat boots into the sensitive issues of society with a coarseness that makes dead baby jokes seem polite. Their problem is that, without any reference points, their irreverence loses its shock value and becomes merely gratuitous and tedious.

Despite its brilliant cover art and title, **We're the Meatmen . . . and You Suck!** runs aground for lack of originality. The puerile forays into morbidity ("One Down Three to Go," about the Beatles), homophobia ("Tooling for Anus"), misogyny ("I'm Glad I'm Not a Girl") and racism ("Blow Me Jah") are too familiar and predictable to be really outrageous. A little more wit would make the Meatmen a more engaging (and hateable) cartoon. One side of the album is live; the other is a reissue of the earlier **Blood Sausage** 7-inch.

Singer Tesco Vee's solo record, on which he's joined by Lyle Preslar and Brian Baker of Minor Threat (both of whom subsequently followed Vee home to join the Meatmen), stands on more solid musical ground. Apparently mellowing with age, he limits his attacks on lesbians, blacks, post-punkers and rock stars. The satire works better because Vee offers himself as an object of parody. A reference point! The only useless cut is the side-long disco version of "Crapper's Delight," which pales before the far more clever rap attacks of the Beastie Boys and Red Hot Chili Peppers.

With a new five-man lineup, **War of the Superbikes** focuses and refines the band's miserable charm, retooling the punk onslaught into a strong, sharp-edged rock sound and presenting a mixed material grill, from utterly inoffensive (the title track and "Abba God and Me") to typically juvenile (the flamencoed "Kisses in the Sunset," "Cadaver Class" and "What's This Shit Called Love," which opens as a demented Presley parody). Just what the doctor ordered! Bonus: spoken-word tripe hidden at the end of each side. [jl/iar]

MEAT PUPPETS

Meat Puppets (nr/Thermidor-SST) 1981
Meat Puppets II (SST) 1983
Up on the Sun (SST) 1985
Out My Way EP (SST) 1986

This Arizona trio has made a career out of defying expectations. The two Kirkwood brothers, Curt (guitar/vocals) and Cris (bass/vocals), along with drummer Derrick Bostrom, burst onto the scene with a convincing above-average thrash sound on their first album, but returned playing radical country-punk on **Meat Puppets II**, a startlingly strong set of stylistic contrasts—loud and soft, fast and slow—all supporting moving, poetic lyrics. The songs are melodic and memorable, the high'n'lonesome singing even more effective in its shoddiness. One of the best albums ever to blend Joe Strummer with Hank Williams, **Meat Puppets II** avoids clichés of any sort in its brilliant evocation of the wide open world of the Southwest. Make no mistake—this is not a hardcore album with some corny twang—it's a fully-realized work in a unique hybrid style.

Up on the Sun removes the Puppets further from hardcore, but doesn't adequately replace the rock'n'roll energy. The lyrics, unlike those on the second album, are nonsensical rambles rather than expressionist word paintings; the playing is uncluttered and melodic but dinky and not really engaging.

The Puppets sound far more involved and enthused on the vastly superior six-track **Out My Way**, again quite unlike anything in their prior repertoire. An utterly crazed rave-up on "Good Golly Miss Molly" merely caps off an ineffable, diverse collection of occasionally funky, occasionally psychedelic, occasionally countryfied rock tunes. [iar]

MEDIUM MEDIUM

Medium Medium EP (nr/Cachalot) 1981
The Glitterhouse (Cherry Red/Cachalot) 1981

This Notts quartet that plays powerful bass-heavy funk debuted with a single in '78, appeared on a compilation album in '79 and signed with Cherry Red in 1980. Their eponymous EP is one of the best (not to mention earliest) modern Brit-funk records, featuring two versions of the hypnotic "Hungry, So Angry," the tension-filled "Further Than Funk Dream" and "Nadsat Dream," all sung by John Lewis in an angst-filled emotive style that, along with the taut, bubbling rhythm section, distinguishes the band.

Unfortunately, **The Glitterhouse**, released later the same year and containing both "Hungry, So Angry" and "Further Than Funk Dream," offers nothing else of equal caliber. The remaining material uses too much aural gimmickry and tends to meander aimlessly without ever matching the urgent groove of the EP. [ds]

MEKONS

The Quality of Mercy Is Not Strnen (Virgin/nr) 1979
The Mekons (Red Rhino/nr) 1980
The Mekons Story (CNT/nr) 1982
The English Dancing Master EP (CNT/nr) 1983
Fear and Whiskey (Sin/nr) 1985
Crime and Punishment EP (Sin/nr) 1986

The Mekons (not to be confused with the Manchester Mekon—both take their name from TV's **Dr. Who**), like the Gang of Four, hail from Leeds and worked some of the same fragmented guitar funk terrain on their first album, an early post-punk landmark. Unfortunately, the screamed vocals obscure both the music and the lyrics: minimalism is one thing, but rank amateurism another. On their eponymous second album, the Mekons move into danceable synth-pop, with protest lyrics attacking bourgeois culture, the army and hollow lives. **The Mekons Story** is an album of outtakes punctuated by inter-track narration.

With only two original members left in the lineup (which, for the record, includes such scene stalwarts as Lu and Steve Goulding), the Mekons returned in 1985 to much international critical adulation with **Fear and Whiskey**, a ragged album with sturdily memorable tunes that mix equal parts of electrified rustic country dance music and cow-rock, with fiddle, piano and harmonica joining the guitars and drums. (A less loopy, more rocking version of John Otway would paint a not-unreasonable comparison.) Sin's label mimics Sun's; the sounds are likewise Americanized. A cover of Hank Williams' "Lost Highway" closes the LP on an appropriate note. Nothing (well, only some things, perhaps) could be further from the Mekons' early noise days. **Crime and Punishment** offers four songs (including the Robyn Hitchcock-like "Chop That Child in Half" and Merle Haggard's "Deep End") from a John Peel session. [gf/iar]

MEMBERS

At the Chelsea Nightclub (Virgin/-Virgin Int'l) 1979
1980—The Choice Is Yours (Virgin/nr) 1980
Radio EP (Genetic-Island/Arista) 1982
Uprhythm, Downbeat (nr/Arista) 1982
Going West (Albion/nr) 1983

At the Chelsea Nightclub finds the Members using punk as a jumping-off point, but that doesn't tell the whole musical story. Incipient instrumental smarts and simple tunes nailed down by infectious, above-average riffs countered the rough-edged delivery and Nicky Tesco's one-of-the-lads vocals. The themes—mainly variations on the suburban kid in the city getting streetwise fast—are mostly framed in mischievous yet endearing (even corny) humor. The album's added bonus is that it contains one of the first, and even now best, white punk ventures into reggae (including, on the US pressing, the subsequent "Offshore Banking Business" single). Thoroughly entertaining.

The second album, however, signaled the advent of a downswing from which the band never really recovered. The material seems thin—a cover of ex-Pink Fairy Larry Wallis' "Police Car" is far and away the most memorable track—and any spark and grit the band might have mustered is sterilized by Rupert Hine's production. (The first LP was produced by Members drummer Adrian Lillywhite's brother, Steve.)

Working with Martin Rushent, the Members' comeback—after a layoff which some mistook for a breakup—sounded for real, first on the teaser EP (one extra track on the US version) and then more substantially on the third LP. Besides the crisp, full sound, the quintet had grown to a septet with a pair of horns, and the music integrated funk and rap in addition to reggae. No longer humorous, lyrics instead alternated social critiques/rallying cries with personal traumas, at which they proved less adept, but the music was more powerful and danceable than ever. Inspired touch: reggaefication of Kraftwerk's "The Model." (About a year after **Uprhythm, Downbeat**'s release in America, it was finally issued—as **Going West**—in the UK. The cassette version has extra tracks.) [jg]

MENTAL AS ANYTHING

Get Wet (Aus. Regular) 1979
Mental as Anything (Virgin/nr) 1980
Expresso Bongo (Aus. Regular) 1980
Cats and Dogs (Aus. Regular) 1981
If You Leave Me, Can I Come Too? (A&M) 1982
Creatures of Leisure (Oz-A&M) 1983
Fundamental (Epic/Columbia) 1986

A kind of Australian Rockpile with a case of the vaudeville giggles, Mental as Anything first surfaced Down Under in 1979 with a sly skiffle-like drinking song called "The Nips Are Getting Bigger" (featured on **Get Wet**, **Mental as Anything**—the equivalent UK release—and **If You Leave Me**) which accurately summarizes their pub-rock earthiness and randy humor. **Get Wet** is certainly a good-natured introduction to a band unafraid to write a love song to a foreign country based on travel ads ("Egypt") or pitch a cheesy instrumental bit with Sam the Sham organ as a "Possible Theme for a Future TV Drama Series."

Combining one song from **Get Wet** and the best of the Australian-only **Cats and Dogs**, the Anglo-American compilation **If You Leave Me, Can I Come Too?** is more of the bouncy same—the band's (un)usual mix of cheek and underlying lyrical sincerity captured in the poignant "Mr. Normal" drawl of singer/guitarist Martin Plaza. The album also features a track produced by Elvis Costello ("I Didn't Mean to Be Mean") in which the rest of the band—guitarist Reg Mombassa, organist Greedy Smith, bassist Peter O'Doherty and drummer Wayne Delisle—work up a good Attractions-like head of steam.

Creatures of Leisure reveals an overwhelmingly downcast band, singing wistful lyrics about romantic discord ("Bitter to Swallow," "Float Away") and a general lack of gumption ("Nothing's Going Right Today," "Spirit Got Lost"). Even the music is depressed, using the same countryish style but playing it with barely a trace of enthusiasm. These boys are down, and can't help but share their burden in the grooves. Without wallowing in self-pity or indulging in any direct declarations of misery, **Creatures of Leisure** is an enormously sad record.

A much better frame of mind prevails on **Fundamental**. Songs like "I Just Wanna Be Happy" and "Live It Up" offer optimistic lyrics about getting past hard times and bad feelings. Other subjects keep things in perspective: in "Hold On," O'Doherty admits a case of the guilts about a ladyfriend; Plaza marvels about public transportation in "Bus Ride." As produced by Richard Gottehrer, the Mentals' music has hit a certain stride that discourages zaniness (a shame), but their sound—still an Australian revision of Nick Lowe—is never less than bouncily appealing. [df/iar]

THE MEN THEY COULDN'T HANG

Night of a Thousand Candles (Imp/nr) 1985
Greenback Dollar EP (Demon/nr) 1986

One of the current rock bands not too unlike the Pogues, this electrified quintet doesn't put a specific ethnic cant to its trad-folkified originals, but does employ similar instruments (e.g., tin whistle, Uillean pipes) and was partially produced by Philip Chevron of MacGowan's clan. Comparisons aside, **Night of a Thousand Candles** (which, incidentally, includes an Eric Bogle song, as does the Pogues' latest) is a fine record, from the tenderness of "Hush Little Baby" to the brutality of "Johnny Come Home." Throughout, TMTCH show abundant spirit and a real flair for tossing the occasional odd component into the songwriting stew. [iar]

MEN WITHOUT HATS

Folk of the 80's EP (Can. Trend) 1980 (nr/Stiff) 1981
Rhythm of Youth (Statik/Backstreet-MCA) 1982
Folk of the 80's (Part III) (Statik/MCA) 1984

From an almost-unknown Stiff EP to a million-selling debut album, Montreal's Men Without Hats made an incredible one-step ascent, without drastically revising their sound. Although **Folk of the 80's** is somewhat rudimentary, Ivan Doroschuk's remarkably obnoxious singing is already in full flower and the songs display his characteristically skewed lyrical perceptions and aggressively bouncy tunes. Reprising "Anarctica" while

94

adding an unlikely and aggravating hit single, "The Safety Dance," and the eminently likable "I Got the Message," **Rhythm of Youth** is slicker but otherwise pretty similar in every aspect save sales volume. Ivan's yelping and theatrical bellowing continue to cry out for the swift and firm application of a two-by-four across the mouth; still, the band's earnest individuality makes it hard to truly dislike the album. The follow-up leaves the formula unchanged, and songs like "Where Do the Boys Go?" and "Messiahs Die Young" are reasonably sprightly and entertaining; other parts drag mercilessly as the band's inflated self-image is delivered pompously to vinyl. [iar]

MERTON PARKAS

Face in the Crowd (Beggars Banquet/nr) 1979
The Singles EP (Beggars Banquet/nr) 1983

If they'd called their LP **Just Another Face in the Neo-Mod Crowd**, no review of it would be needed. An utterly unmemorable group, from the nondescript vocals and tame playing (guitar and piano so polite as to be biteless even at high volume) to the dull songs (a cover of "Tears of a Clown" not excepted). They do deserve two points for the name, a pun combining the band's London neighborhood and the essential outer garment of Mod garb. Ha, ha. (The group did earn some posthumous notoriety when keyboardist Mick Talbot became Paul Weller's partner in the Style Council.) [jg]

METAL BOYS

Tokyo Airport (Fr. Celluloid) 1979

This splinter of Metal Urbain modifies the formula to include more (fragmentary) English lyrics and electronic processing; the overall effect sounds considered and industrial—if just as intimidating—in its approach to the texturing of noise. *Formidable.* [jg]

METAL URBAIN

Les Hommes Mort (Fr. Celluloid) 1980
L'Age d'Or (Fr. Fan Club) 1985

Shouted vocals (in French), distorted slash'n'twang punk guitars, ticking percussion—that's what characterizes these fiery young Gauls, who undoubtedly were France's most extreme "progressive" punks at the time. This is harsh and forbidding music, but the group's ultimate place in history will be assured more than anything by their having cut the first single in the now-extensive Rough Trade catalog. [jg]

METEORS

Teenage Heart (EMI/PVC) 1979
Hungry (Hol. EMI) 1980

This Dutch sextet is kind of raunchy for such a modern combo: Hugo Sinzheimer's vocals are like Bowie in truck-driver drag, and the band could be Lene Lovich's backup with more guitar and motorcycle jackets. In fact, Lovich picked the lover's pledge, "It's You, Only You," from **Teenage Heart** and recorded it for her own **No-Man's-Land**. Then again, the Meteors also offer an anthem of lust frustrated, "(One Hand) on the Wheel," whose UK title

and the chorus are "My Balls Ache." Lots of punch and melodic smarts, but juvenile when they turn to swagger'n'shock tactics.

On **Hungry**, the Meteors shed some of their musical rough edges in favor of more sophisticated arrangements facilitated, no doubt, by Conny Plank's production. Though the material isn't as immediately appealing as on their first LP, it's more consistent, and the lyrics (save a couple of missteps) indicate growth, with less gratuitous sleaze and even occasional eloquence limning the underside of life. [jg]

METEORS

In Heaven (Lost Soul/nr) 1981
Meteors (Ace/nr) 1981
Wreckin' Crew (ID/nr) 1983
Stampede (Mad Pig/nr) 1984
Curse of the Mutants (Dojo/nr) 1985
Monkey's Breath (Mad Pig/nr) 1985
Madness EP (Dojo/nr) 1985
Horrible Music for Horrible People by This Horrible Band (Dojo/nr) 1986

Playing psychobilly (billydelic?) with more instrumental technique than the Cramps is no great accomplishment, since Lux's gang has more flash, trash-passion and sheer heart in one off-key guitar twang or crazed chortle than these three Brits could manufacture in a dozen albums. But the Meteors seem determined to even the score through sheer quantity. [jg]

METHOD ACTORS

Rhythms of You (Armageddon/nr) 1981
Dancing Underneath EP (Armageddon/DB) 1981
Little Figures (Armageddon/nr) 1981 (Armageddon/Press) 1982
Live in a Room! EP (nr/Press) 1983
Luxury (nr/Press) 1983

The Method Actors hail from the Dixie avant-pop capital of Athens, Georgia, where they made their concert debut on Halloween, 1979. Like some fellow Athenians, they dealt in minimalist dance/trance rock. They also made a lot of noise for just two guys. The seven-track 10-inch **Rhythms of You** is a crisp, aggressive capsulization of the Actors' act, a danceable Wire in the stark contrast between David Gamble's thundering drums and Vic Varney's perky chicken-scratch guitar (and bass). "No Condition" is particularly riveting, its psycho-Ramones drive heightened by Varney's choogling guitar and the pair's vocals, one a droll singspeak and the other a madhouse wail.

Dancing Underneath is a 12-inch variation of the first EP, subtracting three tracks but adding the new "E-Y-E," which recalls the experimental dub funk of Public Image's **Metal Box**, thanks to Gamble's hard, shifting syncopation and Varney's disorienting overdubbed guitar conversation.

In England, where the Method Actors received rather ecstatic press, **Little Figures** was originally released as a double album. Songs like "Commotion," a locomotive number with a catchy bass figure and quasi-Eastern guitar interjections (à la Keith Levene), and "Bleeding," with its clipped-bass funk rhythm and dub vocal effects, reinforce the PiL comparison. But the Actors add the exotic clang of steel drums to "Halloween"; "I'm in

the Mood for Love" (a Varney original) has an eerie poppish melody underlined only by bass guitar before breaking into a hammy "Volga Boatmen" chorus. The American version of **Little Figures**, a one-record distillation with ten of the original seventeen cuts, is recommended for the slightly less adventurous. (This version, to complicate discographical matters, was subsequently released in the UK as well.)

Although the Actors first made their reputation as live performers, **Live in a Room!**—recorded at Atlanta's 688 Club—is a disappointing documentary of them on stage. (It must be noted that this is not the original band: Gamble had been replaced by ex-Swimming Pool Q Robert Schmid.) The addition of saxman Stan Satin and occasional guitarist/bassist Michael Richmond (on loan from Love Tractor) fills out their sound without weighing it down. Unfortunately, bootleg-style sound quality dulls the group's manic edge.

Retaining the maximum strength lineup featured on the live record, the Method Actors' next (and final) release was as a quartet. **Luxury** includes a bizarre rocking rendition of the Velvet Underground's "All Tomorrow's Parties" as well as Varney's songs (some co-written with others). Satin's aimless (and ceaseless) sax is an unwelcome addition to the sound, while Varney's falsetto vocals provide ludicrous counterpoint to the rugged beat music. [df/iar]

ANTHONY MEYNELL

See *Squire.*

MICRODISNEY

Everybody's Fantastic (Rough Trade/nr) 1983
We Hate You South African Bastards! EP (Rough Trade/nr) 1984
Microdisney in the World EP (Rough Trade/nr) 1985
The Clock Comes Down the Stairs (Rough Trade/Big Time) 1985

Originally a duo from Cork, Microdisney practice a musical form that combines heavily orchestrated smooth pop with potent songwriting. A sublimely seductive paradox, the music goes down easy but invariably returns to haunt the intellect.

After moving to London and recruiting three more members, Cathal Coughlan (vocals/lyrics) and Sean O'Hagan (guitar/music) recorded **Everybody's Fantastic**, thirteen gently atmospheric songs that touch the heart and the mind with resonant guitar and Coughlan's passionate brogue. Starkly romantic ("Dolly," "I'll Be a Gentleman") and ardently political ("Come on Over and Cry," "Before the Famine"), it's a record that commands attention.

Virtually nonexistent commercial response to their first LP prompted the release of **We Hate You South African Bastards!**, a compilation of early singles and demos recorded as a duo that assured Microdisney's surivival while making an unequivocal statement against apartheid.

The Clock Comes Down the Stairs suffers from improved production: Coughlan's vocals, curiously relieved of Irish accent, are set deep within a mix of overwhelming instrumentation. "Birthday Girl,"

"Horse Overboard" and "Past" are pleasant enough, but verge on the generic. Gone are Coughlan's heartfelt protests and O'Hagan's sharp melodic chords, making this complacent background muzak—a far cry from the compelling impact of **We Hate You**. (The tape has five extra songs.) [ag]

MIDNIGHT OIL

Midnight Oil (Aus. Powderworks) 1978
Head Injuries (Aus. Powderworks) 1979
Bird Noises EP (Aus. Powderworks) 1980
Place Without a Postcard (Aus. CBS) 1981
10,9,8,7,6,5,4,3,2,1 (CBS/Columbia) 1983
Red Sails in the Sunset (CBS/Columbia) 1985

A quintet that originally found a following in the rowdy surf crowd frequenting Sydney-area bars, Australia's Midnight Oil went on to become a national phenomenon, and its music grew far beyond its hard-rock roots. But that categorization never quite fit in the first place; hearing their watershed (**10,9,8,7,6,5,4,3,2,1**) and then reviewing their previous output, the natural query of "how did they make that leap?" becomes "what took them so long?"

Their own iconoclasm is the primary answer. Lead singer Peter Garrett both symbolizes and embodies it: well over six feet tall and bald as a cue ball, he gave up a law career to sing rock'n'roll. His angst/anger-ridden vocals have nothing in common with the standard styles of hard-rock singers, nor do the band's lyrics share any of the genre's fixation on refried love themes. Midnight Oil's songs are frequently political, yet just as often are couched in extremely personal terms, be they about romance (rarely), self-doubt, hopes and fears and so on. And despite its share of semi-normal hard-rock, complete with blistering guitar solos, their eponymous debut album also includes strange notions about chord progressions and arrangements that would eventually flower: "Dust" is a bluesy riff stated on two basses an octave apart, backed by organ and drums.

No doubt the group's insistence on democratic songwriting and generally doing things its own way had something to do with their refusing a major-league deal for five years. Unfortunately, that also meant a lack of money for studio experimentation, and most of their independent-label work sounds like demos, lacking the firm command of a proper producer.

That democracy also retarded the band in working out the complexities of songs and arrangements, including adapting the music to odd lyrical meter (and/or vice versa). **Head Injuries** makes some progress on that front, and the songwriting—still largely done by various teams in the group—seems to have matured. Several listenings reveal a clutch of songs able to transcend the limitations of their presentation, assisted by Garrett's impassioned vocals and the group's overall intensity. What seem at first to be arranging gaffes eventually take on an air of almost integral idiosyncracy. The EP continues that development and also features the anomalous but delightful Shadows-like instrumental, "Wedding Cake Island."

Place Without a Postcard is an unexpected dud, song/soundwise, despite having been produced in London by mainstream veteran Glyn Johns. Yet James Moginie (the most prolific songwriter) began to jell his distinctive guitar sound and creatively explore keyboards, thereby at least partly setting the stage for the group's international introduction.

The strong political views expressed on **10,9,8,7,6,5,4,3,2,1** may have been a sticking point outside Australia (where the local **Rolling Stone** named it album of the year, and Garrett has since stood for national elected office). All the same, Oil's politics are frequently more personal than those of, say, the Clash, and when not, they're more articulate. Increased use of synthesizer handsomely complements the fivesome's most cohesive songwriting and arranging yet, and while no two tracks are more than vaguely similar, it's all completely unified. (Some credit must go to producer Nick Launay, who procured a crisp, if slightly odd, sound.) From the restrained, desperate hopefulness of "Outside World" to the marvelously rampaging near-hysteria of "Only the Strong" to the danceable-yet-anthemic fist-shaking of "Power and the Passion," **10,9,8,7,6,5,4,3,2,1** is nothing less than a masterpiece.

Red Sails in the Sunset is entirely political in content and modern in style. An ambience of explosive potency is conveyed through the venomous lyrics and the barely restrained guitar-rock sound. Some of the topics confronted in songs may be obscure to people in the northern hemisphere ("Jimmy Sharman's Boxers"? "Shipyards of New Zealand"?), but there's no mistaking the universal musical language. "Best of Both Worlds" is particularly gripping; "Kosciusko," despite clumsy lyrical references, has a tense atmosphere that works.

Midnight Oil is obviously a different breed of rock group. Their records are far more listenable and popular than those by many other politically-motivated bands, but no less committed or intelligent.

[jg/iar]

MIGHTY WAH!

See *Wah!*.

MILK 'N' COOKIES

See *Ian North*.

MILKSHAKES

Talking About the Milkshakes (Milkshakes/nr) 1983 & 1986
14 Rhythm & Beat Greats (Big Beat/nr) 1983
After School Session (Upright/nr) 1983
Nothing Can Stop These Men (Milkshakes/nr) 1984
Milkshakes Play 20 Rock & Roll Hits of the '50s and '60s (Big Beat/nr) 1984
Brand New Cadillac EP (Big Beat/nr) 1984
In Germany (Wall City/nr) 1984
Showcase (nr/Brain Eater) 1984
They Came They Saw They Conquered (Big Beat/Pink Dust-Enigma) 1984
Three Knights of Thrashe (Milkshakes/nr) 1984

Ambassadors of Love (Milkshakes/nr) 1984

MILKSHAKES & PRISONERS

The Last Night at the MDC Club (Empire/nr) 1986

Once a Canterbury punk band called the Pop Rivits, as the (also "thee") Milkshakes this foursome quickly became leaders of the trash/garage movement when they switched over to a wonderful, demented guitar-based brew of '60s beat, demi-punk, R&B and Crampabilly. In the years since, they've released *numerous* records on various labels. Judging from what I've heard, the Milkshakes offer no danger of disappointment: jump in anywhere and have a party! [tr]

DANIEL MILLER

See *Silicon Teens*.

MILTOWN STOWAWAYS

Tension Melee (NZ Unsung) 1983

Funky bass, choppy guitar, smooth horns and strangled vocals make this New Zealand sextet a challenging musical proposition. The political lyrics are strongly worded, but not preachy or prosaic. This album isn't exactly my idea of a good time, but indicative of great skill and abundant imagination. When it works, it's impressive. [iar]

MINISTRY

With Sympathy (nr/Arista) 1983
Work for Love (Arista/nr) 1983
'Twitch' (Sire) 1986

Chicago singer/writer/keyboard player Alain Jourgensen is the essence of modern-dancing Ministry. On **With Sympathy** (**Work for Love**, the British edition, is a resequence with one track replaced), A.J. and a drummer partner (joined by various sessioneers and co-produced by ex-Psychedelic Fur Vince Ely) play sophomoric yuppie-funk, filled with numbing repetition, brutish singing and scanty, derivative ideas. Most heinously, "I Wanted to Tell Her" chants the title lyric like a litany, as does "Work for Love," while adding moronic lyrics to the numbing two-chord vamp. If second-rate dance retreads with none-too-bright words sound appealing, Ministry will suit you just fine. I'm afraid, however, neither sympathy nor love are among my feelings about this band.

'Twitch', largely produced by Adrian Sherwood, employs a far different sound, a murky swamp in which vocals take a back seat to enormous, Cabaret Voltaire-style rhythm onslaughts. It's a welcome change—although the results still aren't to my taste, I imagine there are intelligent people who relish this kind of stuff. **'Twitch'** isn't half as obnoxious or aggravating as any of Ministry's previous records. Will wonders never cease? [iar]

MINK DEVILLE

Mink DeVille (Capitol) 1977
Return to Magenta (Capitol) 1978
Le Chat Bleu (Capitol) 1980
Coup de Grace (Atlantic) 1981
Savoir Faire (Capitol) 1981
Where Angels Fear to Tread (Atlantic) 1983

Sportin' Life (Polydor/Atlantic) 1985

Willy DeVille and pals could, on a good night, be the coolest cats found on the New York underground scene ca. '76-'77, despite occasional stylistic sidetracking. After being "discovered," producer Jack Nitzsche got them on the lean, tough R&B beam for a first LP that sweats and smokes through and through like a classic of such fully and lovingly assimilated music should.

Unfortunately, **Return to Magenta** is more of the same but less; on the first LP, the cover of Moon Martin's "Cadillac Walk" was one of many highlights, but here Martin's inferior "Rolene" is pretty much it. **Le Chat Bleu**'s arrival was welcome mainly because it ended Willy's prolonged absence from recording, but it confirmed that stagnation had set in. The band was, by then, a couple of Minks plus some sessionmen, and overall it seemed Willy was looking to become the soul crooner of his dreams without providing the songs to fuel ours (despite some collaborative songwriting with Doc Pomus, hitsmith for Joe Turner, Dion, the Drifters, etc.).

That DeVille had definitely lost touch with the trash/sleaze aesthetic (not to mention Louie X. Erlanger's lowdown gee-tar) is plainer still on **Coup de Grace**. Despite a new, young band and a reunion with Nitzsche (Mink saxist Steve Douglas had produced the third LP), the magic is still largely absent. Tracks like "Maybe Tomorrow" offer traces of the old bite almost as a concession.

Where Angels Fear to Tread, produced by Ron and Howard Albert, is a fine record of new DeVille originals, starting with the soulful and sweet "Each Word's a Beat of My Heart." It's an uncluttered and uncomplicated tribute to DeVille's forebears—Sam Cooke, Phil Spector, the Drifters, Joe Tex, James Brown—with additional forays to Spanish Harlem and other wondrously nostalgic timewarps. DeVille's songwriting and singing are as strong as ever, burning with sincerity and warmth. Simply, elegantly excellent. **Sportin' Life** keeps up his standards with a set of brand new oldies that effortlessly transport you back to the era of sweet soul music. "Something Beautiful Dying" (note the Righteous Brothers reference) is tenderly melancholic; "Little by Little" tries barrelhouse rockabilly; "Italian Shoes" is classic bad dude strutting. Appropriate production and a sharp backing band make this first rate.

Savoir Faire collects tracks from the first three albums. [jg/iar]

MINNY POPS

Drastic Measures, Drastic Movement (Hol. Plurex) 1979 & 1982
Sparks in a Dark Room (Bel. Factory Benelux) 1982

SMALTS

Werktitels EP (Hol. Plurex) 1982

POSTE RESTANTE

Poste Restante (Hol. Plurex) 1983

Even in 1979, Minny Pops didn't seem drastic in the purest sense but rather deliberately, almost clinically extreme. The Dutch foursome's most salient characteristic on record is dissonance, even sheer noise—valid artistic devices in the proper hands, but it takes vision and inspiration, of which the Pops seem to possess little. Whether they're having a go at industrial clang or setting pop clichés and oldies in jarringly alien musical contexts, even their best comes up short of what others (e.g., Throbbing Gristle, 1/2 Japanese) have achieved in the same area. No doubt they've applied themselves diligently to make this music, but the net result lacks spark and invention.

(Minny Pops' first LP, released on the band's Plurex label, Holland's most important and active indie, was reissued in 1982 with the addition of a bonus 45.)

Glimmerings of something better flicker on the Smalts EP. Its syncopated percussion and keyboards/synth noises (including an arresting accordion/harmonica-type sound) are like a soundtrack in search of a movie, but effective within its limits. Smalts was, in fact, two members of Minny Pops exploring new avenues in preparation for creating the musical setting for a stage production entitled *Poste Restante*. The resulting LP of that name involved the whole band, plus others; although they didn't write all the material, Minny Pops perform everything except some vocals (mostly declaimed, not sung). Out of context, and entirely in Dutch, whatever meaning it has is limited to the vaguely unified feel and the knowledge that it's ostensibly a drama about travel. [jg]

MINUTEMEN

Paranoid Time EP (SST) 1980
The Punch Line (nr/SST) 1981
What Makes a Man Start Fires? (SST) 1983
Buzz or Howl Under the Influence of Heat (SST) 1983
Double Nickels on the Dime (SST) 1984
The Politics of Time (nr/New Alliance) 1984
Tour-Spiel EP (nr/Reflex) 1985
My First Bells 1980-1983 [tape] (SST) 1985
Project: Mersh EP (SST) 1985
3-Way Tie (for Last) (SST) 1985

San Pedro, California's greatest musical export clearly understood the concept of brevity. The trio's six albums and three EPs pack an astonishing number of songs, most of which (the early releases, at least) clock in at under a minute. In that brief time, they took apart rock, jazz and funk and put the pieces back together in a jagged collage. Although the Minutemen refused to write verses and choruses, based on their belief that rock'n'roll as we know it is a lethargic dinosaur, each of their songs is a satisfying composition.

The Minutemen saga began in 1980 as a four-piece called the Reactionaries that played regular length songs. Later that year, they slimmed down (numerically speaking) and adopted their new name and radical modus operandi. They stuck to that twisted idea of dada with a groove until the end, and with one out-of-chronology exception, their records kept getting more ambitious *and* better.

The 7-inch **Paranoid Time** EP

offers dogmatic politics redeemed by idiosyncratic Wire-type songs. Each abbreviated blurt of rhythm serves as a backdrop for the rants of bassist Mike Watt and guitarist D. Boon. The best is the apocalyptic "Paranoid Chant" in which Boon screams, "I don't even worry about crime anymore." **The Punch Line** is more complex, musically and lyrically. The band loosens up with more funk, off-kilter rhythms and enigmatic twists in which songs seem to fall apart but don't quite. As proof of the musicians' seriousness, the 12-inch 45 includes an insert entitled *Fundamentals of Design*, which waxes philosophic about "The Order of Harmony," "The Order of Balance" and "The Order of Rhythm." Actually, the record is evidence enough, as it reveals three imaginative musicians capable of playing music that holds together without a center.

What Makes a Man Start Fires? throws jazz and blues elements into the blender, and features the Minutemen's first semi-dramatic song ending—that is, the first on which they do something other than just stop playing. The songs tend toward near-epic length—only one of eighteen is under a minute. On this album, the Minutemen show their instrumental depth, as they shift effortlessly from one fragmentary clash of styles to another. **Buzz or Howl** is the trio's most poetic record, and the one on which they try the least to make the pieces add up, with the loosest improvisations and Boon and Watt screaming their lyrics.

Double Nickels on the Dime slaps 45 numbers onto four sides of vinyl. The unifying concept is driving in a car, but the record is really held together by the band's unflagging commitment to idiosyncrasy. The quirky songs are about Michael Jackson, the band's history, WW III and virtually everything else under the sun. Each is different and somehow good. With this much room to work, the Minutemen don't attempt to bludgeon listeners with lyrics, and deliver gems like "If we heard mortar shells we'd cuss more in our songs and cut down the guitar solos."

As if the Minutemen's abundant output left unjustifiable gaps, they issued **The Politics of Time**, a collection of unused tracks that vary widely in recording and performance quality. The 7-inch **Tour-Spiel** consists of four covers: Van Halen's "Ain't Talkin' 'Bout Love," Blue Oyster Cult's "The Red & the Black," Creedence Clearwater Revival's "Green River" and the Meat Puppets' "Lost." Like their other records, no matter what shape they take, this sounds above all like the Minutemen.

My First Bells is a retrospective cassette—62 cuts!—collecting the contents of the first four releases listed above, plus singles and compilation contributions from the same era. Essential.

Project: Mersh (the title is a sardonic reference to commercialism—"I got it! We'll have them write hit songs" says Boon's cover painting) consists of six imperfect tracks, including Watt's autobiographical "Tour Spiel" as well as the endlessly looped, psychedelicized "More Spiel" and a cover of Steppenwolf's "Hey Lawdy Mama." Half employ guest trumpet;

one even has synth. Typically brilliant and intelligent? Yes. Better presented and more accessible? Somewhat. A compromise of any sort? Hardly. A fine record.

3-Way Tie (for Last) was ironically released the same week in December 1985 as Boon's tragic death in an Arizona car crash ended the Minutemen. Indicating now-moot artistic independence or divergence, the sides are marked "D." and "Mike." Boon's collection combines three of his tunes (including the gripping Vietnam veteran tribute, "The Price of Paradise," and a Nicaragua protest, "The Big Stick") with straight readings of the Meat Puppets' "Lost" (again) and John Fogerty's "Have You Ever Seen the Rain," plus a composition by Watt and then-Black Flag bassist Kira. Watt's more diverse ten-track side has two by Boon, a spoken word piece named "Spoken Word Piece," four more co-written with Kira, Roky Erickson's "Bermuda" and another killer take on the Cult's "The Red & the Black."

As of mid-'86, SST was promising to issue another LP of unreleased studio material. [jl/iar]

MI-SEX

Graffiti Crimes (Aus. CBS) 1979
Computer Games (CBS/Epic) 1980
Space Race (CBS/Epic) 1980
Shanghaied (Aus. CBS) 1981
Where Do They Go? (nr/Epic) 1984

Credit must be go to this New Zealand band for their international hit single, "Computer Games," which preceded the glut of similar-sounding British chart entrants by a year or more. Unfortunately, it was Mi-Sex's only shining hour.

The band's first LP, **Graffiti Crimes**, had been released in Australia before the single was recorded; the song was added and the LP retitled for release in the US and UK. Problem: the earlier material that fills the album sounds nothing like "Computer Games" and lacks both electronic catchiness and overall punch, making it a misleading disappointment for those hooked by the single.

Despite the sci-fi graphics and an attempt to become a genuine techno-rock band as opposed to dabblers, **Space Race** is an equally forgettable follow-up, offering nothing remotely commercial. **Shanghaied**, released only in Australia, sounds more confident and less self-consciously clonelike, but is still only pleasantly mediocre, and does nothing to dispel the band's one-hit onus.

Where Do They Go?, compiled from several antipodean releases, allows Mi-Sex to regain its dignity, if not chart position. A blend of reggae, commercial rock and light-heartedness that could pass for a rougher, less glib Men at Work, the album is engaging if not memorable. [iar]

MISFITS

Beware the Misfits EP (Cherry Red/nr) 1980
Three Hits from Hell EP (nr/Plan 9) 1980
The Misfits Walk Among Us (nr/Ruby) 1982
Evil Live EP (nr/Plan 9) 1982 & 1984
Wolf's Blood (nr/Plan 9) 1984
Legacy of Brutality (nr/Plan 9) 1985

Although considered part of the hardcore punk scene, New Jersey's Misfits date back to the first CBGB

and London punk surge. Drawing their sound from the Ramones and the Damned and their look from horror movies and Kiss, the Misfits first released a string of singles on their wonderfully-named Plan 9 label. Two of their better US-only maxi-singles, "Bullet" and "Horror Business," are compiled on the English **Beware** EP and epitomize what makes the Misfits great: a combination of hooky power-chording, weird, horrific lyrics and singer Glenn Danzig's distinctive basso roar. (For a musical genre in which tone and articulation don't count for much, Danzig's power and control are awesome.)

After years as a strictly underground force, the Misfits seized on the emergence of hardcore in the '80s and grafted horror-punk onto slam-thrash. As a result, **Walk Among Us** practically wallows in psychotronic shock imagery with songs like "Mommy, Can I Go Out and Kill Tonight?" and "Astro Zombies." Unfortunately, aligning themselves with the speedrock crowd, the 'Fits replaced the leisurely whomp-whack of their early singles with a faster, stiffer beat that robs many of the songs of their innate tunefulness. The **Evil Live** EP is a 7-inch which catches the boys on good 1981 nights in New York and San Francisco, drawing mostly from **Walk Among Us**. One cut includes guest vocals by Black Flag's Henry Rollins.

Wolf's Blood finds the Misfits at the point of self-parody; performances are competent enough, but the music has deteriorated to generic hardcore/speed-metal, loaded with gratuitous lyrical references to death, blood, ghouls, etc. (A German edition adds the 45, "Die Die My Darling.") The band broke up shortly after its release. Aficionados should dig up **Legacy of Brutality**, a posthumous collection of outtakes and alternate versions, including "Halloween" and Danzig's "Who Killed Marilyn?" solo single. Recorded over the four years prior to **Walk Among Us**, it is somewhat uneven but does preserve a few of the Misfits' finest moments, including "Angelfuck" and "She." [rnp/dgs]

MISSING PERSONS

Missing Persons EP (nr/Capitol) 1982
Spring Session M (Capitol) 1982
Rhyme & Reason (Capitol) 1984

Notwithstanding singer Dale Bozzio's outrageous auto-sexploitation and the overall commercial-record-industry-hype packaging that permeates the group, Missing Persons are one positive symptom of the accommodation between new and old in rock. Designed to shift product, but retaining high musical standards and an adventurous outlook all their own, Missing Persons fall between genres, at once offending and intriguing intelligent sensibilities.

Originally built on a core of Bozzio, her husband—drummer/keyboardist Terry (once a Zappa employee and a member of would-be supergroup U.K.)—plus guitarist Warren Cuccurullo, Missing Persons changed their name from U.S. Drag and were given a boost by producer Ken Scott who recorded and released their debut EP; it became a hit when picked up by

Capitol. In the latter form, it contained both "Words" and "Destination Unknown," songs that also turned up on the first LP.

Spring Session M (an anagram of the band's name) is a slick, clever piece of modern rock, using synthesizers and guitars in a hybrid style that has come to be very familiar in the '80s. What sets Missing Persons apart from other state-of-the-arters, however, is Bozzio's non-clichéd singing—tough/smart with a bemused, occasionally philosophical outlook, and a characteristic hiccough hitch that recalls Lene Lovich's early vocal gymnastics. Especially for a debut album, Bozzio's voice exudes confidence to spare, and enough personality to invest the band's novel tunes with an appropriate attitude as required.

Continue to suspend your disbelief for a few lines more: although it takes a while to become accustomed, **Rhyme & Reason** is an equally fine record. The lyrics of "Give," in what has weirdly become a minor pop music trend, amount to an ethical exhortation to selflessness, attached to dynamic rock backing. Elsewhere, "Right Now" and "Surrender Your Heart" address romance with a little sensitivity, attractive melodies and sophisticated, full-blooded instrumentation. Bozzio sings with less affectation but consistent skill and subtlety. At its worst, the album offers appealing vacuity. Ignore the trappings and enjoy the music. [iar]

MISSING PRESUMED DEAD

How's Your Bum? (Sequel/nr) 1979
Revenge (Sequel/nr) 1980

For a five-piece-plus-vocalist, MPD put out a rather modest amount of volume, which— considering the sketchiness of the melodies—makes their initial impact fairly unstartling, almost mundane. The drumming could be merely an energetic use of empty boxes and pie tins, judging by the sound. Yet the songs become more agreeable on subsequent listenings, best at a bit higher volume to get more from the interesting use of guitars and basses (nice plucking and plonking textures), as well as dollops of sax. All of this in service of Paul Hartnett's lyrics of life and love gone sour in the modern age. These albums create a thoughtful yet acrid atmosphere; the music is, however, too reserved and unspectacular to cause much of a stir. [jg]

MISSION OF BURMA

Signals, Calls, and Marches EP (nr/Ace of Hearts) 1981
VS. (nr/Ace of Hearts) 1982
The Horrible Truth About Burma (New Rose/Ace of Hearts) 1985

Boston's late Mission of Burma was one of the most important American bands outside the major-label record industry, playing challenging but thrilling rock that is both intellectually and emotionally engaging. Staking out post-punk turf similar to that of Romeo Void, MoB's records never leave melody or structure behind; they just meander around it sometimes.

The EP has two sides (musically speaking): aggressive/strident in some spots, inviting/attractive elsewhere. Standing out among the six tracks is one tremendous song, "That's When I Reach for My

Revolver," as well as a powerful but pretty instrumental, "All World Cowboy Romance."

VS. is more unremittingly intense, a loud, vibrant assault that never becomes unpleasant. While the lineup—guitar, bass, drums, tape manipulation—doesn't inherently stake out any original stylistic ground, neither does Burma proffer clichés; every track has individual character. On first listen, these records sound very British; on further investigation, they're all American.

The posthumous live album compiles performances in four US cities on Burma's final tour. Besides a merciless rendition of the Stooges' "1970" and nine dynamic minutes of Pere Ubu's "Heart of Darkness," **The Horrible Truth** offers eight originals in several stylistic veins. Some of the tracks are intense and captivating, while others are sloppy, lacking the focused punch of their best.

Members of Burma continue to be active in various bands, including Volcano Suns and Dredd Foole and the Din. [iar]

See also *Birdsongs of the Mesozoic.*

MR. PARTRIDGE

See *XTC.*

M&M

See *Martha and the Muffins.*

MODERN ENGLISH

Mesh & Lace (4AD/nr) 1981
After the Snow (4AD/Sire) 1982
Gathering Dust EP (4AD/nr) 1983
Ricochet Days (4AD/Sire) 1984
Stop Start (WEA/Sire) 1986

Colchester's Modern English undertook a drastic change of direction after its first album: **Mesh & Lace** is an oppressively pretentious (sarcastic?) load of monotonous droning and shouting by a precious art band; **After the Snow** is a flawed but rewarding batch of hard-edged, melodic dance songs. The group has pursued the latter style ever since. Instead of the muddy production that favored only the drummer on **Mesh & Lace**, the second record has both sparkling sound and overtly normal musical intentions. Not everything on **After the Snow** is as striking as the wonderful "I Melt with You," but as a first step on a new musical path, it's quite an improvement.

Ricochet Days, an attempt to reconcile the band's abiding commitment to artistic expression with the lure of growing American stardom, is rather equivocal, offering several finely wrought slices of catchiness ("Hands Across the Sea," "Rainbow's End") as well as slightly more obscure efforts. Greater intricacy nicely tints all the material; pristine production by longstanding collaborator Hugh Jones adds to their appeal. Still, Modern English remains precariously perched on a fence between making a musical statement and aiming for commercial easy street. That decision can't be postponed indefinitely.

With the release of **Stop Start**, it's obvious which way Modern English is leaning. It may be a bit early to write them off as boring has-been sell-outs (like, for instance, Simple Minds), but they're

certainly not going anywhere particularly challenging. Bad sign: the refrain of "Ink and Paper," co-written by the band and erstwhile Rubinoo (!) Tommy Dunbar, is too reminiscent of "Born to Run" to be a coincidence. Put these guys on the endangered species list.

Gathering Dust consists of five non-LP tracks from Modern English's pre-pop era, originally released in 1980 and 1981. Atmospheric, dense, aggressive and abrasive. [iar]

See also *This Mortal Coil.*

MODERN EON

Fiction Tales (DinDisc/nr) 1981

Liverpudlians of the early Echo school, Modern Eon plays cold rock music that pushes anxiety as much as rhythm. Although not an easy album to like, **Fiction Tales** does convey originality and stylishness as well as flashes of accessibility; occasional use of odd instrumentation and a good drummer make this more than just a routine genre exercise. [iar]

MODERN LOVERS

See *Jonathan Richman and the Modern Lovers.*

MODERN MAN

Concrete Scheme (MAM/nr) 1980

Produced by fellow Scot Midge Ure, Modern Man is much like a second-string Rich Kids. The vocals are like Ure's but a tad stiffer, the plangent guitars can also snarl—even the melodies are similar. Withal, not too poor, for a side, but on the flip the quintet's catchiness, brevity and solid (if borrowed) musical identity seems to evaporate. [jg]

MODERN ROMANCE

Adventures in Clubland (WEA/Atlantic) 1981
Trick of the Light (WEA/Atlantic) 1983
Party Tonight (Ronco/nr) 1983
Burn It! (RCA/nr) 1985

Formerly doing business as minor-league punk parodists the (Leyton) Buzzards, Geoffrey Deane and David Jaymes switched styles radically without altering their outlook and became a UK chart sensation. **Adventures in Clubland** is fake disco-salsa, with enough beat to satisfy the most demanding feet and enough smirking to prove they don't believe a second of it. For proof, sample "Bring on the Funkateers" or "Ay Ay Ay Ay Moosey." Regardless—or perhaps because—of the insincerity, this is good fun.

A subsequent split left Jaymes in sole command but hardly shorthanded, and he took the band for another joyride, hitting an infectious happy-feet high on "Best Years of Our Lives," rhumba-ing through "High Life," swinging in big-band land on "Don't Stop That Crazy Rhythm" and so on well into the night. (Well, for 40 minutes at least.) Again, a good time is assured for all.

Party Tonight is an everything-you'd-ever-want-to-hear-by-Modern Romance compilation. [jy/iar]

MO-DETTES

The Story So Far (Deram/nr) 1980

Four women—an American, a

Swiss and two Britons—made up the London-based Mo-dettes. Not as poppy as the Go-Go's or as radical as the Slits, the Mo-dettes worked a middle ground, offering feminist consciousness but avoiding polemics and overseriousness. This competent album has its charming moments, but also suffers from a plainness that makes the lesser songs tedious and the better ones not as convincing as they might have been. What the Mo-dettes needed was a really clever producer. [iar]

MODERN EON

MONOCHROME SET

Strange Boutique (DinDisc) 1980
Love Zombies (DinDisc/nr) 1980
Eligible Bachelors (Cherry Red/nr) 1982
Volume, Contrast, Brilliance (Cherry Red/nr) 1983
Jacob's Ladder EP (Blanco y Negro/nr) 1985
The Lost Weekend (Blanco y Negro/nr) 1985

Beginning with a series of arty rock singles, the Monochrome Set took a sharp swing toward lightweight pop when they hit LP form. **Strange Boutique** mixes uncommon source material (polkas, etc.) into cabaret material (à la **Village Green** Kinks). Fortunately, the highly controlled results are untainted by seriousness, and even without much to say, the quartet says it well.

Love Zombies expands the cabaret stylings while limiting the bizarre material, producing a smoother and more accessible sound. The melodies are stronger with Bid's vocals brought up to spotlight lyrics that take sharp, light jabs at emotional traps and social mores.

Eligible Bachelors strips the music down to essential elements—clean, bouncy melodies and gently satirical verse, performed with deceptive facility.

Leading off with the suave pop of "Jacob's Ladder," **The Lost Weekend**—produced by John Porter—has such a light touch that it almost floats away in spots. Nostalgia—from the '30s, '50s and '60s—colors most of the songs, variously suggesting "When I'm 64" crossed with recent XTC and a bikini beach movie soundtrack. Clever and entertaining, although only the second side makes for truly compelling listening.

Volume, Contrast, Brilliance compiles early singles and significant album tracks. [sg/iar]

MONSOON

Third Eye (Mobile Suit Corporation/nr) 1983

A different pop concept to say the least, but one that works marvelously. Producer/writer/instrumentalist Steve Coe, along with his collaborator, Martin Smith, create (with some outside assistance, mostly on percussion) raga-rock along the lines of the Beatles' George Harrison-led excursions ("Within You, Without You," especially). Delivered in a very lovely voice by Anglo-Indian actress Sheila Chandra, alternately languid and kinetic songs (English lyrics and pop structures, hybrid instrumentation) like "Wings of the Dawn (Prem Kavita)" and "Shakti (The Meaning of Within)" meld intriguing sounds to memorable melodies, making

Third Eye a wondrous, if insufferably gimmicky pop achievement. [iar]

See also *Sheila Chandra.*

MOOD

Passion in Dark Rooms EP (nr/RCA) 1983

Disposable synth-rock. This British trio's five songs, originally released on singles, comprise a tedious 12-inch that is far more technological than original. (For Culture Club collectors: Roy Hay guested and Steve Levine produced.) [iar]

MOODISTS

Engine Shudder (Red Flame/nr) 1983
Thirsty's Calling (Red Flame/nr) 1984
Double Life EP (Red Flame/nr) 1985

Originally from Australia, the Moodists are graduates of the thump'n'grind school of gothic punk. Combining dense metallic bass and razor-sharp guitar riffs with singer Dave Graney's demonic growl, the band is capable of a most unholy din. Dark and ominous, their music can at times be surprisingly melodic.

The seven-song **Engine Shudder** is not the Moodists at their most effective. The tracks are devoid of coherence and slip readily into redundancy. Only "Gone Dead" hints at a promising future, thanks to Graney's layered vocals and Chris Walsh's bass work.

Thirsty's Calling is a remarkable improvement. The addition of a second discordant guitar and judicious production makes this music for nightmares. Setting vocals and guitars further back in the mix, the rhythm section comes into their own on "That's Frankie's Negative" and the standout, "Machine Machine." Grimly primal, this music—in no uncertain terms—breathes life into pop's forbidding alter-ego, a region where many dare to tread, but few prove this successful.

The Moodists' reign of terror continues on the six-song EP. Bass and voice are up-front this time, giving the tracks full-bodied menace. "Double Life," "Six Dead Birds" and "Can't Lose Her" are wonderfully desperate songs and by far the Moodists' best to date. Following the EP, the band underwent personnel and label changes, returning in '86 with the "Justice and Money Too" single—light, bluesy pop augmented with strings and piano. They may have lost their venom, but not the ability to craft stunning tunes. [ag]

R. STEVIE MOORE

Phonography (nr/Vital) 1976 (nr/HP Music) 1978
Four from Phonography (nr/HP Music) 1978
Stance EP (nr/HP Music) 1978
Delicate Tension (nr/HP Music) 1978
Everything You Always Wanted to Know About R. Stevie Moore but Were Afraid to Ask (Fr. New Rose) 1984
What's the Point?!! (nr/Cuneiform) 1984
Verve (Hamster/nr) 1985
Glad Music (Fr. New Rose) 1986

The son of a top Nashville session bassist, R. Stevie Moore began doing his own one-man home re-cordings in the early '70s. Over the course of years spent perfecting his technical and conceptual skills, Moore's individuality, wry pop and musique concrète excursions have developed into an awesome—and seemingly bottomless—well of talent just waiting to be unleashed on the masses. In recent years, Moore (now living in New Jersey) has self-released cassettes of his work via mail-order; the two 1984 albums draw (in part) their contents from those tapes. Suffice to say, if you like what you hear on the discs, there's plenty more of equal quality where that came from.

Phonography (issued twice with different artwork) consists of his very early efforts, done between 1974 and 1976. Some of it is fairly rudimentary, but the Bonzo Dog Band-like "Goodbye Piano" displays Moore's incipient brilliance, and a massed-guitars rendition of the **Andy Griffith Show** theme is classic.

Stance is a three-song 12-inch, running around fifteen minutes. Recorded in '76 and '77, top-to-bottom improvement is obvious, from the moody, mostly instrumental "Ist or Mas"—an interpretation of awakening (theme for a ballet perhaps?)—to "Manufacturers," a rollicking jazzy rocker.

Delicate Tension is excellent: great songs of astonishing variety, all tied together by his idiosyncratic, gentle perceptions of life and smooth, versatile voice. There are hints of Zappa, Rundgren, Townshend, McCartney and countless others; Moore's limitations, if indeed he has any, have yet to be encountered.

Moore's tape club's issue is staggering in sheer volume, variety and consistency of quality. (As of mid-'86, his catalogue includes over 150 titles!) More like radio shows than straight collections of music, he includes anything and everything on the tapes, and they collectively provide an in-depth self-portrait of a truly prodigious talent.

Everything You Always Wanted to Know is a two-record compilation of tracks—with historical liner notes (in English) by Robert Christgau—drawing on Moore's discs and tapes from over a decade's worth of recording. Although disjointed in spite of Moore's skillful efforts to compile it in some rational fashion, it provides proof positive of the man's remarkable gift to do virtually any type of music and do it well. More concise and better conceived, the one-disc **What's the Point?!!** provides an ideal introduction to Moore, with such gems as "Part of the Problem," "Puttin' Up the Groceries" and "Bloody Knuckles."

Released by a small UK label, the **Verve** compilation quickly became a rarity; **Glad Music**, a proper studio album recorded in late 1985, reprises "Part of the Problem" and adds a dozen more examples of Moore at the top of his creative powers. There's real C&W played with mock-seriousness ("I Love You So Much It Hurts"), an unnervingly precise synth-flavored version of the Association's "Along Comes Mary" and witty, hand-clapping rock'n'roll ("Shakin' in the Sixties"). Delightful! That the world at large hasn't yet recognized and lionized R. Stevie Moore is criminally neglectful of a giant talent. [iar]

JOHNNY MOPED

Cycledelic (Chiswick/nr) 1978

Johnny Moped's ludicrously silly falsetto rendition of Chuck Berry's "Little Queenie" sets the tone for this album by a seemingly drunken bunch of grungy simpletons whose band genealogy (detailed on the record sleeve) involves some members of the Damned. [iar]

ANTHONY MORE

Flying Doesn't Help (Quango/nr) 1979
World Service (Do It/nr) 1981
The Only Choice (Parlophone/nr) 1984

Anthony More (aka Moore) was a founding member of the progressive trio Slapp Happy in the early '70s; following that band's merger with Henry Cow, More went his own way around 1975, subsequently producing solo records at erratic intervals. His three most recent releases are stunning, fully realized works of a highly idiosyncratic innovator who combines art and rock into a far-reaching, weird and wonderful set of styles, from the atonal to the hook-laden. More imparts all his songs with a non-conformist's perspective that defies easy comprehension.

Flying Doesn't Help displays More's melodic stance, with such beautiful and haunting creations as "Judy Get Down" and "Lucia"; his wit surfaces in sardonic pieces like "Caught Being in Love" and "Girl It's Your Time." Building dense sonic forests filled with jagged splinters and dry, incongruously delicate vocals, the results fall somewhere between Peter Gabriel, John Cale, David Bowie and Kevin Ayers. An extraordinary record that reveals itself a little further each time it's played.

World Service (which, unlike **Flying**, offers musician credits) takes a decidedly less attractive route, better displaying the anti-music aspect of More's work; dour singing and bitter lyrics make it a challenging record that's as brilliant but not as easily enjoyed as the first. "Broke'n Idol," despite glum intent, contains the record's strongest melody. In contrast, "Fat Fly" is unrelentingly bleak; the light relief is provided by atonal background guitar. **World Service** isn't unpleasant; rather, it explores different ground with the same caustic eye and inventive mind.

With ex-Fingerprintz guitarist Jimme O'Neill in tow and ex-Slapp Happy bandmate Dagmar Krause providing backing vocals, More lightens the mood considerably on **The Only Choice**. He incorporates African rhythms on a few cuts, found sounds on others, and presents a lyrical mix of wry observations on ills of the modern world ("Industrial Drums," "Find One Voice") plus fascinating outlooks on communication and relationships (and not simply romantic ones). The often-understated music is consistently likable but a bit less invigorating than his best. Nonetheless, More's varied talents, craft and incisiveness combine to make it a rewarding album. [iar]

ELTON MOTELLO

Victim of Time (Can. Attic) 1979
Pop Art (Edge/Passport) 1980

Best known for an obnoxious

1978 single ("Jet Boy Jet Girl") that coupled the backing track of Plastic Bertrand's "Ca Plane Pour Moi" with smarmy lyrics about fellatio, Elton Motello, an Englishman who had worked in the studio with the Belgian Bert, escaped that juvenility and became a half-baked quirky pop-rocker. Each album—the first, a collection of singles and other items recorded during 1977 and 1978; the second, a fully conceived and executed band effort—has worthwhile tracks that flatter the artist (if not his minor songwriting talent).

Victim of Time leads off with seven minutes of "Jet Boy Jet Girl," but also boasts a funny ode to a drunken father ("He's a Rebel") and great versions of "Pipeline" and the Small Faces' "Sha La La La Lee" (again using Bertrand's backing track). The Ramones rock is functional and, when he's not sinking to topics like "Teen Pimp" and "Artificial Incemination" [sic], Motello's jovial manner makes the record entertaining. Proceed, but with caution.

Pop Art is a wholly different affair—synth-pop that aspires to be weird for weird's sake, but with occasional success. The best track is a totally syncopated version of the Who's "I Can't Explain"; other numbers work New Musik/M dance-pop terrain to good effect. [iar]

MOTELS

Motels (Capitol) 1979
Careful (Capitol) 1980
All Four One (Capitol) 1982
Little Robbers (Capitol) 1983
State of Shock (Capitol) 1985

Rising up from Los Angeles' early new wave underground to become MOR stars, the Motels quickly abandoned the world that launched them. At first committed to calculated oddness, they now make bland, almost colorless sophisti-pop records. Both their debut and **Careful** present the Motels' music on a take-it-or-leave-it basis, presumably on the assumption that it would be uncool to attempt persuasion. Martha Davis croons with just a trace of husky sensuality, prevented from getting too involved by relentlessly quirky material and jagged backing. **Motels** includes "Anticipating" and "Porn Reggae," icy songs about sex; **Careful** features "Danger," which flirts with emotion without succumbing.

All Four One was produced by Val Garay (Ronstadt, Kim Carnes) who simultaneously pulled the Motels away from the rock fringe and, to his credit, made a successful career out of a crumbling low-commercial-potential outfit. Though much of the material is still irritatingly affected, you can bet everyone noticed that the LP's big hit, "Only the Lonely," is an old-fashioned romantic ballad.

Adding ex-Stooges keyboardist Scott Thurston to the lineup (which already includes onetime Iggy drummer Brian Glascock), **Little Robbers** nonetheless continues the profitable process of selling the Motels as a mainstream torch song enterprise. "Suddenly Last Summer" and others are so atmospheric that you'll just want to take a nap. At this point, the Motels are essentially a one-woman show—Davis might as well junk the band and go solo.

State of Shock, bombastically overproduced with a huge drum sound by Richie Zito, is dreadful, losing a few sophisticated, seductive tunes to runaway commercial ambition. [jy/iar]
See also *Pop*.

MOTHMEN

Pay Attention (On-U Sounds/nr) 1981
One Black Dot (Do It/nr) 1982

Sort of psychedelic and sort of danceable (in a soulless way), the Mothmen just plod along with all-too-few interesting touches. Bob Harding's plaintive vocals are the most distinctive thing here, but they're not enough. If this were 1969, this quintet would be my bet for turning into Yes. [ds]

MOTOR BOYS MOTOR

Motor Boys Motor (Albion/nr) 1982

Strange sense of, uh, humor: the cover and enclosed poster is a freak-show photo of a black man's face with lots of little snakes coming out of his mouth. The foursome (two guitars, bass, drums) do a song called "Here Comes the Flintstones," but they should have done the show's actual theme—this ditty ain't happening. Nothing much here is, despite the energetic punk-cum-boogie musical mode and Beefheartian overtones. Interesting, but doesn't come near justifying its existence. [jg]

MOTORS

Motors 1 (Virgin) 1977
Approved by the Motors (Virgin) 1978
Tenement Steps (Virgin) 1980
Greatest Hit (Virgin/nr) 1981

Formed by two ex-members of Ducks Deluxe—Andy McMaster and Nick Garvey, both singers/writers/multi-instrumentalists—plus two younger pub vets—Bram Tchaikovsky and Ricky Slaughter—the Motors seemed like a hit machine from the outset. On record, they made wide-screen, brilliantly arranged and energetically performed grandiose rock-pop, drawing on their longtime experience and solid talents to become a full-blown chart contender with nary a gimmick or pretty face (far from it) to use for teen appeal.

Motors 1, produced by Robert John Lange, is a fresh, exciting record, light-years more subtle and three-dimensional than the rock'n'roll retreads the band's members had been playing prior to the Motors. The engrossing and muscular "Dancing the Night Away"—all six minutes of it—leads off the LP but is unmatched by anything that follows. **Approved By** is a better effort, containing the fruits of the Motors' attack on the singles chart ("Airport" and "Forget About You" both went Top 20) and exhibiting all of the band's strengths: catchy melodies, brilliant arrangements and exciting, energetic use of rock instrumentation.

The Motors effectively disbanded after the second album, having tired of touring (and possibly each other). Garvey and McMaster continued working together using the group name, eventually engaging Jimmy Iovine to produce their next album in New York. **Tenement Steps**, the unfortunate result of far too much time

spent in the studio, is an appalling, overblown mess, reeking of self-indulgence and artistic confusion. The chorus of the best-known track, "Love and Loneliness," sounds exactly like Steve Still's "Love the One You're With"—and that's as good as this record gets.

Greatest Hit has all of the above-mentioned songs as well as the rest of the Motors' best work. Neophytes would do well to start (and end) here. [iar]

See also *Nick Garvey, Bram Tchaikovsky.*

JUDY MOWATT

Black Woman (Island/Shanachie) 1979
Only a Woman (Greensleeves/ Shanachie) 1982
Working Wonders (nr/Shanachie) 1985

Partly because Rastafarianism is intrinsically patriarchal, the number of important women reggae performers can still be counted in single digits. Singing behind Bob Marley, the I-Threes (Marcia Griffiths, Rita Marley, Judy Mowatt) were for a long time the only visible female presence in roots music. While they've all enjoyed successful solo careers, Mowatt has made the most significant strides, writing and producing her own material.

On **Black Woman**, she covers three Wailers songs and dedicates an original to Marley. The album amply displays her talents as a composer as well as performer, and brought her international acclaim. The quiet militancy of **Only a Woman** is offset by an engaging vocal style—strong and clean—that recalls American R&B. By the time **Working Wonders** was released, she was being called (by *Reggae Beat* magazine) the queen of reggae. Featuring a variety of producers and material, the LP suffers from its crossover efforts, but Mowatt's singing is more assured than ever. [bk]

ALISON MOYET

Alf (CBS/Columbia) 1984

Many felt that Alison Moyet's soulful vocals were the best thing about Yazoo, an oddly-conceived partnership with ex-Depeche Moder Vince Clarke. As a solo artist, her amazing pipes are supported by smooth synth-and-drums dance music created by full-service producers Tony Swain and Steve Jolley, who co-wrote the material and played on the LP as well. Moyet's star turn yields mixed results: consistently great singing and bland sound leaves songwriting the only variable, which it unfortunately is. Other than "All Cried Out," the coyly tasteless "Love Resurrection" and Lamont Dozier's magnificent "Invisible," there aren't many tunes in the winners column. What made Yazoo work was great writing; judging by **Alf**, maybe Moyet's partnership with Clarke wasn't such a weird idea after all. [iar]

MUD HUTTERS

Factory Farming (Defensive/nr) 1981

Take one of those brain-starved young boys out of a Dickens novel, one who's seen a lot of weirdness. Age him, and have him describe what he thinks he remembers (making sure there's a hypo of tranquilizer at the ready) in front of a doofy

100

rock'n'roll band. Get the music to complement his accounts by making a bunch of funny sounds around it with a synthesizer or other keyboards, by stopping abruptly, etc. If he doesn't veg out, record it and press on vinyl. I wouldn't buy it, though. [jg]

MUNCHENER FREIHEIT

Umsteiger (Ger. CBS) 1982

This two-guitar quartet, whose name means Munich Liberty, could have gone three ways on **Umsteiger** ("transfer"). The group has a definite knack for power pop with exceedingly good Beatlesque harmonies. They are also capable of slightly unusual touches in the arrangements. They even go for the offbeat sound entirely befitting a band led by an ex-member of fringe band Amon Düul II. But instead of giving their all to any one of these approaches, they try to mix all three, making this an unsatisfying album. The lyrics, which are all in German, even include a reworking of Dylan's "It's All Over Now, Baby Blue." [jg]

COATI MUNDI

The Former Twelve Year Old Genius (Virgin/nr) 1983

Coati Mundi—aka Kid Creole sidekick "Sugar Coated" Andy Hernandez—has done a lot of odd musical projects in his time (including a production job for Germany's Palais Schaumburg!) and his solo album is no less idiosyncratic in lyrical outlook (if not content). In addition to the clever title reference to Stevie Wonder, the irrepressibly funny genius also parodies "Grand Master Flush and the Fluffy Five" and "Kurtis Bluff" on the rap jape "Everybody's on an Ego Trip." While the album cleverly—and occasionally buoyantly—mixes soul, salsa and disco, it suffers from Hernandez's simply trying too hard. [jy]

PAULINE MURRAY AND THE INVISIBLE GIRLS

Pauline Murray and the Invisible Girls (Illusive/nr) 1980
Searching for Heaven EP (Illusive/nr) 1981

Fresh out of Penetration, the early punk band for which she was lead vocalist, Pauline Murray joined forces with producer Martin Hannett's occasional agglomeration, the Invisible Girls, which in this particular incarnation included Buzzcocks drummer John Maher. The album features subtle pop that is closer in spirit and execution to British folk-rock than to the Beatles or Sex Pistols. Murray's singing is too bright and lively to handle the more downbeat material, but the band's ability to pattern exciting sounds around her brings out her voice's inherent passion, while the soft but dense rock creates a mood of chilling agitation.

Searching for Heaven repeats the album's accomplishments but varies notably on "Animal Crazy," which introduces a dislocated disco beat that turns it into an interesting dance music variant. [sg]

MUSIC REVELATION ENSEMBLE

See *James Blood Ulmer.*

MUTABARUKA

Check It (Hightide/Alligator) 1983
Outcry (nr/Shanachie) 1984

As another dub poet, Mutabaruka (born in Jamaica as Allan Hope) inevitably inspires comparisons to Linton Kwesi Johnson, but where LKJ's poems are often ironic and his delivery knife sharp, Mutabaruka's work is more direct, thick with dread. Unlike Dennis Bovell's gorgeous formal arrangements on Johnson's LPs, Mutabaruka is more spontaneous. His poems dictate the musical direction—the rhythms jerk the band along. Suffice to say both artists derive from the same traditions of Jamaican poetry and music; if you like one, chances are you'll like the other.

Mutabaruka's two available albums are equally strong. **Check It**, a bold debut, contains his first three singles: "Naw Give Up," "Everytime I Hear de Soun'" and "Hard Time Loving." **Outcry** continues the poet's verbal attack, while showing the influence of his dramatic concert appearances. (He performs in manacles.) Music and lyrics sound more linked than on the prior LP, and the band seems to be working with the poet rather than just backing him up.

Mutabaruka has also produced other West Indian poets, with two recent compilations (**Word Soun' 'ave Power** and **Woman Talk**) to his credit. [bk]

MX-80 SOUND

Hard Attack (Island/nr) 1977
Out of the Tunnel (nr/Ralph) 1980
Crowd Control (nr/Ralph) 1981

A weird post-metal art band from Indiana, MX-80 center their sound around Bruce Anderson's slashing, trebly guitar riffing and Rich Stim's deadpan, often indecipherable mumble. As a five-piece (with two drummers, no less), they released a 7-inch EP on the local Gulcher label, impressing Island Records enough to sign them, but the resulting **Hard Attack** never came out in the States and attracted little attention aside from some critical raves. A move to San Francisco (shedding one drummer in the process) brought them to the attention of that city's Ralph Records, home of the Residents and other offbeat types.

Out of the Tunnel may well be MX-80's high-tide mark, particularly on the concurrent single, "Someday We'll Be King" b/w "White Night"; on these two sides, their formula of convoluted, breakneck melodies, cross-fed musical genres and Anderson's white-hot soloing nears critical mass. Unfortunately, the follow-up, **Crowd Control**, proved virtually unlistenable—a messy, depressing collection of metallic dirges best characterized by their atonal slaughter of the theme from Brian DePalma's film, *Sisters.* [rnp]

NAILS

Hotel for Women EP (nr/City Beat-Jimboco-PVC) 1981
Mood Swing (RCA) 1984
Dangerous Dreams (RCA) 1986

Formed as the Ravers in Boulder, Colorado, the Nails moved to New York in the late '70s and established themselves on the local club circuit. Although recorded as a sextet, the most notable item on the four-song **Hotel for Women** is the bizarre minimalism of "88 Lines About 44 Women," a sardonic romantic history recited in quirky couplets backed by a dinky electronic drone.

The album features a fleshed-out version of that number, as well as a swell remake of the Hombres' classic "Let It All Hang Out" and seven new murky, moody songs that bring rhythm to the fore and vaguely recall Wall of Voodoo without the Southwestern flavor. [iar]

NAKED EYES

Burning Bridges (EMI/nr) 1983
Naked Eyes (nr/EMI America) 1983
Fuel for the Fire (EMI/EMI America) 1984

Following closely in the wake of the far less wholesome Soft Cell, this vocalist-and-synthesist duo from Bath had the good sense to a) have hitmaker Tony Mansfield as their producer and b) cover a classic pop tune, Bacharach/David's "Always Something There to Remind Me." Thus armed, the pair's assault on America was enormously successful. **Naked Eyes** (almost the same LP as **Burning Bridges**) contains a second hit, "Promises, Promises," and another good number, "Voices in My Head." **Fuel for the Fire** has "(What) In the Name of Love" to recommend it, but little else. [iar]

NAKED RAYGUN

Basement Screams EP (nr/Ruthless) 1983
Throb Throb (Homestead) 1985
All Rise (Homestead) 1986

Chicago's Naked Raygun is one of those encouraging new punk bands that bloomed in the Midwest long after thrash had apparently isolated the punk aesthetic in its own circumscribed ghetto, where it would never again challenge the musical values of regular folk. Lump Raygun in with Hüsker Dü, Man Sized Action, Big Black and Breaking Circus and you'll be oversimplifying, but you'll have your finger on a movement of sorts. All of these bands expand the current boundaries of punk and cast aside some of its trappings to bring punk back into contact with the mainstream. If none of them ever attains huge success, all at least appeal to adventurous people who don't have mohawks.

Naked Raygun (like most of the other bands mentioned) has an unabashed love for the naive arty experimentation of Wire and the Buzzcocks. The **Basement Screams** EP is a hodgepodge of underproduced, underconceived songs with a lot of Misfits-type paramilitary chanting; energetic and articulate but not directly compelling. **Throb Throb**'s songs are much better, its drive more urgent and John Haggerty's piercing guitar lines a sonically expansive, sharp force. Even at low volume, the album is loud.

The best track, "I Don't Know," is a grippingly melodic art-punk anthem that turns on singer/plumber Jeff Pezzati's anti-idol wail, "What poor gods we do make." A potent, impressive album.

All Rise keeps up the all-out assault level, with dynamic production by Iain Burgess making the guitars roar with speaker-shredding distortion. Pezzati's subtly vindictive lyrics (e.g., "Mr. Gridlock" and "The Strip") voice their critiques in an oblique, ironic fashion generally outside the capabilities of punk auteurs. **All Rise** may be a bit short on melodies (something hinted at in "Knock Me Down"), but Raygun is obviously getting better all the time. Their **Flip Your Wig** may not be far off. Watch for this band. [jl/iar]

WAZMO NARIZ

Things Aren't Right (Illegal/IRS) 1979
Tell Me How to Live (nr/Big) 1980

Chicagoan Wazmo Nariz mixed witty double entendres and a semi-jaundiced, semi-naive view of the mysteries of sex with solid songwriting and unusual vocal gyrations, backed by an excellent band. The result was offbeat Midwestern pop—"Tele-tele- telephone" and "Checking Out the Check-Out-Girl." **Tell Me How to Live** varied Nariz's style with parodies (the Presleyesque "Don't Say Always, If You Mean Never") and anthems ("Welcome to the Eighties, Ladies"). Despite a wealth of talent and wild humor, Nariz fell between niches—too bizarre to be pop, too pop to be avant-garde— and the band dissolved amid financial worries and critical apathy. [sg]

NASMAK

Nasmak Plus Instruments/Instruments Plus Nasmak (Hol. Plurex) 1980
Indecent Exposure 1 [tape] (Hol. Plurex) 1981
Indecent Exposure 2 [tape] (Hol. Plurex) 1981
Indecent Exposure 3 [tape] (Hol. Plurex) 1982
Indecent Exposure 4 [tape] (Hol. Plurex) 1982
Indecent Exposure 5 [tape] (Hol. Plurex) 1982
Indecent Exposure 6 [tape] (Hol. Plurex) 1982
4our Clicks (Hol. Plurex) 1982
Heart Ache Blow Up EP (Hol. Plurex) 1982

This prolific Dutch group started off as a punky quintet with a flair for melodrama and deliberately offbeat quirks, yet were intent on breaking serious artistic ground even then, as **Nasmak Plus Instruments** shows. Their declaration of artistic commitment evidently resulted in the exit of one member and, subsequently, the six **Indecent Exposure** cassettes (subtitled "The Smell Remains"). Nearly an hour apiece, they show occasional flashes of genuine creativity, but each bogs down in its own self-indulgence. Any resemblance to the Residents is superficial at best; Nasmak lacks the wit and spark of the Unfab Four and seems incapable of humor, even when that's their intent.

The melodrama remains in the lyrics, as does a punk-derived penchant for stark, punchy bass/drums riffs with spare but nasty guitar and gruff English vocals. Nasmak's

defining characteristic is the way they write songs and then work at denuding them of melody, replacing much of it with sonic spaces and disc(h)ord(s). Intriguing, but still seeking an apt musical voice. The last two discs are the best to sample, since they are leaner and more disciplined, if still a touch misguided. [jg]

NAZ NOMAD AND THE NIGHTMARES

See *Damned*.

NECESSARIES

Big Sky (Sire/nr) 1981
Event Horizon (Sire/nr) 1982

These two albums are almost the same; the original release was withdrawn, given a partial overhaul, a new title and a relaunch. Although the band was from New York, and included ex-Modern Lover bassist Ernie Brooks, both LPs are UK-only. (Chris Spedding was a member, but had split by the time of these recordings.)

The Necessaries' high-power pop puts the best attributes of rock (crazed, distorted guitars, loud drums) to the service of melodious, intelligent songwriting. Like the early Motors or Records, the Necessaries start with catchy, solid tunes and then give 'em full electric treatment. Rough but sensitive, **Big Sky/Event Horizon** is an impressive outing from a criminally neglected band. [iar]

BILL NELSON

Northern Dream (Smile/nr) 1971 (Butt/nr) 1981
Quit Dreaming and Get on the Beam (Mercury/nr) 1981
Sounding the Ritual Echo (Mercury/nr) 1981 (Cocteau/nr) 1985
Das Kabinett (The Cabinet of Dr. Caligari) (Cocteau/nr) 1981 & 1985
The Love That Whirls (Diary of a Thinking Heart) (Mercury/PVC) 1982
La Belle et la Bête (Cocteau/PVC) 1982 (Cocteau/nr) 1985
Flaming Desire and Other Passions EP (nr/PVC) 1982
Chimera EP (Mercury/nr) 1983
Savage Gestures for Charms Sake (Cocteau/nr) 1983
Vistamix (nr/Portrait) 1984
Trial by Intimacy (The Book of Splendours) (Cocteau/nr) 1984
2fold Aspect of Everything (Cocteau/nr) 1985
The Summer of God's Piano (Cocteau/nr) 1985
Getting the Holy Ghost Across (Portrait) 1986

BILL NELSON'S RED NOISE

Sound-on-Sound (Harvest) 1979 (Cocteau) 1985
Revolt into Style EP (Cocteau/nr) 1983

From hippie folk singer to awesome rock guitarist to high-tech art-venturer, Bill Nelson's musical career—now spanning the better part of two decades—has consistently shown style, character and exemplary attention to quality if occasional indulgent excessiveness. Beginning with a homemade solo album released by a local Yorkshire record store, through a six-album stint leading Be-Bop

Deluxe, then the short-lived experimental group, Red Noise, and finally as a wholly independent solo act (again), Nelson has made lots of brilliant music, and has also worked with some of the most interesting purveyors of modern sounds, producing and playing on numerous records.

Northern Dream is a lovely piece of amateur work, mixing some electric lead guitar with a melodic folk sense—sort of early Neil Young with an English accent. Very impressive, given the circumstances, and not without genuine merit. **Northern Dream** led to Be-Bop Deluxe and a major-label contract; that band succumbed to audience expectations and business problems, becoming an unfortunate symbol of guitar showboating and retarded creative development. We fast-forward to the formation of Red Noise after the dissolution of Be-Bop, which had forced Nelson into the confining role of guitar pyrotechnician. Retaining Be-Bop's keyboard player but outlawing guitar solos, Nelson attacked the future with gusto, drawing together lyrical modernism and subtly infiltrated synthetic sounds. The songs are the weak link—despite good ideas, some are half-formed and not up to his usual standards. **Sound-on- Sound** has its moments, but is essentially a work in progress.

Also in progress during Red Noise's brief existence was Nelson's solo work. Although not issued until 1981, **Quit Dreaming and Get on the Beam** was recorded, piecemeal, at various times and places in early 1979. Unaccompanied save for his brother Ian on sax (and all of Red Noise on one cut), Nelson relieved the self-consciousness of Red Noise's technocracy with more varied subjects and styles. There are more keyboards, but his avoidance of guitar is less forced, and there's even an old-fashioned solo on one number. Although a little disjointed, **Quit Dreaming** is a mature record of real substance and style. Included in the first 10,000 copies was a bonus LP, **Sounding the Ritual Echo (Atmospheres for Dreaming)**, which consists of synthesizer/tape instrumental fragments; interesting if unfocused. The fifteen pieces sound like audio sketches for later works.

Das Kabinett (The Cabinet of Doctor Caligari) was written and recorded as the score for a stage presentation by the Yorkshire Actors Company. Released on Nelson's own label, the record consists of eighteen instrumental pieces, each designed to accompany a particular scene in the story. Musically stunning, it's a hard concept for rock fans used to song structure (and words) to grasp, but Nelson does manage to impressionistically convey some of the plot.

The Love That Whirls—which also included a bonus record, **La Belle et la Bête (Beauty and the Beast)**, the score for another dramatic production by the same company—was Nelson's finest work yet. Preponderantly synthesized and showcasing great songs, he dabbles in a variety of styles—Oriental, techno-pop, dance rock, artsy—all with confidence and success. His most accessible work outside of Be-Bop, it's really Nelson's long-overdue breakthrough, opening many eyes and ears to his talents. (**Das Kabinett** and **La Belle et la Bête** were reissued in 1985 as a double-album set.)

The 12-inch **Flaming Desire** EP consists of an extended version of the title song (an LP track) and five leftovers from the **Love That Whirls** sessions, some also available on UK 45s.

Chimera is an important release, documenting Nelson's acknowledged influence by Japan's Yellow Magic Orchestra, most notably drummer Yukihiro Takahashi, who plays on four of the six tracks. Also joining the previously hermetic artist is (the group) Japan bassist Mick Karn and others, making tracks like "Acceleration" and "Glow World" invigorated and dynamic. Again playing a lot of guitar, Nelson is in fine form, singing better than ever and writing strong, fascinating songs in a number of different modes. (All of **Chimera** wound up on the American **Vistamix**, joined by four prior creations, including "Flaming Desire" and "Empire of the Senses.")

Nelson's next major new album was **Getting the Holy Ghost Across**, ten fully-produced numbers ranging in length from under one minute to nearly nine. The sound is vintage Nelson— percolating rhythms, layered synths and guitars, passionately cool vocals— and the songs are warmly accessible, with proper lyrics and likable melodies; the wiggly synths and hornwork on "Heart and Soul" even link Nelson faintly to funk. Perhaps marking the length of time that has passed since Be-Bop, "The Hidden Flame" has a fiery guitar solo amidst the keyboards.

Savage Gestures for Charms Sake is an expendable collection of one-man studio instrumentals that are evocative and lovely, but not gripping. The sumptuously-packaged **Trial by Intimacy** is a boxed set containing four individually-titled records (**The Summer of God's Piano**, also released on its own, **A Catalogue of Obsessions**, **Pavillions of the Heart and Soul**, **Chamber of Dreams**), all previously unreleased solo instrumentals: ambient pieces, improvisations, experiments, incidental mood music and odds and ends. The **2fold Aspect of Everything** is a two-disc (**Eaux d'Artifice** and **Confessions of a Four-Track Mind**) compilation of obscurities— B-sides, remixes, demos and other non-LP matter. [iar]

See also *A Flock of Seagulls, Ippu-Do, Skids, Yukihiro Takahashi, Units.*

NENA

Nena (Ger. CBS) 1983
99 Luftballons (Epic) 1984
It's All in the Game (Epic) 1985

German pop sensation Nena hit it big internationally in 1984 with a nuclear protest song, "99 Luftballons." Boasting the attractive voice of Gabriela "Nena" Kerner and a jolly modern sound, Nena's catchy songs tend towards bubblegum simplicity, but are undeniably engaging, whether sung in English or German. **Nena**, the band's homeland debut, is monolingual, but does contain "99 Luftballons" as well as the equally wonderful "Nur Geträumt" and "Leuctturm," all melodic and bouncy hits that mix rock

strength with pure pop arrangements. However, the record is not consistent, and has a lot of draggy songs that don't make any lasting impression.

The first Anglo-American album translates the hits and other cuts (offering "99 Red Balloons" as well as the German-language original, smoothly converting "Nur Geträumt" into "Just a Dream") while also preserving several more of the original LP's tracks unchanged and appending new material (from a second German LP) to flesh out a stronger, but still flawed, program.

Although no serious stylistic changes were made in the interim, **It's All in the Game** (sung entirely in English, translated by Lisa Dalbello) is fairly irrelevant, lacking any great songs to carry along the rest which are merely forgettable. Guest sax work by David Sanborn is innocuous; an overall resemblance to mid-period Abba suggests where this lot might be headed if they have a future. [iar]

See also *Stripes.*

NERVUS REX

Nervus Rex (Dreamland) 1980

One of the few artistic successes on producer Mike Chapman's short-lived Dreamland label, **Nervus Rex** epitomizes the bubblegum side of new wave pioneered by Blondie. The pace is brisk and the touch light on predictable yet pleasing throwaways like "Go Go Girl" and "The Incredible Crawling Eye." As a perfect point of reference, the New York band includes a lively cover of Shocking Blue's giddy early '70s hit, "Venus." Flimsy but fun.

Guitarist/singer Lauren Agnelli went on to become one-third of neo-beat folkniks, the Washington Squares. [jy]

NEW AGE STEPPERS

New Age Steppers (On-U Sound/nr) 1980 (Statik/nr) 1982
Action Battlefield (On-U Sound-Statik/nr) 1981
Crucial 90 [tape] (Statik/nr) 1981
Threat to Creation (Cherry Red/nr) 1981
Foundation Steppers (On-U Sound/nr) 1983
Victory Horns (On-U Sound/nr) 1983

Producer Adrian Sherwood is the only constant in this ever-changing jam session that has included members of the Slits, Public Image, Raincoats, Pop Group and Rip Rig & Panic in a wild melting pot of synthesized post-rock and reggae, transmuted through dub studio techniques. In practical terms, it amounts to variations on a theme or, more accurately, a rhythm. Everything is built on top of a slow, steady reggae base, but what's heaped on varies from electronic no-wave noise to pretty, melodic singing. It's weird, but occasionally very nice, and consistently unpredictable.

New Age Steppers varies widely, from entrancing to repulsive, with lots of synthesizer babble and overlong dub mixes. A few of the songs stand out, but it's an effect they're reaching for, not hit singles, so you take the whole package, not bits and pieces. Intriguing, but not entirely successful.

Action Battlefield (repackaged, along with the first LP, on the cassette-only **Crucial 90**) is much better—more organized and song-oriented; Ari of the Slits sings lead on all the tracks and her voice, while not exactly pleasant, adds a comforting personality and continuity. Not as weird or chaotic as its predecessor, **Action Battlefield** is strange but appealing.

Which is not true of **Threat to Creation**, recorded jointly with reggae band Creation Rebel. The LP has almost no vocals, little structure and no discernible direction. When it isn't understated meanderings, it's self-indulgent art-noise that could please only undiscriminating fans of Public Image, whose Keith Levine [sic] takes half of the guitar chores. [iar]

See also *Dub Syndicate.*

NEW ASIA

Gates (Situation 2/nr) 1982

Of more discographical than musical interest, **Gates** is a passel of grating, noisy tracks from a recording project (not a band) led by Ian Little, a Phil Manzanera protege who has become a noted and successful producer. Other participants include Manzanera and former Hitmen Ben Watkins and Pete Glenister. [jg]

See also *Youth and Ben Watkins.*

NEWCLEUS

Jam on Revenge (Sunnyview) 1984
Space Is the Place (Sunnyview) 1985

A couple of songs from this album were successful, so it would be misleading to call the youthful Newcleus a one-hit wonder. But the only track that's worth talking about is "Jam on It," a hip-hop celebration of the joys of juvenilia. Innocent but not gooey, the song takes rap off the street and cleans it up for mass consumption without emasculating it. The clincher is a lightweight synthesized bass lick that's the bounciest bottom (excuse me) since Chic's "Good Times." Over this, treated voices tweet nonsense syllables and the kids just have a good time. Unfortunately, the band never regained the magic of this rap classic, so the 12-inch of it is the definitive Newcleus purchase. [jl]

COLIN NEWMAN

A-Z (Beggars Banquet/nr) 1980 provisionally entitled the singing fish (4AD/nr) 1981
Not to (4AD/nr) 1982

A-Z was actually meant to be Wire's fourth album, but EMI didn't see it that way. As a consequence, it became Newman's solo LP, demonstrating that he was indeed the prime creative force in the group, but also suggesting that perhaps ex-partners Lewis and Gilbert might have stemmed the excesses of producer Mike Thorne (who, as he'd done with Wire) both runs the console and adds keyboards. On **A-Z** (as before) he helps create spacious, sensuous soundscapes, but often ends up overcrowding them with keyboards. Newman delivers his willfully oblique lyrics with a strangely detached urgency; the overall effect at times suggests being drugged and locked in a room with an inquisitor shouting

senseless questions. But **A-Z**'s triumph is that it shows how even simple pop-rock devices can be rearranged and/or modified to devastating effect.

On **the singing fish**, Newman experiments by building up textures and melodies with an interesting assortment of instruments (all played and produced by him) in twelve different ways ("Fish 1," etc.). It isn't the tuneless or monotonous "art" you'd expect from this sort of no-vocals venture either—it's thinking man's muzak which, unlike "ambient" Eno-isms, doesn't dissipate before your very ears upon close listening. Newman is at once more clinical **and** more playful than ever before.

Not to is a return to the instrumental format of **A-Z**, with a significant change: Thorne is absent. Ex-Wire drummer Robert Gotobed and Desmond Simmons remain (with Simmons' guitar/arranging role expanding) and Simon Gillham picks up the bass, giving it an identity of its own. Wire and **A-Z** leftovers are interspersed between newer songs, and the feeling suggests what post-**Pink Flag** Wire might have been without Thorne: minimalist threads rather than sheets of sound; thorny, sometimes atonal, dissonant and rhythmically disjointed, but somehow more personally engaging. Newman himself seems vulnerable—bitter, wistful, showing less lyrical self-assurance, like Ray Davies' art-rock cousin. [jg]

See also *Dome, Desmond Simmons.*

NEW MODEL ARMY

Vengeance (Abstract/nr) 1984
No Rest for the Wicked (EMI/Capitol) 1985
Better Than Them EP (EMI/nr) 1985

A trio vigorously lauded by supporters as the new Clash, New Model Army are long on principle and maintain a fervent, unyielding political stance. Taking their primary inspiration from early punk roots, though less abrasive and more melodic, NMA breathe life into the genre, providing a most effective medium for singer/guitarist Slade the Leveller (né Sullivan) to deliver his politcally charged messages. The eight angry, vehement cuts on the first LP rely equally on Stuart Morrow's acrobatic bass lines and Slade's accusatory cockney rants. Although the intensity wanes towards the end, it's an arresting debut.

Morrow left prior to the release of **No Rest for the Wicked**. Despite his presence on it, the LP lacks the determined ferocity of its predecessor. Some potentially great songs ("My Country," "Grandmother's Footsteps," "No Rest") are forceful enough to have belonged on **Vengeance**; other tracks swap enthusiasm for overindulgence and suffer as a result. "Better Than Them" is a surprising acoustic foray but meanders interminably; the preachy "Shot 18" is simply ridiculous. Without appropriate musical backing, Slade's harsh protests lose their impact, leaning dangerously towards hollow sloganeering.

The EP ventures deeper into acoustic territory. A double-pack 45—an LP track plus three new items—shows the group at ease in these surroundings, but sacrifices the remainder of their vitality in the process. The new songs have the heartfelt honesty that was becoming questionable on **No Rest for the Wicked**. If they pursue it, New Model Army could very well do for acoustic folk what they did for early punk. [ag]

NEW MUSIK

Straight Lines EP (nr/Epic) 1980
From A to B (GTO/nr) 1980
Anywhere (GTO/nr) 1981
Sanctuary (nr/Epic) 1981
Warp (Epic/nr) 1982

New Musik's Tony Mansfield (writer, producer, vocalist, keyboardist, guitarist) has never been overly enamored of trendy trappings of music or image, which is why his band, never fashionable, had only minor UK hits. (As a freelance producer, however, Mansfield has had no such trouble.) Nonetheless, in attempting to recast and/or rediscover pop-rock through modern technology, New Musik helped launch the style as a commercial force in America, where its debut single, "Straight Lines"—predating Gary Numan's US hit with "Cars"—nearly crossed over from the dance clubs to the mass market as an import. (The 10-inch EP also includes its follow-up and both B-sides.)

New Musik's sound is immediately appealing: full and spacious, with vocals, acoustic guitars, synths and other keyboards plying melodious ditties impeccably deployed and ingeniously enhanced at the mixing console. What's most telling about this new musik is that it's sensuous but not sensual, energetic but not violent, calling up a sort of bittersweet, melancholic feeling, but never redolent of the gloom-doom syndrome. Which makes the band either a breath of fresh air or an overly polite, sterile waste of time.

Yet, surprisingly enough, the lyrics are almost all about loneliness, alienation, and humanity's inability to cope with the modern world—but worded simply, and exclusively in terms of ideals (safety, identity, luxury), abstractions (lines, numbers, motion) and/or metaphors (often to do with the ocean and travel). Though hardly immortal poesy, when put in context with the music, core phrases can be most evocative.

From A to B contains three strong singles (one, "This World of Water," is brilliant) unmatched by those on **Anywhere**, but otherwise there's little difference in quality or style between the two. **Sanctuary** takes the best of both, making it a near-apotheosis of ear candy. **Warp**, however, is somewhat transitional. Band involvement in the studio had apparently increased, adding a new rhythmic component with no effective niche, and more acute (and pessimistic) lyrics are accompanied by a paucity of new melodic ideas.

Mansfield's subsequent life as a pop producer has yielded hits for Naked Eyes, Captain Sensible, Mari Wilson and others. [jg]

NEW ORDER

Movement (Factory) 1981
1981—1982 EP (nr/Factory) 1982
Power, Corruption and Lies (Factory) 1983 (nr/Qwest) 1985
Low-life (Factory/Qwest) 1985

Following the bizarre 1980 death of Ian Curtis, the three remaining members of Joy Division transmuted into New Order, adding guitar/synth player Gillian Gilbert before recording **Movement**. Largely accomplishing what Joy Division set out to do, New Order has sold millions of records and earned boundless critical enthusiasm playing a heady and uncompromising mix of dreamy meanderings and unforgettable techno-dance music, taking off from "Love Will Tear Us Apart," alleviating some of Curtis' lyrical suffering while retaining the depth and unique musical personality he outlined. Produced by Martin Hannett, **Movement** wisely sidesteps the comparisons to Joy Division by downplaying the vocals and emphasizing electronics; it may lack the former band's sheer sharpness of vision, but maintains a fascination with decay and paradox, showcasing excellent guitar and synthesizer work.

The **1981—1982 EP** consists of five songs taken from British 45s, and showcases some of New Order's pop-styled work, especially the magnificent "Temptation" and "Procession." Coincidentally, New Order was already showing remarkable facility for making uncommon—but highly popular—singles, issuing a huge UK smash, "Blue Monday." (Long unavailable on album, the song was later added to the cassette version of **Power, Corruption and Lies**.)

New Order's second album is an utter masterpiece, from the cryptic (but decipherable if you work hard at it) artwork to the eight lengthy tracks of state-of-the-creative-art electronic dance music. Blending moody strains of pseudo-strings with seemingly misplaced guitar bits and coldly kinetic rhythms, plus artless but engaging vocals and syncopated effects, deceptively simple tracks like "Age of Consent" and "Leave Me Alone" convey intense sensations that you can't easily shake. An emotionally and physically moving record by one of the era's most important bands.

New Order was formally introduced to America through the auspices of Quincy Jones, currently in the spotlight as Michael Jackson's producer, whose Qwest label put out **Low-life** and reissued **Power, Corruption and Lies**. One of the finest LP's of 1985, **Low-life** starts out with an ironic electronic ballad, "Love Vigilantes," that is utterly unlike anything the band has ever tried but succeeds brilliantly. "The Perfect Kiss" is very poppy, with lush synth strains and perfectly inappropriate froglike (!) sound effects. The other six tracks are almost as appealing, tentatively exploring other stylistic areas without abandoning the essential New Order sound. [sg/iar]

See also *Paul Haig*.

NEW ORDER

The New Order (Fr. Isadora) 1977

NEW RACE

The First and the Last (Statik/nr) 1983

Early American punk fanzines had little to write about, which is probably why the first New Order got a lot of press. But just because the group featured Ron Asheton (Stooges guitarist), Scott Thurston (Stooges keyboardist and future Motel) and Dennis Thompson (MC5 drummer) didn't mean its music had to be worthwhile. The album is full of misplaced guitar breaks, heavy metal sludge and little or no passion. Some things look great on paper, but on vinyl this one stinks.

New Race, a 1981 one-Australian-tour aggregate of Asheton, Thompson and three former members of early Australian punk band Radio Birdman (including guitarist Deniz Tek and singer Rob Younger), fares a lot better on an album recorded live and then studio-improved (with an added guitarist on two numbers and a backing vocalist on three). Production, sound and playing are all real good (except for the intros and the applause you may not think it's a concert album at all) and the energy level is impressive. The material includes the MC5's "Looking at You" (given a blistering seven-minute-plus rave-up), Birdman tracks and one (ugh!) topical number, "November 22, 1963," written by Asheton and Destroy All Monsters singer Niagara. **The First and the Last**, while not an essential historic document, remains a powerfully charged rock'n'roll album with some searing moments. [cpl/iar]

NEW YORK DOLLS

New York Dolls (Mercury) 1973
In Too Much Too Soon (Mercury) 1974
New York Dolls (Mercury/nr) 1977
Lipstick Killers [tape] (nr/ROIR) 1981
Red Patent Leather (Fr. Fan Club) 1984
Best of the New York Dolls Mercury/nr) 1985
Night of the Living Dolls (nr/Mercury) 1986
Personality Crisis EP (Kamera/nr) 1986

The New York Dolls had the style, attitude, rawness and audacity to reinterpret the notion of punk as it had existed in the '60s and to create a decidedly '70s over-the-edge new reality prior to punk. Although they made only two proper albums and were a meaningless relic by the time the Sex Pistols played their first gig, the Dolls singlehandedly began the local New York scene that later spawned the Ramones, Blondie, Television, Talking Heads and others. A classic case of the whole being greater than the sum of its parts, the Dolls were much more than just a band. Their audiences emulated them and formed groups. Detractors' venom inspired countless teenage rebels. Their signing to a major label set an example of commercial feasibility; their subsequent failure to shift product turned the record industry anti-punk for years.

After building a reputation on seedy late-night New York stages, the Dolls' awful magnetism netted them a label contract. Todd Rundgren took the production reins, and delivered a great-sounding document with all the chaos intact. A genuine rock classic, **New York Dolls** contains "Personality Crisis," "Looking for a Kiss," "Trash" and other wondrous slices of gutter poetry punctuated by David Jo Hansen's slangy howl and Johnny Thunders' sneering guitar. No home should be without one.

The legendary Shadow Morton produced the second album; though the results don't match Rundgren's, the Dolls come roaring through nonetheless. There are fewer originals, but the songs they covered have never been the same. "Stranded in the Jungle," "Showdown," "Bad Detective" and "Don't Start Me Talking," reflecting the band's live repertoire at the time, affirm the Dolls' R&B roots.

Johansen, Thunders and guitarist Syl Sylvain have all gone on to solo careers of some note; bassist Artie Kane and drummer Jerry Nolan were in various minor bands before disappearing entirely. (A minor footnote: In 1983, Fan Club released **The Legend of the Corpse Grinders**, capturing a band that included Kane for a year. Another LP called **Children of the Dolls** compiles assorted post-Dolls 45s.) In 1977, Mercury repackaged both albums together with new artwork and liner notes by Tony Parsons. ROIR issued a cassette-only collection of 1972 demos, produced by then-manager Marty Thau. Except for the appearance of original drummer Billy Murcia (whose overdose death in London, noted in Bowie's "Time," considerably helped build the Dolls' legend), **Lipstick Killers** is of archival value only, underscoring the enormity of Rundgren's accomplishment on the first record. Another bit of archaeology, **Red Patent Leather** captures the fading Dolls on a New York stage in 1975 during a brief era when a pre-Pistols Malcolm McLaren managed them. The set includes a bunch of otherwise unvinylized numbers (e.g., "Daddy Rolling Stone," "Something Else," "Pirate Love") but is not exactly a peak performance.

Indicative of the Dolls' enduring relevance to young people, both English and American Mercury have recently issued compilation albums. **Night of the Living Dolls** manages to uncover a heretofore unreleased take of Morton's "Give Her a Great Big Kiss," a tune the Dolls used to play. [iar]

See also *Heartbreakers, David Johansen, Sylvain Sylvain, Johnny Thunders*.

NEXDA

Nexda EP (Hol. Plurex) 1982

It's all so obscure, from who Nexda are (is?) to what they're about. The songs are named three-digit numbers, like "121," which don't seem to figure in the lyrics (such as can be made out, even though they *are* in English, not Dutch). This frustrating obliqueness smacks of sheer willfulness, rather than any attempt to leave the musical situations created here open to interpretation. The synth, sax and percussion conjure atmospheres of an automated jungle, despair, etc. But why so standoffish? [jg]

NICO

Chelsea Girl (nr/Verve) 1967 (MGM/nr) 1971 (Polydor/nr) 1974
The Marble Index (Elektra) 1969
Desertshore (Reprise) 1971
The End (Island) 1974
Drama of Exile (Aura/nr) 1981
Do or Die! [tape] (nr/ROIR) 1982
The Blue Angel (Aura/nr) 1985
Behind the Iron Curtain (Dojo/nr) 1986

NICO & THE FACTION

Camera Obscura (Beggars Banquet/Beggars Banquet-PVC) 1985

KEVIN AYERS/JOHN CALE/ENO/NICO

June 1, 1974 (Island) 1974

A fashion model and bit player in Fellini's **La Dolce Vita**, the German-born Nico (Christa Paffgen) was plunged into the maelstrom of rock when Andy Warhol introduced her to the Velvet Underground, whom she then joined. **Chelsea Girl**, her maiden voyage on a solo musical career, is of interest mainly for its links to the band Nico had just left. Five songs were written (but not recorded) by Velvet Undergrounders; three others were written or co-written by a very young Jackson Browne. The material, however, is sabotaged by tepid arrangements and weak production. Highlight: the hypnotic "It Was a Pleasure Then," where Nico's sepulchral voice is accompanied only by feedback guitar (undoubtedly by Lou Reed).

The Marble Index was a substantial improvement. Producer John Cale took Nico's disturbing poetry and set it to even more disturbing music; the result is one of the scariest records ever made. Unlike **Chelsea Girl**, in which Nico tried to adapt to an outmoded chanteuse tradition, **The Marble Index** blasts her off to her own universe. Regardless of whether more credit is due her or Cale, the album is powerfully effective.

The Nico-Cale collaboration continued on **Desertshore**. Here the disjunctive imagery is set to slightly less gothic arrangements than before, proving Nico's chanting (she doesn't "sing" any more than she writes "songs") can be as chilling **a cappella** as it is accompanied by a horror-movie soundtrack.

Three years later—Nico doesn't quite bang'em out—she and Cale turned up with Roxy Music guitarist Phil Manzanera and Brian Eno on synthesizer for **The End**. The title track is the Doors epic, which Nico had also recorded just previously on the all-star **June 1, 1974** album. With one exception, the rest of **The End** is original material, with the emphasis on Nico's voice and eerie, foot-pumped harmonium rather than on distracting sound effects. The exception, "Das Lied der Deutschen" (or "Deutschland über Alles"), is enough to make you run out and buy war bonds.

Seven years later, Nico re-emerged without Cale but with a conventional rock band on **Drama of Exile**. This jarring blend hurts everyone involved; adding insult to injury, bassist/producer Philippe Quilichini filters Nico's voice for a tinny effect. Her psychotic writing is still fascinating, and preferable to aimless versions of the Velvet Underground's "Waiting for the Man" and David Bowie's "Heroes."

In 1985, joined by two sidemen and Cale as producer, Nico resurfaced with the odd but exciting **Camera Obscura**. This modernization program includes both the nearly vocal-less title track's meandering semi-random improvisation and an attractively sombre version of "My Funny Valentine," with stops in between for fascinating blends of Nico's unique singing

and post-noise industrial music. With **Camera Obscura** she raises her artistic average this decade to a respectable 50 percent.

Do or Die!, recorded live throughout Europe, is a lengthy sampler of Nico's work minus the production flourishes of her studio albums. Another concert set, the two-LP **Iron Curtain** was recorded (1985) in Warsaw, Budapest and Prague with a band that included Eric Random and a drummer from the Blue Orchids. **The Blue Angel** is a retrospective compilation that even includes Velvet Underground material.   [si/iar]

STEVE NIEVE

See **Elvis Costello**.

NIGHTINGALES

The Nightingales EP (Cherry Red/nr) 1982
Pigs on Purpose (Cherry Red/nr) 1982
Hysterics (Ink-Red Flame/nr) 1983
The Crunch EP (Vindaloo/nr) 1984
Just a Job (Vindaloo/nr) 1984
In the Good Old Country Way Vindaloo/nr) 1986

Trebly guitar scrubs and busy drumming, both at hyperthyroid pace, support the snide, self-mocking, self-pitying, annoyed, despairing, sarcastically scathing and generally intelligent (if not always intelligible) tirades of one Robert Lloyd. (Dry wit, too.) The boy has a lot of mind to give the world a piece of.

On the first EP, the melodies are memorable if minimal, and the playing seems just a touch out of control. **Pigs on Purpose** shows a bit more instrumental skill (despite bad mastering) and more varied tempos and textures. The Fall would seem to be a major influence, not only in the abrasive, paradoxically unobtrusive guitar work but Lloyd's singing/ranting, which owes something to Mark E. Smith's vocal/lyrical style. **Hysterics** marks a label change and much improved production; tone colors are expanded with the use of banjo, trombone and viola. A greater assortment of musical styles is also demonstrated: bass parts borrowed from reggae, an inside-out Bo Diddley beat on "Ponces All" and a flirtation with country & western ("The Happy Medium"). The **Crunch** EP features the contrast of tightly controlled chaos **and** some of Lloyd's more melodic vocals. Released during a period of numerous personnel shifts (they were briefly a sextet), the Nightingales manage to avoid sounding transitional; there's plenty of drive and power on these tracks. Highly recommended.

On **Country Way** the Nightingales are smart enough not to attempt a straightforward country album. Many bands lacking a real identity might make such an error, but the 'Gales are able to embellish their own sound with country and bluegrass elements. Lyrics are more smart-arse than ever (see "Part Time Moral England" and "I Spit in Your Gravy"), while the playing gets downright hot on "The Headache Collector." Highly recommended, even—or maybe especially—for those who hate country & western. (**Just a Job** is a compilation of **The Crunch**, non-LP singles and a track from **Hysterics**.)   [jg/dgs]

NINE BELOW ZERO

Live at the Marquee (A&M/nr) 1980
Don't Point Your Finger (A&M) 1981
Third Degree (A&M/nr) 1982

The underrated Nine Below Zero had progressed from being a cautious but promising above-average R&B cover band to performing fresh, confident originals at the time it broke up in 1982. Releasing a live album as a debut is a tad unusual, but **Live at the Marquee** captures NBZ's tightness and enthusiasm. The material is mostly old tunes, including powerful versions of the Four Tops' "I Can't Help Myself" and Sam the Sham's "Woolly Bully."

Don't Point Your Finger, produced by old pro Glyn Johns, was a transitional album. Though the majority of songs are originals (most written by singer/guitarist/founder Dennis Greaves), they sound authentically old (e.g., "One Way Street," "I Won't Lie" and "Three Times Enough").

The band updated its sound on **Third Degree** with wonderful results. Greaves successfully infiltrates his beloved R&B roots with elements of traditional rock'n'roll, pop and even a touch of reggae ("Easy Street SE 17"), all infused with a healthy shot of punky energy ("Eleven Plus Eleven," "Tearful Eye," "True Love Is a b Crime" and the terrific "Wipe Away Your Kiss.")   [ks]

See also **Truth**.

999

999 (UA/nr) 1978
Separates (UA/nr) 1978
High Energy Plan (nr/PVC) 1979
Biggest Prize in Sport (Polydor) 1980
Biggest Tour in Sport EP (nr/Polydor) 1980
Singles Album (UA/nr) 1980
Concrete (Albion/Polydor) 1981
13th Floor Madness (Albion/nr) 1983
Face to Face (Labritain/nr) 1985

Despite a large recorded output and an avoidance of typecasting, 999 has never amounted to anything more than a dispensable, ordinary band of moderate ability. Variously posing as mutant bubblegum, rocky art-school cleverness, heavy metal and quirky pop, 999's problem has always been a lack of adequate talent to invest their music with originality or memorableness. To be fair, though, they have managed a few good sides along the way and also deserve credit for endurance and persistence.

999 introduced the band, dressed in kicky, colorful clothes and working with power-pop producer Andy Arthurs, yet it's not a pop album. The music's harmless but charmless, although the vocals are occasionally winning, as on "Me and My Desire" and the whiny "Emergency."

For their second effort, 999 enlisted soon-to-be-a-superstar producer Martin Rushent, and **Separates** does have a lot more going for it. The band's playing is harder and tighter, with better focus, although the semi-hit "Homicide" benefits more from a clever arrangement than intrinsic quality. Other good tunes include the taut "Feelin' Alright with the Crew" and an all-out rocker, "High Energy Plan." Still undistinguished, but improving. (**High Energy Plan** is an

American revision, with two tracks deleted and two 45 cuts added.)

Biggest Prize in Sport teamed 999 (temporarily a five-piece, having added a second drummer to aid the injured Pablo Labritain) with producer Vic Maile, resulting in a disc that is trebly and lifeless, except for the poppy title track, which sounds like a cockney Ramones.

Hoping to stir up some domestic interest, 999's American record company issued a six-song live mini-album, **Biggest Tour in Sport**, recorded in 1980 in the US. The sound's good and hot; selections include "Homicide," "Emergency" and "Feelin' Alright with the Crew."

Not to be outdone, their English label whipped up a collection—in chronological order—of 999's singles, starting with "I'm Alive" (1977) and running through "Waiting" (1978), including both sides of each—fifteen tracks in all. If you need to find out about 999, **Singles Album** is the record to have, containing all their esssential (i.e., good) material.

Concrete could almost be mistaken for an Inmates record, thanks to two pointless covers ("Li'l Red Riding Hood," "Fortune Teller") and a mundane guitar-rock sound that is totally characterless.

13th Floor Madness was slagged off in the press as soft disco, but the self-released **Face to Face** is a pleasant surprise, offering melodic rock with a certain charm (despite occasional gaffes and witlapses). The band's original lineup, still together after all these years, is not exactly getting better by leaps and bounds, but the songs here are their most likable in a long time—a few could even be characterized as memorable—and bits of invention keep them moving along.   [iar]

NINE WAYS TO WIN

Nine Ways to Win (Duke) 1983

Another characterless modern dance duo (a singer and a keyboard player), Nine Ways to Win are clever, smooth and engaging on their first LP, released on Genesis' label. Avoiding the hermetic sound endemic to such endeavors by using a lot of supporting players, Jonathan Hughston and David Ferguson create some moderately memorable tunes and a greater number of utterly forgettable ones.   [iar]

NITECAPS

Go to the Line (Sire) 1982

A winning combination: a four-piece not unlike an American Rumour, plus the fab Uptown Horns, produced by Langer/Winstanley, all spearheaded by the unlikely Jahn Xavier, who, as "X-sessive," was once a Voidoid behind Richard Hell.

How pleasant a shock it is to find the selfsame lad helming a crackerjack band (multi-racial, and including sometime NY Dolls bassist Peter Jordan); who would have expected this baby-faced imp to open his mouth and give forth a full, throaty growl like a cross between Joe Jackson and Otis Redding? **And** have the songs and sincerity to back it up? White soul rarely sounds this good, and the 'Caps are capable of following a supercool arcane cover of a Wilmer & the Dukes tune with an original that sounds just as authentic. Other than a less-successful medley of a pair by the Easybeats and Zombies, the music is almost entirely penned by Xavier, who also wields a mean guitar. X-sessive has grown up impressive. [jg]

NITS

Tent (Hol. Epic) 1979
New Flat (Hol. CBS) 1980
Work (Hol. CBS) 1981
Omsk (Hol. CBS) 1983
Kilo EP (Hol. CBS) 1983

R.J. STIPS

U.P. (Hol. CBS) 1981

Considering how lightly most Dutch rock's been taken, the derivativeness of the Nits' first three albums comes as no surprise. Influences ranging from the Beatles to Talking Heads abound, as do resemblances to tongue-in-cheek pop synthesists like 10cc and fellow Dutchmen Gruppo Sportivo. (Robert Jan Stips, who produced most of Gruppo's albums and oversaw part of **Tent** and all of **New Flat**, later became a Nit for **Omsk** and **Kilo**.)

Too often it seems (especially on **Tent**) that the Nits are being cute, clever, even tidy just for their own sakes. On **New Flat**, the occasional arty touch provides a welcome contrast, and the melodies are snappy enough not to be dismissed out of hand. On **Work**, however, the lyrics are too self-consciously arty and the music too inconsequential to carry them.

Omsk and **Kilo** show the Nits finding their voice—or voices. The band's brighter, poppier side is strengthened by Stips, but it's the moodier songs, mostly by Hans Hofstede, that come to the fore. Already adept at sketching little emotional postcards, on these two discs Hofstede moves into a style not unlike recent Elvis Costello— though hardly as bilious—and the keyboard-dominated (*not* overrun) settings are effective/affecting, even haunting.

Stips' own album is a curious blend of pop-rock and jazz syncopations, a unified, distinctive style that starts out intriguing and winds up irritating. [jg]

KLAUS NOMI

Klaus Nomi (RCA/nr) 1982
Simple Man (RCA/nr) 1982
Encore! (RCA/nr) 1983

One of the 1980s' most profoundly bizarre characters to emerge through rock music, the late Klaus Nomi specialized in unexpected mixes of vocal styles in anomalous settings. His awesome falsetto and dramatic tenor were equally applied to classical music and rock'n'roll, producing startling records that ramble wildly from high-pitched operatic vocals accompanied by a synthesized orchestra to ultra-stylized pop and warped interpretations of rock oldies. Nomi's records stretch from hauntingly beautiful (Purcell's stunning "Cold Song") to hysterically funny (a somber reading of "Can't Help Falling in Love," a languid dissection of "The Twist") to straightforward Sparks-like big band rock ("Simple Man"). His final album, a compilation that also includes a live performance, is the one to get, an

utterly unique creation that defies you not to fall under its wonderful spell. [iar]

NORMAL

See *Dome, Robert Rental and the Normal, Silicon Teens.*

IAN NORTH

Neo (Aura/nr) 1979
My Girlfriend's Dead (nr/Cachalot) 1980
Rape of Orchids (nr/Neo) 1982

MILK 'N' COOKIES

Milk 'n' Cookies (Island/nr) 1977

Multifarious North (singer, guitarist, synthesist, producer and songwriter) was the leader of Long Island's finest contribution to wimp rock, Milk 'n' Cookies, who were playing dingy New York bars in their cute baseball uniforms when a visiting tycoon took them to England in hopes of making them a hit machine in the Anglo-pop sweepstakes. The band's LP— recorded in 1975 but unreleased for two years—is full of catchy melodies, twee lyrics and energetic fizz-pop guitar hooks. Awfully early for the power pop revival, it never was very popular; however, fans of bands like Shoes and Sparks might appreciate its preciously naive charms.

North's subsequent solo career has taken several turns. Living in England for a while, he led a new wave band called Neo which collapsed after recording an unreleased album. North salvaged and revised various studio efforts (with two different lineups) to piece together **Neo**, actually a pretty good record. The overall timbre is modern rock with melody and bitterness; some of the songs are excellent. The problem is North's pretentiously unnatural deep voice.

Returning to New York, North began recording unaccompanied, producing the two most recent discs at home on simple equipment, using synthesizers as a major sonic component (and the only one on **Rape of Orchids**). **My Girlfriend's Dead** contains some good songs played dully; the four-song 12-inch **Rape of Orchids** is simply sub-Gary Numan tedium. [iar]

NOVEMBER GROUP

November Group EP (Food for Thought/Modern Method) 1981
Persistent Memories EP (nr/Brain Eater) 1983
Work That Dream EP (A&M) 1985

Boston's November Group starts with a powerful rhythm section, and then adds Kearney Kirby's synthesizers, sporadic guitar and Ann Prim's stern vocals to make slick, modern dance music utterly devoid of warmth. The first record is more suited to marching than dancing or listening. **Persistent Memories** shows more diversity and less formula, and introduces a promising factory number, "Put Your Back to It." The far more accomplished **Work That Dream**, recorded by the duo in Frankfurt with German musicians, takes another intriguing swipe at "Put Your Back to It." The other tunes are less distinguished, but all are functional for club play. [iar]

GARY NUMAN

The Pleasure Principle (Beggars Banquet/Atco) 1979
Telekon (Beggars Banquet/Atco) 1980
Living Ornaments '79 (Beggars Banquet/nr) 1981
Living Ornaments '80 (Beggars Banquet/nr) 1981
Dance (Beggars Banquet/Atco) 1981
I, Assassin (Beggars Banquet/Atco) 1982
New Man Numan (TV/nr) 1982
Warriors (Beggars Banquet/nr) 1983
Berserker (Numa/nr) 1984
White Noise—Live (Numa/nr) 1985
The Fury (Numa/nr) 1985

TUBEWAY ARMY

Tubeway Army (Beggars Banquet/nr) 1978 (Fame/nr) 1983
First Album (nr/Atco) 1981

GARY NUMAN & TUBEWAY ARMY

Replicas (Beggars Banquet/Atco) 1979
The Plan 1978 (Beggars Banquet/nr) 1984

Gary Numan rose to prominence originally with a frigid synthesizer dance hit, "Are Friends Electric?" His basic sound—subsequently very influential in the dance music and new romantic spheres—began with precise, antiseptic synthesizer handling much of the instrumental work, and topped it with lobotomized deadpan vocals singing science-fiction lyrics, a combination that is sometimes abrasive but frequently charming.

Tubeway Army (released in America three years later as **First Album**) features primitive electronics and production that showed some flair, though guitars dominate and compositions are locked into the three-minute post-punk structure.

Replicas, which uses synth as its dominant instrument, includes "Are Friends Electric?" and reached Number One in Britain. A composite of material from J.G. Ballard novels to Germanic iciness and '60s pop, the album forged a style that was stunningly new at the time but now sounds hopelessly dated.

The Pleasure Principle, Numan's first release under his own name, contains the international hit "Cars" and continued Numan's maturing love affair with the synthesizer. His interest in technology showed itself to be increasing in both the lyrics and the music.

Telekon brought guitar noticeably back into the mix. The songs raised Numan's despondent romanticism to new heights (depths?), permeated by doom and synthetic syncopation.

Living Ornaments '79 and **Living Ornaments '80** capture Numan's tours for those years, and were issued separately as well as in a special boxed set. (And all three were, by plan, quickly deleted.) Performances give energy to the songs, and Numan's live voice is frequently more impassioned than his studio persona's. The 1979 LP features synthesizer pyrotechnics by Ultravox's Billie Currie that are unmatched on the 1980 recording.

Dance was Numan's first album following the disbanding of his backup group and his retirement

from touring. The album exposed a flair for ironic lyrics and a most undanceable set of dance tunes, downplaying the beat and showing new interest in melodics.

Unfortunately, **I, Assassin** suggested that Numan had hit a stylistic quandary, as it tended back toward his hits but lost his style in the wake of new fashion. Whereas **Pleasure Principle** was the vanguard of the future, the equally professional **I, Assassin** borders on nostalgia.

Subsequently stumped for a way to revive his flagging career, Numan made the roundly dismissed, almost laughable **Warriors**. He was much better served by the TV best-of and, surprisingly, a collection of pre-synthesizer riff-rockers dating from 1978 that were previously unreleased. The dozen guitar-based demos on **The Plan** are punky but clear and non-aggressive, providing an unassuming setting for Gazza's characteristically deadpan voice and ridiculous lyrics, free of the formulaic setting that typified his early hits, some of which clearly had their beginnings in this material. (A number of the songs turned up, re-recorded with more keyboards, on **Tubeway Army**.) Funny stuff that holds up quite well and proves he hasn't always been a bozo. [sg/iar]
See also *Dramatis*.

NUNS

The Nuns (Butt/Posh Boy-Bomp) 1980

For a brief moment in the late '70s, the Nuns seemed as if they might be the catalyst for a successful new wave/punk scene in San Francisco—their early days were praised by the media, and they had a rabid local cult following. But time quickly passed them by. Aggressive musicianship and demanding vocals—especially Jennifer Miro's ice-cold, intense singing—make their only album (which the group reformed to record) is well worth hearing. Lyrically, the Nuns spoke about the decadent side of life as well as anyone, with such tales as "Wild," "Child Molester" and "Suicide Child." [cpl]

N.Y.C. PEECH BOYS

Life Is Something Special (Island) 1983

With a colorful Keith Haring graphic on the cover, the interracial Peech Boys (starring singer/guitarist Bernard Fowler (who's since sung with Philip Glass and others) and keyboardist Michael de Benedictus, co-producer with Larry Levan) emerged from the downtown club scene, cross-cultural loyalties obvious. A funk band with rock instincts, or a rock band adapting itself to urban dance music? Whatever the modus operandi, this album stands as an enjoyable pioneering hybrid, early proof that the two sounds can not only co-exist peacefully, but can mingle creatively. [iar]

JUDY NYLON AND CRUCIAL

Pal Judy (On-U Sound/nr) 1982

SNATCH

Snatch EP (Fetish/nr) 1980
Snatch (Pandemonium/nr) 1983

Abandoning New York for London, no-waver Judy Nylon teamed with Pat Palladin to form Snatch, ultimately making the German-inspired sound collage "R.A.F." with Brian Eno, which appeared on the B-side of his "King's Lead Hat" 45. The **Snatch** EP features Nylon and Palladin teaming up for a pseudo-Tom Waits blues drone called "Shopping for Clothes" and the softly electronic ballad, "Joey," as well as "Red Army," which imitates the technique and style of "R.A.F." Clever and inventive, the work has gentle strength, bitter humor, and a thoroughly jaundiced worldview.

Pal Judy, which she and Adrian Sherwood co-produced, grafts the blues poetics and electronic compositional structures of Snatch onto fairly straightforward rock music. The result—a moody, adeptly created and performed record suggestive of Patti Smith— smacks of modernized cocktail- lounge music (in the best tradition of that genre.) Nylon's originals are acrid and funny in their scope, but the record is stolen by her laconic, opiated rendition of "Jailhouse Rock." [sg]

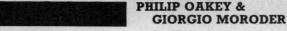

PHILIP OAKEY & GIORGIO MORODER

See *Human League.*

EBENEZER OBEY

Je Ka Jo (Virgin/nr) 1983
Miliki Plus (Virgin/nr) 1983
Juju Jubilee (nr/Shanachie) 1985

Along with King Sunny Adé, Chief Commander Ebenezer Obey dominates the juju music genre, that beautiful, spiritual and eminently danceable combination of traditional chants, hymns, African highlife, rock and country-western. An easy way to think of juju is as inverted Western pop: interlocking guitars function as rhythmic instruments while numerous drummers take on the melodic responsibilites. Born in Lagos in 1942, Obey joined his first professional band, the Fatai Rolling Dollars, in 1958. By 1963 he had formed his own group, and has since released almost 90 singles and albums.

Obey calls his personal style the "miliki (enjoyment) sound." Beginning where noted juju entertainer I.K. Diaro left off, Obey has drawn in such Western elements as multiple guitars and a Hawaiian steel guitar soloist, adding them to the traditional rhythmic fundament. Songs tend to reflect Obey's strong Christian beliefs as well as the common problems (often economic) of everyday life.

No record could do justice to the endlessly intense melodic and rhythmic variations heard during one of Obey's all-night concerts. (His touring band is 15 members strong.) Most juju albums contain side-long songs, but even those rarely put across the scope of a single number. **Je Ka Jo** and **Miliki Plus** are similar to Obey's many Nigerian records; **Jubilee** is a sampler package—edited versions of eight tunes—presenting Obey's progression from grassroots juju to ever-more-sophisticated compositions. Unfortunately, it suffers from a severe case of enjoyment interruptus. [rg]

RIC OCASEK

See *Cars, Suicide.*

HAZEL O'CONNOR

Breaking Glass (A&M) 1980
Sons and Lovers (Albion/A&M) 1980
Glass Houses (Albion/nr) 1980
Cover Plus (Albion/nr) 1981
Smile (RCA/nr) 1984

Something of a jane-of-all-trades (including, during one dog-days period, a soft-core porn flick), Coventry-born O'Connor first came to prominence as protagonist of the film *Breaking Glass*, which was more or less a new wave remake of *A Star Is Born*. The soundtrack LP consists wholly of O'Connor's songs. She tailored them to the plot—to a frustrating extent, their "onstage" performance by O'Connor's rock heroine *was* the plot—and they are stagey, overstated, even cornball. Her few savvy lyrics are buried amid exhortatory sloganeering almost hippyish (rather than punky) for its fuzzy mystical tinge. The backing is dominated by sax supported by keyboards, with muted guitar and assorted psychedelic touches.

This set the stage for the style

O'Connor sought on **Sons and Lovers**; released from theatrical demands and having accrued her own ongoing band, she still honed the same musical style (and kept the soapbox handy when her store of failed romance lyrics ran down.) **Sons and Lovers** marches along (literally) at an even headier and less varied pace; her vocal style nearly caricatures itself, not unlike Siouxsie Sioux doing an endless, mechanical stutter. Underneath this, the credible band (including her guitar-playing brother Neil, formerly of the Flys, and saxman Wesley Magoogan, later of the Beat) struggles to enhance her promising melodies even as it runs roughshod over them.

Tony Visconti, who'd surrendered the producer's chair to Nigel Gray for **Sons and Lovers**, returned for **Cover Plus**, on which he successfully moderates O'Connor's more extreme tendencies. At long last, not every song is an anthem; the title track was a Top 10 hit by virtue of a good melody given the poppier treatment it merited. Yet strangely enough, O'Connor seems a little lost, as if excessive idiosyncrasy were essential to her identity. [jg]

OCTOBER FACTION

See *Black Flag.*

OH-OK

Furthermore What EP (nr/DB) 1983

After hearing so many art bands buried in their own sense of self-importance, it's refreshing to bask in the modesty of Athens' Oh-OK. Like R.E.M. (with whom they share a family tie), the humble four put their elliptical ideas over as much by being good guys as anything else. The songs on **Furthermore What** offer dreamy melodies, ringing guitars (this *is* the New South) and quirky, minimal arrangements that hover just outside the pop realm. David McNair's angular drumming and Lynda Stipe's pumping bass give the music drive; Linda Hopper's breathy singing and Matthew Sweet's Athenian economical guitar space things out up top. This kind of modesty rarely ascends to greatness, but Oh-OK is distinctly a fresh pleasure. [jl]

OINGO BOINGO

Oingo Boingo EP (nr/IRS) 1980
Only a Lad (A&M) 1981
Nothing to Fear (A&M) 1982
Good for Your Soul (A&M) 1983
Dead Man's Party (MCA) 1985

DANNY ELFMAN

So-lo (MCA) 1984

This eight-piece LA outfit (with a three-man horn section) works very hard at being America's answer to XTC in a transparently Devo-esque manner, but the studied wackiness/quirkiness sounds awfully forced and usually manages to hide solid cleverness behind overproduction and ludicrous hamminess.

The EP, all ten inches of it, is the band's most succinct engagement. The four cuts belie the size of the lineup—a trio might have made these long slices of mild perversity. The album that followed, however, plays up OB's flaws, letting contrived bits diminish the impact of demi-clever lyrics and thoroughly competent music. The only track that stands out is "On the Outside," and it succeeds because it sounds normal. Despite obvious talent, **Only a Lad** is a waste.

Taking a turn toward synth-funk (as either a commercial ploy or an amused art statement), **Nothing to Fear** is more likable, yet still sounds phony. A couple of the tunes, especially the title cut, are forceful enough to be exciting. When not pushing pressurized dance rock, Oingo Boingo revert to their previously established lighter style, and the horns play it subtle rather than brassy. Better, but still a derivative disappointment.

Electronic music veteran Robert Margouleff produced **Good for Your Soul** and trimmed some of the usual excess, giving Oingo Boingo a streamlined and powerfully-driven attack. The timely "Wake Up! (It's 1984)" and "Who Do You Want to Be" are among the most invigorating and engaging things the band has ever done. There's still significant quantities of chaff, but on this outing the wise-guy dance-rock largely works.

Singer, chief songwriter and Oingo Boingo leader Danny Elfman made **So-lo** with five members of the band, but it offers a slightly different, more synthesized outlook. "Gratitude" is a brilliant construct combining Elfman's best melody and absurd vocals in one wacky tour de force; other tracks (a ballad, a rave-up, etc.) are more like the band's work. Displaying Wall of Voodoo B-movie aspirations, Elfman unfortunately lacks the focus or vision to counteract his grandiose, theatrical instincts.

Dispersing rumours of defunction, Oingo Boingo returned with their least obnoxious record yet. **Dead Man's Party** benefits from one bona fide soundtrack single ("Weird Science") and a couple of other strong songs ("Stay," a soulful "Help Me," the Devoesque title track). [iar]

OK JIVE

Life at the Blue Chonjo Sky Day & Night Club (Epic/nr) 1982

These expatriate South Africans managed to come up with a unique sound on their album, despite having borrowed an awful lot of it from African and Caribbean pop. Characterized by tight, choppy ultrarhythmic interplay between two guitarists and a female lead singer's initially charming (but ultimately monotonous) voice, the group's perky ethnic dance music lacks enough dynamic material to make it work for a whole album. In short, the sound is pleasing, but the songs are boring. Pity they didn't include their first (Joe Jackson- produced) single, "On Route," which not only sounds great, but goes somewhere, too. [ds]

SONNY OKOSUN

Mother and Child (Oti/nr) 1983
Liberation (nr/Shanachie) 1984
Which Way Nigeria? (Jive Afrika) 1984

A decade younger than Fela Kuti, Nigeria's Sonny Okosun grew up on the Beatles and Elvis Presley rather than the country-western twang that influenced Sunny Adé, or the funk explosion that gripped

Fela. He and his group blend high-life, reggae, funk and various African beats into an international style, an Afro-rock that dovetails nicely into his politics.

On **Liberation**, "Tell Them" spiritedly invokes (in English) martyred freedom-fighters around the world; other songs mix Yoruba and English. **Which Way Nigeria?** is more of the same, and also quite good. The horn-happy sound is both accessible and eminently danceable, and has served him well through a career that spans over a dozen albums. Since scoring a major political hit in 1976, with "Fire in Soweto," his music has taken a softer turn. [rg]

101ERS

Elgin Avenue Breakdown (Andalucia/nr) 1981

Before there was a Clash, Joe Strummer was in a gritty, R&B-styled London pub band. The 101ers broke up after a short career, issuing only one incredible 45, "Keys to Your Heart" (included here), while in existence. This album, five years after the fact, combines three previously unreleased 1975/1976 demo sessions and a live performance captured on cassette. It's an essential artifact for Clashologists, spreading hints of things to come all over the place; as an energetic slice of simple, raucous rock'n'roll, it's worth every penny as well. [iar]

ONE THE JUGGLER

Django's Coming EP (Regard/nr) 1983
Nearly a Sin (Regard/Regard-RCA) 1984

Mixing Bowie's **Ziggy Stardust** era with doses of T. Rex and Mott the Hoople, One the Juggler update acoustic-based glam-rock into the '80s, with occasional success. "Passion Killer" is one tune Adam Ant should have written, acoustic guitars colliding with poseur vocals and throaty sax in a cool and catchy explosion; "Damage Is Done" *really* sounds like old Bowie/Mott the Hoople. The rest of the record is mixed, with some of the derivation more ludicrous and pointless than clever and agreeable. **Nearly a Sin** is nearly good. [iar]

ONLY ONES

The Only Ones (CBS/nr) 1978
Even Serpents Shine (CBS/nr) 1979
Special View (nr/Epic) 1979
Baby's Got a Gun (CBS/Epic) 1980
Remains (Fr. Closer) 1984

Singer Peter Perrett and ex-Spooky Tooth drummer Mike Kellie comprised the prominent half of the Only Ones. The quartet drew on Perrett's romanticism and artful decadence and Kellie's musical skills and long experience. This contrast of youth and seasoned professionalism helped gain the Only Ones quick prominence, but only one song, "Another Girl, Another Planet," earned them any lasting acclaim.

The Only Ones (including that ace song) is the best of their three original albums. Perrett's languid vocals and songs provide the character and focus, but the band's skills carry it off handsomely. **Even Serpents Shine** varies little from its predecessor and contains some

captivating material, but lacks anything as great as "Another Girl, Another Planet." **Special View** picks tracks off both these albums and adds the two sides of an early single done originally as a demo—a fair condensation of the band's work to date.

Although finally realizing simultaneous release in the US and the UK with **Baby's Got a Gun**, the Only Ones' commercial success was still too slight to sustain them; despite three albums of at least adequate quality, they called it quits in 1981. [iar]

ORANGE JUICE

You Can't Hide Your Love Forever (Polydor/nr) 1982
Rip It Up (Polydor/nr) 1982
Texas Fever EP (Polydor/nr) 1984
The Orange Juice (Polydor/nr) 1984
In a Nutshell (Polydor/nr) 1985

ZEKE MANYIKA

Call and Respond (Polydor/nr) 1985

The insufferably coy Orange Juice, leaders of the Scottish pop revolution, typified a UK trend toward clean, innocent looks that unfortunately spilled over into the music. Emphasizing their "unspoiled" raggedness, the band began with clumsy tunes about insecurity and romantic rejection. Singer Edwyn Collins mumbles and croons like a slowed-down Ray Davies. **You Can't Hide Your Love Forever** is supposed to be charming, but isn't.

Surprisingly, **Rip It Up** (not named after the Little Richard tune) explores the first album's ingenuousness in greater depth with thought-provoking results. Though young love remains the theme, tension has replaced cuteness; on the title track, "Louise, Louise" and others, Collins responds angrily to being treated like a chump. He's still a bit of a narcissistic crooner, but **Rip It Up**'s more realistic approach is far more appealing and rewarding.

Escalating musical differences and other internal conflicts caused the band to split prior to the release of **Texas Fever**, leaving Collins and drummer Zeke Manyika to carry on as a duo. Salvaged from the original band's final sessions, the EP further refines the standards set on **Rip It Up**. There's an implicit Western theme, but most of the songs have a quirky, exotic Afro-funk feel, fleshed out with stellar guitar work by Collins and Malcolm Ross (later of Aztec Camera). Their talents make "Punch Drunk," "A Place in My Heart" and "Sad Lament" memorable.

Collins and Manyika teamed with producer pal Dennis Bovell for **The Orange Juice (The Third Album)**, which contains some of Edwyn's strongest songs: the melodically haunting "What Presence?!," the sadly biographical "Lean Period" and "Artisans," a garage rave-up.

Embittered by their commercial failure, Zeke and Edwyn called it quits. **In a Nutshell** is a posthumous compilation that contains the very best of this often overlooked band, from their early days on Postcard ("Falling and Laughing," "Poor Old Soul") through the last days on Polydor (tracks from the third LP).

Manyika and Collins continue to be musically active. With singer

Paul Quinn, the latter has recorded a pair of fine singles (including a cover of Lou Reed's "Pale Blue Eyes") in a country-western setting, while the former, fronting his band Dr. Love, released the wonderful **Call and Respond** in 1985. [jy/ag]

ORCHESTRAL MANOEUVRES IN THE DARK

Orchestral Manoeuvres in the Dark (DinDisc/nr) 1980
Organisation (DinDisc/nr) 1980 (Virgin/nr) 1985
O.M.D. (nr/Virgin-Epic) 1981
Architecture & Morality (DinDisc/Virgin-Epic) 1981
Dazzle Ships (Telegraph-Virgin/Virgin-Epic) 1983
Junk Culture (Virgin/Virgin-A&M) 1984
Crush (Virgin/Virgin-A&M) 1985

Moving from electronic tape experiments to highly polished synthesizer pop and beyond, Liverpudlians Andy McCluskey and Paul Humphreys (with other full-time members, including—very significantly—a corporeal acoustic drummer) are among the most successful practitioners of electro-pop, as first demonstrated by a delightful string of singles. Abandoning their formula after two albums, however, OMD proved capable of far more ambitious creations not wholly beholden to any one type of technology.

Orchestral Manoeuvres in the Dark exhibits stylish electro-pop comparable to Ultravox's music. Aided by Dalek I's Andy Gill, McCluskey and Humphreys build the songs up from computer- generated rhythms, and while the album does not create any new forms, it polishes the synthesizer song into a full-bodied medium. Thanks to a knack for melodies and hooks, notable attractions are the catchy "Electricity" and "Messages."

Organisation (which includes an excellent bonus single of early tape experiments and live tracks) features a human drummer and ethereal synthesizer techniques that suit the depressive subject matter of "Enola Gay" and the like, and pays attention to variation in the tunes (a problem that mars the first LP). With nods to John Foxx and David Bowie, OMD overlays melodies to dramatic effect—and the performance is excellent.

O.M.D. is an American compilation of songs from the two British albums, including both "Enola Gay" and "Electricity." Recommended.

Architecture & Morality struggles with new techniques, and includes two magnificent, ethereal hit singles: "Joan of Arc" and "Souvenir." While OMD is again willing to experiment with sound, much of the album sounds more naturalistic than electronic; an intriguing and highly inventive use of the technology.

The conceptual **Dazzle Ships** overreaches by a mile, succumbing to excessive found-tape gimmickry in lieu of adequate songwriting. It does contain the striking "Genetic Engineering" (which integrates a Speak and Spell toy to make a point) and "Radio Waves," as well as some amazing sounds and a powerful atmosphere to recommend it. Impressive but not a good place to start.

Junk Culture is much stronger, pulling away further from sparkling

107

pop while retaining smart melodies in far denser and newly dance-based styles. "Tesla Girls" incorporates scratch production to great effect while using science as a clever lyrical base (shades of Sparks); the rhythm-heavy "Locomotion" and the more fanciful "Talking Loud and Clear" are likewise ace tracks.

Despite its easygoing ambience and a shortage of really memorable songs, **Crush**—OMD's least stylized, most mainstream album— isn't half-bad. "So in Love" and "Secret" are the obvious romantic singles, but the record has more serious moments as well: the topical "88 Seconds in Greensboro," "Women III" (an ambiguous consideration of feminism) and "Bloc Bloc Bloc," wherein McCluskey sings some truly stupid lyrics with only a trace of embarrassment. **Crush** often borders on tedium, but there's an ineffable quality that keeps it within the bounds of acceptability.

OMD's international breakthrough, which **Crush** started, culminated in "If You Leave," a dull ballad from the *Pretty in Pink* soundtrack which became a Top 10 American single. [sg/iar]

ORIGINAL MIRRORS

Original Mirrors (Mercury/Arista) 1980
Heart-Twango & Raw-Beat (Mercury/nr) 1981

Steve Allen, a strong crooner in the Bryan Ferry mold, started his own band after Deaf School bit the dust; it didn't worked out well at all. The Original Mirrors seemed entranced by the kind of pop-opera bombast that characterized Deaf School at their worst; self-discipline was never a high priority. For every rockin' moment that crystallizes passion into something comprehensible, there are ten others of sprawling excess. [jy]

JOHN OTWAY AND WILD WILLY BARRETT

John Otway & Wild Willy Barrett (Extracked/nr) 1977 (Polydor/nr) 1977
Deep & Meaningless (Polydor/nr) 1978
Way/Bar (Polydor/nr) 1980
Deep Thought (nr/Stiff) 1980
I Did It Otway EP (Stiff/Stiff America) 1981
I Did It Otway (Can. Stiff Canada) 1981
Gone with the Bin (Polydor/nr) 1981
Head Butts EP (Empire/nr) 1982

JOHN OTWAY

Where Did I Go Right? (Polydor/nr) 1979
All Balls and No Willy (Empire/nr) 1982
Gleatest Hits (Strikeback/nr) 1986

This charming nutter from Aylesbury, best heard in the company of his multi-instrumental sidekick/musical interpreter Barrett, is tough to evaluate on record. The more help he has making records apart from Barrett, the more lost he gets. He is somewhat mercurial too, scraping bottom on those thankfully rare occasions when he takes himself seriously. And so much of what he's about just doesn't translate to vinyl—though seeing him even once enhances listening to even the relatively duff tracks.

Otway renders (once or twice per LP) someone else's material—from "Green Green Grass of Home" to Alfred Noyes' "The Highwayman"!—with daffily inspired abandon. He can write hysterically infectious ditties (like "Really Free") or likably folky and sentimental tunes, though these can be a little drippy. There's little pattern for rule-of-thumb judgment, save that Barrett-less he comes off bland (**Where Did I Go Right?**) or energetic but less effective (**All Balls and No Willy**). The most consistent records are the first album and **Way/Bar** (or **Deep Thought**, which is half the latter plus assorted cuts). The **Gone with the Bin** compilation is a neat (if incomplete) summation, but prospective fans are referred to the **I Did It Otway** EP (four of the six cuts non-LP) as an inexpensive toe-wetter. (The Canadian release of the same name is a full-length album—with the same cover done all in red rather than green— containing four added tunes.) [jg]

OUR DAUGHTERS WEDDING

Digital Cowboys EP (EMI America) 1981
Moving Windows (EMI America) 1982

This snappy New York electro-pop trio's indie single "Lawnchairs" became a dance-floor favorite, combining a good beat with lyrics of bemused paranoia ("lawnchairs are everywhere"). **Digital Cowboys** makes the mistake of trying to redo "Lawnchairs" with a real drummer and badly rephrased vocals. An innocuous one-hit wonder. [rnp]

OUTCASTS

Self Conscious Over You (Good Vibrations/nr) 1979

Once reckoned the most popular punk outfit in Belfast, the Outcasts never quite developed their assets as did the rivals that passed them by. On the quartet's LP, they faintly suggest a young, punky Slade, but they're neither intensely raucous enough, nor are their songs—save for the title tune—catchy or cogent enough to make them memorable. [jg]

AUGUSTUS PABLO

This Is Augustus Pablo (Jam. Tropical) 1973 (nr/Heartbeat) 1986
Ital Dub (Trojan/nr) 1975
King Tubbys Meets Rockers Uptown (Jam. Clocktower) 1976 (nr/Shanachie) 1984
Original Rockers (Greensleeves/Shanachie) 1979
Africa Must Be Free Dub (nr/Ras) 1979
Rockers Meets King Tubby in a Firehouse (nr/Shanachie) 1981
East of the River Nile (nr/Shanachie) 1981
Earth's Rightful Ruler (nr/Shanachie) 1983
Thriller (Vista/nr) 1983 (Echo/nr) 1985
King David's Melody (nr/Alligator) 1983
Rising Sun (Greensleeves/Shanachie) 1986

A reggae original, dubmeister Augustus Pablo is as closely identified with his instrument—the melodica—as jazz musicians are with theirs. Pablo (Horace Swaby) was a Kingston pianist when he borrowed a melodica and learned to play it. The simple instrument's unusual sound caught the ears of local record producers, who hired him to give their dub treatments some exotic color. Soon he was composing, arranging and producing his own instrumental tracks; now the reedy, vaguely Middle Eastern sound of Pablo's melodica is immediately recognizable—a plaintive cry in the desolate dub landscape.

Pablo's earliest available recordings are mainly session work. Both **Ital Dub** and **King Tubbys Meets Rockers Uptown** (widely considered a dub classic) are as much showcases for King Tubby's mixing as for Pablo's playing. His own debut, **This Is Augustus Pablo**, is much better, distinguished by strong presence and lively playing. So is **Original Rockers**, a collection of singles he doctored. The selection is diverse, and Pablo's production (particularly the drum sound) is bright and snappy. For the uninitiated, either of these two offers a perfect place to start.

His recent work is, to some extent, of a piece, with little variety and few distinguishing characteristics. **Africa Must Be Free Dub** is an adequate companion to an LP made by singer Hugh Mundell, a young Pablo protégé who was murdered. **Rockers Meets King Tubby in a Firehouse**, while compelling, features less melodica than usual. **East of the River Nile** is quintessential Pablo, and perhaps his most consistent LP. **Earth's Rightful Ruler** includes a real rarity—a vocal—along with a new version of Pablo's first record, "Java." **King David's Melody**, a singles collection, has the evenness of sound and style of an album. It's a bit sleepy, but lovely all the same.

Pablo's latest release, **Rising Sun**, marks a change in direction. Mixed by Scientist, the overall sound is less distinctive than Pablo's other work. Many of the tunes are up-tempo and disappointing, even though some of the playing—particularly on "Pipers of Zion"—is superb. While a stylistic departure is often refreshing, one hopes this is a transitional album, not a glimpse of things to come. [bk]

PALAIS SCHAUMBURG

Das Single Kabinett EP (Ger. Zick-Zack) 1981
Palais Schaumburg (Kamera/nr) 1982
Lupa (Ger. Phonogram) 1982
Parlez-Vous Schaumburg? (Ger. Phonogram) 1984

Palais Schaumburg is an eccentric, intelligent pop band of frequently shifting personnel from Hamburg, Germany. While their eclectic records display obvious oddball/new wave influences, they seem to have also listened to their share of jazz and 20th-century European composers. **Das Single Kabinett** is a six-track mini-LP of stripped-down, danceable electro-pop, with vocals and synthesizer work owing more than a little to the Residents. The concluding "Aschenbecher" features tight ensemble playing and complex chords, proving the band knows what it's doing. No run-of-the-mill egghead weirdness here.

Palais Schaumburg, their first LP, is a strong collection of smartly-arranged dance tracks, with sounds and harmonies that get more bizarre as the album progresses. Their only record released in England and the last before lead singer Holger Hiller left the group, it is highly recommended.

Produced by Kid Creole associate Andy (Coati Mundi) Hernandez, **Lupa** shows a major change in the band's sound, as prominent vibes and horns mix with odd synth textures to give the LP a clear jazz feel. Throughout it all, they exhibit a Pere Ubu-cum-XTC quirkiness, and at times sound like a hip German Weather Report. Whether or not that's something the world needs is another story, but **Lupa** is an interesting, unique album.

Making another about-face, they released **Parlez-Vous Schaumburg?**. Incorporating some Latin tinges, a punchy horn section and ersatz big-band soundtrack arrangements (on a Fairlight no doubt), it is—idiosyncracies notwithstanding—their most accessible record, at times sounding like Shriekback's experimental side. [dgs]

See also *Holger Hiller*.

PALE FOUNTAINS

Pacific Street (Virgin/nr) 1984
...from across the kitchen table (Virgin/nr) 1984

Although they have precious little to say, this Scottish quartet takes an incredibly long time to get it out. Overdramatic to the point of absurdity, much of the Fountains' music falls somewhere between fake jazz and soul, with occasional digressions into pop and folk.

Pacific Street has few redeeming qualities other than Mick Head's soulful crooning and the imaginative use of super-amplified acoustic guitar. The eight weighty songs borrow from a wide variety of stylistic sources, failing to elaborate on any. The only fully-developed idea is the pop tune "Reach."

The Fountains manage to pull off more than one good number on their second LP. "Shelter" is a reckless rocker, as is the boisterous "27 Ways to Get Back Home" and the breezy "Jean's Not Happening." Elsewhere, the same indulgences that made **Pacific Street** intolerable reassert themselves. It's plain to see

that acoustic pop/folk is the band's strong suit—they should abandon the pretentious soul and jazz forays. [ag]

ROBERT PALMER

Clues (Island) 1980
Maybe It's Live (Island) 1982
Pride (Island) 1983
Riptide (Island) 1985

It's not surprising that this stylish rock dilettante—whose '70s dabblings included excursions into R&B, funk, reggae and Little Feat-backed rock'n'roll—should catch up with post-punk in the '80s. What is remarkable is that on **Clues**, his sixth solo LP, he manages to come up with two tracks as sublime as "Johnny and Mary" and "Looking for Clues," which are heady, intricate and danceable at the same time. Also commendable is the job he does on a couple of collaborations with Gary Numan, injecting more life into them than one would think possible. Still, **Clues** retains an irritating stylistic disparity (heavy metal track/Beatles cover), as if Palmer were afraid his going wholeheartedly into anything new might alienate his audience.

Two years on, Palmer's dilemma is even more apparent on **Maybe It's Live**, a sidestep tentative down to its title and half-live/half-studio format. Combining inferior concert versions of old material, blah new stuff and another collaboration with Numan, the LP continues Palmer's indecisive course.

Without any big-name collaborators, Palmer again delivers a weirdly mixed bag on **Pride**, venturing into electro-disco with the herky-jerky, overbearing "You Are in My System" while affecting a charming calypso flavor in other spots. There's also a reprise of the unsettling undercurrents of "Johnny and Mary" on "Want You More." Palmer's voice is such that the less he tries, the better he sounds: when the going gets hot, his singing becomes overwhelming and irritating.

Palmer's next move was into the vile but hitbound Power Station, a part-time all-star band with two Duran Durannies and a Chicster, produced by Bernard Edwards. When the group opted to tour, however, he bailed out, retaining Edwards and Tony Thompson from the brief collaboration to finish **Riptide**, a bombastic funk record with such tripe as "Addicted to Love," a song whose main value lies in its parody potential. [ds/iar]

See also *Power Station*.

PANIC

13 (Hol. Ariola) 1978

Fairly standard punk-pop; whatever else might have been wrong with their production—like no bass—at least Panic made sure the vocals were out front. The Dutch trio-plus-shouting vocalist puts the tunes and humorous lyrics first, which helps compensate for some of the sloppiness. Inspirational verse: "No one to marry when you're 13...I wanna be 16!" [jg]

TAV FALCO'S PANTHER BURNS

Behind the Magnolia Curtain (Rough Trade) 1981
Blow Your Top EP (Rough Trade/Animal) 1982

Sugar Ditch Revisited EP (New Rose/Frenzi) 1985
Now! [tape] (nr/Frenzi) 1985

For folks who prize unspoiled simplicity in rock'n'roll, and especially in rockabilly, Tav Falco's Panther Burns may be the ultimate. Drenched in echo, Falco goes through a familiar repertoire of Presley-derived whoops, mutters and coos, while an amateurish backing band that includes Alex Chilton grinds away laboriously like high-school rockers struggling through their first rehearsal. The deliberately slowed-down tempo and brazen sloppiness invest **Behind the Magnolia Curtain** with an intriguing conceptual purity, but the rawness turns prolonged exposure into a painful experience.

The four songs on **Blow Your Top** provide more of the same frayed recklessness. Thanks to cleaner sound and playing that verges on being professional, this set almost has commercial potential. (See "Love Is My Business" for proof.) It's still a long way from Falco's sweaty hysteria to the well-oiled appeal of the Stray Cats, though.

Falco recorded **Sugar Ditch Revisited** at Sam Phillips' Memphis studio with "Lx" Chilton and a few other Panther Burnsmen; the six tracks are well-played, well-sung, well-recorded, under control and somewhat underwhelming. The countrybilly spirit and sincerity is there, but the performances start and stop without ever really heating up, and the absence of chaos leaves the simple (if esoteric in origin) material to stand alone, which it doesn't do all that well, until the frisky finale, "Tina, the Go Go Queen." The **Now!** tape, released on Falco's label, Frenzi, consists of seven numbers recorded live in Memphis, 1984. [jy/tr]

PARACHUTE CLUB

The Parachute Club (RCA) 1983
At the Feet of the Moon (RCA) 1984

On their first LP, this fine Canadian septet—a soulful, low-tech match for labelmates M+M—displays a strong rhythmic consciousness (timbales and congas rather than synth thwack). Boasting a phenomenal singer (Lorraine Segato) and produced on the first LP by M+M/Eno collaborator Daniel Lanois, the Club gets positively inspirational on the joyous "Rise Up," while also addressing specific topics like nuclear war, sexism and hunger with intelligent lyrics and inventive, colorful music. Folk of the '80s, indeed!

At the Feet of the Moon, produced by ex-Materialist Michael Beinhorn, bounces to a much funkier beat, with muscular drumming, strong bass and substantial electronic intrusion. (There's a truncated Beinhorn remix of "Rise Up" pasted on the second side—it's out of place but welcome.) Segato's voice, while equally magnificent, gets less prominence; coupled with more functional/less unique music, this record isn't nearly as captivating as its predecessor. [iar]

GRAHAM PARKER AND THE RUMOUR

Howlin Wind (Vertigo/Mercury) 1976
Heat Treatment (Vertigo/Mercury) 1976

Live at Marble Arch (Vertigo/nr) 1976
Stick to Me (Vertigo/Mercury) 1977
The Pink Parker EP (Vertigo/Mercury) 1977
The Parkerilla (Vertigo/Mercury) 1978
Squeezing Out Sparks (Vertigo/Arista) 1979
Live Sparks (Vertigo/Arista) 1979
The Up Escalator (Stiff/Arista) 1980
High Times (Vertigo/nr) 1980
Pourin' It All Out (nr/Mercury) 1985

GRAHAM PARKER

Another Grey Area (RCA/Arista) 1982
The Real Macaw (RCA/Arista) 1983
Anger: Classic Performances (nr/Arista) 1985

GRAHAM PARKER AND THE SHOT

Steady Nerves (Elektra) 1985

Before Elvis Costello and Joe Jackson, there was Graham Parker, redefining the singer/songwriter category for rock'n'roll audiences suspicious of the James Taylors and Carly Simons. With his raspy, Van Morrison-influenced vocals and soul-on-fire tunes, this diminutive Englishman burst on the scene just before the punk explosion and showed how to be personal without sacrificing power.

Produced by Nick Lowe, **Howlin Wind** is a classic debut album, full of fine ideas fleshed out with ragged enthusiasm. Parker acknowledges his roots throughout, singing such original R&B boppers as "White Honey" and "Lady Doctor" with sly wit and masterfully reconstructing rockabilly on the angry "Back to Schooldays," complete with guest twangin' by Dave Edmunds (who recorded the song himself on **Get It**). Evidencing an equally powerful sensitive side, Parker checks in with the reflective "Between You and Me" and "Don't Ask Me Questions," the latter a chilling wail of anguish.

On **Howlin Wind** (and all subsequent LPs through **The Up Escalator**), Parker received formidable backing from the Rumour: Brinsley Schwarz (guitar) and Bob Andrews (keyboards), both ex-Brinsley Schwarz band members; Martin Belmont (guitar), ex-Ducks Deluxe; Stephen Goulding (drums) and Andrew Bodnar (bass), both ex-Bontemps Roulez. Often compared to Dylan's erstwhile cohorts, the Rumour displays the same self-assurance and finesse as the Band, but rocks harder. Despite a checkered recording career on its own, the Rumour was always a stellar support group.

Heat Treatment is essentially a continuation of **Howlin Wind**; although it has two fewer songs, each is punchier than the earlier LP. For spirited soul, there's "Hotel Chambermaid" and "Back Door Love." Parker's serious tunes are also more intense: "Turned Up Too Late" delivers a devastating romantic rejection; the anthemic "Fools' Gold," one of his finest achievements, affirms the need to search for the best, however elusive—it's inspiring and unaffected.

The oft-bootlegged **Live at Marble Arch** promo LP (produced by Nick Lowe) contains live renditions of tracks from these first two discs; original copies are impossible to locate, but counterfeits have been widely circulated in both

England and America.

With the vastly improved music scene as a catalyst, Parker evidently felt the need to assert himself more strongly on **Stick to Me**, but the resulting overstatement and stylistic diversity couldn't be contained comfortably on one LP. Nonetheless, many tracks taken individually are undeniably compelling. The title cut is a soaring declaration of dedication in the face of a hostile world; in Ann Peebles' "I'm Gonna Tear Your Playhouse Down," Parker unleashes exhilarating nastiness. But one need only look at Side Two to sense the confusion: it begins and ends with raucous throwaways designed to compensate for the massive epics in the center. No amount of party fun, however, could clear the air after the overblown theatrics of the seven-minute "Heat in Harlem." Parker is sabotaged by his own indecision.

In classic contract-fulfilling tradition, Parker cranked out a two-record set, **The Parkerilla**: three live sides plus a second studio version of "Don't Ask Me Questions." Adequate but musically unnecessary, it did the legal trick, and Parker was free to switch to a different American label. The sour-grapes "Mercury Poisoning" (1979) was his first release on Arista, which declined to put its name to the promo-only grey 12-inch one-sided single, now also a rare collector's item.

Squeezing Out Sparks resolved Parker's stylistic dilemma. It's his toughest, leanest and most lyrically sophisticated LP; in a way a sad loss of innocence. Eschewing the lighter soul elements of his earlier work, Parker adopts a harsh, nearly humorless tone that suggests cynicism instead of anger. (Regardless, critics generally loved it and sales were decidedly improved over previous efforts.) "Discovering Japan" and "Nobody Hurts You" are sizzling, passionate rockers; for better or worse, the album's centerpiece is "You Can't Be Too Strong," an anti-abortion ballad full of disturbing imagery and emphatic phrasing. In his eagerness to forge a coherent style, Parker neglects to vary the emotional tone.

A novel promo album featuring live versions of every song in the same running order as on the studio version, plus two other live cuts, was issued to radio as **Live Sparks**, further strengthening the band's concert reputation.

Parker somehow lost his sense of purpose on **The Up Escalator**. Although retaining the intense, driven approach of **Squeezing Out Sparks**, the material on this album falls short, possessing fury without context, which results in unsatisfying overkill. Individually, "No Holding Back," "Devil's Sidewalk" and "Love Without Greed" crackle nicely; collectively, they produce a hollow roar. Those looking to assign blame will notice the increasing influence of the king of rock melodrama, Bruce Springsteen, who even joins in vocally on the bloated "Endless Night." Also, the departure of Bob Andrews must have added to the changing situation.

The rest of the Rumour followed Andrews through the exit prior to **Another Grey Area**, which actually constitutes a minor comeback, avoiding the noisier extremes of **The Up Escalator**. A band of New York session musicians provides

precise though unspectacular accompaniment; Parker co-produced with Jack Douglas. Interestingly, the harder-rocking tracks are the least effective: "Big Fat Zero" and "You Hit the Spot" seem little more than half-hearted gestures. In contrast, ballads like "Temporary Beauty," "Dark Side of the Bright Lights" and "Crying for Attention" have a graceful and unforced ring of sincerity never before heard on a Parker LP. Though **Another Grey Area** seldom overwhelms, it does indicate that, after six studio albums, Parker is still waiting to take chances.

The Real Macaw is a chance he probably shouldn't have taken. Songs like "You Can't Take Love for Granted" and "Life Gets Better" reach Parker's required level of intensity; the production and playing do not. David Kershenbaum gives Parker the kind of sparse, colorless setting he used to create for Joe Jackson, and the musicianship is unnecessarily understated. The end product: a disc that is watered-down and should have been harder.

Steady Nerves rights the balance, blending the pop veneer of **The Real Macaw** with a tougher band attack. Reunited with firebrand guitarist Brinsley Schwarz, Parker turns in a bracing series of characteristically pithy performances, from the cheerfully raunchy "When You Do That to Me" to the gorgeously romantic "Wake Up (Next to You)" to "Break Them Down," a classic GP fist-waver. A solid album that bodes well. (The CD has an extra song, "Too Much Time to Think.")

High Times and **Pourin' It All Out** are (English and American, respectively) greatest hits packages of songs cut with the Rumour. **Anger** collects tracks from Parker's Arista (US) albums. [jy]
See also **Rumour**.

PARROTS

The Parrots EP (Desert Island-Attrix/nr) 1980

A quartet that made promising noises on the **Vaultage 78** compilation of Brighton bands fizzles on its EP. Intelligent lyrics and a nascent pop sensibility are couched in ska and reggae rhythms, but a lack of character and drive, especially in the vocals, renders it merely inoffensively bland. [jg]

PASSAGE

Pindrop (Object/nr) 1980
For All and None (Night & Day-Virgin/nr) 1981
Degenerates (Cherry Red/nr) 1982
Enflame (Cherry Red/nr) 1983
Through the Passage (Cherry Red/nr) 1983

Keyboardist/vocalist/composer/producer Dick Witts *is* the Passage, regardless of lineup shifts (at first a quartet, now a trio). A former percussionist with a noted classical orchestra, Witts and his fellow Mancunians make records that defy pigeonholing, evoking comparisons to Keith Emerson and Weather Report on one hand and Wire, Gang of Four and Joy Division on the other. The reviewer who sat them smack between early Soft Machine and the Fall may have come the closest of all.

Unlike the Softs, Witts uses a goodly assortment of keyboards—strictly for delivering and coloring

the music, without obligatory solos. And while the Passage boasts no brilliant Robert Wyatt parallel at the traps, the drums are also an effective part of the music (as when fluttering like a heartbeat). Witts is no strident caterwauler like Mark E. Smith, and if his socio-politically oriented lyrics do reduce complexities to catchphrases, they also promptly expand upon them—generally avoiding egregious didacticism or exhortation—articulately and strikingly. Witts frequently uses sensationalism, but as an effective device, not just for shock value.

The songs are often surprisingly memorable. The two most recent productions show improved clarity and cogency, and tracks like "XOYO" (from **Degenerates**) couple the usual unlikely lyrics with surprisingly conventional, even commercial, hooks.

Through the Passage is, sadly, a disappointing compilation. It does include "Devils and Angels" and "Taboos," two worthy 45s never before on LP, but the other selections haven't got the collective intensity of any of the original albums. [jg]

PASSIONNEL

See *Alex Gibson.*

PASSION PUPPETS

Beyond the Pale (Stiff/Stiff-MCA) 1984

The Passion Puppets play reasonably concise melodic guitar rock with a strong rhythmic component. The sound is consistently attractive—nearing U2 or the Alarm in spots—but there are no distinguishing features or memorable songs on their bland album. [tr]

PASSIONS

Michael and Miranda (Fiction/nr) 1980
Thirty Thousand Feet Over China (Polydor/nr) 1981
Sanctuary (Polydor/nr) 1982

Introduced on **Michael and Miranda**, the Passions appeared to be part of the post-punk movement, characterized by spare arrangements, stark vocals and fairly unmelodic—though lyrically interesting—songs. Subjects like unhappy love ("Oh No, It's You") and frustrated attempts at relationships and communication ("Palava"), along with "Obsession," "Suspicion," fear ("Man on the Tube") and neuroses ("Absentee") make the world on **Michael and Miranda** a particularly anxious one.

Thirty Thousand Feet Over China is less bleak, though still tainted with anger, deceit and suspicion. With a new producer, Nigel Gray, and a new bass player, the Passions sound smoother and more melodic ("Someone Special," "Runaway" and the nicely poppy "Bachelor Girls"). Lyrics are as sharp and offbeat as ever—check the clever, almost tongue-in-cheek "I'm in Love with a German Film Star."

Between **Thirty Thousand Feet** and **Sanctuary**, the Passions released a single, "Africa Mine," arguably their best song. It's a pretty, haunting, bitter and impassioned condemnation of colonialist exploitation but could really be applied to greed by any name.

"Africa Mine" foreshadowed the sound of **Sanctuary**, which is smooth without being bland, sophisticated without being smug, and pretty without being soppy. Barbara Gogan shows growing confidence as a singer; her new expressiveness and the addition of a synthesizer serve to fill in and soften what used to be rough edges. The soaring title track is especially memorable. [ks]

PAYOLAS

Introducing Payolas EP (nr/IRS) 1980
In a Place Like This (IRS) 1981
No Stranger to Danger (A&M) 1982
Hammer on a Drum (A&M) 1983

PAUL HYDE AND THE PAYOLAS

Here's the World for Ya (nr/A&M) 1985

Vancouver, British Columbia was the site of one of Canada's most volatile early punk explosions, but only a couple of bands have managed to spread their fame much beyond the city limits. The Payolas are one of those, and for a while managed to retain some of the scene's fire after signing to an American label.

The gatefold 7-inch EP—four songs, two of them redone for the first album—was recorded by an early four-piece lineup, produced by guitarist Bob Rock to sound like a high-voltage cross between the New York Dolls, Clash and Ramones.

An impressive debut, **In a Place Like This** is political (but not preachy), offering sophisticated punk with reggae seasoning, which makes it reminiscent of the Clash without getting derivative about it. Musical variety, lyrical quality and youthful power add to the album's strong impact.

No Stranger to Danger, expertly produced by Mick Ronson (who had not previously distinguished himself in that role), shows enormous progress—from an able but inexperienced adolescent band to a tremendously skilled and creative heir to Mott the Hoople. (If that connection doesn't register, Ronson was a late member of Mott and worked extensively with ex-leader Ian Hunter afterwards.) The judicious addition of contemporary keyboards, the band's vastly improved singing and a more-melody/less-thrash outlook make every track a treat.

Sticking with Ronno, **Hammer on a Drum** takes a large step away from the youth and energy of the band's beginnings. Singer Paul Hyde selectively affects a near-perfect vocal imitation of Ian Hunter (who also appears on the record, furthering the Mott relationship). It's slick and engaging, but sorely lacking in believable personality. It may not be fair to expect any group to remain true to its (perceived) principles, but getting this fogeyish so fast is neither commendable nor flattering.

Here's the World for Ya, produced by big-time mainstreamer David Foster, is even less invigorating. For this boring and bland synth-rock record, the band feels obliged to thank members of Rush and Loverboy. Rock on! [iar]

PENETRATION

Moving Targets (Virgin/nr) 1978

110

Coming Up for Air (Virgin/Virgin Int'l) 1979
Race Against Time (Clifdayn/nr) 1979

Inspired into existence by the Sex Pistols, Penetration emerged from northern England in 1977 with a great punk single, "Don't Dictate." Led by singer Pauline Murray, brash amateurism had been converted into competent musicianship by the time of **Moving Targets**, released at first on glow-in-the-dark gimmick vinyl that was far noisier than illuminating. Playing mostly originals (written by Murray collaborating with others in the band), but including Patti Smith's "Free Money" and the Buzzcocks' "Nostalgia," Penetration's debut LP mixes expansive creations and direct punk-outs, all done with style and originality. Unlike other LPs by young bands of this era, **Moving Targets** still sounds surprisingly fresh years later.

Coming Up for Air, produced poorly by Steve Lillywhite, isn't nearly as good, despite some swell tracks. Where the first record was almost consistently exciting, only "Shout Above the Noise," "On Reflection" and "Lifeline" have the same melodic, dramatic intensity. The band had evidently run out of good songs, and the muffled sound only exacerbates the mishmash.

An officially-sanctioned bootleg, **Race Against Time** consists of a side of demos and a live side. The studio work predates the band's album sessions and is pretty boring; the live material, recorded in Newcastle mostly in 1979, is energetic and well-played.   [iar]

See also *Pauline Murray and the Invisible Girls*.

PERE UBU

The Modern Dance (Phonogram/ Blank) 1978 (Rough Trade) 1981
Datapanik in the Year Zero EP (Radar/nr) 1978
Dub Housing (Chrysalis) 1978
New Picnic Time (Chrysalis/Rough Trade) 1979
The Art of Walking (Rough Trade) 1981
390 Degrees of Simulated Stereo (Rough Trade) 1981
Song of the Bailing Man (Rough Trade) 1982
Terminal Tower: An Archival Collection (Rough Trade/ Twin/Tone) 1985

Originally from Cleveland, Pere Ubu combined disorienting—often dissonant—rock and urban blues in a stunningly original and outlandish mix, but never lost an urgent, joyous party atmosphere. Lead singer David Thomas' plebian warble is the most noticeable feature of their sound, coloring all of Ubu's proceedings in a bizarre light; casual listeners might, as a result, overlook the band's powerful, polished musicianship. One of the most innovative American musical forces, Pere Ubu is to Devo what Arnold Schoenberg was to Irving Berlin.

The Modern Dance includes two songs remade from early 45s Pere Ubu had released on their Hearthan label. Focusing on themes of alienation and adolescent angst, the album cuts a precarious middle ground between art-rock and Midwestern garage pop. **Datapanik in the Year Zero** is more successful, collecting five of the original Hearthan tracks, including the dynamic,

paranoiac "30 Seconds Over Tokyo." Dark, challenging material.

Dub Housing takes a quantum leap in production and material. Eerie guitar and keyboard work by Tom Herman and Allen Ravenstine, respectively, rivets Thomas' otherworldly vocals to a dark vision at once surreal and lodged in claustrophobic real life. Uncompromising music and solid songwriting, especially on the obsessive drone, "Codex." Highly recommended.

New Picnic Time shifts toward brighter, more open sound and a deformed blues ethic. Still bearing an air of disaster, Thomas' lyrics develop story-songs that increasingly focus on common elements of everyday life, drawing more in line with his strong religious beliefs. The factors combine into a bizarre music reminiscent of Captain Beefheart.

The Art of Walking features increasing interest in musical development, tending toward ambient use of sound to create new aural landscapes, as well as more creative use of dissonance.

390 Degrees of Simulated Stereo overviews Pere Ubu's development through a collection of live recordings, featuring their best songs from the 1976—1979 era, including "30 Seconds Over Tokyo," "My Dark Ages" and "Heart of Darkness." Recommended.

Song of the Bailing Man brings Pere Ubu firmly into the art rock fold, with the addition of Anton Fier (Feelies, Lounge Lizards) and Mayo Thompson (Red Crayola). With clean production and spare sound, Pere Ubu abandoned the chaotic inspiration that charged their earlier work, replacing it with an unaccustomed restraint that sounds out of place.

Terminal Tower is, as billed, an archival collection with lyrics and abundant liner notes. Many of these eleven essential Ubu tracks—from "Heart of Darkness" and "The Final Solution" to "Not Happy" and "Lonesome Cowboy Dave"—are otherwise hard to find; two are alternate mixes.   [sg/iar]

See also *Red Crayola, David Thomas, Tripod Jimmie*.

LEE PERRY

Roast Fish Collie Weed and Corn Bread (Jam. Upsetters)
Scratch on the Wire (Island/nr) 1979
The Return of Pipecock Jackxon (Hol. Black Star Liner) 1980
The Upsetter Collection (Trojan/nr) 1981
Mystic Miracle Star (nr/ Heartbeat) 1982
History, Mystery and Prophecy (Island/Mango) 1984
Heart of the Ark Vols. 1 & 2 (Seven Leaves/nr) 1982
Megaton Dub Vols. 1 & 2 (Seven Leaves/nr) 1982
Reggae Greats (Island/Mango) 1984

LEE PERRY AND THE UPSETTERS

Super Ape (Island/Mango) 1976
Scratch and Co.: Chapter One the Upsetters (nr/Clocktower)
The Upsetter Box Set (Trojan/nr) 1985
Some of the Best (nr/Heartbeat) 1986

JAH LION

Colombia Colly (Island/Mango) 1976

Certainly eccentric, possibly mad, Lee Perry is reggae's most influential producer, with a career that spans the entire history of the music. He started at Coxsone Dodd's Studio One label, first as a talent scout, then as producer. Moving on to other labels, he recorded hit after hit for Jamaican artists, assembling the original Wailers and producing their earliest —some say best—tracks. Perry has also done extensive solo work, composing, arranging and singing his own records. With the help of a studio band, the Upsetters (named for one of his aliases), Perry has forged a style that's idiosyncratic and revolutionary—full of shifting, echoey rhythms and weird sound effects. His characteristic sound is unique—extended grooves layered like fog, with odd vocals and percussion shimmering in the dense mist.

Perry became an Island house producer in the '70s and a major influence on new wave bands with an affinity for reggae. (The Clash covered "Police and Thieves," a tune he co-wrote with Junior Murvin, on their first LP; Perry later did some production for the band.)

His early work as both producer and performer is well chronicled. **Some of the Best** contains many fine recordings, including "People Funny Boy" and others that make plain American R&B's essential link to reggae. **The Upsetter Collection** has "Return of Django," a UK hit, and the Gatherers' "Words of My Mouth," the rhythm track of which Perry would use again and again. **Chapter One** features a dub of Junior Byles' "Curly Locks," Ricky and Bunny's "Bush Wed Corn Trash" and others co-produced with Brad Osbourne. All three compilations are lively, vital and consistent.

Perry's Island releases are also notable. **Colombia Colly** (billing him as Jah Lion) is one of the best, showing him in stylistic transition and getting weirder, with a cover of Peggy Lee's "Fever" and one cut that features a creaking door. **Super Ape**, from the same year, is more conventional, a dub LP that emphasizes the Upsetters' playing. Perry's personality is evident, though subdued. The number of engineers credited on **History, Mystery and Prophecy**, Perry's last Island LP, suggests the label might have been attempting to smooth out the roughness. The sound is too clean, static and unexciting.

Perry's Island years also yielded two almost identical compilations—**Scratch on the Wire** and **Reggae Greats**. Both feature "Police and Thieves," as well as "Roast Fish and Cornbread" and "Soul Fire" (from the brilliant Jamaican-only **Roast Fish Collie Weed and Corn Bread** LP), but neither is essential.

His other LPs vary in quality. **The Return of Pipecock Jackxon** derives from Dutch sessions during which Perry reportedly experimented with LSD and destroyed the studio. Needless to say, it's brilliant. So is **Mystic Miracle Star**, which he made with the Majestics. Surprisingly straightforward, with few sound effects, it is still full of his characteristic production signatures. Less impressive are the two

so-so volumes of **Heart of the Ark** (compilations of Perry-produced singers); worse, the two **Megaton Dub** volumes are so lackluster that one authority wondered in print whether Perry had actually produced them.

Two notable '85 releases bring us up to date. On "Judgment in a Babylon," a startling Jamaican 12-inch, Perry accuses Island Records boss Chris Blackwell of being a vampire who killed Bob Marley. Although libelous and crazy, it must be heard. In a more historical vein, **The Upsetter Box** makes three classic out-of-print LPs (**African Blood**, **Rhythm Shower** and **Double 7**) available again. Pricey but worthwhile, the set features appearances by U-Roy, I-Roy and others, and marks Perry's return to Trojan, the label that will release his next LP, **Battle of Armagideon**.   [bk]

MARK PERRY

Snappy Turns (Deptford Fun City/nr) 1981

GOOD MISSIONARIES

Fire from Heaven (Deptford Fun City/nr) 1979

Launched by the adventurous Mark Perry following the breakup of Alternative TV, the Good Missionaries unfortunately aren't anything special. The band recalls Frank Zappa at his most self-indulgent; the music meanders without form or reason. Maybe creating this chaos was enjoyable for the people involved (including Henry Badowski), but that doesn't justify the record's release. File under "Failed Experiments."

Perry's subsequent solo outing belies its title by dishing up more of his semi-tortured recitation of what-a-bloody-world-it-is to the tune of . . . well, no recognizable tune at all.   [cpl/jg]

See also *Henry Badowski*.

PET SHOP BOYS

Please (Parlophone/EMI America) 1986

Chapter 53 in the Most Unlikely Chart-Topping Bands of All Time Record Book: Pet Shop Boys, a duo of ex-*Smash Hits* journalist Neil Tennant and Chris Lowe, have disproven the longstanding belief that rock-crit bands (other than the Pretenders, that is), by definition, never have mass appeal. **Please** is a slick, set of anonymous easy-listening disco tracks, brilliantly, soullessly produced (mostly by Stephen Hague), with ridiculous, overbearingly smug lyrics recited by Tennant, who speak-sings suspiciously like a young Al Stewart. The in-joke references and self-amused esoterica strewn throughout songs like "West End Girls" and "Opportunities" should have precluded their general popularity, but evidently the laxative-smooth synth backing has some utilitarian value for people. Ghastly, depressing and offensive.   [iar]

PHANTOM, ROCKER & SLICK

See *Stray Cats*.

PHOTOS

The Photos (CBS/Epic) 1980

Post-Blondie pop in punk clothing, the Photos were a competent male trio backing Wendy Wu's distinctive visage and Ronnie Spectorish voice. Unfortunately, Wu and her Worcestershire compatriots lacked the presence and sheer sauciness to compensate for inane lyrics and likable but forgettable tunes. There are some smart touches—like the punk-cum-strings (!) reworking of Bacharach/David's "I Just Don't Know What to Do with Myself." Early UK pressings included a bonus disc of the Photos' developmental **Blackmail Tapes**, proving that the band could actually work up a sweat while remaining amiably dull. [jg]

PHRANC

Folksinger (Stiff/Rhino) 1985

Looking like a crew-cut Matt Dillon on the cover of her first album, Phranc is an otherwise tradition-minded descendant of such '60s protest singers as Bob Dylan, Phil Ochs, Joan Baez and Tom Paxton. The topical songs, performed with simple beauty on acoustic guitar, address various subjects and personalities of current interest, from women athletes to Marvel's comic book about the Pope to "Female Mudwrestling" to Los Angeles' celebrity coroner, Thomas Noguchi. Taking one too many cues from Dylan, there's an unnecessary reading of his chilling "Lonesome Death of Hattie Carroll" and several similar originals. Phranc's not a timeless melodicist, but her wry lyrical observations and attractive singing makes **Folksinger** a worthy effort. [iar]

CHARLIE PICKETT AND THE EGGS

Live at the Button (nr/Open) 1982
Cowboy Junkie Au-Go-Go EP (nr/Open) 1984

CHARLIE PICKETT

Route 33 (Making Waves/Twin/Tone) 1986

Pickett may have led *the* new wave bar band; on the Eggs' records, these Floridians throw original tunes in with covers of wildly varying notoriety, shake it all up and pour out their fiery stuff. That Pickett's own tunes often compare favorably to those he choses to cover makes their scarcity on the live LP disappointing, and using three tunes by the Pirates (during and after Johnny Kidd) and two by the Flamin' Groovies on one album is a bit much, even if Pickett's slide work and the nasty ensemble nearly makes numbers like "Slow Death" sound newly minted.

For their long-awaited second vinyl outing the Eggs took to the studio and cut five songs, including "Overtown," a great number about the Miami riots and "Marlboro Town," a dopey "Louie Louie" adaptation that was a hit single for Charlie's cousin Mark Markham two decades ago. Even without the special charge they get onstage, the Eggs reel off true-blue high-energy rockers, further establishing guitarist John Salton as a first-rate student of Thunders, Fogerty and Sky Saxon. It's hard to believe this band isn't as big a global legend as it deserves to be.

Eggless, but joined by such grunge talents as ex-Panther Burns guitarist Jim Duckworth and Maureen Tucker, Charlie is still burning with unquenchable rock'n'roll fire on **Route 33**. The material is almost entirely Pickett's; Minneapolis legend Chris Osgood produced it to resemble an old Stones' album from a real ethnic American perspective. A little bit blues, a little bit country, and strictly bullshit-free, the album is a straightforward electric charge from a real heartlands original. [jg/iar]

JEFFREY LEE PIERCE
See *Gun Club.*

PIGBAG

Dr. Heckle and Mr. Jive (Y/Stiff) 1982
Lend an Ear (Y/nr) 1983
Pigbag Live (Y/nr) 1983
Favourite Things (Y/nr) 1983

Pigbag played only instrumentals, as befits a sextet with a four-piece brass-and-reed section. The music is mostly uptempo, Latin-tinged jazz-funk and good fun for the length of a single; "Papa's Got a Brand New Pigbag," included on the first album, was a big dancefloor hit. Stretched out over an album, though, the band's writing limitations become stultifyingly clear. **Dr. Heckle and Mr. Jive** contains three variations on the "Papa" formula and a couple of slower cuts that reveal a band with technical know-how and nothing to say. Following a second studio album and a poorly-received live set, Pigbag called it a day. **Favourite Things** is a retrospective. [si]

PIL
See *Public Image Ltd.*

PINK INDUSTRY

Forty-Five EP (Zulu/nr) 1982
Low Technology (Zulu/nr) 1983
Who Told You, You Were Naked (Zulu/nr) 1983
New Beginnings (Zulu/nr) 1985

With many of their Liverpool compatriots (Echo, Frankie, Pete Burns) gone on to worldwide fame and fortune, these two stalwarts —singer Jayne Casey and bassist/keyboardist Ambrose Reynolds (actually a onetime member of Frankie), adding a guitarist after the first album—continue to evade commercial success as Pink Industry (following the dissolution of Casey's Pink Military). Far from being simply credible by association, PI makes highly pleasing music that is original, fragile, attractive, ethereal and haunting. [iar]

PINK MILITARY

Blood and Lipstick EP (Eric's/nr) 1979
Do Animals Believe in God? (Eric's/nr) 1980

A minor chapter in the explosion of new Liverpool bands, Pink Military was formed by Jayne Casey after Big in Japan folded in 1978. Their album, recorded after two years and numerous lineup changes, is an eclectically derivative (yet amusing) hodgepodge that is neither stunningly original nor disgustingly clichéd. [sg]

PIRANHAS

The Piranhas (Sire/nr) 1980

The Piranhas hailed from England's south coast—a charming, idiosyncratic quintet with thick accents, funny lyrics and a jaundiced attitude that led to such neurotic numbers as "Getting Beaten Up," "I Don't Want My Body" and "Green Don't Suit Me." The music is mostly good-natured ska, in the general direction of early Madness and Bad Manners, though a number of the tracks fall well outside the genre, some recalling spy-movie soundtracks from the '60s. The Piranhas are likable, but smart enough to be a lot more than mere fun. [iar]

HONEST JOHN PLAIN
See *Lurkers.*

DER PLAN

Normalette Surprise (nr/Optional) 1981
Die Letze Rache (Ger. Ata Tak) 1983
Japlan (Jap. Ata Tak) 1985

The only American release by this Dusseldorf *neu deutsche welle* band pairs three bonus songs on one side with a full-length album on the other. Whimsical and dissonant, in spots very much like the Residents, der Plan incorporates toylike instrumental sounds, tape cut-ups, sing-song vocals, TV theme music and Spike Jones sound effects to create a diverting excursion into the weird and wonderful. Must be heard to be believed. [tr]

PLANET PATROL

Planet Patrol (21-Polydor/Tommy Boy) 1983

Modern hip-hop meets classic soul: Arthur Baker and John Robie supply the songs, music(ians) and production, while the five members of Planet Patrol add skillful Motown-style vocals that especially recall the Temptations in their prime. The four new songs are both soulful and exciting, with synth percussion and scratch-mix tricks interweaving with the inspiring singing. On two covers—Gary Glitter's "I Didn't Know I Loved You (Till I Saw You Rock and Roll)" and Todd Rundgren's "It Wouldn't Have Made Any Difference"—the stylistic traffic jam gets mighty bizarre, but still works. A neat record that should have been more influential. [iar]

PLAN 9

Frustration (nr/Voxx) 1982
Dealing with the Dead (nr/Midnight) 1984
I've Just Killed a Man I Don't Want to See Any Meat (nr/Midnight) 1985
Keep Your Cool and Read the Rules (nr/Pink Dust) 1985

Outside of its art college, Rhode Island hasn't exactly been a watershed for modern rock music. But the state has a group to be proud of in Plan 9, whose **Frustration** is exciting garage psychedelia. Four guitars provide a swirling, mesmerizing effect that recalls the best of the late '60s and gives able support to Eric Stumpo's emotional vocals. The only drawback is that there are no original songs here, just covers of hopelessly obscure gems from the '60s.

By contrast, **Dealing with the Dead** features eight original songs as well as a '60s sound so convincing that you'll swear you can smell incense burning. Stumpo's vocals are great, a whiny growl crossbreeding Michael J. Pollard and John Kay; the massed guitars and Debora D's atmospheric keyboards increase the sense of deja entendu even further. Far more convincing than a lot of other similar-minded outfits, Plan 9 knows just how to launch a magic carpet ride to the center of your mind. Diabolical.

I've Just Killed a Man is a steamy live album recorded as a six-piece in Boston, Washington D.C., New Haven and Providence. A trio of ace covers—including the MC5's "Looking at You"—and a guest appearance by head Lyre Jeff Conolly on add extra excitement to the spirited fun.

Keep Your Cool covers a lot of stylistic ground, including the film noir ambience of "Street of Painted Lips" sung by Debora D, an unclassifiable rollicking instrumental ("King Nine Will Not Return") and various stripes of '60s rock, suggesting everything from Steppenwolf to Spirit. The band's songs are solid, if some are a little undeveloped, the two covers righteously arcane. Only complaint: a hint of restraint on Side One. [cpl/iar]

PLASMATICS

New Hope for the Wretched (Stiff/Stiff America) 1980
Beyond the Valley of 1984 (nr/Stiff America) 1981
Metal Priestess EP (Stiff/Stiff America) 1981

New Hope for the Wretched, "produced" by Jimmy Miller, represents the Plasmatics' first stage—mere artless gimmickry as conceived by the group's manager and lyricist, ex-porn entrepreneur Rod Swenson. Former sex-show queen Wendy O. Williams hoarsely talks/shouts/heavy-breathes lyrics jumbling the psychotronic film aesthetic (sex, violence, gratuitous grotesqueries) accompanied by a band playing with no subtlety whatever at punk speed and volume, reprising the "best" bits of the 'Matics' preceding proto-hardcore indie singles (e.g., Williams buzzsawing a guitar in half). Entertaining for its sheer crassness perhaps, though hardly listenable.

Beyond the Valley of 1984, though, *is* quite listenable, if only intermittently memorable. Swenson's lyrics aspire to nightmares of apocalypse and superhuman lust and degradation. The music is likewise heavier, but clearer and not without flashes of finesse: punchy drums courtesy of guest Neal Smith (ex-Alice Cooper), good guitar squeals from Swenson's main writing collaborator, Richie Stotts and even a culture-shock backing-vocals appearance by the girl-group Angels.

Metal Priestess—25 minutes at a sub-LP price—is the best buy of the lot: smokin' live versions of two of **Beyond the Valley**'s best, not to mention proof that Williams *can* sweetly carry a tune, as grim as it is ("Lunacy"). The record also notably captures the Plasmatics before the completion of their heavy metal metamorphosis. (See the band's subsequent **Coup d'Etat** and Williams' solo albums for those grisly details.) [jg]

PLASTIC BERTRAND

Plastic Bertrand AN1 (Sire/nr) 1978
Ca Plane pour Moi (nr/Sire) 1978

J'te Fais un Plan (Bel. RKM) 1979
L'Album (Can. Attic) 1980
Greatest Hits (Can. Attic) 1981
Plastiquez Vos Baffles (Can. Attic) 1982

One of the first punk gag records and still one of the greatest, "Ca Plane pour Moi" was a major European hit in late '77 and early '78, launching the career of blond Belgian pretty boy Roger Jouret—aka Plastic Bertrand. Scuttlebutt at the time claimed Bertrand was the invention of some anonymous French studio pranksters; in fact, Jouret had already played drums in an earlier Belgian punk trio called Hubble Bubble (whose one LP was notable only for a trashy cover of the Kinks' "I'm Not Like Everybody Else"). Together with producer/songwriter Lou Deprijck, he created the persona of Plastic Bertrand, a jolly satire on the safety-pin image and jackhammer crunch of punk.

"Ca Plane pour Moi" ("This Life's for Me") is truly great dumbness—Bertrand singing verbose, seemingly nonsensical French lyrics over a classic three-chord Ramones roar with Spectorish saxes and a winning falsetto "oooh-weee-oooh" on the chorus. **Ca Plane pour Moi** (the US title of **Plastic Bertrand AN1**, released first in Belgium, then in England) also contains more of the hilarious same—a spirited remake of the Small Faces' "Sha La La La Lee" and "Wha! Wha!," wherein Bertrand does barnyard animal imitations.

The follow-up album, **J'te Fais un Plan**, has two limp reggae entries actually recorded in Jamaica (the title song and "Hit 78") and a sugary-sweet ballad called "Affection" dedicated to Jonathan Richman. More interesting is the ten-minute electro-disco number "Tout Petit la Planete," a blatant Kraftwerk cop tarted up with a nagging hook and a rich synthesizer sound predating by two years the synth-pop confections of the Human League and O.M.D.

L'Album is only for the true P-Bert devotee, its tighter formulaic new wave pop distinguished by a catchy vanilla-funk rap track, "Stop ou Encore," which bears a passing similarity to Blondie's "Rapture." The **Greatest Hits** album collects his big European successes with a pair of bonus live tracks. [df]

See also *Elton Motello*.

PLASTICLAND

Color Appreciation (Bam-Caruso/Pink Dust) 1985
Wonder Wonderful Wonderland (Bam-Caruso/Pink Dust) 1985

Following several 7-inch releases on their own label, this time-warped psychedelic quartet from Milwaukee, Wisconsin began issuing wonderful albums of original paisley retro-rock. Both **Color Appreciation** (with a Pretty Things' tune amidst such band creations as "Euphoric Trapdoor Shoes," "Rat-Tail Comb" and "Pop! Op Drops") and **Wonder Wonderful Wonderland** (featuring such giddy items as "Grassland of Reeds and Things," "Processes of the Silverness" and "Fairytale Hysteria") are charming, whimsical, stylish, witty, and utterly entertaining. [iar]

PLASTICS

Welcome Plastics (Island/nr) 1981
Plastics (nr/Island) 1981

HAJIME TACHIBANA

H (Jap. Yen-Alfa) 1982
Hm (nr/Ralph) 1984
Taiyo-Sun (Jap. School) 1985

The Plastics' discography contains three Japanese LPs, at least one of which is significantly better than their Western release, **Welcome**. (**Plastics** is the US equivalent.) An art-pop quintet comprising four men and a female singer, Plastics' cues comes from American pop culture of the '60s in general and the B-52's in particular. Jumpy and clever, nervous and kitschy, they take Western ideals of technology and commercialism and give them an Asian flavor. A great, original band; as noted, however, this is not their best record.

Following Plastics' breakup at the end of 1981, Tachibana put down his guitar in favor of exploring jazz sax, resulting in **H**, a diverting album which is wacky but not silly—his commitment to this musical path is no less sincere for its synthesis with what he helped develop in Plastics.

Three years on, his saxisms on **Hm** are artier and less lightheartedly playful—but not too much of either; **Hm** is still fun. Primitive drums (or were they copped from a '40s B-movie conga line production number?) are often used to underpin "outside" jazz sax charts and solos, interlarded with quieter numbers minus bass and drums in which pretty melodies are stated. Odd but ingratiating. [iar/jg]

PLIMSOULS

Zero Hour EP (nr/Beat) 1980
The Plimsouls (nr/Planet) 1981
Everywhere at Once (Geffen) 1983

PETER CASE

Peter Case (Geffen) 1986

LA's Plimsouls are another band that got sucked up by the record companies' power pop madness in the Knack's wake. Following a short independent recording career, they signed with a big label and made one fine LP that didn't sell, and that was nearly the end of that.

Heaps of promise are already evident on the cheap-sounding **Zero Hour** 12-inch EP. Fronted by sharp-voiced Peter Case (formerly Paul Collins' bandmate in the Nerves), the Plimsouls toss out enough cutting harmonies and nifty guitar licks to recall **Beatles VI**, although their spirit is totally fresh and beyond nostalgia, the aggression modern.

That promise is fulfilled on their first major-label LP, which trims only the raggedest edges to showcase vibrant, hummable tunes like "Now." The Plimsouls' affection for '60s soul also gets a tumble via the use of a horn section and a hot cover of "Mini-Skirt Minnie."

The band's relationship with Planet soured soon after the LP stiffed, and the Plimsouls left the label to make a wonderful independent 12-inch called "A Million Miles Away." Showing enormous commercial and personal resilience, they subsequently joined the Geffen roster and produced **Everywhere at Once**, re-recording that memorable single alongside a batch of similarly strong new ones, all bubbling with undiminished fire and melody. Lyrics, however, show signs of frustration: "How Long Will

It Take?," "My Life Ain't Easy," "Play the Breaks." Case subsequently went solo, issuing an album in 1986. [jy/iar]

PLUGZ

Electrify Me (nr/Plugz) 1979
Better Luck (nr/Fatima) 1981

Guitarist/singer Tito Larriva—now in the Cruzados—led this early LA band. The Plugz play sharp and punky rock'n'roll with a strong sense of pop structure on the varied **Electrify Me**. The title track is mildly reggaefied; there's also a cover (in Spanish) of "La Bamba" as well as some folky things, all sticking close to the band's essentially unadventurous core.

Better Luck is more pop/folk/countryish—Rank and File meets Tom Petty. More mainstream, it displays a promising rock talent enervated to the point of tedium. (The Plugz subsequently contributed three very divergent songs to the *Repo Man* soundtrack.) [tr]

See also *Cruzados*.

POET AND THE ROOTS

See *Linton Kwesi Johnson*.

POGUES

Red Roses for Me (Stiff/Enigma) 1984
Rum Sodomy & the Lash (Stiff/Stiff-MCA) 1985
Poguetry in Motion EP (Stiff/Stiff-MCA) 1986

The Pogues, a motley London-based agglomeration (lately an octet) of erstwhile punk rockers (singer/songwriter Shane Mac-Gowan was in the unlamented Nips; guitarist Philip Chevron led Dublin's Radiators from Space) and knockabout folkies, play traditional (and MacGowan's stylistically antiquated originals) Irish, English and Australian folk songs, their basic reverence tempered only by rock spirit and tempos. While both albums have their fine moments (especially the Elvis Costello-produced second), their folk orientation should have precluded the outpouring of praise rock critics heaped on them. (For those that want it, there are certainly enough genuine folk artists in Great Britain who play this music with more knowledge and credibility.) Something of a Tom Waits-like figure, MacGowan writes songs of London life that are gritty and realistic; the band plays them with rudimentary acoustic instrumentation. Only bassist Cait O'Riordan, who became Costello's fiancée in early '86, uses an amp.

Far better than either album, however, is the Costello-produced 12-inch **Poguetry** EP: three new MacGowan songs, plus an instrumental reel. Mixing zydeco with Gaelic soul, "London Girl" is a rousing singalong, an urban travelogue that sounds like the hit of Kevin Rowland's dreams; "A Rainy Night in Soho" is a beautiful Van Morrison-like waltz played on piano with tasteful horns and strings; "The Body of an American" is a drinking song that most closely resembles the Pogues' general busker sound, with uilleann pipes, martial drums and jolly tin whistle. (Collectors' note: Stiff also issued the EP as a 7-inch pic disc.) [iar]

POINTED STICKS

Perfect Youth (Can. Quintessence) 1980

Modestly appealing pop punk, produced by fellow Vancouverite, Payolas guitarist Bob Rock, from a band whose earlier 45 ("What Do You Want Me to Do?" b/w "Somebody's Mom") boded far better. The faint stirrings of imaginative pop on Side Two don't go far enough, either, and Nick Jones' mischievous Everly Brothers-ish voice can't carry it alone. [jg]

POISON GIRLS

Chappaquiddick Bridge (Crass/nr) 1981
Total Exposure (Xntrix/nr) 1981
Where's the Pleasure (Xntrix/nr) 1982
I'm Not a Real Woman EP (Xntrix/nr) 1983
7 Year Scratch (Xntrix/nr) 1984
Songs of Praise (Xntrix/CD Presents) 1985

The Poison Girls—a middle-aged woman who wittily calls herself Vi Subversa plus a male backing band—are highly politicized musical agitators employing rock (minimalist at the start, highly diverse and sophisticated of late) as their means for registering social and sexual protests. Lyrics are clever and subtle, making points with intelligence rather than sloganeering.

Chappaquiddick Bridge is a studio recording with a bonus flexidisc bluntly entitled "Statement." Leaving the Crass camp for their own label, **Total Exposure**—pressed on clear vinyl and fitted in a transparent plastic sleeve—is a live album with some of the same songs. The earlier LP offers an easier introduction, thanks to a somewhat varied approach that doesn't carry over in concert.

With their musical skills much improved, **Where's the Pleasure** balances intellectual integrity with audio listenability and achieves a measure of success on musical merit alone. Largely ignoring the governmental politics of the first two discs, **Where's the Pleasure** deals almost solely with sexual matters, using music that's more refined and vocals that are crystal clear. Subversa's weary, whisky-and-tobacco-stained voice is a husky but serviceable instrument that perfectly suits the material and lends a tragic, poetic air to the record.

Even more accessible is the wonderful **I'm Not a Real Woman** EP—four varied songs that utterly abandon punk for a rock-cabaret sound, Celtic folk singing and poetic recitation. At her funniest, Subversa employs a Noel Coward-like delivery to offer her sharp lyrics.

Songs of Praise is even more skillful and attractive. Vi is in fine voice, having proven to be a talented and unique singer; the band stretches further into areas of sublime, suave rock and funk scarcely imaginable at the group's outset. Lyrics are likewise subtler and more intriguing, setting this album somewhere between Marianne Faithfull, John Cale and Ian Dury. [iar]

POLECATS

Polecats Are Go! (Vertigo/nr) 1981
Make a Circuit with Me (nr/Mercury) 1983

This young, stylish London trio virtually disappeared after releasing **Polecats Are Go!**, a gem of a rockabilly revival album. Producer Dave Edmunds applies the same polish he brought to the Stray Cats, and these 'Cats truly sparkle. Piano, saxophone and careful vocal harmonies ice the usual neo-rockabilly cake of trebly guitars, acoustic bass and driving drums. A bizarrely-conceived stab at David Bowie's "John I'm Only Dancing" doesn't quite come off; otherwise, this mix of oldies and originals parties like crazy.

Their American label passed on the LP but patched together a seven-cut disc from singles (the glossy title track, a version of T. Rex's "Jeepster" and "John I'm Only Dancing") and album tracks. The band was gone by then, but it was a nice gesture. [si]

POLICE

Outlandos d'Amour (A&M) 1978
Regatta de Blanc (A&M) 1979
Zenyatta Mondatta (A&M) 1980
Ghost in the Machine (A&M) 1981
Synchronicity (A&M) 1983

POLICE ET AL.

Brimstone & Treacle (A&M) 1982

STEWART COPELAND

Rumble Fish (A&M) 1983
The Rhythmatist (A&M) 1985

STING

The Dream of the Blue Turtles (A&M) 1985

Though neither bassist/singer Sting nor veteran guitarist Andy Summers would have gone in this direction individually, they became intrinsic to drummer Stewart Copeland's notion of being new wavers in 1977, when it was still pretty new. As a band, the three worked in earnest to stake out their own musical turf, even probing a few of rock's boundaries. Their considerable abilities eventually yielded the Police sound: rock and reggae interlocked in proportions varying from number to number, further spiced with musical influences like Summers' quasi-classical harmonic overtones and Sting's reggae-into-jazz vocalisms.

Outlandos d'Amour is the brisk, brash initial Police barrage of bright, featherweight tunes (like "Roxanne," "Born in the 50's," "Can't Stand Losing You") and deceptively clever riffs and rhythms. It's pithy, infectious and seductive, sometimes all at once. Only a silly joke in dubious taste and Sting's pair of "let's own up" diatribes are irksome, but those can be ignored—musically, they aren't bad anyway.

Sting came up short of material on **Regatta de Blanc**, and only one of Copeland's attempts at taking up the slack is truly spot-on, funny and catchy. All the same, "Message in a Bottle" is an all-around gem, and if Sting's other material isn't stellar, the performances are: effective vocal emoting and instrumentally sparkling tours de force like the title track (which also shows the virtue of space in music). The sound was further enhanced for **Zenyatta Mondatta**, and that same instrumental excellence brightens much of the record, but too much of the album relies on just that. The more

direct cuts are too cute for words (hence "De Do Do Do . . . ") but, like bubblegum (the music and the candy), they stick with you.

Ghost in the Machine was critically considered the milestone marking the threesome's arrival as Major Artistes, but this critic begs to differ. Aside from a half-step forward (mainly Sting's saxual experimentation) the record shows the Police taking several giant leaps in the direction of the rock mainstream at the expense of at least half the songs (which are, in and of themselves, okay to pretty good).

Synchronicity (or at least "Every Breath You Take") pitched the Police into the ranks of commercial rock superstars, but most of the record simply can't be taken seriously by anyone but a chowderhead and/or indiscriminate fan. The "humor" is flat, the "experiments" with jazz shadings and electronic touches more yawn-provoking than mood- evoking; in the end, it seems just an overgrown platinum molehill. Sting's "love me—I'm the sexy, intellectual and vulnerable man of the '80s" off-the-record image is hard to divorce from his songs, especially when he whines about being "The King of Pain." And Iron Maiden regularly churns out epics as gripping as "Synchronicity II." The Police have clearly become the bloated dinosaur they once complained about. But "Every Breath You Take" *is* every bit a classic, a surf-music rhythm line utterly transmogrified, relentlessly driving Sting's declaration of love/hate/obsession. So skip the LP and get the 45, which even edits out the song's draggier bits.

As a movie, *Brimstone and Treacle* has lots of mystical mood, with Sting effective as a rogue busy smudging the line between good and evil. The soundtrack album consists of one Go-Go's track, a Squeeze item, two choral pieces and some miscellaneous music by Sting, with and without his two compatriots, successful only on the evocative title instrumental and the band's resurrection (from Sting's early days in Last Exit) of the smoldering "I Burn for You."

On another soundtrack excursion, Stewart Copeland left the Klark Kent disguise home and did the music for *Rumble Fish* as himself, writing, producing and playing everything but horns and strings. Surprisingly, the atmospheric instrumentals downplay drums. Some are structured enough that they could use lyrics; an actual song co-written and vocalized by ex-Wall of Voodooer Stan Ridgway is easily the standout. Copeland's second solo record is the soundtrack to his African safari video. Described on the sleeve as "a curious blend of musical snatches from Tanzania, Kenya, Burundi, Zaire, the Congo and Buckinghamshire," **The Rhythmatist** is variously a rock album with Africanisms layered on and a rock interpretation (or imitation) thereof. The blurry line between what is genuine and what Copeland has made of whole Anglo-American cloth is disturbing to say the least, and there's obviously real African music where this dubious rock star contraption came from, but the record is lovely and invigorating nonetheless, especially thanks to Copeland's collaborator, vocalist Ray Lema.

In 1985, with the Police on hiatus,

Sting came up with a multi-platinum solo album. Enlisting a seasoned band of top black American players, Sting attempted to sophisticate himself by introducing jazz trappings to a new batch of songs, including "If You Love Somebody Set Them Free," "Love Is the Seventh Wave," "Fortress Around Your Heart" and the unbelievably stupid "Russians." Despite the illustrious company, however, Sting alone is little different than Sting with the Police: his pretensions and smugness still dominate, and his voice is still his voice. [jg/iar]

See also *Fripp & Summers, Klark Kent.*

POLYPHONIC SIZE

Live for Each Moment/Vivre pour Chaque Instant (Fr. New Rose) 1982
Mother's Little Helper EP (nr/Enigma) 1982

Polyphonic Size is Belgian; their album was produced by Strangler Jean-Jacques Burnel who also contributed bass and vocals. Unlike Burnel's other work outside the Stranglers (his first solo LP, production for Japan's Lizard), this has none of his usual aggression. Instead he delicately captures Polyphonic Size's lovely synthesizer art-pop. Sung primarily in French by a man and a woman backed by simple (not rudimentary—this is carefully constructed and subtle) electronics, this resembles Orchestral Manoeuvres' lighter work. Excepting some perky numbers that lean toward Japanese synthesists like Plastics, a low-key approach— gentle, almost tender singing and languid tempos— makes **Live for Each Moment** as relaxing as a hot bath, but without the ennui, thanks to a resolute commitment to pop song structures. A very pretty record.

Mother's Little Helper has five songs, including a humorous electronic re-interpretation (not unlike the Flying Lizards) of the Rolling Stones classic after which the record is named. [iar]

POLYROCK

Polyrock (RCA) 1980
Changing Hearts (nr/RCA) 1981
Above the Fruited Plain EP (nr/PVC) 1982

Polyrock isn't the only group from New York to explore a new-sensibility dance music, but they were one of the first few to gain artistic credibility, mostly via the involvement of Philip Glass (with Kurt Munkacsi) as their producer. On **Polyrock**, the band combines minimalist repetition with electro-pop and smart, aware songs, then strips it all down to skin and bone for extremely single-minded dance music. Fascinating in its extremity, the album functionally presents a series of Pavlovian clues disguised as very good dance music.

Changing Hearts follows the same basic pattern but loosens up the sound, occasionally breaking away from austere dance music for a taste of straightforward pop, including a reworking of the Beatles' "Rain." Otherwise, Billy and Tommy Robertson write some of the most vulnerable songs this side of David Byrne, with solid (if lean) performances and production.

Following the departure of Tommy Robertson (leaving the band

a much-improved five-piece), his singer/guitarist brother produced **Above the Fruited Plain**, five tracks with more character and melody than any previous Polyrock work. [sg]

POP

The Pop (Arista/Automatic) 1977
Go! (Arista) 1979
Hearts and Knives EP (nr/Rhino) 1981

Essentially a hard-rock/power pop outfit, LA's Pop acquired some hip status through an actively pro-local scene stance as well as attitudes shared with more overtly rebellious colleagues. Their do-it-yourself debut LP shows them equally adept at pounding out fierce rockers and lovingly constructing softer, more melodic tracks, with occasionally eccentric production touches, linking both in the anthemic "Down On the Boulevard." As good as the Raspberries' **Starting Over** but more urgent, and less studiedly nostalgic or obviously derivative.

Go!, produced by former Spark Earle Mankey, shows how the band moved with the times, modifying British modern pop notions to suit themselves. Not quite as humor-conscious (for better and worse) as XTC, the Pop employ a strangely detached intensity that gives a fillip to each track. There isn't any one brilliant number (although "Under the Microscope" comes close), yet **Go!** is entertaining straight through.

Two years later, however, without the guitar and arranging talent of Tim McGovern (who had joined the pre-stardom Motels), and the support of a major label, the remaining foursome sound somewhat chastened for not having played it safer—and they do. On **Hearts and Knives**, they're a blander version of their former selves, serving up pleasant, lightweight originals and a lame Stones cover that's limply out of character. [jg]

IGGY POP

The Idiot (RCA) 1977
Lust for Life (RCA) 1977
TV Eye Live (RCA) 1978
New Values (Arista) 1979
Soldier (Arista) 1980
Party (Arista) 1981
Zombie Birdhouse (Animal) 1982
I Got a Right (nr/Invasion) 1983
Choice Cuts (RCA) 1984

STOOGES

The Stooges (Elektra) 1969 & 1977 & 1982
Fun House (Elektra) 1970 & 1977 & 1982
No Fun (Elektra/nr) 1980

IGGY AND THE STOOGES

Raw Power (CBS/Columbia) 1973 & 1981
Metallic K.O. (nr/Import) 1976

IGGY POP & JAMES WILLIAMSON

Kill City (Radar/Bomp) 1978

Iggy Pop (James Osterberg) embodied everything punk stood for when punk rock exploded in England in the mid-'70s, but Iggy had begun performing in Middle America nearly a decade earlier. He is still performing, serving up much the same arrogant honesty that put him in the punk pantheon.

The Stooges (the debut LP by Iggy's self-willed band) sounds like nothing else released in 1969. Its moronic lyrics and three-chord "tunes" clearly anticipate the lowest-common-denominator populism of '70s punk. Tempos are a bit draggy, but all the ingredients for what followed are present. One of the most superficially artless records ever made.

By contrast, **Fun House** knowingly sucks the listener into its raucous vortex. This ingeniously constructed album starts out menacingly ("Down On the Street") and builds relentlessly to its apocalyptic conclusion ("L.A. Blues"). Iggy's singing—much more expressive than on **The Stooges** —veers from sullen petulance to primal scream on songs of adolescent solipsism. **Fun House** comes as close as any one record ever will to encapsulating what rock is, was and always will be about. Inspired touch: Steven Mackay's saxophone. (**No Fun**, issued between reissues of the originals, consists of tracks from both Stooges albums.)

Raw Power is another masterpiece, featuring the stinging lead guitar of James Williamson in a reorganized Stooges. With Williamson as co-author, Iggy's songs are more musical (i.e., a sense of structure emerged) in their sex-and-death conflation ("Gimme Danger," "Death Trip"). The title track and "Search and Destroy" are only two of **Raw Power**'s tunes to achieve classic status for staring into the abyss. Heavy metal in every sense, the album marked the end of the Stooges as a band concept—Iggy hereafter received solo billing—and effectively, the first stage of Iggy's career.

Metallic K.O. is a seminotorious, semi-legal document of the Stooges' last concert, in 1974. The band staggers toward entropy as Iggy maliciously baits the crowd (which responds in kind). Only six songs, but more than your money's worth of bile. Highlight: a version of "Louie, Louie" you've never heard before.

As a solo artist, Iggy resurfaced under the influence of David Bowie, **The Idiot**'s producer and co-writer. Instead of flailing all over the place, he conserves his energy on numbers like the funky (!) "Sister Midnight" and the menacing "Funtime." The album's tone is generally subdued ("Nightclubbing," "Baby," "Dum Dum Boys"), lumbering along in medium gear. It's disturbingly effective, but of mixed parentage.

Iggy reasserted himself on the rapid follow-up, **Lust for Life**. More upbeat than its predecessor, the album swaggers along to Iggy's confident delivery of the title track, "Success," the powerful "Turn Blue" and other self-analytic tunes. Jim Morrison's influence is noticeable on a few songs, but the clear-eyed vision is Iggy's own.

Kill City was salvaged from the period between the Stooges' breakup and Iggy's redemption via Bowie. The songs plod, the sound is bad and the vocals—recorded on weekend leaves from the hospital where Iggy was residing at the time—are buried. The strung-out music has a voyeuristic appeal if you enjoy wallowing in others' degradation; otherwise, nasty stuff. (After **Kill City** had gone out of print, **I Got a Right** reissued half of

it, adding a side of 1973/4 rehearsal tapes—including a version of the title tune—that are rough but intense and worthwhile.)

The dreadful **TV Eye Live** was a contract-breaker and sounds like it. Half the tracks—recorded on 1977 US tours—include Bowie on keyboards; they sound bad. The others sound worse. Iggy is uninspired throughout. Forget this quickie.

Realigning with Williamson, Iggy signed to Arista and released **New Values**, a no-nonsense collection of hard rockers. His increasingly sophisticated lyrics abound in mordant humor ("I'm Bored," "Five Foot One," "New Values").

Soldier features a supergroup of sorts (Glen Matlock, Ivan Kral, Steve New, Barry Andrews, Klaus Kruger) riffing along to Iggy's mostly bitter rants. **Party** continues in this vein, vacillating between self-deprecation ("Eggs on Plate") and obnoxiousness ("Rock and Roll Party," "Sincerity," etc.). Two non-original oldies—"Sea of Love" and "Time Won't Let Me"—also get perfunctory treatment.

After the aesthetic dead-end of the Arista albums, **Zombie Birdhouse** marked a welcome shift in strategy. No longer singing so much as rap-chanting, Iggy turns surprisingly (by being public) cerebral for a crazy blend of sociological ("The Villagers") and philosophical ("Eat or Be Eaten") discourse, pseudo-folk ("The Ballad of Cookie McBride") and topical documentary ("Watching the News"). Spare musical accompaniment underscores the album's ascetic nature. He's come a long way since the Stooges, but **Zombie Birdhouse** reveals that Iggy is far from the end of his creative tether.

Addenda: Following a resurgence of interest resulting from Bowie's hit version of their collaborative "China Girl" (which Iggy sang on **The Idiot**), his two RCA albums were culled for the fast-buck **Choice Cuts**. The cover helpfully notes the inclusion of the song of the hour, and prominently notes Bowie's songwriting and production credits. [si/iar]

See also *New Order/New Race*.

POP GROUP

Y (Radar/nr) 1979
For How Much Longer Do We Tolerate Mass Murder (Y-Rough Trade) 1980
We Are Time (Y-Rough Trade/nr) 1980

Abrasive, militant British punks raging against racism, oppression, hunger and anything else that's a world problem; as usual, there's no solution, only anger. This Bristol band synthesizes Beefheartian structures and tribal dance beats to create a didactic soundtrack that barely lets you breathe. Their two primary albums are alternately brilliant and intolerable. (**We Are Time** is a hodgepodge of outtakes, live tracks and assorted miscellany.)

Despite the shortcomings of their own records, the Pop Group made their influence strongly felt both as credible minimalists ahead of their time and because of the members' subsequent musical ventures: Bassist Simon Underwood helped found Pigbag and multi-instrumentalist Gareth Sager formed Rip Rig & Panic. [gf]

See also *Pigbag, Rip Rig & Panic, Mark Stewart and the Maffia.*

PORK DUKES

Pork Dukes (Wood/nr) 1978 (Butt/nr) 1979

Whoever these four no-good rotters masquerading behind pseudonyms were, they had good reason to hide. Except for musings by such children of the revolution as the Meatmen's, the Pork Dukes' pink-vinyl LP is the most vulgar, offensive, rude, disgusting, infantile, noxious load of puerile rubbish ever released commercially. In its defense, for those who can stomach it, the music is competent and the lyrics pretty funny. One can only pray this was done for laughs . . . [iar]

POSITIVE NOISE

Heart of Darkness (Statik/nr) 1981
Change of Heart (Statik/Sire) 1982
Distant Fires (Statik/nr) 1985

The title of Positive Noise's second album signifies the drastic change that had taken place after the group's debut LP as a result of the departure of Ross Middleton, the band's singer/leader/lyricist who left in mid-1981 to form Leisure Process with studio saxophonist Gary Barnacle. The Scottish band began as a five-piece (including two other Middleton brothers) and in late 1980 recorded **Heart of Darkness**, which is pretty dire—a badly produced mishmash of art-funk, Skids-like cheering, PiL noise and assorted pretentious nonsense. It suffers from indecisive direction as much as a lack of originality.

For **Change of Heart**, guitarist Russell Blackstock also assumed the vocal chores, and Positive Noise transmuted into a slick electronic dance machine, churning out precise rhythms with anxious, semi-melodic vocals. Gone is the audio clumsiness and uncertain footing of the first LP; Positive Noise's niche is definitely in club music. They've put out some excellent singles since then and a new album in 1985. [iar]

POSTE RESTANTE

See *Minny Pops*.

WILL POWERS

Dancing for Mental Health (Island) 1983

I've encountered many a strange record in my day, and rock seems capable of stretching to include virtually any bizarre concept anyone cares to bring to it, but this album clearly deserves a weird league all its own. Simply outlined, it consists of photographer Lynn Goldsmith reciting motivational self-improvement exhortations and emotional psychodrama, mostly in (synthetically altered) seemingly male voices, over busy dance music co-written variously by Sting, Steve Winwood, Tom Bailey, Nile Rodgers and Todd Rundgren and performed by an uncredited crew, all ostensibly produced by Goldsmith. A phenomenal exercise of super-ego, this is both a Great Artistic Achievement and an unbelievably smug heap of horse puckey. [iar]

POWER STATION

The Power Station (EMI/Capitol) 1985

This part-time supergroup (whose name would be "Kraftwerk" in German) agglomerates Andy and

John Taylor—the guitar/bass axis of Duran Duran—with ex-Chic drummer Tony Thompson and singer Robert Palmer. (Plus Bernard Edwards as producer.) On paper, a promising idea—especially in light of the Durannies' funk pretensions and Simon Le Bon's vocal inadequacies—but, on vinyl, a miserable, boring explosion of overbearing drums pounding (you thought the drums were mixed high on **Let's Dance**?) through tuneless, formless "songs." While Power Station's slickly functional dance-funk is just minor on the softer numbers, the ultimate realization of the concept, "Some Like It Hot," offers a numbingly industrial take on electro-funk made truly execrable by Palmer's contemptible singing. But that's *nothing* compared to the excruciating jam/destruction of Marc Bolan's "Bang a Gong (Get It On)," matching an appalling lack of originality (why didn't they also swing through "Johnny B. Goode" while they were getting to know one another?) with utter disdain for and desecration of the song's melody, tempo and boppy charm. Repugnant.

Incidentally, when the band that swore it would not tour hit the road, it was without Palmer, replaced for disputed reasons by the even less talented Michael Des Barres, adding another chapter to his Chequered Past. [iar]

PRAGVEC

No-Cowboys (Spec/nr) 1981

Bizarre, kitschy doodlings in a semi-pop mode by a London band loosely formed around four members, including singer/ guitarist Susan Gogan. Pleasant if you don't pay too much attention. [iar]

115

PREFAB SPROUT

Prefab Sprout EP (Kitchenware/nr) 1983
Swoon (Kitchenware/Epic) 1984
Steve McQueen (Kitchenware/nr) 1985
Two Wheels Good (nr/Epic) 1985

Smart and sophisticated garden-pop-jazz—imagine Aztec Camera meets Steely Dan with absurdist lyrical inventions and close-formation female backing vocals—Newcastle's Prefab Sprout is essentially the creation of singer/ songwriter Paddy McAloon. Performed by a trio joined by a guest drummer, the EP and **Swoon** (no overlapping tracks) evince a unique and ingenious wit—the album's "Cue Fanfare" is about chess champ Bobby Fischer— supported by light and mellifluous music in a number of refined styles. Remarkable and enticing.

Steve McQueen (titled **Two Wheels Good** in the US) was produced with a fine hand by Thomas Dolby, who also plays on it as a fifth group member. Although it starts slowly, it soon becomes obvious they've improved considerably on the previous record. The adult gossamer pop includes the remarkably airy "When Love Breaks Down" (guest produced by Phil Thornally, suggesting the band has a strong stylistic backbone), the obscure but lovely "Appetite" and the mesmerizing "Goodbye Lucille £1." "Blueberry Pies" sounds like a lost Sade tune; "Horsin' Around" is as cavalier as its title. Brilliant! [iar]

PRESSURE COMPANY

See *Cabaret Voltaire.*

PRETENDERS

Pretenders (Real/Sire) 1980
Extended Play EP (nr/Sire) 1981
Pretenders II (Real/Sire) 1981
Learning to Crawl (Real/Sire) 1984

Although bands fronted by ex-music critics have generally been doomed to culty oblivion, the Pretenders—formed in London by Ohio-born Chrissie Hynde—are major league stars in both America and England. Despite the tragic deaths of guitarist James Honeyman Scott in 1982 and bassist Pete Farndon (after leaving the group) a year later, the nucleus of Hynde and drummer Martin Chambers have pressed on, overcoming the group's disasters with incredible strength and resilience. At this point the Pretenders seem able to continue and succeed as long as Hynde cares to exercise her unique talents as a songwriter and vocalist.

After several brilliant singles (starting off with a Nick Lowe-produced Kinks' cover, "Stop Your Sobbing"), the long-awaited **Pretenders** proved that the 45s were only the beginning. The band's several strengths—Hynde's husky voice and sexually forthright persona, Chambers' intricately syncopated (but never effete) rock rhythms, Scott's blazing, inventive guitar work—invested numbers like "Tattooed Love Boys," "Mystery Achievement" and the songs released originally on singles—"Kid," "Brass in Pocket," "Stop Your Sobbing"—with instantly identifiable character and obvious rock excitement. Needless to add, the LP was a great creative achievement and an enormous hit.

Mind-boggling success caught the Pretenders short of material, and producing a follow-up proved no small challenge. Eighteen months of touring and freaking out left little time for writing or recording; the stopgap EP compiles both sides of two singles and a live version of "Precious." The record's fine as a placeholder, but made redundant when both A-sides turned up on the subsequent album.

Pretenders II would have been a real stiff (creatively) were it not for those selfsame 45 cuts ("Message of Love" and "Talk of the Town"), the latter being one of the best things the band has ever done. Of the other ten cuts, only a handful match the quality of the first album, with self-consciousness and repetition marring Hynde's writing and performance. An air of uncertainty—whether to play up the obvious arena side or to explore restrained ballads and more complex, subtle arrangements—stymied them, and resulted in a confusing melange of conflicting directions.

Scott's death and Farndon's departure, coupled with Hynde's pregnancy, kept the band out of action for most of 1982, releasing only one 45 ("Back On the Chain Gang" b/w "My City Was Gone") with Billy Bremner guesting on guitar and future Big Countryman Tony Butler on bass. The band's net output for the following year was also a single, the wistful, sentimental "2000 Miles."

Judging by its title, **Learning to Crawl** might have been a petrified,

116

self-pitying record, but that's hardly the case. In a startling return to prime form, a revitalized Hynde and Chambers lead two new Pretenders through a collection of characteristic songs, including all three aforementioned single sides and such new grippers as "Middle of the Road" and "Time the Avenger," which are the easy equal of anything Hynde has written or recorded. The only thing lacking is the complexity in the drumming, replaced here by forthright beats that are nothing special. But free of the misjudgment that ankled the second album, the Pretenders again prove both their mettle and talent.

Unrelated to the music but typical of the inescapable private life drama that seems to guide the band, Hynde subsequently took time off to marry Simple Minds' singer Jim Kerr and raise two children, creating another long wait between records. But with **Learning to Crawl** as proof of her—and the band's—flexibility and stamina, it's a safe bet that the next Pretenders album will also be great. [iar]

PRINCE

For You (Warner Bros.) 1978
Prince (Warner Bros.) 1979
Dirty Mind (Warner Bros.) 1980
Controversy (Warner Bros.) 1981
1999 (Warner Bros.) 1982

PRINCE AND THE REVOLUTION

Purple Rain (Warner Bros.) 1984
Around the World in a Day (Paisley Park) 1985
Parade (Paisley Park) 1986

Writing critically about Prince at this stage is rather academic. However, it's impossible to overstate his impact on the direction and sound of music, and much of that influence predates **Purple Rain**. As an artist, Prince's trailblazing cross-fertilization of numerous stripes of "black music" and "white music" has led the way for much (and much-needed) erosion of the color distinction that crept back into pop music in the '70s. As a writer, producer and behind-the-scenes string puller (for the Time, Sheila E., Vanity 6, etc.), he has further infiltrated the world's musical consciousness, adding numerous new voices to the charts in characteristic but rarely repetitive variants on his own work.

While Prince's catalogue is mottled with misogyny and excessive/tasteless sexuality, it also contains a huge amount of extraordinary music, stunning in its originality and easy grasp of numerous forms and styles, made even more impressive by the fact that all of his albums (before **Purple Rain**) involved virtually no one other than Prince, whose multi-instrumental talent is awesome.

Prince's impressive but unexceptional first two albums began to attract the attention of new wave funk fans. It's an oversimplification to call the hybrid R&B/disco/pop-rock (with Hendrixy guitarisms) akin to a blend of Blondie, Bootsy and Blowfly, but while other artists bare their hearts, Prince would rather bear his genitals. On **Dirty Mind**, for example, the "Head" in question is below the belt and the sibling games of "Sister" are X-rated. If the ultra-sex obsession doesn't put you off, **Dirty Mind**'s

catchy tunes (like the unforgettable ambience and melody of "When You Were Mine," later covered to great effect by Cyndi Lauper), sly lyrics and strong production, coupled with Prince's trademark falsetto, make for a winning combination.

Controversy acknowledges Prince's expanded audience. While the sexual (ahem) thrust of **Dirty Mind** is often redeemed by his seemingly ingenuous ingenuity, **Controversy** pushes flash with little substance, and sounds like he's straining for approval. Lyrically, Prince's ambivalence manages to get "Ronnie, Talk to Russia," "Annie Christian" and "Jack U Off" all on one side.

His increased maturity shows on the ambitious **1999**, its four sides filled with some great music (the first side has three of his best-ever songs: "1999," "Little Red Corvette" and "Delirious") and enigmatic clues about the star's assorted mysteries. Prince displays even greater skill—plus an overt absorption of electro-dance music—and (thankfully) some restraint, but not throughout. Sexuality is still on gratuitous display; flashy indulgences stretch some tracks beyond justification (the album needn't have taken two discs). The problem is that Prince's mastery of mannerisms can't cover his superficiality, but then his dazzling talent can keep you from noticing.

Purple Rain is Prince's first album to use a band in the studio; it's also his most varied. One of the few multi-platinum albums to deserve such acclaim, it has a little of everything, from the spare rhythms of "When Doves Cry" to the sweeping balladry of the title track. Prince can't avoid a few dashes of vulgarity here and there, but for whatever reason, tones it down considerably, singing of romance where copulation used to be the whole shooting (er . . .) match. A masterpiece from a mercurial, chameleonlike talent.

Around the World in a Day is a clear-cut effort to confound his millions of new fans. Where **Purple Rain** exorcised some of his childhood ghosts, the startling flower-power psychedelia here returns to Prince's two major obsessions—sex and god. As such, it's a wildly mixed accomplishment. On one hand, paisley pop tunes like "Raspberry Beret" are wonderfully engaging and memorable; at the other end, his heavenly dialogue in "Temptation" is beyond appalling. It's hard to shake the feeling that Prince is basically showing off his chameleonic muscle, but **Around the World in a Day** certainly proves his ability to master whatever style he feels like trying.

Parade—music from Prince's second film, *Under the Cherry Moon*—is, by comparison, an underwhelming if artful collection of restrained songs in a number of only sporadically interesting styles: mild psychedelia not unlike "Raspberry Beret," but neither as catchy or colorful; skeletal funk that makes "When Doves Cry" sound positively Spectoresque; spare theatrical show tunes and instrumentals with little impact; and subtly arranged rock, which provides the record's most entertaining tunes, "Girls & Boys" and "Mountains." Prince seems to be stripping his music down to its most elemental while

attempting some heretical mixing gambits. Perhaps **Parade** will prove in the future to be an important innovation; for the present, however, this experiment is an opaque, uninvolving failure. [jg/iar]

See also *Andre Cymone, Morris Day, Sheila E, Jesse Johnson's Revue, Mazarati, Time.*

PRINCE CHARLES AND THE CITY BEAT BAND

Gang War (Greyhound/Solid Platinum) 1981
Stone Killers (Virgin/ROIR) 1983
Combat Zone (Virgin/nr) 1984

Boston funk flautist Charles Alexander leads the City Beat Band through eight long Gap Band-styled party grooves on **Stone Killers** (released first in America on cassette only and then in England on vinyl). The music is infectious and unassailably danceable; the semi-rap lyrics vary from juvenile and obnoxious—"Big Chested Girls"—to simplistic and funny—"Cash (Cash Money)." **Combat Zone** is a more ambitious LP. Several real songs mix an aggressive blend of Mayfield/Chicago soul and modern stylings; elsewhere, he parties hardy and even tries a notable scratch-funk revision of "Jailhouse Rock." [iar]

PETER PRINCIPLE

See *Tuxedomoon.*

PROCESS AND THE DOO-RAGS

Too Sharp (CBS/Columbia) 1985

Having found considerable leering success with the sexploitation Mary Jane Girls, Rick James continues his musical outreach program with this humorously-named male vocal quintet. They sing, James handles virtually everything else, listing his name (as writer, producer, arranger and performer) a dozen times on the back cover. Except for the familiarity of the lyrical conceits ("Serious Freak," "Dance the Way You Want," etc.), it's an enjoyable detour, an agreeably modern soul record disguised as hot dance-funk. [iar]

PROFESSIONALS

I Didn't See It Coming (Virgin/nr) 1981

The Professionals—alias Paul Cook and Steve Jones—have done very little to maintain a high profile in the years since the Sex Pistols broke up. They haven't been inactive—what with recording some final tracks as the Sex Pistols, backing people like Joan Jett and Johnny Thunders and doing lots of production work—but this album, the release of which was delayed for the better part of a year, is their only solo longplayer together so far.

With Paul Meyers (bass) and Ray McVeigh (guitar), the trademark Cook/Jones rock crunch stretches over wide terrain, and the songs are neither Pistols' retreads nor trusty punk oldies. Not all of it is good, but "The Magnificent" (a song seemingly aimed at John Lydon, complete with parodic Public Image guitar), "Payola" and the anthemic "Kick Down the Doors" are just some of the tracks that bear repeated spins.

Confidential to cinema fans:

Cook and Jones can be seen in several movies, including the Pistols' *Great Rock'n'Roll Swindle* and *Ladies and Gentlemen, the Fabulous Stains.* [iar]

PROPAGANDA

Calling on Moscow EP (nr/Epic) 1980

Originally called the Passengers, this British quartet was deemed by their US label to be apt representatives of the acceptable sound of new wave, so *voilà!*—a 10-inch EP—four tracks of forgettable, mildly humorous rock'n'roll. Whee. [jg]

PROPAGANDA

A Secret Wish (ZTT-Island) 1985
Wishful Thinking (ZTT-Island/nr) 1985

Germany's Propaganda—two men and two women—play intricate, almost orchestral synth-based rock of little inherent excitement. As encouraged by Trevor Horn and Paul Morley, each divergent track is a huge stylized production number, but none offer much in the way of listening pleasure. The band's character— when any is present— derives mainly from gimmickry (gory English S&M lyrics on "Duel," Art of Noise-styled mix hysterics on its invigorating instrumental doppelganger, "Jewel.") **A Secret Wish** includes contributions from Steve Howe, David Sylvian, Glenn Gregory and others, but you'd never notice from listening. **Wishful Thinking** is an album of remixes and reworkings of previously released material. [tr]

PSYCHEDELIC FURS

The Psychedelic Furs (CBS/Columbia) 1980
Talk Talk Talk (CBS/Columbia) 1981
Forever Now (CBS/Columbia) 1982
Mirror Moves (CBS/Columbia) 1984

This London band, whose lineup has varied substantially around a core of three, debuted with an album that mixed a drone-laden wall of noise (two guitars, sax and/or keyboards) with an odd adaptation of the quieter Bowie **Low**-style sound. The impact is shallow, due less to the profusion of producers than to the lyrics rasped by Richard Butler in his bored, asthmatic drawl.

Talk Talk Talk, produced by Steve Lillywhite, displays surprising melodiousness in a newly crystallized style amalgamating the Velvet Underground, **Highway 61** Dylan and even **Revolver** Beatles, all given a fresh face and a driving beat. The wall of noise is sculpted to bring its components into sharp relief, and Butler shows he can toss off memorable imagery with mock-casual aplomb. The catchy opening track, "Pretty in Pink," served as the titular inspiration for a 1986 film and soundtrack album of the same name.

On **Forever Now**, Butler writes to his strengths. Though the Furs had lost two key members, the others' increased sophistication— shored up by wisely-chosen session help (somber cello, horns, Flo & Eddie)—is orchestrated by Todd Rundgren in a major production coup, best exemplified by the brilliant single, "Love My Way."

Mirror Moves is the Furs' (Butler, his bassist brother Tim and guitarist John Ashton) most commercially-minded record. In collaboration with Keith Forsey as producer and deputized drummer, the LP contains a full side of memorable rockers written and played in the group's inimitable style. "The Ghost in You," "Here Come Cowboys," "Heaven" and "Heartbeat" may not be profound or timeless, but they do show occasional perspicacity and exceptionally well-ordered playing and production.

Note: The first three LPs have different track sequences in the US and UK releases. Also, two tracks were subbed for a controversial cut on the first LP and one altered and retitled on the third. [jg/iar]

PSYCHIC TV

Force the Hand of Chance (Some Bizzare/nr) 1982
Dreams Less Sweet (Some Bizzare/nr) 1983
Berlin Atonal Vol. 1 (Ger. Atonal) 1984
N.Y. Scum Haters (Temple/nr) 1984
Berlin Atonal Vol. 2 (Ger. Atonal) 1984
25 December 1984—A Pagan Day (Temple/nr) 1985
Those Who Do Not (Ice. Gramm) 1985
Themes II (Temple/nr) 1985
Mouth of the Night (Temple/nr) 1985

An album that appears to be devoted to an obscure faith known as "The Temple ov Psychick Youth" might be accepted on face value— after all, various cults have produced albums of devotional music to spread their gospel among rock fans—however, when the musicians behind the project are two ex-members of Throbbing Gristle (Genesis P-Orridge and Peter Christopherson) aided by a onetime Alternative TV-er (Alex Fergusson), it becomes much harder to judge where religious sincerity ends and elaborate put-on begins. Adding to the confusion, Stevo, who runs Some Bizzare (the label that originally abetted the group), is quoted on the back cover of their first album: "A naive person can open his eyes in life, but someone with his eyes open can never end up naive." Just who's kidding who here?

Force the Hand of Chance, regardless of its sincerity or utter lack thereof, is an amazing package: two records (one purported to be the partial soundtrack of a four-hour videocassette), a poster/booklet, pictured costumes, symbology and mail-order merchandise offerings. Musically, the main disc is a weird assortment of quiet ballads, screeching white noise, simple pop and more, with lyrics by P-Orridge that drift over terrain not all in keeping with the mystical concept. At times, form far outweighs function and some songs become merely effect without substance; others stand up nicely on their own regardless of the accompanying baggage. The adjunct record, **Psychick TV Themes**, uses real and imagined ethnic instruments from various exotic cultures to produce instrumentals that range from crazed to cool, intense to ephemeral —something like Eno's ambience filtered through Spike Jones' sensibility.

Dreams Less Sweet is another remarkable record, no less appealing for its equally abundant bizarrity. From the sweet vocal pop of "Hymn 23" or "White Nights" to the pan-ethnic soundscapes and soundtracks that employ everything from English horn to Tibetan thighbone (as well as a lot of found sounds), PTV display an ineffable mastery of avant-garde dadaism as well as traditional musicmaking. Like tuning into a radio station overrun by university-educated acid-freaks, **Dreams Less Sweet** provides a thoroughly unpredictable and unsettling, yet utterly profound experience.

PTV has since continued to release disturbing live albums, featuring different lineups around the P-Orridge-Christopherson- Fergusson core. **Berlin Atonal Vol. 1**, recorded at a festival in December 1983, matches a grisly side of speaker- shredding, grinding, excruciating chaos by PTV with a side by percussionist Z'ev. The limited edition (5,000) **N.Y. Scum Haters**—an all-PTV onslaught, captured at Danceteria in November 1983—is better organized and recorded, more varied and sporadically more musical. There's still a lot of fearsome noise, but there's also some respite from the mania. **Berlin Atonal Vol. 2** is shared with a band called La Loora. **Mouth of the Night** is music to accompany a dance company. [iar]

PUBLIC IMAGE LTD.

Public Image (Virgin/nr) 1978
Metal Box (Virgin/nr) 1979
Second Edition (Virgin/Island) 1980
Paris in the Spring (Virgin/nr) 1980
The Flowers of Romance (Virgin/Warner Bros.) 1981
Live in Tokyo (Virgin/Elektra) 1983
This Is What You Want . . . This Is What You Get (Virgin/Elektra) 1984
Commercial Zone (PiL) 1984
Album/Cassette (Virgin/Elektra) 1986

The Sex Pistols were a tough act to follow, even for Johnny Rotten. After that band's entropic dissolution, Rotten reclaimed his civilian surname, Lydon, and started Public Image Ltd., supposedly more a way of life than a mere band, "rock" or otherwise.

PiL's opening salvo, **Public Image** (aka **First Issue**) couldn't seem to make up its mind between more-or-less straight rock (the unnaturally likable "Public Image") and musical endurance tests. "Annalisa" could be a Led Zeppelin backing track, but other cuts ("Theme," "Fodderstompf") are excruciating and/or self-indulgent. PiL knew they wanted to annoy, but were still working out the best way to do it.

They found it on **Metal Box**, a brilliant statement, from packaging —three 12-inch 45s in an embossed circular tin—to performance. Jah Wobble's overpowering bass sets up throbbing lines around which Keith Levene's guitar and keyboards flick in and out. Lydon wails, chants and moans impressionistic lyrics. It's disturbing, captivating and a milestone in new wave's brief but dense history.

A limited edition, **Metal Box** wasn't cheap to produce, so it was reissued as **Second Edition**: the same music on two LPs in a gatefold sleeve. **Second Edition** benefits from printed lyrics and funhouse photos, but **Metal Box** has superior sound—this is **tactile** music—and a running order that makes better sense.

The live **Paris in the Spring** offers no new material, and may even have been released primarily to stifle a bootleg from the same concert. The band plays well, with drummer Martin Atkins more noticeable than on **Metal Box**; the Parisian audience is barely perceptible. All cover type (title, songs, etc.) is in French. Get the joke?

On **The Flowers of Romance** the band shows a healthy desire not to repeat itself. With bassist Wobble gone, PiL relies on other resources; compared to this, **Metal Box** could be played in supermarkets. Lacking a bass, the "band" centers its "songs" around drum patterns and little else. Lydon's romantic imagery dabbles in ghostly apparitions ("Under the House") and Middle East chic ("Four Enclosed Walls"). He also serves up customary rants against hangers-on ("Banging the Door"), women ("Track 8") and Britain ("Go Back," "Francis Massacre"). But the music is so severe as to lend credence to a record executive's statement that **The Flowers of Romance** is one of the most uncommercial records ever made—at least within a "pop" context.

Never a comradely bunch, PiL seemed to unravel beyond repair when Levene left in 1983. The band had just scored a surprise comeback demi-hit with "(This Is Not a) Love Song." Lydon rounded up some unknown New Jersey accompanists and went to Japan. Only two of the ten tracks on **Live in Tokyo** are new songs; the faceless recruits are shoved in the back of the sonic mix; the album stretches about 45 minutes of material over two 12-inch 45s without **Metal Box's** punch. Forget this one.

PiL started work on **This Is What You Want** before Levene's departure. His guitar parts were wiped off the finished product, now spiked only by Lydon's glum caterwauling. Levene saw to the release of his own version of the session tapes under the name **Commercial Zone**; the music here is considerably more interesting —perhaps even more lively. By taking PiL seriously as a career, Lydon has committed heresy against punk anomie. At least he's still excruciating.

The same can't be said for the eminently listenable **Album** (or **Cassette**, depending on your format of choice), which is either the worst sell-out of Lydon's career or the first popular-oriented PiL album ever. Dispensing with noise, free-form aggression and anti-music production, a stack of uncredited musicians play powerful, highly organized, prickly-but-accessible rock (and, on the brilliant "Rise," demi-pop) while Lydon masterfully bleats in near-tuneful harmony on top. The studio sound (courtesy Lydon and Bill Laswell) is live and virile; the seven bluntly-titled songs ("FFF," "Home," "Ease") are as intelligent and captivating as any in PiL's past. **Album**. Great. [si/iar]
See also *Afrika Bambaataa, Brian Brain, Jah Wobble.*

PUNISHMENT OF LUXURY

Laughing Academy (UA/nr) 1979

In its (few) better moments, Newcastle's Punilux resembled a cross between Roxy Music and a drunken edition of early XTC. The rest of this album is synth- sweetened heavy metal riffing from a minor talent turned sophomoric and sour. Favorite line: "Vanity has bum ways."　　　　　　　　　　[mf]

PURPLE HEARTS

Beat That! (Fiction/nr) 1980

While this LP shows them to be too derivative to be taken seriously, Purple Hearts were still one of the most sincere (or at least convincing) neo-mod bands. At points they closely approximate '65/'66 Who and Stones (and even endow a '66 Bowie single with more credibility than the original.) Almost analogous to early Badfinger.　　[jg]

JIMMY PURSEY

Imagination Camouflage
　　(Polydor/nr) 1980
Alien Orphan (Epic/nr) 1982

JAMES T. PURSEY

Revenge Is Not the Password
　　(Turbo/nr) 1983
The Lord Divides (Eskimo
　　Green/nr) 1983

Gone solo, the earnest Sham 69 mouthpiece took a turn for the artier, leaving behind some of his plain-spoken charm and much of his obstreperousness, too, in favor of more emotional and creative depth and range. Slide guitar, sax and even synthesizers broaden the instrumental palette of **Imagination Camouflage** and, while there aren't any excellent songs, they're almost all good ones (aided in composition and performance by renegades from Generation X).

Unfortunately, **Alien Orphan** goes almost too far. Musically, it turns from the stagey rock of its predecessor into a goulash of electro-rock-funk-jazz often held together by fluid, graceful bass riffing, guitar and keyboard used only as embroidery. It seems to forget the notion of songs as songs, not elaborate aural concoctions. Still, it's swell background music—a meticulously constructed soundscape—and other than the parts that *do* try to be poignant or obvious, most of it does connect eventually, one way or another. [jg]

PYLON

Gyrate (Armageddon/DB) 1980
Pylon!! EP (Armageddon/nr) 1980
Chomp (nr/DB) 1983

This influential and highly-rated Athens, Georgia combo came on like a cross between the B-52's and Gang of Four. Atop thin, almost brittle, metallic guitar, bass and no-nonsense driving drums—which all mesh into stark but inviting dance rhythms—Vanessa Briscoe artlessly shouts/talks/gargles celebrations of life and innocent warnings/ wonderings about restrictions on freedom. Though limited in material—the first two records contain about four really good songs all told; the rest are merely okay or repetitive—Pylon is fraught with possibilities for development. The 10-inch **Pylon!!** EP has two of their best, including the dance-club staple, "Cool."

Promise notwithstanding, **Chomp**, produced by Chris Stamey and Gene Holder (both then of the dB's), was the quartet's swansong. More ambitious in scope, Pylon incorporates a psychedelic drone in spots and sometimes sounds less anxious and strident than before.

The album includes both melodic (!) sides of a great preceding single ("Crazy" b/w "M Train") and other cool slices ("Beep," "Gyrate") of floor-shaking art.　　[jg/iar]

Q-FEEL

Q-Feel (Jive) 1983

These tiresomely upbeat British techno-poppers recall the giddy chirp of Pilot, getting down to their appointed dance-music chores with much polish and absolutely no soul. The popular club single contained here, "Dancing in Heaven (Orbital Be-Bop)," is a descendant of "Pop Muzik," lacking only that song's charm and originality.　　[iar]

QUANDO QUANGO

Pigs & Battleships (Factory/nr) 1985

This Anglo-Dutch quartet has become popular on dance-floors (if not record stores) on both sides of the Atlantic with a masterful assortment of big-beat grooves. Latin and jazz-tinged funk shares the spotlight with reggaefied disco. Orchestration is primarily busy percussion beneath bass, keyboards and horns, with mostly tuneless, chanted vocals of lyrics that aren't exactly poetry. Playing and production are uniformly sharp, but Quando Quango would be best served with 12-inch dance mixes; an entire LP's worth becomes redundant and forgettable.　　[dgs]

QUICK

Mondo Deco (nr/Mercury) 1976
Alpha/Beta EP (nr/Quick Fan
　　Club) 1978

After losing his grip on the Runaways, Kim Fowley discovered the Young Republicans, five male Californians he rechristened the Quick. They aspired to be an adolescent version of Sparks, playing melodic, Anglophilic tunes verging on bubblegum (like, but not as good as, Milk 'n' Cookies). Guitarist/songwriter Steven Hufsteter was pretty much the man in charge, and his limited talents shunted the Quick into a fairly tight mold; **Mondo Deco** is now more of an amusing artifact than it seemed at the time.

Alpha/Beta, a 10-inch souvenir of the group's unsuccessful attempt to court Elektra Records in 1977, came out early the following year through the band's fan club and showed they could draw on far more power than had previously been indicated. They're still basically Anglo/effete but, even on a version of "Somewhere Over the Rainbow," the Quick could manage real punch.　　[iar/jg]

See also *Cruzados, Three O'Clock.*

QUINCY

Quincy (CBS/Columbia) 1980

Abetted in their escape from the Bowery circuit by CBGB's owner, signed to a major label and produced by the talented Tim Friese-Greene, Quincy tried to make pleasant but predictable fare like "Critics' Choice" and "Roamin' Catholic" work in a crisp, slightly Carsish, neo-pop setting, but were too faceless to merit any daylight notice.　　[iar]

ROBERT QUINE/FRED MAHER

Basic (EG) 1984

New York guitar master Quine

(Voidoids/Lou Reed) and ex-Material drummer Maher have here recorded a mesmerizing no-frills celebration of the sound of the electric guitar. Over the pro forma mechanized rhythm patterns suggested by the title, the pair lay down their riffs and then Quine embroiders them—magically. Don't look for memorable tunes or even clever tricks—this is a player's album, amazingly pure though not so simple. Warning: Quine and Maher are credited jointly with guitars, bass and drum programs, so don't assume that Quine plays all the guitar.   [mf]

See also *Jody Harris and Robert Quine, Richard Hell, Lou Reed*.

MAXIM RAD

Times Ain't That Bad (Fr. Dreyfus) 1980

Odd fella, this Rad; not all of the strange verbal juxtapositions can be ascribed to gaps in his grasp of English (I mean, "White Action, African Lemons"?). Rad seems to *want* to be outré and often is, though he's more compelling when direct. He gets a surprising amount of mileage out of a simple rock'n'roll/R&B format, thanks to darting, dirty-twanging guitar and hyperactive, fretless bass lines. His vocal style offers hints of Tom Verlaine and Richard Hell alongside Van Morrison and Jackson Browne. After a breakdown like this, you could be excused for thinking Rad's just plain confused; what makes him worth hearing is that, *au contraire*, he's pretty darn engaging.   [jg]

RADIATORS FROM SPACE

TV Tube Heart (Chiswick/nr) 1977

RADIATORS

Ghostown (Chiswick/nr) 1979

London independent label Chiswick discovered these early Irish punk frontiersmen in Dublin; although never a commercial success, the Radiators from Space proved to be a wonderful musical find. Their recording career, which actually predated the debut vinyl of such first wavers as the Clash and Elvis Costello, evinces talent and intelligence far beyond many forgotten bands of that generation.

TV Tube Heart may not have been revolutionary, but energetic delivery of clever and melodic songs about such soon-to-become-hackneyed topics as the music press and club denizens make it a much better survivor of its era than many now hopelessly dated artifacts. From the outset, Radiators from Space showed themselves to be a better breed of punk.

Ghostown, produced by Tony Visconti, is nearly a power pop record with some unsettling flaws damaging another batch of good tunes. One item is almost identical to later Boomtown Rats (although who recorded it first is unclear); another is a trite '50s homage that seems out of place. **Ghostown** does have its moments, though, and several tracks have the same wonderful feel as the second Fingerprintz LP. Obviously a band with great untapped potential, the Radiators were a surprisingly sophisticated bunch whose records are worth hearing.

In 1985, leader Philip Chevron surfaced in consort with Elvis Costello as a producer and performer; he then went on to join the Pogues.   [iar]

RADIO BIRDMAN

Radios Appear (Sire) 1978
Living Eyes (Aus. WEA) 1981

The Saints' international success sent American and English labels scurrying to Australia. Radio Birdman is what they brought back. The sextet (who could have used a capable producer) owed a lot to the Stooges and their predecessors; the band went so far as to co-write a song with Ron Asheton and to record a Roky Erickson number. Rounding off **Radios Appear** with a sendup/tribute to "Hawaii Five-O,"

Radio Birdman did make its contribution. Over the years, their importance as Aussie punk pioneers—through ex-members' work with the likes of New Race and the Screaming Tribesmen and as a positive scene influence—has come to be better understood.   [iar]

See also *New Order/New Race, Screaming Tribesmen*.

RADIO STARS

Songs for Swinging Lovers (Chiswick/nr) 1977
The Holiday Album (Chiswick/nr) 1978
Two Minutes, Mister Smith (Moonlight/nr) 1982

Radio Stars generally had more good ideas than they knew what to do with. On their two original albums they play fast-moving pop/rock with heavy overtones and a penchant for bizarre lyrical matter. On **Songs for Swinging Lovers** (even the cover is a poorly executed great idea), they come on like a 1977 version of singer Andy Ellison's legendary '60s psychedelic pop outfit, John's Children; faster and louder, but still decidedly off-center. Bassist Martin Gordon, fresh from a stint in Sparks (a band many compared to John's Children), supplies the odd ditties, covering such topics as rotting corpses, rapists and macaroni'n'mice casseroles. He even adds a jingle for the group's label, "Buy Chiswick Records." If Gordon's way with a tune had always been up to his words, the band might have lived up to its name. But the quality of the material is too inconsistent to sustain interest for a whole album—too much is dull, repetitive riffing.

The Holiday Album suffers from much the same malady as its predecessor: too many throwaways. For that reason, **Two Minutes, Mister Smith**, a posthumous compilation of singles and choice album tracks, is *the* Radio Stars album to own. The group's heights were almost all achieved on singles, especially the brilliant "From a Rabbit," a kitchen-sink pop production number of the highest order, included here.   [ds]

RAINCOATS

The Raincoats (Rough Trade/nr) 1979
Odyshape (Rough Trade) 1981
The Kitchen Tapes [tape] (nr/ROIR) 1983
Moving (Rough Trade/nr) 1984

The Raincoats introduced four English women parked on the fringes of conventional pop music. Or are they just an avant-garde edition of the Roches? The harmonies are there and the lyrics are esoteric and philosophical, eschewing predictable sentiments, but the music comes together only in spurts. A cover version of "Lola" plays havoc with that song's gender enigma. The rest of the songs just play havoc.

On **Odyshape**, the scope of the band's sound expands; the mingling of snappy acoustic and jangly electric guitars provides saner contrast to the violin shrieks. There's even a poignant song about a girl who's "Only Loved at Night." But the Raincoats are still not an easy listen.

The Kitchen Tapes captures a December 1982 New York show supported by three other demimonde musicians. The playing, while still a bit low on the virtuosity index, shows refinement and development. In spots, the Raincoats spin a shimmery curtain of lovely sound; elsewhere, pan-cultural percussion supports fascinating vocal arrangements. But their potential for cacophony (better organized than before, but boisterous nonetheless) will keep you alternately straining to hear and jamming your fingers in your ears. **Moving** reprises some of the material from the live cassette.

[gf/iar]

RAIN PARADE

Emergency Third Rail Power Trip (Zippo/Enigma) 1983
Explosions in the Glass Palace EP (Zippo/Enigma) 1984
Beyond the Sunset (Island/Restless) 1985
Crashing Dream (Island) 1986

Like most of the bands implicated in the West Coast psychedelic revival (paisley underground, if you insist), Rain Parade has a better ear for style than for substance. Most of the genre's bands tend to make very deft, subtle music but have nothing to say; in Rain Parade's favor, they know the nuances of form better than anyone else. And if the Velvet Underground- meets-the Lemon Pipers pop sound tells more about who they like than who they are, at least the Paraders have good taste.

Emergency Third Rail Power Trip is a gentle record with neatly crafted songs and mildly trippy textures. However, the retreat into style prohibits all listener identification, and while the songs make good background music, as foreground they're a snore. **Explosions in the Glass Palace** is a somewhat misleading title: there are, in fact, no explosions on this EP. But the sound is filled out and less generic. The record has a dreamlike quality to it—where the band once sounded lethargic, it now waxes hypnotic. The psychedelic touches, rather than offering a running historical narrative filled with inside jokes, give the pop structures some depth. Not a glandular jolt, but a nice quiet listen.

Crashing Dream, Rain Parade's major label debut, has one simply beautiful song ("Depending on You"). Another ("Mystic Green") sounds uncannily like the Records, while "Don't Feel Bad" hybridizes two Beatles songs (you figure out which). The album's flimsy but attractive, competent technique in search of a spine and a direction. **Beyond the Sunset** is a live album recorded in Japan.

[jl/iar]

See also *Kendra Smith, Windbreakers.*

RAINY DAY

See *Kendra Smith.*

RAISE THE DRAGON

Deliverance EP (IRS) 1984

At his smoothest, Richard Spellman sings like a debonair blend of David Bowie and Bryan Ferry (loud, his voice is quite less appealing); Sean Lyons provides attractive, fragile guitar threads. With backing from five sessionmen, including erstwhile Rumour bassist Andrew Bodnar, the pair spin both lovely, melodic tunes ("The Blue Hour") and tedious light dance-rockers ("Deliverance" and "Raise the Dragon"). An ill-advised cover of "Hold On (I'm Coming)" is laughable.

[iar]

PHILIP RAMBOW

Shooting Gallery (EMI/Capitol) 1979
Jungle Law (EMI/nr) 1981

Yet another singer who owes a considerable debt to Van Morrison, former Winkies leader Philip Rambow so far hasn't fulfilled the promise of his appealing hot- coals-in-mouth singing style. On **Shooting Gallery** he's casual rather than driven—bouncy numbers like "Don't Call Me Tonto" and "The Sound and the Fury" could be downgraded fairly easily to fluff pop.

Jungle Law turns the heat up considerably, boasting sharper musicianship, memorable material and impassioned singing. The tunes seem drawn from life, especially "Snakes and Ladders" and "Beyond the Naked and the Dead." Phil Rambow may not be capable of matching the white-hot histrionics of Elvis Costello or Graham Parker, but **Jungle Law** proves he can make a direct, emotionally credible record.

[jy]

RAMONES

Ramones (Sire) 1976
Leave Home (Sire) 1977
Rocket to Russia (Sire) 1977
Road to Ruin (Sire) 1978
It's Alive (Sire/nr) 1979
End of the Century (Sire) 1980
Pleasant Dreams (Sire) 1981
Subterranean Jungle (Sire) 1983
Too Tough to Die (Beggars Banquet/Sire) 1984
Animal Boy (Beggars Banquet/Sire) 1986

RAMONES ET AL.

Rock'n'Roll High School (Sire) 1979

With no more than four chords and one manic tempo, the Ramones blasted open the clogged arteries of mid-'70s rock, reanimating the music. Their genius was to recapture the short/simple aesthetic from which pop had strayed, adding their own caustic sense of humor and minimalist rhythm guitar sound. The result not only spearheaded the original new wave/punk movement, but also drew the blueprint for more recent hardcore punk bands.

Ramones almost defies critical comment. The fourteen songs, averaging barely over two minutes each, start and stop like a lurching assembly line. Singer Joey Ramone's monotone is the perfect complement to Johnny and Dee Dee's guitar/bass pulse. Since the no-frills production sacrifices clarity for impact, printed lyrics on the inner sleeve help even as they mock another pretentious convention—although the four or five line texts of "Now I Wanna Sniff Some Glue," "I Don't Wanna Walk Around with You" and "Loudmouth" become anti-art of their own. Like all cultural watersheds, **Ramones** was embraced by a discerning few, slagged off as a bad joke by the uncomprehending majority. It is now a classic.

The slightly glossier **Leave Home** is cut from the same cloth: another Ramones' dozen (fourteen hits) under a half hour in length. The band's warped Top 40 aspirations emerge on "I Remember You" and "Swallow My Pride," sandwiched between such anthems as "Gimme Gimme Shock Treatment" and "Pinhead." Like "Let's Dance" on **Ramones,** "California Sun" relates

the band to the pandemic moronity that has always informed the best rock'n'roll.

Rocket to Russia is the culmination of the Ramones' primal approach. Virtually all fourteen tracks (including golden oldies "Do You Wanna Dance?" and "Surfin' Bird") are well-honed in execution, arrangement and songwriting wit. Clean production streamlines toe-tappers like "Cretin Hop," "Teenage Lobotomy" and "Rockaway Beach," and emphasizes Joey's increasingly expressive singing on the "ballads," "I Don't Care" and "I Wanna Be Well." The album also contains the Ramones' naive attempt at a hit single, "Sheena Is a Punk Rocker."

"Sheena" only scraped the charts, and drummer Tommy Ramone (né Erdelyi) left, to be replaced by ex-Voidoid Marky Ramone (né Marc Bell). The Ramones had spewed out well over forty tracks (including a couple of 45 B-sides) inside of two years. They emerged next with **Road to Ruin**, a surprisingly (but understandably) downbeat collection. Desperate to join the mainstream, the band lengthened its material, even breaking the three-minute barrier on "I Wanted Everything" and "Questioningly," a touching love (!) song. Despite the perky "I Wanna Be Sedated," "Don't Come Close" and (oldie) "Needles and Pins," **Road to Ruin** is a bit lackluster; earlier rave-ups, unlike "I'm Against It" and "Go Mental," never sounded forced. A rethink seemed in order.

Meanwhile, the band lent their musical and dramatic talents to the movie *Rock'n'Roll High School.* The soundtrack album includes two new compositions (one the theme song), an eleven-minute live medley of five previously-recorded tunes plus the Ramones backing the Paley Brothers ("C'mon Let's Go") and co-star P.J. Soles (on a second version of "Rock'n'Roll High School"). Appropriate songs by various artists fill out the record.

Anyone whose appetite for live Ramones was whetted by the film soundtrack should seek out **It's Alive**, a two-disc London concert recording (with Tommy drumming) that pretty much reprises their first three albums.

The next Ramones LP, **End of the Century**, features intimidating production by the legendary Phil Spector. The band responds with a good brace of songs whose polish and (relative) wordiness show them outgrowing punk. Dubious bonus: Joey warbling "Baby, I Love You."

On **Pleasant Dreams**, the Ramones moved away from their pioneering minimalism and into heavy metal territory, although distinctive lyrics insured they hadn't lost their grasp of teenage angst. But with **Subterranean Jungle** the Ramones got back to where they once belonged: trashy '60s pop adjusted to current taste. That means not only a couple of acid-age oldies ("Time Has Come Today," "Little Bit o' Soul") but original tunes with male protagonists hung up on girls and themselves. It also means easing off the breakneck rhythm that was once Ramones dogma. **Subterranean Jungle** is an underrated item in the band's canon.

With **Too Tough to Die**, the Ramones—sporting a new drummer and reunited with Tommy Erdelyi as

the record's co-producer—got serious about stealing back some thunder from the hardcore punk scene they'd inspired. The sound is more ferocious than ever, and they dip back into quick-hit song lengths. Some by-now predictable macho sentiments (the title track, "I'm Not Afraid of Life") are offset by the token dose of sensitivity ("Howling at the Moon," guest-produced by Eurythmician Dave Stewart). But the Eddie Cochranesque "No Go" that closes the album shows the Ramones haven't lost their sense of humor.

The Ramones' big release in what was for them an otherwise quiet 1985 was "Bonzo Goes to Bitburg," a UK-only 45 assailing Ronald Reagan for the itinerary of his German vacation. That song, retitled "My Brain Is Hanging Upside Down," also turned up on **Animal Boy**. Produced by Jean Beauvoir, the Ramones sound a bit more like a straight rock band than ever before (mostly in the drum sound and articulated rhythm guitar.) The animal-theme record has typically entertaining entries (current drummer Richie's "Somebody Put Something in My Drink" and a wistful ballad, "She Belongs to Me") as well as other notable songs. Dee Dee (the LP's main songwriter) affects a quasi-British accent to sing "Love Kills," a Pistols-styled tribute to Sid'n'Nancy just in time for the film, while the nostalgically terse "Eat the Rat" is the closest brush with hardcore the Ramones have made in years.

[si/iar]

RANDY RAMPAGE

Randy Rampage EP (Can. Friend's) 1982

Early D.O.A. bassist Rampage —with assists from ex-D.O.A. drummer Chuck Biscuits and former members of California's Dils and Avengers—shows he can almost approximate solid, even (gasp) "musical" punk rock, if he'd just tighten up his wig (and get a producer).

[jg]

ERIC RANDOM

Earthbound Ghost Need (New Hormones/nr) 1982

ERIC RANDOM & THE BEDLAMITES

Time-Splice (Doublevision/nr) 1985

This experimental multi- instrumentalist (and Cabaret Voltaire associate) dabbles in a wide variety of styles, hopping around from art-noise to reggae to jazz to non-Western idioms. But instead of merely regurgitating these genres, Random gives them unusual arrangements, adding odd and eerie synths, guitar, percussion, etc. Both of his albums follow this pattern, but **Time-Splice** features much cleaner production and sharper playing. **Earthbound Ghost Need** (title derived from Wm. Burroughs' *Naked Lunch*) includes a version of Ravel's *Bolero* that would have left Bo Derek in a much different mood. Production, arrangements and styles seem to take priority over songwriting, but Random is a talented artist.

[dgs]

RANK AND FILE

Sundown (Rough Trade/Slash-Warner Bros.) 1982

R

120

Long Gone Dead (Slash-London/Slash-Warner Bros.) 1984

Rank and File was formed in Austin, Texas, even though three of its original members were Californians who had played in San Diego's Dils and San Francisco's Nuns. R&F's distance from those early punk outfits is more than geographical: These four fellows play delicately crafted cowboy rock. (Imagine if Marshall Crenshaw had grown up listening to Hank Williams rather than Buddy Holly.) David Kahne—whose name on a cover is reason enough to buy an LP—produced **Sundown**, giving Rank and File squeaky clean sound for their tuneful and tasty pop numbers that also benefit from pretty harmonies and confident playing. Effortlessly enjoyable.

But, alas, too good to last. **Long Gone Dead** retains only half the band—brothers Chip and Tony Kinman (the main creative force on **Sundown**, writing almost all the songs)—joined by a bunch of temporaries like Tom Petty drummer Stan Lynch. Although it's hard to identify the source of the problem, **Long Gone Dead** has all the right ingredients, but only a skimpy portion of the first album's evocative magnificence. Perhaps it's Jeff Eyrich's production, which is fussier than Kahne's and partially obscures the Kinmans' melody-laden writing and rich vocals. Lacking **Sundown**'s lost and lonesome prairie feel, **Long Gone Dead** is appealing but disappointing. [iar]

RATIONAL YOUTH
Cold War Night Life (Can. YUL) 1982
Heredity (Capitol) 1985

Although this Canadian synthesizer trio occasionally lapses into lyrical pomposity, for the most part Rational Youth serves up fresh sounds and workable songs that show lots of promise. A bit like early Human League (but not grim), **Cold War Night Life** is a well-produced LP from talented technicians with minds *and* hearts. **Heredity** blends in more guitar for increased commercial appeal, but maintains a certain down-to-earth spunkiness that distinguishes Rational Youth from other post-Duran tech-pop bands. [iar]

RAW POWER
Screams from the Gutter (nr/Toxic Shock) 1985

In an interesting bit of Euro-American hardcore fraternity, this album by an Italian punk band—five guys from Reggio—was recorded in Indiana and issued by a California label. Raw Power play genre creations (like "Hate," "Nihilist," "Bastard," "My Boss") with fiery punk venom and helpfully sing them in English. [iar]

RAYBEATS
Roping Wild Bears EP (Don't Fall Off the Mountain/nr) 1981
Guitar Beat (Don't Fall Off the Mountain/PVC) 1981
It's Only a Movie! (Greensleeves/Shanachie) 1983

With so many current musicians having a strong sense of rock'n'roll history as well as an overriding interest in style, the emergence of groups like the all-instrumental Raybeats was inevitable. These four refugees from the New York City no-wave avant-garde have backgrounds that include stints with the Contortions and 8-Eyed Spy. But, lo and behold, they make frothy rock dance pieces, reminiscent of the tightly structured formats artists like the Ventures, Duane Eddy and the Shadows played many years ago. The simple melodies are defined by sparkling guitars, junky organ and wailing sax—a golden opportunity for most educated bands to condescend. But these fellas don't, because they obviously enjoy what they're playing, which makes them absolutely lovable. (Note: the UK and US versions of **Guitar Beat** differ by two tracks.) [jy]

See also *Jody Harris*.

ROGER C. REALE AND RUE MORGUE
Radio Active (London/Big Sound) 1978

With infectious melodies and clearcut hooks, this has to be classified as pop, but Reale's rough, tough vocal style makes it difficult to do so; that contrast is what makes the record so appealing. Connecticut's Reale has a knack for melody that's best exhibited on "High Society" and "Kill Me," but all the tracks hold up well. There's even a surprisingly good cover of the Troggs' "I Can't Control Myself." Reale might not have the sexual leer of Reg Presley, but he comes close. [cpl]

REAL KIDS
Real Kids (Bronze/Red Star) 1978
Outta Place (nr/Star-Rhythm) 1982
All Kindsa Jerks Live (Fr. New Rose) 1983
Hit You Hard (Fr. New Rose) 1983

TAXI BOYS
Taxi Boys EP (nr/Star-Rhythm) 1981
Taxi Boys EP (nr/Bomp) 1981

REAL KIDS/TAXI BOYS
Girls! Girls! Girls! (Fr. Lolita) 1983

The Real Kids were one of Boston's earliest new wave bands; their debut album is chock-full of dynamite tracks that take the trashier aspect of the Rolling Stones and couple it with the high-power guitar approach of the Ramones. Frontman and onetime Modern Lover John Felice not only provides tough guitar and distinctive lead vocals, but also has a knack for writing clear, infectious melodies. Spin "All Kindsa Girls," "She's Alright" or "My Baby's Book" for proof.

Poor sales of the first Real Kids LP resulted in Felice becoming a roadie for the Ramones, but he subsequently returned to Boston and formed the Taxi Boys. That group's two EPs (each with a different lineup) carry on the Real Kids tradition—high energy '60s garage-band rock. The production of the records might be crude, but Felice is in fine form on both. (The Bomp release is a 12-inch, the earlier one a 7-inch pressed on pink vinyl.)

Reactivating the Real Kids with a new and improved lineup, Felice made **Outta Place**, a dandy of an album. Harder yet still pop-oriented, with stellar production by Andy Paley, the record is strengthened by consistently good material and plenty of rock'n'roll spirit. After releasing the LP in France, that country's New Rose Records kept the Real Kids' recording career going, issuing another sharp studio record, **Hit You Hard**, and the live-in-Paris **All Kindsa Jerks Live**, which recaps Felice's song catalogue onstage with fiery enthusiasm. The Lolita release is a Real Kids/Taxi Boys compilation. [cpl/iar]

RECORDS
Shades in Bed (Virgin/nr) 1979
The Records (nr/Virgin) 1979
Crashes (Virgin) 1980
Music on Both Sides (Virgin/Virgin International) 1982

Like the Motors, the Records were reborn pub-rockers, making a quantum leap into the present by leaving their history behind and starting afresh with finely honed pop craftsmanship and the heavy record company support they had never previously enjoyed. While the Motors went for grandiose production numbers, the Records—led by ex-Kursaal Flyer drummer Will Birch—made sharp, tuneful confections that offered maximum hooks-per-groove in a classic Anglo-pop style not unlike the Hollies, with similarly brilliant harmonies and ringing guitars.

Shades in Bed (retitled **The Records**, resequenced and dressed in a completely different cover for America) is a wonderful LP, featuring song after song of pure pop with clever lyrics and winning melodies. Almost every track could have been a single; "Starry Eyes" and "Teenarama" were actually released, which left "Girls That Don't Exist," "Affection Rejected" and "Girl" as untested chart material. The English album included a bonus 12-inch, **High Heels** (an untitled 7-inch in the US), of the Records' renditions of four classic tracks, including the Kinks' "See My Friends" and Spirit's "1984."

Crashes, produced mainly by Craig Leon, showcased a revised lineup, Jude Cole having taken Huw Gower's guitar slot. (Gower eventually wound up in David Johansen's band ca. 1982.) Nothing here can match the first LP's charm except for two tracks produced by Mick Glossop—"Man with a Girl Proof Heart," written while Birch was still a Kursaal Flyer, and "Hearts in Her Eyes," which was done better by the Searchers later that year. At best a weak rehash of **Shades in Bed**, **Crashes** is passable, but hardly a great follow-up.

After a two-year recording gap, **Music on Both Sides** introduced a new five-piece lineup, with guitarist Dave Whelan and singer Chris Gent joining the surviving core of Birch, bassist Phil Brown and guitarist John Wicks. Birch produced this muddled but pleasant album that sounds like **Rubber Soul** with a crappy rock singer. Not a great parting shot, although less fey and precious than their early work. [iar]

See also *Huw Gower*.

RED CRAYOLA
Parable of Arable Land (nr/International Artists) 1967 & 1980 (Radar/nr) 1978
God Bless the Red Crayola and All Who Sail on Her (nr/IA) 1968 & 1980 (Radar/nr) 1979

Soldier-Talk (Radar/nr) 1979
Three Songs on a Trip to the U.S.A. EP (Recommended/nr) 1984

ART & LANGUAGE AND THE RED CRAYOLA
Corrected Slogans (nr/Music Language) 1976 (Recommended/nr) 1982
Kangaroo? (Rough Trade) 1981

RED CRAYOLA WITH ART & LANGUAGE
Black Snakes (Sw. Rec-Rec) 1983

MAYO THOMPSON
Corky's Debt to His Father (Glass/nr) 1986

Red Crayola first surfaced on Texas' International Artists label during the psychedelic era of the mid-'60s, with **Parable of Arable Land** and **God Bless the Red Crayola and All Who Sail on Her**. Rather unusual even for that time, the group faded into limbo until turning up to do sessions in 1976 with the Art & Language organization, which yielded the demos collected on **Corrected Slogans**; the album parallels somewhat the serious/silly music of Robert Wyatt. Largely acoustic in nature, **Corrected Slogans** has extremely simple songs, operatic vocals and complex lyrics that are satirical and/or political. It qualifies as rock only by association.

Radar Records, exhilarated by the critical success of Pere Ubu's dada punk, reissued **Parable of Arable Land** in 1978 and **God Bless** in 1979. Mayo Thompson and partner Jesse Chamberlin reformed Red Crayola to make **Soldier-Talk**, aided by Lora Logic and the entirety of Pere Ubu. Uniting Red Crayola's flower-power garage music with modernistic, fragmented arrangements and a fierce, broken beat, the album centers around cynical military themes. A challenging work.

Kangaroo?, reuniting Red Crayola with Art & Language, tones down the chaos for a musical discussion of Soviet Communist ideals and history, including the gentle, poignant instrumental, "1917." More in the style of avant-garde theatre music than rock, the LP is like Brecht out of Vivian Stanshall, with impressive results. **Black Snakes** has more of Thompson's dramatic vocals and features Ubuite Allen Ravenstine on sax and synth. The cornerstone tracks are "The Sloths," a prolix acid fable, the puerile "Ratman, the Weightwatcher" and "A Portrait of V.I. Lenin in the Style of Jackson Pollock." If you've read William Kotzwinkle, you'll certainly enjoy **Black Snakes**. [sg/iar]

RED CROSS
Red Cross EP (nr/Posh Boy) 1980
Born Innocent (nr/Smoke 7) 1982

REDD KROSS
Teen Babes from Monsanto (nr/Gasatanka) 1984

Despite being young—all members were under twenty when they started—Red Cross was a notable force on the Southern California punk scene with their first EP—terrific teen pop-punk numbers with a total devotion to modern camp and junk culture. Half the six tracks—"S & M Party," "I Hate My School" and "Annette's Got the Hits"—are near-classics.

Born Innocent doesn't have any tracks that reach the heights of the EP, but overall it's equally simple, sloppy and charming. It would be difficult to dislike Red Cross, as they innocently sing about their cultural icons—Charlie Manson (going so far as to cover Manson's "Cease to Exist"), Linda Blair, Patty Hearst, et al. It's especially nice to discover a group that doesn't take itself seriously and just enjoys playing.

With original Red Cross drummer Ron Reyes already in and out of Black Flag, the brothers McDonald remain the only permanent members of the band, recently rechristened Redd Kross for legal reasons. The seven-song, Geza X-produced **Teen Babes from Monsanto** retains the same wickedly funny spirit, covering Kiss ("Deuce"), the Stones ("Citadel"), Stooges ("Ann") and Bowie ("Savior Machine"), adding "Linda Blair 1984" as the sole original. The music—a wild'n'zany blend of rock and punk—isn't particularly special, but the inherent craziness (and a great cover) saves the day. K-Tel for wackos. [cpl/iar]

RED GUITARS

Slow to Fade (Self Drive/nr) 1984
Tales of the Expected (Virgin/nr) 1986

On their major-label debut, Hull's Red Guitars sound briefly like Cockney Rebel (from whom they borrow the refrain of "Sweetwater Ranch"), as well as Lloyd Cole, Bowie, Aztec Camera and Dream Academy. The quintet's light songs are pretty flimsy; guitarist Robert Holmes' vocals are likewise second-rate. While delicate and varied, arrangements and production alone can't make up for the record's inherent lack of *raison d'être*. [iar]

RED HOT CHILI PEPPERS

The Red Hot Chili Peppers (nr/Enigma-EMI America) 1984
Freaky Styley (EMI America) 1985

Awesomely powerful and remorselessly sarcastic, this California quartet melds floor-shaking rock-funk to wickedly clever songs like "True Men Don't Kill Coyotes," "Baby Appeal" and "Get Up and Jump." The Chili Peppers, who aren't above a little self-obsessed boasting or earnest political protest, play a thoroughly entertaining mutation of George Clinton, Was (Not Was), Peter Wolf, Kurtis Blow and Wall of Voodoo. Shake it, but make sure you pay attention at the same time!

Founding guitarist Hillel Slovak, who had missed the Peppers' debut LP during a stint with What Is This, returned to the fold in time for the second outing. Sagely engaging Clinton to produce, the Peppers made **Freaky Styley** more outrageous but easier to swallow as utilitarian dance-rock as well. A version of Sly Stone's "If You Want Me to Stay" shows they can play it straight; "Yertle the Turtle," based on a Dr. Seuss character, proves their dadaist sensibilities remain in full force. Other bits of rhythmicized doggerel—"Catholic School Girls Rule," "Thirty Dirty Birds," "Black-eyed Blonde"—keep tongue in cheek, mind in the gutter. Not a

record you'll be proud to own, **Freaky Styley** is nonetheless a ton of funk fun. [iar]

See also *What Is This*.

RED LORRY YELLOW LORRY

Talk About the Weather (Red Rhino/nr) 1985
Paint Your Wagon (Red Rhino/nr) 1986

If you loved Joy Division, you'll like Red Lorry Yellow Lorry. The Lorries similarly inhabit a bleak world in which swirling guitar figures and pretentious, gloomy lyrics are the only comforts. While Joy Division were the unchallenged lords of these nether regions, RLYL work the territory with enough savvy and intelligence (not to mention a cool supressed-acid-rock guitar sound) to make it work. **Talk About the Weather** ultimately succumbs to its own murky tunelessness, but not without a fight.

After that LP, RLYL recorded a great single, "Chance," which, with its distorted organ drone and rushed tempo, sounded as though the band had located its own true voice. However, **Paint Your Wagon** borrows enough from Ian Curtis and Joy Division that you'd think it had been released by Factory (ca. 1981), especially on cuts like "Head All Fire" and "Save My Soul." Despite this disappointing follow-up to such a promising debut, Red Lorry Yellow Lorry is still a band to watch. [jl/dgs]

RED NOISE

See *Bill Nelson*.

RED ROCKERS

Condition Red (nr/415) 1981
Good as Gold (CBS/415-Columbia) 1983
Schizophrenic Circus (CBS/415-Columbia) 1984

New Orleans' Red Rockers not only sound a bit like early Clash on their debut album, they match political conviction word for word, through songs like "Guns of Revolution," "White Law" and "Dead Heroes." But the Rockers lack the Clash's wit, and their humorlessness makes the record more preachy than passionate.

Thus armed with expectations, **Good as Gold** came as something of a surprise, starting with the first track. Gone was the raging rhetoric, replaced by a startlingly pretty pop song, "China," filled with articulate, ringing guitars and John Griffith's newly smoothed-up vocals. With ex-Stiff Little Fingers drummer Jim Reilly in the lineup, Red Rockers switched to melodic pop-rock, much like 415 labelmates Translator but with more emphasis on electric drive and generally less-exceptional songwriting. **Good as Gold** is consistently good and "China" deservedly became a hit single, but the band failed to really catch on commercially and returned with an equally bewildering follow-up, **Schizophrenic Circus**. Seemingly an attempt to become America's Alarm, the LP—produced by Rick Chertoff—goes nouveau-country and encompasses both the anthemic, folky "Blood from a Stone" (covering the Hooters) and a totally unnecessary remake of "Eve of Destruction." Danger sign: too

little original material of any significant quality. [iar]

REDS

The Reds (A&M) 1979
Stronger Silence (Kingdom/Ambition) 1981
Fatal Slide (Can. Stony Plain) 1982

Philadelphia's Reds perfected a hard-hitting, theatrical style that makes the music jump off the record and pin you to the wall. Suggesting an educated alternative to the Stooges, or a double-time interpretation of the Doors, this quartet played only at peak intensity, much like a dumb heavy metal band. However, the Reds don't exaggerate the flourishes or crescendos as, say, Black Sabbath would; instead, they move on rapidly to the next explosion, punk style. This breakneck hybrid is topped off by the tormented vocals of Rick Schaffer, who never seems to be fully in control of himself. Their A&M outing suffers from overstatement: too much sound and fury, not enough power. The more recent efforts harden the attack to simulate the effect of getting hit with a tossed brick, while highlighting the clean, surprisingly graceful musicianship. **Stronger Silence** features "The Danger" and "Driving Me Crazy"; **Fatal Slide** includes "Five Year Plan" and "Gone Too Far." [jy]

REDSKINS

Neither Washington nor Moscow (Decca/nr) 1986

Along with the Style Council, Test Dept. and Billy Bragg, the Redskins are at the forefront of British rock's Socialist movement. Led by guitarist Chris Dean (whose alter-ego, X. Moore, is an *NME* scribe), the trio augments an R&B-influenced sound with keyboards and a horn section, covering much the same musical terrain as the first Dexy's album (but marred by erratic production and mastering). Most of the songs are simple and catchy, and almost all the titles end in exclamation points! More important to the comrades than tunes, however, are lyrics—each song is a call to arms for the oppressed to rise up. Though doctrinaire, the Redskins are dead honest, committed to what they're doing, and make some good music. There aren't many bands around these days with those qualities. [dgs]

LOU REED

Lou Reed (RCA) 1972
Transformer (RCA) 1972 (RCA International/nr) 1981
Berlin (RCA) 1973
Rock n Roll Animal (RCA) 1974
Sally Can't Dance (RCA) 1974
Lou Reed Live (RCA) 1975
Metal Machine Music (RCA) 1975
Coney Island Baby (RCA) 1976
Rock and Roll Heart (Arista) 1976
Walk on the Wild Side: The Best of Lou Reed (RCA) 1977
Street Hassle (Arista) 1978
Live Take No Prisoners (Arista) 1978
The Bells (Arista) 1979
Growing Up in Public (Arista) 1980
Rock and Roll Diary 1967—1980 (Arista) 1980
The Blue Mask (RCA) 1982
Legendary Hearts (RCA) 1983
Live in Italy (RCA/nr) 1984
New Sensations (RCA) 1984
City Lights: Classic Performances (nr/Arista) 1985

Mistrial (RCA) 1986

Since he formed the Velvet Underground in 1966, Lou Reed's career has spanned several major rock upheavals, but he has always managed to be a leader not a follower, despite an iconoclastic resistance to fashion. A highly principled free-thinker, Reed has provided inspiration, direction and songs for bands with a taste for the seamier side of the rock sensibility.

Reed's influence began with the Velvet Underground's predilection for forbidden fruit—drugs, bizarre sex, suicide—in its lyrics, and raging chaos in its music. How could punk (much less the Jesus and Mary Chain) have ever occurred without "Sister Ray" or "Heroin" as touchstones? In his solo work, Reed has strayed far into heavy metal territory and experimental noise, as well as restrained, seemingly normal rock, but always with a rebellious attitude, probing honesty and unselfconscious abandon. He has managed to remain relevant throughout, serving as a guide for all sorts of unconventional music makers.

Lou Reed, recorded in England with session players like Steve Howe and Rick Wakeman (both of Yes!), includes previously unreleased Velvet Underground material (some of which turned up much later on **VU**) and the first incarnation of "Berlin." Effortlessly alternating nihilism with ironic wistfulness, the music is surprisingly lean and no-nonsense, getting Reed's solo career off the ground with a flourish.

The existence of a New York cafe society in the early '70s led to an alliance between Reed and David Bowie, who co-produced **Transformer** with Mick Ronson. Joining the legion of androgynous glam-rockers, Reed penned "Walk on the Wild Side," a chronicle of the Warhol crowd that—issued as a single—became a genuine subversive hit. Although **Transformer**'s music is a bit too campy, the LP is nonetheless a classic .

Fresh from his work with Alice Cooper, Bob Ezrin produced **Berlin**, using such players as Jack Bruce and Steve Winwood. While lyrically intense and haunting, the music is understated, almost plain. But Reed's tragic tales, like "Caroline Says" and "Sad Song," pack an intense emotional charge and **Berlin**, in spite of itself, is one of his best. (Not recommended for depressives or would-be suicides.)

Rock n Roll Animal captures Reed onstage in New York with an unbelievably bombastic heavy metal band powered by guitarists Steve Hunter and Dick Wagner. Playing a collection of elongated hits ("Sweet Jane," "Rock'n'Roll," "Heroin") at stun volume, Reed proves he can sound as neanderthal as any arena band of the day, but his songs and singing make it powerful. **Sally Can't Dance** attempts a mainstream sound with boring songs that lack fire; although a commercial success, it's one of Reed's most forgettable efforts, marking the beginning of a bad period in his career. To mark time, his next release was **Lou Reed Live** (more **Rock n Roll Animal**), followed by the truly deviant **Metal Machine Music**, four sides of unlistenable noise (a description, not a value judgment) that angered and disappointed all but the most devout

Reed fans. If he was simply looking to goad people and puncture perceptions, **Metal Machine Music** was a rousing success.

Coney Island Baby and **Rock and Roll Heart** proffer the same unambitious restraint as **Sally Can't Dance**; the new wrinkle is Reed's revelatory lyrics. After years of describing a depraved life-style with a hint of defensive pride, Reed began to open up and admit personal pain and doubts. A new creative vista mired in a musical rut.

Street Hassle shows Reed somewhat revitalized—or at least moved to action—by the onslaught of his young punk apostles. More aggressive sound and new-found vocal strength power songs like "Real Good Time Together" and the scathing "I Wanna Be Black." The band is exciting, and every path pursued bears fruit.

Another live album, **Take No Prisoners**—recorded at New York's Bottom Line—gives Reed a chance to try his hand at being a standup comedian. The four sides include only two or three songs each, the band vamping endlessly while Reed banters with the crowd, offering sharp opinions and cutting comments on a variety of subjects. Although not a great musical accomplishment, it's one of the funniest and most entertaining live albums of all time.

Reed continued to expose his sensitive side on **The Bells** and **Growing Up in Public**, using driving rock and delicate melodicism to back thoughtful lyrics and impassioned singing. A triumphant success, **The Blue Mask** uses almost no instrumental overdubs to get a spontaneous feel from a basic backing trio (including guitarist Robert Quine) and features some of Reed's strongest writing in years. The portraits he paints are miserable characters living outside society, and it's not clear whether or not they're fictional.

Walk on the Wild Side, **Rock and Roll Diary** and **City Lights** are compilations—the first of his RCA albums and the second mixing Velvet Underground material (almost two sides' worth) with a spotty bunch of tracks from both RCA and Arista records. The latter has excellent liner notes. There are other English and European retrospectives as well.

Reed found new acclaim with the band he enlisted for **The Blue Mask**; adding drummer Fred Maher to the core of Quine and bassist Fernando Saunders completed a perfect touring/ recording unit that Reed lost no time in exploiting. **Legendary Hearts** could just as well have been credited to the Lou Reed Band—every song is fully developed and confidently delivered in a manner suggesting a tight, well-rehearsed unit. It ranks with any Reed record all the way back to the Velvets in substance and stands out as his strongest work in style, using the group as a powerful lens that magnifies his themes and obsessions down to the finest detail. Picking an ideal moment to sum up his career to date, Reed recorded **Live in Italy** with the same band— two albums of material divided almost evenly between Velvets-era and solo work.

It seemed almost too good to continue. For his next record, Reed decided to play all the guitar himself, yet **New Sensations** is anything

but self-indulgent. Forsaking the two-guitar sound just throws Saunders' distinctive fretless bass playing and Reed's spare arrangements into higher relief, and they merit the attention. As do the songs, which prove that a middle-aged rock songwriter can have plenty to offer.

Mistrial is an essentially styleless observation of the times in which we live, simply played as variable-strength rock with Lou on guitar and Saunders (with some outside assistance) doing the rest. Reed's 1986 concerns are television ("Video Violence"), the state of world affairs ("The Original Wrapper," in which a credible funk track sets the stage for Reed to demonstrate his abilities as an urban wordsmith), emotional violence ("Don't Hurt a Woman," "Spit It Out") and personal realities ("Mama's Got a Lover" and a moving, memorably beautiful pair that close the album: "I Remember You" and "Tell It to Your Heart"). Although many of the melodies are too spare and casual to make any enduring impression, lyrics are obviously what's important here; by this point, Reed's albums have a higher (lower?) purpose than mere toe-tapping or bus-stop humming. [iar/mf]

REELS

The Reels (Back Door/Polydor) 1979
Quasimodo's Dream (Aus. Polygram) 1981
Beautiful (Aus. K-Tel) 1982

Singer David Mason sounds like a deep-echo Elvis Costello with a nagging cough. The songs have a wacky Madness edge and the band leaps into them with the speeding ska fury of classic 2-Tone. The suspicion that you've heard it all before does not diminish the eccentric, energetic joy of this Australian quintet's only US/UK release. The Reels' resounding lack of success in this hemisphere can probably be attributed to murky production too idiosyncratic for American radio and the fact that the English had already done this sort of thing better. [df]

RE-FLEX

The Politics of Dancing (EMI/Capitol) 1983

I can't tell them apart from the Fixx or Inxs or any other likeminded outfit with "x" in their name, but England's Re-Flex display a knack for penning strong melodies and playing walloping dance grooves, best exemplified on the title track and "Hurt." The quartet's debut LP was capably produced by John Punter. [tr]

RELUCTANT STEREO-TYPES

The Label (WEA/nr) 1980

This Birmingham outfit played likable reggaefied rock/pop much like another band of the same city and era, the Beat. Similarities include pointed-but-subtle lyrics that avoid clichés while covering political topics, prominent horn work, boppy dance rhythms and high musical standards. Differences include a more free-form, lesssoulful approach and stricter adherence to reggae rhythms on most tunes. Comparisons aside, **The**

Label is an ace record by a skilful, inventive band. [iar]
See also *King*.

R.E.M.

Chronic Town EP (nr/IRS) 1982
Murmur (IRS) 1983
Reckoning (IRS) 1984
Fables of the Reconstruction (IRS) 1985
Lifes Rich Pageant (IRS) 1986

Who would have expected an American musical revolution to be launched from Athens, Georgia? R.E.M.'s rough-hewn guitar pop, introduced on a stunning indie single ("Radio Free Europe") in 1981, has put them in the vanguard of a major movement that relies on homegrown, populist rootsiness rather than transatlantic inspiration. Blending Pete Buck's Byrdsian guitar playing with Michael Stipe's hazy, sometimes melancholic (but never miserable) vocals and impressionistic lyrics and a strong, supple rhythm section (Bill Berry and Mike Mills), R.E.M. plays memorable songs with unprepossessing simplicity and emotional depth. R.E.M. has remained as intelligent and committed to artistic expression (not just their own) as early boosters had hoped.

The five-song **Chronic Town** EP, co-produced by Mitch Easter, continues the sound (if not all the rushed excitement) of the single, and boasts the remarkable "1,000,000" and the equally memorable "Carnival of Sorts (Boxcars)." Although not released as such in the UK, some of **Chronic Town** surfaced on a 1983 EP coupled with tracks from **Murmur**.

Murmur is a masterpiece, containing all the essential components of truly great serious pop music. From "Catapult" to "Pilgrimage" to a reprise of "Radio Free Europe," Stipe inscrutably (but evocatively) mumbles his vocals with unmistakable passion, while the band spins haunting webs of guitar rock that are heavy with atmosphere. A completely satisfying collection that served as a guidepost for many of the bands who chose to follow R.E.M. back to the South for inspiration.

Doomed to disappoint by comparison to the debut, **Reckoning** is not quite as consistent, although it contains enough equally great music to maintain R.E.M.'s reputation for excellence. "Harborcoat," "So. Central Rain (I'm Sorry)," "(Don't Go Back to) Rockville" and "Pretty Persuasion" are all wonderful, and display not only clearer production (Easter and Don Dixon) but a less hurried pace and more articulate singing.

Fables of the Reconstruction (aka **Reconstruction of the Fables**), produced in London by Joe Boyd, finds R.E.M. largely neglecting catchy melodicism and driving rhythms for reflective, languidly meandering numbers that lack focal points and seem to start and finish with the structured inexorability of a light switch. A number of the songs are flat-out boring, and the album in toto is vague and colorless. **Fables**, however, is not without its positive accomplishments. Although scarcely in a league with their best work, "Can't Get There from Here," "Driver 8" and the raucous "Auctioneer (Another Engine)" have familiar attributes. Otherwise, the album has little to recommend it. [iar]
See also *Fleshtones*.

RENALDO AND THE LOAF

Songs for Swinging Larvae (Do It/Ralph) 1979
Arabic Yodelling (nr/Ralph) 1983
Streve and Sneff [tape] (nr/Ralph) 1984

RESIDENTS & RENALDO AND THE LOAF

Title in Limbo (nr/Ralph) 1983

Only the Residents' label would bother to sign a duo as deeply weird as Renaldo and the Loaf—in real life two Englishmen named David Janssen and Brian Poole (the latter *not* of '60s swingers the Tremeloes). Their bizarre studio-doctored vocals, cut-and-paste arrangements, jerky robot rhythms and alien instrumentation (among the pair's noisemakers: scalpel, metal comb, hacksaw blade, biscuit tins) suggest that Renaldo and the Loaf was evolved in the Residents' image. Unfortunately, **Songs for Swinging Larvae** has all the madness and none of the coherence of the Residents' nutty concepts, its offbeat wit stampeded instead by rampant disorienting eclecticism. Guaranteed to clear the room of your choice.

Arabic Yodelling is roughly more of the same, a collection of Rube Goldberg home-brewed insanity recorded over a two-year period. A bit less weird for weird's sake (although hardly in danger of mass appeal), it keeps the blindly whimsical faith the Residents themselves have partially outgrown. **Title in Limbo**, the group's joint effort with their American soul brothers, however, is not at all enticing. **Streve and Sneff** is an American reissue of a pre-**Larvae** cassette the band had previously distributed on their own. [df/iar]

ROBERT RENTAL AND THE NORMAL

Live at the West Runton Pavilion (Rough Trade) 1981

Emerging from the do-it-yourself school of synthesizer playing, Robert Rental teamed up with the Normal (aka Daniel Miller, head of Mute Records) for this one-off show, reproduced on a one-sided album. The compendium of noises involved bears relation to music only by inference, though it *is* an impressive display of live electronics, tape loops and devices, similar in scope and approach to avant-garde electronic events of the '60s. Rental and the Normal are firmly rooted in rock, however, and this half-record proffers more ideas per minute than can be found anywhere except the more esoteric recordings of Cabaret Voltaire. [sg]
See also *Thomas Leer*.

REPLACEMENTS

Sorry Ma, Forgot to Take Out the Trash (nr/Twin/Tone) 1981
The Replacements Stink EP (nr/Twin/Tone) 1982 & 1986
Hootenanny (nr/Twin/Tone) 1983
Let It Be (Zippo/Twin/Tone) 1984
The Shit Hits the Fans [tape] (nr/Twin/Tone) 1985
Tim (Sire) 1985
Boink!! (Glass/nr) 1986

Lots of folks say that Minneapolis' Replacements are the best rock'n'roll band in the world, and when it all clicks—volume, rawness, speed (pace **and** ingested substances), energy and passion—they're right. But lots of times, when the band can't be bothered to play their own songs or finish whatever they're playing, when they really just want to be difficult, they're possibly the worst.

They get written off a lot as sloppy, but that's just an easy thing people say who don't see beyond the chaos. Chris Mars drums like he's possessed; Tommy Stinson is a spoiled teen (he was twelve when the band started) but thumps a mean bass-line; buffoonish Bob Stinson's likely to wear a dress (or less) onstage but can alternate between ripping metal leads and achingly tender melody lines that prove he's got a heart (if not a brain). And Paul Westerberg—too terrified to sing his soft songs—hides behind the band's noise. The Mats (short for Placemats) are one of those classic rock'n'roll combos whose music, looks and personalities fit together perfectly, the stuff of which legends are made. The lore surrounding them is already pretty thick.

The musical evidence was there on the first album, eighteen songs following the usual loud/fast rules with titles like "Shut Up," "Kick Your Door Down" and "Shiftless When Idle." But they showed some depth on the slow, bluesy ode to J. Thunders, "Johnny's Gonna Die." Their EP went for pure driving thrash and produced some gems, including "Dope Smokin Moron," "Kids Don't Follow" and "God Damn Job." **Stink** landed them in the hardcore ranks, even though the music and lyrics are much sharper than most, mixing equal parts arrogance and self-deprecating humor.

On **Hootenanny** they combined blues, power pop, folk, country, straight-ahead rock, surf (or, more accurately, ski) and punk in a way few hardcore bands could even imagine, and people started taking notice. **Stink**'s "Fuck School" gave way to "Color Me Impressed," a soaring power pop number about being bored at hip parties, proving a wisdom beyond their years, and sounding pretty incongruous next to "Run It," a paean to beating red lights. Westerberg reached into his bag of solo heartstoppers for a naked-yet- never-sappy confession of loneliness, "Within Your Reach."

With **Let It Be**, the Mats became "stars," at least on the independent club/college radio circuit. The LP was more focused, boldly carrying out what they'd only tried on **Hootenanny**. They blended power pop and country shuffle on "I Will Dare" and raved-up on novelty rockers like "Tommy Gets His Tonsils Out" and "Gary's Got a Boner." Loneliness gave way to total emptiness on "Unsatisfied."

Critics trampled each other in a rush to claim discovery rights. Sire signed them and Twin/Tone celebrated with a cassette-only live tape—stolen from some kid bootlegging an Oklahoma show—which showed the feckless Mats at their most messed-up, playing—or at least starting to play—covers from R.E.M. to the Stones; Thin Lizzy to X.

Although there is no consensus on the issue, the Replacements did make the transition to major-labeldom with their artistic integrity intact. It looked for a while as if Alex Chilton would get the nod, but ex-Ramone Tommy Erdelyi ended

up producing **Tim** (great title, that), retaining all the raggedness and devil-may-care rock'n'roll spirit that makes the Replacements great. These Westerberg tunes are among his best ever, from the melancholy bar ballad, "Here Comes a Regular," to the obnoxiously mean-spirited anti-stewardess slur, "Waitress in the Sky." His raging insecurity shines through on "Hold My Life" ("because I just might lose it . . .") and "Bastards of Young"; he celebrates college radio in "Left of the Dial" and considers the romantic possibilities of public transportation on "Kiss Me on the Bus." A stupendous record.

Boink!! is an eight-song UK condensation of their pre-**Let It Be** catalogue, with the added bonus of an otherwise unreleased Chilton-produced cut, "Nowhere Is My Home." [ep/iar]

RESCUE

Messages EP (nr/A&M) 1984

Cleverly produced by Tony Mansfield, this American quintet sounds decidedly British on these five nifty dance-rock tunes. Although nothing else matches up to it, the title track—with powerful drumming and a weedy synth figure—points up the band's strengths: crafty, original songwriting and a likable singer in guitarist Paul McGovern. [iar]

RESIDENTS

Meet the Residents (nr/Ralph) 1974 & 1977 & 1985
The Residents Present the Third Reich 'n Roll (nr/Ralph) 1975 & 1979
Fingerprince (nr/Ralph) 1976
Duck Stab/Buster & Glen (nr/Ralph) 1978
Not Available (nr/Ralph) 1978
Eskimo (nr/Ralph) 1979
Nibbles (Virgin/nr) 1979
Diskomo/Goosebump EP (nr/Ralph) 1980
The Residents Commercial Album (Pre/Ralph) 1980
Mark of the Mole (nr/Ralph) 1981
The Tunes of Two Cities (Ralph) 1982
Intermission EP (London/Ralph) 1982
The Residents' Mole Show (no label) 1983
Residue of the Residents (Ralph) 1983
George & James (Korova/Ralph) 1984
Whatever Happened to Vileness Fats? (Ralph) 1984
Assorted Secrets [tape] (Ralph) 1984
Ralph Before 84: Volume One (Korova/nr) 1984
The Census Taker (nr/Episode) 1985
The Big Bubble (Black Shroud-Ralph) 1985
The Eyeball Show—Live in Japan (Torso/Ralph) 1986

RESIDENTS & RENALDO AND THE LOAF

Title in Limbo (Ralph) 1983

What's a Resident? Epithets abound, but anent actual identities, anyone who knows ain't talking. Cineastes transplanted—so the story goes—from Shreveport, Louisiana to the San Francisco Bay area who also dabble in musical experiments, the foursome (trio? duo? *solo*?—one guy does almost all the

"singing," aside from guest vocalists) has woven a remarkable cloak of secrecy. Aside from the avowed purpose of avoiding misleading and potentially divisive individual credits, this creates an attention-getting mystique which, when the limited speculation on same has been exhausted, leaves absolutely nothing to contemplate but the music itself.

The Residents have led Ralph Records from cottage industry to self-sufficient label, able to sell artistically ambitious *oeuvres* without selling themselves out. They're also paradigmatic of limited technical and compositional ability marshalled, along with wit and imagination, in the service of works seeking to trample sacrosanct icons and the boundaries of rock.

They evidently haven't the talent to write distinctive melodies that don't sound utterly bizarre. When they try, the results invariably sound like someone else's—albeit distinctly distorted or perverted—which is probably one reason why the dissection and reassembly of various bits of rock tradition was their early forte. Also, their approach owes great debts to the early groundbreaking of both Frank Zappa and Captain Beefheart. (It's even been argued—granted, somewhat whimsically—that the storied N. Senada, a poet/saxist who allegedly collaborated with the Residents during his brief sojourn in the Bay Area, is really Beefheart.) All that said, the Residents are superior synthesists, and the derivations of their work can't deny the entertainingly provocative nature of their best achievements.

The first four efforts by the then-unnamed group were album-length tapes, including one which was sent (with no name on it) to a record company in the hopes of a deal and sent back to the quartet's return address care of "Residents." Hence the moniker.

N. Senada's contribution, the concept of phonetic (re)organization, was adapted by the Residents on their vinyl LP debut, **Meet the Residents**, which after alleged legal threats by the Beatles' record label, was reissued in '77 with graphics not so savagely parodic of the similarly named Beatles LP (and with improved sound). The record is sometimes a goofy sophomoric giggle, sometimes a striking, off-the-wall twist of musical mind. The Residents had arrived, but weren't yet sure quite where they were.

On **The Residents Present the Third Reich 'n Roll** the band transforms hooky bits from '60s Top 40 hits into two ridiculous, funny, scary and just plain jaw-dropping- weird side-long suites, "Swastikas on Parade" and "Hitler Was a Vegetarian," intended as "revenge" for the brainwashing of American youth into acceptance of rock's trivialization (or something like that). The LP was reissued with partially censored graphics in '79 (the original showed a carrot-toting Nazi officer who bore a distinct resemblance to Dick Clark).

Fingerprince returned to the first LP's contrast of very short tracks with one lengthy one, but in considerably higher gear: imagine a meeting of the minds of Frank Zappa and Steely Dan in a very

avant mood—with the results processed through a computer programmed by a paranoid schizophrenic with a sense of humor. (Snakefinger, who had played outrageous guitar on their early tapes and 45-only version of the Stones' "Satisfaction"—which makes Devo's subsequent try sound like the 1910 Fruitgum Co.—also guests here.)

Duck Stab was originally released as an EP—the group at its most consistently accessible so far—but was enlarged to album size by the **Buster & Glen** half (also succinctly catchy and humorous). This was evidently cut as a lightweight diversion from the sessions for the more crucial conceptual masterwork, **Eskimo**. The project may have gotten out of control, since its release was postponed a year. Instead, out popped **Not Available**, which supposedly had been recorded just after **Meet the Residents**—and which, according to "the theory of obscurity," was not intended for release. Hooey? If new, it's the culmination of various ideas the band had cultivated; if genuinely old, a lasting influence on Residentiala to come. I'd say the latter, since most everything said to have been recorded after it seems more refined in execution, if not so grand in sweep. Can you imagine a vast epic in five sections told with the recitative cadence of nursery rhymes (a Residents vocal-part trademark) but sounding as though played by E.T. and family?

With help from ex-Mothers keyboardist Don Preston and drummer Chris Cutler of Henry Cow/Art Bears fame, **Eskimo**'s broad, electronically spacey sonic contours form a backdrop for what the Residents would have you believe is a re-creation of Eskimo life and culture (instrumental, but with printed narration on the jacket to explain the "stories.") It's brilliant and—yep—chilling, their most (but not totally) serious undertaking yet, evocative if not quite authentic. Some of its sections were reprogrammed as "Diskomo" and coupled on an EP with a Residential look at Mother Goose.

The Residents then went incredibly unserious and recorded an album of forty one-minute songs, some with anonymous celebrity assistance. (Fred Frith is credited, but Lene Lovich and XTC's Andy Partridge, among others, aren't.) **The Residents Commercial Album** is a gimmick, and the inspiration brought to bear on its challenge of brevity is hit-and-miss, with too many tracks mere fragments, deservedly and otherwise.

The Mole trilogy began auspiciously with **Mark of the Mole**, a murkily limned but engrossing story of the Moles, forced out of their home into sharing one with the Chubs, and the ensuing conflict between the "underground" and slick complacency. A thin story, but musically harrowing. Unfortunately, **The Tunes of Two Cities** suggested that the Residents had painted themselves into a corner. The narrative isn't advanced and, although its context is fleshed out, it's simply not enough. The Residents seek to convey the cultural contrast in musical terms, alternating the Moles' abrasive, industrial grind with the Chubs' offbeat yet unctuous cocktail jazz. Neither the device nor its execution, notwithstanding some swell sax work by Norman Salant, can justify a whole album.

This should have been a sign that the Residents' camp was in disarray. Despite the acquisition of hotshot LA management, the Residents began to reel first from internal dissension and later several desertions from the Ralph brain trust, if not the group itself. (A subject about which *nobody's* talking—and where do you draw the line, if there is indeed a line to draw?)

The 1983 live **Mole Show** LP is the Residents' own authorized bootleg of the show's groundbreaking presentation at LA's Roxy Theatre in late '82. (The band also toured Europe.) It scopes down the two extant installments and adapts them for live performance. This makes it hard to follow unless you're already well-versed in the two LPs, and it's aurally limited in the way you'd normally expect a live record of complicated studio music to be. That said, it's surprisingly good—and the Residents do find a charming way of squirming out of having presented an unfinished work. But it's still an evasion. (**Intermission** is exactly as billed—"extraneous" music from the show, and the first Residents record unable to stand on its own.)

Residue collects Resident leftovers, rarities and unreleased versions. It too sidesteps the Mole issue, but is at least exciting and entertaining (if a bit uneven and unintegrated), relying notably on the Residents' patented warpage of rock clichés.

That's more than can be said of their collaboration with likeminded English weirdos Renaldo and the Loaf; this is the first Residents record I wish had never been released. Who's at fault isn't totally clear (it can't all be Renaldo), but the record is far less than the sum of its parts; only one track is truly worthy of the Residents. The rest deserves to be dumpsterized and forgotten.

Not content with one incomplete ambitious venture, the Residents then launched another: the American Composers Series, an attempt to lionize their favorite writers by interpreting their work. The first (and, so far, only) volume of the projected sixteen-year (!) undertaking, **George & James**, matches up a side each of George Gershwin and James Brown (live at the Apollo, no less—with crowd sounds) and is an excellent, typically bizarre success.

After that came two soundtrack albums, one of a Residents short film and the other of a Hollywood feature. Although hardly the records you'd expect to offer hope for a bright Residential future, that's just what they do. The long-rumored *Vileness Fats* was intended to be a full-length music video back in 1972, but was later abandoned. But I simply can't believe that the music was recorded over a decade ago; the songs may date from then, but the recording sounds of recent vintage. And it's a good, if not major, addition to the group's canon.

Even better is the certifiably current **The Census Taker**, which subverts more soundtrack music genres than you can shake a stick at in brilliant Residential fashion. (Could this be the band's mode of entry into the real world?)

Billed as "Part Four of the Mole Trilogy," **The Big Bubble** finds the Residents (not the band pictured on the cover) portraying a group called Big Bubble, made up of cross-bred Mole/Chubs called Zinkenites. In the story, this group is trying to reestablish Mole language and traditions, so it seems the tale is far from over. It sounds like Snakefinger's guitar on some tracks, but there's little else of great interest. Everything sounds forced and/or rehashed. These recent albums raise the question: While we wait for the end (or at least part three) of the trilogy, will the Residents trivialize themselves, however artfully? Will they become the house band on *Saturday Night Live*? To be continued . . . ? [jg/dgs]

See also *Snakefinger*.

MARTIN REV

Martin Rev (nr/Infidelity) 1980
Clouds of Glory (Fr. New Rose) 1985

The keyboard half of controversial New York psycho-electronic duo Suicide proves only slightly more melodic on an eccentric eponymous solo outing—all keyboards and rhythm machines, with only the occasional grunting vocal. The rich layering of synthesizer effects—at least compared to the brute minimalism of Suicide—is close to the articulate electronic orchestration of the Ric Ocasek-produced **Suicide** album also released in 1980. The simple floating melody and disco rhythm-box ping of "Mari" also suggest the mantric pop quality of Suicide's near-hit 12-inch single, "Dream Baby Dream." More typical of **Martin Rev**, though, is the hellish pumping of "Nineteen 86" and "Jomo"'s industrial racket; the only thing missing is Suicide singer Alan Vega's mad bark.

Half a decade later, Rev returned with the like-minded **Clouds of Glory**, pressed on red vinyl. Musical styles may have finally caught up with this minimalist electro-rhythm pioneer, but he sticks resolutely true to course here, dispensing with vocals and layering weird sound effects over sturdy sequencer lines. The gently attractive "Whisper" would have made a very pretty song were Rev to give it lyrics. [df/iar]

KIMBERLEY REW

The Bible of Bop (Armalanta/Press) 1982

Like ex-bandmate Robyn Hitchcock, Kimberley Rew survived the end of the Soft Boys to produce further forays into melodious '60s folk-rock and psychedelia, as the eight tracks (seven previously released) on this 45-rpm mini-LP prove. Working with the dB's, ex-Soft Boys and Waves, Rew doesn't pursue weirdness as avidly as Hitchcock does, but the singer/guitarist/keyboardist has a neat winner with **The Bible of Bop**. Rew's next venture was a full-time career with the rock-popping Katrina and the Waves. [iar]

REZILLOS

Can't Stand the Rezillos (Sire) 1978
Mission Accomplished . . . but the Beat Goes On (Sire/nr) 1979

REVILLOS

Rev Up (Snatzo-DinDisc/nr) 1980
Attack (Superville/nr) 1983

Scotland's Rezillos were a blast of fresh air compared to the more serious bands of new wave's first charge. They were partial to an overhauled '60s look (e.g., foil miniskirts, pop-art fabrics) and songs with titles like "Flying Saucer Attack" and "Top of the Pops." **Can't Stand the Rezillos** is an action-packed document of their pop/-camp approach. Thrashings of the Dave Clark 5's "Glad All Over" and Gerry & the Pacemakers' "I Like It" surround "(My Baby Does) Good Sculptures," a typically loopy original.

The band flew apart not long after their album debut, leaving the live **Mission Accomplished** as an unsatisfactory memorial. Besides duplicating six tunes from **Can't Stand**, the record is plagued by near-bootleg-quality sound. Otherwise the performance is a rave-up from start to finish, with five new originals and versions of the Kinks' "I Need You," Cannibal & the Headhunters' "Land of 1000 Dances" and even Sweet's "Ballroom Blitz."

Fortunately, singers Fay Fife and Eugene Reynolds regrouped with new musicians as the Revillos, who took the Rezillos' promise even further. **Rev Up** is filled with pastiches of '60s genres—"Bobby Come Back to Me," "On the Beach," "Secret of the Shadow," "Motorbike Beat"—and the obligatory non-originals—"Cool Jerk," "Hungry for Love," "Hippy Hippy Sheik" [sic]. The only foul touch is retitling the Rock-a-Teens' "Woo-Hoo" as "Yeah Yeah" and pawning it off as an original. But **Rev Up** is hilarious. [si]

See also *Shake*.

RICH KIDS

Ghosts of Princes in Towers (EMI/nr) 1978 (Fame/nr) 1983

After being squeezed out of the Sex Pistols, bassist/singer Glen Matlock formed the Rich Kids with guitarist Midge Ure and drummer Rusty Egan (both of whom later collaborated on Visage, with Ure eventually going on to join Ultravox), plus one Steve New. During their tempestuous year-long alliance, the Rich Kids managed only this one album, ludicrously misproduced into a muffled mess by Mick Ronson. Despite abysmal sound, the band's talent emerges, and **Ghosts** is an extraordinary album of daring experimental rock-/pop that has two utterly brilliant pieces (the title track and "Marching Men") plus a few others nearly as good. While the predominant guitar work is occasionally mundane, there are enough novel ideas and convincing songs to make this uniquely flavored project survive the audio bloodbath and emerge victorious. [iar]

See also *Ultravox, Visage*.

JONATHAN RICHMAN AND THE MODERN LOVERS

Jonathan Richman & the Modern Lovers (Beserkley) 1977 (nr/Rhino) 1986
Rock'n'Roll with the Modern Lovers (Beserkley) 1977 (nr/Rhino) 1986
Back in Your Life (Beserkley) 1979 (nr/Rhino) 1986
The Jonathan Richman Songbook (Beserkley/nr) 1980
Jonathan Sings! (Rough Trade/Sire) 1983

Rockin' and Romance (Rough Trade/Twin/Tone) 1985
It's Time For (Rough Trade/Upside) 1986

MODERN LOVERS

The Modern Lovers (Beserkley) 1976 (nr/Rhino) 1986
Live (Beserkley) 1977
The Original Modern Lovers (Bomp) 1981

At the outset of his career, Jonathan Richman was considered a radical trailblazer, precociously exploring minimalist rock years before such behavior became popular (or even acceptable). Not only was his unique approach enormously influential on later bands, early members of the Modern Lovers went on to become successful in such groups as Talking Heads and the Cars. Over the course of his recordings, however, Richman's predilection for childlike whimsy replaced the angst-ridden emotionalism of his first songs, and he eventually lost his flock by refusing to remain the same character he had been a decade earlier.

The first Modern Lovers album was cobbled together by Beserkley supremo Matthew King Kaufman out of demos, the bulk of which had been produced by John Cale in 1971 when it looked as if the band would be signed by Warner Bros. Despite the fragmentary nature of its parts, **The Modern Lovers** is surprisingly coherent, and contains all of Richman's classic creations: "Roadrunner," "Pablo Picasso," "Girl Friend," "She Cracked," etc. The stark, simple performances highlight an adenoidal New England voice that lacks everything technical but nothing emotional. One of the truly great art-rock albums of all time.

Although released shortly after *The Modern Lovers*, **Jonathan Richman & the Modern Lovers** was recorded five years later with a totally different band, and has little in common with it. Not realizing the time frame, many people took this as a sign of artistic inconsistency, and were put off by such silliness as "Abominable Snowman in the Market" and "Hey There Little Insect." The record is, in fact, pretty great, blending guilelessness with heart-wrenching honesty, e.g., "Important in Your Life." Enough of Richman's early approach carries over to temper the silliness, and it's a thoroughly charming, low-key album.

Rock'n'Roll takes Richman significantly further away from seriousness; mixing traditional folk songs and lullabies with originals that would do Mister Rogers proud ("Ice Cream Man," "Rockin' Rockin' Leprechaun"), the sarcastically titled album stretched the ability of his adult fans to join in the fun. Some abiding wittiness—like "Dodge Veg-O-Matic"—improved matters, but the LP left many wondering where Richman was heading.

Live, recorded in England, is full of the silliest songs in his repertoire—featherweight and best suited for very young people. **The Jonathan Richman Songbook** is a compilation.

Back in Your Life was recorded (after a long layoff) with two different bands, the regular Modern Lovers and a vocals/glockenspiel ensemble. The songs are totally over the top, as fanciful and ridiculous as possible.

There's nothing remotely connected to the Modern Lovers' rock'n'roll work; comparisons to Groucho Marx's musical ventures are more relevant. Impossible to hate, this record merely defies honest enthusiasm.

Four years later, the same is fortunately not the case on **Jonathan Sings!**, an utterly wonderful album showcasing a fully revitalized Richman with an altogether new outlook. Audibly bursting with love, Richman eloquently (in his own clumsy way) sings of "That Summer Feeling," exclaims "You're the One for Me" and rejoices at having "Somebody to Hold Me." Elsewhere, he defends the wisdom of infants in "Not Yet Three," offers a new look at world travel ("Give Paris One More Chance") and even extolls the joys of "This Kind of Music." The new Modern Lovers—two women and three men—have a strong but understated presence that keeps Richman exciting without getting in his way. Simply put, **Jonathan Sings!** is one of the most uplifting albums in memory, and Richman's best since the first Modern Lovers album.

On a roll, Jonathan kept right on charming through the next two albums. **Rockin' and Romance** (retaining two Modern Lovers from **Sings**) is a spartan, casually- produced (to the point of sonic obscurity) affair, but songs about "The Beach," "Vincent Van Gogh" (number two in Richman's Great Painters series), baseball ("Walter Johnson," "The Fenway"), travel ("Bermuda") and other winning topics are all filled with Richman's remarkable wit and intelligence. Who else could write a paean to bluejeans that discusses the relative merits of various brands without being mistaken for a commercial? Slight demerits for the shoddy sound quality, but no complaints whatsoever about the music.

It's Time For reunites Richman with erstwhile Modern Lover guitarist Asa Brebner. The audio fidelity is better; the inclusion of an accordionist, producer Andy Paley's guitar work and Richman's sax tooting makes for an unusual (for Richman), busier-than-ordinary rock sound. ("Yo Jo Jo" is a crazed instrumental rave-up, the most electric thing he's done this decade.) Richman's lyrical concerns are more general than in the recent past: for every "Double Chocolate Malted" (which has a strangely cranky tone to it) or "Corner Store" there are two songs (e.g., "It's You," "When I Dance," "Just About Seventeen," "This Love of Mine") that are less specific and to a degree less captivating. A confusing (confused?) album, **It's Time For** has the aura of a transitional project.

The demos dredged up for **The Original Modern Lovers** date from 1973 and were produced by Kim Fowley. The LP includes two versions of "Roadrunner," plus "Astral Plane," "Girlfren" and "She Cracked," as well as some otherwise unrecorded numbers. Despite thin sound it offers slightly different approaches than what surfaced on the first album. Shoddy but relevant. [iar]

See also *Necessaries, Real Kids, Talking Heads.*

STAN RIDGWAY

The Big Heat EP (Illegal/nr) 1985
The Big Heat (IRS) 1986

It's no coincidence that the lyrics on this album are printed on the inner sleeve in prose format; ex-Wall of Voodoo singer Ridgway's a pulp

novelist at heart. Delivered with his exaggerated side-of-the-mouth delivery and instrumentation that reaches for maximum film noir ambience, the songs recount amazing stories of crime, war and bizarre characters in a highly engaging and uncommon fashion. **The Big Heat** is a rare record—one that will have you as interested in the lyrical action as its substantial musical attributes. [iar]

RIKKI AND THE LAST DAYS OF EARTH

Rikki and the Last Days of Earth (DJM/nr) 1978

RIKKI SYLVAN

The Silent Hours (Kaleidoscope/nr) 1981

Rikki and the Last Days of Earth made a couple of 45s and one roundly ignored album; Sylvan's subsequent solo venture doesn't do much to improve his credibility. Vocals that fall between Gary Numan and David Sylvian, predictable technocratic songs ("I Am a Video," "Into the Void") and arty but generally bland rock with occasionally prominent synthesizer make **The Silent Hours** a derivative, dull exercise. [iar]

MARC RILEY WITH THE CREEPERS

Creeping at Maida Vale EP (In Tape/nr) 1984
Cull (In Tape/nr) 1984
Gross Out (In Tape/nr) 1984
Shadow Figures EP (In Tape/nr) 1984
Fancy Meeting God! (In Tape/nr) 1985
Warts 'n' All (In Tape/nr) 1985
Four A's from Maida Vale EP (In Tape/nr) 1986

Guitarist/keyboardist Riley was booted out of the Fall in 1982, reportedly over an unseemly penchant for pop. His prolific output as a solo artist, however, only slightly deserves such categorization. Although Riley shares his former band's taste for deadpan vocals and distorted guitar and keyboard sounds, freed of Mark Smith's clutches he exhibits more melodic, structured songwriting and has one foot firmly rooted in the garage punk tradition.

All three EPs are taken from sessions for John Peel's radio program and feature one of Riley's favorite lyrical gambits—taking the piss out of other groups. **Creeping at Maida Vale** is a great little record, with four strong songs, including "Location Bangladesh," a clever stab at bands who travel the world for exotic video locales. **Four A's**, equally enjoyable, contains "Bard of Woking," aimed at the people's-poet pretensions of one Style Councillor. The **Cull** compilation is Riley's strongest vinyl offering; **Creeping** takes up one side while the other reprises prior, vaguely Velvets-ish singles. **Gross Out**, while not breaking any new musical ground, does contain one of Riley's finest moments ("Gross"). **Fancy Meeting God!** is an energetic, sometimes catchy and often hilarious LP, unfortunately losing a little zip by the end. Had it been edited together with **Gross Out**'s highlights, the sum would have been much greater than the parts.

Warts 'n' All is a fun greatest-hits run-through recorded live in Amsterdam. As entertaining for Riley's between-song banter as it is for great songs (including Eno's pre-ambience "Baby's on Fire"), it can serve as a very good introduction to unacquainted.

Although Riley and his mates certainly don't have to be compared to the Fall, what they do have in common is the ability to release records of quality in rapid-fire succession. The Creepers (as they are now known) seem on the verge of becoming a major force on the independent scene. [dgs]

RIP RIG & PANIC

God (Uh Huh-Virgin/nr) 1981
I Am Cold (Virgin/nr) 1982
Attitude (Virgin/nr) 1983

MARK SPRINGER

Piano (Illuminated/nr) 1984

An offshoot of the Pop Group, Rip Rig & Panic was a jazz-funk fusion band that left new wave behind musically but retained an irreverent sensibility. Named after a Roland Kirk LP, the band appropriately featured saxophone/piano free-for-alls. They were not as anarchic as their jazz inspirations, though; repetitive bass licks (Sean Oliver) and stable percussion (Bruce Smith) are great aids for more right-wing listeners.

The band's most appealing aspect is its high-spiritedness. Beyond absurd titles, Rip Rig & Panic leap around stylistically from (short) track to track. Tranquil piano (Mark Springer) solos and silly chats provide respite from screeching sax (Gareth Sager), Arabic and Far Eastern touches and hard-edged vocals (Neneh Cherry and, on **God**, ex-Slit Ari Upp). **Attitude**, the band's most accessible album, comes closest to normal songs while maintaining a zany eclecticism. Far from forbidding, Rip Rig & Panic keep the show rolling with deft musicianship and oddball humor. In late 1983, they reorganized as Float Up CP. [si]

See also *Float Up CP.*

TOM ROBINSON BAND

Power in the Darkness (EMI/Harvest) 1978 (Fame/nr) 1982
TRB Two (EMI/Harvest) 1979
Tom Robinson Band (Fame/nr) 1982

TOM ROBINSON

North by Northwest (Panic/IRS) 1982
Cabaret '79 (Panic/nr) 1982
Atmospherics EP (Panic/nr) 1983
Hope and Glory (Geffen) 1984

SECTOR 27

Sector 27 (Fontana-EMI/IRS) 1980

Tom Robinson escaped from the ashes of Cafe Society, a lightweight London outfit produced by Ray Davies, in 1975 to become a highly visible rock bandleader, championing various radical causes through music. Signed to EMI in the wake of that label's disastrous liaison with the Sex Pistols, Robinson's avowed homosexuality and uncompromising political stance made him an extremely controversial figure. Luckily, a brilliant (nontopical) first single, "2-4-6-8 Motorway," and a riveting first album made the band

internationally successful, affording the singing bassist the opportunity to be a real rock activist—spearheading Rock Against Racism and other organizations—rather than merely a complainer. But a myopic outlook and limited musical range drew Robinson into a morass of sloganeering and overbearing self-righteousness (especially on-stage) that forced a major career rethink after only two albums.

Power in the Darkness contains track after track of impassioned, heartfelt political anger, funneled through articulate lyrics and Danny Kustow's raging guitar figures. The memorable songs seethe with honest conviction and convert rock energy into anthemic power. (The American release at the time contained a bonus seven-song disc, compiling live tracks from an English EP and both sides of the "Motorway" single.)

TRB Two was produced by Todd Rundgren and basically encores the style and content of its predecessor, but with a more mainstream sound and fewer rough edges (not really an improvement). Robinson's alternate approach—slower numbers played at a bouncy shuffle perfect for in-concert singalongs—*does* improve with Todd's treatment. This brace of polemics isn't as striking as Robinson's first, but fans of **Power in the Darkness** won't find anything obviously missing here (except perhaps drummer Dolph Taylor and keyboardist Mark Ambler, who had both been replaced).

After the TRB collapsed under its own weighty baggage, Robinson formed Sector 27; its focus was more on personal relationships than politics. With a new lineup—notably including a bassist which allowed Robinson to concentrate on singing—the restrained album has some winning songs, although none with the immediacy of his previous outings.

North by Northwest—recorded in Hamburg with only producer Richard Mazda and a drummer—is Robinson's most mature and subtle album. Featuring material co-written with Peter Gabriel and a cover of a Lewis Furey song, Robinson explores various sophisticated settings and succeeds in making a pleasantly slight record, marred only by an agonized (and agonizing) song of love lost, "Now Martin's Gone."

Cabaret '79 is a live recording made shortly after the original TRB's dissolution; it includes Robinson's confrontational signature tune, "Glad to Be Gay," as well as a reading of Noel Coward's "Mad About the Boy," which resulted in some legal problems between Robinson and Coward's estate. **Tom Robinson Band** is a useful compilation (with notes by the artist) of the band's best tracks, drawing on singles and EPs from items like "Don't Take No for an Answer," "Glad to Be Gay" and "Motorway." Turning over a new page, Robinson then began a succesful era of straightforward commercial rock, captured on the **Atmospherics** EP (parts of which were incorporated onto the subsequent LP) and **Hope and Glory**. He's certainly capable of writing and recording skillfully routine rock; it just doesn't make for very interesting listening: "War Baby" and a terrible version of

Steely Dan's "Rikki Don't Lose That Number" were hits (for undiscernable reasons). Robinson's sincerity and commitment are obvious, but mediocre singing and bland arrangements keep **Hope and Glory** from being anything but ordinary. [iar]

TABU LEY ROCHEREAU

Tabu Ley (nr/Shanachie) 1984

TABU LEY ROCHEREAU WITH FRANCO

Omona Wapi (nr/Shanachie) 1984

Singer Tabu Ley Rochereau and guitar hero Franco are, respectively, the leading celebrities in their musical style. Soukous ("having a good time") is a shimmering, perky and ridiculously danceable pan-African sound. On **Tabu Ley**, the sexy soul singer adds a horn section, organ and backing vocalists to the sweet melodies, acoustic guitars and Afro-Cuban rhythms that define Congolese music. With comfortable naiveté, Rochereau sings (in both Zairean and French) of making love and money. **Omona Wapi** ditches a lot of the excess baggage, emphasizing instead—along with Rochereau's sweet vocals—three interlocking guitarists led by Franco's ululating lines. [rg]

ROCKATS

Live at the Ritz (Island) 1981
Make That Move EP (nr/RCA) 1983

LEVI AND THE ROCKATS

Louisiana Hayride (Rockhouse/Posh Boy) 1981

LEVI

The Fun Sessions EP (nr/PVC) 1983

The Rockats, hybrid English/American rockabilly specialists, were formed by singer Levi Dexter, whose appreciation of '50s American rock infused the band with a real traditionalist ethic. They made only one record together before splintering; bassist Smutty Smiff has since kept the Rockats' name alive. **Louisiana Hayride**, recorded live in Shreveport, Louisiana in 1979, bristles with feeling, but lacks something in recording quality, especially as regards the mix. And if there was an audience at that gig, no one bothered telling them to clap.

Live at the Ritz, cut in New York over a year later, is a much slicker affair—a premonition of the Stray Cats but without a magnetic personality like Brian Setzer. With Levi gone and a new lineup in place, the playing's fine, the sound quality is great and the tunes all sound like Johnny Cash should be singing 'em. (One of the new members—guitarist Tim Scott—went on a few years later to make an EP of unpleasant dance-rock under his own name.)

Make That Move, with a new guitarist and drummer in the quintet, attempts to effect a stylistic escape. Produced by Mike Thorne, one side isn't rockabilly at all, using keyboards to build an energetic but characterless soup. On the flip, the overbearing "Go Cat Wild" contains more drums than on all of the Stray Cats' records put together. Only the title song and "Never So Clever" recapture the band's original sound

with a glimmer of the old spirit.

Dexter, for his part, sticks to the straight and narrow on **The Fun Sessions**. Sharing production with Richard Gottehrer and employing a basic 'billy trio, he hiccoughs his way through five cool tracks exploding with understated energy. Not innovative by any means, but I'll take his earnest copies over the Rockats' boring originals any day. [iar]

See also *Tim Scott.*

ROCKPILE

Seconds of Pleasure (F-Beat/Columbia) 1980 (Demon/nr) 1984

Rockpile's sole moment in the spotlight is at least as exhilarating as anything Nick Lowe or Dave Edmunds has done on his own. As usual, this is rock'n'roll with the accent on "roll." Obvious influences include the Everly Brothers ("Now and Always") and Chuck Berry (his own "What a Thrill"). The blues "A Knife and a Fork" and the medium-tempo "When I Write the Book" are rare respites. **Seconds of Pleasure** has the extra bonus of guitarist Billy Bremner singing the rollickin' "Heart" and "You Ain't Nothin' but Fine." Throughout, the band delivers the hard-partying, good-time music we've come to expect from Lowe and Edmunds, together or (now, sadly) apart.

The LP originally included a 7-inch single, **Nick Lowe & Dave Edmunds Sing the Everly Brothers**, with their renditions of "Take a Message to Mary," "When Will I Be Loved" and two more classics. [si]

See also *Billy Bremner, Dave Edmunds, Nick Lowe.*

NILE RODGERS

Adventures in the Land of the Good Groove (WEA/Mirage) 1983
B-Movie Matinee (Warner Bros.) 1985

Guitarist Nile Rodgers co-produced David Bowie's best—uh, best-*sounding*—album. So does the runaway success of **Let's Dance** mean Rodgers is a musical mastermind? Chic's string of hits (the group's own as well as productions for others) suggests the answer is yes; his first solo LP, however, begs to differ. Rodgers proves he can make a fair-to-middling one-man Chic (no mean feat), but a visionary he's not—unless you define vision as smug sexism. The neatest touch on the record is the mass of chorus vocals sung with a drum machine "at P.S. 111 playground right after school," according to the sleeve notes. A pity the song ("Yum-Yum") is the album's most offensive meditation on the desirability of "poontang."

Complete with 3-D cover (but no glasses), **B-Movie Matinee** reflects Rodgers' cinematic tastes, offering such promising referents as "Plan-9," "Doll Squad" and "The Face in the Window." Unfortunately, while the music is unassailable (especially Jimmy Bralower's precision drumming and Rodgers' snappy guitar work), the thankfully smug-free lyrics aren't half as good as the titles. Nonetheless, a state-of-the-art dance record. (And the dreamy ballad, "Wavelength," is lovely.) [mf/iar]

ROLL-UPS

Low Dives for Highballs (Bridge House/nr) 1979

These popsters from South London anomalously emerged in the midst of the mod revival, on a mod label no less. They go in a lot of different directions but are saved by spunky individuality that lets them build a niche of their own. Lea Hart (almost all the songwriting) sings like a cocky cockney crossed with a dollop of—it's true!—Donald Fagen, and melds his guitar to Jeff Peters' in dual-axe moves Brian May didn't have in mind when he wrote the book. Add on an assortment of non-electronic keyboards, and you've got a swell pop recipe for songs ranging from a 10cc-ish look at adulterous "Blackmail" to shock-horror destruction as epic as any punk's. [jg]

ROMANELLI

Connecting Flight (Polydor/21) 1982

Bridging the gap between Vangelis' film soundtracks and current synth-rock, multi-keyboardist Romanelli created this album of boring high-tech instrumentals with three sidemen, including drummer Rusty Egan (Rich Kids, Visage, etc.). [iar]

ROMAN HOLLIDAY

Roman Holliday EP (nr/Jive) 1983
Cookin' on the Roof (Jive) 1983
Fire Me Up (Jive) 1984

Typical of the ability of English pop to absorb virtually any musical style so long as the band dresses colorfully, the seven-man Roman Holliday succeeded by playing fired-up jumpin' jive in sailor caps. The five-song EP, an American teaser compiled from UK singles, is great fun, containing "Stand By," "Motor Mania" and "Don't Try to Stop It." Dead catchy and brilliantly produced (by Peter Collins), if utterly disposable.

Cookin' on the Roof expands the EP to ten numbers but with no accompanying increase in entertainment. The new tracks are largely over-stylized and under-ingenious. Music this derivative and gimmicky requires pinpoint accuracy in hitting just the right balance of new and old; the filler isn't bad, just dispensable in light of their better efforts.

Following a top-to-bottom rethink by the band, **Fire Me Up** sounds nothing like its predecessor. Looking like rockabilly sharpies and soft-pedaling the horns and jazz in favor of synths and modern rock'n'roll, Roman Holliday's bland new direction is strictly yesterday's news. Useless. And the Mutt Lange-written single, "One Foot Back in Your Door," which leads off the LP, is really bad bombast. [iar]

ROMANTICS

The Romantics (Epic/Nemperor) 1980
National Breakout (Epic/Nemperor) 1980
Strictly Personal (Epic/Nemperor) 1981
In Heat (Epic/Nemperor) 1983
Rhythm Romance (Epic/Nemperor) 1985

Once upon a time, Detroit's Romantics were the band the Knack

always wanted to be, hammering out a few essential chords while the singer wailed out inconsequential lyrics, usually about girls (of course). They played fast, loose and tough, but unlike the Knack, weren't obnoxious. This is the kind of band that would have been happy jamming to "Louie, Louie" or "La Bamba" all night if they hadn't been able to devise their own alternatives.

The Romantics' self-titled debut and **National Breakout** capture that era beautifully. Silly red leather suits notwithstanding, **The Romantics** shows the boys at their most raucous, crashing through "What I Like About You" (their best-ever track) and other dance-floor pips. The optimistically titled second LP continues in the "Twist and Shout" vein, highlighted by "Tomboy" and "Stone Pony."

Strictly Personal, the panicky response to disappointing sales, finds the Romantics switching from powerful pop to soulless arena-rock. All broad, exaggerated gestures and no charm. Sad. **In Heat** wiped away the tears, elevating the band into the Top 10 with the execrable "Talking in Your Sleep" and the far-more likable "One in a Million." Having hit the heights, drummer/singer Jimmy Marinos left the group; the others hung in to make **Rhythm Romance**, another likably dumb batch of pop songs culminating in a credibly rootsy version of "Poison Ivy." [jy/iar]

ROMEO VOID

It's a Condition (nr/415) 1981
Never Say Never (nr/415-Columbia) 1982
Benefactor (CBS/415-Columbia) 1982
Instincts (CBS/415-Columbia) 1984

DEBORA IYALL

Strange Language (CBS/415-Columbia) 1986

Walloping big-beat riffs with snaky sax and darkly intelligent lyrics characterize this Bay Area dance/think combo. Native American artist-and-poet-turned-vocalist Debora Iyall uses her smoky, conversational voice to wax reflective on love and lust in these modern times; consistent with the band's name, she sings not only of situations where love is absent, but also of when it *should* be absent.

It's a Condition introduced Romeo Void's unique blend of jazz, funk, rock and confrontational poetry in its formative stages, the music a bit tentative and unfocused, especially in contrast with Iyall's hard-edged lyrics. **Never Say Never**, a four-song EP co-produced by Ric Ocasek, gained the group significant airplay and sales, leading to the link between San Francisco independent 415 and the CBS megalith. Consequently, it's no surprise that a truncated version of "Never Say Never" opens up **Benefactor**; as it turns out, that song proved to be more of a stylistic mold than might be considered healthy.

The most fully realized record of the bunch, **Instincts** boasts rich, full-blooded production, top-notch playing and reprises of various stylistic avenues. "Just Too Easy" resembles "Never Say Never" and pairs Ben Bossi's sax sax work with Iyall's sardonic, spoken monologue; "A Girl in Trouble (Is a Temporary

127

Thing)" touches a poppier, more melodic side; "Six Days and One" reverts to a spare, mainly rhythmic approach. Mixing strength with beauty, Romeo Void makes very special dance music for the mind.

A strange blend of unlikely people creating rather unsurprising music, Iyall's solo album was produced by Pat Irwin (once a Lydia Lunch collaborator in 8-Eyed Spy). The cast includes Irwin (clarinet, sax, guitar, synth), Richard Sohl (pianist in the original Patti Smith Group) and others; Ben Bossi (sax) and Aaron Smith (drums) of Romeo Void also participate. Iyall obviously takes her poetry seriously; unfortunately, Irwin (co-writer of six tunes here) leads the musicians through underwhelming, blandly faceless rock backing that pointedly lacks Romeo Void's atmospherics.   [rnp/iar]

KEVIN ROWLAND AND DEXYS MIDNIGHT RUNNERS

See *Dexys Midnight Runners.*

ROXY MUSIC

Roxy Music (Island/Reprise) 1972 (Polydor/Atco) 1977
For Your Pleasure . . . (Island/ Warner Bros.) 1973 (Polydor/Atco) 1977
Stranded (Island/Atco) 1973 (Polydor/nr) 1977
Country Life (Island/Atco) 1974 (Polydor/nr) 1977
Siren (Island/Atco) 1975 (Polydor/nr) 1977
Viva! (Island/Atco) 1976 (Polydor/nr) 1977
Greatest Hits (Polydor/Atco) 1977
Manifesto (Polydor/Atco) 1979
Flesh & Blood (Polydor/Atco) 1980
The First Seven Albums (EG-Polydor/nr) 1981
Avalon (EG-Polydor/Warner Bros.) 1982
The High Road EP (EG-Polydor/ Warner Bros.) 1983
The Atlantic Years 1973—1980 (EG-Polydor/Atco) 1983

ROXY MUSIC/BRYAN FERRY

Street Life (EG/nr) 1986

Arguably the most influential rock group of the '70s, Roxy Music's impact has become more obvious in the years since the original punk return-to- the-basics ethos gave way to a growing interest in style and fashion and art. The "new romantic" movement and the synth fops would have had no historical traditions to follow were it not for the pioneering efforts of Bryan Ferry, Brian Eno, Phil Manzanera, Andy Mackay, Paul Thompson and their various cohorts. Even though Roxy Music grew pale and rather timid in its later years, the recorded work (not to mention the countless side projects that all the various members have produced or participated in) stands as a seminal wellspring of nonconformity and successful art-pop experimentation.

With the release of their first LP, the fledgling Roxy Music revolutionized rock—trashing concepts of melodic conservatism, ignoring the prevalence of blues- based and otherwise derivative idioms and denying the need for technical virtuosity, either vocally or instrumentally. The flamboyantly bedecked poseurs presaged such couture iconoclasts as the New York Dolls and all that followed them; the music mixed all sorts of elements into a newly filtered original sound that set the stylish pace. The tracks— classics like "Re-make/ Re-model," "2 H.B.," "If There Is Something" and (on later versions) "Virginia Plain"—are amateurish but highly developed, blunders of brilliance that took some getting used to. The use of kitsch graphics also proved to be often imitated; a landmark LP.

For Your Pleasure . . . refines and magnifies Roxy's style with equally amazing material like "Do the Strand," "Editions of You" and "In Every Dream Home a Heartache." Another classic record. **Stranded**, the first LP after the departure of Brian Eno, introduces violinist Eddie Jobson to the fold and pursues a more subtle sound, favoring slower and quieter songs such as "Mother of Pearl," "Sunset" and "Psalm," while still finding room to rock on the chaotic "Street Life."

Roxy's best LP, **Country Life**, ran into trouble over its revealing cover photo—some American copies were shrink-wrapped in opaque green plastic; later the cover was changed to remove the undies-clad models and leave only the foliage. Regardless, the ten tracks are exemplary and of consistent strength—almost a greatest-hits album of new material. Highly recommended.

Siren was the final studio album of Roxy's first incarnation. There are some great tracks ("Love Is the Drug," "Both Ends Burning," "Sentimental Fool"), but an overabundance of forgettable numbers substantially diminishes its value. Roxy then went on sabbatical, with only the one-disc live document (**Viva!**) and the essential **Greatest Hits** collection issued during the two-year gap.

Reactivating Roxy Music, Ferry, Manzanera and Mackay made three group LPs with various part-time sidemen, but it wasn't the same. Although there are brilliant tracks ("Dance Away," "Over You," "Angel Eyes," etc.) on each of the albums, the overly refined low-key approach bears only passing resemblance to the unpredictable rock weirdness of their best work. (An otherwise needless compilation, **The Atlantic Years**, consolidates the best of **Manifesto** and **Flesh & Blood** onto one disc, adding two earlier cuts from **Greatest Hits**.) Fortunately, these records neither embarrass nor contradict the Roxy legacy; this era (subsequently proving to be the group's last) is separate and, though not equal, at least estimable.

Addenda: In 1981, the band's English management and label repackaged all of Roxy Music's studio albums to that point—seven in all—as a boxed set; add in **Avalon**, and you've got the works. Mixing selections from the band with Ferry's solo career, **Street Life** offers 20 tracks on two discs. **The High Road**, recorded live in Glasgow, offers four oddly chosen tunes and a running time approaching half an hour as a ten-person lineup walks through Neil Young's "Like a Hurricane," John Lennon's "Jealous Guy" and two of Ferry's tunes. The playing is, of course, great and the sound magnificent—only the band's crucial personality is lacking.

Roxy Music finally called it a career after 1983. Ferry resumed his solo work again with a new album in mid-'85; Manzanera and Mackay formed a new trio called the Explorers.   [iar]

See also *Brian Eno, Explorers, Bryan Ferry, Savage Progress, Yukihiro Takahashi.*

RUBBER RODEO

Rubber Rodeo EP (nr/Eat) 1982
Scenic Views (Phonogram/ Mercury) 1984
Heartbreak Highway (Phonogram/ Mercury) 1986

Armed with the slogan "It don't mean a thang if it ain't got that twang" inscribed in the vinyl, the six-song **Rubber Rodeo** 12-inch helped announce/advance the development of country-punk. The band hails from Rhode Island, but that doesn't stop it from forging a mix of synthesizer, fiddle, organ, pedal steel guitar and drums that's different and fun. The originals (especially "How the West Was Won") are bouncily tuneful and heartfelt; a cover version of Dolly Parton's "Jolene" comes off a bit like Heart without the arena pomp. Weird but worth it.

Following a three-song 12-inch most notable for its inclusion of the theme from "The Good, the Bad and the Ugly," Rubber Rodeo signed to a major label and recorded a debut album under the supervision of Hugh Jones (Echo and the Bunnymen, Damned). Unfortunately, along the way to **Scenic Views**, Rubber Rodeo misplaced their personality and emerged a plain-sounding dance-rock group (mild pedal steel coloration notwithstanding). Only the vocals—by Trish Milliken and Bob Holmes, sometimes together—serve to distinguish it from any routine MTV outfit. Only "The Hardest Thing" recalls the band's early Great Plains ambience; it also happens to be the LP's strongest song.

Heartbreak Highway (produced by Ken Scott) is much better, but still leaves one wishing the band's records were more colorful and gimmicky. Rubber Rodeo's urban cowpoke image remains stronger than its musical personality, although some of the songs (most notably the title track, "Maybe Next Year," a radical cover of the grotesquely sappy "Everybody's Talkin'" and an instrumental called "The Civil War") have a redeemingly jaunty air of good-humored kitschiness.   [iar]

RUBINOOS

The Rubinoos (Beserkley) 1977
Back to the Drawing Board (Beserkley) 1979
Party of Two EP (Warner Bros.) 1983

The adolescent Rubinoos' inclusion on Beserkley's highly selective roster may have been related to the fact that guitarist T.V. Dunbar had a brother in Earthquake, the label's charter band. Or it may simply have been that someone noticed they were a great, fresh-sounding pop band with talent far beyond their tender years. A clear, no-frills approach, solid original songs and convincing vocals (from Jon Rubin, the group's namesake) made them eminently likable, and earned the band a moderate national hit with Tommy James' "I Think We're Alone Now." Their first album, which included the single, also boasted a great white-soul tune called "Hard to Get" and a lightly raucous rave-up, "Rock and Roll Is Dead." Although a bit bland, **The Rubinoos** doesn't have one bad song, half-baked performance or dumb lyric. Slight but fun.

Their second album, aptly named for the band's near brush with the big time, found them a bit more mature but less self-assured. Except for one superb Raspberries soundalike, "I Wanna Be Your Boyfriend," the record seems too anxious to please, and suffers from noticeable timidity and fewer memorable songs.

Reduced to a duo of Rubin and Dunbar, the Rubinoos drifted back into view four years later with **Party of Two**, a disposable EP of five slick pop songs produced and played by Todd Rundgren and Utopia. All the right components are in place—melodies, harmonies, meaningless lyrics, etc.—but there's no youthful spark left to ignite any serious excitement.   [iar]

RUDIMENTARY PENI

Rudimentary Peni EP (Outer Himalayan/nr) 1981
Farce EP (Crass/nr) 1982
Death Church (Corpus Christi/nr) 1983

This London hardcore trio from the Crass family was forced to dissolve by illness. The eponymous EP is pretty rough going: the band is fairly tight but tuneless. Nick Blinko's screeching vocals obscure heartfelt lyrics and more than one track is ruined by wrong-speed mastering. A wider variety of rhythms than most of their ilk offer suggested promise, however, and the second EP corrects most of the problems. On **Death Church**, things all come together and venomous lyrics rip through loud and clear (as they should, given titles like "Vampire State Building" and "Alice Crucifies the Paedophiles"); while the songs are not exactly hook-laden, this is quite melodic for the genre. Tempos run from moderate metal through Pistols-style thrash to hyper-drive blur. An intelligent, exciting and highly recommended album.   [dgs]

RUEFREX

Flowers for All Occasions (Stiff/MCA) 1986

Ruefrex is one of the growing legion of nouveau guitar bands whose existence proves how influential (and inimitable) U2 really is. This forgettable album, produced by Mick Glossop, fits alongside the earnest and overblown pomp of the Alarm, Zerra I, the Waterboys, etc. The drums sound annoyingly huge, and lead vocalist Allan Clarke is a breast-beating Richard Jobson type. On the rare occasion songs display some subtlety, you know just when the big climax will occur—they have energy, but no idea how to use it. To make things worse, "Even in the Dark Hours" proves that '70s-length guitar solos aren't totally dead. Avoid this one.   [dgs]

RUMOUR

Max (Vertigo/Mercury) 1977

Frogs Sprouts Clogs and Krauts
(Stiff/Arista) 1979
Purity of Essence (Stiff/Hannibal)
1980

It's tempting to compare the Rumour's relationship with Graham Parker to the Band's with Bob Dylan: Highly respected but unsuccessful bar band (Brinsley Schwarz and Ducks Deluxe versus the Hawks) hooks up with talented singer/songwriter (Parker versus Dylan) to create some of the decade's best music ('70s versus '60s). Of course Parker is not Dylan, and **Max**, the Rumour's first LP on their own, is not **Big Pink**, although they would obviously have loved it to be. Often enough, the Rumour (Brinsley Schwarz, Bob Andrews, Martin Belmont, Andrew Bodnar, Steve Goulding) captures the *sound* of the Band, minus Robertson's lyrical profundity. What's really strange is that the Rumour is far more natural and interesting as a minor-league Band (on great tracks like "Hard Enough to Show," "Mess with Love" and a sublime Band-like arrangement of Duke Ellington's standard "Do Nothing 'Till You Hear From Me") than when attempting to forge their own identity on the subsequent albums. **Max** may not be terribly original but it is utterly enjoyable.

Frogs, on the other hand, seems to be an attempt to recast the Rumour in a vein that conforms more with Stiff's offbeat image. As a clever pop-oriented band, they succeed mainly in *sounding* stiff, with only a couple of songs ("Emotional Traffic," "All Fall Down") standing out from other failed experiments.

Purity of Essence succeeds in recapturing some of the looseness of **Max**. The band had been reduced to a quartet with the departure of Bob Andrews, whose voice—the group's best—and keyboards are missed. Even so, the album has its moments, although they mostly come on non-original material. Still, while lacking a real frontman and strong material of its own, the Rumour is talented enough to make enjoyable (if not hit) records. The question is whether they should continue to do so, or find another talented frontman and return to a situation where their musical skills are put to best use.

The Rumour also backed Garland Jeffreys on his **Rock & Roll Adult** live LP and have worked—as a whole or individually—on other projects since parting ways with Graham Parker after **The Up Escalator**. In 1985, Brinsley Schwarz rejoined Parker. Belmont has been part of Nick Lowe's ensemble for several years.   [ds]

RUNAWAYS

The Runaways (Mercury) 1976
Queens of Noise (Mercury) 1977
Live in Japan (Mercury/nr) 1977
Waitin' for the Night (Mercury)
1977
And Now . . . the Runaways
(Cherry Red/nr) 1979
Flaming Schoolgirls (Cherry
Red/nr) 1980
Little Lost Girls (nr/Rhino) 1981
The Best of the Runaways
(Mercury) 1982
I Love Playing with Fire (Laker-
Cherry Red/nr) 1982

People still have violently divided opinions when it comes to the Runaways' place in the musical universe. To many, they were the first all-girl (instrument-playing) rock band to matter, spiritual godmothers to the Go-Go's and Bangles, and seminal punk rockers to boot. Others see them as nothing more than a pre-packaged peepshow whose heavy metal-cum-glitter approach was dated from the very start.

Here are the facts: teenagers Joan Jett (whose love of T. Rex and Suzi Quatro inspired her to learn guitar) and drummer Sandy West decided to form a band with encouragement (and eventual management) from Kim Fowley. The band that recorded **The Runaways** was a combination of raw garage-band playing and brassy, high-school-bad-girl sexuality typified by their unofficial anthem, "Cherry Bomb."

By the time **Queens of Noise** (a decided improvement over the debut) was released, trouble was fomenting; although Cherie Currie was the "official" lead singer, Jett wound up taking the microphone on six of the ten songs. Things came to a head when, after a tour of Japan (documented on the **Live in Japan** album), Currie and bassist Jackie Fox quit the band. Vicki Blue was hired as a new bassist, and Jett took over the reins for good.

Except in Japan, the Runaways never made any real commercial inroads—many saw them as inept puppets—merely another Fowley hype—and refused to take the music seriously. **Waitin' for the Night** did nothing to alter that. The album came out just as modern-day punk was emerging, and Jett (if not the rest of the band) readily latched onto the scene to the extent that Steve Jones of the Sex Pistols contributed one song ("Black Leather") to **And Now . . . The Runaways**. But West and guitarist Lita Ford wanted to go in a more heavy metal direction, and the album would prove to be their last.

Posthumous notes: **Flaming Schoolgirls** is a substandard compilation of live tracks and studio outtakes, while **Little Lost Girls** is actually **And Now . . . The Runaways** re-released as a picture disc. **The Best of the Runaways** and **I Love Playing with Fire** are additional recaps of various material. As for the band members, Lita Ford has become a big metal star under her own name; West and Blue have been active but out of the national spotlight; Laurie McAllister (who held down the bass spot in the waning months) ended up in another all-girl Fowley project, the Orchids. After failed attempts at making it both as a solo act and with her sister Marie, Currie married Toto guitarist Steve Lukather. And we all know where Joan Jett's love of rock'n'roll got her.   [rnp]

RUN—D.M.C.

Run—D.M.C. (Profile) 1984
King of Rock (Profile) 1985
Raising Hell (Profile-
London/Profile) 1986

This three-man rap band from Hollis, Queens were the first to succeed in doing what no other black artist (with the exception of Grandmaster Flash, briefly) had done before: make white people listen to rap in large numbers. Having established themselves with the rap audience via several smart and witty singles ("Sucker M.C.'s" and "It's Like That"), "Rock Box"—included on the first album—was the pioneering step that lifted them into a league all their own. Melding a simple bass riff to the thunderous rhythm tracks that provide the entire accompaniment for their early raps, the coup de grace is blazing rock guitar, played by Eddie Martinez (for a while an adjunct member of Blondie). The combination is perfect—verbal acuity and theatrical drama matched by an inexorable pounding beat *and* the unavoidable power of electric guitar—and the single was huge, setting the stage for a whole meeting of the races that has helped chip away the barriers that kept "black music" and "white music" segregated all through the '70s.

Run—D.M.C. contains all their early hits and is an utterly essential rap record not just for rap fans. Even though the repetitious rhythms get tiring if you're not in the dancing mood, the funny, perceptive interwoven raps remain captivating centers of attention, and just trying to catch everything they fire off can become a full-time hobby. **King of Rock** takes some chances—like a reggae/rap blend—while repeating the functional formula of "Rock Box" on the title track, which simply inverts the riff and recasts the rap. Currently peerless in their field, Run (Joe Simmons), D.M.C. (Darryl McDaniels) and ace dj/musician Jam Master Jay (Jason Mizell) have enormous potential, and this seems like only the beginning.

Producer (with Russell Simmons) Rick Rubin adds his characteristic rock-funk touches to **Raising Hell**, like the "My Sharona" riff in the Beastie Boyish "It's Tricky" and the cover of Aerosmith's rap-like "Walk This Way" (with Steve Tyler and Joe Perry contributing). On the downside, most of the rhymes are nothing special, making the commendable racial consciousness of "Proud to Be Black" stand in strong contrast to the litany of typical "I'm Run/He's DMC" raps, the commercial culturalisms contained in "My Adidas" and the predictable words to "Dumb Girl." Overly spartan music—simple beats (some of which sound positively acoustic) and Jay's percussive turntable action for backup—hurt some of the tracks (especially since they've proven themselves equal to more active and complex arrangements); in addition, the daring duo's sharp verbal gymnastics don't really get started until the second side. More familiar than inherently exciting, **Raising Hell** could still use some more heat.   [iar]

RUTS

The Crack (Virgin/Virgin
International) 1979
Grin & Bear It (Virgin/nr) 1980

RUTS D.C.

Animal Now (Virgin/nr) 1981
Rhythm Collision Vol. 1
(Bohemian/nr) 1982

On **The Crack**, the Ruts meld the Pistols' instrumental attack with leader Malcolm Owen's Strummeresque bellow; while less inspired than either of those bands, the Ruts started out with far more finesse (including nimble bass). True to their early association with reggae collective Misty in Roots (sponsor of their first 45), the Ruts often incorporated reggae riffs—adeptly, not heavy-handedly, and without missing a single roughshod 4/4 stride. Simple, straightforward political lyrics are heartfelt but not strident.

Grin and Bear It is odds'n'sods, and sounds it, but contains an assortment of minor gems (including the non-Virgin debut 45, live sides, etc.), highlighted by brilliant career-high-point single "Staring at the Rude Boys." In short, a fitting tribute (as intended) to Owen, dead of an OD four months previously. As Ruts D.C. (for da capo) the remaining three made saxist/keyboardist Gary Barnacle a full member. On **Animal Now**, personal themes of self-doubt and angst ("Despondency," anyone?) get equal airing with the usual attacks on hypocrisy and social manipulation. Often gripping, but undercut by a tendency to infuse intrusive jazz-funk touches.

Minus Barnacle (who departed for session work and Leisure Process), the trio cut **Rhythm Collision**, an LP of funk-inflected reggae in ready-made dub form, akin in concept to Dennis Bovell's **I Wah Dub**. It's a sharp, sometimes powerful, sometimes catchy piece of work, with saxist Dave Winthrop (ex-Secret Affair) and one Mitt (harmonica) supplying additional shades to the dark-hued mood.   [jg]

S

SADE

Diamond Life (CBS/Portrait) 1984
Promise (Epic/Portrait) 1985

The recent trend towards mild jazz/Latin-inflected pop music (Carmel, Everything but the Girl) has found its most successful proponent so far in this talented singer. A stunningly beautiful Nigerian raised in England, Sade Adu writes (the lyrics are hers alone, the music mostly co-written with Stuart Matthewman, the sax/guitar player in her trio) and performs mellifluous, thoughtful tunes with aplomb and jazz leanings that seem to derive from a wholly different era. Despite the music's obvious stylization, Sade's almost colorless voice exudes little personality; her strength is a cool timbre that conveys dispassionate wisdom.

Somehow avoiding both nostalgia and schmaltz, **Diamond Life** is an anomaly: nothing about it would turn off Andy Williams fans, but self-consciousness legitimizes it to the rock audience. "Hang on to Your Love," "Sally," "Smooth Operator" and "Your Love Is King" are the standouts, evoking chic nightclub society of the '60s. (In fact, the first of those includes the very noticeable sound of glasses clinking.) The perfect soundtrack to your Laurence Harvey dreams, and a very alluring pop record.

Sade's follow-up, **Promise**, is slightly drier and less cozy, but the nine songs are every bit as good. Economical arrangements make every carefully-placed rim shot and guitar twang count on such excellent songs as "Is It a Crime" and "Sweetest Taboo."   [iar]

SAD LOVERS AND GIANTS

Cle EP (Last Movement/nr) 1981
Epic Garden Music (Midnight Music/nr) 1982
Feeding the Flame (Midnight Music/nr) 1983
In the Breeze (Midnight Music/nr) 1984

This quintet was from Watford —near London, but evidently insulated from that city's turbulent trendiness. Sad Lovers sound like a cross between R.E.M. and a garage-spawned analogue of **Dark Side of the Moon**. Tristan Garel-Funk plays jangly guitar, almost all of it arpeggio chorded (think Byrds/Searchers), and David Woods adds texture and melody with sax and keyboards, eventually growing more sophisticated in sound and shading, if not technique. The songs canter at new wave uptempo or a more brooding mid-speed, but the music is moody and contemplative, regardless. Vocals, by one Garce, aren't trendily emotive, instead possessing the kind of quiet gravity that makes overstatement unnecessary, even with lyrics of hurt or anger.

Epic Garden Music is pretty much what its self-satiric title suggests, but also boasts several excellent crystallizations of the group's style. **Feeding the Flame**, after an abrasive opening, is a much quieter, less immediate and ultimately more distressing record. **In the Breeze** consists of alternate versions of some tracks plus a few unreleased rough gems; it's almost as essential as the first LP, although the three songs the two discs share are presented in earlier, rawer takes here. The group dissolved in late '83. [jg]

SAINTS

(I'm) Stranded (Harvest/Sire) 1977
Eternally Yours (Harvest/Sire) 1978
Prehistoric Sounds (Harvest/nr) 1978
Paralytic Tonight Dublin Tomorrow EP (Fr. New Rose) 1979
Prehistoric Songs (Fr. Harvest) 1981
The Monkey Puzzle (Fr. New Rose) 1981
Out in the Jungle . . . (Flicknife/nr) 1982
A Little Madness to Be Free (Fr. New Rose) 1984
Live in a Mud Hut (Fr. New Rose) 1985

CHRIS BAILEY

Casablanca (Fr. New Rose) 1983
What We Did on Our Holidays (Fr. New Rose) 1984

Every decade's snotty kids are the same, as Australia's Saints handily prove. These so-called modern punks emerged in '77 with a raw, driving sound recalling the Pretty Things of the early '60s. On **(I'm) Stranded**, Chris Bailey sings with the same irritable snarl that band's Phil May had back when he was considered competition for Mick Jagger. The rest of the Saints respond in kind, issuing sheets of rough, gray rock'n'roll noise, including the title track, a pioneering international punk hit.

Eternally Yours refines the attack without diminishing the impact, boasting tighter playing and even a horn section. Highlights include "Know Your Product," a cynical outburst, and "Run Down," the kind of putdown bands like this have to do well to maintain credibility.

On **Prehistoric Sounds**, Bailey and guitarist Ed Kuepper strain against stylistic limitations. Slicker than before, the band sometimes resembles a punk Chicago and conveys a feeling of general discontent.

The French-only **Paralytic Tonight Dublin Tomorrow** EP has hornwork on several of its five tracks, but the rip-roaring energy drive turns the Saints into something more like a punked-up Chicago *blues* band.

Prehistoric Songs collects highlights from the preceding albums along with various singles. Hearing a bunch of their ragged cover versions in succession can be unsettling, but it's also thrilling, in a sick way, to witness "River Deep, Mountain High," "Kissin' Cousins," "Lipstick on Your Collar" and Otis Redding's "Security" being put through the meatgrinder. Not for the fainthearted (or tradition-minded).

Chris Bailey re-emerged in 1981 with **The Monkey Puzzle** and a new band of Saints. Although the tone isn't nearly so abrasive, the devotion to rootsy no-nonsense rock'n'-roll remains. See the buoyant cover of "Dizzy Miss Lizzy" for details.

Out in the Jungle . . . finds Bailey at his most polished, handling brooding ballads and horn-laden rockers with impressive aplomb. Although still a superlative growler, much of the exhilarating edge of previous Saints classics has been unduly muted by professionalism. Brian James of the Lords of the New Church guests on guitar.

Bailey recorded his first solo album, **Casablanca**, in Paris;

accompanying himself only on simple guitar (acoustic/electric, doubletracked in spots) he sings like a folk/blues troubador. The songs are mixed in quality—from a straight reading of Jimmy Reed's "(Take Out Some) Insurance on Me Baby" to the pretty "Wait Till Tomorrow"—and, lacking domineering rock power to drive them, have a tendency to drift a bit. Nonetheless, some tracks are quite strong, gaining urgency from the stark, unprepossessing presentation.   [jy/iar]

See also *Laughing Clowns*.

RYUICHI SAKAMOTO

One Thousand Knives (Hol. Plurex) 1982
B-2 Unit (nr/Alfa-Island) 1980
Merry Christmas, Mr. Lawrence (Virgin/MCA) 1983
Illustrated Musical Encyclopaedia (10-Virgin/nr) 1986

RYUICHI SAKAMOTO WITH ROBIN SCOTT

Left Handed Dream (Epic) 1981

RYUICHI SAKAMOTO FEATURING THOMAS DOLBY

Field Work EP (10-Virgin/nr) 1986

Sakamoto, keyboardist for Yellow Magic Orchestra, recorded **One Thousand Knives** four years before it was released by Dutch independent label Plurex. While remaining a member of YMO, he made **B-2 Unit** with the help of Dennis Bovell and XTC's Andy Partridge. Though not extracting as much from them as might be expected, Sakamoto did turn in an effort of decidedly oddball venturesomeness.

But **Left Handed Dream** truly sees him flower, more obviously integrating his British collaborators. Though he plays at least a little of everything, Sakamoto gets help not only from his YMO mates but also chums like singer Robin Scott (who gets co-billing) and Adrian Belew. All this without losing himself; the record is uniquely—even at times off-handedly—scintillating, going from fractured, slippery funk to grave, darkly atmospheric stuff pitting percussion against drone.

Merry Christmas, Mr. Lawrence is the soundtrack to a film starring Tom Conti, David Bowie and Sakamoto himself. Instrumental except for a David Sylvian vocal on "Forbidden Colours," Sakamoto performed the entire excellent album singlehandedly.   [jg]

SALVATION ARMY

See *Three O'Clock*.

SANDII AND THE SUNSETZ

Eating Pleasure (Alfa/nr) 1980
Heat Scale (Alfa/nr) 1981
Immigrants (Sire/nr) 1982

Produced by Yellow Magic Orchestra's Harry Hosono, this is modern pop-rock with a female vox, but there's a twist: never before has anything seemed so bland yet so ineffably and naggingly offbeat. I forget what attracted me enough to wonder what it was about in the first place. (Indecipherable lyrics don't help.)   [jg]

SAVAGE PROGRESS

Celebration (10-Virgin/nr) 1984

Led by bassist/songwriter Rik Kenton—one of the two bassists on the first Roxy Music album over a decade earlier—Savage Progress plays dance-rock with much the same loose and funky feel as the Thompson Twins. The quartet incorporates glints of various Third World musics, adding character to the otherwise plain melodies and banal lyrics. Vocalist Glynnis sings like a member of Bananarama; the band (whose lineup fields bass, keyboards and percussion) is facile and flexible, making easy transitions from the calypso of "Falling" to the eerie Arabia of "My Soul Unwraps Tonight" to the Bow Wow Wow-styled "Heart Begin to Beat." By not allowing themselves to become too involved in any of these flavors, Savage Progress remains light and likable, but they will need stronger songs to keep from being just a well-produced shell of appealing styles. [iar]

TENOR SAW

Fever (Jam. Blue Mountain) 1985
Tenor Saw/Coca Tea Clash (Witty/nr) 1986
Tenor Saw Meets Don Angelo: The Golden Hen EP (Uptempo/nr) 1986

One of the best new reggae singers, Tenor Saw released several 12-inch singles in 1985 (notably "Ring the Alarm" and "Roll Is Called"), and has appeared on albums paired with other singers. Unfortunately, his first full-fledged LP, **Fever**, is a middling effort. The playing is fine and Saw's immediately distinctive voice is rich, but the material is weak. On the best tracks ("Pumpkin Belly" and "Eenie Meenie Minie Mo") he does some weird vocal improvisation against synthetic bass lines; the rest of the record is bland and typical. [bk]

SCARS

Author! Author! (Pre-Charisma/nr) 1981
Author! Author! EP (nr/Stiff) 1981

If this Scottish band's post- psychedelia didn't lean so far toward pomp-rock, its highly melodic writing would be vastly more infectious. Ho-hum words and a disconcerting tendency to sound like early '70s Alice Cooper don't help; fully fleshed-out production of a colorful guitar-based sound and the band's own bravura do. The EP features three from the album plus an extra song that shows the Scars' best side. [mf]

SCENICS

The Scenics (Can. Bomb) 1979

A weird Toronto trio with traces of the Velvet Underground, Pere Ubu, Television, Talking Heads and other similarly high-minded outfits. Highlight of the album: an unrecognizable (pre-Billy Idol) version of Tommy James' "Mony Mony." [iar]

PETER SCHILLING

"Major Tom (Coming Home)" EP (WEA/Elektra) 1983
Error in the System (WEA/Elektra) 1983
Things to Come (WEA/Elektra) 1985

Back when German music was affectionately referred to as "kraut-rock," it seemed as if spacey progressive experimentalism was the only kind of music Teutonic youth could play. Since that era, the nation's stylistic scope has widened considerably and been exported to global popularity as well. So there's something nostalgic and heart-warming about the sci-fidom of Peter Schilling's left-field hit single, "Major Tom (Coming Home)," which essentially copies the story of David Bowie's "Space Oddity" into a modern electro-pop setting. The 12-inch offers the single four ways: English, German, instrumental and an eight-minute John Luongo remix. The song sounds best *auf Deutsch*.

Error in the System contains "Major Tom (Coming Home)" sung in English, a plodding, otiose instrumental called "Major Tom Part II" and a German version of "Silent Night, Holy Night" (with new lyrics), as well as fake reggae and a bunch of needless "Major Tom" sounda-likes. Throughout, Schilling's almost accentless multi-tracked vocals are blandly sweet, and the metronome- powered electro-bubblegum pleasant if shallow. A full album of this synthetic weight-lessness is more than enough; briefer doses aren't at all painful.

Things to Come proves the narrow limits of Schilling's appeal. At best, a few songs echo his hit; otherwise, it's a tedious and unoriginal bore. [iar]

IRMIN SCHMIDT

See *Can*.

FRED SCHNEIDER AND THE SHAKE SOCIETY

See *B-52's*.

BRINSLEY SCHWARZ

Brinsley Schwarz (UA/Capitol) 1970
Despite It All (UA/Capitol) 1970
Silver Pistol (UA) 1972 (Edsel/nr) 1986
Nervous on the Road (UA) 1972
Please Don't Ever Change (UA/nr) 1973
New Favourites (UA/nr) 1974
Original Golden Greats (UA/nr) 1974
Fifteen Thoughts (UA/nr) 1978

Many pub-rock bands of the early '70s served as launching pads for English musicians whose fame and fortune increased enormously with the advent of new wave. Along with Ducks Deluxe, Brinsley Schwarz easily takes the cake as a hotbed of talents just waiting for the right moment to burst forth. Although largely unheralded (and commercially ignored) at the time, its five members—Nick Lowe, Ian Gomm, Brinsley Schwarz, Bob Andrews and Billy Rankin—have surely proven their skill and importance many times over since the band dissolved in 1975. Lowe's solo career and membership in Rockpile, not to mention his voluminous production credits, have made him a constant presence, a revered elder in the Church of Cool. Gomm's solo albums are more in keeping with the Brinsleys' laid-back, easy-listening countrified pop. Confirmed sidemen Schwarz and Andrews both served in the Rumour (with and without Graham Parker) and have each produced and

played alongside many other spot-light stars as well. Rankin played in a band called Tiger and has drummed on loads of records by likeminded rockers. (He and Schwarz also joined future Rumour member Martin Belmont in the last incarnation of Ducks Deluxe.)

The music on Brinsley Schwarz's albums seems at once totally removed and perfectly in keeping with the individuals' later escapades; little hints of the future keep cropping up amid the genial, American-flavored rock and mild pop. There's "Ju Ju Man," a cover included on **Silver Pistol** that Dave Edmunds later recorded for his **Get It**, backed by Lowe, Rankin and Andrews. The first appearance of Lowe's "(What's So Funny 'Bout) Peace, Love and Understanding" is on **New Favourites**; it's since become a classic item in Elvis Costello's repertoire. Lowe's brush with American chart success, "Cruel to Be Kind," was co-written with Gomm and doesn't sound very different from some of the Brinsleys' richer pop numbers. Much of the Rumour's crisp Van Morrison swing is present in tracks like "Surrender to the Rhythm" (on **Nervous on the Road**). You get the point.

In a nutshell, while some of the music on these albums is either dull or wimpy beyond belief—and check those embarrassing hippie pictures!—they contain enough wonderful stuff to make Brinsley Schwarz's records well worth discovering.

Of discographical interest: the first two LPs are also available as an American twin set (**Brinsley Schwarz**) released in 1978. **Original Golden Greats** and **Fifteen Thoughts** (kudos to the latter's art director) are compilations of tracks from the band's entire career; there's some duplication, but both have gems not otherwise found on any album. Brinsley Schwarz also contributed five cuts to the 1972 live compilation, **Greasy Truckers Party**. [iar]

See also *Ducks Deluxe, Nick Lowe, Graham Parker, Rockpile, Rumour*.

ROBIN SCOTT

See *M, Ryuichi Sakamoto*.

TIM SCOTT

Swear EP (Sire) 1983

Ex-Rockat guitarist Scott pounds out some of the dumbest dance-rock ever on this five-songer, produced by Richard Gottehrer. Joined by ex-Holly and the Italians bassist Mark Sidgwick and drummer Lewis King (plus Jane Wiedlin's vocals on one song), Scott's inadequacy as a singer and writer are made abundantly clear on the moronic title song and "Good as Gold"; elsewhere, he's just a bland and forgettable rocker. [iar]

SCRAPING FOETUS OFF THE WHEEL

Hole (Self Immolation-Some Bizzare/Self Immolation-ZE-PVC) 1984
Nail (Self Immolation-Some Bizzare/ Self Immolation-Some Bizzare-Homestead) 1985

YOU'VE GOT FOETUS ON YOUR BREATH

Deaf (Self Immolation/nr) 1981
Ache (Self Immolation/nr) 1982

Thank goodness for rock'n'roll —otherwise, what excuse would there be for people like Jim Thirlwell (aka Clint Ruin, aka Frank Want, aka Scraping Foetus off the Wheel, aka Foetus Over Frisco, aka Phillip and His Foetus Vibrations, aka You've Got Foetus on Your Breath, etc.)? Although undeniably talented, it's virtually impossible to pin down just what he does; suffice to say his projects are all characterized by rudeness, irreverence, abrasion, unpredictability and an incredible grasp of music-making's never-ending possibilities.

The only thing to do with *Hole* is jump in and pray you survive. The LP (which includes a bonus disc of previous issue in the US) has a little of everything: industrial cacophony ("Clothes Hoist"), high political drama ("I'll Meet You in Poland, Baby"), spare crypto-blues ("Sick-Man"), demented surf music ("Satan Place"), something sick built on a swing beat ("Water Torture"), the *Batman* theme and lots more. The rhythms here would make Test Dept. proud, the lyrics might distress Frank Zappa and it's all played at a confusion level that makes Christmas Eve at Harrods seem placid. Simply put, you've never heard *anything* like this before.

Nail is another delicious voyage into Foetus' crazed imagination. From the soundtrack-styled opening ("Theme from Pigdom Come") through a generally cinematized concept collection of high-octane rants—sort of Birthday Party with a sense of humor meets latter-day Pink Floyd—SFOTW goes about his usual business, layering sound on sound, insult on injury. An apparently nonexistent instrumental entitled "!" is the LP's definitive existential high point, but there's plenty of clever lyrical competition on such vehement audio orgies as "The Throne of Agony" and the '40s-jazzy "Descent into the Inferno." [iar]

SCREAMING BLUE MESSIAHS

Good and Gone EP (Big Beat/nr) 1984
Twin Cadillac Valentine EP (WEA/nr) 1985
Gun-Shy (WEA/Elektra) 1986

One part Scottish, two parts English, this fierce trio is appropriately named. Not adverse to howling until blue in the face, they could very well be the prophesied saviours of static '80s pop. The Messiahs take their love of Americana and render it into an unrecognizable hybrid of psychobilly, R&B, garage grunge and lethal punk energy.

Blistering would be a euphemistic description for **Good and Gone**— singer/songwriter Bill Carter shrieks and wails his way through these six tracks in a merciless attack. The crudely worded "Someone to Talk To" (supposedly culled from a Marine drill chant), "Happy Home" and a cover of Hank Williams' "You're Gonna Change" give the Messiahs a roguish sort of appeal. Daring, foolhardy and just plain good fun.

On the title track of **Twin Cadillac Valentine**, the jagged edges have been smoothed down and the tune wanders amid sterile production. The three other tracks are raucous live versions of previously issued songs and provide the EP's only real signs of life.

Gun-Shy suffers from the same restraint. Occasional glimpses of the old form seep through, but never gain the momentum needed to sustain the effort. Our potential saviours seem to have strayed from the path of righteousness for the moment. Be on guard, however, for when the Messiahs return, it will likely be with a vengeance.   [ag]

SCREAMING MEEMEES

If This Is Paradise, I'll Take the Bag (NZ Propeller) 1982

For all the offbeat get-up, packaging and names, this Auckland foursome plays relatively conventional pop-rock (though some of it with a fashionably quirky sound). Strengths: tunefully boyish vocals, melodies that pull you in a after a few listens and a lack of fuss and worry—even when the Meemees *are*, according to the lyrics, worried— that's refreshingly ingenuous but not cutesy. The ringing guitars recall the sound of Stuart Adamson when he was in the Skids but again minus the tension. Added bits of keyboards help fill out the sound. A dash more substance and these guys—very popular at home—could graduate to world class.   [jg]

SCREAMING TRIBESMEN

Move a Little Closer EP (What Goes On) 1985
Date with a Vampyre EP (What Goes On) 1985

One of Australia's better current quasi-punk bands, the Tribesmen have issued a pair of international EPs, one as a trio, the other as a quartet, with only singer/guitarist Mick Medew appearing on both. **Move a Little Closer** presents four slices of melodic Seedsy garage grunge that reeks of both the '60s and the '80s; neglecting the gimmicky, trite title cut, **Date with a Vampyre** does boast three excellent, well- produced slices of artfully memorable rock-pop.   [iar]

SCRITTI POLITTI

Works in Progress EP (St. Pancras-Rough Trade/nr) 1979
4 A-Sides EP (St. Pancras-Rough Trade/nr) 1979
Songs to Remember (Rough Trade/nr) 1982
Cupid & Psyche 85 (Virgin/Warner Bros.) 1985

Originally an arty conceptual trio from Leeds, Scritti Politti underwent a number of drastic developmental changes on the way to becoming, ultimately, just a vehicle for singer Green Gartside. By the time Scritti Politti released its long-awaited first album in 1982, Green had pulled the band through a phase of haunting synth-pop ("The Sweetest Girl") and into a souled-out revamp of early T. Rex, minus Bolan's unique sword- and-sorcery outlook. **Songs to Remember** is an unassumingly warm and charming set, with boppy beats, quirky tunes and abundant catchy goodwill. While Green's obvious songwriting mastery and affecting voice makes every song appealing, a few— "Asylums in Jerusalem," "Faithless"

and "The Sweetest Girl"—are absolutely wonderful.

Subsequently shedding the pretense of a band, Green moved himself to New York, where he turned to high-sheen soul music as his life's work. With producer Arif Mardin, Material drummer Fred Maher and other heavyweights, the entirety of Green's output for the following two years turned up on a 1984 12-inch, establishing him as a truly brilliant pop craftsman. "Wood Beez (Pray Like Aretha Franklin)" and "Absolute" are stunning, both in terms of traditional musical excellence and up-to-date modern stylings and sound.

Green consolidated his triumph by including both songs on **Cupid & Psyche 85**, only the second Scritti Politti album in six years. Recorded and produced in the main with Maher and keyboardist David Gamson but featuring numerous other musicians, the painstakingly well-crafted record is unfailingly pleasant. Nonetheless, only "The Word Girl" approaches the engaging excellence of the two singles.   [jw/iar]

SECRET

The Secret (Oval-A&M/nr) 1979

A British duo, aided here by three added musicians, the Secret pursued roughly the same muse as Sparks, playing quirky, uptempo inventions with witty lyrics and intricate arrangements. Lacking any real character, though, their album succeeds in tweaking the intellect and making toes twitch, but falls short of substantial impact on either front.   [iar]

SECRET AFFAIR

Glory Boys (I Spy-Arista/Sire) 1979
Behind Closed Doors (I Spy-Arista/Sire) 1980
Business as Usual (I Spy-Arista/nr) 1982

Secret Affair were the mod revival's top dogs because they forged a distinctive sound that didn't simply pick up where the Jam (or Who) left off. Ian Page's mellifluous vocals and Dave Cairns' plangent guitars spearheaded the band's enthusiastic drive, hampered only by occasionally stiff drumming; the consistently above-average tunes of **Glory Boys** are given an extra fillip by the sporadic addition of horns. What grates, though, is the pushy, overstated rhetoric, especially in light of the movement's brief, fad-like existence.

The instrumental attack on **Behind Closed Doors** is tighter and the lyrics—though still pretentious—arty on a more personal level. At least half of the songs are excellent. By the time of **Business as Usual**, though, the Affair was a big fish in an evaporated neo-mod pond. The group could hardly maintain its self-important image, and with it went the creative spark. The album, while smoother than ever before, is as journeyman-like as its title suggests.   [jg]

SECRETS

The Secrets (Why Fi) 1982

This Midwest American quartet (whose name, for some reason, is supposed to have an asterisk following it) made their debut in 1979 with a single released on a Kansas City, Missouri independent label.

Three years later, their LP, co-produced by Stan Lynch of Tom Petty's band, leads off with "It's Your Heart Tonight," the single's A-side. A bit older and more stylish perhaps, the new-lineup Secrets still play brilliant power pop, with instantly memorable songs, sparkling vocal harmonies and crisp rock'n'roll instrumentation. Ten could-be-hits on one disc.   [iar]

SECTION 25

The Key of Dreams (Bel. Factory Benelux) 1982
Always Now (Factory/nr) 1982
From the Hip (Factory/nr) 1984

Blackpool's Section 25 follows in the Joy Division tradition, anchoring their songs to basso depresso vocals and upfront drums, backed by synthesizers and guitar. Though lacking that band's intensity, they have nicely reproduced the atmosphere. Self-produced, **The Key of Dreams** presents nine examinations of paranoia and anxiety, using lurking glissandi, curious touches of Doorsish piano and Oriental philosophy. **Always Now** works away from imitation of Joy Division, giving greater emphasis to musical technique outside the parameters of rock. Producer Martin Hannett thickens the sound, bringing new body to Section 25's work. **From the Hip** takes after New Order a bit and explores two alternate paths—pastoral mood pieces featuring soothing ambient synthesizer and faint guitar, and driving electronic dance music with a light touch—both of which succeed to great effect. It's their best album (and "Reflection" could be a hit single)—a distinguished example of where modern synthesizer music is going.   [sg/iar]

SECTOR 27

See *Tom Robinson Band.*

SELECTER

Too Much Pressure (2-Tone/Chrysalis) 1980
Celebrate the Bullet (Chrysalis) 1981

The Selecter—an interracial, multi-national seven-piece—emerged from the same Coventry scene that gave birth to the Specials; founder Neol Davis was in on the creation of the 2-Tone label, which ignited the entire neo-ska movement in England. The first 2-Tone release was a Specials 45; its flipside, an instrumental credited to and entitled "The Selecter" which had, in fact, been recorded by Davis and Specials drummer John Bradbury some months earlier. When the A-side became a hit, interest in the Selecter also grew, and Davis was obliged to recruit a band.

With the gifted Pauline Black handling most of the lead vocals, the Selecter sounded like no other band in the genre; they employed the same upbeat rhythms, but added a much poppier and individual touch, much of it due to Black's style and influence.

Too Much Pressure is bursting with great songs like "On My Radio," "Three Minute Hero," "Time Hard" and the title track. Davis wrote much of the material, but contributions from other sources—within and without the lineup—added further variety. The playing hops along, with a horn section

added in spots, but the spark throughout is Pauline Black, who shines with enormous vocal talent.

Celebrate the Bullet has little of the first LP's brilliance; although the performances don't lack anything tangible, the songwriting is vastly less inspired and none of the anti-trendy cleverness so vital to the previous album's uniqueness can be discerned. The Selecter dissolved soon after; Black did several solo singles and some acting.   [iar]

WILL SERGEANT

See *Echo and the Bunnymen.*

SERIOUS YOUNG INSECTS

Housebreaking (Aus. Native Tongue) 1982

At times, this Australian trio resembles the Police—intricate, subtle rhythms smoothly interwoven with fluid guitar and bass lines—but these guys (as the band's handle might indicate) have more whimsical ideas than ol' Sting. There's a song called "I Want Cake" which is simply the title chanted, mantra-like, over a pulsing dance instrumental. Other tunes—"Parents Go Mental," "Why Can't I Control My Body?"—play up an XTC-like side, although there are evident traces of the Jam and others as well. The Insects' playing is excellent and their tunes well-developed. **Housebreaking** is a strange record, but one worth finding.   [iar]

BRIAN SETZER

The Knife Feels Like Justice (EMI America) 1986

While his ex-bandmates headed straight from the Stray Cats into tired arena rock, guitarist/singer/songwriter Setzer did a few sideman projects and then unleashed this strong, varied album that further illustrates his multi-dimensional talent. His range here includes unembellished frontier rock ("The Knife Feels Like Justice"), wistful balladry ("Boulevard of Broken Dreams"), Cochranesque rock'n'roll ("Radiation Ranch"), soulful power pop (the autobiographical "Chains Around Your Heart"), rock bluegrass ("Barbwire Fence") and lots more. With tasteful restraint, Setzer checks his wilder instincts, avoiding showy guitar work, verbal grandstanding or self-parody; maturity and subtlety are the two most unexpected, welcome components of **The Knife Feels Like Justice**.   [iar]

SEX GANG CHILDREN

Song and Legend (Illuminated/nr) 1983
Beasts (Illuminated/nr) 1983
Live in London and Glasgow (Corpus Christi/nr) 1983
Ecstasy and Vendetta Over New York [tape] (nr/ROIR) 1984
Re-enter the Abyss (Dojo/nr) 1985

ANDI SEX GANG

Blind! (Illuminated/nr) 1985

Alongside Specimen and others, Sex Gang Children helped lead the Batcave movement, a largely meaningless collection of bands dedicated to dressing up like old Alice Cooper, clinging to a raunchy post-Bowie outlook, writing lyrics that virtually define pretentious pseudo-literary bullshit and adopting names guaranteed to keep radio censors on their toes. Certainly not the worst of the horrid lot, the Sex Gang Children bear an obnoxious and uncanny resemblance to Adam and the Ants, with nothing remotely original or interesting to offer. The *best* feature of the band is a vague sense of song structure. So unless war whoops, overactive echo, pounding percussion and songs about "German Nun," "Kill Machine" "Cannibal Queen" and "Shout and Scream" (all on **Song and Legend**) sound enticing, skip this band entirely.

Beasts is a compilation of singles, slightly overlapping the first LP. **Ecstasy and Vendetta** captures the Sex Gang Children flailing away onstage in the Big Apple at the end of 1983. About half the material comes from the first studio album; the performance is blurry, over-wrought and horrible. [iar]

SEX PISTOLS

Never Mind the Bollocks, Here's the Sex Pistols (Virgin/Warner Bros.) 1977 (Virgin/nr) 1985
The Great Rock'n'Roll Swindle (Virgin/nr) 1979
Some Product Carri On (Virgin/nr) 1979
Flogging a Dead Horse (Virgin/nr) 1980
The Heyday [tape] (Factory/nr) 1980
The Mini Album EP (Chaos/nr) 1985
The Original Pistols Live (Receiver/nr) 1985
After the Storm (Receiver/nr) 1985
Live Worldwide (Konexion/nr) 1985
Best of the Sex Pistols Live (Bondage/nr) 1985
Anarchy in the UK Live (UK/nr) 1985
Never Trust a Hippy (Hippy/nr) 1985
Where Were You in '77 (77/nr) 1985
Power of the Pistols (77/nr) 1985

Although their importance—both to the existence of new wave music and more generally to pop culture—can hardly be overstated, the Sex Pistols did not make their stand primarily on albums. In fact, discography notwithstanding, the Pistols made only one actual studio album during their brief fourteen-month existence (November 1976 to January 1978). In a textbook McLuhanesque example of the media being the message, the Pistols' impact was not the result of any vast commercial success, and—against the general rock tide—released most of their efforts on 7-inch singles.

Fulfilling an essential and immaculate role as martyrs on the new wave altar by logically self-destructing rather than falling prey to standard rock'n'roll conventions (and politely waiting until no one was paying much attention before descending into typical wasted rock-stardom), the Pistols and manager/instigator/provocateur Malcolm McLaren challenged every aspect and precept of modern music-making, thereby inspiring countless groups to follow their musical and social cue onto stages the world over. A confrontational, nihilistic public image and virulent nihilistic socio-political lyrics set the tone that still guides punk groups today. And, just to confound their enemies, the Pistols made

totally unassailable electric music that sounds just as exciting and powerful today as it did a decade (!) ago.

Populated by such classics as "Anarchy in the UK," "God Save the Queen" and "No Feelings," **Never Mind the Bollocks, Here's the Sex Pistols** is a wonderful, essential piece of rock music. Prototypical punk without compromise, it includes almost everything you need to hear by the Sex Pistols. Oddly, at the time of its release, the LP was a disappointment when compared to the sky-high expectations the band had created. Four of the tracks had already been released as singles and many others had circulated on well-known in-progress bootlegs like the legendary **Spunk**. Now, of course, as the best recorded evidence of the Pistols' existence, it almost defies criticism. Paul Cook, Steve Jones, Johnny Rotten (Lydon) and Sid Vicious (plus Glen Matlock, the main architect and author of the Pistols' music, who was sacked early on, allegedly for liking the Beatles) combined to produce a unique moment in rock's history, and **Bollocks** is the proof. (The American release has one extra track, a different running sequence and altered artwork.)

The Great Rock'n'Roll Swindle, the soundtrack to an amazing bio-pic about the band posthumously banged together semi-coherently from a number of abortive film projects, exists in three forms—a one-disc album of highlights and two slightly different full-length two-record collections. In any case, it's a semi-connected batch of songs by various bands (not just the Pistols) that's chock-full of surprises, fun and strange goings-on. There are regular Pistols tracks—some with vocals by Sid, Steve Jones and Eddie Tudor taking the place of the departed Rotten—as well as live performances, studio outtakes, symphonic renditions, a surprisingly great disco medley, McLaren's first foray into the world of singing and much more. A bit light-hearted (and lightheaded) but with loads of sharp music. The single-record extract has most of the prime material, but either full dose is highly recommended.

Some Product Carri On is for diehards only, scraping the barrel for radio interviews and commercials— audio verité for people whose interest in the Pistols has more to do with sociopathic fascination than pop culture. However otiose it may be, the album shows careful assembly and is wickedly funny in spots—good for one embarrassing listen then straight into the trash compactor. **Some Product** is completely expendable, quite unlike **Flogging a Dead Horse**, which—wretched back-cover scatology aside—provides the commendable service of compiling seven ace 45s (both sides of each) into one handy introduction to the world of the Sex Pistols. From "Anarchy in the UK" to "The Great Rock'n'Roll Swindle," all of the Pistols' greatest moments are featured. If you don't have a complete set, this record catches you right up; for newcomers, the LP is a must-have. **The Heyday** is a cassette-only collection of interviews with Lydon, Cook, Jones and Vicious.

In 1985, a veritable flood of new Sex Pistols records—legal, dubious

and plainly unauthorized—hit record shops. **The Mini Album** consists of a half-dozen early studio outtakes, probably from the same supply as those issued on **Spunk**. **The Original Pistols Live**, with liner notes by producer Dave Goodman, records a 1976 gig. **Live Worldwide** is a compendium of a dozen live cuts, presumably from various gigs. Many others, most of them also concert recordings, followed. [iar]

See also *Chequered Past, Malcolm McLaren, Public Image Ltd., Professionals, Rich Kids, Sid Vicious*.

SHAGGS

Philosophy of the World (nr/Third World) 1969 (nr/Red Rooster) 1980
Shaggs' Own Thing (nr/Red Rooster) 1982

There's always room for dada in rock, and the three Wiggins sisters from New Hampshire virtually define ingenuous amateurism on their first album, a home-brew job originally released in 1969. In a startling treatise that tears down every skill-related barrier that generally precludes musically unskilled children from making records, it boasts that perennial candidate for worst song of all time, "My Pal Foot Foot." **Philosophy of the World** is truly inspired awfulness: incompetent drumming totally unrelated to the song under attack, two not-quite- tuned guitars and clumsy vocals offering Hallmark card platitudes. In toto, a triumph!

After reissuing the Shaggs' first album, NRBQ's Red Rooster label saw to the creation of another batch of tunes, this time making a concerted effort to achieve a semblance of musical acceptability. To that end, another Wiggins was brought in to play bass, the selection of material encompasses some non-originals and both the sound and playing is several hundred times improved. (The benchmark is a swell remake of "My Pal Foot Foot.") **Shaggs' Own Thing** gives up a lot in terms of ear- wrenching misery, achieving instead a simple Jonathan Richman-like sweetness—a piece of true rock primitivism. [iar]

SHAKE

Shake EP (Sire/nr) 1979

When the Rezillos split into vocal and instrumental factions, the latter became Shake. A trio led by guitarist Jo Callis (who'd penned 90 percent of the Rezillos' originals), Shake over-reacted to their ex-bandmates' frivolity by playing their loud'n'fastisms deadpan on this 10-incher. Second mistake: Callis let the other two write. Third mistake: dull sound. Smart move: breaking up. Smarter move (for Callis): joining the Human League. [jg]

SHAKIN' PYRAMIDS

Skin 'Em Up (Cuba Libre-Virgin/nr) 1981
Celts and Cobras (Cuba Libre-Virgin/nr) 1982
Shakin' Pyramids (nr/Rock'n'Roll) 1983

Few neo-rockabilly combos are as down-home folksy as Scotland's Shakin' Pyramids. This trio not only avoids electricity, they barely condone musical instruments, having

started out as a pair of busking acoustic guitarists and a singer/harmonica player.

The corrupting touch of fame lured them into adding electric guitar, acoustic bass and a spot of drums to **Skin 'Em Up**. The album pounds furiously, putting your average megawatt metal band to shame. Songs—mostly non-originals—zip by at a blinding rate; the record's only flaw is its brief running time. Then again, if brevity be the soul of this music, the Shakin' Pyramids are a rockabilly Ramones.

Like the Ramones, the Pyramids have a growth problem. **Celts and Cobras** offers a higher percentage of their own songs, but accompanied by piano, accordion, electric bass and even—gack!—a string section. More dismaying is the band's descent into schlock-pop consciousness: instead of Eddie Cochran and Link Davis tunes, we get the Everly Brothers and Gene Pitney. The band still rocks, but they'd better figure out where they're going.

The American release (whose cover pictures and sleeve lists them as a quartet) distills the two albums, featuring mainly originals. [si]

SHAKIN' STREET

Vampire Rock (Fr. CBS) 1978
Shakin' Street (CBS/Columbia) 1980

Led by singer Fabienne Shine and her songwriting partner, guitarist Eric Lewy, Shakin' Street emerged from obscurity in France thanks to American producer/manager Sandy Pearlman, who procured an international recording deal for the band.

Shakin' Street's debut album, **Vampire Rock**, recorded in London but released only in France, is an impressive, raucous and wild rocker, with English lyrics that touch a number of bases, from sharp to silly. Shine's accented singing, which at times recalls Grace Slick, is a powerful asset; the twin-guitar roar sounds almost uncontrollable.

The band's eponymous second effort was recorded in America, with ex-Dictator Ross the Boss replacing one of the guitarists. Playing simple, direct hard-rock-cum-metal, the album offers nothing original, save for a strong song recut from **Vampire Rock** ("No Time to Lose") and one truly great number, "Susie Wong," which supports a haunting melody with subtly arranged electric/ acoustic instrumentation. [iar]

SHAM 69

Tell Us the Truth (Polydor/Sire) 1978
That's Life (Polydor/nr) 1978
Adventures of the Hersham Boys (Polydor/nr) 1979
The Game (Polydor/nr) 1980
The First, Best and Last (Polydor/nr) 1980

The archetypal working class ramalama dole-queue band, deliverers of socio-political bromides over blazing guitars, Sham 69 had a bad case of arrested development. Their populist slogans were ultimately chanted like football cheers, but taken far less seriously. Arguably Sham's best single, "Hurry Up Harry" is about the importance of "going down 'a pub." Lead singer/lyricist Jimmy Pursey seemed earnest enough, but the band was too simpleminded to amount to anything of lasting musical import, despite enormous UK popularity.

The first LP sidesteps the issue of decent production by having one side with none at all and the other recorded live. The sound, oddly enough, isn't so much derived from the Clash and Pistols as it is from the Dolls, Heartbreakers and Ramones. (It's hard to judge how much of that is by design and how much is due to sheer incompetence.) More than any of those, Pursey's cockney yelling tabbed him as the anykid who could, but it's also true that almost any kid could have written the LP in his sleep.

That's Life offers more of the same while enlarging on an idea heard briefly on **Tell Us the Truth**, using "slice of life" dialogues (kid vs. parents, boy and girl, boy and girl's boyfriend, etc.). Pursey lets on that he has bigger ambitions as he plays the cockney wideboy imitating Bob Dylan on one cut. This dross is brightened only by "Hurry Up Harry" and the anthemic "Angels with Dirty Faces."

Pursey worked up some "poetic" lyrics for **Hersham Boys**; this, plus the increased use of keyboards (played by Pursey's co-producer, Peter Wilson) meant that Sham was nearing the stage of early Boomtown Rats. But who could take his words seriously if he cried them like a fishmonger?

By **The Game**, Sham's playing and lyrics had sharpened to the point of respectability, but there are few tunes likely to induce serious groove wear; a case of too little too late. The **First, Best and Last** compilation does include some non-LP singles (but not the first, on Step Forward) plus a limited-edition bonus live EP. The non-45 tracks weren't chosen (from admittedly slim pickings) to display Sham at its smartest, but the part about being the last is true.   [jg]

See also *Angelic Upstarts, Cockney Rejects, Jimmy Pursey, Wanderers.*

SHANGO

See *Afrika Bambaataa.*

FEARGAL SHARKEY

Feargal Sharkey (Virgin/Virgin-A&M) 1985

Following a slow start—three singles, only one of which ("Never Never" with Vince Clarke's Assembly) was any good—Sharkey's ascent from ex-Undertone to chart-topping singing sensation was accomplished with relative alacrity thanks in large part to producer Dave Stewart (of Eurythmics). Sharkey's solo album is an uneasy pairing of his distinctive vocals and tame, mainstreamish arrangements of material from diverse sources. "A Good Heart" (by Lone Justice's Maria McKee, but as yet unrecorded by her own band) is a sturdy piece of slightly soulful pop; "You Little Thief" (by Benmont Tench of Tom Petty's band) is similarly memorable. "Love and Hate" resembles late-period Undertones, while Feargal's version of "It's All Over Now" is simply a mistake.   [iar]

SHEENA AND THE ROKKETS

Sheena and the Rokkets (Jap. Alfa) 1979
Sheena and the Rokkets (nr/A&M) 1980

An ingenious Japanese technopop quartet with a female singer and a taste for Anglo-American rock'n'roll of the '60s, the Rokkets' Japanese debut contains over-the-top readings of "The Batman Theme," James Brown's "I Got You" and a truly nutty version of "You Really Got Me," as well as impressive originals like "Radio Junk" and "Rocket Factory." A perfectly wonderful blend of cultures and musical sensibilities, sung in Japanese and fractured English.

The American release, reprising five songs, is a very different record. Some tunes, cut originally in Japanese, were redone with English vocals; others sound like the results of completely new sessions. Overall, it lacks the carefree zaniness that imbues the Japanese album with its bubbling infectiousness. More serious, less entertaining.

[iar]

SHEILA E.

Sheila E. in The Glamorous Life (Warner Bros.) 1984
Sheila E. in Romance 1600 (Paisley Park) 1985

Multi-talented Sheila Escovedo—percussionist, singer, composer, producer, actress (well . . .)—made quite an entrance under Prince's wing on **Glamorous Life**. The frenetic nine-minute title tune, filled with rhythms, hooks and insidious lyrics, is the best-known item, but the other five tracks display other equally appealing sides of Sheila's musical personality. Probably due to his non-involvement in the songwriting, Prince's touch is light, his influence relatively subtle.

No one could easily miss the erotic content of the first LP, but **Romance 1600** is far hornier, with coy titles like "Toy Box" and "Bedtime Story" driving home the point without a grain of subtlety. Otherwise, the album centers around the overextended "A Love Bizarre." Sheila and Prince (guitar, bass, vocals) stretch this minor tune to over twelve minutes, leaving all but the most mechano-minded drifting off the dance floor and out the door. If you're listening at home, forget it! Luckily, Side Two is tons better—"Yellow" and "Romance 1600" go a long way towards redeeming the excessive mess on Side One.   [iar]

PETE SHELLEY

Sky Yen (Groovy/nr) 1979
Homosapien (Genetic/Genetic-Arista) 1982
XL1 (Genetic/Genetic-Arista) 1983
Heaven and the Sea (Mercury) 1986

As creative linchpin of the Buzzcocks, Manchester's Pete Shelley perfected a pop style based on intellectualizing his emotional responses, often to humorous effect. But, as with the group, he is strongest making singles, apparently hard-pressed to sustain his energy throughout an entire album.

Shelley's first solo LP, **Sky Yen**, was actually recorded in 1974, long before the Buzzcocks, and demonstrates an early interest in Germanic electronic music. An exercise in simpleminded drone electronics conducted on a single oscillator rather than full-fledged electronic instruments, the album is a collectors' item of minor interest.

The post-Buzzcocks **Homosapien**, including the hit single of the same name, is a dance album, with

Shelley clearly taking the reins and eliminating the guitar/drums combination as axis of his songs. A turn to electronics doesn't signal a surrender to them, though; the songs, not the technique, remain paramount. Shelley seems to draw influence from a wide group of sources (such as the Doors and Marc Bolan), and the album cleverly sidesteps the trap of monotony that sometimes afflicted the Buzzcocks. (There are differences between the UK and US versions: the latter replaces "Pusher Man," "It's Hard Enough Knowing" and "Keats' Song" with "Love in Vain," "Witness the Change" and "In Love with Somebody Else." Fine. The more Shelley the better.)

Shelley reintroduces guitar on **XL1** and downplays the electronics to create more direct, urgent dance music. "Telephone Operator" is equal to "Homosapien"; the LP also contains other solid examples of clear-headed songwriting—"If You Ask Me (I Won't Say No)" and "You Know Better Than I Know," for instance—that allow strong rhythms to predominate without obscuring the abundant musicality. The tape version in both countries is different: the American adds dub mixes of "Homosapien" and another track; the English an extra LP's worth of remixes.

Heaven and the Sea serves up more of Shelley's reflective soul-searching, but without much relish. Except for the percussion-laden "No Moon," the songs are fairly routine and Stephen Hague's mundane production does little to distinguish any. Shelley is becoming a specialized taste—fans will appreciate this record as much as any of his prior solo releases, unbelievers won't be especially affected.   [sg/iar]

SHIRTS

The Shirts (Harvest/Capitol) 1978
Street Light Shine (Harvest/Capitol) 1979
Inner Sleeve (Capitol) 1980

These six Brooklynites were playing Top 40 covers in local bars until they happened onto the Bowery club circuit in 1975. Abandoning the boroughs for a career in Manhattan with original material, the Shirts became a popular if unhip fixture, and eventually wound up making three albums of totally bland hoping-for-the-mainstream rock. Singer Annie Golden has had some individual success—in the movie of *Hair*, with a solo single in 1984 and on Broadway—but the band is little more than a bad memory. Each of the albums has an enjoyable song or two, but there's nothing remarkable about any of them.   [iar]

SHOCKABILLY

The Dawn of Shockabilly EP (Rough Trade/nr) 1982
Earth vs. Shockabilly (Rough Trade/nr) 1983
Greatest Hits EP (nr/Red) 1983
Colosseum (Rough Trade/nr) 1984
Vietnam (Fundamental Music) 1984
Heaven (Fundamental Music) 1985

Crazed rockabilly-tinged remakes of "Psychotic Reaction" and two Yardbirds classics isn't a bad idea, especially if gonzo guitar and drums like those on **The Dawn of Shockabilly** are brought to bear on 'em. Taking the same tack on "A Hard Day's Night" and a country oldie, adding silly organ also makes

a funny kind of sense. But guitarist Eugene Chadbourne's nonsense vocals (stupidly muffled, or in silly cartoon character styles, with at least two or three different voices per track) ruin the whole thing. Eugene shouldn't be careful with his axe, but with his mouth.

Greatest Hits takes one track each from the two preceding English records and adds a quartet of stunning live cuts, including the amphetaminized "Bluegrass Breakdown" and a nearly unrecognizable version of the Doors' "People Are Strange." **Vietnam** is a relatively grand affair, with a huge tour-diary poster and material by Arthur Lee, John Fogerty, John Lee Hooker and the Beatles mercilessly savaged by Chadbourne and his two henchmen.

Heaven takes the terrible trio further into the realms of the truly weird. Only three covers (Bolan, Lennon and a mystery), but such inspired originals as Eugene's "How Can You Kill Me, I'm Already Dead" and "She Was a Living Breathing Piece of Dirt" more than make up the difference. On that (bum) note, Shockabilly ceased to exist.

Occasionally listenable, often more stupid than funny, Shockabilly was, if nothing else, absolutely unique.   [jg/iar]

See also *Eugene Chadbourne.*

SHOES

Black Vinyl Shoes (nr/Black Vinyl) 1977 (Sire/PVC) 1978
Present Tense (Elektra) 1979
Tongue Twister (Elektra) 1981
Boomerang (nr/Elektra) 1982
Silhouette (Demon/nr) 1984

This brilliant power pop quartet from Zion, Illinois began by recording at home on a 4-track, which resulted in a self-released LP that attracted national attention and, eventually, a major-label contract. John and Jeff Murphy, Gary Klebe and drummer Skip Meyer blend electric guitar—loud, distorted, multi-tracked—with breathy, winsome vocals to create melodic rock made most impressive by the presence of three equally talented singer/songwriters.

Black Vinyl Shoes was recorded in a living room; the intricately layered guitars and vocals make that hard to believe. The songs, telling tender tales of failed romance, are catchy and instantly likable. The band also put the record in an impressive package and distributed it as a vinyl demo; in fact, it's one of the finest homebrewed releases ever, and is a much more valid piece of music than many productions by well-known bands with far greater technical resources. After the small initial pressing sold out, the album was licensed to PVC and reissued with wholly different artwork.

(**Black Vinyl** is actually not Shoes' first album. A prior longplayer, **Un dans Versailles**, was recorded by the Murphy brothers with a previous drummer and privately issued in a minute quantity around 1975. Charming but a bit rough, it sounds like a less-developed attempt at what was to come. Shoes also recorded—but never released—an album's worth of excellent tunes in 1976 under the working title **Bazooka**.)

After signing to Elektra, Shoes recorded **Present Tense** in a full-scale English 24-track studio with a professional producer, but ended up sounding pretty much the same as before, only with much greater audio fidelity. Given the chance to experiment and open up their sound, Shoes opted to hold fast—lots of vocals, lots of melody, lots of fuzzed-out guitars. Another triumphant LP that probably could have been made at home without losing any appreciable amount of charm or appeal—it's Shoes' talent, not studio technology, that matters here.

Tongue Twister succcessfully maintains the quality level of **Present Tense**, but Shoes are clearly standing still creatively. Their style is honed as far as it's going to go, and they're sticking with it. **Boomerang**, recorded near the band's home base without a strong outside producer, suffers from inconsistent song quality and an overanxious feeling, no doubt brought on by the band's failure to catch on commercially. (Early pressings of **Boomerang** included a 12-inch live EP, **Shoes on Ice**, recorded at the Zion Ice Arena in 1981, offering six of the band's best tunes as proof of their ability to play them well live.)

Parting company with their label, Shoes retired to the studio they had built in Illinois and continued writing and recording. A trio of Murphy, Murphy and Klebe made the next Shoes album, **Silhouette**, released only in Europe via various licensing arrangements. The sound (incorporating more keyboards and subtler dabs of guitar) is typically exquisite, and the songs (four by each member) are fine examples of the band's seemingly effortless pop suss. A fine, relaxed return that reasserts Shoes' considerable talent. [iar]

SHOES FOR INDUSTRY

Talk Like a Whelk (Fried Egg/nr) 1981

Bristol's Shoes for Industry is one of those bands apparently so distressed by the world that you have to wonder how they go on living. Anchored by a thumping rhythm section, frontman Basset Davies anxiously declaims such heavy works as "Violent Stabbing with a Knife" as well as the overtly silly "Invasion of the French Boyfriends." Much ado with little result. [jy]

SHOP ASSISTANTS

Shop Assistants EP (Subway Organisation/nr) 1985
Safety Net EP (53rd & 3rd/nr) 1986

Along with the Jesus and Mary Chain, Edinburgh's Shop Assistants are part of a trend away from the terribly twee pop Scotland was nurturing five years ago. Four lasses and a lad (including two drummers), Shop Assistants are raw, catchy and utterly without pretense. These two EPs combine some of J&M's white-noise pop with Buzzcocks- influenced buoyancy, and—when necessary—tuneful delicacy (see **Safety Net**'s "Somewhere in China"). The four-track debut is promising; **Safety Net** is nothing short of brilliant. [dgs]

SHRIEKBACK

Tench EP (Y/Y America) 1982
Care (Y/Warner Bros.) 1983
Jam Science (Arista/nr) 1984
Knowledge, Power, Truth and Sex EP (Ger. Arista) 1984

The Infinite (Kaz/nr) 1984
Oil and Gold (Arista/Island) 1985

Barry Andrews was a founder of XTC and later the organist in Robert Fripp's League of Gentlemen. David Allen was coincidentally replaced in Gang of Four by League bassist Sara Lee. Together with guitarist/vocalist Carl Marsh and a drum machine, Andrews and Allen formed Shriekback, a cagey dance band with solid rhythms and insidiously weird vocals. The playing is top-notch, a slithering swamp snake that oozes cool malevolence on **Tench**'s six tracks. Shriekback abounds in originality and creativity, if not warmth. Notwithstanding several changes in personnel, Allen and Andrews have remained the band's core, preserving its spirit of prickly iconoclasm.

Care, their first LP, is an intelligent, well-produced, spirited record demonstrating what every XTC fan knew all along—Andrews is one of rock's most original and musical keyboard players. Over Allen's slinky, oblique bass lines, Andrews provides subtle shadings and clever doodles that move in and out of the mix, making this perfect for both dancing and scrutiny. Most bands with this much talent would be content to showcase their chops, but Shriekback can write a good song too, especially the brilliantly haunting "Lined Up," a funk concoction that sets an impossible standard for inferior but like-minded bands.

Jam Science doesn't quite match **Care** for sheer invention, but is nonetheless a solid, confident LP. More prominent use of drum machines, female backing vocals and string synths give the record a slick Euro-disco feel. (Released by UK Arista, this LP should not be confused with an unauthorized release of the same name on Dutch Y, which contains most of the same songs but in unfinished form. The German EP, with four of the proper album's tracks, is legit.)

Shriekback is very big on remixes. Most of their singles offer non-album versions plus additional alternative mixes. Several of these (along with some originals) are available on **The Infinite**, a compilation drawing from **Tench** and **Care**.

Oil and Gold goes for a much harder sound, with booming, sometimes overpowering guitar and drums (most evident on "Nemesis," a big dance club hit and the only song ever written which makes prominent use of the word "parthenogenesis" in the lyrics.) When they do go for the more ethereal colors found on **Care**, the results are pretty boring ("This Big Hush," "Faded Flowers"). After the LP was released, Marsh left the group, and was replaced for an American tour by former Voidoid guitarist Ivan Julian. [iar/dgs]

SHRINK

Shrink EP (Oval-A&M/nr) 1979

Charlie Gillett, aside from being one of the most astute writers to chronicle rock'n'roll's development, was also clever enough to spot the talents of, among others, Lene Lovich and Holly and the Italians early. His own Oval label, however, also had this clod. Shrink's prior single (written by the Secret, labelmates who also produced this EP) was okay glam-rock, but 20

minutes of his dull rock-cum-guitar-noise heroics alternating with quiet, studiously eccentric mush on this 10-inch disc is intolerable. Talk about studied weirdness—the cover photo shows his stage persona, a bizarrely-clad character with half a head of hair and the rest of his noggin and face sprayed with metallic paint, toting a Flying V guitar. Keep the cover for a laugh and pitch the record. [jg]

SIDEWAY LOOK

Sideway Look (Virgin/nr) 1984

This Scottish quintet writes solid nouveau pop songs and plays them with a mix of guitars and keyboards. (Did I mention accordion?) The arrangements haul in everything—from controlled guitar feedback to mellow horns—which makes the album highly varied in sound, but Brian Smith's posey vocals—a dramatic Bowie/Eric Burdon delivery—occasionally seem out of place. Smoothly capable on everything from mild soul to straightforward guitar-based dance rock (and managing to drop hints of everyone from Big Country to Haircut One Hundred), Sideway Look look ready to have a hit, but it might be in any one of their styles. [iar]

SIGUE SIGUE SPUTNIK

"Love Missile F1-11" (Parlophone/ Manhattan) 1986

Spurred no doubt by former Generation X bandmate Billy Idol's solo stardom, Tony James formed this mega-hype mess as some sort of latter-day version of Malcolm McLaren's great rock'n'roll swindle. So far, SSS has proven far more adept at getting ridiculous haircuts and attracting labels and press coverage (much of it highly unfavorable) than making or selling records, and this debut single (a three-version 12-inch) shows why. Produced by Giorgio Moroder, the track starts with a speedy monotonic bass riff, and then piles on sound effects, scratch mix maneuvers and a pinch of a song. Mildly entertaining but utterly redundant, and not half as outrageous as it ought to be, "Love Missile" hardly seems like the work of any Next Big Thing. [iar]

SILENT RUNNING

Shades of Liberty (Parlophone-EMI/EMI America) 1984

If Belfast bands have become known for passionate intensity, someone forgot to tell this quintet. Their album (retitled **Emotional Warfare** in its US edition) contains slick humdrum dance-rock with only Peter Gamble's Bonoesque bellowing to suggest (not generate) any enthusiasm. The pounding "Emotional Warfare" is as good as it gets, and that's not very. [iar]

SILICON TEENS

Music for Parties (Mute/Sire) 1979

Whether you realize it or not, Daniel Miller has probably been as responsible as anybody (save Robert Moog) for the rise of synthesizers in modern rock, via his Mute Records, a groundbreaking single (as the Normal) and production work for Depeche Mode and many others. The illusory Silicon Teens (despite the personnel

list on the sleeve) is a pseudonymous Miller studio project, offering fourteen percolating synth versions (with vocals) of such rock'n'roll classics as "Memphis, Tennessee," "Judy in Disguise," "You Really Got Me"—you get the idea. There are several originals as well, but the title says it best: a good time is guaranteed for all. The approach here is more conservative and reverent than David Cunningham's more devolutionary Flying Lizards, but the two concepts are not that far apart. (And I'm not sure who did it first.) [iar]

See also *Robert Rental and the Normal.*

DESMOND SIMMONS

Alone on Penguin Island (Dome/nr) 1981

On his own record (which Simmons singlehandedly wrote and performed), this Colin Newman cohort fell in with the austere minimalism of Newman's former Wire colleagues, Graham Lewis and B.C. Gilbert, who produced **Penguin Island**. Simmons is more song-oriented than they are, but seemingly mistook reduction for redaction; despite some good songs here, they've been cut to the bone, made somewhat alien and abstract. A few even sound as though they were recorded underwater. All the same, a moving, high, lonesome quality does come across, as on the melodica- dominated instrumental title track. Patience is rewarded, but you may feel he made you work too hard. [jg]

SIMPLE MINDS

Life in a Day (Zoom/PVC) 1979 (Virgin/nr) 1982
Real to Real Cacophony (Arista/nr) 1980 (Virgin/nr) 1982
Empires and Dance (Arista/nr) 1980 (Virgin/nr) 1982
Sons and Fascination/Sister Feelings Call (Virgin/nr) 1981
Themes for Great Cities (nr/Stiff) 1982
Celebration (Arista/nr) 1982 (Virgin/nr) 1982
New Gold Dream (81-82-83-84) (Virgin/Virgin-A&M) 1982
Sparkle in the Rain (Virgin/Virgin-A&M) 1984
Once Upon a Time (Virgin/Virgin-A&M) 1985

Scotland's Simple Minds once took a lot of (mostly) undeserved criticism for being arty and pretentious, but in their early days, the mix of serious/philosophical lyrics with danceable rhythms supporting oblique musical structures did make them something of an acquired taste. Often dense, occasionally discordant and gloomy, Simple Minds' music also stretches to commercial pop, an area they've pursued with increasing enthusiasm and success of late.

Life in a Day largely recalls Roxy Music, but also touches lightly on several forms, including pop, psychedelia and an adventurous tense/terse style they explored on subsequent albums. "Sad Affair" is modish; "All for You" has disturbing overtones of the Doors and early Jefferson Airplane; "No Cure" sounds like the Buzzcocks-meet-the-Who; "Chelsea Girl" is delightful '60s pop, complete with full orchestration.

With **Real to Real Cacophony,** the band lives up (or down) to the album's clever title. Excepting a couple of standouts like "Carnival (Shelter in a Suitcase)" and the haunting instrumental "Film Theme" (Simple Minds are one of the few bands that can and do create worthwhile instrumentals with real skill), **Real to Real Cacophony** is just like the band in the title song; "Real to real cacophony/Echo, echo on endlessly."

The minute the needle sets down on **Empires and Dance**'s "I Travel," it's obvious that Simple Minds have reorganized and changed direction; while not completely successful, the album is extremely atmospheric and promising, including some good dance tunes and a few more quasi-psychedelic ones ("Kant-Kino" and "Room").

Celebration is a compilation of tracks from the first three albums.

Sons and Fascination/Sister Feelings Call—two discrete albums originally released as one work, then reissued separately—is Simple Minds' first really good record. While still experimental, the group sounds more comfortable in the semi-funky, semi-dancey, semi-electronic groove introduced on **Empires and Dance**. "The American," "20th Century Promised Land" and "Love Song" are all top-drawer examples of modern dance music and "Theme for Great Cities" is another fine instrumental.

Themes for Great Cities takes the best material from **Real to Real Cacophony, Empires and Dance** and **Sons and Fascination**, presenting the band much more strongly than the individual records originally did. (One notable omission: "20th Century Promised Land.")

New Gold Dream (81-82-83-84) takes another great step forward. The songs are stronger and the sound shows a definite thawing, mellowing trend, while retaining its majestic power. "Promised You a Miracle" (soulful and dramatic dance tune), "Glittering Prize" (warm, pretty ballad) and the panoramic title track stand out. A memorable, mature record marked by compassion and sensitivity.

Working with producer Steve Lillywhite, **Sparkle in the Rain** is another fine, affecting record with textured, intricate rhythmic rock and Jim Kerr's personable singing. Simple Minds sound firmly in control of their sound, equally capable of grand gestures and subtle nuance. The first side is great, featuring four of their best songs: "Speed Your Love to Me," "Book of Brilliant Things," "Up on the Catwalk" and "Waterfront." The flipside is less exhilarating, but does include a cover of Lou Reed's "Street Hassle."

At this point, Simple Minds' story gets complicated. Jim Kerr married Chrissie Hynde in 1984. The following year, the band had its first £1 US hit with "Don't You (Forget About Me)." Bassist Derek Forbes quit to go solo. They appeared at Live Aid. Jim and Chrissie had a baby. And their first post-stardom LP is the most appalling sell-out in recent memory. Produced by Jimmy Iovine and Bob Clearmountain, **Once Upon a Time** is virtually unlistenable, a perversion of the group's sound specifically and unpleasantly geared for American radio. To be fair, none of the tracks sound like the *Breakfast Club* theme (Kerr being far too intelligent to allow that), but "Sanctify Yourself," "Alive and Kicking," "Oh Jungleland" (great title), etc. are wretched, transparent stabs at the Sound of Today's Album Rock Radio, bearing only passing resemblance to Simple Minds' prior work.   [ks/iar]

SIMPLY RED

Picture Book (Elektra) 1985

From the soul-funk-America school of Manchester musical thought comes Simply Red: raspy singer Mick "Red" Hucknall, a couple of ex-Durutti Column members and three other blokes, including a trumpet player. Mixing original tunes with eclectically-selected covers, **Picture Book** sounds like a lot of contemporary UK soul: a slick, earnest imitation that compensates for its irrelevance by attempting as many different substyles as possible. Leading with the well-intentioned but clumsy "Moneys Too Tight (To Mention)" ("They're talking about Reaganomics/Lord, down in the Congress" and "Did the earth move for you, Nancy?") and putting Talking Head's "Heaven" to sleep permanently, Simply Red are simply dull.   [tr]

SINCEROS

The Sound of Sunbathing (Epic/Columbia) 1979
Pet Rock (Epic/Columbia) 1981

Having played together (under a different name) in the mid-'70s, the Sinceros' first break was that the group's rhythm half backed Lene Lovich on **Stateless** and toured with her; they carried some of her bizarritude back with them onto **The Sound of Sunbathing**. Basically a vehicle for guitarist/singer Mark Kjeldsen, the band's other historical claim is that Sinceros keyboardist Don Snow replaced Paul Carrack in Squeeze.

The debut LP has two great tracks—a quirky bit of silliness called "Take Me to Your Leader" and a Joe Jackson soundalike, "Little White Lie." Otherwise, it's an amiable pop record with little character. **Pet Rock**, produced by Gus Dudgeon, removes any trace of oddness, and is strictly MOR for old-timers.   [iar]

SIOUXSIE AND THE BANSHEES

The Scream (Polydor) 1978 (nr/Geffen) 1984
Join Hands (Polydor/nr) 1979 (nr/Geffen) 1984
Kaleidoscope (Polydor/PVC) 1980 (nr/Geffen) 1984
Juju (Polydor/PVC) 1981 (nr/Geffen) 1984
Arabian Knights EP (nr/PVC) 1981
Once Upon a Time/The Singles (Polydor/PVC) 1981 (nr/Geffen) 1984
A Kiss in the Dreamhouse (Polydor/nr) 1982 (nr/Geffen) 1984
Nocturne (Wonderland-Polydor/Geffen) 1983
Hyaena (Wonderland-Polydor/Geffen) 1984
The Thorn EP (Wonderland-Polydor/nr) 1984
Tinderbox (Wonderland-Polydor/Geffen) 1986

In 1976, Siouxsie Sioux (née Susan Dallion) and Steve Severin were part of the clique of steady Sex Pistols fans known as the Bromley Contingent. As Siouxsie and the Banshees, the nascent punk rock stars debuted at the 100 Club's legendary 1976 punk festival; aided by future Ant guitarist Marco Pirroni and future Pistol Sid Vicious (on drums!), the motley crew bashed through a lengthy free-form rendition of "The Lord's Prayer," stopping only when they became bored.

From such uncertain beginnings, Siouxsie and the Banshees evolved within two years into a highly popular band, regularly appearing on the charts despite the group's brooding, abrasive style. **The Scream** capsulized the first-generation sound of the Banshees: Siouxsie's icy, sometimes tuneless wail swooping over the brutish rhythms of bassist Severin and drummer Kenny Morris and the metal-shard roar of John McKay's guitar. The songs are relentlessly grim, albeit often sardonic (as in "Carcass" and their version of the Beatles' "Helter Skelter"). The only break in style is "Hong Kong Garden," an almost upbeat song that, as a 45, punched its way into the UK Top 10.

But **The Scream** seems positively cheerful in light of its follow-up, **Join Hands**, a plodding, depressive album notable only for the commission of their "Lord's Prayer" butchery to vinyl. Two days into a tour to promote the album, Morris and McKay abruptly walked out of the band. Guitarist Robert Smith from opening act the Cure and ex-Slits drummer Budgie were drafted to complete the tour. Budgie subsequently signed on as a permanent Banshee and the group proceeded to record **Kaleidoscope** without a guitarist to call their own. (Guest stars John McGeoch of Magazine and ex-Pistol Steve Jones alternated guitar duties on the LP.) **Kaleidoscope** marked a bilateral move away from the group's original wall of noise; many of the songs are softer and more melodic (e.g., "Happy House" and the flower-powery "Christine"), and there is an increased use of framing concepts ("Red Light" is built around the whirr-click of a camera auto-winder). Shortly afterward, McGeoch officially joined the band and they toured America for the first time.

Finally a full-fledged band again, the Banshees released **Juju**, their strongest and most satisfying record to date. Siouxsie's voice had developed into a surprisingly subtle instrument, and the technical prowess added by Budgie and McGeoch brought power and complexity to songs like "Spellbound" and "Arabian Knights."

Also released in 1981, **Once Upon a Time** assembled all of the band's singles (including the otherwise non-LP "Staircase (Mystery)" and "Israel") on one record. The American **Arabian Knights** EP reprises the contents of a British 12-inch plus one extra tune.

A Kiss in the Dreamhouse finds the Banshees veering back into the more experimental terrain of **Kaleidoscope**, letting their jarring, near-pop style pass through some pretty strange permutations (like the deviant neo-bop of "Cocoon" and the medieval recorder stylings of "Green Fingers").

Nocturne is a two-LP live set recorded (with no overdubs) at the Royal Albert Hall in late 1983. Robert Smith is the featured guitarist on a full-course selection from the band's repertoire, stretching back to "Switch" and "Israel," but also drawing heavily from **Dreamhouse**. Awesome.

With Smith again rounding out the lineup, **Hyaena** starts off with the utterly magnificent "Dazzle," a haunting blend of industrial-strength drumming and symphonic backing, with some of Siouxsie's best singing ever. The album is much more melodic, light and inviting than any of the band's others, going so far as to touch on an earlier extra-curricular excursion into jazzy stylings ("Take Me Back") and allowing piano to dominate "Swimming Horses." The Beatles' "Dear Prudence," a big 1983 hit single for the Banshees, also helps leaven the traditional dark intensity.

Smith was subsequently forced to flee, as being a full-time member of two major groups had taken its toll on his health. Former Clock DVA guitarist John Carruthers replaced him. Already maintaining a rather low 1985 profile, the Banshees were set back a bit further when Siouxsie broke her kneecap during a show.

At a point where some were ready to write the band off as aging, lazy veterans, they came back in early '86 with **Tinderbox**, one of their strongest LPs in years. Carruthers fits in well, his rich playing stylistically similar to both Smith's and McGeoch's; the rhythm section is as steady as ever. The big plus is punk's original princess herself—Siouxsie's voice has never been so warm and tuneful as it is on tracks like "The Sweetest Chill," "Cannons" and the great single, "Cities in Dust."

Not bad for a band whose initial intent at that 1976 debut was to annoy the crowd enough to get thrown off the stage.   [tr]
See also *Creatures, Glove.*

SISTERS OF MERCY

Sisters of Mercy EP (Merciful Release/Brain Eater) 1983
The Reptile House EP (Merciful Release/Brain Eater) 1983
First and Last and Always (Merciful Release/Elektra) 1985

The all-male Sisters from Leeds began by playing what they jokingly called heavy metal, which it sort of was, but not punk-metal. (An odd feat with a rhythm generator—the band has always been drummerless.) Andrew Eldritch is the band's focus: as lyricist, chief melodist, producer (pre-LP, sometimes with Psychedelic Fur John Ashton) and lead singer in a deep, aptly gothic voice.

Although their pre-LP body of work amounted to several albums' worth of tracks, only two songs were used on the album. As with most of their early work, the eponymous 12-inch EP, particularly its excellent "Alice," suffers from sub-par sound. The sound got better and the group's identity began to come into its own by Reptile House. (You might say it grew claws.) With the issue of "Tempest of Love" (available only as a single), the Sisters extended their reach to include *danceable* doom-rock.

The album, produced by Dave Allen (Associates, Cure), at last attains the group's long-sought clarity and sophistication and, ergo, is nearly sublime in its pristine bleakness. Although somewhat distanced from the original metal jumping-off point, the incorporation of power poppish guitar and dancey rhythms does nothing to place the group within either category; their sonic integrity somehow remains intact. Eldritch's vocals, like Jim Morrison plus David Bowie and slowed down to half-speed, are as gloomy as ever.

None of this is meant to be taken seriously—the group are anti-fashionists who've cultivated an elaborate conscious posture, making themselves more successful than their album. A German live bootleg gives some indication of their true intention: it consists mainly of oldies—from the Stooges to the Stones; Dolly Parton to Hot Chocolate. [jg]

SKAFISH

Skafish (Illegal/Illegal-IRS) 1980
Conversation (nr/IRS) 1983

Indiana's Jim Skafish is one of the oddest eggs ever to wander into the shopping mall of rock music. Visually androgynous and, well, unattractive, Skafish builds his songs on neurotic angles of romance, suicide and growing up different that are most pessimistic. Yet, by couching them in sprightly tunes delivered with great geniality, he creates an unnerving dynamic. His band is skilled and supple; his first album, despite all its personality flaws, is clear and fascinating rather than grim or depressing.

Skafish lunges off in a different direction on the disappointing **Conversation**, which starts with a mundane disco track, "Secret Lover," notable only for his voice's jarring unsuitability to the genre. With the exception of two loud rockers and a few blandouts, the rest of the record follows stylistic suit. What's worse, the lyrics aren't even very interesting. [iar]

SKELETON CREW

Learn to Talk (Recommended/Rift) 1984

Its three-man lineup quickly trimmed to a less-extravagant two, Skeleton Crew regaled audiences in America, Europe and Japan with its unique and functional mix of rhythmically twisted rock, electric and acoustic noise, wittily interpolated taped voice fragments and "fake folk music." Most of the latter had a distinctly East European flavor, though one New York gig consisted entirely of folk music from around the world. Guitarist Fred Frith alternated playing conventional and homemade guitars, six-string bass, violin and keyboards while occasionally singing in a high-pitched voice. Tom Cora busied himself on cello as well as four-string bass and devices; both worked kickdrums with their feet as their fingers flew. They had enough material for maybe three good albums, but this one fine LP will serve for posterity. [mf]
See also *Fred Frith.*

SKIDS

Wide Open EP (Virgin/nr) 1978
Scared to Dance (Virgin/nr) 1979
Days in Europa (Virgin/nr) 1979
The Absolute Game (Virgin/nr) 1980
Joy (Virgin/nr) 1981
Fanfare (Virgin/nr) 1982

The Skids' rise and fall revolved almost wholly around Richard

Jobson—singer, writer, creative dilettante. Emerging from Scotland as a promising punkish quartet playing literate and challenging rock music with anthemic proclivities, under Jobson's increasing leadership the Skids became more and more pretentious and less and less a band, finally evaporating into the mist after a miserable fourth LP, recorded as a duo. The first three albums, however, offer a precious body of inspiring and unique rock'n'roll with obvious Scottish blood. In hindsight, it's easy to see what role guitarist Stuart Adamson (now a star in his own right with Big Country) played in defining the Skids' sound at the band's outset.

Wide Open, a four-song 12-inch on red vinyl, contains two inspired successes in "The Saints Are Coming" and "Of One Skin," both of which also appear on the similarly excellent **Scared to Dance**. Using loud guitar and semi-martial drumming for its basis, Jobson's hearty singing sounds like an eighteenth century general leading his merry troops down from the hills into glorious battle. Two other standouts on the LP ("Into the Valley" and "Hope and Glory") maintain the style but are different enough to keep things exciting. (The US release substitutes two tracks and has an alternate song order.)

Bill Nelson produced the Skids' (with a new drummer and bassist) second album, **Days in Europa**, but the match-up proved problematic. In polishing and refining the band's sound even a little, he smoothed off the vital edge. There's less gusto in the grooves, although some songs (like "Working for the Yankee Dollar," "Charade" and "Animation") shine through regardless.

The lineup remained stable for **The Absolute Game** while a new producer took over the helm. Mick Glossop did a good job presenting Jobson's widening vision amidst semi-grandiose arrangements, but the blooming Jobson ego had led the band a long way from its early forthrightness. Parts of **The Absolute Game** are just arty pretense, but the inclusion of substantial, engaging material makes it a reasonable addition to the collection. **Strength Through Joy**, a bonus album of finished studio outtakes, came with early pressings. Interesting, but not essential.

After a few more changes in the lineup, only Jobson and bassist-cum-multi-instrumentalist Russell Webb remained Skids. Joined by an all-star guest cast of ten, they made **Joy**, a failed concept album about Scotland. To call it bad is curt but realistic.

Fanfare, released after the group finally (mercifully) ceased, is an excellent compilation of singles and album tracks that serves as the perfect introduction to the Skids' magic.

Afterlife: Adamson formed Big Country and furthered the Skids' pan-ethnic experimentation in service of arena metal; Jobson, after several wanky albums of pretentious poesy, formed the Armoury Show, and has followed his former bandmate back into the rock'n'roll fray. [iar]
See also *Armoury Show, Big Country.*

SKREWDRIVER

All Skrewed Up (Chiswick/nr) 1977

In 1977, Blackpool skinheads Skrewdriver were different from their primal punk contemporaries in outlook and dress, preferring hardnosed working class style and self-indulgent hedonist ethics to trendy nihilism and social awareness. Their back-to-basics LP plays at 45 rpm and includes an odd choice of material in the Who's "Won't Get Fooled Again." Periodic rumours of Skrewdriver's reformation and new recording projects continue into the '80s. Unfortunately, the band also acquired a reputation as National Fronters, causing a fracas when gossip sheets accused Madness' Suggs of being a friend. [iar]

SLAPP HAPPY

See *Henry Cow.*

SLAUGHTER AND THE DOGS

Do It Dog Style (Decca/nr) 1978
Live at the Belle Vue (Rabid/nr) 1979
The Way We Were (Thrush/nr) 1983

SLAUGHTER

Bite Back (DJM) 1980

This Manchester punk group released the first 45 on that city's pioneering independent label, Rabid Records, and were regular giggers at London's famed Roxy Club, managing to appear in the punk documentary Don Letts filmed there. Unfortunately, Slaughter and the Dogs were more timely than talented, and **Bite Back**, their lone internationally-issued LP, is totally undistinguished guitar-based rock noise, produced by ex-Mott the Hoople drummer Dale Griffin. [iar]

SLICKEE BOYS

Hot and Cool EP (nr/Dacoit) 1976
Separated Vegetables (nr/Dacoit) 1977 (nr/Limp) 1980
Mersey, Mersey Me EP (nr/Limp) 1978
Third EP (nr/Limp) 1979
Here to Stay (Ger. Line) 1982
Cybernetic Dreams of Pi (nr/Twin/Tone) 1983
Uh Oh . . . No Breaks! (nr/Twin/Tone) 1985

Washington, DC's Slickee Boys have been scene stalwarts for a decade; they've developed over the years from a punky rock'n'roll band with an affection for classic English forebears into a far more individualistic and American band with lots of their own ideas.

Hot and Cool is a 7-inch EP with one original (by leader/guitarist Kim Kane) joining arcane covers like "Psycho Daisies" and "Brand New Cadillac." The German-only **Here to Stay** recapitulates the contents of that and the two subsequent EPs, plus a couple of independent singles. Guileless, earnest, occasionally embarrassing, bizarre in its selection of covers (from Talking Heads to the Grass Roots), often exciting in its basic enthusiasm, **Here to Stay** is an unprepossessing, entertaining collection of homemade records by a developing band.

On **Cybernetic Dreams of Pi** the Slickee Boys play brawny, good-natured power pop. Songs like "When I Go to the Beach" (jolly surf parody), "Pushin' My Luck" and a breezy version of Status Quo's

ancient "Pictures of Matchstick Men" may be a bit glib, but are loads of fun nonetheless. **Uh Oh . . . No Breaks!** finds the quintet plundering their own vaults for material to re-record. No matter: all thirteen tracks display the same vim and charm of their first record, but scads more skill and smarts. Melodies, hooks and energy to spare, variety and clever lyrics—these boys may not be the *dernier mot*, but they *are* worthwhile. [iar/jy]

SLITS

Cut (Island/Antilles) 1979
Retrospective (Y-Rough Trade/nr) 1980
Return of the Giant Slits (CBS/nr) 1981

Lurching into existence during the original 1977 explosion of pre-commercial London punk, the all-female Slits wrested the anyone-can-make-a-band-so-why-not-do-it-yourself ethos away from the traditionally no-women-allowed rock brotherhood and unselfconsciously paraded their stunningly amateur rock noise with support from bands like the Clash. While on the road as part of a punk package tour, the Slits were immortalized in all their primitive glory in *The Punk Rock Movie.* Looking back at the group's tentative beginnings now, it's clear that while the Slits may have been truly awful, they weren't much worse than many of their male contemporaries, and undoubtedly a damn sight better and smarter than some. It was probably fortunate, however, that several years elapsed before the Slits got around to recording a debut album; by the time they reached the studio, Viv Albertine, Ari Upp and Tessa, joined by drummer Budgie (later of Siouxsie and the Banshees) had become reasonably competent players. Spare and rudimentary, but bursting with novel ideas and rampant originality, **Cut**—produced brilliantly by Dennis Bovell—forges a powerful white- reggae hybrid that serves as a solid underpinning for Ari Upp's wobbly, semi-melodic vocals.

"**Retrospective**" (so-called; the LP has no real title) is a coverless, no-info-provided authorized bootleg consisting of early (pre-reggae) studio doodles and live tracks that should really have stayed in the can (or wherever).

Return of the Giant Slits, released originally with a bonus 45 featuring an extra track and an interview with the band (both appended to the cassette version) turned toward African, rather than Jamaican rhythms, and attempted to make the Slits slightly more commercially accessible. [iar]
See also *New Age Steppers.*

SLOW CHILDREN

Slow Children (Ensign) 1981
Mad About Town (Ensign) 1982

Although originally a full-sized Los Angeles club band, by the time of these two LPs, Slow Children had diminished to a duo: Pal Shazar (vocals) and Andrew Chinich (vocals/guitar), with the aid of producers/players Jules Shear and Stephen Hague and others, including Translator drummer David Scheff. Signed after relocating to England, Slow Children's first album was available in the UK almost a year before a revised version appeared in America. **Slow Children** includes their dance semi-hit, "Spring in Fialta," a heavy but skittish beat layered with anxious synth noises and Shazar's dramatic synth vocals. The album isn't otherwise much like that track, but one constant factor is intellectually bright lyrics that seem too good for the music.

Mad About Town has a strong second side, with energetic tunes supporting more smart words; the first side, however, is distinctly underwhelming, failing to anchor ideas with grabby musical settings. By and large, Slow Children make records that are more suited to reading than listening. [iar]

SLY & ROBBIE

See *Sly Dunbar*.

SMALTS

See *Minny Pops*.

KENDRA SMITH/DAVID ROBACK/KEITH MITCHELL

Fell from the Sun EP (Rough Trade/Serpent-Enigma) 1984

VARIOUS ARTISTS

Rainy Day (Rough Trade/Llama) 1983

Gathering most of the nouveau Los Angeles pop family tree for a vinylized mix'n'match collection of classic covers, **Rainy Day** is Rain Parader David Roback's project. And a glorious achievement it is: Bangle Susanna Hoffs makes you love her even more, singing "I'll Be Your Mirror" and "I'll Keep It with Mine"; Michael Quercio of the Three O'Clock does "Sloop John B" and "Rainy Day, Dream Away"; Roback sings and plays mind-bending acid guitar on an excerpt from the Who's "A Quick One"; former Dream Syndicate bassist Kendra Smith also excels on "Flying on the Ground Is Wrong" and Alex Chilton's "Holocaust." All told, a brilliantly conceived and executed piece of interpretative source-material nostalgia.

With drummer Keith Mitchell and guitarist Juan Gomez, Roback and Smith subsequently formed a quartet known as Clay Allison. The group issued a single, but dropped a member and shed the name before adding two new songs to fill out **Fell from the Sun**. Smith's vocals perfectly meld with the subtle mood music—a pleasant drone with translucent elegance that resembles the Velvet Underground at their most restrained. Lovely and touching.

Latest reports have Smith and Roback working as a duo named Opal. [iar]

PATTI SMITH

Horses (Arista) 1975

PATTI SMITH GROUP

Radio Ethiopia (Arista) 1976
Easter (Arista) 1978 (Fame/nr) 1983
Wave (Arista) 1979

Patti Smith was already an established poet and playwright on the New York underground literary scene when she expanded her repertoire to include rock criticism (her work appeared mostly in *Creem*

and *Rolling Stone*) and public performance, first reading her poetry and then singing with minimalist musical accompaniment provided by Lenny Kaye, professional rock writer and (then) amateur guitarist. Sharing Tom Verlaine's fascination with nineteenth century decadent literati like Rimbaud, Baudelaire and Verlaine (the original), Smith drifted into the fledgling New York rock underground, becoming an enormously popular performer/ figure. A debut single ("Piss Factory") was privately released, featuring Smith, Kaye and pianist Richard Sohl. By the time Smith signed to Arista in 1975, Ivan Kral had joined her group, sharing guitar and bass chores with Kaye, and drummer Jay Dee Daugherty had been lured away from Lance Loud's Mumps.

Horses, produced by John Cale, broke a lot of stylistic ground, thanks to Smith's wild singing and disconcerting lyrics, but it also showcased inspired amateurism in the playing and an emotional intensity that recalled the Velvet Underground at its most powerful. Too idiosyncratic to be generally influential, **Horses** is a brilliant explosion of talent by a challenging, unique artist pioneering a sound not yet fashionable or, by general standards, even acceptable.

With **Radio Ethiopia**, the Patti Smith Group made an effort to drop **Horses**' clumsiness in favor of a more refined, organic sound and grander artistic pretensions. Smith plays a lot of guitar on the album, and producer Jack Douglas renders the proceedings with great seriousness. Tracks like "Ask the Angels" and "Pumping (My Heart)" have a nearly routine rock sound, made special largely by Smith's untrained but expressive voice and, of course, her highly individual songwriting.

Bruce Brody replaced Richard Sohl for **Easter**, and Jimmy Iovine produced the album, which contains the band's big hit single, "Because the Night," co-written by Bruce Springsteen. Having proven that they could play as well as most bands, the PSG set out to make something of their sound; Iovine did a fine job. By this point a much more mature singer, Smith sounds confident and striking and the band keeps pace.

After the success of **Easter**, **Wave** stumbles, evidently due to overconfidence. Todd Rundgren's production seems to have been an error in judgment. Smith's lyrics are at their most self-indulgent; although songs like "Dancing Barefoot" and "Frederick" are accessible and memorable, much of the record is unfocused, half-baked and insufferable. A misguided cover of the Byrds' "Do You Want to Be (A Rock 'n' Roll Star)" rings phony and hollow.

Smith's musical career ended after **Wave**; she moved to Detroit and married ex-MC5 guitarist Fred Smith. The two have stayed far from the spotlight—and the press—since. [iar]
See also *Lenny Kaye Connection*.

T.V. SMITH'S EXPLORERS

The Last Words of the Great Explorer (Kaleidoscope/Epic) 1981
Channel Five (Expulsion/nr) 1983

Tim Smith was the leader of the Adverts, who clung on long enough

to make two albums. After they expired, Smith formed the Explorers—originally a trio, but expanded to a five-piece by the time of their first album. A far cry from the stripped-down guitar drone of the Adverts, **The Last Words** uses synthesizer and slick musicianship to mold an engaging dance album that benefits from Smith's strong voice and inventive songwriting. There are touches of Sparks, the Only Ones, Duran Duran (figuratively speaking; DD came after) and others, making it a great record from an unexpectedly gifted performer. [iar]

SMITHS

The Smiths (Rough Trade/Sire) 1984
Hatful of Hollow (Rough Trade/nr) 1984
Meat Is Murder (Rough Trade/Sire) 1985
The Queen Is Dead (Rough Trade/Sire) 1986

You'd be perfectly within your rights to hate the Smiths. With the possible exception of the Violent Femmes, no act since Jonathan Richman has raised blatant self-absorption to such a high level. Mancunian singer Morrissey and company stand for the traditional values of selfishness, self-pity and the unbearable anguish of love. His melancholy romantic sensibility makes Elizabeth Barrett Browning sound like Nelson Algren.

The key to the Smith's enormous success is the no-nonsense band's offsetting Morrissey's flightiness with classic Modern Lovers-style riff-rock. Johnny Marr's spare, hooky guitar creates a seriously compelling underground pop sound with a simplicity more telling than all of the singer's unwanted confessions.

The Smiths boasts ten near-perfect tunes (eleven on the US edition, which adds "This Charming Man"), over which Morrissey sings about the bittersweet agonies of coming out. He overindulges to the point of sounding almost like a parody of a lounge singer, but goes far enough to make it sound more daring than forced. With lines alternately funny ("Hand in glove/The sun shines out of our behinds") and clunky ("Does the body rule the mind/Or does the mind rule the body/I dunno"), the album dares you to resist it and then makes it very difficult to do so.

The English-only **Hatful of Hollow** is a generous collection of singles and early live-on-the-radio takes. It doubles **The Smiths**' best cuts and beats its lesser material. It also adds the tremeloed single "How Soon Is Now?," which takes the heaviest art-rock dance groove since U2's "Pride (in the Name of Love)" and throws the lines "I am the son/and the heir/Of a shyness that is criminally vulgar" in its path. Quite a formidable obstacle, but the groove wins out. The Smiths in a nutshell.

Meat Is Murder is both less frilly and less appealing than prior efforts. Morrissey is nearly as dry as the rest of the band, and the whole thing sounds two-dimensional. And while anyone at all disposed toward melancholy can accept some of his indulgences in that direction, who can forgive the vegetarian self- righteousness (that's right) of the title track? The US edition adds "How Soon Is

Now?" to the program.

Bassist Andy Rourke left the Smiths in April 1986 and was replaced by Craig Gannon, an early guitarist in Aztec Camera. [jl]

SNAKEFINGER

Chewing Hides the Sound (Virgin/ Ralph) 1980
Greener Postures (Do It/Ralph) 1981
Manual of Errors (nr/Ralph) 1982
Against the Grain (nr/Ralph) 1983

Although his music career began in the early '60s and he recorded two albums with English pub-rockers Chilli Willi and the Red Hot Peppers, guitarist Phil "Snakefinger" Lithman is best known for his association with the Residents and his resultant Ralph Records solo career. On songs like "Sinister Exaggerator" and their savage reworking of "Satisfaction," Snakefinger's deranged slidework and upside-down solos—trickily playing the wrong notes in the right places—adds a deviant and immediately recognizable edge.

Snakefinger's first solo outing was "The Spot," a cutely weird little single that ended up on **Chewing Hides the Sound**. But his first two albums pointed up Snakey's major weakness as a solo artist: even with copious musical and technical input from the Residents, he just isn't that weird (for a Ralph act, that is). Skeletal arrangements and over-reliance on clichéd rhythm-box beats don't help, either. Nonetheless, swell subsequent singles ("Man in the Dark Sedan" and Kraftwerk's "The Model") became modest underground hits.

Around the time of **Greener Postures**, Snakefinger hit the club circuit with a backing band variously known as Bast and the Dead Residents. The presence of steady company (including Beefheart alumnus Eric Feldman) makes **Manual of Errors** an improved listening experience; juxtaposed against (relatively) straight rock backing, Snakefinger's innate weirdness comes across as even more subversive.

Against the Grain is an intelligent compilation of his Ralph work and provides the perfect entry to this unique guitarist's demi-warped world. Everything you'd want to hear is here—from "The Spot" through "Beatnik Party"—plus a great unreleased track, "I Love You Too Much to Respect You." [rnp/iar]

SNATCH

See *Judy Nylon*.

SNEAKERS

Sneakers EP (nr/Carnivorous) 1976
In the Red EP (nr/Car) 1978

The 7-inch **Sneakers** EP—six songs engineered by Don Dixon—marked the first vinyl appearance of a seminal but little-heard band containing North Carolina rock scene VIPs Chris Stamey, Will Rigby and Mitch Easter. To get the folklore out of the way, Stamey and Rigby later founded the dB's; Stamey went on to a solo career; Don Dixon became a busy producer (working with R.E.M., among many others); Easter is also a well-known producer, fronts Let's Active and operates Mitch's Drive-In Studio, one of the hotbeds of new American rock.

S

The 12-inch **In the Red**, made after Stamey had relocated to New York, was really a reunion of sorts. Here, instigators Stamey and Easter combine their Angloid pop/rock with brooding, quasi-baroque clavinet, the saunter of a Parisian *boulevardier*, even some avant-gardish desperation, all with an air of sophistication received in innocence. [jg/iar]

See also *dB's, Let's Active, Chris Stamey.*

SOFT BOYS

A Can of Bees (Two Crabs/nr) 1979 & 1984 (Aura/nr) 1980
Underwater Moonlight (Armageddon/nr) 1980 (Can. Attic) 1980
Two Halves for the Price of One (Armageddon/nr) 1981
Invisible Hits (Midnight Music/nr) 1983
Live at the Portland Arms [tape] (Midnight Music/nr) 1983
Wading Through a Ventilator EP (De Lorean/nr) 1984

From Canterbury they came circa 1977: a brilliant songwriter leading a two-guitar band that revered the Byrds, the Beatles and Syd Barrett's Pink Floyd most of all. Some called it the start of a psychedelic revival, but the Soft Boys' verve and wild-eyed sincerity made it more of a post-psychedelic awakening.

The Boys' earliest non-45 recording was their last to be released and contains three otherwise unissued cuts. Featuring an early lineup, **Wading Through a Ventilator** shows a promising weirdness that sets it apart from what most everyone else was doing in 1977, but reveals singer/guitarist Robyn Hitchcock as a still-embryonic songwriter. He got off a few good ones on **A Can of Bees**, by which time guitarist Kimberly Rew had joined the band, but the rest declines disappointingly into grating medium-metal power pop. That same year (1979), the Soft Boys recorded an uncharacteristically all-acoustic live tape that was later sold by mail to buyers of **Invisible Hits** as **Live at the Portland Arms** and contains the most bizarre assortment of cover versions imaginable. But then cover versions were always one of the band's strong suits, from Hitchcock's intense reading of John Lennon's "Cold Turkey" on the first LP to his hilarious ravings on "That's When Your Heartaches Begin" (on the tape). Also of historic interest are two Syd Barrett numbers: "Astronomy Domine" on **Two Halves for the Price of One**, a grab-bag of material (some recorded live) mixed in both chronology and quality, and "Vegetable Man" on the Canadian issue of **Underwater Moonlight**.

The core of the Soft Boys canon are **Invisible Hits** (recorded in 1979) and **Underwater Moonlight**. Some form of insanity prevented the timely release of the former; it shows Hitchcock at his best—maturely immature and crazily serious—as he races from hearty lust ("Let Me Put It Next to You") to vulnerable harangue ("Empty Girl," "Blues in the Dark"). Few other albums capture the humor, pathos, anger and grotesquerie of man/woman so well.

Underwater Moonlight is one of the new wave's finest half-dozen albums and unquestionably its most unjustly underrated one. "I Wanna Destroy You" is a rant against war and intolerance; "Insanely Jealous" builds to a frenzy—twice; "I Got the Hots for You" contains some of the funniest erotic lines ever written. This album has everything— melody, power, wit, laughs and heart, not to mention a great guitar sound.

Hitchcock remains one of the most unique songwriters to have emerged from the new wave (whatever, in retrospect, that was). He reunited with the original Soft Boys rhythm section of Andy Metcalfe and Morris Windsor for his latest solo recordings, which stand with his best work. Rew went on to form Katrina and the Waves. [mf]

See also *Robyn Hitchcock, Katrina and the Waves, Kimberley Rew.*

SOFT CELL

Non-Stop Erotic Cabaret (Some Bizzare/Sire) 1981
Non-Stop Ecstatic Dancing EP (Some Bizzare/Sire) 1982
The Art of Falling Apart (Some Bizzare/Sire) 1983
Soul Inside EP (Some Bizzare/Sire) 1983
This Last Night in Sodom (Some Bizzare/Sire) 1984

Singer Marc Almond and keyboardist David Ball performed a minor miracle in 1981, taking an obscure soul song and turning it into a most atypical synthesizer tune, coming up in the process with a worldwide smash hit that rode *Billboard*'s chart for almost a year. "Tainted Love" (recorded originally by Gloria Jones) is as passionate and desperately sleazy as Kraftwerk is cool and clean. The Almond/Ball originals on **Non-Stop Erotic Cabaret** don't always cut so deeply, but all offer decadent fun. Among them: "Sex Dwarf," highlighted by a nagging synthesizer riff, and "Say Hello, Wave Goodbye," blatant though stirring sentimentality. Almond's breathy, insinuating vocals and Ball's surprisingly varied electronic and acoustic keyboards (kudos to producer Mike Thorne) never part pat.

Non-Stop Ecstatic Dancing, half an hour (six tracks) of dance mixes, intends primarily to divert and manages to overcome its basic filler role. Highlights include a languid version of "Where Did Our Love Go?" and the unforgettably neurotic "Insecure . . . Me?"

It's too bad Almond and Ball didn't part ways before descending into the embarrassing self-parody of **The Art of Falling Apart**. With Ball's keyboards growing progressively cooler, Almond tries ever more desperately to invoke a sleazy atmosphere and just ends up sounding silly. The nadir—indeed, the worst Soft Cell effort of all time—is the pitiful ten-minute Jimi Hendrix medley of "Hey Joe," "Purple Haze" and "Voodoo Chile (Slight Return)" that comes on a bonus 12-inch 45. It's like a five-year-old trying to read Shakespeare. **Soul Inside** is a collection of odds and ends, including a version of "You Only Live Twice (007 Theme)," two remixes and a live radio session.

This Last Night in Sodom contains further fruitless flailing, as titles like "The Best Way to Kill" and "Mr. Self Destruct" attest. After this,

Soft Cell broke up once and for all. Outside of one solo album, little has been heard from Ball; Almond has released a number of records. [jy]

See also *Marc Almond, Dave Ball.*

SOLID SENDERS

Solid Senders (Virgin/nr) 1978

After leaving Dr. Feelgood, guitarist Wilko Johnson formed a likeminded quartet which lasted only long enough to record this one album. (Johnson subsequently made solo records and formed a 1982 band with Lew Lewis.) Based in R&B, but with other evident influences (reggae, blues, pop), **Solid Senders**—a studio disc plus a bonus live 12-inch — downplays Johnson's frenetic guitar brilliance in favor of a group approach, which leaves sonic room for John Potter's keyboards to share the spotlight. Old-fashioned, but extremely lively. [iar]

SONIC YOUTH

Sonic Youth EP (nr/Neutral) 1982
Confusion Is Sex (nr/Neutral) 1983
Kill Yr. Idols EP (Ger. Zensor) 1983
Bad Moon Rising (Blast First/Homestead) 1985
Death Valley 69 EP (Blast First/Homestead) 1985
EVOL (Blast First/SST) 1986

Latter-day rock'n'roll revolutionaries have shown a marked tendency toward swift burnout. They reveal their raw vision to the world; the world—being the philistine place that it is—turns away; the musicians move on. Sonic Youth, unlike so many of the noise bands that formed in New York in the early part of this decade, has had the fortitude to stick it out and develop its ideas beyond the original stances. As a result, the band has gotten better and better, and can now articulate its rough sounds with chilling beauty.

The debut EP proves that a reliance on artsy posturing can get boring in an awful hurry. Rigidly defined beats and disembodied poetic vocals eviscerate Sonic Youth's principal weapon—jangling, ringing, dissonant guitar noise. This disc is no fun.

Confusion Is Sex gives the guitars freer rein, and the result is a happily anarchic and intense mess. The tortuous "She's in a Bad Mood" captures its subject matter like few songs before it, and a crude cover of Iggy's "I Wanna Be Your Dog" proves that the artistes can rock. The record alternates between pulse and drone; its quiet spaces quickly get cluttered with weirdly tuned, percussive guitars, often bowed or struck with a drumstick.

Kill Yr. Idols reprises two tunes from **Confusion Is Sex** and adds three similarly twisted tracks. Like **Confusion**, this EP is dark and haunting, particularly on "Early American," where the guitars ring like macabre bells.

Bad Moon Rising brings Sonic Youth into the light, and shows a quantum developmental leap. The sounds are still harsh—feedback, distortion and dissonance—but the group uses them to create a variety of effects and moods. Like many records made in 1984 and 1985, the album is a statement about America and, while avoiding the ennoblement of the mythological common man, does capture both the beauty

and creepiness of the frontier west of the Bowery. "Death Valley 69," recorded with Lydia Lunch, sounds like X on a bad trip, and puts the band's screaming guitars into a straight rocker. The rest of the disc is more painterly and less propulsive; the band gets its explosiveness from the quiet sections, where interwoven guitar parts hint at jarring disorder. (Creedence fans should remain calm—Sonic Youth does not cover the song from which the record takes its name.) The **Death Valley 69 EP**, its title track a reprise from the LP, also culls one track each from the previous three discs, along with the heretofore unissued anarchy of "Satan Is Boring."

The material on **EVOL** is presented in more basic song structures, giving the band more accessibility and versatility than ever before without diluting their brutal strength one iota. Command of their resources is so great than they can make rackety shards of atonal guitars sound almost catchy on tracks like "Green Light," while "Shadow of a Doubt" and the end of "Expressway to Yr Skull" (listed as "Madonna, Sean and Me" on the back cover) both take raw, jagged sounds and blend them into a peaceful stillness. **EVOL** is a very impressive album wherein Sonic Youth makes the leap from great noise band to great band.

For fanatics and collectors, there have also been legitimate limited edition live albums and cassettes, as well as bootlegs. [jl/dgs]

SORE THROAT

Sooner Than You Think (Hurricane/nr) 1979

An interesting though mediocre band, Sore Throat started as punks, yet quickly developed attributes that were both sophisticated and precocious, using horns and dance rhythms long before their voguishness began. Sore Throat's lone album displays the sextet's broad range—from slow ballad to high-energy rocker—as well as a plain set of songs, but, unfortunately, no particularly absorbing moments. More impressive for its prescience than content, file under "Promising but a Few Years Early," next to Deaf School. [iar]

SORROWS

Teenage Heartbreak (Epic/Pavillion) 1980
Love Too Late (nr/Pavillion) 1981

The mid-'70s New York club scene had a large population of Anglo-pop bands, playing Merseybeat root music as accurately as possible. The Sorrows were formed in 1977 from the remains of the Poppees, a minor member of the skinny tie brigade; two years later the Sorrows had a major-league record deal.

Teenage Heartbreak, a dozen melodic originals, isn't bad, blending all the right ingredients with enough aggression to shun wimpiness. In another time and place, the Sorrows might have been a nonsalacious Knack.

The coup on **Love Too Late** is the production credit—Shel Talmy, the man behind all the early Kinks/Who records. Disappointingly (although the same thing happened when Talmy produced surfrockers Jon and the Nightriders), the sound is not exceptional, and the record is basically similar to the group's first outing. [iar]

SOULSONIC FORCE
See *Afrika Bambaataa*.

SOUND

Jeopardy (Korova/nr) 1980
From the Lions Mouth (Korova/nr) 1981
All Fall Down (WEA/nr) 1982
Shock of Daylight EP (Statik/A&M) 1984
Heads and Hearts (Statik/nr) 1985
In the Hothouse (Statik/nr) 1985

It's hard to understand why this Liverpool quartet can't find commercial success. Although inconsistent, at their best the Sound's excellent neo-pop bears favorable comparison to the Psychedelic Furs and Echo and the Bunnymen. **Jeopardy** has a stark, beautiful quality, the material given direct exposure rather a production bath. Adrian Borland's vocals are sincere and gripping; the musical attack is both subtle and aggressive. **From the Lions Mouth** builds on that firm foundation with a fuller sound that recalls U2. Unfortunately, **All Fall Down** is dismal, offering material, performances and production that lack flair, emotion and direction.

Shock of Daylight—a six-song mini-album—is a strong return, building melodic, dramatic songs on a gutsy bass/drums drive, overlaying guitar, keyboards and even brass to create an attractively textured and varied sound. Following that triumph, however, it was time for another setback: Despite intermittently winning presentation, most of the songs on **Heads and Hearts** aren't very good, and Borland's singing drifts too often towards self-important histrionics. [cpl/iar]

SOURIS DEGLINGUEE

La Souris Deglinguee (Fr. New Rose) 1981

This Parisian punk quartet had a Vietnamese lyricist/guitarist; their songs (all sung in French) concern topics like rebellion, racism and political freedom. A swell translation of American and English rock idioms, they combined the best musical aspects of early Clash, New York Dolls, Eddie and the Hot Rods and the Stray Cats. Now defunct, la Souris Deglinguee ("The Collapsing Mouse" or thereabouts) made great, energetic rock that's forceful and fun. They were easily good enough to compete internationally, but never became known outside their homeland. [iar]

SOUTHERN DEATH CULT
See *Cult*.

SPANDAU BALLET

Journeys to Glory (Reformation-Chrysalis/Chrysalis) 1981
Diamond (Reformation-Chrysalis/Chrysalis) 1982
True (Reformation-Chrysalis/Chrysalis) 1983
Parade (Reformation-Chrysalis) 1984
The Singles Collection (Chrysalis) 1985

Viewed at the start by some as adventurous and trendsetting, Spandau Ballet's ludicrous garb and chic disco were both dubious new wave developments, leading to much replication. Head poseur Tony Hadley and his four cohorts found great club success with a heavily rhythmic brand of distant funk-rock dolled up with synthesizers and stentorian singing. Produced by Richard James Burgess, **Journeys to Glory** contains one great dance hit—the tightly-compressed riffer, "To Cut a Long Story Short," and a batch of retread variations thereon. **Diamond** added horns and several other reformulated moves, producing a few more estimable British chart smashes ("Chant No. 1," "Paint Me Down"). Possessing only limited talent themselves, Spandau opened the floodgates to a wave of superior electrodance bands who had little trouble creatively eclipsing them.

Spandau's next two albums found them abandoning synthesizers and high-pressure funk for schmaltzy pop with soul pretensions. Working with the production team of Tony Swain and Steve Jolley, the fivesome made **True** and **Parade**, the first yielding several attractive blends of energy, melody, warmth and stylishness ("Communication," "Lifeline") as well as some of the sappiest MOR in memory ("True," which became an enormous hit.) Generally less wimped-out, **Parade** nonetheless continues the bland chart fare, with the poles best represented by "Revenge for Love" (good) and "Only When You Leave" (egregiously mellow).

Amidst a legal tumult between Spandau and Chrysalis, the label issued a worthwhile collection of the band's singles. [iar]

SPARKS

Halfnelson (nr/Bearsville) 1971
Sparks (Bearsville) 1971 (Warner Bros./nr) 1975
A Woofer in Tweeter's Clothing (Bearsville) 1972 (Warner Bros./nr) 1975
Kimono My House (Island) 1974
Propaganda (Island) 1974
Indiscreet (Island) 1975
Big Beat (Island/Columbia) 1976
Introducing Sparks (CBS/Columbia) 1977
No. 1 in Heaven (Virgin/Elektra) 1979 (Fame/nr) 1982
Best of Sparks (Island/nr) 1979
Terminal Jive (Virgin/nr) 1979
Whomp That Sucker (Why-Fi-RCA) 1981
Angst in My Pants (Atlantic) 1982
Sparks in Outer Space (Atlantic) 1983
Pulling Rabbits Out of a Hat (Atlantic) 1984

Ron and Russell Mael—two enormously talented wiseacres from Los Angeles—have influenced numerous bands through their own records and outside projects; it's possible to trace many contemporary musical trends back to the pair's prescient and/or trailblazing efforts. And while their recording career has the consistency of chunky peanut butter, some of their albums are truly wonderful in a number of stylistic modes. Sparks remain unpredictably capable of greatness each time they enter the studio.

As an art-rock quintet called Halfnelson, Sparks made their earliest, misanthropic efforts to appeal to the neurotic nouveau pop segment of 1971 America via a debut album produced by Todd Rundgren. First released as **Halfnelson** (by Halfnelson), it was promptly withdrawn, repackaged and reissued as **Sparks** (by Sparks). That original band—sort of Marlene Dietrich meets the Stooges—included Earle Mankey, later a producer (and artist) of some note and merit, and his brother Jim. The album is a subtle and brilliant exposition of unique talent, displaying the Maels' remarkable facility for bizarre, dadaist lyrics and Russell's scarifying falsetto. **A Woofer in Tweeter's Clothing** refined, energized and improved on the first LP, and is one of Sparks' triumphant achievements; a demented blueprint of incomprehensible weirdness. Many hated them, few heard them, but none who did forgot them on the basis of this utterly individual effort. (The first two LPs were subsequently packaged together and reissued in Britain.)

Moving to London and recruiting an all-new set of sidemen, keyboardist Ron and singer Russell hooked up with producer Muff Winwood and made a series of singles (many included on the first two Island albums) that turned them into enormously popular glam-pop teen idols. Mixing prolix and profoundly funny wordplay with killer hooks and a solid guitar-and-piano-based sound, Sparks were the forerunners (and to some extent instigators) of the skinny tie Anglo-pop revival that swept America a few years later. After two brilliant and incredibly formulaic albums (**Kimono My House** and **Propaganda**), the gimmickry wore thin; **Indiscreet**, produced pompously by Tony Visconti, has some terribly boring, unbelievably overblown numbers amidst the succinct pop smashes. Sparks were outgrowing bubblegum.

The Maels, their lock on the top of Britain's charts ended, fired their band and returned to America to begin a very bad career patch, starting with **Big Beat**. Despite a bit of momentum (and perhaps material) left over from their previous work, it's basically a poor homecoming. (The band for this record included Tuff Darts leader Jeff Salen on guitar, ex-Milk 'n'Cookies bassist Sal Maida and drummer Hilly Michaels.) The subsequent **Introducing** LP, recorded with LA session men, is far worse; Sparks' creative low-point.

The group's complex saga then began to involve Giorgio Moroder, who produced **No. 1 in Heaven**, converting the one-time pure-guitar-poppers into a driving Eurodisco synthesizer machine, pounding out repetitive drum-laden dance grooves. Only semi-successful, musically speaking, it does deserve credit for predating the entry of countless other rock groups onto the high-tech dance-floor. **Terminal Jive**, the only Sparks album not released in the US, tempers the funk but suffers a serious personality loss, the result of the Maels' co-writing too much of the material with others.

Leaving the disco behind, Sparks next began an alliance with a Moroder associate, German producer Mack. They recorded **Whomp That Sucker** in Munich with their first steady band since **Indiscreet**: David Kendrick, Leslie Bohem and Bob Haag (who also work on their own as Gleaming Spires). The songs reclaim some of their early pop wit, but with a maturity and dignity not previously typical. It's an improved but still transitional record, leading them out of the creative woods, but not yet operating at peak power, despite some really swell numbers.

Angst in My Pants, however, *is* their triumphant return, a full-fledged top-notch collection of tunes with offbeat humor, winning melodies and excellent arrangements, displaying the benefits of touring and working within a proper band context album. It's the first Sparks album that belongs in their hall of fame alongside **Woofer** and **Kimono**. The self-produced **In Outer Space** features then-Go-Go Jane Wiedlin duetting with Russell on two songs, and is a mixed creative success, with a shortage of stunning lyrics and songs that drag presenting the biggest obstacles. Remarkably (but wisely) sticking with the same band, the equally inconclusive **Pulling Rabbits Out of a Hat** has better material but less personality and again only a handful of standout tracks.

Ron and Russell have (together) done numerous projects for other artists, including production and collaborative songwriting (or just lyrics). Their clientele has included Telex, Lio and the Go-Go's. [iar]
See also *Bijou, Telex*.

SPEAR OF DESTINY

Grapes of Wrath (Burning Rome-Epic/nr) 1983
One Eyed Jacks (Burning Rome-Epic/nr) 1984
World Service (Burning Rome-Epic/nr) 1985

Following the stormy existence of their Theatre of Hate, singer/guitarist Kirk Brandon and bassist Stan Stammers launched Spear of Destiny, which has so far issued three albums. **Grapes of Wrath**, produced by Nick Launay, unveils a straightforward guitar/bass/drums quartet; Andy Mackay-like saxophone work serves as the sole distinguishing tonal component. Brandon's songs are a drag—spare, dirgey things with hopeless quasi-Scottish melodies and self-important, insignificant lyrics. Slight Nick Cave tendencies don't add enough extremism to salvage these effortlessly ignorable tracks.

One Eyed Jacks introduces a different, larger lineup (including ex-Tom Robinson Band drummer Dolph Taylor); the superior results lean alternately towards Big Country and Adam Ant. A basically inept vocalist with nothing in the way of a natural instrument, Brandon sings everything like he's rousing the troops for a final assault, a tactic that overpowers the flimsy tunes. Lacking a feel for full-blown majesty (like Richard Jobson), he's too zealous for his own good.

Co-produced by SOD and Rusty Egan, **World Service** is again hindered by Brandon's horrifically bad singing. On "Rocket Ship," he misses notes continually; on "Come Back," he makes the words sound almost unpronounceable. The operatic melody of the title track exposes all of his aural inadequacies at once. Soulful backing by a stellar vocal trio on three songs underscores the problem. [tr]

SPECIALS

The Specials (2-Tone) 1979 (Fame/nr) 1984
More Specials (2-Tone) 1980
Ghost Town EP (2-Tone) 1981

SPECIAL A.K.A.

The Special A.K.A. Live! EP (2-Tone/nr) 1980
In the Studio (2-Tone) 1984

Coventry's Specials spearheaded the ska revival in 1979, with leader/keyboard player Jerry Dammers also serving as head of 2-Tone, the band's pioneering label, which altered pop culture by releasing records by Madness, the Beat, Selecter and Bodysnatchers.

Produced by Elvis Costello, the Specials' debut LP also boasted the assistance of an elder statesman of bluebeat, trombonist Rico Rodriguez, an original member of the Skatalites. With the double lead vocals of Terry Hall and Neville Staples, guitarists Lynval Golding and Roddy Radiation and an impeccable rhythm section composed of John Bradbury and Sir Horace Gentleman, the Specials were widely acclaimed as the most exciting band to emerge in 1979, and their impact has continued well into the '80s. **The Specials** contains such classic 2-Tone (as the sound came to be called) numbers as "Doesn't Make It Alright," "Too Much Too Young," "A Message to You Rudy" and (on the American edition) the hit single "Gangsters." Mixing socially and politically aware lyrics with infectious dance rhythms, **The Specials** served as a virtual blueprint for many bands to follow. A few months later, the band released a hot 7-inch EP recorded live in London and Coventry that includes "The Guns of Navarone" and a side-long medley of covers dubbed "Skinhead Symphony."

Unfortunately, their momentum foundered with the release of **More Specials**, on which the group abandoned the fresh sound of their debut in favor of a more turgid experimental approach. (It does, however, contain some prime material: "Enjoy Yourself" and, only in the US, "Rat Race.") Rumours of internal strife abounded, and though the Specials managed to release the angry **Ghost Town** 12-inch—which went straight to number one in riot-torn Britain—shortly thereafter the original band succumbed to infighting. Hall, Staples and Golding split off to form the Fun Boy Three, and other members drifted off as well. It became clear that the Specials name had become merely a vehicle for whatever Dammers was up to, and it was three (reportedly arduous) years before he completed the "group's" third album, ironically titled **In the Studio**. Working with several steady associates (notably vocalists Stan Campbell and ex-Bodysnatcher Rhoda Dakar, in addition to loyal drummer John Bradbury) plus a large pool of sessioneers, Dammers filled the album with disarmingly varied, largely unstylized (nothing you would really call ska) essays on serious political topics ("Racist Friend," "Free Nelson Mandela," "Alcohol") leavened by the lighthearted "(What I Like Most About You Is Your) Girlfriend." Striking but troubled, the music's easygoing bounce belies the overweening polemicism. [jw/iar]

See also *Colour Field, Fun Boy Three, Selecter.*

SPECIMEN

Batastrophe EP (nr/Sire) 1983

Specimen was a leading exponent of the Batcave glam-punk non-movement; their demi-album (an American compilation of UK singles, all on the London label) blends T. Rex, Adam Ant, Ziggy Bowie, Gary Glitter and Tommy Steele into a reasonably innocuous breed of loud chart-pop played for all the inherent B-movie melodrama possible. "The Beauty of Poisin" and "Returning from a Journey" are both catchy tunes with big beats; the other four are swell, but not as memorable. [iar]

CHRIS SPEDDING

Chris Spedding (RAK/nr) 1976
Hurt (RAK/nr) 1977
Guitar Graffiti (RAK/nr) 1979
I'm Not Like Everybody Else (RAK/nr) 1980
Friday the 13th (nr/Passport) 1981
Mean and Moody (See for Miles/nr) 1985

One of the top rock session guitarists of the '70s, Chris Spedding has had a truly aberrant solo career. A veteran of numerous outfits starting in the '60s and the creator of several early solo albums, Spedding became known as a member of the Sharks, who made two rock'n'roll LPs in the wake of Free. After Sharks split up, Spedding released a succession of LPs that combine exquisite rock guitar with lackluster vocals and songs so vapid as to be virtually nonexistent. The "highlight" of **Chris Spedding** is a novelty item called "Guitar Jamboree" which features Spedding aping various guitar heros in a show of chameleonlike virtuosity. We pick up the story later in 1976, however, when he teamed up with the then-unrecorded Vibrators for a great single, "Pogo Dancing," the first punk dance record.

Hurt, Spedding's next LP, is a more solid follow-up, thanks to Chris Thomas' crisp production. The material is generally better, and there's one outstanding number, the ominous "Lone Rider."

Guitar Graffiti finds Spedding meandering again, producing a crass attempt to cash in on his new wave credibility (honestly established through his seminal alliances with the Sex Pistols and the Cramps, for whom he produced demos, and the Vibrators). The worthwhile track is "Hey, Miss Betty," the only one produced by Thomas; the song is a rocking homage to '50s bondage queen Betty Page.

In 1979, Spedding surprised everyone by joining the Necessaries, a New York band that included former Modern Lover Ernie Brooks. Though he kept a low profile—refusing featured billing within the group—the combination of his dark pop ditties and leader Ed Tomney's preppie sensibility never melded. Spedding added brilliant leads to Tomney's material, but his songwriting still lacked coherency, and in some instances he abandoned guitar for keyboards. Spedding split without fanfare after less than a year (he was gone by the time the Necessaries made their LP in 1981), returning to England to record **I'm Not Like Everybody Else**, an album of his Necessaries-era material.

In 1981, PVC released **Friday the 13th**, a live set with Spedding joined by former Sharks (and occasional Talking Head) bassist Busta Cherry Jones and New York drummer Tony Machine. Featuring a selection of songs from all the above-listed albums, **Friday the 13th** was released primarily as an ersatz retrospective of his RAK material. Showing off Spedding's guitar work in the context of some extended soloing, it's the best of the lot. [tr]

See also *Necessaries, Vibrators.*

SPHERICAL OBJECTS

Past and Parcel (Object Music/nr) 1978
Elliptical Optimism (Object Music/nr) 1979
Further Ellipses (Object Music/nr) 1980
No Man's Land (Object Music/nr) 1981

This Manchester group was centered around Steve Solamar, a terrible singer with an intensely personal viewpoint. His songs concern typical subject matter, but utter lack of self-consciousness invests his writing with more openness and introspection than you're probably hoping to hear.

The five Objects of **Past and Parcel** play simple rock that's lightweight but pleasant; Solamar's overbearing vocals spoil it. **Elliptical Optimism** has the same lineup and a more textured sound, featuring organ (prominently) and trumpet (occasionally). The songs are instrumentally inventive, while the vocals are less abrasive but no more interesting.

Further Ellipses takes a danceable turn, playing it smooth and rhythmic with more horns and synthesizer and less guitar. Solamar's singing continues to resemble David Thomas' but sounds too forced to be believably weird. The musical development is impressive, the songs are good, but the same old problem persists.

No Man's Land, which announces itself to be the final Spherical Objects album, has a different lineup from the previous three and sounds it. Gone are the keyboards and horns, replaced by rudimentary guitar/bass/drums plus patches of Solamar's wailing harmonica. There are some very pretty songs that are slowed down to add emotion, but overall the initial impression isn't as strong as **Further Ellipses**. A strange way to go out, **No Man's Land** is a record that slowly reveals itself to be quite lovely in spots. [iar]

SPITBALLS

Spitballs (Beserkley) 1978

Not a band, but a wonderful novelty album done at the height of Beserkley's prominence and activity. **Spitballs** employed everyone on the label's roster at the time—the Modern Lovers, Greg Kihn Band, Earthquake, Rubinoos and Sean Tyla—to record (in various permutations) fifteen rollicking cover versions of songs from the '60s. The resulting LP is a joyous celebration of the participants' roots, a thoroughly enjoyable collection of great songs performed with affection and élan. Samples of the repertoire: "The Batman Theme," "Chapel of Love," "Boris the Spider" and "Bad Moon Rising." [iar]

SPIZZ

Spizz History (Rough Trade/nr) 1982

ATHLETICO SPIZZ 80

Do a Runner (A&M) 1980

SPIZZLES

Spikey Dream Flowers (A&M) 1981

Whatever vocalist Spizz's incarnation—as Spizzoil, Spizzenergi, Spizzles, Athletico Spizz 80—he'll always be best remembered for one genuine novelty hit, 1979's "Where's Captain Kirk?" The charm and wit of that single was nowhere to be found on the subsequent **Do a Runner**, which was mired in the band's predilection for science fiction imagery. If it seems tough to conceive an album of time warps, time machines and almost nine minutes of "Airships," imagine how tough it would be repeat that formula; **Spikey Dream Flowers** offers robots, deadly war games and incessant runaway guitar with no place to go.

Spizz History compiles tracks from various Spizz eras. It includes "Where's Captain Kirk?" as well as "Soldier Soldier," a version of Roxy Music's "Virginia Plain" and a 1982 single, "Megacity," to recommend it; otherwise Spizz needs to recharge his batteries. [gf]

SPK

Information Overload Unit (Ger. Normal) 1980
Leichenschrei (Side Effects/Thermidor) 1982
Auto-Da-Fé (Ger. Walter Ulbricht) 1983
Machine Age Voodoo (WEA/Elektra) 1984

This Australia-based band—now a male/female couple—has variously explained their acronym as Surgical Penis Klinik, System Planning Korporation and Sozialistisches Patienten Kollektiv. Their music has likewise varied from industrial metal noise to sophisticated and moderately restrained dance-rock with strange attributes. The first two albums are pretty rugged going—the three favorite instruments seem to be drum machine, a synth set on white noise, and feedback. Fans of Throbbing Gristle and early Cabaret Voltaire might be interested, as would anybody with hard-to-eject party guests.

Auto-Da-Fé is so devoid of information (no track listing even) that it makes New Order records look encyclopedic. The approach is somewhat softened from prior work; while hardly poppy, synth melodies and dance beats in a style resembling D.A.F. are present. Lyrics are often vulgar and/or morbid, but the results aren't half as shocking as they seem to imagine.

Machine Age Voodoo might be mistaken for a more adventurous Blondie with Kraftwerkian tendencies; an interesting hybrid of mainstream disco and experimental electronic aggression.

SPK has recently gained notoriety for their Einstürzende Neubauten- influenced performance practices. One London gig ended in a riot when officials stopped them ten minutes into the show for violating fire regulations. (They were featuring onstage welding at the time.) [iar/dgs]

SPLIT ENZ

Mental Notes (Aus. Mushroom) 1975

Mental Notes (Chrysalis) 1976
Dizrhythmia (Chrysalis) 1977
Frenzy (Aus. Mushroom) 1979 (A&M) 1982
The Beginning of the Enz (Aus. Mushroom) 1979
The Beginning of the Enz (Chrysalis/nr) 1981
True Colours (A&M) 1980
Waiata (A&M) 1981
Time and Tide (A&M) 1982
Enz of an Era—Greatest Hits 1975-1982 (Aus. A&M) 1982
Conflicting Emotions (A&M) 1984

New Zealand's Split Enz began their recording career in pleasantly uncommercial fashion, writing gently eccentric tunes that echoed the softer side of **Foxtrot**-era Genesis. Consisting of demos, Mushroom's **The Beginning of the Enz** chronicles those earliest days and finds Tim Finn's bittersweet singing style starting to work its magic.

For **Mental Notes**—their first proper album—the Enz took shape as a sprawling seven-piece, including spoons player Noel Crombie. They had grown overtly weird and flamboyant, with many tunes resembling little, distorted symphonies. The effects don't always work, simply because flakiness carried past a certain point can't be taken seriously on any level. The Genesis parallel holds here as well.

By the time Roxy Music's Phil Manzanera produced the second **Mental Notes**, the Enz were ready for the world beyond Oz. Bizarre carnival costumes and distorted upsweep hairdos served as attention-grabbers. Tim Finn's wistful voice adds a sweet patina to disoriented and lyrically offbeat outings like "Stranger Than Fiction" and the morbid "The Woman Who Loves You."

Dizrhythmia made a distinct lurch toward the mainstream, thanks primarily to the departure of co-leader/guitarist Phil Judd, replaced by Tim's sibling Neil. With Tim in full command, the melodically intricate material went from coldly quirky to genuinely appealing, even cute. Highlights: the dizzy "Bold as Brass" and "Crosswords," at once bristling and ornate.

Financial woes subsequently forced the band to work on a diminished budget. With Neil Finn contributing songs and vocals as well as guitar, the Enz cut **Frenzy**, poppier still and less elusive than before. It's hampered by cheap sound, but "I See Red" creates a delightfully tuneful whirlwind, and "Mind Over Matter" re-creates the warmly majestic quality of the best of **Dizrhythmia**. The US/UK version of the LP differs from Mushroom's by half.

The second LP to be called **Beginning of the Enz** is a distillation of tracks from Chrysalis' **Mental Notes** and **Dizrhythmia**.

With **True Colours**, the Enz staged a full assault on America. They had become a cuddly pop band with sweet vocals, crackerjack melodies and hardly any strangeness. Fortunately, the material is genuinely first-rate, including the bouncily contagious "I Got You" and "I Hope I Never," a plainly melodramatic number suitable for Barbra Streisand. (As a marketing ploy, the LP was pressed on laser-etched plastic and packaged in variously-colored covers.)

Although **Waiata** has gorgeously haunting tracks like "Iris" and "History Never Repeats," as well as adorable ones like "Clumsy," there's a hint of blandness around the edges. The Enz show no desire to surprise here, and seem on the verge of becoming a hipper Bee Gees.

Happily, **Time and Tide** restores the passion, adding a new sense of wonder to the palatable melodies. "Dirty Creature" (of habit), "Hello Sandy Allen" and "Make Sense of It" all merit inclusion in the Enz hall of fame, blending a gentle beauty with vaguely unsettling otherworldliness.

Conflicting Emotions is the band's swansong, and it's hard to imagine a grander exit. Keeping the ethereal melodies intact, the Enz finally build up the physical side of the music to equal strength. The playing is tough and direct like never before; "Bullet Brain and Cactus," "I Wake Up Every Night" and others drive hard without obscuring the wholesome moralism of the lyrics. The message? Try to lead a good life. Who could quarrel with that? [jy]

See also *Tim Finn, Phil Judd, Swingers.*

SPLODGENESSABOUNDS

Splodgenessabounds (Deram/nr) 1981
In Search of Seven Golden Gussets (Razor/nr) 1982

A fiercely tasteless joke band led by singer Max Splodge, the rest of the crew on the eponymous debut sports names like Miles Runt Flat and Pat Thetic Von Dale Chiptooth Noble. The record, which includes an order form for such delectables as "moulded bum logo badge," is concerned with various bodily functions and scatological maladies (not to be confused with scat melodies!) with only the scantest trace of humor. Except for some clever song titles, this is utterly worthless tripe. [iar]

MARK SPRINGER

See *Rip Rig & Panic.*

SQUEEZE

Squeeze (A&M) 1978
Cool for Cats (A&M) 1979
6 Squeeze Songs Crammed into One Ten-Inch Record EP (nr/A&M) 1979
Argybargy (A&M) 1980
East Side Story (A&M) 1981
Sweets from a Stranger (A&M) 1982
Singles—45's and Under (A&M) 1982
Cosi Fan Tutti Frutti (A&M) 1985

DIFFORD & TILBROOK

Difford & Tilbrook (A&M) 1984

Squeeze's songwriting team of Glenn Tilbrook (melody) and Chris Difford (words) has been compared favorably to Lennon and McCartney; that's not only a reflection of their abilities but also an indication of how little real craftsmanship is found in rock'n'roll these days. Like their supposed models, Difford and Tilbrook are blessed with enormous talent which has often enabled them to get by on less-than-full expense of effort. What has often passed for ingenuity in Squeeze has in fact been little more than glibness. When the competition's weak, it's sometimes hard to tell the difference.

A classic premature debut, **Squeeze** finds the lads barreling through inconsistent material, a situation exacerbated by John Cale's cluttered production. However, "Take Me I'm Yours" and "Bang Bang" (both produced by the band) show spirit and potential.

With **Cool for Cats**, Squeeze entered their adolescence. Primary vocalist Tilbrook, a sweet triller, and gruffer Difford show greater confidence at the mike and together create arresting odd harmonies to go with their bent pop tunes. Wonderful cuts abound, including "Slap and Tickle," a sleazy synth rocker; "Cool for Cats," a modern pub-rock romp; and "Up the Junction," three minutes of working-class heartbreak that outdoes McCartney for pathos.

6 Squeeze Songs was an effort to establish the band in the US market, a well-chosen mini- greatest hits.

Squeeze grew up on **Argybargy**. Tilbrook and Difford had found their style and were settling into it, creating finely etched pop music with increasing intricacy. Here, the humor outweighs pretense. "If I Didn't Love You" is wryly awkward; "Farfisa Beat," is a delightful throwaway; "Pulling Mussels (from the Shell)" teaches a herky-jerky lesson in catchy cleverness. Any lack of commitment is outweighed by the variety and freshness of the material.

If the Beatles parallel holds, **East Side Story** is Squeeze's **White Album**. Produced by Elvis Costello and Roger Bechirian (apart from one cut by Dave Edmunds), it's jammed with fourteen songs that touch on everything from soul to country to psychedelia. Although each tune qualifies individually as a glittering little gem, the album lacks coherence. Still, it's meant to be a dazzling tour de force, and it is. Highlights: "Someone Else's Heart," a Difford excursion into sentiment reminiscent of the Zombies; "Mumbo Jumbo," which reflects Costello's influence; and "Messed Around," a slick piece of fake rockabilly with echoes of early Cliff Richard.

On **Sweets from a Stranger** the band pulls back slightly from the elaborate excesses of **East Side Story** without any loss of class. "When the Hangover Strikes" conducts a leisurely trip into Cole Porter land, while "I've Returned" soars on the strength of an exuberant Tilbrook vocal and ringing guitars. But again, the record has little cohesion.

Because Squeeze concentrated on making albums rather than singles after **Cool for Cats**, their singles compilation, released soon after the band's dissolution was announced, serves little purpose, pleasant though it is. The choice of songs like "Is That Love" and "Black Coffee in Bed"—one of Difford and Tilbrook's worst ever—for singles seems totally arbitrary. Thus, there's little sense of occasion here. "Annie Get Your Gun," the one new track, isn't even very good.

As it was their decision to disband Squeeze and continue writing and performing together, Difford and Tilbrook surprised no one by releasing an album of songs that, except for being funkier and even more boring than Squeeze, basically sounds no different from the band's latter efforts. Joined by the rest of a Squeezelike lineup (drums/bass/keyboards) and occasional horns and strings, the dull duo try to sound like Hall and Oates, but lack the cynical instincts to engineer such a slick veneer, and songs like "Action Speaks Faster," "Love's Crashing Waves" and "Picking Up the Pieces" are simply turgid, lifeless workouts.

After two years of unsatisfying divorce, Tilbrook and Difford reconvened Squeeze with original pianoman Jools (now Julian) Holland, drummer Gilson Lavis and a new (occasionally fretless) bassist, Keith Wilkinson. Laurie Latham produced the subsequent **Cosi Fan Tutti Frutti** LP, a bland collection that generally repeats the **Difford & Tilbrook** laxo-soul approach to much the same (non-)effect. "Last Time Forever," while sonically impressive, is a regrettably somber development for this once-giddy band. [jy/iar]

See also *Paul Carrack, Jools Holland, Harry Kakoulli, Sinceros.*

SQUIRE

...Get Smart! (Hi-Lo/nr) 1983
The Singles Album (Hi-Lo/nr) 1985

ANTHONY MEYNELL & SQUIRE

Hits from 3000 Years Ago (Hi-Lo/nr) 1981 & 1984

Woking neo-mods Squire never got a major-label LP contract, so leader Meynell gets top billing on **Hits from 3000 Years Ago**, presumably since he put it out himself, wrote all fourteen tracks (eleven demos, three live, all played by Squire) and sings all but three. The band is remarkable for avoiding image-mongering and "us vs. them" polemics; they love the music, plain and simple. Most of this really sounds as though it was recorded around 1965. **...Get Smart!** presents a dozen sprightly new love songs sung and played by Meynell, his drummer brother and guest horn and keyboard players. The glorious pop stylings eschew replication of any specific genres, instead holding to an ingenuous squeaky-clean approach that, by default, recalls the Beatles, Turtles and Herman's Hermits. Hummable and charming. [jg/iar]

SQUIRREL BAIT

Squirrel Bait (Homestead) 1985

Louisville, Kentucky's answer to Hüsker Dü, Squirrel Bait are young, fast and energetic, with a thick guitar punky sound and a properly hoarse shouter in Peter Searcy. The eight songs on their debut are roughly melodic, but the sonic attack is the main flag carrier, and they've got enthusiasm to burn. (Footnote: at its oddest juncture, **Squirrel Bait** resembles the Groundhogs.) Solid, promising, exciting stuff. [iar]

STADIUM DOGS

What's Next (Magnet/nr) 1978

This south coast quintet at first sounded like early XTC but rethought its aims and became an instant "new wave" band. **What's Next** resembles a punky 10cc—briefer and sillier, but more glib than clever. [jg]

CHRIS STAMEY

It's a Wonderful Life (Albion/DB) 1983
Instant Excitement EP (nr/Coyote) 1984

CHRIS STAMEY GROUP

Christmas Time (nr/Coyote) 1986

One of the guiding lights and progenitors of the Southeast's nouveau-pop explosion, Chris Stamey led North Carolina's pioneering Sneakers before moving to New York, recording ultra-pop records on his own label, playing with Alex Chilton and forming the dB's. Recorded while Stamey was still in that band, **It's a Wonderful Life** (subtitled, on the back cover in reverse type, "It's a Miserable Life") takes him far afield from the offbeat pure pop he is best known for. Joined by longstanding compatriots Ted Lyons and Mitch Easter, Stamey plays mesmerizingly moody and somber tunes ("Winter of Love," "Depth of Field," "Oh Yeah!") and aggressive demi-pop ("Never Enters My Mind"). Elsewhere, he warps the lyrics of "Tobacco Road" over a nearly all-drums background ("Get a Job"), offers cynical humor about urban life in a jarring, percussive setting ("Brush Fire in Hoboken") and plays a quiet piano piece with tape effects (the aptly-named "Still Life £3"). The only relatively straightforward pop song is the bitter "Face of the Crowd." Overall, a strange and unsettling album, filled with fascinating adventures and subcurrents of profound unhappiness.

Following his decision to opt out of the dB's—on the eve of their finally recording an American album—Stamey instead made his own **Instant Excitement**, an odd but more upbeat hodgepodge encompassing both a homely reading of John Lennon's "Instant Karma," an idyllic love song ("When We're Alone"), a frisky country-rocker and an instrumental opus, "Ghost Story." Produced by Don Dixon, the songs are somewhat more typical of Stamey's original pop outlook, played with little attempt to impose a style in the studio. Eclectic and a little casually half-baked but likable and, in spots, utterly touching.

The delightful **Christmas Time** mini-album introduces Stamey's new combo (actually the same people credited on **Instant Excitement**) and marks a brief reunion with his old one, the dB's, who get cover credit as "special guests." Recalling a long-lost tradition, the original songs are all seasonal—"The Only Law That Santa Claus Understood," "You're What I Want (for Christmas," "Snow Is Falling," even a new acoustic version of the unexpectedly appropriate "It's a Wonderful Life." Even more resonantly, the attractive title track sounds a lot like Brian Wilson's reflective mode. [iar]

STARGAZERS

Watch This Space (Epic/nr) 1982

If your idea of rock'n'roll stretches to encompass be-bopping pseudo-swingtime, then the nostalgic Stargazers—one of London's '80s throwbacks—may be for you. Five young men dressed in powder blue Buddy Holly jackets adorn the LP's front cover; the music inside combines elements of early '50s rock in the Bill Haley mode with the shoutalong big band jive of Cab Calloway. It's fine if you're into such campy silliness; however, if either the Stray Cats or Joe Jackson's **Jumpin' Jive** digression leaves you cold don't make this date. (That's a beautiful Bentley on the cover, though.) [iar]

STARJETS

Starjets (Epic/Portrait) 1979

Spunky if unoriginal, this Belfast quartet showed some promise, but not enough to really count. The album is fairly straight rock'n'punk, with added melody and restraint (plus some clever touches, like Beach Boys harmonies), but not as poppy as the Undertones. The lyrics rerun predictable subject matter—school, camaraderie, war, stardom—and the music's not strong enough to divert on its own merits. Likable but lost. (Footnote: some of Starjets later wound up in the Adventures.) [iar]

WALTER STEDING

Walter Steding (nr/Red Star) 1980
Dancing in Heaven (Animal) 1982

The idea of an avant-garde punk violinist may be intriguing; as one of the genre's few proponents, Walter Steding is not. Aside from Robert Fripp's enlivening, energetic appearance on "Hound Dog," the first side of this New Yorker's self-titled debut LP offers little more than self-conscious preppie punque. The second half is mainly aimless processed fiddle scraping. Producer Chris Stein provides superficial technical polish, but one can only wonder why he bothered.

For his second outing, on Stein's label, Steding recruited a larger band and several part-time helpers. Despite an apparently sincere resolve to master pop forms, he still has little to say and even less wherewithal to say it. [mf]

STEEL PULSE

Handsworth Revolution (Island/Mango) 1978
Tribute to the Martyrs (Island/Mango) 1979
Caught You (Island/nr) 1980
Reggae Fever (nr/Mango) 1980
True Democracy (Wiseman Doctrine/Elektra) 1982
Reggae Sunsplash '81 (nr/Elektra) 1982
Earth Crisis (Wiseman Doctrine/Elektra) 1984
Reggae Greats (Island/Mango) 1984
Babylon the Bandit (WEA/Elektra) 1985

In the late '70s, this young black Birmingham sextet found an affinity with the righteous rebellion of white new wavers and built its early reputation largely by touring British punk venues (as documented on live anthology records from Manchester's Electric Circus and London's Hope and Anchor). Steel Pulse's crossover appeal derives in large part from its young, modern thoughtfulness—not to mention the group's incredible strength as one of the very best self-contained reggae units in the world.

Steel Pulse's virtues include a gorgeous, multi-textured musical palette, especially on the first album and much of **Caught You**, intelligent lyrics (most notably on **Handsworth Revolution**, and also on **Tribute to the Martyrs**), a wondrous, sinuously propulsive beat and sweet lead vocals by Selwyn "Bumbo" Brown, who also has a nice quasi-scat style. Criticisms: the music, while always ear-enriching and heartfelt, lacks consistently memorable tunes. Also, there's been an increasing tendency toward preachy, trite lyrics (on **Caught You** and **Reggae Fever**), surprising since songwriting guitarist David Hinds has already shown he can do better.

If **Caught You** (retitled **Reggae Fever** in America) is Steel Pulse at its most pop-oriented, **True Democracy** has the band reaching for the most common denominator. Steel Pulse's best falls between the two extremes. Which brings us to **Earth Crisis**, where tasty use of synth and sharp production makes it their finest, most consistent album since **Tribute to the Martyrs**. As for the documentary festival album, **Reggae Sunsplash '81**, Steel Pulse has an entire side, but never quite shakes a frustrating stiffness and artificiality. Pass it up. **Reggae Greats** is a compilation.

With the release of **Babylon the Bandit**, however, it was clear that the band's professed ideals were no longer jibing with their attempts to crack the (American) market. Protest lyrics swathed in slick, upwardly-mobile production are difficult to consider seriously. [jg/bk]

TOM STEVENS

See *Long Ryders*.

MARK STEWART AND THE MAFFIA

Learning to Cope with Cowardice (Plexus/nr) 1983
As the Veneer of Democracy Starts to Fade (Mute/nr) 1985

Teamed with dubmeister Adrian Sherwood, ex-Pop Grouper Stewart produces what could best be described as avant-garde reggae on **Learning to Cope with Cowardice**. Making a wide left turn past Sly and Robbie, the disc is dark and forbidding, with a plethora of ghostly, off-center sounds floating in and out of nowhere, rarely paying heed to musical convention. At times, things get gimmicky enough to resemble a demo disc for effect units, but **Cowardice** is a rewarding album with political consciousness.

Stewart's convictions push further to the fore on **As the Veneer of Democracy Starts to Fade**. This time abandoning reggae for a disorienting marriage of big-beat drums and dissonant electronics that is not unlike early Cabaret Voltaire, several tracks feature taped authoritarian voices that you probably thought only existed in your nightmares.

Stewart is a talented and daringly experimental artist who should be mandatory listening for anyone who thinks using synthesizers only means sounding like the Human League. [dgs]

STIFF LITTLE FINGERS

Inflammable Material (Rough Trade) 1979
Nobody's Heroes (Chrysalis) 1980
Hanx! (Chrysalis) 1980
Go for It (Chrysalis) 1981
Now Then . . . (Chrysalis/nr) 1982
All the Best (Chrysalis/nr) 1983

Ulster political punks Stiff Little Fingers began as exciting if narrow-minded sloganeers, led by raw-voiced singer/guitarist Jake Burns. SLF's debut album, Rough Trade's first LP release, includes such classic protest punk as "Suspect Device" and "Alternative Ulster," but the music is pretty much routine ramalama. By **Nobody's Heroes**, they had changed labels, acquired a new drummer and developed a bit more subtlety in terms of music and lyrics. The record's best track, "Wait and See," audaciously thumbs a collective nose at the band's detractors; a roughed-up version of the Specials' "Doesn't Make It Alright" proved them to be developing interests beyond punk's limited ken. A live set, **Hanx!**, served as a premature greatest hits collection, containing powerful renditions of their best material in a well-recorded concert environment before an enthusiastic audience.

Go for It broke Stiff Little Fingers' mold. On it they emerged as a different sounding band. Burns' voice is smoother and less anguished; the music, while no less energetic and committed, is more diverse and sophisticated. The title track, a memorable martial guitar instrumental, shows how far they'd come, bearing scant resemblance to their early rabble-rousing roughness. Other numbers draw on reggae stylings for variety.

Now Then . . . continues the exploration of more accessible musical turf and is full of solid rock songs that pair energy and melody with clever guitar play. With new drummer Dolphin Taylor from the Tom Robinson Band, SLF sounds better than ever. Their political consciousness remains undiminished, but subtler and stronger lyrics effectively replace inchoate rage with on-target criticism.

Following the group's dissolution, the retrospective **All the Best** was released, containing 30 tracks on two albums. [iar]

STING

See *Police*.

STINKY TOYS

Stinky Toys (Polydor/nr) 1977

The concept of a French punk band with a female singer seemed remarkably promising when Stinky Toys first began playing gigs in London in late 1976. A year later, this record came as a major disappointment, consisting as it does of uninspired sub-Rolling Stones rock'n'boogie with terrible vocals by Elli Medeiros. [iar]

R.J. STIPS

See *Nits*.

STOOGES

See *Iggy Pop*.

RICHARD STRANGE

The Live Rise of Richard Strange (nr/ZE-PVC) 1980
The Phenomenal Rise of Richard Strange (Virgin/nr) 1981

This former Doctor of Madness made two albums of a thematic work similar in concept to the rise and fall of a demagogue chronicled by the Kinks in **Preservation Act 2**, but less meticulously plotted and more thoughtful in content. Only **Live Rise**'s vocals were recorded onstage at Hurrah in New York. (The backing tracks had been cut previously and played back for the performance.) Aside from the obvious sound/production quality upgrade, the second (all-studio) version drops three numbers and adds five to flesh out the concept, and sports beefier back-up (stronger guitar plus some super sax work courtesy of ex-Secret Affair Dave Winthrop.) Strange emerges as a significant artist in the vein of Ziggy-era Bowie, but tougher and minus the androgyny.

[jg]

STRANGLERS

IV Rattus Norvegicus (UA/A&M) 1977 (Fame/nr) 1982
No More Heroes (UA/A&M) 1977
Black and White (UA/A&M) 1978
The Stranglers EP (Jap. UA) 1979
Live (X Cert) (UA/nr) 1979
The Raven (UA/nr) 1979 (Fame/EMI America) 1985
IV (nr/IRS) 1980
The Meninblack (Liberty/Stiff) 1981
La Folie (Liberty/nr) 1981 (Fame/nr) 1983
The Collection 1977-1982 (Liberty/nr) 1982
Feline (Epic) 1983
Aural Sculpture (Epic) 1984
Great Lost (Jap. UA) 1983
Great Lost Continued (Jap. UA) 1983

J.J. BURNEL

Euroman Cometh (UA/nr) 1979

D. GREENFIELD & J.J. BURNEL

Fire & Water (Ecoutez Vos Murs) (Epic/nr) 1983

HUGH CORNWELL & ROBERT WILLIAMS

Nosferatu (Liberty/nr) 1979

The Stranglers have been enormously popular since bursting on the scene in 1977 with one of the first new wave albums, preceding both the Clash and the Sex Pistols to the racks by several months. Ten years and no personnel changes later, the Stranglers are still going strong, churning out periodic hit singles and credible albums.

Their first album was produced by Martin Rushent (who continued to work with them through 1979's live LP). **Rattus Norvegicus** includes both sides of the awesome debut single, "London Lady" and "(Get a) Grip (on Yourself)," as well as other blunt gonad-grabbers like "Hanging Around" and "Sometimes." The violently emotional lyrics and bitterly spat vocals are supported by Jean-Jacques Burnel's almost impossibly deep-throated bass grunts and Hugh Cornwell's slashing guitar, with contrasting jolly organ sounds by Dave Greenfield providing the only relief from otherwise relentless aggression. A great album.

No More Heroes continues in the same vein, but drops any hint of restraint that may have been in force the first time around. Rude words and adult themes abound, with no punches pulled, from the blatant sexism of "Bring on the Nubiles" to the sarcastic attack on racism ("I Feel Like a Wog") to the suicide of a friend ("Dagenham Dave").

Despite the virulence, however, the music is even better than on the debut, introducing pop stylings that later became a more common aspect of the Stranglers' character. **No More Heroes** is easily the Stranglers' best album.

Tricked out with gray-swirl vinyl and a limited edition bonus 45 (three tunes, including a wonderfully gruff version of "Walk on By"), **Black and White** lacks only good songs. Except for "Nice 'n' Sleazy," most of the tracks are merely inferior rehashes of earlier work, making this an easily forgettable outing.

Four gigs in '77 and '78 provided the basis for **Live (X Cert)**. The material is all familiar, but the high-tension ambience and some choice bits of Cornwell-versus-the-audience banter make it an effective dual-function live/greatest hits album.

Borrowing a gimmick from the Rolling Stones, original copies of **The Raven** sported a 3-D cover panel. Inside, a political consciousness (first unveiled on **Black and White**) takes full flower, permeating songs like "Nuclear Device," "Shah Shah a Go Go" and "Genetix." Freed from the relative mundanity of human relationships, which formed the basis of most of the Stranglers' previous lyrics, **The Raven** adopts a global perspective, stretching out to include a scathing put-down of LA entitled "Dead Loss Angeles." One other song, "Duchess," pioneered another new direction—catchy, level-headed melodic pop totally outside the group's general sound.

With no records released in America for two years, the Stranglers signed with IRS Records, who assembled **IV**, a mongrel consisting of half of **The Raven** and some non-LP singles, plus one totally new track, "Vietnamerica."

The Meninblack, previewed on a song of the same name from **The Raven** (and **IV**), is a hypothetical soundtrack/concept album (concerning aliens with godlike powers) that is essentially a critique of organized religion. There's a fair amount of non-vocal instrumental content, lots of synthesizers and other keyboards, tricky special effects and little of the Stranglers' usual thrust. Although radically different, **The Meninblack** is a departure for nowhere.

On their next LP, the Stranglers returned to topicality and forthrightness, while continuing their melodic pop explorations. **La Folie** offers a striking juxtaposition of attractive backing and scathing lyrics. Subtle, effective, mature and energetic.

Following a change in British labels, a catalogue compilation called **The Collection** appeared in 1982, including almost everything you'd want from the preceding albums, plus a couple of bonus sides from singles. A great introduction for neophytes and a record that should be of interest to anyone not owning absolutely everything the band has done.

Signing to Epic accomplished two things: a chance for the Stranglers to musically free themselves of past baggage and a consistent release schedule in America. **Feline** is restrained and dignified, but also lackluster and boring. (The US edition adds the appropriately low-key 1981 single, "Golden Brown.") **Aural Sculpture** is far better, containing

several strong tracks: "Skin Deep," melodic rippling-organ pop that recalls "Duchess," and "Ice Queen," a simpleminded allusion to cinematic irony that has lots of neat hooks and a pleasing chorus, punctuated by brassy brass. Additionally, "Uptown" melds powerful acoustic guitar to a fractured melody and comes out like a Pete Shelley song that wasn't. Although not a fully satisfying record, **Aural Sculpture** has enough quality merchandise to make it a worthwhile purchase.

Solo work: In the group, Burnel's gravel-bottom bass and guttural vocals played a crucial role on the early, maximum-aggression records. For his 1979 solo album, Burnel made a self-indulgent political statement, complete with historical maps, slogans and polemic songs like "Euromess" and "Deutschland Nicht über Alles." Using a rhythm box and playing almost all the instruments himself, Burnel invests **Euroman Cometh** with neither musical direction nor engaging ideas, making it about as much fun as sitting through a political science lecture.

Teaming with bandmate Dave Greenfield, Burnel's second album "forms the musical basis for the film 'Ecoutez Vos Murs' by Vincent Coudanne." **Fire & Water** takes two approaches—typical soundtrack ambience, relying on doomy keyboard effects, and songs, some with vocals. "Rain & Dole & Tea" is sung in Phil Spector fashion by a multitracked female vocalist; "Nuclear Power (Yes Please)" actually quotes Albert Einstein in a remarkably clumsy science lesson; "Detective Privée" is a sensuously murmured French number. Not heinously awful, but not likely to inspire repeated listenings either.

For *his* first extracurricular outing, Cornwell co-wrote, co-produced and co-performed an album with American drummer Robert Williams. The collaborative compositions on **Nosferatu** offer substantive lyrics, but the atonal performances sound even more dour than the early Stranglers. Two members of Devo put in guest appearances, and there are some Devo-like effects worked in, but if not for an incongruous cover of Cream's "White Room," there wouldn't be any light relief at all. While it's nice that the pair (with some assistance from Ian Underwood) has the instrumental prowess to do it all themselves, **Nosferatu** requires more from the listener than it deserves (or returns), and both men have made much more entertaining records separately since.

[iar]

See also *Lizard, Polyphonic Size, Taxi Girl, Robert Williams*.

STRAWBERRY SWITCH-BLADE

Strawberry Switchblade (Korova/nr) 1985

Glamourdolls (matching polkadot dresses, colorful hair streamers, blood-red lipstick) Jill Bryson and Rose McDowell do all the vocals, songwriting and guitar work; seven sessionmen (and an orchestra) provide the bubblegummy electro-pop backing that makes lightweight creations such as "Since Yesterday" and "Secrets" so unavoidably charming and catchy.

[tr]

STRAY CATS

Stray Cats (Arista/nr) 1981
Gonna Ball (Arista/nr) 1981
Built for Speed (nr/EMI America) 1982
Rant n' Rave with the Stray Cats (Arista/EMI America) 1983

PHANTOM, ROCKER & SLICK

Phantom, Rocker & Slick (EMI America) 1985

Disenchanted with modern new wave, Brian Setzer bagged his trendy New York group, the Bloodless Pharaohs, formed a rockabilly trio, and abandoned New York for England. The Stray Cats wowed 'em with exotic Long Island appeal, spearheading a rockabilly revival that naturally became absorbed into new wave. Is there a moral here?

Unlike some neo-rockabillies, the Stray Cats don't care about painstaking reconstructions of moldy old recordings. They diddle around with non-originals, while Setzer's own early songs tackle topical events ("Storm the Embassy," "Rumble in Brighton"). Setzer's extended guitar soloing sometimes seems descended from jazz rather than rockabilly, but there's no faulting his skill or the group's spirit.

Gonna Ball, released about nine months after **Stray Cats**, finds the band moving into R&B turf. Musical veterans like Ian Stewart and Lee Allen help fill out the sound; a strong producer, like Dave Edmunds on the first album, would have helped even more. Setzer is a better guitarist than singer, and some of **Gonna Ball**'s songs resemble the music rockabilly was revolting against.

Combining the best of both British albums and adding one new cut, **Built for Speed** is a good introduction to the band. The US, generally not known for humoring nostalgic musical throwbacks, sent it into the Top 5. The Stray Cats must have been doing something right.

If chart success is the yardstick, they continued to do that something on **Rant n' Rave**, the trio's first identical and simultaneous US/UK release, and also their last record together. Again produced by Dave Edmunds, the effervescent rock'n'roll teen rebellion of "(She's) Sexy & 17" leads the stylistic parade (with one exception—the beautiful soul ballad, "I Won't Stand in Your Way," with vocal backing by Fourteen Karat Soul) and the rest of the record falls neatly in line, recalling Eddie Cochran, Carl Perkins and the whole rockabilly-into-early-rock'n'roll era. Sure it's formulaic and derivative as hell, but timelessly enthralling and truly entertaining as well. The Stray Cats broke up in late 1984; while his bandmates teamed up with guitarist Earl Slick and issued a run-of-the-mill rock album the following year, Brian Setzer worked with the Honey Drippers and released his first solo LP in early 1986.

[si/iar]

See also *Brian Setzer*.

PETE STRIDE/JOHN PLAIN

See *Lurkers*.

STRIPES

The Stripes (Ger. CBS) 1980

German post-Blondie rock of the most rudimentary variety, the Stripes take better to updated Gidgetude than fake petulance, telling virtually the same joke thirteen times with only minor variations (notwithstanding the two American-written tunes, one by Hall and Oates, no less). Kicker: the quartet's singer and prime asset went on to earn much greater fame a few years later in a far-superior band bearing her (nick)name, Nena. [jg]

STYLE COUNCIL

A Paris EP (Polydor/nr) 1983
Introducing the Style Council EP (nr/Polydor) 1983
Cafe Bleu (Polydor/nr) 1984
My Ever Changing Moods (nr/Geffen) 1984
Our Favourite Shop (Polydor/nr) 1985
Internationalists (nr/Geffen) 1985
The Lodgers EP (Polydor/nr) 1985
Home & Abroad (Polydor/Geffen) 1986

After six years spent growing up in public with the Jam, Paul Weller felt the need to function within a more relaxed, less restrictive framework. That in mind, he enlisted the services of former Merton Parkas/Dexys keyboard player Mick Talbot to form the Style Council, with all other needed instruments to be supplied by guests. Promising that the band would be nothing if not unpredictable, they then proceeded to issue a single, "Speak Like a Child," that sounded much like where the Jam left off. Another single, the funky "Money-Go-Round," preceded the four-song **A Paris** EP, the sleeve of which shows the duo carefully posed with the Eiffel Tower in the background, looking like a Giorgio Armani ad. Highlighted by the catchy "Long Hot Summer," the material is light, breezy summertime soul, owing as much to Weller's pretensions of some sort of continental flair as it does to obvious referents like Curtis Mayfield. **Introducing the Style Council** combined both singles with the contents of the UK EP, although some of the numbers were remixed. Not released in England, it sold better there as an import than it did in the country of its issue.

Cafe Bleu and **My Ever Changing Moods** are equivalent LPs with slightly different tracks. (The US version replaces two minor cuts with the UK hit, "A Solid Bond in Your Heart.") A scrambled assortment of soul, bebop, cocktail jazz, rap and whatever else Weller could think of, it's simply too schizophrenic to be a good album, although it does show integrity—this band is unlikely to be guided by public demand. Two tracks—"Headstart for Happiness" and "The Paris Match" (this time featuring Everything but the Girl)—are improved versions of previously released material, and "My Ever Changing Moods" gave Weller the first US Top 30 single of his career.

The Style Council's second album was also released in alternate trans-Atlantic forms. **Internationalists** has a different cover than **Our Favourite Shop** and omits the latter's title song. Though still rather varied, the album is much more coherent than its predecessor.

There are still clinkers: "The Stand Up Comics Instructor" is clever but awkward, and the rhumba-shuffle of "All Gone Away" would sound at home in a dentist's office. However, tracks like "Walls Come Tumbling Down!," "Come to Milton Keynes" and "Boy Who Cried Wolf" more than tip the scales in the record's favor. As ever, it's undeniable that Weller means every word, but the continuing trend towards a crystalline, antiseptic sound is unfortunate.

It was obvious that *Absolute Beginners* was not going to be without a contribution from Weller, so the band rewrote "With Everything to Lose" from the second album (itself already a direct lift from "Long Hot Summer") and came up with "Have You Ever Had It Blue." Shortly thereafter, the Style Council issued a live album, **Home & Abroad**, a squeaky-clean, all-too-accurate collection of songs drawn from both albums as well as singles. (The UK CD adds two tracks.) Considering that the Style Council often put live version on their flipsides (see **The Lodgers** EP), this set seems to be mostly for those who absolutely must have everything Weller puts his name to.

The Style Council are, so far, a good singles band, an even better live act and about as unpredictable as anyone currently making pop records. Already more successful in the US than the Jam ever were, they appear to have a free ticket to English success—ironically, the situation that led Weller to dissolve the Jam. [dgs]

POLY STYRENE

See *X-Ray Spex*.

SUBHUMANS

The Day the Country Died (Spiderleg/nr) 1982
From the Cradle to the Grave (Bluurg/nr) 1984
Worlds Apart (Bluurg/nr) 1986

More punk protest against almost anything from a run-of-the-mill British quartet. While the drums scamper along, the bass pogos in and around the guitar's dull roar while this "singer" guy shouts his head off about everything wrong with the world. More's the pity—it sounds like they almost have an idea here and there, but are prejudiced against being too clever. The guitarist does play spiffy animal-wail solos, though. [jg]

SUBURBAN LAWNS

Suburban Lawns (nr/IRS) 1981
Baby EP (IRS) 1983

This eccentric California quintet made a minor splash in 1979 with an independent single, "Gidget Goes to Hell," a spirited, twisted variation on the '60s *Gidget* movies. But the group's jittery industrial pop comes off highly ordinary on **Suburban Lawns**, a sub-Devo mesh of hiccoughing vocals, angular tunes with tiresome stop-start rhythms and a high, weedy guitar/organ sound.

Reduced to the quartet of Su Tissue, Frankie Ennui, Chuck Roast and a bizarrely-named bassist, the Lawns returned with a much better outlook on **Baby**. Richard Mazda produced the five songs, including the alluring "Flavor Crystals" and a batch of muscular syncopated dance creations that evade rhythmic pursuit. [df/iar]

SUBURBAN STUDS

Slam (Pogo/nr) 1978

Laboring through these seventeen tracks of mostly stereotypical punk thrash, you might begin to suspect the Studs were a put-up job. Yet buried in the midst of **Slam** is a diamond in the rough: "I Hate School" sounds like a hybrid of the Sex Pistols and the Heartbreakers having a rave-up. Then you begin to notice other flashes of dumb cunning . . . [jg]

SUBURBS

The Suburbs EP (nr/Twin/Tone) 1978
In Combo (nr/Twin/Tone) 1980
Credit in Heaven (nr/Twin/Tone) 1981
Dream Hog EP (nr/Twin/Tone) 1982 (Mercury) 1983
Love Is the Law (Mercury) 1983
Suburbs (A&M) 1986

One of Minneapolis' major musical resources, the Suburbs have maintained the same lineup since debuting on vinyl (as did the extraordinary Twin/Tone label) via a 1978 nine-song 7-inch red vinyl EP of above-average punkish rock'n'roll.

With their first album, the Suburbs began displaying signs of incipient greatness; singer Beej Chaney's ominous, neurotic calm providing perfect counterpoint for the band's enthusiastic playing; guitarist B.C. Allen adding tension with scrabbly rhythm and violent lead. The songs unpredictably explore real-world subjects like "Hobnobbin with the Executives" and "Cig Machine."

After demonstrating what they could do on **In Combo**, the Suburbs proved how well they could do it with the double-album, **Credit in Heaven**, a slickly-delivered opus that refines the band's approach and fairly bubbles over with creative concepts, great playing and bizarre songs. The comparisons to Bryan Ferry—cool in the eye of the storm—are amplified by Chaney's blase delivery, but the music—powered by Hugo Klaers' ultra-busy drumming—is something else, blending cool funk with nervous disco and jazzy aplomb. A stunner, and highly recommended, regardless of religious persuasion.

Things heated up for the Suburbs in '82, when they started attracting significant club play for a 12-inch of the song "Waiting." They included that track on the **Dream Hog** EP (in original and extended remix form), along with two sharp new white-funk tunes (one of them about dance music) plus a restrained near-ballad, and then signed to Mercury, who promptly reissued it before sending the 'Burbs into the studio to cut a new album.

The result of that maneuver, **Love Is the Law**, is easily their best vinyl chapter, a powerful and personality-laden set of songs that incorporate more rock than usual as well as horns and some of their most offbeat lyrics. "Rattle My Bones" is brilliantly demento bebop; the superb "Love Is the Law" has the most memorable hook in the repertoire; "Hell A" took one of its verses from a Los Angeles phone booth scrawl. **Love Is the Law** is a great, great album.

Making the probably inevitable Prince connection via the production guidance of Robert Brent

(better known as the Revolution's drummer, Bobby Z), the Suburbs came roaring back three long years later with another powerful record, albeit one whose character is less firmly held in its musical approach than its lyrics. Gone is the antsy, skittish urgency of yore; **Suburbs** is utterly listenable (but not overwhelmingly unique), with equally subtle nods to the 'Burbs crypto-funk and Prince's happy-feet dance rock. Thankfully, Chaney and Poling's nastily humorous lyrics — notably on "Every Night's a Friday Night" (. . . in hell), "America Sings the Blues" and "Superlove"—are as clever as ever. [iar]

SUBWAY SECT

See *Vic Godard & the Subway Sect, JoBoxers*.

NIKKI SUDDEN (& DAVE KUSWORTH)

See *Swell Maps*.

SUICIDAL TENDENCIES

Suicidal Tendencies (nr/Frontier) 1983 (nr/Caroline) 1986

Every once in a while, a band previously lost in the mire of some genre emerges from the crowd ineffably better than and different from their competition. Sucidial Tendencies—a California quartet voted Worst Band *and* Biggest Assholes in *Flipside* magazine's 1982 readers' poll—could have been just another hardcore band, but they're not. This LP benefits enormously from clear production (by Glen E. Friedman), tight, careful playing— fast and blurry in spots if you don't keep up, but not indistinct—and singer/lyricist Mike Muir, whose intelligence and forceful personality invest songs like "Fascist Pig" and "Suicide's an Alternative" with wit and wisdom. Suicidal Tendencies' other strength is an ability to vary the tempo, a gambit best used on the chilling "Institutionalized," a half-sung, half-recited alienation number which powerfully encapsulates all the punk sociology of *Repo Man* and *Suburbia* in four minutes. Don't miss this one. (The 1986 reissue is on—get this!—compact disc.) [iar]

SUICIDE

Suicide (Bronze/Red Star) 1977 (nr/Red Star) 1981
1/2 Alive [tape] (nr/ROIR) 1981

ALAN VEGA AND MARTIN REV

Suicide (ZE) 1980

A mainstay of the New York rock underground since the early '70s, the two-man Suicide (prefiguring Yazoo, Soft Cell, Blancmange, Tears for Fears, etc.) mixed Alan Vega's blues-styled vocals and Marty Rev's synthesizer, originally a broken-down Farfisa organ they couldn't afford to repair. Escaping the dingy clubs of Manhattan, Suicide went on to cause riots in Europe while on tour supporting Elvis Costello. They provided a soundtrack for Werner Fassbinder's film, *In a Year of Thirteen Moons*, and always provoked extreme reactions. Often confrontational in nature, they produced an unequaled, obsessively American electronic music that scarcely resembles other singer/keyboards outfits.

Suicide (1977) is a nearly perfect relic of mid-'70s Manhattan attitudes, a portrait of society grinding down to self-destruction. Rev's powerful minimalist repetition catapults Vega's pained and constantly cracking voice through indictments of Viet Nam mentality ("Ghost Rider"), broken romance ("Cheree," "Girl") and holocausts both public and personal ("Rocket USA," "Frankie Teardrop"). Stolid and restrained, the record simmers with repressed emotion and excellent, unusual performances. Four years later, the LP was reissued with "I Remember," "Keep Your Dreams" and "96 Tears" added, as well as a flexi-disc of Suicide live in Brussels. Recommended, though clearly not for everyone.

Suicide, the confusingly titled Vega/Rev LP, was produced by the Cars' Ric Ocasek, who smoothed the sound out to an almost socially acceptable level. (These same sessions produced the duo's zenith, 1980's anthemic "Dream Baby Dream," issued as a 12-inch single.) Rev's use of electronics had grown more subtle and complex, while Vega's vocals seem tethered and uneasy. "Harlem" is a stunning melange of urban despair and tortured musicianship, and is the album's most affecting number.

The tape-only **Half-Alive** pairs one side of live material and one side of studio outtakes. Released after Suicide's dissolution, it offers no breakthroughs, but stands simply as a tribute to a fine, underrated band. The live side demonstrates how much fun Suicide were in concert, despite sloppiness and Vega's antagonism toward audiences. [sg]

See also *Martin Rev, Alan Vega*.

ANDY SUMMERS

See *Fripp & Summers*.

SUNNY JIM BAND

Maximum Pain (Ger. Vertigo) 1980
Jay (Ger. Vertigo) 1982

This quartet consists of two Brits, a Frenchman and a Dutchman based in Cologne who once contracted (but wound up not going) to tour Iron Curtain countries. They play tight, assured, angular rock'n'roll and reggae, with smart-enough arrangements and some above-average lyrical ideas. Unfortunately, like their melodies, the words are too often half-baked, not quite complete or satisfying.

Despite its title, the first album suffers from stiffness, as if they're unwilling to let go. The second LP, produced by Steve Nye (Roxy Music, Japan, etc.), loosens them up a bit. Although the hooks are again generally a hair short of the mark, excerpts would make an eyebrow-raising EP. [jg]

SWANS

Filth (nr/Neutral) 1983
Cop (K.422/nr) 1984
Raping a Slave EP
    (K.422/Homestead) 1985
Greed (K.422/PVC) 1986

Play the Velvet Underground's "Sister Ray" at half-speed—go ahead, do it—and you've got Swans plus a sense of humor and the possibility that, if you just adjust the speed control, everything will get good. Take away the sense of humor and the speed control, and you've got Swans. In all probability, you've also got either a high threshold for

crunching pain or a splitting headache. Well, that's Swans. Downtown New York arties, friends of the infinitely more imaginative Sonic Youth, Swans trudge through dragging tempos, 2/2 meters and low frequency mush, all the while howling about alienation and despair. Listening to Swans isn't like banging your head against a wall; it's like banging your head against the side of a swimming pool—underwater.

Filth is all that it promises to be: squalor without catharsis (now there's an LP title!) The group is so conceptually strapped to its sludge m.o. that this album is actually more formulaic than Kajagoogoo. **Cop** features new album and song titles, a new label, a trimmed-down lineup and new cover art. What it lacks are new ideas. *Boom. Crunch. Boom. Crunch. Boom. Crunch.* Where Sonic Youth makes great music that's painful to listen to, Swans offer pain without reason.

The 1985 EP, **Raping a Slave** (retitled **Swans** in the US), offers few changes in the actual sounds they incorporate, but makes things more interesting by using them in unexplored ways. A marked improvement over previous discs, and a good lead-in to **Greed**, where everything finally gels. New weapons are added to the Swans' arsenal, along with a variety of seemingly inconceivable approaches: The harrowing "Fool" is almost all piano and (sung!) vocals; several songs feature female background singers (serving more as an instrument than harmony.) The closing "Money Is Flesh" has a two-note trumpet part played ad nauseum. Each track is a complete work in itself, enthralling and narcotizing. Swans, yes, but they'll always be one of rock's ugliest ducklings. [jl/dgs]

RACHEL SWEET

Fool Around (Stiff/Stiff-Columbia) 1978
Protect the Innocent (Stiff/Stiff-Columbia) 1980
...And Then He Kissed Me (CBS/Columbia) 1981
Blame It on Love (CBS/Columbia) 1982

The proverbial little girl with the big voice, Rachel Sweet burst out of Akron, Ohio in her early teens under the watchful eye of producer Liam Sternberg. An integral component (along with Lene Lovich) of the second Stiff Records signing blitz, Sweet recorded an impressive debut on which Sternberg figured prominently as both writer and producer. In its original English release, **Fool Around** is a great-sounding record that has Sweet voicing Sternberg's vision of the hip girl-child. The American version—remixed, re-ordered and with two different tracks—has much less vitality.

Protect the Innocent shows Sweet forsaking Sternberg's new wave-cum-country sensibility, muddling about in search of a focal point. Dolled up in black leather and singing songs that run the gamut from Lou Reed's "New Age" to Elvis' "Baby, Let's Play House" to the Damned's "New Rose," Sweet seems the victim of somebody's half-assed marketing goof.

...And Then He Kissed Me is Sweet's third horse change in the middle of a career busy going nowhere, a Spectorian stab at MOR rock. Devoid of the freshness that

was her most obvious asset, the LP contains her first genuine American hit, "Everlasting Love," a duet with teen dream Rex Smith.

Blame It on Love shows signs of revitalization. Though it sounds Tom Petty-influenced, Sweet wrote the entire album's worth of catchy material. She may never regain the youthful charm of her debut LP, but at least this LP shows her regaining control over her musical direction. If she can steer away from the temptations of MOR, Sweet could still become a woman to watch. [jw]

SWELL MAPS

A Trip to Marineville (Rather-Rough Trade/nr) 1979
Jane from Occupied Europe (Rather-Rough Trade/nr) 1980
Whatever Happens Next... (Rather-Rough Trade/nr) 1981
Collision Time (Rather-Rough Trade/nr) 1982

NIKKI SUDDEN

Waiting on Egypt (Abstract/nr) 1982 & 1986
The Bible Belt (Flicknife/nr) 1983

NIKKI SUDDEN & DAVE KUSWORTH: JACOBITES

Jacobites (Glass/nr) 1984
Shame for the Angels EP (Pawn Hearts/nr) 1985
Robespierre's Velvet Basement (Glass/nr) 1985
Pin Your Heart to Me EP (Glass/nr) 1985
When the Rain Comes EP (Glass/nr) 1986
The Ragged School (nr/Twin/Tone) 1986

England's Swell Maps proved that a group of intelligent, fearless, versatile people can record five LPs (counting the double **Whatever Happens Next...**) and produce little of any value.

A Trip to Marineville, which came with a bonus four-song EP, finds our embryonic cartographers dabbling in Pistols-styled punk and more experimental noise-making, using unorthodox implements. Despite their energy and tenacious desire to produce something new, the package simply does not contain enough ideas that work. The following **Jane from Occupied Europe** shows the band's confidence waxing while its will to organize wanes. Since it's the *desire* to organize sound that fills the gap left when avant-gardists throw the rules away, this proved to be Swell Maps' undoing.

By the time of the interminable **Whatever Happens Next...**, mainly a collection of homemade cassette demos, Swell Maps were rambling and floundering. **Collision Time** consists of about half of **Jane from Occupied Europe** plus an assortment of singles. Though promising at the outset, Swell Maps succumbed to preciousness and self-indulgence with depressing speed.

Nikki Sudden, the band's singer and guitarist, subsequently released two solo albums which basically offer more of the same. But the fecund Jacobites—a trio (plus friends) of Sudden, guitarist Dave Kusworth and ex-Swell Maps drummer Epic Soundtracks (Sudden's

brother)—sing an altogether different tune. With Kusworth co-writing the songs, Sudden has rid himself of all references to Swell Maps.

All of the Jacobites' records have a similar romantic format consisting of seductive acoustic guitar, a thumping muffled rhythm section and Sudden's whining Dylanesque vocals. The Jacobites pillage their idols (Stones, Neil Young, Dylan), but with such loving devotion—as on "Fortune of Fame" (**Shame for the Angels**), "Where Rivers End" (**Robespierre's Velvet Basement**) and others—their motives transcend any appearance of carbon-copy revivalism. **The Ragged School** is an American compilation of Jacobites tracks. With this band, Sudden may at last fulfill the promise the Swell Maps never did.

[mf/ag]

SWIMMING POOL Q'S

The Deep End (Armageddon/DB) 1981
The Swimming Pool Q's (A&M) 1984
Blue Tomorrow (A&M) 1986

The Athens, Georgia sound of the B-52's and Pylon—a singular fusion of collegiate-ham artiness and post-punk desperation—also typifies the snappy debut by Atlanta's Swimming Pool Q's, but the Q's add a few interesting wrinkles of their own. While "Big Fat Tractor" favors familiar "Rock Lobster" whimsicality, "Rat Bait" is an exhilarating chip off Captain Beefheart's block with jarring rhythm and growling guitar. In "Stick in My Hand," the Q's apply a heavy blues throb and aggro-folk vocal harmonies (guitarist Jeff Calder and organist Anne Richmond Boston) to a story of Southern religious fanaticism. What's more, they have a great sense of black humor, like the comic masochism of "I Like to Take Orders from You."

With new-found responsibilities as major-label artists, the Q's play it more seriously on their second album, blending intelligent, evocative lyrics with a roaring folk-into-rock sound. When Boston sings "The Bells Ring," you feel like you're on the Trailways bus with her, escaping from romance with a Walkman turned up full-blast. When Calder sings "Pull Back My Spring," you can tangibly sense the tension. Armed with excellent, semi-regional songs and great flexibility in arranging and singing them, the band fills the album with honest, heartfelt music that has inherent strength not reliant on volume or dance beats.

Blue Tomorrow is even better, evidencing the band's growing confidence and burgeoning songwriting skill. Mike Howlett's production adds the audio definition and power their records previously lacked; the Q's take the opportunity to stretch their stylistic range further afield than ever before. Boston's vocals are exquisite—Linda Ronstadt meets Wanda Jackson and Sandy Denny—and songs like "Now I'm Talking About Now," "Pretty on the Inside" and "More Than One Heaven" show them off to best effect. (For aficionados, a brand new version of "Big Fat Tractor" demonstrates how far they've traveled since that first LP.) [df/iar]

SWINGERS

Counting the Beat (Carrere/Backstreet) 1982
Picking Up Strangers (Aus. Mushroom) 1982

SWINGERS ET AL.

Starstruck (A&M) 1983

Leading this trio up from Down Under, ex-Split Enz guitarist/composer Phil Judd rejects his earlier, convoluted melodicism for a still-quirky but more compact, abrasive approach, with phenomenal results. Judd's eccentric mental mixmaster spews out the clichés of mid-'60s Anglo-rock (Beatles, Stones, Who, Kinks) wackily updated, unreal and askew. His Dave Davies-as-young-schizo vocals (often abetted by gibberish falsettos) deliver lyrics almost too too rock-song banal to believe, surrounded by twangy guitars that resemble so many layers of electrified rubber bands. The band performed selections from both their LPs in the 1982 Australian movie, *Starstruck*, the soundtrack album of which contains Swingers tracks not found on **Counting the Beat**. [jg]

See also *Blam Blam Blam, Phil Judd*.

SYLVAIN SYLVAIN

Sylvain Sylvain (RCA) 1979

SYL SYLVAIN AND THE TEARDROPS

Syl Sylvain and the Teardrops (RCA) 1981
'78 Criminals (Fr. Fan Club) 1985

To hear Syl Sylvain nowadays, you'd never guess he was once a member of the dreaded, subversive New York Dolls. For one thing, he's an absolutely winsome singer, the perfect punk-with-a-heart-of-gold who seems to be striking an "aw, shucks!" pose at the mike. For another, his records are glistening, rocking pop with no hard edges, plenty of ingratiating melodies and lots of pizazz. One of the fun things about Syl is trying to spot all the elements his eclecticism has absorbed. Over the course of these two LPs, he borrows from salsa, Tom Petty, Phil Spector, Gary Lewis and the Playboys and many more.

Sylvain's solo debut features the breathless "14th Street Beat," an ode to the Big Apple; the more focused follow-up heightens the romantic angle with such tunes as "I Can't Forget Tomorrow," "Just One Kiss" and "It's Love." Pure charm.

'78 Criminals is a compilation of singles Sylvain did with various bands—including the Criminals —following the Dolls' collapse. [jy]

RIKKI SYLVAN

See *Rikki and the Last Days of Earth*.

DAVID SYLVIAN

Brilliant Trees (Virgin/nr) 1984
Alchemy—An Index of Possibilities [tape] (Virgin/nr) 1985
Words with the Shaman EP (Virgin/nr) 1985

Sylvian's first solo record expands and refines Japan's approach with assistance from bandmates Jansen and Barbieri and such modern-music luminaries as Holger Czukay, Riuichi Sakamoto

and Jon Hassell. Japan fans should wholeheartedly enjoy **Brilliant Trees**, which closely resembles some of the band's final efforts. [iar]

See also *Riuichi Sakamoto*.

SYSTEMATICS

Rural EP (Aus. M Squared) 1980

This Australian pair seem utterly determined to be outre, but unlike most others with the same goal, they have the talent to be strikingly oddball: synth with all the texture of processed cheese hums a bright little tune while the vocalist rhapsodizes over a female freak ("She's my little revulsion"), a guitar does nimble abstract-jazz figures to accompany the musings of a blithely suicidal mutant (no legs or shoulders). Then there's a number about a mutation-inducing agent designed to remove toes. Cleverly done, and grimly amusing in its way. [jg]

HAJIME TACHIBANA

See *Plastics*.

YUKIHIRO TAKAHASHI

Saravah! (Jap. Toshiba-EMI) 1977
Neuromantic (Alfa) 1981
Murdered by the Music (Statik/nr) 1982
What, Me Worry? (Alfa/nr) 1982
What, Me Worry? EP (Jap. Yen-Alfa) 1982
Time and Place (Jap. Yen-Alfa) 1983
Wild and Moody (Cocteau/nr) 1985

BEATNIKS

The Beatniks (Statik/nr) 1982

The outside projects of Yellow Magic Orchestra drummer/vocalist Takahashi (not to mention his colleague, Riuichi Sakamoto) suggest that there's something amiss with the band's format; his solo work is far more amusing than YMO's, even when the other members are involved. (They've contributed half an album's worth to his solo LPs and play on lots more; Sakamoto even appears on the pre-YMO **Saravah!** LP.)

Takahashi's albums are far less programmatic and predictable than YMO's. He'll go from a reggae-style version of "Stop in the Name of Love" to a new-romantic soap opera to tongue-in-cheek pop powered by galloping synths to poignant soul-searching to a loopy update of Duane Eddy guitar instrumentals. He also uses guitar and other instruments more prominently. Most of the guitar work is by YMO pal Kenji Omura, although Bill Nelson's e-bow graces much of **What, Me Worry?** and Phil Manzanera, bringing fellow Roxy Musician Andy Mackay's sax and oboe along for the ride, is on much of **Neuromantic**.

The two 1982 albums are pleasant surprises, with playing and material that's at once aggressive and arty; **Murdered by the Music** (from 1980 but unreleased in the West for two years) is the more goofy and eclectic. The **What, Me Worry?** EP features three tracks from the LP of the same name—one with Japanese lyrics this time—plus another bright original and a sprightly cover of an old German tune.

Selecting those songs that best combine melody and muscle, **Time and Place** is a strong live set mostly interpreting his previous repertoire but also adding some new things (plus a version of Bacharach/David's "The April Fools"). The band giving it all a unified feel is keyboardist Keiichi Suzuki, Bill Nelson, ex-Plastic Hajime Tachibana and drummer David Palmer. Interestingly, Takahashi doesn't drum—he sings, plays keyboards and guitar.

Wild and Moody is an LP of pretty songs—mainly romantic though a little lyrically offbeat—dressed (but not tarted up) in electro-dance clothing. Nothing awesome, but nearly all of it delightful.

The Beatniks are a duo of Takahashi and Suzuki; they split all of the playing (including some twittery synth) and singing. Suzuki's vocals are better than Takahashi's (which often resemble an overly echoed mumble), but the lyrics, written not by YMO-associate Chris Mosdell or Peter Barakan (as on the latter three albums) but merely translated into

English, are moodier but less cogent than those on Yuki's solo LPs. [jg]

TALKING HEADS

Talking Heads: 77 (Sire) 1977
More Songs About Buildings and Food (Sire) 1978
Fear of Music (Sire) 1979
Remain in Light (Sire) 1980
The Name of This Band Is Talking Heads (Sire) 1982
Speaking in Tongues (Sire) 1983
Stop Making Sense (EMI/Sire) 1984
Little Creatures (EMI/Sire) 1985

JERRY HARRISON

The Red and the Black (Sire) 1981

Talking Heads—three conservative-looking refugees from the Rhode Island School of Design—first appeared on the New York Bowery circuit in mid-1975, playing on a CBGB bill headlined by the Ramones. From the outset, it was clear that, although the Heads shared an attitude and commitment to self-expression with the other bands then on the New York scene, they were charting a course all their own. That individuality, coupled with a strong adventurous streak, has resulted in both critical and commercial success for their group albums and some spin-off projects as well.

The impossibly high-strung David Byrne (who has mellowed somewhat over the years), leads the Heads, his neurotic but insightful perceptions focusing the group's sensibility. The core of Talking Heads additionally consists of bassist Tina Weymouth, an early incidence of new wave's occasionally non-sexist outlook, drummer Chris Frantz (now her husband) and keyboardist/guitarist Jerry Harrison, an ex-Modern Lover who joined the trio in time for their first album. Together, and enlarged at times by temporary adjunct members, the Heads have produced intellectual dance music and artistic pop of different sorts, finding numerous rewarding levels on which to function.

Talking Heads: 77 is an astonishing debut with uncomplicated, almost low-key music supporting tense, bizarre lyrics, sung by Byrne in a wavering voice. He sounds downright uncomfortable admitting rather than proclaiming the words, but that only adds to the edgy appeal of such songs as "The Book I Read," "Psycho Killer" and "Uh-Oh, Love Comes to Town."

The Heads began a relationship with Brian Eno on their second album, essentially taking him on as a temporary fifth member. On **More Songs About Buildings and Food** (as well as the two succeeding LPs), they worked, at first adding elements to the basic framework and then ultimately subsuming the foundation into a wholly new approach. Here, the use of acoustic and electronic percussion fills previous spaces, and the inclusion of Al Green's "Take Me to the River" evinced the band's deep interest in "black music" and provided them with their first glimpse of mainstream popularity. The material isn't as startlingly fresh or satisfying as on the first LP, but some of the tracks work fine.

The collaboration with Eno shifted into high gear on **Fear of**

Music, moving rhythm to the front on "I Zimbra," and foreshadowing the band's new direction. It's a tentative step—most of the album sounds like a refinement on **More Songs**—but it draws further away from their spartan origins.

Remain in Light incorporates various outside players (Adrian Belew, Nona Hendryx, a horn section) and makes a fully realized Great Step Forward. Funk and African influences meet electronics and intellectual artiness to produce intricate, occasionally stunning tapestries that almost abandon song structure but do make a new kind of sense. "Houses in Motion" and "Once in a Lifetime" are among the Heads' finest achievements, and the relationship with Eno seems at its peak. But trouble was apparently brewing, and the Heads spent the next year pursuing solo projects, leaving the group on hold and revoking Eno's guest membership.

The Name of This Band is a two-record live album, showcasing the group's best material as well as recapitulating the stages in its development. Side One (1977) and Side Two (1979) feature the basic quartet in the early days; Sides Three and Four (1980 and 1981) capture the augmented lineup, with Belew, Hendryx, Bernie Worrell, Busta Jones and others adding a brilliant funky flavor. The Heads' second concert record is **Stop Making Sense**, the one-disc soundtrack to their documentary feature film of the same name. Not only are the performances uniformly excellent, but the selection—from "Psycho Killer" to "Once in a Lifetime" to "Burning Down the House"—neatly recaps the various periods of their career in a concise, cohesive setting.

Speaking in Tongues, a perfectly realized synthesis of budding pop instincts, powerful atmospherics and solid dance tunes, contains some of the Heads' best work, e.g., "Burning Down the House" and "Girlfriend Is Better." Having experimented with communal music-making, the Heads reclaimed tight control and, while there are numerous guest players, it is the Heads' album all the way. Uncovering new areas of ambition, the group commissioned noted modern artist Robert Rauschenberg to design a novel package for the record (also issued with a Byrne painting on a more traditional sleeve.)

Nine simple songs played with relative restraint and the fewest sidemen they've employed in a long time, **Little Creatures** is ostensibly the Heads' back-to-the-minimalist-roots rock'n'roll album, an escape from pan-culturalism and artistic grandiosity. (It's not.) Byrne's songs are as straightforward and non-Headsy as he can make them; considerations of mundane topics (sex, babies, television) join his typically oblique character studies and essays on being and nothingness. Were the flimsy songs sturdier, the album might have been more creatively successful; as realized, **Little Creatures** merely sounds careless and insignificant. (To be fair, "Road to Nowhere" and "Walk It Down" are the winners in a weak crop.)

All of the Heads have participated in extracurricular musical activities. Lacking a hit single (like the Tom Tom Club) or a Broadway production (Byrne), few got to hear

to hear the fruits of Jerry Harrison's efforts during the band's 1981 sabbatical. On **The Red and the Black** he continues to explore the pan-ethnic, cross-rhythmic music of **Remain in Light**, not a surprise, since many of the auxiliary Heads (like Belew, Worrell and Hendryx) also appear on Harrison's record. The results are fairly funky, albeit in a relaxed, slow-motion way. [iar/rnp]

See also *David Byrne, Tom Tom Club*.

TALK TALK

Talk Talk EP (nr/EMI America) 1982
The Party's Over (EMI/EMI America) 1982
It's My Life (EMI/EMI America) 1984
The Colour of Spring (EMI/EMI America) 1986

Talk Talk's debut is slick and professional but lifeless, sounding as though it were programmed by record company execs to be a synth-rock Foreigner. At the time earning some comparisons to Duran Duran, Talk Talk does have a double name, a common producer (Colin Thurston) and a similarly superficial veneer, but lacked Duran's panache. Most of Talk Talk's songs are full of melodramatic angst and amateurish lyrics (which might have been overlooked had the band not foolishly included a lyric sheet). The EP previewed **The Party's Over** with four selections from it.

Things took a turn for the better on **It's My Life**, although Talk Talk still isn't an essential component of modern culture. The title track handily wins the 1984 Roxy Music soundalike award; other synth-powered dance tracks like "Dum Dum Girl" reveal Mark Hollis to be a truly mixed-up vocalist. Now that Talk Talk seems capable of making reasonably interesting (and varied) records, their creative future looks a lot brighter.

The Colour of Spring finds producer Tim Friese-Greene collaborating with Hollis as a songwriter and keyboard player, joining Talk Talk's two other members (drummer Lee Harris and bassist Paul Webb) and a lot of other musicians. Except for "Life's What You Make It" and a gritty guitar solo on "I Don't Believe in You," the first side is gruelingly slow and soporific; Side Two is sporadically more energetic, but the languid pacing still makes it an endurance challenge. [ks/iar]

TALL DWARFS

Canned Music (NZ Flying Nun) 1983

This New Zealand duo uses acoustic and electronic instruments as well as sound effects and tape tricks to produce eccentric, unpredictable and mostly charming creations that resemble the inventive home-brew work of R. Stevie Moore. **Canned Music** has seven songs and a ghastly back cover. [iar]

TROY TATE

Ticket to the Dark (Sire/nr) 1984
Liberty (Sire/nr) 1985

Armed with an impressive resumé—Shake, The Teardrop Explodes, Fashion—singer/guitarist Troy Tate released his first solo album in 1984. Working with various

musicians from his past associations (including ex-Teardrop David Balfe), Tate uses his attractively husky voice and substantial songwriting skill, as well as deft sound effects and complex arrangements, to put across ten melodic songs that approach modern pop from several different directions. The most memorable tracks on **Ticket to the Dark** are "Safety Net," "Love Is . . ." and "Thomas," but virtually all are well worth hearing. An exceptionally good record. [iar]

TAXI BOYS

See *Real Kids*.

TAXI GIRL

Seppuku (Mankin-Virgin/nr) 1981

Stranglers Jean-Jacques Burnel (producer) and Jet Black (drums) are involved with this record; otherwise Taxi Girl appears to consist only of a British singer, a guitarist named Mirwais and a keyboard player. Whoever they are, **Seppuku** comes off as a pretentious load of pseudo nonsense, with suave and arty arrangements and playing hampered by lifeless songs. The bored vocals only mirror the effect this LP has on the listener. [iar]

TOT TAYLOR AND HIS ORCHESTRA

Playtime (Easy Listeners/nr) 1982

TOT TAYLOR

The Inside Story (Easy Listeners/nr) 1984

Playtime, a minor gem by ex-Advertising man Taylor, consists of revisionist Tin Pan Alley-style ditties. The piano, bass and drums are augmented by guitar and even occasional dribbly synthesizer, as well as the more traditional horns and strings. Taylor's modestly clever wordplay is more whimsical and self-parodic than his models'. Also, you almost don't notice that his ingratiatingly unassuming humor is often subtly slipping a happy mask over observations on the grayness, tedium and loneliness of the modern day-to-day. We are "Living in Legoland."

His second album (no orchestra, mostly Tot alone) is another delightful grab-bag. Although not the equal of **Playtime** (and shorter, too), if you love one you'll want both. Taylor's penchant for whimsical, wacky pop-rock is complemented here by increased indulgence of his incurable romanticism; his flaky charm is even equal to his choice of Cole Porter's "All of You" as the album's closing song. [jg]

BRAM TCHAIKOVSKY

Strange Man, Changed Man (Radar/Polydor) 1979
The Russians Are Coming (Radar/nr) 1980
Pressure (nr/Polydor) 1980
Funland (Arista) 1981

Bram Tchaikovsky was a group as well as Peter Brammell's nom de rock, but it was the lack of a similarly strong second creative force in the band that proved to be its undoing. The ex-Motors guitarist/bassist/vocalist had the talent to make his band work for a while, but couldn't maintain its quality alone.

Strange Man, Changed Man sounds fresh and punky (if rather trebly), an energetic mixture of the Byrds, Springsteen and, not surprisingly, the Motors. (Nick Garvey, one of Bram's ex-bandmates, co-produced.) The LP includes three fine singles ("Girl of My Dreams," "I'm the One That's Leaving," "Sarah Smiles"); the rest of the material has also worn remarkably well.

Expanding from a trio to a quartet and doing the production themselves, Bram (the band) came up with a sophomore effort (**The Russians Are Coming**, retitled **Pressure** for the cold war USA) that is an improvement soundwise but far less consistent songwise, with writing divided among various combinations of the members.

Subsequent personnel shifts left Bram (the man) with neither satisfactory writing partners nor an alternate (or harmony) vocalist to shore up his own shortcomings. An attempt to pursue several ill-advised directions makes **Funland** (production again by Garvey) lifeless. The only times Bram's tepid vocals cut loose are on an old Motown tune, the oft-covered "Breaking Down the Walls of Heartache," and a Motors B-side, "Soul Surrender," which was recorded as an afterthought by Bram, Garvey and deputized drummer Hilly Michaels. [jg]

THE TEARDROP EXPLODES

Kilimanjaro (Mercury) 1980
(Mercury/nr) 1980
Wilder (Mercury) 1981

Charming despite frequent bouts of pretentiousness, Julian Cope—The Teardrop Explodes' singer/songwriter/frontman—led the Liverpool group through two albums before pushing on to a solo career. Cope's influences include everyone from Scott Walker to the Doors to Tim Buckley, but Teardrop's sound was better than the sum of its parts. The group's problem was Cope's scattershot approach—his songs are filled with too many amorphous, meaningless and just plain silly images—and his lack of a good editor.

Kilimanjaro is the more focused of the two; next to it, **Wilder** sounds like a debut, as whatever restraining influence the band had on Cope was removed, leaving him to write all of the songs unaided. **Kilimanjaro** was released twice in the UK (the second version added a single, "Reward," and a totally different cover). The American release uses the first cover but switches the sequencing and swaps two cuts. In any form, it's a lush, mesmerizing, appealing album, whose only problem (other than the lyrics) is that the songs tend to float together with little individual character. But the ones that do stand out are terrific: "Poppies in the Field," "Treason," "Reward" and "When I Dream," the last providing a brush with American radio success. Most of the songs have a childlike, dreamy quality.

While better-defined musically, **Wilder** is more confused lyrically, though it still carries the band's unique atmosphere. Cope's flat voice and sometimes turgid lyrics serve as instruments used for sonic value to provide color, especially on "Bent Out of Shape," "Seven Views of Jerusalem" and "The Culture Bunker." [ks]

See also *Julian Cope, Troy Tate*.

TEARDROPS

Final Vinyl (Illuminated/nr) 1980

Buzzcocks bassist Steve Garvey was a Teardrop; the rest of this Manchester-based organization had some ties to the Fall and other local legends. **Final Vinyl** is very inconsistent—too much mucking about in the studio ruins the decent tracks with spurious talking and noises—but there is some fine music here that hovers between the Buzzcocks and the Sex Pistols. [iar]

TEARS FOR FEARS

The Hurting (Mercury) 1983
Songs from the Big Chair (Mercury) 1985

In this highly industrialized age, efficiency remains a highly valued commodity, so there is something socially responsible about the burgeoning duo population in pop music. The trend towards pairs of pale, fashionable youngsters making hugely popular self-contained (often synthesizer-based) records has increased the number of potential bands by at least a factor of two. Bath's Tears for Fears, one of the better creators of nouveau intellectual pop—of the highly listenable variety, not the challenging work-for-your-culture sort—make clever, memorable records with startling, thought-provoking lyrics about alienation, psychological analysis and failed romance. That they avoid formula and repetition is an added bonus.

The Hurting introduces Roland Orzabal and Curt Smith (the band includes two low-profile sidemen as well) and their intensely dour, introspective worldview. Orzabal's songs—largely derived from primal scream theory and other aspects of modern psychology—discuss only somber topics of deep pain and sorrow. Like their titles ("The Hurting," "Mad World," "Start of the Breakdown," "Watch Me Bleed"), the songs are more often depressed than angry. Odd fare for hit records with teenybop appeal to be sure, but occasionally anxious vocals and the eclectic, often remarkable music belie the dark thoughts being conveyed. It's disconcerting to find yourself humming along with such misery, but **The Hurting** is an excellent, mature record.

Over two years in the making, **Songs from the Big Chair** finds Tears for Fears less miserable, more capable of expressing anger and on their way to major international stardom. "Head Over Heels" (grand pop), "Everybody Wants to Rule the World" (haunting pop) and "Shout" (gruff rock)—all co-written by Orzabal with others in the group—are the best three out of eight. The music is more ambitious and sophisticated, making for a few numbers that go on too long without generating much of an impact, but the strong entrants are excellent. (The UK tape release adds six tracks.) [iar]

TEENAGE HEAD

Teenage Head (Can. Goon Island) 1979
Frantic City (Can. Attic) 1980
Some Kinda Fun (Can. Attic) 1982

TEENAGE HEADS

Tornado EP (nr/MCA) 1983

This hard-rockin' quartet from Toronto owes more than its name to the Flamin' Groovies—their records are full of non-stop crazed rock'n'-roll songs about cars, parties, girls, booze and general wanton fun, all imbued with the original Groovies' unreconstructed spirit. With nods to Eddie Cochran, Chuck Berry, Gene Vincent and other rock pioneers, Teenage Head races along, guitars blazing, through numbers like "Ain't Got No Sense," "Kissin' the Carpet," "Teenage Beer Drinking Party" and "Disgusteen." If they were smarter and more sarcastic, T. Head might have more in common with the old Dictators; as it stands, their sound, while hardly original, is perfect for parties held in gymnasiums. The first three records may not be hip, but they are solid, sweaty and convincingly salacious.

Given a pluralizing, sanitizing "s" for **Tornado**, their American debut—six new songs that aren't particularly invigorating—the group lowers its hysteria level in an ill-advised stab at maturity and commercial hard-rock acceptability, dropping from Canada's would-be Van Halen to a junior-league Loverboy in one easy step. [iar]

TEENAGE JESUS AND THE JERKS ET AL.

No New York (nr/Antilles) 1978

TEENAGE JESUS AND THE JERKS

Teenage Jesus and the Jerks EP (nr/Lust/Unlust) 1979

Teenage Jesus pushed the anything-goes/anyone-can-do-it philosophy of punk about as far as it would stretch without breaking. Formed by onetime CBGB waitress Lydia Lunch and saxophone/conflict artist James Chance, TJ and the Jerks went beyond minimalism and atonality into what Lunch proudly called "aural terror"; the band cranked up a musical death knell over which she screamed her lyrics of fear, pain and unpleasantness. Chance quit to form the equally abrasive but funkier Contortions; the Jerks soldiered on as a trio, leaving their sonic bloodbaths on the **No New York** anthology and two Bob Quine-produced singles ("Orphans" and "Baby Doll") that are preserved on the eponymous EP. Lydia ranks as one of the most creatively untalented guitarists of all time; her blistering walls of noise, while completely lacking in melody or taste, possessed an unremitting atavistic ferocity akin to latter-day King Crimson. Never a band to waste the audience's time, Teenage Jesus specialized in twenty-second songs and ten-minute sets (which many witnesses at the time still considered about nine minutes too long.)

Lydia went on to form numerous other bands and musical alliances. Drummer Bradley Field popped up briefly as a bongo player for the Contortions; bassist Jim Sclavunos became the drummer in Lydia's subsequent band, 8-Eyed Spy. [rnp]

See also *James Chance, 8-Eyed Spy, Lydia Lunch*.

TELEPHONE

Telephone (Fr. Columbia-EMI) 1977
Crache Ton Venin (EMI/nr) 1979
Au Coeur de la Nuit (Virgin/nr) 1980
Telephone! EP (Virgin/nr) 1982
Un Autre Monde (Virgin/nr) 1984

Telephone's biggest contribution to rock culture was proving to a stodgy French record industry that a local band could succeed singing teenage protest lyrics in their native tongue. As far as the rest of us are concerned, Telephone's sound is more Stonesy hard-rock than Pistols punk thrash. They are quite good at it, though, investing their crunchy guitar boogie with cutting punk force while singer Jean-Louis Aubert shoots as much Jaggeresque venom as possible into the soft curves of a romance language.

Both the band's first LP, produced by Mike Thorne, and **Crache Ton Venin**, produced by Martin Rushent in his pre-Human League days, are recommended for their spunk and energetic garage sound. The **Telephone!** EP, produced by Bob Ezrin, has six songs delivered mostly in lightly accented English that show development into subtler, more modern territory, like "The Cat," a slinky number sung by female bassist Corinne Marienneau and accented by bawdy trombone.

Glyn Johns produced **Un Autre Monde**, on which Telephone shifts sideways and back. Marienneau gets more chances to sing (in French) formless numbers that have neither personality nor energy, while Aubert's turns in the spotlight again recall the Glimmer Twins. A boring mess. [df/iar]

TELEVISION

Marquee Moon (Elektra) 1977
Adventure (Elektra) 1978
The Blow-Up [tape] (nr/ROIR) 1982

Live, they were the ultimate garage band with pretensions—Television's influences were Coltrane and Dylan as well as Roky Erickson—but on record they achieved a polish that added genuine strength. The group evolved from the Neon Boys and initially consisted of Tom Verlaine (guitar/vocals), Richard Lloyd (guitar), Billy Ficca (drums) and Richard Hell (bass). Hell left, later forming the Heartbreakers with Johnny Thunders, and ex-Blondie bassist Fred Smith took over his slot. Thus constituted (and significantly reduced in fringe aggression), Television recorded "Little Johnny Jewel," a privately-pressed single which many regard as a turning point for the whole New York scene.

TV signed to Elektra and released **Marquee Moon** in 1977. A tendency to "jam" onstage caused detractors to refer to them as the Grateful Dead of punk, but it was the distinctive two-guitar interplay (along with Verlaine's nails-on-chalkboard vocals) that set them apart. Verlaine's staccato singing in songs like "Prove It" and "Friction" is impressive, and the long workout on the title track showed a willingness to break away from the solidifying traditions of their more self-conscious contemporaries.

Adventure was, contrary to its title, smoother and more controlled than its predecessor, but did not want for good material. "Glory," "Foxhole" and the beautiful "Days" showed the band to have a firm grip on their songwriting. Television lasted about another year before splintering. A posthumous tape-only compilation of live performances shows the band's rawer side and includes such concert cover staples as "Knockin' on Heaven's

Door," "Satisfaction" and the 13th Floor Elevators' classic "Fire Engine" (inexplicably listed as "The Blow Up" and credited to Verlaine, though the song is mentioned by its true name and source in the liner notes). Verlaine and Lloyd have both released solo albums; Ficca became a Waitress. Richard Hell went on to form other bands under his own name after leaving the Heartbreakers.   [jw]

See also *Heartbreakers, Richard Hell, Richard Lloyd, Tom Verlaine, Waitresses.*

TELEVISION PERSONALITIES

. . . And Don't the Kids Just Love It (Rough Trade/nr) 1981
Mummy Your Not Watching Me (Whaam!/nr) 1982
They Could Have Been Bigger Than the Beatles (Whaam!/nr) 1982
Then God Snaps His Fingers (Whaam!/nr) 1983
The Painted Word (Illuminated/nr) 1983
Chocolat-Art (Ger. Pastell-Principe Logique) 1985

Drawing their inspiration from '60s British pop and psychedelia, London's TV Personalities are an amateurish, haphazard band whose records offer nothing in the way of slick musicianship but loads of brilliantly adapted pop-art weirdness. They started out wide-eyed and Jonathan Richman-like but have evolved into (and beyond) rambling, jagged space noise and various stripes of psychedelia.

The first album is altogether charming in its guileless version of Carnaby Street pop given a modern neurotic outlook. The cover sets the time frame with a collage that fits together *The Avengers'* Mr. Steed and Twiggy. From a Kinksish tale of boyish admiration ("Geoffrey Ingram") to the lyrically acute "I Know Where Syd Barrett Lives," simply and softly played guitars, bass and drums support coy vocals sung with a strongly adenoidal accent by Daniel Treacy. Haunting melodies and abundant wit make the record bizarre but wonderful, far more eccentric and original than the solemn neo-mod rehashers.

Moving from succinct pop art and flower power to trippy psychedelia, the mixture of keyboards and low-budget studio effects help make **Mummy Your Not Watching Me** very different. Although some of the numbers follow the pattern of the first album ("Painting by Numbers" and "Lichtenstein Painting"), others meander through mild mind expansion, in homage to acid rockers like Pink Floyd. The standout in this vein is "David Hockney's Diaries," a song which demonstrates the problem inherent in adorableness trying to be spacey. The shoebox production removes any grandiosity they may have intended, and what's left sounds mixed up and silly. If it weren't for the redeeming pop tunes, **Mummy** would have been a real disappointment.

Released concurrently with the announcement of the band's dissolution (a temporary situation, as it turned out), **They Could Have Been Bigger Than the Beatles** includes reprises of some previously recorded songs as well as a pair of '60s ultra-mods the Creation's best numbers—"Painter Man" and "Making Time"—given affectionate and

respectful (if incompetent) treatment. The album offers sixteen tracks of should-have-been-good nostalgic art-rock, but sacrifices a lot of charm with an overly heavy guitar sound. Best cut: "The Boy in the Paisley Shirt."

The Painted Word lists a four-man lineup and actually features a group photo (albeit a dark, fuzzy one) on the front cover. Musically, the TVPs have drifted off into spare, droning psychedelia and ultra-restrained rock that's hauntingly beautiful, like the Velvet Underground's most delicate moments. The songs all seem to be originals, and effectively convey a melancholic sense of futility, even when superficially addressing relatively jolly topics. Surprisingly serious, but excellent.

Chocolat-Art (sarcastically subtitled "A Special Tribute to James Last") was recorded live as a trio in Germany, and features simple but effective performances of such TVP classics as "Silly Girl," "I Know Where Syd Barrett Lives" (appending "I know where Paul Weller lives—'cause he's a hippie, too") and "Look Back in Anger." They're not always quite in tune, but you know they mean well. Parochial listeners will understandably lose patience with the group's unabashed amateurishness, but the Television Personalities say what they mean and mean what they say, with integrity and an intangible quality that makes them unique and wonderful.   [iar]

TELEX

Looking for Saint Tropez (Sire/nr) 1979
Neurovision (Sire) 1980
Sex (nr/PVC) 1981
Birds and Bees (Interdisc/nr) 1982

This Belgian synth trio specializing in suave Euro-disco is at once a bland dance machine and a reasonably clever techno-pop team. Deadly slow adaptations (with processed vocals) of "Rock Around the Clock" and Plastic Bertrand's "Ca Plane pour Moi" make **Looking for Saint Tropez** noteworthy; the originals, while faster, are mundane and one-dimensional.

Neurovision takes the same approach, giving Sly Stone's "Dance to the Music" the full Telex treatment amidst a batch of boring originals. (If their use of synthesizers weren't as dull as technically possible, their records might be a lot better.) **Sex** adds a novel element by employing Ron and Russell Mael of Sparks as lyricists; the collaboration resembles their own band's work with Giorgio Moroder in form, if not content. Unfortunately, Telex's languid creations lack the spunk to keep up with the warped wordplay of "Sigmund Freud's Party," "Exercise Is Good for You" and "Carbon Copy." (**Birds and Bees** replaces three of **Sex**'s tracks with subsequent singles.)   [iar]

TENPOLE TUDOR

Eddie Old Bob Dick and Gary (Stiff) 1981
Let the Four Winds Blow (Stiff) 1981
Swords of a Thousand Men (Can. Stiff) 1981

This wonderful, over-the-top crew of drunken rowdies is led by the inimitable Eddie Tudorpole, whose wobbly vocals lend the proper air of debauchery to the band's

hard-driving arias. **Eddie Old Bob Dick and Gary** contains such classy trash as "Wunderbar," "3 Bells in a Row" and "Swords of a Thousand Men," replete with bizarre concepts, catchy melodies and loopy singing. The great tracks co-exist with some real dogs, but when Tenpole Tudor are on the mark, their good humor and rock energy are undeniably infectious. Their second release, **Let the Four Winds Blow**, takes the band (up or down isn't an issue) to a new plateau, working flippant pseudo-country ("Throwing My Baby Out with the Bathwater"), mock-funk ("Local Animal"), even ersatz ballroom schmaltzola ("Tonight Is the Night"). The Canadian-only **Swords of a Thousand Men** picks the best tracks from both LPs and wraps them in the artwork from the second. Not for the uptight or supercilious, but John Otway fans will understand.   [iar]

10,000 MANIACS

Human Conflict Number Five EP (nr/Mark) 1982 (nr/Christian Burial-Press) 1984
Secrets of the I Ching (nr/Christian Burial-Press) 1983
The Wishing Chair (Elektra) 1985

10,000 Maniacs survive in provincial upstate New York by playing deceptively challenging new pop music. Singer Natalie Merchant's innocent girl voice skips lightly over gentle melodies, while bassist/guitarist Steven Gustafson, bassist/guitarist John Lombardo and drummer Jerome Augusyniak provide the body of the music with unobtrusive reggaefied grooves. But on closer inspection, all is not so cozy. Warped guitars slice in and out, and Merchant's fragmented lyrics gently evoke images of a decaying society bent on violent self-destruction.

Human Conflict Number Five is simple and a little underbaked, but it advances 10,000 Maniacs' trademarks: Merchant's voice and lilting Caribbean grooves. **Secrets of the I Ching** offers a much deeper look at the band. It serves up tastes of Latin and Spanish in the lyrics, and ranges from screeching noise over a pop hook to almost psychedelic power calypso. Both records present difficult ideas in a very palatable manner, without compromise.

The band's major label debut codified their sound more than before, largely dispensing with everything but traditionally-minded electric folk. Comparisons to Fairport Convention help somewhat, although the sensibility and cultural references are truly small-town Americana. Merchant's reflective, impressionist lyrics and clear singing shines on new songs like "Can't Ignore the Train" and new versions of three tunes originally done on **Secrets of the I Ching**. Honest and enthralling music.   [jl/iar]

TEST DEPT.

Beating the Retreat (Some Bizzare/nr) 1984
The Unacceptable Face of Freedom (Ministry of Power-Some Bizzare/nr) 1986

TEST DEPT. AND THE SOUTH WALES STRIKING MINERS CHOIR

Shoulder to Shoulder (Some Bizzare/nr) 1985

Like that other notable contemporary band of philosophical noise-makers, Einstürzende Neubauten, Test Dept. eschew all musical tradition to play stunning ultra-percussion with an industrial bent. Like their Teutonic soul brothers, Test Dept. use large metallic objects and power tools to add stark modern realism to the drum overload, but also bring more structure and rhythm to the assault.

Beating the Retreat—two 12-inch EPs comprising a single-length album—adds occasional vocal effects (not singing) that do little to vary the din, which is simply awesome in its intensity and single-mindedness. Several startling tracks take a wholly different approach, offering sparse ambient sound and effects that blithely incorporate real instruments like cello and harp.

Shoulder to Shoulder, proving the band's political commitment and activism, gives half of its running time to the 90-member Welsh choir. In a truly strange exercise, the two forces collaborate on one track.

The Unacceptable Face of Freedom, with an unwieldy fold-out cover Hawkwind would have been proud of, is a powerful record, both in its potent musical attack and ongoing political convictions. Real drums seem to have replaced most of the steel-bashing, and the instrumentation also includes Fairlight orchestras, taped voices (speaking and singing), sequencers and bagpipes. Observations about the state of British life are angrier than ever—"Statement" features a miner giving a first-hand account of picket-line police brutality, and recurring military themes in the music drive home the point even harder. Test Dept. is now firmly established as one of England's most important bands.   [iar/dgs]

TEX AND THE HORSEHEADS

Tex and the Horseheads (nr/Bemisbrain-Enigma) 1984
Life's So Cool (Stiff/Enigma) 1985

One of the wilder cow-punk bands, Tex and the Horseheads are spiritual kin to the Gun Club. And while they lean toward a very punky image (lead singer Texacala Jones dresses like a female Stiv Bator; on the first album, the bassist's name is Smog Vomit and the drummer is Rock Vodka), their playing is fairly coherent. Mixing mutant blues (even a cover of Jimmy Reed's "Big Boss Man") into the country-rock blender, Tex and the Horseheads have a convincingly strong sound, but are a few pints short on material.

The John Doe-produced **Life's So Cool** is much better, an out-of-control blues-rock riot that recalls **Exile on Main Street**. It starts with an uncredited quote from the traditional instrumental "Cat's Squirrel" and then goes on to such topics as drinking, fornicating and tangling with the law in songs that are substantial and thoughtfully developed. Texacala's singing shows great improvement; exciting guitarist Mike Martt and bassist J. Gregory Boaz add complementary vocals. A very impressive showing with enough bite and spit to satisfy anyone. [iar]

THAT PETROL EMOTION

Manic Pop Thrill (Demon/nr) 1986

The O'Neill brothers left the memory of the peerless Undertones behind with few prospects for their musical future. While Feargal Sharkey underwent his transformation into a mature, clean-cut, intellectual pop chanteur, they laid low, quietly scorning the business that had shattered their teenage dreams. Thankfully, they've now returned with an excellent new quintet that builds on their past accomplishments without revisiting them. Sean (ne John) O'Neill and Derry homeboy Reamann O'Gormain both write and play guitar; brother Damian has switched to bass; a drummer and American singer Steve Mack complete the lineup. **Manic Pop Thrill** is a reasonably apt title for these angry, articulate rock melodies that span the continuum from sweet balladry to PiL/Fall-like noise. Mack is a fine, controlled shouter in the Keith Relf/Steve Marriott tradition; the band's combination of slide guitars, Bo Diddley beats, wild harmonica wailing and rave-up energy recalls nothing so much as the early Stones, Yardbirds and Velvet Underground. That there's no hint of nostalgia or revivalism here suggests that, even with all the crap that masquerades as music, some things about rock'n'roll will never die. [iar]

THE THE

Soul Mining (Some Bizzare/Epic) 1983

MATT JOHNSON

Burning Blue Soul (4AD/nr) 1981 & 1984

When Matt Johnson—in his guise as the The—is in prime form, his pop creations are excellent (despite an eerie vocal resemblance to Ian Anderson of Jethro Tull). Unfortunately, he also displays horrid tendencies toward studio self-indulgence, making worthless, wanky instrumentals. On **Burning Blue Soul**, Johnson (produced on two tracks by Dome) meanders tiringly through formless "songs" with laughably precious lyrics. **Soul Mining** contains "Uncertain Smile" and "This Is the Day," both attractive, warm and nicely arranged with understated eloquence. But it also has its share of snores. [iar]

THEATRE OF HATE

He Who Dares Wins Live in Leeds (SS/nr) 1982
He Who Dares Wins Live in Berlin (Burning Rome/nr) 1982
Westworld (Burning Rome/nr) 1982
Revolution (Burning Rome/nr) 1984
Live at the Lyceum [tape] (Burning Rome/nr) 1984
Theatre of Hate EP (Stiff/nr) 1985
Original Sin Live (9 Mile/nr) 1985

Although singer/guitarist Kirk Brandon's heart and conscience were obviously in the right place, Theatre of Hate's recorded work—unremittingly morose and often strident—was rarely as good as the band's enthusiastic press notices

made it out to be.

Mick Jones (then of the Clash) produced the studio LP, **Westworld**, capturing the full extent of ToH's urgency, especially in the ominous, chilling, "Do You Believe in the Westworld." But, despite a variety of interesting arrangements, the mix is muddy and, while the feeling is strong, Brandon's vocals aren't. What good does a conscience do if you can't express it understandably? "Do You Believe" is the LP's strongest track, concerning the US, China, Russia, the world and the aftermath of a neutron bomb explosion. Brandon sounds understandably agitated, and the effect resembles punked-up Sergio Leone. The only other track of any note is the haunting "Love Is a Ghost." **He Who Dares Wins** (live in Berlin), produced by manager Terry Razor, has thick, dense sound, but reasonably clear vocals. The muscular rock sound, intense atmosphere and teetering sax gives it an edgy excitement.

Brandon shut down the Theatre of Hate in 1982 and formed a new band, Spear of Destiny. The posthumous Stiff EP compiles four early tracks; there have been a number of live releases as well. [ks/iar]
See also *Spear of Destiny*.

THEYR

Mjotvidur Maer (Ice. Eskimo) 1982
The Fourth Reich (Shout/nr) 1982
As Above . . . (Shout/Enigma) 1982

Theyr (an approximation of untranslatable characters) has released several albums in their native Iceland; **As Above . . .**, issued in the US and UK, copies the artwork from **Mjotvidur Maer** but has little in common with its content. Musically harsh but never strident, Theyr shares stylistic ground with bands like Killing Joke, the Fall and A Certain Ratio, plus the Residents and urban funksters, but they still have an identity all their own, forged with indifference to trends going on elsewhere. Distinctly modern, full-blooded and powerful, Theyr's biggest shortcoming is their lyrics, which are awful and pretentious. [iar]

THIN WHITE ROPE

Exploring the Axis (Zippo/Frontier) 1985

Although it starts out slow and winds up boring, the middle of **Exploring the Axis** exposes a fiery blend of guitar rock with a slight country tinge and incipient songwriting strength. Something between a ragged and raw Wire Train and the Meat Puppets, Davis, California's Thin White Rope have the ability to nail some exciting, original music, but often as not miss the point. Promising but confused. [tr]

THIS HEAT

This Heat (Piano/nr) 1979 (Recommended/nr) 1983
Deceit (Rough Trade/nr) 1981
This Heat with Mario Boyer Diekuuroh [tape] (Fr. Tago Mago) 1982

In 1976, Charles Hayward of Gong (and Phil Manzanera's Quiet Sun) joined with Charles Bullen and Gareth Williams to form This Heat. Though arising from art rock and the British school of fusion jazz, This Heat quickly developed into an

experimental band largely dependent on tape loops and production tricks.

This Heat covers two years in the band's history, featuring both live and studio cuts. They use guitar, clarinet, drums and keyboards, permutated with loops, phasing and overdubs, breaking down patterns into only faintly connected musical moments that include artificial skips and looped end-grooves. Though insolent and withdrawn, the music is adventurous and, in its own peculiar way, engrossing.

The punnily-titled **Deceit** is more coherent and raucous, yet avoids the dismal drones and cacophony of other "experimental" groups. Free of clichés, the music blends politics and intelligence, steering clear of artifice and trendiness. Austere, brilliant and indescribable.

This Heat with Mario Boyer Diekuuroh compiles tapes from 1977/8, featuring studio sessions with the Ghanian drummer who greatly influenced their perceptions of rhythm. [sg]

THIS MORTAL COIL

It'll End in Tears (4AD/Valentino) 1984

Not so much a band as a studio party, This Mortal Coil combines the prodigious talents of members of the Cocteau Twins, Modern English, Dead Can Dance, Xmal Deutschland and others in the 4AD label stable to produce atmospheric vignettes, drawing material from such diverse sources as Alex Chilton, Tim Buckley and Colin Newman, as well as penning new songs. The album mixes a few instrumentals with lush vocal performances, and though all rather agreeable, most of it wouldn't disturb a sleeping infant. [dgs/iar]

DAVID THOMAS AND THE PEDESTRIANS

The Sound of the Sand and Other Songs of the Pedestrians (Rough Trade) 1981
Vocal Performances EP (Rough Trade/nr) 1982
Variations on a Theme (Rough Trade/Sixth International) 1983
More Places Forever (Rough Trade/Twin/Tone) 1985

DAVID THOMAS & HIS LEGS

Winter Comes Home (Re/nr) 1982

DAVID THOMAS AND THE WOODEN BIRDS

Monster Walks the Winter Lake (Rough Trade/Twin/Tone) 1985

The Pere Ubu vocalist's first solo album is something of a surprise. Thomas' lyrics and unusual compositions bring strangenesss out of the mundane—imparting magic to everyday objects and activities—aided by an eclectic bunch: Richard Thompson, Anton Fier, Chris Cutler, Eddie Thornton, Philip Moxham and others. Each demonstrates hitherto unguessed aspects of their talents, and Thomas' otherworldly voice—animal noises transmuted into human speech—has never been more expressive. A high point of avant-garde-folk-blues- jazz-rock, the only title that fits Thomas' cultural synthesis.

Variations on a Theme, which prominently features Richard Thompson, again mixes a bit of everything—including country, jazz and blues—into Thomas' own unique style. Probably the most musically sedate and "normal" record he's ever done, only two tracks recall Pere Ubu's general looniness. Throughout, Thomas demonstrates genuine fascination with his subject matter, as well as an invariably novel perspective. A good follow-up, and one indicative of enormous artistic reach.

Winter Comes Home—which gives front cover billing to ex-Henry Cows Chris Cutler and Lindsay Cooper—mixes intellectual stand-up comedy with winning performances, all recorded live in Munich in 1982. Cooper's bassoon perfectly suits Thomas' tastefully strident vocal excursions. Most notable is the title track, essentially a shaggy-dog story.

Thomas is reunited with Ubu bassist Tony Maimone for **More Places Forever**. Along with Cutler's drums and Cooper's one-woman woodwind section, Thomas has all the backdrop he needs to gather us into his little world and cast his spell. He displays his love for things like insects and sunshine, and in "New Broom" follows some dust on its journey. Ubu fans finally get to hear the track for which **Song of the Bailing Man** was titled.

The new band assembled for **Monster Walks the Winter Lake** is almost an Ubu reunion, with Maimone joined by Allen Ravenstine on synths and Paul Hamann producing. The low-key music moves more slowly than usual, with cello and strangely- played accordion often the predominant instruments. Lyrics are more philosophical, with recurring monster metaphors; the four-part, eleven-minute title track is a real treat.

A song stylist in the truest sense of the word, David Thomas is one of rock's few *truly* one-of-a-kind artists. [sg/dgs]

THOMPSON TWINS

A Product of . . . (T/nr) 1981 (Fame/nr) 1983
Set (T/nr) 1982 (Fame/nr) 1984
In the Name of Love (nr/Arista) 1982
Quick Step & Side Kick (Arista/nr) 1983 (Fame/nr) 1985
Side Kicks (nr/Arista) 1983
Into the Gap (Arista) 1984
Here's to Future Days (Arista) 1985

The name notwithstanding, there are no twins and no Thompsons in this once-obscure, now globally known modern pop band. Originally configured as a loose collection of players—as many as seven—led by singer/synthesist/songwriter Tom Bailey, the Twins eventually pared down to just Bailey, Alannah Currie and Joe Leeway and became one of the world's leading purveyors of occasionally adventurous, invariably danceable modern chart fare.

All six musicians credited on **A Product of . . .** manage to play some percussion in addition to their primary instruments—sax, guitar, keyboards, etc. The cleverness and variety of the tracks, however, eliminates any potential monotony that might have resulted from the heavy reliance on rhythm. And although the music is designed to incite maximum motion, there isn't one track that skimps on lyrical, melodic or structural depth. The album isn't uniformly wonderful, but the textures and sounds make it pleasurable and energizing.

Set adds one member, a full-time bassist, but is otherwise not very different—in cast or in content—from its predecessor. Exemplified by such great numbers as "In the Name of Love" and "Bouncing," Bailey and his cohorts prove that it is possible to make totally listenable dance music that doesn't beg suspension of critical faculties. Producer Steve Lillywhite and Thomas Dolby also pitch in, making **Set** a very nice record indeed. (The Thompsons' first exposure in America came via **In the Name of Love**, which consists of two tracks from the first LP and eight from the second.)

Building on the dance sound of "In the Name of Love" (in fact, quoting it on the first track, "Love on Your Side"), the Twins emerged mature, motivated and commercially focused on their third album, **Quick Step & Side Kick**. (The American release strangely changes the title and rearranges the tracks a tad. The British cassette includes a bonus side of remixes.) Demonstrating varied and skilled songwriting and extraordinary self-contained music-making (the three play almost everything you hear on keyboards), the album bounces from start to finish, but no two tracks have much in common other than a good mood and a strong beat.

Consolidating their stardom, **Into the Gap** is a virtual greatest hits album, containing "Hold Me Now," "Doctor Doctor," "You Take Me Up" and "Sister of Mercy," all of which were radio, chart and club staples for many months. The Twins' strength is their avoidance of repetition; the songs vary widely in tempo, style, instrumentation, subject matter and vocal arrangements (all three sing). Although everyone can't like all of their songs, the Thompson Twins have an ineffable appeal that makes them a welcome pop archetype for the '80s.

By the point of **Here's to Future Days**, co-produced by Bailey and Nile Rodgers, the machine is starting to run down a bit. "Lay Your Hands on Me" is brilliant, but "Don't Mess with Doctor Dream" is boring. "King for a Day" is cute but overly familiar, "Tokyo" is corny. And who needed to hear a new version of the Beatles' "Revolution"? **Future Days** is not significantly inferior to the Twins' best albums, but it lacks some of their freshness and vitality.

In April 1986, at the end of a six-month world tour, Joe Leeway left the band to go solo; Bailey and Currie announced they would continue as the Thompson Twins. [iar]

TRACEY THORN

See *Everything but the Girl.*

THREE JOHNS

Some History EP (CNT Productions/nr) 1983
Men Like Monkeys EP (CNT Productions/nr) 1983
A.W.O.L. EP (Abstract/nr) 1984
Do the Square Thing EP (Abstract/nr) 1984
Atom Drum Bop (Abstract/nr) 1984
Death of the European EP (Abstract/nr) 1985
Brainbox (He's a Brainbox) EP (Abstract/nr) 1985
The World by Storm (Abstract/nr) 1986

This trio from Leeds—*actually comprising three fellows named John*—specializes in discordant socio-political guitar punk with trembling falsetto vocals. Their preference for a rhythm machine over a live drummer creates a unique tension in the overall sound.

Some History compiles two singles (from 1982 and 1983) on one 12-inch, and is very much indicative of the trio's approach. Save for a surfacing maniacal edge, the two succeeding EPs stake out more of the same turf. The singing John's whining vocals would grate in large doses, but brevity—four songs each—keeps these two records from becoming downright annoying.

The Johns plunge headfirst into dance rock on **Do the Square Thing**. Lyrically oblique and riddled with innuendo, the title track is, for these thrashers, an extraordinarily slick piece of extended dance-floor fodder. Surprisingly, it makes a stronger impression than their usual dirges.

Characteristics that might be tiresome if abused are kept judiciously in check on the first LP, **Atom Drum Bop**. The vocals don't wander unnecessarily, guitar lines are blindingly sharp and melodic, and the production is crystalline. "Teenage Nightingales to Wax," "Firepits," "Do Not Cross the Line" and the odd ballad, "No Place," all help make this the Johns' most fully realized endeavor.

Two further four-song EPs both evince continued growth towards tuneful pop. Without losing any of their bite, the A-sides offer incisive comments on some pretty heady subject matter: America's destructive influence on Continental heritage ("Death of the European") and yuppiesque self-centered apathy ("Brainbox"). The B-sides are more jagged, and just as strong.

The World by Storm, released with a limited edition 7-inch live EP, is highly recommended. The Johns have honed their craft to seeming perfection: it will be difficult for them to improve on tunes like "King Car," "Torches of Liberty," "Demon Drink" and the pre-LP single, "Sold Down the River." [ag]

THREE O'CLOCK

Baroque Hoedown EP (nr/Frontier) 1982
Sixteen Tambourines (nr/Frontier) 1983
Arrive Without Travelling (IRS) 1985

SALVATION ARMY

The Salvation Army (nr/Frontier) 1982

One of the brightest lights of new American pop-psychedelia, LA's Salvation Army debuted with an album that was liable to inspire young bands all around the world to join in the fun. The melodies have the ethereal quality of a young Syd Barrett; the music is a blend of all the most colorful '60s sounds, showing the influence of such groups as the Byrds, Move, Hollies, Music Machine and others.

Following legal action by the real Salvation Army, the group was forced to change its name, and became the Three O'Clock. The five songs on **Baroque Hoedown** have poppier vocals and equally engaging music. The addition of ex-Quick

drummer Danny Benair also brought the group a harder edge. Don't miss their cover of the Easybeats' "Sorry."

Sixteen Tambourines is even better—an incredible full-length collection of chiming, memorable power pop tunes played and sung as if each track were likely to get played on every radio station coast-to-coast. Slick and inventive production by Earle Mankey delivers the songs (most co-written by guitarist Louis Gutierrez and bassist Michael Quercio) in utterly engaging style. Best numbers: "On My Own," "Jet Fighter," "And So We Run." Absolutely charming and remarkably memorable.

In 1985, the Three O'Clock signed to IRS and released their second album. **Arrive Without Travelling** isn't quite as delightfully twinky as its predecessor, but it does contain enough characteristically lightheaded material ("Her Head's Revolving," "Simon in the Park") to maintain the group's standing as preeminent paisley popsters. [cpl/iar]

See also *Kendra Smith.*

3 VOICES

3 Voices (NZ Unsung) 1983

A one-off big band project from New Zealand, this album is modern-abrasive (as opposed to old-fashioned abrasive), with bleating horns, meta-tonal vocal arrangements and rhythms that trundle from near-reggae to near-rock. Weird and not entertaining. [iar]

THROBBING GRISTLE

Second Annual Report (Industrial/nr) 1978 (Fetish/nr) 1979 (Mute/nr) 1983
D.o.A. (Industrial/nr) 1979 (Fetish/nr) 1981 (Mute/nr) 1983
Twenty Jazz Funk Greats (Industrial/nr) 1979 (Fetish/nr) 1981 (Mute/nr) 1983
Heathen Earth (Industrial/nr) 1979 (Fetish/nr) 1981 (Mute/nr) 1983
Throbbing Gristle's Greatest Hits (nr/Rough Trade) 1980
Funeral in Berlin (Ger. Zensor) 1981
24 Hours [tape] (Industrial/nr) 1981
Mission of Dead Souls (Fetish/nr) 1981 (Mute/nr) 1983
Five Albums (Fetish/nr) 1982
Thee Psychick Sacrifice (Illuminated/nr) 1982
Editions Frankfurt—Berlin (Illuminated/nr) 1983
Once Upon a Time (Live at the Lyceum) (Casual Abandon/nr) 1983

Raised on William S. Burroughs and Philip K. Dick, and inhabiting a science-fiction-now world of industrial depression, Throbbing Gristle produced some of the most confrontational and unpleasantly fascinating music of recent years, ostensibly as a means to radicalize the listener into abandoning bourgeois romanticism for a realistic view of life.

Second Annual Report (the band's first) uses mournful synthesizer drones to paint a grimly powerful vision of post-industrial, mid-depression England.

D.o.A. is brighter in tone and more polished in technique. Less cohesive than the previous album, **D.o.A.** places greater emphasis on live material, found tapes and individual productions by separate

members of the band. The music is aggressively anti-melodic, but the spirit is powerful and the surprises plentiful. Recommended for the strong.

Twenty Jazz Funk Greats breaks away from **D.o.A.**'s stark bleakness in an attempted truce between their radical attitudes and pop music, removing the cutting edge from their calculated chaos but offering more accessibility.

Heathen Earth is a return to form, adding savagery to the mix, expanding Gristle leader Genesis P-Orridge's obsession with the profane juxtaposition of everyday symbols and motifs. The music is clean, vicious, sharp and occasionally displays the band's transition to energetic, if still outré, rock.

Greatest Hits, subtitled "Entertainment Through Pain" (an apt description of the band's approach), collects material from the first four albums. Recommended for a solid overview.

Funeral in Berlin and **Mission of Dead Souls** are live albums. The first features all previously unreleased material; the latter is a recording of the band's final show in San Francisco. Those who desire a lot more Throbbing Gristle live should check out **24 Hours**, a collection of two dozen C-60 cassettes packed in a suitcase and containing most of the group's live shows. (Rough Trade reportedly also offered a suitcase set of 33 tapes around the same time. Did anyone actually buy one of these?) In 1983, however, Rough Trade bowed to marketing pressures and made those 33 cassettes available individually. **Five Albums** is more reasonably sized, a boxed set reissuing all the albums that had previously been on Fetish.

Although Throbbing Gristle has been defunct now for many years and its members scattered into Psychic TV and Chris & Cosey, new records—most of them live (how can there be anything left?)—are still being released. [sg/iar]

See also *Chris and Cosey, Psychic TV.*

JOHNNY THUNDERS

So Alone (Real/nr) 1978
In Cold Blood (Fr. New Rose) 1983
Diary of a Lover EP (nr/PVC) 1983
New Too Much Junkie Business [tape] (nr/ROIR) 1983
Hurt Me (Fr. New Rose) 1984
Que Sera, Sera (Jungle/nr) 1985

For his first solo LP, the legendary New York Dolls/Heartbreakers guitarist enlisted the aid of ex-Pistols Paul Cook and Steve Jones, some of the Hot Rods, the Only Ones and even old-timers Steve Marriott and Phil Lynott. Choosing material representative of all his prior musical phases and aided immeasurably by co-producer Steve Lillywhite, Thunders turns in reasonably strong performances, perfectly employing his gutter guitar and New York sneer in a number of (musical) veins, including greasy R&B and a tender ballad. Not since the Dolls' two records has he sounded so lucid and involved—**So Alone** is Johnny Thunders at his best.

Thunders didn't release anything else under his own name for five years after that. The LP-plus-EP **In Cold Blood** returned him to the racks, combining five newly-recorded studio tracks—with just a drummer and Walter Lure—that

152

don't amount to much with a poor live Boston show taped in 1982. (**Diary of a Lover** consists of the five studio cuts plus a subsequent item.) At **Cold Blood**'s best, Thunders pounds out a stinging "Green Onions" that suggests his guitar skills aren't gone yet.

Narrated in New Yawkese by the artist, **New Too Much Junkie Business** offers live, demo and live-in-the-studio recordings from 1982, co-produced by Jimmy Miller with a variety of players helping out on renditions of everything from the Dolls' era "Jet Boy" and "Great Big Kiss" to numbers that overlap **Diary of a Lover**. Most notable is "Sad Vacation," a tribute to Sid Vicious. That song also appears on the French-only **Hurt Me**, alongside renditions of some of Thunders' best songs as well as "Eve of Destruction" and "It Ain't Me Babe."

Que Sera, Sera comes complete with a batch of solid new songs, a steady rhythm section (Keith Yon and Tony St. Helene), an illustrious cast of guest stars and a surprisingly easygoing, clearheaded outlook. Variety is a watchword: Stonesy pseudo-reggae ("Cool Operator"), sneering sexist raunch ("Little Bit of Whore"), restrained reality ("Short Lives," wherein JT denounces the live-fast-die-young credo), familiar Dollsy be-bop ("Tie Me Up" and "Endless Party," co-written with David Jo) and a hot uptempo instrumental ("Billy Boy") mix gaily. In fact, the most wasted thing about this LP is the unnecessary cover shot of Thunders looking like the not-so-living dead. [iar]

See also *Heartbreakers*.

THURSAFLOKKUR

Gaeti Eins Verid . . . (Ice. Bit) 1982

This is the fourth album by an inventive Icelandic jazz-rock group. Where many of their contemporaries go the dense, Fall-noise route, Thursaflokkur play like a hip Blood, Sweat & Tears: upbeat, light drums supporting generally reserved electric piano, guitar (capable of wild solos at times) and bass, with strong vocals that can get a little overpowering. Exotic even if the content is not especially esoteric. [iar]

TIGERS

Savage Music (Strike/A&M) 1980

So what if three of these Tigers were former members of old bands like Juicy Lucy and Van der Graaf Generator? The London fivesome sound as credible as the other ska/reggae bands that cropped up in the Specials' wake, and more fun than most: tart lyrics delivered with good humor, catchy reggae making distinctive use of synth as lead instrument, even some energetic, pop-tinged R&B. Hardly immortal, but highly entertaining. [jg]

'TIL TUESDAY

Voices Carry (Epic) 1985

Boston's underground scene has spawned some excellent, adventurous bands, but 'Til Tuesday is not one of them. "Voices Carry," the quartet's mega-hit, is an adequate (if clumsy) song that utilizes the full extent of singer/bassist Aimee Mann's limited vocal capabilities; the rest of their Mike Thorne-produced album is surprisingly unstylish, bland and unengaging. [iar]

TIME

The Time (Warner Bros.) 1981
What Time Is It? (Warner Bros.) 1982
Ice Cream Castle (Warner Bros.) 1984

Prince's first major male spin-off effort, Minneapolis' Time was an exceptionally fertile launching pad for several careers: vocalist Morris Day, who walked away with the *Purple Rain* film, Jesse Johnson, who went on to front his own Prince soundalike outfit, and Jimmy Jam and Terry Lewis, who became an awesomely succesful freelance writing-production team, scoring hits with Janet Jackson, Cherrelle, Patti Austin, the S.O.S. Band and many others.

The Time's albums alternate between straight, infectious dance-funk tunes and extended jams punctuated by all sorts of silly business. Day's personality informs the songs, filling them with sharp-dressed sex-machine jive, but occasionally allowing a glimpse of the self-effacing chump who realizes that having an onstage valet to hold the mirror for on-site preening is a satire on that selfsame smugness. **Ice Cream Castle** is the best of the three, six tracks including several killer dance grooves. (The Time performed "Jungle Love" in a memorable *Purple Rain* club sequence.) But they've still mainly got loving on the brain: with Prince downplaying overt sexuality in his own records, the Time sings "If the Kid Can't Make You Come" and "My Drawers." To cap off this divergent LP, "Ice Cream Castles" is fine bubble-gum funk-pop.

See also *Morris Day, Jesse Johnson's Revue*.

TIMES

Pop Goes Art! (Whaam!/nr) 1981
This Is London (Artpop!/nr) 1983
I Helped Patrick McGoohan Escape (Artpop!/nr) 1983
Hello Europe (Artpop!/nr) 1985
Go! with the Times (Ger. Pastell-Principe Logique) 1985

Led by singer/songwriter Edward Ball, these psychedelic poseurs neatly recapture the lightweight pop sounds of swinging England, circa 1967, in a seamlessly integrated genre lift. Not as fringe weird or inventive as the Television Personalities, when the Times spin out tunes like "Goodbye Piccadilly" and "The Chimes of Big Ben" on **This Is London**, you'll swear it's the paisley-colored '60s all over again. The Times aren't totally unconnected to the present: "Whatever Happened to Thamesbeat" shows lucid insight into the neo-mod revival with pointed lyrics.

The earlier, low-budget **Pop Goes Art!** includes the marvelously kitsch "I Helped Patrick McGoohan Escape" as well as appropriately-devised creations like "Biff! Bang! Pow!" and the title track. If you don't mind that the Times are totally derivative and enjoy the style they lift, the group is a great example of nostalgia that succeeds on its own merits. [iar]

TIME ZONE

See *Afrika Bambaataa.*

TIN HUEY

Contents Dislodged During Shipment (Warner Bros.) 1979

This sextet of eccentrics from Akron, Ohio (hometown of Devo—something in the water supply, perhaps?) were more eclectic and musicianly than their local colleagues. The Hueys' stunning should-have-been-a-hit version of the Monkees' "I'm a Believer" (included on the album) was inspired by Robert Wyatt's re-arrangement, and the band owes a nod to Frank Zappa as well. Yet their blend of blues, jazz and progressive rock is hilariously unique, offering up a warped vision of Middle America. For Tin Huey, "weekends in my Lay-zee Boy" (from "Hump Day") might be punctuated by the discovery of a car filled with doll heads ("Puppet Wipes"); a surreal "Chinese Circus" comes to town; they even admit to fantasies of technological megalomania ("I Could Rule the World If I Could Only Get the Parts"—later the title of a mini-LP by the Waitresses).

After Tin Huey's artistically fruitful (but commercially hopeless) one-album career ended, various members went on to pursue other projects, the most notable of which are guitarist Chris Butler's creation, the Waitresses, and multi-horn wizard Ralph Carney's Swollen Monkeys. [jg]

See also *Waitresses.*

TIN TIN

See *Stephen Duffy.*

TIREZ TIREZ

Etudes (Object Music/nr) 1980 (Aura/nr) 1981
Story of the Year (Bel. Crepuscule) 1983

Their French name to the contrary, this trio hails from the New York area and borrows far too much from early Talking Heads to be accused of originality. Singer Mikel Rouse shows promise, but **Etudes** (their third release) is so rhythmically monotonous that it's hard to take for a full run-through. [jy]

TOM TOM CLUB

Tom Tom Club (Island/Sire) 1981
Close to the Bone (Island/Sire) 1983

Tom Tom Club provides light refreshment for Talking Heads Tina Weymouth (bass) and her husband Chris Frantz (drums). Although their albums appear during lulls in Heads activity, the first gained its own momentum with two popular dance tracks: "Wordy Rapping-hood" and "Genius of Love." Weymouth and her three sisters' airy vocals sound delightfully innocent over steady but unthreatening rhythm. **Close to the Bone** continues in the same whimsical and sensitive vein (e.g., "Pleasure of Love"). Both records skirt cloyingness, saved by the Tom Tommers' self-conscious ness. Even former art school students can have fun sometimes. [si]

TONES ON TAIL

Tones on Tail (Situation Two/nr) 1983
'Pop' (Beggars Banquet/Beggars Banquet-PVC) 1984

Freed of the inept artistic pretensions of singer Pete Murphy, the guitarist and drummer (later joined by the bassist) of Bauhaus remained in touch after the split and formed Tones on Tail, a generally interesting experiment in various styles. **Tones on Tail** is a full-length album

made up of the band's early (1982/3) singles. It careens from languid, whispered rock to jumpy light funk to spare atmospheric soundtracks and offers very little songwriting content—scanty ideas in service of largely pointless studio fiddling. But while **'Pop'** also has some draggy recidivist Bauhaus tendencies, it also has real songs of modern music that show taste, delicacy and moderate imagination. "Lions," for instance, works an attractively light synth-samba sound while proffering lines like "Lions always hit the heights/'Cause to kill it's always the easy way out." (I said they weren't *completely* cured.) The multi-movement "Real Life" blends acoustic guitar picking with hushed vocals, angry lyrics and weird sound effects—neo-Yes? There's also a song titled "Slender Fungus." [iar]

See also *Love & Rockets.*

WINSTON TONG

See *Tuxedomoon.*

TORCH SONG

Wish Thing (IRS) 1984

This enigmatic English trio plays ethereal synth-dance music—an instrumentally subtle creation given most of its character by singer Laurie Mayer's delicate voice. "Don't Look Now" and "Sweet Thing" are appealing, airy concoctions; a demento version of "Ode to Billy Joe" seems calculated to shock and/or offend but is nonetheless amusing. Intriguing and substantial. [iar]

TOTO COELO

"I Eat Cannibals" EP
(Radialchoice/Chrysalis) 1982

These five English ladies made one great novelty single, "I Eat Cannibals," produced by ace pop hack Barry Blue. In America, the group's name was mysteriously changed to Total Coelo and the song released on a 12-inch, in two versions with an added number. Over a big mock-tribal beat, the five winningly chant the nonsense lyrics, making it a memorable exercise in silliness.

In 1986, one Coeloite surfaced in the Cherry Bombz, a new outfit with Terry Chimes and other ex-members of Hanoi Rocks. [iar]

TOURE KUNDA

Casamance au Clair de Lune (Celluloid) 1984
Amadou Tilo (Celluloid) 1984
Live Paris—Ziguinchor (Celluloid) 1984
Natalia (Celluloid) 1985

The surprising international mass appeal of Senegal's Toure brothers—Ismail, Sixu Tidiane and Ousmane—must be attributed in large part to their soothingly mellifluous voices, tones that wash over the listener like warm milk. Like traditional griots, many of their songs deal with simple reflections on nature and family life, but Toure Kunda also experimented with Western technology—electrified instruments—even before they fell under the sway of Celluloid house producer Bill Laswell. They progressed from the relatively basic drums and voices of **Casamance** to electric guitars and such on **Amadou Tilo**. With **Natalia**, the horn section is more apparent than before, and keyboardist Bernie

153

Worrell, percussionist Aiyb Dieng and a flock of synthesizers make appearances. All in all, pretty wonderful stuff. [rg]

TOURISTS

The Tourists (Logo/nr) 1979
Reality Effect (Logo/Epic) 1979
Luminous Basement (RCA/Epic) 1980
Tourists (RCA International/nr) 1981

In light of Dave Stewart and Annie Lennox's relatively inventive and adventurous subsequent work as Eurythmics, the Tourists were remarkably low on vitality or originality, playing instead a redundant rehash of '60s American acid and folk-rock. Symptomatic of the group's shortcomings, their crowning achievement was scoring a hit with an utterly dull remake of Dusty Springfield's "I Only Want to Be with You."

Lennox, who proved to be a much more expressive singer, here sings with strength but no character; duets with guitarist Peet Coombes resemble the worst of the Jefferson Airplane. Otherwise the group recalls It's a Beautiful Day, the Byrds, Mamas and Papas, the Who and others. If the Tourists had had a personality to call their own, they probably wouldn't have known what to do with it, they were so busy aping others. It's a shame, because some bands have successfully absorbed and adapted these same musical prototypes with much greater élan; at their best, the Tourists could only imitate.

The 1981 LP called **Tourists** is a compilation of previous album tracks; the US edition of **Reality Effect** combines the "best" contents of the band's first two British releases. Since Eurythmics' success, there have been other repackages of Tourist material. [iar]
See also *Eurythmics*.

FRANK TOVEY

See *Fad Gadget*.

TRACIE

Far from the Hurting Kind (Respond/A&M) 1984

Paul Weller discovered Tracie Young in 1982 by announcing a talent hunt in *Smash Hits*; he selected the 17-year-old from the hordes that responded and set about fashioning her into a chart-bound blue-eyed soul singer in a rebirth of England's great pre-fab pop traditions of the early '60s. And, not unlike the idol-making of *Expresso Bongo*, the main component lacking was significant —or at least developed—talent. Tracie has improved since her tentative beginnings, but this airy Weller-produced LP is still tepid and tedious; the songs (including four by the impresario and one by Costello) are rendered indistinguishable by Young's colorless singing and bland arrangements. At its best, a few Motownish tunes show signs of life but never capture more than a fraction of the excitement they aim for. A noble experiment, perhaps, but not a successful one. [iar]

TRANSLATOR

Heartbeats and Triggers (CBS/415-Columbia) 1982
No Time Like Now (CBS/415-Columbia) 1983

Translator (CBS/415-Columbia) 1985
Evening of the Harvest (CBS/415-Columbia) 1986

Formed in Los Angeles, this talented quartet's career got rolling only after moving to San Francisco and signing with 415 Records there. Translator's music encompasses elements of venerable folk-rock but also modern sounds, novel ideas and cool deadpan pop—simply put, diversity makes Translator fine and often fascinating. Singing guitarists Steven Barton and Robert Darlington have a wide stylistic arsenal and the ability to write varied songs of quality and endurance. **Heartbeats and Triggers**, produced by the peerless David Kahne, is a great debut album with very few weak tracks.

No Time Like Now contains another batch of melodic and rocking tunes played with ringing guitars and attractive harmonies; unfortunately, a lot of them don't wash. While "Un-Alone," "Break Down Barriers" and the title track keep the musical faith, "L.A., L.A." is a trite, gimmicky digression and "I Hear You Follow" is too reserved; others are equally unprepossessing or simply plain. Stick with the first album.

Translator, produced by Ed Stasium (Ramones), is for the most part a return to form. "Gravity" is as good as anything they've done; other tunes maintain a tasteful, invigorating blend of vocals, rhythm guitars and intelligent songwriting. The biggest problem here is time: for a third album, they're not really going anywhere new creatively, and commercial success still seems well over the horizon.

Perhaps that frustration explains the radically different album that followed: **Evening of the Harvest's** one-take guitar rock scarcely resembles prior Translator music. To be fair, this is not your average numbskull arena rubbish—most tracks retain the band's melodicism intact—but each is careful to include a (credited) spot of riffing, and some of the songs are pretty dire. [iar]

TRANSMITTERS

And We Call That Leisure Time (Heartbeat/nr) 1981

One-time Glaxo Babies vocalist Rob Chapman leads the Transmitters, an interesting enigma of riveting lyrics and free-form minimalism on guitar, bass, drums and squawking sax. The Transmitters walk a very fine line between accessibility and weirdness; easy to appreciate but hard to like. Chapman's a talented singer and writer, and the music might be really good if it weren't so one-dimensional. File under "Eager- to-please-Pere Ubu-offspring." [iar]

TREES

Sleep Convention (nr/MCA) 1982

A one-man synth army from San Diego, California, Dane Conover (here dubbed Trees) offers a wonderful collection of modern musical ideas and clever tunes that efficiently combine up-to-date electronics with old-fashioned rock instruments, tossing in inventive production and intelligent, provocative lyrics as well. **Sleep Convention** is one of my favorite albums—a stunning debut showing

remarkable originality and talent that promises great things ahead as well as much immediate enjoyment. That this record died the commercial death is not just incomprehensible, it's criminal. [iar]

TRIFFIDS

Treeless Plain (Hot-Rough Trade/nr) 1984
Raining Pleasure (Hot-Rough Trade/nr) 1984
Field of Glass (Hot-Rough Trade/nr) 1985
Love in Bright Landscapes (Hol. Hot-Megadisc) 1986

Although now relocated to London, this quintet hails originally from Perth, Australia. Their musical influences, however, are strictly American. Occasionally augmenting standard rock instrumentation with strings, trumpet and pedal steel, the Triffids manage a spacious country blues-meets-Television sound.

Raining Pleasure is a lightweight, lilting album with some nice songs and more-than-competent playing, but self-righteous lyrics decrying promiscuity and alcohol are pretty much ruinous. The preachy "Property Is Condemned" is almost worthy of a TV evangelist's seal of approval.

Treeless Plain and **Field of Glass** both have more bite—"My Baby Thinks She's a Train" (from the former) sounds like the best song Tom Verlaine never wrote. (Singer/songwriter David McComb's voice bears similarity to both Verlaine and Jim Morrison.) Most of the Triffids' best material is on **Love in Bright Landscapes**, a Dutch compilation. [dgs]

TRIO

Trio (Mobile Suit Corporation/nr) 1982
Live im Frühjahr 82 [tape] (Ger. Mercury) 1982
Trio EP (Mercury) 1982
Trio and Error (Mercury) 1983
Bye Bye (Ger. Mercury) 1983

Originally issued in Germany in 1981, Trio's Klaus Voorman-produced debut album was updated to include their European million-seller, "Da Da Da ich lieb dich nicht du liebst mich nicht aha aha aha." (With the lyrics redone in English, the song was popular in dance clubs outside Germany as well.) Compared to the rest of the album, though, the minimalist hit sounds nearly symphonic; **Trio** is basically guitar and drums behind monotonal (but bilingual) vocals. Lyrics are obsessed with lousy relationships and steeped in black humor—sometimes just blackness without the humor. But the band's brutally primitive sound announces itself first.

The cassette-only **Live im Frühjahr 82** essentially reprises the album, emphasizing guitar for a hot sound, and includes between-song raps *auf Deutsch*. The **Trio** 12-inch EP consists of five tracks from the album of the same name (including six-plus minutes of the English-language "Da Da Da") plus a later single, "Anna."

After that tentative step, Trio's American label took the plunge with **Trio and Error**, which *also* includes "Da Da Da"; the new material—almost all in English—is a little more musical and only a little less downbeat. But the naiveté is charming.

With **Bye Bye**, Trio departed roughly the same as they entered: simple, witty and sarcastic in two languages. A '50s revivalist spirit informs the crazed guitar work of "Ich lieb den Rock'n'Roll" and a constipated "Tutti Frutti"; for those with longer memories, Trio thoughtfully includes an (almost) reverent version of "Tooraloolooraloo." Full-scale production on "Out in the Streets" renders it the most routine-sounding track Trio recorded; others (e.g., the catchy "Immer noch einmal") are as deliciously spartan as ever. [si/iar]

TRIPOD JIMMIE

Long Walk off a Short Pier (nr/Do Speak) 1982
Warning to All Strangers [tape] (no label) 1986

A trio starring ex-Pere Ubu guitarist Tom Herman, Tripod Jimmie inhabits a world of hypertense vocals and simple, rough, aggressive rock noise, in an underground '80s revision of the power trio concept. Recorded "live on the shores of Lake Erie," **Long Walk's** eleven numbers show traces of Television, Ubu and Talking Heads, all essentially similarly-minded organizations. Powerful and disquieting. [iar]

TOM TROCCOLI'S DOG

See *Black Flag*.

TROUBLE FUNK

Drop the Bomb (Sugar Hill) 1982
In Times of Trouble (D.E.T.T.) 1983
Saturday Night. Live! (Island) 1985

Trouble Funk belongs to Washington, DC's go go scene, for years the best-kept secret in "black music." Go go is a throwback to greasy, percussive, endless-groove funk that sacrifices structure, production and slickness for loose community involvement. The bands—basically rhythm sections with a few frills on top—do their thing while the musicians and audience yell a whole lot of nonsense (like "Let's get small, y'all" or "Drop the bomb!") The funk is solidly Southern, with a strong James Brown flavor and tons of sloppy percussion. In no other North American music does the cowbell play such a major role.

Chuck Brown, godfather of go go, developed it from drum breakdowns which he used in clubs to link Top 40 covers. Not surprisingly, he found people were grooving more on these bridges than the songs. Go go has grown concurrently with hip-hop, and offers a group alternative to beat-box isolationism. The unsophisticated grooves began to break out nationwide in '85, and Trouble Funk promise to be one of the genre's leaders.

Drop the Bomb is a seminal go go album because it was released by Sugar Hill, home of the uptown rap set. Virtually all prior go go releases were on Washington's local T.T.E.D. (aka D.E.T.T.) label. Bronx dj's used to find the discs and soak the labels off 'em to keep audiences (and competitors) from finding out what they were playing; **Drop the Bomb** gave everyone a chance to get go go. It also produced two classic tracks: the title tune and the monster 12-inch, "Hey Fellas." Both are wet, sticky and great for dancing. Spin them and you're part of the party.

The double-LP **In Times of Trouble** is like two separate albums. Two sides are studio material that has nowhere near the juice of the debut. The other two are long live jams that sum up the scene. The band maintains a low-tech groove, and the four lead singers move the jam along with a lot of assistance from the crowd. It's not like the Godfather of Soul's side-long live medleys because Trouble Funk doesn't do any songs. It's just a hot bottom, some rolling percussion, a couple of tag phrases and a lot of audience participation. The ultimate funk spirit of these sides is intoxicating.

T-Funk-3 continues the fun with six long, generic demi-instrumentals (and a couple of shorter shards) wisely cut live, in front of an enthusiastically cooperative Saturday night crowd. Cue it up and move! [jl/iar]

TRUE SOUNDS OF LIBERTY

See *T.S.O.L.*

TRUE WEST

True West EP (nr/Bring Out Your Dead) 1983
Hollywood Holiday (Fr. New Rose) 1983
Drifters (Zippo/PVC) 1984
Hand of Fate (Red Rhino/CD Presents) 1986

True West may be part of the new psychedelic underground, but the Davis, California quintet has definitely got a sound and style all its own. Drawing inspiration from Syd Barrett (the band's first release was a single of his "Lucifer Sam," reprised on the EP) and Roky Erickson, they play a frenetic, dense drone with crazed guitars and dramatic vocals.

Co-produced by guitarist Russ Tolman and Dream Syndicater Steve Wynn, **True West** is a marvelous, rough record—five slices of chaos that kick nostalgia out in favor of powerful rock with a dark, threatening ambience. Echo-laden sound gives tunes like "Hollywood Holiday" and "Steps to the Door" an unsettling noise level that considerably heightens tension. **Hollywood Holiday** has the entire contents of the EP plus three more sophisticated tracks subsequently recorded with a new rhythm section. (And a spiffy cover snap of Jimmy Cagney as well.)

For their first full-length album, **True West**—sporting a not-so-good new drummer—trot out nine new songs (reprising "And Then the Rain" from the French LP) that showcase Gavin Blair's vocals as much as Tolman's inventive, original guitar work. A strikingly good record that escapes the strictures of neo-psychedelia by incorporating folk-rock ambience, **Drifters** retains just enough raw-edged aggression to keep things from getting unacceptably melodic. "Look Around" is the clear standout, but other numbers—"Shot You Down" and "Hold On," for instance—also marry engaging sound and arrangements to solid songwriting. [iar]

TRUTH

Five Live EP (IRS/nr) 1984
Playground (IRS) 1985

Leaving behind the constricted scope of skinny-tie R&B revivalists Nine Below Zero, singer/guitarist Dennis Greaves formed the Truth and proceeded to follow the Style Council's lead in updating '60s soul (Hammond organ, doo-wop vocal backing, shingaling rhythms) for an audience that is unlikely to know or care about the originals. **Five Live** is an introductory EP; **Playground** is a fine album of intelligent, tasteful originals (especially "Exception of Love"; "I'm in Tune," an exciting rave-up; and the title track, a straight rocker) played with real character and a minimum of self-consciousness. [iar]

TRYPES

The Explorers Hold EP (nr/Coyote) 1984

What's in a name? The Trypes, Willies, Yung Wu—and, to an only slightly lesser extent, the Feelies—are all aggregations of the same post-hippie suburban spudheads from New Jersey. The bands all sound different, although they all play some Feelies songs and share a fascination with layered guitars, drones and the music of Brian Eno and the Velvet Underground.

The Trypes are the quietest, most introspective of the bunch, and **The Explorers Hold** is a placid, constantly shifting landscape of sounds. The emphasis is on coloration, not beat; yet, for all its subdued calm, there's an explosive tension bubbling underneath the music. The muted guitars threaten but never give way to riotous mayhem. Only on the cover of George Harrison's "Love You To" do drummer Stan Demeski's hyperkinetic tom-tom patterns come to the fore, making the Trypes a loud psychedelic folk band. The quieter songs, complete with woodwinds and keyboards, are hauntingly beautiful. [jl]

T.S.O.L.

T.S.O.L. EP (nr/Posh Boy) 1981
Dance with Me (nr/Frontier) 1981
Change Today? (nr/Enigma) 1984
Revenge (Enigma) 1986

TRUE SOUNDS OF LIBERTY

Beneath the Shadows Alternative Tentacles) 1982

California's T.S.O.L. exploded out of Long Beach to become a premier hardcore band in the area. Their first vinyl foray, in 1981, was a tough, politically inspired five-song EP that bristles with excitement. Ron Emory's thrashing guitar provides a steady foundation for Jack Greggors (credited on the sleeve with "mouth and other organs") to sing over. These fine songs, like "Abolish Government/Silent Majority," are super hot.

Moving from Posh Boy to Frontier, T.S.O.L. also made other changes. For one thing, Greggors changed his name to Alex Morgon; more importantly, the group turned away from politics and joined the horror/shock-rock movement. Along with a cover depicting the grim reaper in a graveyard, the lyrical themes of **Dance with Me** are largely those of B-movie scare flicks, and nearly as much fun. Unlike many other bands who have proven useless at this genre, T.S.O.L succeed because their brutal, razor-edge sound is always musically convincing, regardless of the subject matter.

Change seems to be T.S.O.L.'s watchword. **Beneath the Shadows** involves a third label, the addition of a keyboard player and a new drummer (plus a vocalist named Jack Delauge in Morgon's place—the same guy?). Oh, and they also sound totally different. Dropping any remaining connection with hardcore, the newly refined approach leaves the group neo-psychedelic, but with lots more rock drive and character than most in the genre. A great record from an always surprising band.

Change Today? keeps the band's string of changes alive, with a new label and two new members in the lineup. (The front cover also reclaims the acronym.) Only guitarist Ron Emory and bassist Mike Roche remain, joined by Joe Wood (guitar/vocals) and Mitch Dean (drums). Fielding a whomping near-punk rock sound, the foursome are aggressive but coherent and lucid, singing shapeless songs that pack a wallop but little lasting substance. Not a bad record, but not their best effort. [cpl/iar]

MASAMI TSUCHIYA

See *Ippu-Do.*

TUBEWAY ARMY

See *Gary Numan.*

MAUREEN TUCKER

See *Velvet Underground.*

TUFF DARTS

Tuff Darts (Sire) 1978

New York's Tuff Darts will probably be best remembered (if at all) as a resumé item for Robert Gordon, who was the glam-punk band's original singer around 1976. Although he did record as a Dart on **Live at CBGB's**, Gordon was long gone by the time the band made an album all its own two years later. (The band was on hold for part of that time while guitarist/leader Jeff Salen played with Sparks.)

The Darts—a junior-league rock band with a penchant for gangster clothes—had a total of two good songs, both of which are included on the LP. Otherwise, the record ranges from simply bad to truly wretched, as on the moronic "(Your Love Is Like) Nuclear Waste." [iar]
See also *Robert Gordon.*

TUXEDOMOON

Half Mute (nr/Ralph) 1980 (CramBoy/nr) 1985
Desire (Pre/Ralph) 1981 (CramBoy/nr) 1985
Divine (Operation Twilight/nr) 1982
A Thousand Lives by Picture (nr/Ralph) 1983
Holy Wars (CramBoy/Restless) 1985
Ship of Fools (CramBoy/Restless) 1986

WINSTON TONG

Theoretically Chinese (Crépuscule/nr) 1985

PETER PRINCIPLE

Sedimental Journey (Made to Measure/nr) 1985

Their albums constitute only a partial discography for this mercurial aggregate of musicians and artists; prior to Ralph, they had released singles and EPs on their own. (Some of these were later reissued by CramBoy.) Pioneers in performance-oriented synthesizer music, Tuxmoon leaven their attack with sax and violin and were one of the first synth bands to use electronic percussion properly, i.e., as a fully integrated substitute for real drums. **Half Mute** is their most fully realized album, a balanced assemblage of pop ("What Use?"), futuristic chamber music ("Tritone") and impressionistic sound collages ("James Whale"). **Desire** is a generally unsatisfying follow-up, save for a sneaky parody of "Holiday for Strings" entitled "Holiday for Plywood." **Divine**, the score for a Maurice Bejart ballet, jettisons the synth beat that makes their best work so attractive. **A Thousand Lives by Picture** is a compilation of tracks previously issued on Ralph.

Tuxedomoon has been based in both San Francisco and Belgium, and continues to eschew the commercial success they likely could achieve. Vocalist Winston Tong has done many outside projects, including a solo album, **Theoretically Chinese**, on Crépuscule. Bassist Peter Principle released his own solo "soundtrack" record on a subsidiary of Crammed Discs, the Belgium-based label that, under an arrangement with the band's own Joeboy label, has been reissuing the group's catalogue and released the new **Holy Wars** album.

By the time of **Ship of Fools**, only Principle and singer/multi-instrumentalist Steven Brown remained from the original lineup. Trading in clever humor for self-conscious artsiness (which was always just beneath the surface anyway), the LP falls flat on its face, especially on the second side, where the band proffers "pieces" rather than songs; titles include "A Piano Solo," "Lowlands Tone Poem" and "Music for Piano & Guitar." Flirting with both light jazz and 20th century classical styles without getting much of a grip on either, the music is about as creative as the nomenclature. [rnp/dgs]

TV PERSONALITIES

See *Television Personalities.*

TV21

A Thin Red Line (Deram/nr) 1981

This neat Scottish quintet sounds at times variously like Haircut One Hundred, U2 and XTC; variety keeps things hopping throughout **A Thin Red Line**. Although basically guitar-oriented, the lineup includes trumpet and synth/organ; the songs are personal and thoughtful. Singer Norman Rodger has a serviceable voice and tries hard; the rest of the band, when the recording quality does them justice (different studios and sessions make for inconsistent sound), are no slouches either. [iar]

23 SKIDOO

Seven Songs EP (Fetish/nr) 1982 (Illuminated/nr) 1985
Tearing Up the Plans EP (Pineapple-Fetish/nr) 1982
Culling Is Coming (Operation Twilight/nr) 1983
Urban Gamelan (Illuminated/nr) 1984

One of England's most daringly experimental post-punk bands, 23

Skidoo are friendly with the members of Cabaret Voltaire; the two outfits once entertained thoughts of merging. But while 23 Skidoo's early avant-dance-floor style was similar to the Cabs', they've always maintained a closer link to both free-form improvisation and non-Western idioms, especially in their recent work.

Seven Songs (which lists eight tracks, has nine and was reissued with three added cuts) is a near-brilliant fusion of funk, tape tricks and African percussion. The band switches gears effortlessly between different-yet-accessible dance tracks like "Vegas El Bandito," the ethnomusicology of "Quiet Pillage" and sound collages ("Mary's Operation"). **Tearing Up the Plans** continues in much the same vein.

On **The Culling Is Coming**, 23 Skidoo gets too obscure for its own good. The first side, recorded live at the WOMAD Festival, is a mishmash of tape loops, random percussion and primitive horn honks which sound like dying animals and add up to third-rate Stockhausen. Side Two utilizes Balinese gamelans (tuned gongs of a sort) and sounds better thought-out. **Urban Gamelan** is a stronger album, livelier and less esoteric. As the title implies, real gamelans aren't used, but glass jugs and CO_2 cylinders are. 23 Skidoo will never enjoy wide-scale popularity, but they are an earnest, disciplined band who make uncompromising music.   [dgs]

20/20

20/20 (Portrait) 1979
Look Out! (nr/Portrait) 1981
Sex-Trap (nr/Mainway) 1982

Originally from Tulsa, Oklahoma, LA's 20/20 started out cute and unthreatening, their lush vocal harmonies announcing their love for the Beatles, Byrds and Beach Boys. That's not to say that Steve Allen and his cohorts aren't interesting in their own right: on their debut, producer Earle Mankey helps the band convert their influences into a striking present-tense form, adding dabs of electronics to dense arrangements. Songs like "Yellow Pills" and "Remember the Lightning" give the impression of being squeezed into a smaller space than is safe—that contents-under-pressure tension adds an exciting edge.

Recorded without Mankey, **Look Out!** is pleasing, but doesn't sparkle the way **20/20** does. More spacious sound exposes the essential banality of the material and shows up the often formulaic nature of the vocal harmonies.

After a lack of commercial acceptance (and the end of the industry's infatuation with skinny-tied power pop bands) cost them their major-label deal, 20/20 dropped out of national sight, but came back in late '82 as a trio with an independent release that unfortunately isn't very impressive. The band subsequently evaporated, but guitarist Chris Silagyi became a well-regarded record producer. [jy]

TWIST

This Is Your Life (Polydor/nr) 1979

This obscure transitional band has loads of fascinating history, the details of which are thus: Guitarist Pete Marsh had been in a schmaltzy duo which evolved into the horribly wimpy Easy Street, a British band signed to Georgia-based Capricorn Records. (Easy Street also included Richard Burgess, who later abandoned easy listening for synthesizer funk, working with Visage, Spandau Ballet and forming Landscape. He's not in this band, but it seemed interesting.) Twist bassist Andy Pask became a member of Landscape while Marsh went on to form pseudo-mystery band Blanket of Secrecy. Drummer Steve Corduner was an ex-member of Nasty Pop.

With guest stars Elvis Costello and Steve Nieve, it's not overly surprising that **This Is Your Life** occasionally resembles **My Aim Is True**. An interesting album with some good songs, it deserved better than it got; despite the uncertain devotion of its members to bouncy rock'n'roll, together they carried it off admirably.   [iar]

SEAN TYLA GANG

Yachtless (Beserkley) 1977
Moonproof (Beserkley) 1978

SEAN TYLA

Just Popped Out (Zilch/Polydor) 1980

From seminal pub-rock bandleader (Ducks Deluxe) to early Stiff signee (his "Texas Chainsaw Massacre Boogie" was the label's fourth release) to the Tyla Gang and a solo career, guitarist Sean Tyla's been around. His three albums (the first two with a steady band of pub compadres) are hard-rocking and honest but not thrilling, despite good playing and Tyla's sincere hoarse vocals. **Yachtless** is the raunchy one, full of lead guitar and aggressive drumming. **Moonproof** takes a subtler attack, introducing acoustic guitar and a more American sound, but no energy loss. **Just Popped Out**, which employs an amazing cast of pub-rock characters (including former members of Ace, Bees Make Honey, Ducks Deluxe, Chilli Willi and the Red Hot Peppers and Man, not to mention Joan Jett and Kenny Laguna!), offers bitter, depressed songs given the best studio treatment of Tyla's career. Comparisons to Bob Seger's gritty rock don't exactly say it, but both share a commitment to personal vision and unfancy, straightforward music.   [iar]

UB40

Signing Off (Graduate/nr) 1980
Present Arms (DEP Int'l/nr) 1981 & 1985
Present Arms in Dub (DEP Int'l/nr) 1981 & 1985
The Singles Album (Graduate/nr) 1982
UB44 (DEP Int'l/nr) 1982
Live (DEP Int'l/nr) 1983
1980—83 (nr/A&M) 1983
Labour of Love (DEP Int'l/A&M) 1983
Geffery Morgan (DEP Int'l/A&M) 1984
The UB40 File (Graduate/nr) 1985
Baggariddim (DEP Int'l/nr) 1985
Little Baggariddim EP (DEP Int'l/A&M) 1985

This integrated Birmingham reggae outfit built its huge following on an independent label (the band's own DEP International, now distributed by Virgin) with non-Rastafarian lyrics concerning social issues (not unlike what many new wave bands addressed) and an ineffable pop sensibility. From the get-go, UB40's music has held appeal far beyond the specialized market; they are the most commercially successful reggae band in the world. Quietly percolating grooves, garnished with sultry horn lines and centered around Ali Campbell's cool, Stevie Wonderesque crooning (with and without sweet harmonies) give UB40 an instantly identifiable sound (or formula, as you will).

On the early albums, even the best of the uneven songwriting—as catchy as it does get—sounds samey and is dominated by the group's style. Contrary to the lyrics' urgency, the music suggests that even when "The Earth Dies Screaming," we'll hear it calmly sipping tea in a hot tub. Until recently the band's tunesmithing seemed to rise to the occasion only for singles (and often, surprisingly, for B-sides).

The Singles Album is UB40's best English-only LP, even though over half of it had already appeared on **Signing Off**. (For the quantity-minded, the latter does include a bonus disc with another 21 minutes of music.) As a matter of fact, any non-fan possessing a couple of UB 45s might hesitate before buying an album by the group.

Present Arms is notable for more prominent use of toasting (which continued on **UB44**) and little else, aside from two solid singles. **Present Arms in Dub**, though, thoughtfully attempts an alternative to the usual dub style, which is generally just vocal-less electronic fiddling of greatly variable quality. Here, UB40 drastically changed the face of its music to the point where some songs are hardly recognizable; it's nearly as though the material were written explicitly for dub treatment. An "A" for effort.

UB44, in addition to minor alterations (more Latin percussion, sparingly applied gurgling synth), displays wider lyrical range and increased verbal acuity, but the only truly striking tune is, naturally, a single ("So Here I Am"). It's not that UB40 have little to offer; it's just that their singles are the brightest spots cut from the same relatively unvarying cloth.

The live album was recorded on tour in Ireland in 1982 and features such tunes as "Food for Thought," "Tyler" and "One in Ten."

In an effort to export some of UB40's success to the States, the group's American label issued **1980—83**, a selection of tracks from **UB44, Present Arms** and early singles. Not a bad set, but not the introduction America wanted. What finally did the trick was a novelty of sorts, but one that addressed the band's shortcomings as songwriters: **Labour of Love** is an LP of cover versions, drawing on reggae (and reggaefied) hits from a number of diverse authors: Neil Diamond ("Red Red Wine"), Jimmy Cliff ("Many Rivers to Cross"), Delroy Wilson ("Johnny Too Bad") and Bob Marley ("Keep on Moving"). The resultant variety and melodic quality makes it UB40's most easily enjoyable album, richly filled with loving tributes played superbly.

Geffery Morgan, entirely new original material, shows a vastly more creative UB40 at work: inventive production, intriguing rock rhythms, powerful and memorable songwriting and new outlooks all combine to make it a great record that remains rooted in reggae but is much more diverse than the form generally allows. "Riddle Me" and "If It Happens Again" are ace reggae/rock hybrids; "Nkomo A Go Go," with a propulsive dance-rock beat and wailing saxophone, shows the full range of UB40's development. A very impressive step forward from a band who already know the formula for success.

The UB40 File is a repackage of **Signing Off** with a second disc consisting of all the singles the band cut that year. (It doesn't require a detective to realize that it merely reissues—and not for the first time—everything on their original label.) Unnecessary, except for completists.

Baggariddim consists of three new recordings (the catchy "Don't Break My Heart," "Mi Spliff" and a charming reggaefied "I Got You Babe" sung with Chrissie Hynde) on an EP plus a seven-song album of dub mixes—with guest toasters—from **Labour of Love** and **Geffery Morgan**. The one-disc **Little Baggariddim** offers the three new items, plus "I Got You Babe" dub and two additional numbers.

[jg/iar]

U.K. DECAY

For Madmen Only (Fresh/nr) 1981
A Night for Celebration [tape] (Decay/nr) 1983
Rising from the Dead EP (Corpus Christi/nr) 1984

This English art/poetry/noise trio comes from the Fall school of dead seriousness. Bleak of both lyric and music, U.K. Decay offers ponderous observations on matters social, political, sexual and theatrical, with most of the vocals intoned atonally from what sounds like a great distance. The music, which at times resembles a grittier Gang of Four or a less organized Public Image, would be much more inviting if not backing humorless lines like "A coolness knows no conscience..."

[iar]

U.K. SUBS

Another Kind of Blues (Gem/nr) 1979
Live Kicks (Stiff/nr) 1980
Brand New Age (Gem/nr) 1980
Crash Course (Gem/nr) 1980
Diminished Responsibility (Gem/nr) 1981
Endangered Species (NEMS/nr) 1982

Best Of (1977-1981) (Abstract/nr) 1982
Flood of Lies (Scarlet-Fall Out/nr) 1983
Demonstration Tapes (Konexion/nr) 1984
Subs Standard (Dojo/nr) 1985
Gross-Out USA (Fall Out/nr) 1985
In Action—Tenth Anniversary (Fall Out/nr) 1986
Left for Dead: Alive in Holland '86 [tape] (nr/ROIR) 1986

CHARLIE HARPER

Stolen Property (Flicknife/nr) 1982

Alongside their contemporaries, the never-say-die U.K. Subs' 1977 punk sounds old-fashioned, yet Nicky Garratt's wall-of-sound rhythm guitar and Charlie Harper's chant/sung vocals make for highly enjoyable charged rock'n'rage that owes more to bands like the MC5 than Sex Pistols. Maybe it's the familiarity of their style that makes the quartet more listenable than, say, the Exploited; whatever the case, the Subs play high-energy, fast-paced punk with a social conscience, and that keeps them one of England's most successful speedrock outfits.

Brand New Age finds the Subs bemoaning alienation in the modern world on the title track and singing their signature tune, "Emotional Blackmail," twice. **Diminished Responsibility** confronts such issues as racism, rioting, gangsters, Paris, prison and urban decay. Harper's songwriting (in collaboration with various members of the band) shows lyrical growth—he's quite capable of incisive lines and spot-on humor—on **Endangered Species**, a fact he almost acknowledges on "Sensitive Boys"; elsewhere, the bleak terrain is littered with better-expressed and subtler observations on the world's ills. Best tune: the touching "Fear of Girls."

Flood of Lies showcases a new lineup and has a great political cartoon of Maggie Thatcher on the cover; the songs are once again more aggressive ("Violent Revolution," "Soldiers of Fortune"), but there's room for some humor as well ("Revenge of the Jelly Devils"). **Gross-Out USA**, their second live album (after **Crash Course**), recapitulates the band's career in fine raucous form with sixteen songs that are offered start-to-finish. just as they happened. **Left for Dead** does the same feat, adding to the Subs' live album legacy with an American tape-only release, recorded with yet another lineup in Holland. The 23 songs overlap only a half-dozen with **Gross-Out**; the performance is typically incendiary and the recording quality not half bad.

Harper's solo effort is worth checking out. Unlike the Subs' all-original music, **Stolen Property** oddly consists of '60s garage band classics such as "Pills," "Louie, Louie," "Hey Joe" and "Waiting for My Man." Harper also made an extracurricular album with some friends under the name Urban Dogs.

[cpl/iar]

See also *Urban Dogs*.

TRACEY ULLMAN

You Broke My Heart in 17 Places (Stiff/MCA) 1983
You Caught Me Out (Stiff/nr) 1984
Forever: The Best of Tracey (Stiff/nr) 1985

Tracey Ullman's musical career is based on her chameleonlike visual characterizations (pictured on both LP jackets) and good taste in choosing songs to record. She hasn't got any particular talent as a singer, but that hasn't prevented her from having hits on both sides of the Atlantic. On **You Broke My Heart in 17 Places**, with producer Peter Collins and a stack of top sessioneers, Ullman (overdubbed like crazy in spots) covers such campy classics as "Move Over Darling" and "Bobby's Girl," as well as more contemporary winners, like "(I'm Always Touched by Your) Presence Dear" and Kirsty MacColl's "They Don't Know." To some extent a commercially-minded snooze, the mix of songs and sounds, relatively free of kitsch and gratuitous nostalgia, makes it a mild treat. **You Caught Me Out** is essentially the same album with a dozen different numbers. Besides co-writing the title track, MacColl again has her back catalogue tapped, this time for "Terry," which Ullman stifles; other jukebox selections here include "Where the Boys Are," "Give Him a Great Big Kiss" and, for anomaly's sake, a terrible version of the Waitresses' "I Know What Boys Like."

Ullman's musical career subsequently stalled out, with only a compilation album to keep her in the bins. She did, however, continue as an actress and was quite good alongside Meryl Streep and Sting in *Plenty*.

[iar]

JAMES BLOOD ULMER

Tales of Captain Black (nr/Artists House) 1979
Are You Glad to Be in America? (Rough Trade/nr) 1980
Free Lancing (CBS/Columbia) 1981
Black Rock (CBS/Columbia) 1982
Odyssey (CBS/Columbia) 1983
Part Time (Rough Trade/nr) 1984
Got Something Good for You (Ger. Moers) 1986

MUSIC REVELATION ENSEMBLE

No Wave (Ger. Moers) 1980

Arguably the most innovative electric guitarist since Jimi Hendrix, Ulmer is certainly worthy of that challenge. With mentor Ornette Coleman, Ulmer introduced many to the avant-garde concept of harmolodics with the release of **Tales of Captain Black**, eight songs of hot funk and boiling rhythms. But the production is somewhat flat, and Coleman upstages him. Still, an eye-opening debut.

Are You Glad to Be in America? is Ulmer's finest album, revealing a staggering understanding of the roots of jazz, dance music, Eastern polyrhythms and harmolodic textures in a lively sound mix, featuring Blood's first vocal efforts. Without Coleman, Blood works with fabled electric bassist Amin Ali and the stunning sax combo of David Murray (tenor) and Oliver Lake (alto); the music fairly crackles.

No Wave is an experimental album recorded with the Music Revelation Ensemble (Ali, Murray, Lake and Ronald Shannon Jackson on drums). It's Ulmer's most inaccessible work, as well as his least focused.

Free Lancing and **Black Rock** are technical masterpieces, making up in precision what they lack in

emotion (as compared to **Are You Glad to Be in America?**). Working to expand his audience, Ulmer concentrates more on electric guitar flash, and actual melodies can be discerned from the improvised song structures (improvisation being one of the keys to harmolodics).

Odyssey takes Ulmer in a novel direction: working with just a drummer (Warren Benbow) and violinist (Charles Burnham), he builds mesmerizing but patchy fabrics of busy guitar, traversing kinetic jazz, blues, pop and rock idioms with relaxed power. Singing in an engaging rustic blues voice, Ulmer essays extremely traditional song forms ("Little Red House" and "Are You Glad to Be in America?" sound like Taj Mahal.) Matching the cheery cover photo, this is easily his most accessible, commercial and likable record. With a firm grip on jazz-rock and progressive music, Ulmer's future possibilities remain boundless.

[gf/iar]

ULTRAVOX

Ultravox! (Island) 1977
Ha!Ha!Ha! (Island/nr) 1977
Systems of Romance (Island/Antilles) 1978
Live Retro EP (Island/nr) 1978
Three Into One (Island/nr) 1980
Vienna (Chrysalis) 1980
Rage in Eden (Chrysalis) 1981
New Europeans (Jap. Chrysalis) 1981
Mini-LP EP (Aus. Festival) 1981
Quartet (Chrysalis) 1982
Monument—The Soundtrack EP (Chrysalis/nr) 1983
Lament (Chrysalis) 1984
The Collection (Chrysalis) 1984

MIDGE URE

The Gift (Chrysalis) 1985

Originally lost in the gap between glam-rock and punk, Ultravox became prime movers of the electro-pop and new romantic movements when they combined synthesizer with the direct and danceable pop music of the new wave.

Ultravox!—produced by Brian Eno, Steve Lillywhite and the group—marries the flamboyance of poseurdom to the cold minimalism of Kraftwerk, with more than a touch of punk's roughness. John Foxx's voice is typically distant, singing lyrics that contain jumbled images expressing passive dislocation (a popular Ultravox theme). While synthesizers are in short supply, the budding Ultravox style can be noted in "Dangerous Rhythm," the oddly passionate "I Want to Be a Machine" and the classic "My Sex."

Ha!Ha!Ha! comes closer to the spirit of punk, filled with tight, straightforward rockers outlining a spirit of alienation and life free of love, companionship and comprehension. Billy Currie's electric violin playing is stunning, and the climactic track, "Hiroshima Mon Amour," introduces full-force synthesizer into Ultravox's music, delineating the boundary between past and future. Recommended.

Systems of Romance, produced by Conny Plank, fuses the band's pop vision with spare, crystalline electronic sound. Focused both lyrically and musically on the fragmentation of experience, the album weaves a sinuous existential mood that suggests dreams and autumn nights. Highly recommended.

157

Vienna, also produced by Plank, was marked by the departure of Foxx and guitarist Robin Simon; ex-Rich Kid guitarist Midge Ure filled out the new lineup. Ultravox's recast sound included a more symphonic use of synthesizer, layered in deep swells for new heights of sonic density. **Vienna** includes Ultravox's best hits: "All Stood Still," "Sleepwalk," "Passing Strangers" and the title track. The new approach proved highly satisfying and successful, spawning a horde of less-inspired imitators collectively referred to as new romantics.

Noting **Vienna**'s success, Island issued **Three Into One**, a compilation of songs drawn from the first three albums, including "My Sex" and "Hiroshima Mon Amour."

Rage in Eden, Ultravox's last outing with Plank, finds Ure sliding into operatic vocals and pretentious lyrics, but the music—again displaying complex synthesizer patterns—is superb, with Currie, Ure, bassist Chris Cross and drummer Warren Cann blending brilliantly.

New Europeans is a Japanese compilation of B-sides from the **Vienna** and **Rage in Eden** period, added to A-sides "The Voice" and "New Europeans." Though the flipsides are hardly top-notch, they are interesting, and the mastering/ pressing provides unbeatable audio quality.

The Australian **Mini-LP** combines two rare tracks from an early flexi-disc ("Quirks" and "Modern Love") with the contents of **Live Retro**, an excellent live 7-inch EP originally released in 1978.

Quartet continues in much the same vein as **Rage in Eden**, but producer George Martin thins out the sound too much, reducing the band to a subordinate role as backing for Ure, whose lyrics are infused with religious overtones. Clear but unsatisfying.

Ultravox self-produced **Lament**, proving themselves quite capable of working without outside supervision. The album contains two of their finest singles, "One Small Day" and "Dancing with Tears in My Eyes," amidst a host of other suave and personable excursions. **Lament** further elevates Ultravox's reputation as one of the few groups to capably incorporate synthesizers and other modern conveniences into a truly unique sound.

The live **Monument** also serves as the soundtrack to a concert videocassette of the same name. **The Collection** is a remarkable compilation of the band's singles (1980 to 1984)—fourteen cuts, including "Sleepwalk," "We Came to Dance," "All Stood Still," "One Small Day"— all stellar examples of craft and creativity. Not a bad introduction to the group's post-Island work.

Except for a slightly increased guitar focus and the large proportion of instrumentals, Ure's one-man solo album (with a little assistance, mostly on bass and vocals) sounds enough like Ultravox in spots to unsettle his bandmates. This could easily be mistaken for a group effort. (Although few would believe *they* would attempt a laidback cover of Jethro Tull's "Living in the Past"—downright bizarre, but not as awful as you might imagine.) "If I Was" has a nice refrain but typically trite lyrics—Ure's uncertainty becomes aggravating—and goes on too long. If nothing else,

this mix of familiar synth-rock and adventurous instrumentals proves that Ure will easily survive the end of Ultravox when it comes; perhaps **The Gift** has hastened that eventuality.

In mid-1986, during sessions for the band's next album, Warren Cann quit. [sg/iar]

See also *Faith Global, John Foxx, Visage*.

UNDERTONES

The Undertones (Sire) 1979 (Ardeck/nr) 1983 (EMI/nr) 1986
Hypnotised (Sire) 1980 (Ardeck/nr) 1983
Positive Touch (Ardeck/Harvest) 1981
The Love Parade EP (Ardeck/nr) 1982
The Sin of Pride (Ardeck/nr) 1983
All Wrapped Up (Ardeck/Ardeck-Capitol) 1983

The best band ever to come from Northern Ireland, the Undertones took a youthful adoration for the glam-rock era and gave it the stripped-down simplicity and energy of punk to create truly wonderful albums of pop/rock (and, towards the end, soul) with a difference. Their body of work evidences rapid creative growth; each album clearly shows a different stage in their development. Their wind-up, as unavoidable as it was disappointing, resulted from the group's lack of sustained commercial success and their inability to shake the public's first impression of them as an Irish Ramones.

Very young when they began, the Undertones started out writing simple, fetching melodies with lyrics about teenage concerns and playing them fast and raw on basic guitars, bass and drums. With Feargal Sharkey's unique, piercing tenor out front, songs on the first album ("Jimmy Jimmy," "Here Comes the Summer," "Girls Don't Like It") are spare and efficient pop gems that are as infectious as measles, suggesting a bridge between teenybop and punk. (The US edition has two songs added from an early single; a limited-edition English 10-inch released at the same time contained those two tracks plus a pair from the LP.)

The Undertones broadened their scope for **Hypnotised**, making the sound clearer and more instrumentally distinct while offering uniquely cast lyrics telling stories and describing characters with impressive skill. Standout tracks include "My Perfect Cousin," the delicate "Wednesday Week" and the gently self-critical "More Songs About Chocolate and Girls." Of the four albums, **Hypnotised** has the best balance of sophistication and innocence.

Positive Touch takes another step forward. It introduces well-placed horns and piano (by Paul Carrack) to the sound and explores much more ambitious ground in reflection of the band's personal and musical maturation. While the songs are not all immediately catchy, they are ultimately rewarding, displaying numerous new sides and levels to the Undertones. An enormous artistic achievement for a band that had been playing rudimentary four-chord riff numbers a scant two years earlier.

The Love Parade EP—actually a 12-inch single with four songs on the B-side—includes three otherwise unavailable live recordings tied together with weird noises and unfathomable dialogue. Most importantly at the time, it showed the band to be newly rooted in '60s soul psychedelia.

Perhaps overly stung by their commercial problems, the Undertones made their final album with more ambition than concentration. **The Sin of Pride** has its brilliant moments—the soulful "Got to Have You Back" (not an original), "Bye Bye Baby Blue," "The Love Parade," "Chain of Love"—but the fear of being thought of as an immature pop band drives them into low-key excursions that drift away tunelessly, and overactive horn charts bury the band's instrumental personality. Also, the sound is disturbingly distant.

The English version of **All Wrapped Up**, the Undertones' posthumous singles collection, has two discs and features all of their A-sides plus seventeen flipsides— 30 magnificent cuts in all. From "Teenage Kicks" right up through "Chain of Love," it's a stirring reminder of what a truly marvelous band they were. The American version has the same gross cover photo but drops one disc and sixteen of the B-sides.

Since the 'Tones broke up, Feargal Sharkey has been the most visible of the five, making one great 1983 single ("Never Never") with Vince Clarke's otherwise stillborn Assembly and then a not-so-great solo 45 ("Listen to Your Father") for Madness' Zarjazz label the following year. He made an additional one-off single, produced by Queen drummer Roger Taylor, before linking up with Eurythmic Dave Stewart and scoring with "A Good Heart." The O'Neill brothers formed That Petrol Emotion. [iar]

See also *Feargal Sharkey, That Petrol Emotion*.

UNITS

Digital Stimulation (nr/415) 1980
New Way to Move EP (nr/Epic) 1983

One of the first American synthesizer-based rock bands, San Francisco's Units started out playing Cabaret Voltaire-style cacophony, but quickly developed an educated electro-pop approach. Lyrically, **Digital Stimulation** is rife with irony and black humor; the spontaneous, creative music complements it well. The Units obviously prefer purer electronic sounds to the pseudo-pipe organ noises employed by many other synth bands, but stop before succumbing to the dreaded noodling disease. The upshot is a dozen sharp pop tunes of estimable value.

Typical of the Units' hard-luck recording career, the band made a second album (**Animals They Dream About**) for 415, with Bill Nelson producing. Although it solidified the early test-run of **Digital Stimulation** into a unique and coherent style wrapped around brutal assaults on American thought, the record was never released, due to a falling-out between the Units and the label. A loss.

In 1983, following the success of an independently-issued 12-inch dance-floor hit ("The Right Man," produced by Tubeman Michael Cotten), the Units signed with Epic

and went to Wales to record, again with Nelson. Incredibly, the resulting album also never saw the light of day, but an EP *was* released, combining "The Right Man" and "A Girl Like You" with three songs from those sessions and a remix by Ivan Ivan. Solidly appealing and catchy dance-rock. [sg/iar]

UNKNOWNS

Dream Sequence EP (Bomp-Sire) 1981
The Unknowns (nr/Invasion) 1982

Liam Sternberg, Ohio's answer to Phil Spector, produced the six tracks for **Dream Sequence** "in an aircraft hangar." California's Unknowns play pure '60s garage rock with Mosrite guitars (displayed and mentioned on the cover for added authenticity), heaps of echo and tremelo, and incorporate various period genres (surf music, Creedence swamp choogle, psychedelia, punk) into their songs. Where **Dream Sequence** is slick but boring, **The Unknowns** album shows them in greater command of their musical vocabulary and adds traces of the Animals, Yardbirds, Blues Project and the Doors to spice things up considerably. A rendition of Buddy Holly's "Rave On" ties up a neat package of heavily stylized nostalgia.

Unknowns leader Bruce Joyner subsequently formed a new band he dubbed the Plantations and released a 1983 LP, **Way Down South**. [iar]

UNREST WORK & PLAY

Unrest Work & Play EP (Art Hole/nr) 1982

It must have been a lot of work for this duo from the southern coast of Britain to play all of this, and unrest is indeed the state of mind it conveys: slathering guitar chords at odds with themselves, feedback whine, vocals that fall into Gregorian chant-like drones (or intoned as though the fellows had bellyaches), intermittent pounding drums. In a way, it's like the Pop Group trying to re-create Fairport Convention in its own image. One of the most disquieting records since Public Image's **Metal Box**. UW&P also made an album, **Informs**. [jg]

UNTOUCHABLES

Live and Let Dance EP (nr/Twist-Enigma) 1984
Wild Child (Stiff/Stiff-MCA) 1985

There were a number of promising local R&B-cum-ska outfits on the LA scene at the time, but it was the worthy Untouchables who caught Stiff's attention and wound up with a label deal on both sides of the Atlantic. **Live and Let Dance** introduced the seven-man band's energetic dance attack with half a dozen exciting numbers, starting with the unforgettably catchy "Free Yourself." (One listen and you'll swear you heard it on a 1980 2-Tone single.) Otherwise, the 12-inch presents solid reggae and ska in the UB40 mold; a live take of the Monkees' "Stepping Stone" clarifies their individuality.

Wild Child reprises "Free Yourself," surrounding it with ten additional strong tracks, including the similarly effective title track, a cool version of "I Spy for the FBI," obscure but also recorded by John

Hiatt) produced by Jerry Dammers, a slice of straight rap-funk ("Freak in the Streets") and a synth-tinged rock tune ("Lovers Again"). Stewart Levine's production could be more full-bodied, but the band's enthusiasm and precision keep the house rocking from start to finish. [iar]

URBAN DOGS

Urban Dogs (Fall Out/nr) 1983

This not-so-super session of U.K. Subs singer Charlie Harper and Vibrators guitarist Knox (plus a rhythm section) plays highly charged riotpunk that sounds like a cross between early Stranglers, early Pistols and early Stooges. Alongside Knox originals (including the Vibes' classic "Into the Future," here retitled "Sex Kick") and a couple of Harper's own raunchy numbers, there are the obligatory covers like Iggy's "I Wanna Be Your Dog" and the Dolls' "Human Being," complete with soundalike Thunders licks. The raunch, spirit and electricity runs high from start to finish, making **Urban Dogs** everything a great punk record should be. [iar]

URBAN HEROES

Age of Urban Heroes (Hol. Ariola Benelux) 1980
Who Said . . . (nr/Handshake) 1980

These Dutchmen have the ability to make sparks fly from what would otherwise be just homely old R&B-flavored rock'n'roll, adding plenty of poppy touches in the arrangements. But their coarse, jocose aggressiveness sometimes overpowers whatever else they have to offer. And they should not have manhandled a great tune like the Equals' "Baby Come Back." [jg]

URBAN VERBS

Urban Verbs (Warner Bros.) 1980
Early Damage (Warner Bros.) 1981

Fascinating but tragically overlooked, Washington, DC's Urban Verbs were an arty quintet whose lead singer is Talking Heads' drummer Chris Frantz's brother. And therein lay the Verbs' problem: while guitarist Robert Goldstein guided the band through striking modern instrumental pieces of depth and quality, Roddy Frantz's urban-alienation lyrics, delivered in a fair approximation of David Byrne's vocal style, typecast the group as second-string Heads. The Verbs' records showed great potential, but this needless flaw prevented them from being taken seriously. [iar]

MIDGE URE

See *Ultravox.*

U-ROY

Dread in a Babylon (Virgin) 1976 & 1983
Natty Rebel (Virgin/nr) 1976 & 1983
Rasta Ambassador (Virgin/nr) 1977
Version Galore (Front Line/nr) 1978
Jah Son of Africa (Front Line/nr) 1979
Crucial Cuts (Virgin/nr) 1983

Just as dub reggae anticipated funk and rock remixes, toasters—chanting reggae dj's—prefigured rap. U-Roy (Ewart Beckford) was one of Jamaica's first dj's to graduate from sound systems to chart success in the late '60s. His signature style is plain and direct: he shrieks

and chants over the instrumental tracks of other hits, interrupting and talking back to the vocals. When he first appeared, such musical antics were unprecedented on record, and he became an immediate sensation. While it can't be said that U-Roy invented toasting, he's considered the godfather of dj's, and an inarguable reggae pioneer.

Because U-Roy isn't very active, his records drift in and out of print. **Version Galore**, which collects many of his first hits, is a must, although far from definitive. Most of his available LPs, in fact, date from the mid-'70s, when he was signed to Virgin and produced by Tony Robinson. Both **Dread in a Babylon** and **Natty Rebel** are excellent samplings of U-Roy's forceful toasting, though the sound and production are smoother, less offbeat and startling than his early work. (**Dread** has the slight edge for featuring the wonderful "Runaway Girl" and "Chalice in the Palace.") **Crucial Cuts** combines some early items with tracks from **Rasta Ambassador** for an odd combination of old and new styles (some hits are re-recordings) that is inconsistent but serviceable. [bk]

U.T.F.O.

"Beats and Rhymes" (nr/Select) 1984
"Roxanne, Roxanne" (nr/Select) 1984

For a brief period in late winter 1984/5, you couldn't leave your house or turn on your radio in New York without hearing some rapper going on about a girl named Roxanne. There was "Roxanne's Revenge," "The Real Roxanne," "Roxanne You're Through," "Roxanne's Mother," "Roxanne's Brother," "Roxanne's Doctor"—even "Roxanne's a Man." Demonstrating the volatility of the dance music market, Roxanne replaced "y'all" as the word most frequently used in raps, and the term quickly passed into urban slang for an unaccommodating woman. Credit for this fad goes to Brooklyn's three-man U.T.F.O. (Untouchable Force Organization), who started it all with "Roxanne, Roxanne," a playful poke at a good-looking girl with the temerity to resist their suave attentions.

From the beginning, Doctor Ice, the Kangol Kid and the Educated Rapper have led a charmed life. After winning a break-dancing contest, they gave up their gig dancing for fried chicken at a fast food joint, went on a European tour with Whodini and ultimately found themselves on the *Phil Donahue Show*, which led to an invite to Dustin Hoffman's daughter's birthday party. Before things could get any weirder, they released a 12-inch of the sharp and fast "Beats and Rhymes," oddly, a better rap than its follow-up, "Roxanne, Roxanne." The latter's lines aren't exceptionally clever, but U.T.F.O. created such strong personae for themselves and the stuck-up Ms. R., while isolating such a familiar problem (girl says no), that teenagers identified with them in a way they could never connect with Run—D.M.C. or other rappers. What the single may have lacked in raw power, it made up for in character.

The Roxanne fad will surely disappear, leaving U.T.F.O. at mortal levels of popularity. But the group is very talented and will maintain

an audience long after the sequel bearers have faded into oblivion. [jl]

See also *Full Force.*

U2

Boy (Island) 1980
October (Island) 1981
War (Island) 1983
Under a Blood Red Sky (Island) 1983
The Unforgettable Fire (Island) 1984
Wide Awake in America EP (Island) 1985

With a unique, passionate sound, individualist lyrical outlook and youthful guilelessness, Dublin's U2 made a big splash quickly. The quartet had released a few praiseworthy singles before **Boy** introduced them to the world at large, via such songs as "I Will Follow," "An Cat Dubh" and "Into the Heart." Powerful and emotional, singer Bono Hewson mixes a blend of rock, Gaelic and operatic styles, with the occasional yowl or yodel to lead the band's attack; electric guitarist Dave "the Edge" Evans largely shuns chords in favor of brilliant lead figures that propel and color the songs. Drummer Larry Mullen and bassist Adam Clayton provide a driving and solid (but sensitive) foundation, completing the musical package, delivered to disc with great skill and invention by producer Steve Lillywhite. An unquestionable masterpiece, **Boy** has a strength, beauty and character that is hard to believe on a debut album made by teenagers.

Although it might have been unreasonable to expect U2 to remain pure and ingenuous indefinitely, **October** seems a bit overblown and oblique in comparison to **Boy**. Already showing signs of becoming a bit of a sensitive *auteur*, Bono's lyrics abandon "Stories for Boys" and adopt "Stranger in a Strange Land." Lillywhite, meanwhile, embellishes the magnificent and direct rock power with found sound gimmicks, piano and abundantly atmospheric sensuality. All that said, **October** has significant virtues—"Gloria," "I Fall Down" and "Is That All?" rank with the group's best work, and several others fall just short, mostly the result of incomplete songwriting efforts. But, in totality, not a great record.

War, on the other hand, *is* tremendous—an emotional, affecting collection of honest love songs ("Two Hearts Beat as One," "Drowning Man") and political protest ("Sunday Bloody Sunday," "Seconds," "The Refugee") given complex and varied, but unfailingly powerful, treatments. The mix is uncomfortably skewed—towards the drums and on, on "New Year's Day," bass—but judicious addition of violin and trumpet supports, rather than detracts, from the band's fire. (Bizarre casting note: the LP's backing vocals are by Kid Creole's Coconuts.)

Taking advantage of U2's growing rep as a commanding live act, **Under a Blood Red Sky** presents them on American and German stages, playing eight dynamic numbers drawn from all three albums, with awesome strength and clarity. Although billed as a mini-LP, the running time exceeds 32 minutes.

Abandoning Steve Lillywhite in the hopes of exploring new audio

terrain, U2 made an unusual selection of producer and recorded **The Unforgettable Fire** with Brian Eno (and his collaborator Daniel Lanois) behind the board. While the record's lyrical theme, largely a commemoration of Martin Luther King, Jr. and personal heroism in general, is both commendable and occasionally articulate, the record's success as an ambitious piece of pop music is more mixed, hitting highs—"Pride (in the Name of Love)," "A Sort of Homecoming," "Wire," the title tune (all on the first side)—as well as an embarrassing low—"Elvis Presley and America." U2's predicament is that their strength is their strength, and the more complex their aspirations, the harder to convey their passion.

One doesn't ordinarily expect epiphanies on a budget-priced record of outtakes and live oddities, but **Wide Awake in America**'s heart-stopping eight-minute live version of "Bad" is among U2's finest recordings, and sent me scurrying back to **The Unforgettable Fire** to hear what else I might have missed. Besides another live track, the EP also contains two worthy-of-release studio cuts: "Three Sunrises" and "Love Comes Tumbling." Even when these guys don't put their best forward, what they've got is still pretty amazing. [iar]

CHERRY VANILLA

Bad Girl (RCA/nr) 1978
Venus d'Vinyl (RCA/nr) 1979

Onetime David Bowie publicist Vanilla left Staten Island behind and spent time in Britain pursuing a recording career, making two inconsistent but surprisingly good albums. Along with guitarist/songwriter Louis Lepore and a loose collection of backup players, Vanilla—who sings passably—works her way through songs woven of her own experiences.

The first album, **Bad Girl**, is a bit on the blunt side—"I Know How to Hook" and "Foxy Bitch" are typical—but the follow-up takes a much subtler approach and neatly balances cleverly arranged, varied music with sensitive, believable lyrics. While Ms. V isn't breaking down any musical barriers, her two albums prove her talent as a writer and performer. [iar]

DAVID VAN TIEGHEM

These Things Happen (Warner Bros.) 1984

In her bid to become the leading terpsichorean patron of avant-rock music, choreographer Twyla Tharp followed projects with David Byrne and Glenn Branca by commissioning a score by Van Tieghem, a multi-instrumentalist mainly known as a drummer with the Love of Life Orchestra and other New York experimental ensembles. Working with many local luminaries, Van Tieghem's music for *Fait Accompli* covers a wide range of styles, from African-tinged rhythms to obscure pop sounds. The interpolation of extraneous bits of found sounds (news, animal noises, etc.) keeps things going when the music threatens to drag, which—given its subordinate role as accompanying earwork—is frequently. [iar]

VAPORS

New Clear Days (UA) 1980
Magnets (Liberty) 1981

One of the first in a breed of fresh-faced bands who fit neatly into the pop charts and accompanying teenybopper trappings while retaining vague new wave credibility, the Vapors started at the top and quickly sank from view. Their first single, "Turning Japanese," was an enormous international hit; their inability to match it made both of their subsequent albums major disappointments. They weren't that bad, though.

New Clear Days follows in the strictly British fashion originated by Ray Davies and continued by Paul Weller and Madness. Some of singer David Fenton's songs show a talented, mature tunesmith at work; unfortunately, they all suffer in light of the awesomely catchy jingle that dominates the record, overshadowing the subtler, more thoughtful material.

Magnets also lacks a peer for "Turning Japanese," although "Jimmie Jones" (about Jonestown) nearly meets the challenge. Unfortunately, Fenton's greater aspirations and budding political conscience are severely out of step with the band's unbreakably commercial music.

Had they not been doomed by their own devices from day one, the Vapors might have proven well worth watching and hearing for a long time to come. [iar]

BEN VAUGHN COMBO

The Many Moods of Ben Vaughn (Making Waves/nr) 1986

This highly entertaining debut comes from a no-frills New York-area rock'n'roll quartet whose previous claim to fame was Vaughn's composition of a brilliant song—"I'm Sorry (But So Is Brenda Lee)"—recorded by Marshall Crenshaw on **Downtown**. (The BVC's own version—a sleepy acoustic country treatment—is less impressive.) Vaughn has a clever way with lyrics (and titles): besides romantic ditties he pokes fun at the tyranny of trendies ("Wrong Haircut," "I Dig Your Wig") and defines down-to-earth suburbanism ("Lookin' for a 7-11," "M-M-Motor Vehicle") that implicitly satirizes Springsteen's epochal New Jersey bombast. The band (bass, drums, accordion) raucously supports Vaughn's unstylized vocals and guitar to make **The Many Moods** a truly enjoyable musical diversion. [iar]

TESCO VEE

See *Meatmen*.

ALAN VEGA

Alan Vega (nr/ZE-PVC) 1980
Collision Drive (ZE-Celluloid) 1981
Saturn Strip (ZE-Elektra) 1983
Just a Million Dreams (ZE-Elektra) 1985

As the vocal half of Suicide, singer Alan Vega was an infuriating electronic shaman. On his own, he creates seductive, '50s-inspired music that succeeds with or without rockabilly revivals. **Alan Vega**'s impact is the result of its spare instrumentation—just the singer plus Phil Hawk on guitar and drums—and deceptively simple songs. "Jukebox Babe" transcends its stuttering lyric and solitary riff to engulf its idiom and then the universe. "Lonely" should be the last word (or moan) on that subject. The rest of the album is similarly zenlike, and no less enjoyable for it.

Collision Drive has a three-piece band and broader musical range. Besides the droning rock'n'roll of "Magdalena 82" and "Magdalena 83," "Outlaw" flirts with heavy metal rhythms and textures; "Viet Vet" is an extended narrative reminiscent of the Doors. Vega's moody lyricism has the poet's touch—sometimes heavy-handed but always his own. This recycling is creative.

Continuing Ric Ocasek's association with Suicide, the tall one produced Vega's third solo album, which mostly abandons the simplicity of his early work in favor of propulsive keyboard-dominated drone-rock, played by Ocasek and a variety of sidemen, including members of Ministry and Greg Hawkes of the Cars. With Vega mumbling like an inarticulate mix of Lou Reed and Jim Morrison, **Saturn Strip** covers a lot of ground. "Video Babe" reasserts Vega's atmospheric rockabilly sensibility (recall "Jukebox Babe") but with very modern accessories, while his offhand cover of Hot Chocolate's "Every 1's a Winner" closes the LP on an enigmatic, inconclusive note.

Just a Million Dreams shows Vega acquiescing in an almost routine rock milieu. He's not exactly Mr Mister (yet), but the backing tracks are so filled with typical synth sounds, electronic rhythms and sizzling lead guitar that they provide little or no musical excitement to stimulate Vega's vocal hysteria. In fact, it's difficult at times to believe that this bland singer is actually Vega. [si/iar]

SUZANNE VEGA

Suzanne Vega (A&M) 1985
Marlene on the Wall EP (A&M/nr) 1986

Like Patti Smith a decade earlier, Suzanne Vega was selected from an "underground" New York scene—in this case, the post-rock folk generation that outgrew new wave for acoustic guitars and sensitively poetic lyrics—and elevated to preeminent status by being the first with a major label record deal. Whether or not that makes her more noteworthy than those left struggling in greater obscurity is immaterial, and irrelevant to the qualities of her first album. Singing in a cool, wispy voice, and accompanying herself on guitar, Vega resembles a mix of Joni Mitchell with Laurie Anderson and Tim Buckley. Producers Lenny Kaye and Steve Addabbo assembled a number of studio players to support Vega in discreet, restrained fashion; the unobtrusive backing presents her songs clearly and pleasingly. **Suzanne Vega** has some memorable material and generally avoids preciousness or wilfull obscurity. She's a talented melodicist, and this album suggests lots of potential for development. [iar]

VELVET UNDERGROUND

The Velvet Underground and Nico (Verve) 1967 & 1985
White Light/White Heat (Verve) 1968 & 1985
The Velvet Underground (MGM) 1969 (nr/Verve) 1985
Loaded (Atlantic/Cotillion) 1970
Live at Max's Kansas City (Atlantic/Cotillion) 1972
Squeeze (Polydor/nr) 1973
1969 Velvet Underground Live (Mercury) 1974
VU (Verve-PolyGram) 1985
Velvet Underground (Polydor/nr) 1986
Another View (Verve) 1986

MAUREEN TUCKER

Playin' Possum (nr/Trash) 1981

The Velvet Underground marked a turning point in rock history. After the release of **The Velvet Underground and Nico** the music could never be as innocent, as unselfconscious as before, knowing the power of which it was capable. The band's first album may have come on a bit cute with its Andy Warhol-designed banana cover—indeed, patron Warhol's name (he also "produced") was splashed around like a talisman—but singer/guitarist Lou Reed's tough songs and the band's equally tough playing owed nothing to anybody. In perverse subject matter ("Heroin," "Venus in Furs"), deceptively simple musical forms and anarchic jamming, the Velvets displayed the rebellious traits new wave bands would pick up on ten years later. Singer Nico's four vocals provide textural context and breathing space between Reed's darker visions.

With Nico gone, **White Light/White Heat** is almost unbearably intense. John Cale recites a gruesome little story ("The Gift") over steamy accompaniment, and Reed sings the praises of amphetamines (the title track)—and that's the light entertainment. The second side consists of extended, feedback-wailing guitar solos ("I Heard Her Call My Name") and graphic porno-junkie tales ("Sister Ray"). The album is as morally black as its cover.

Something had to change, and when the Velvet Underground next surfaced, they sounded like a different band. Cale's departure (replaced by Doug Yule) might have played a part, but remaining *auteur* Reed has since shown himself capable of wide mood swings. The music on **The Velvet Underground** is quiet, melodic, gentle even when it turns up the juice ("What Goes On," "Beginning to See the Light") and—who would have believed it?—moving ("Jesus," "I'm Set Free"). Only "Murder Mystery," with its double-tracked chatter, is guilty of self-indulgence.

The group started on a fourth, unreleased album before switching record companies. Sixteen years later, songs from those sessions finally surfaced officially on **VU**. They show the Velvet Underground stoking the rock'n'roll fire that blazed forth on **Loaded**: "Foggy Notion" is a timeless rave-up of classical simplicity (though typically kinky subject matter). Reed recycled half of **VU**'s material on his early solo albums, but it's charming to hear them played forcefully by a functioning band.

By 1970, the Velvet Underground was into a wholesome overdrive. **Loaded** was superficial compared to the preceding albums, but does include the anthemic "Sweet Jane" and "Rock and Roll." Personality conflicts, however, resulted in Reed leaving the group before the record's release; Yule took some of the vocals and most of the credit. **Loaded**'s sweetness-and-light music was the Velvets' death throes.

With its creative force gone, the band shuffled along for two more years and even released a British album, **Squeeze**, with no original members. For new doses of the real thing, fans had to be content with live recordings of past glories. **Live at Max's Kansas City** is a low-fi document of the Velvets' last hurrah in the Big Apple. The band is tight but mellow; three of the four songs taken from the first album were originally sung by Nico.

The two-record **1969** is more interesting in its extended view of the group and choice of material. As on the **Max's** LP, the post-Cale band is generally relaxed—a far cry from the musical entropy of the first two albums. The Velvet Underground got its groundbreaking out of the way early.

In 1986, Polydor released a five-album boxed set, reissuing the first three original albums and **VU**, adding a bonus record of nine previously unavailable tracks, including an early "Rock and Roll," an instrumental "Guess I'm Falling in Love," a studio take of "We're Gonna Have a Real Good Time Together" and two versions of "Hey Mr. Rain." Sensibly, **Another View** was also issued separately.

In 1981, the Velvets' female drummer, Maureen (Mo) Tucker, released a one-woman album on her own Trash Records. Its frantic guitar playing and cluttered sound

could have come straight from sessions for the first Velvet Underground album, if you can imagine that band playing "Slippin' and Slidin'," "Bo Diddley" and other oldies. [si]

See also *John Cale, Nico, Lou Reed.*

VENUS AND THE RAZORBLADES

Songs from the Sunshine Jungle (Spark/Visa) 1978

This one's hard to explain. Kim Fowley had helped assemble the Runaways; Venus was a second (less stable) project along the same lines, finding young Los Angeles punks with promise and fashioning them into a band. Including, variously, guitarist Steven T. (with whom Fowley wrote the group's material), fourteen-year-old female wunderkind Dyan Diamond, Roxy Music bassist Sal Maida (sessions only) and others, Venus and the Razorblades managed a short but unsightly career. This posthumous record, cobbled together from miscellaneous tapes Fowley had produced, is their legacy—well-played, noisy-but-safe melodic punk that owes more to California wholesomeness than to Bowery decadence. [iar]

TOM VERLAINE

Tom Verlaine (Elektra) 1979
Dreamtime (Warner Bros.) 1981
Words from the Front (Virgin/ Warner Bros.) 1982
Cover (Virgin/Warner Bros.) 1984

Television was the satisfying result of a clash between two disparate styles. Leader Tom Verlaine was the dreamer, playing sinuous guitar and singing in the strangled, intense voice of a young poet. Guitarist Richard Lloyd and the rhythm section of Billy Ficca and Fred Smith tended more to classic, bash-it-out rock'n'roll. When Verlaine went solo, many assumed he'd simply float off into the ozone.

Surprisingly, he managed to preserve Television's delicate balance and even add new elements on his first solo LP. Two tortured, driving mini-epics—"The Grip of Love" and "Breakin' in My Heart," a classic from TV's live sets—blend flesh and spirit perfectly. The vividly desperate "Kingdom Come" has the honor of being covered by David Bowie (on **Scary Monsters**)—how's that for an endorsement? There's even a playful nonsense song, "Yonki Time," indicating Verlaine is using his freedom to grow.

Alas, with **Dreamtime**, Verlaine narrows his scope, seeming to retreat into the isolation of the familiar. There are taut, anxious tunes ("Down on the Farm"), lilting ones ("Without a Word") and an abundance of exquisite guitar licks, but it's too predictable. A performer who trades in passion can't afford *not* to surprise.

Words from the Front shows more daring, although—like its predecessor—it suffers from inconsistent material. "Postcard from Waterloo" proves that Verlaine can be as romantic as Barry Manilow without sacrificing keenness. "Days on the Mountain" provides perhaps the ultimate in lightheaded ecstasy, with its fluttering guitar skillfully imitating the ascension into heaven.

In some ways, **Cover** constitutes

a return to the style of Verlaine's first LP. The songs are short and to the point, without the sometimes florid expansivess of his previous two efforts. On the other hand, brevity doesn't discourage Verlaine from floating into the ozone—he just does it quicker. For every "Lindi-Lu," a fine jerky rocker, there's two like "Swim," a gentle evocation of airheadedness.

Whether this enormously talented artist will end up a cliché or a genius remains to be seen. [jy]

VIBRATORS

Pure Mania (Epic/Columbia) 1977
V2 (Epic/nr) 1978
Batteries Included (CBS/nr) 1980
Guilty (Anagram/nr) 1983
Alaska 127 (Can. Dallcorte) 1984
Fifth Amendment (Ram/nr) 1985

KNOX

Plutonium Express (Razor/nr) 1983

Like the Stranglers, the Vibrators were considerably older than the other bands comprising the London punk scene in 1977. A rudimentary quartet with a knack for insidiously catchy songs, the Vibrators—after a brief alliance with Chris Spedding, whom they backed on the first punk novelty record, "Pogo Dancing"—established themselves with a stream of clever pop singles that captured the minimalist energy (but not inchoate rage) of their peers.

Pure Mania—with its soon-to-be-a-cliché color-Xerox cover—is a treasure trove of memorable ditties that strip down pop in a parallel to the Ramones' streamlining of it. A brilliant record, cheerful in a loopy way and filled with great fragmentary tunes and innocuously threatening lyrics.

V2, recorded in the Vibrators' briefly adopted home base, Berlin, features new bassist Gary Tibbs (later a Roxy Musician and Ant) and a more ambitious agenda. While it includes some material not that different from the debut LP, it's too pretentious and overblown, following too many different cul-de-sacs to hang together.

As the Vibrators continued their intermittent semi-existence, CBS issued a retrospective, **Batteries Included**, with such classic tunes as "Judy Says" and "Yeah Yeah Yeah." As both of the Vibes' original LPs have long been deleted, it's an essential punk album.

Alaska 127 features the entire original lineup (Knox, Eddie, Pat Collier and John Ellis), playing routine but likable rock that has good sound and a bit of the old melodic acuity, but none of **Pure Mania**'s underground ambience or innocent excitement.

Knox has recorded solo and done an album with Charlie Harper of the U.K. Subs as the Urban Dogs. Pat Collier has become a successful producer. [iar]

See also *Urban Dogs.*

VICE SQUAD

No Cause for Concern (EMI/nr) 1981
Live in Sheffield [tape] (Live/nr) 1981
Stand Strong Stand Proud (EMI/nr) 1982
Shot Away (Anagram/nr) 1985

It's easy to understand why Vice

Squad was one of the most successful new punk bands. Their music is powerful, lyrics bitterly intense, and they had—until she departed, following a dispute over animals' rights—a major focal point in lead singer Beki Bondage. **No Cause for Concern** is a passable debut; **Stand Strong Stand Proud**, however, is a first-rate punk effort with a driving, punchy sound and Beki's demanding voice sending chills down the spine. Also, the material is better developed, showing Vice Squad to be evolving without sacrificing their original ideas.

Following Bondage's departure to form Ligotage, the Squad pressed on, but without the same level of success. [cpl]

SID VICIOUS

Sid Sings (Virgin/nr) 1979
Love Kills NYC (Konexion/nr) 1985

A classic piece of campy horribleness, **Sid Sings** is a miserable-sounding live record of one of Sid's (pre-death) New York rent-party gigs. The ex-Pistol is teamed with ex-Doll Jerry Nolan's band, the Idols, for a pathetic performance of punk standards. Depressing and morbid. **Love Kills NYC** is a similar record, issued six years later during the blizzard of irrelevant Pistols vinyl. [iar]

HOLLY BETH VINCENT

See *Holly and the Italians.*

VIOLENT FEMMES

Violent Femmes (Rough Trade/ Slash) 1983
Hallowed Ground (Slash) 1984
The Blind Leading the Naked (Slash) 1986

One of the most remarkable and original bands in recent memory, the Violent Femmes burst out of Madison, Wisconsin playing acoustic instruments and singing intense, personal songs with remarkable candor and love. At first described as a punk version of the Modern Lovers, the Femmes—Gordon Gano (vocals, guitar, songs), Brian Ritchie (bass), Victor De Lorenzo (drums)—have proven to be strictly unique. On the skeletal first album, Gano's articulate passion and maladjustment combine with the charged (but not very loud) playing to convey an incredible sense of desperation and rage. "Blister in the Sun" and "Kiss Off" are typical of the anger seething in the grooves, while "Gone Daddy Gone" and "Please Do Not Go" show a more upbeat side still rooted in extreme individuality and super-ego. The disc's best couplet: "Why can't I get just one fuck?/Guess it's got something to do with luck."

Hallowed Ground takes a much different approach, displaying Gano's religious fervor and a connection with traditional American folk music. (He has since launched a simultaneous side project, Mercy Seat, to perform strictly gospel music.) The cast includes a banjo picker and autoharp strummer, as well as a horn'n'clarinet section; the material encompasses tragic balladry ("Country Death Song"), old-timey spirituals ("Jesus Walking on the Water," "It's Gonna Rain"), mild be-bop ("Sweet Misery Blues") and demented jazz-funk ("Black Girls"). Not as pointed as the first album, it nonetheless showcases an inquisitive and amazing band committed

161

to self-expression, regardless of the consequences.

The cleverly titled third LP was produced by Talking Head Jerry Harrison with conscious mainstreaming intent. Of course, the Femmes at their most commercial are still pretty radical, although "I Held Her in My Arms" does sound unnervingly like Bruce Springsteen. As if to prove their orneriness, a vituperative attack on "Old Mother Reagan" and the similarly anti-authoritarian "No Killing" demonstrate an undying rebellious spirit. But it's another type of spirit that invests the bluesy "Faith" and the Stonesy "Love and Me Make Three," keeping god in the grooves alongside Marc Bolan, who gets worked over with a misbegotten Headsish version of "Children of the Revolution." The Velvet Underground fares better on "Good Friend," a Femmes original that uncannily echoes Lou Reed.

[iar]

VIPERS

Outta the Nest! (nr/PVC) 1984

Rather than discuss the relevance or validity of the entire garage-rock-cum-psychedelic revival—y'know, the bands who dress up like it's 1967 and play tambourines and fuzzed guitar—I'll just note that New York's Vipers are one of the leading lights of said movement. Suffice to say **Outta the Nest** sounds precisely like your (best/worst) memories of mid-'60s American rock, from the Seeds to the Standells to the Shadows of Knight.

The Vipers write good tunes that sound properly dated and play them with equally stylized vim. The production could be better, but that's not the idea. As they sing in the lead-off track, "Nothing's from Today."

[iar]

VIRGIN PRUNES

A New Form of Beauty 2 EP (Rough Trade/nr) 1981
A New Form of Beauty 4 "Din Glorious" [tape] (Rough Trade/nr) 1982
...If I Die, I Die (Rough Trade/nr) 1982
Over the Rainbow (Fr. Baby) 1985
Love Lasts Forever EP (Baby/Touch and Go) 1986

Dublin weirdos with androgynous names and a predilection for semi-melodic rock and conceptual lyrics, the VP's have been prolific, releasing a tape-only album and several 45s before getting around to a proper debut LP. The 10-inch **A New Form of Beauty 2** contains two ominously dark and abrasive assaults plus a quieter abrasive doodle; the cassette features highlights from a Dublin gallery performance, mixing early PiL-style semi-songs with all sorts of taped sounds to very unsettling effect. Produced by ex-Wire man Colin Newman, **If I Die** has hard-edged but delicate pop ("Ballad of the Man") as well as challenging, long-winded opuses with skewed, angular instrumentation and ponderous vocal recitations ("Baudachong," "Caucasian Walk"). A complex band of many minds, the Prunes stake out unique ground, straddling art and mundanity with style and skill. Difficult but fascinating modern music. **Over the Rainbow** is an odds and ends compilation.

[iar/dgs]

VISAGE

Visage (Polydor) 1980
The Anvil (Polydor) 1982
Fade to Grey—The Singles Collection (Polydor) 1983
Beat Boy (Polydor) 1984

Formed around cult-figure fop Steve Strange, Visage began as a part-time group uniting the formidable talents of Ultravox's Midge Ure and Billy Currie, Magazine's Dave Formula and ex-Rich Kid drummer Rusty Egan for the ultimate in dance-oriented new romanticism. **Visage** is filled with rich humor and sound puns in addition to solid musicianship on guitars and synthesizers; how could anyone not crack a smile over the Ennio Morriconesque homage to Clint Eastwood, "Malpaso Man," or the self-mocking "Visa-Age"? Added to the humor, the fine music automatically deflates Strange's colorful pretensions.

Unfortunately, those pretensions dominate **The Anvil**, where Strange attempts to wring every mannered drop of angst and meaning out of his lyrics and vocals. Luckily, the rest of Visage perform as strongly as ever, although in a far darker mood than before.

Continuing their strictly-dance version of Heaven 17-styled electro-funk, **Beat Boy** finds Visage (comprising, this time, Strange and Egan joined by the Barnacle brothers and Andy Barnett) readier to rock, using plentiful guitar on the endless title track and elsewhere to color the inexorable rhythms and repetitious, vapid lyrics. The songs are incredibly (and annoyingly, if you're paying attention) long, but there are still eight of 'em, with a total party time of over 45 minutes.

Fade to Grey is the most concise proof of Visage's merit, compiling nine catchy slices of dance-rock (two remixed for the occasion) and an otherwise unreleased (and utterly unnecessary) cover of "In the Year 2525." "Pleasure Boys," "We Move" and "Night Train" are among the best efforts, showing that conciseness can surely be an asset.

[sg/iar]

VITAMIN Z

Rites of Passage
(Phonogram/Geffen) 1985

On the only memorable track this wimpy synth-rock trio can deliver, singer Geoff Barradale does an appallingly close approximation of Marc Almond; the lyrics, however, are so stupid that no one could ever mistake "Burning Flame" for Soft Cell. A strange collection of sidemen played on **Rites of Passage**, including ex-Ant Chris Hughes and ex-Roxy Music guitarist Neil Hubbard, but it's a lost cause: these no-talents are dead in the water.

[iar]

VIVABEAT

Party in the War Zone (Charisma) 1980

This one-hit (well, almost one) California guitar-plus-synthesizer sextet sounds like Sparks played at half speed. Their big number, "Man from China," is a foursquare dance track with a catchy riff that is whistled for novel effect. Otherwise, the LP is a stiff.

[iar]

WAH!

Nah=Poo—The Art of Bluff (Eternal/nr) 1981
The Maverick Years '80—'81 (Wonderful World/nr) 1982

MIGHTY WAH!

Hope EP (Eternal/nr) 1983
Come Back EP (Eternal-Beggars Banquet/nr) 1984
A Word to the Wise Guy (Eternal-Beggars Banquet/nr) 1984
Weekends EP (Eternal-Beggars Banquet/nr) 1984
The Way We Wah (WEA/nr) 1984

One of the significant groups of the second Liverpool scene, Wah! (and numerous titular variations thereon) functions as a vehicle for extrovert Pete Wylie. On **Nah=Poo**, Wylie and crew sound like Emerson, Lake and Palmer with hipper (though equally flamboyant) arrangements. He sings melodramatically on stirring but superficial material like "The Death of Wah!" and "Seven Minutes to Midnight." Wylie may—as he intimates—be a fraud, but at least he's an entertaining one.

A Word to the Wise Guy—a full album and a bonus single—contains more of Wylie's flighty excursions into soul, pop, funk and anything else he happens across. Although not very consistent, it's an unpredictable and generally likable collection. The 12-inch **Come Back** has two versions of that ace track (also on the LP) plus a couple of other items. **Weekends** contains an alternate version of that album track as well as a demo for it and two other odds and ends from Wylie's sprawling career.

The Way We Wah is a retrospective of Wylie's single successes, from "7000 Names of Wah," "Hope" and "Story of the Blues" to his reading of Johnny Thunders' "Can't Put Your Arms Around a Memory."

[jy/iar]

WAITRESSES

Wasn't Tomorrow Wonderful? (ZE-Polydor) 1982
I Could Rule the World If I Could Only Get the Parts EP (nr/ZE-Polydor) 1982
Make the Weather EP (Polydor/nr) 1983
Bruiseology (Polydor) 1983

Founder/composer/guitarist Chris Butler invented the Waitresses; fellow Akronite Patty Donahue gave the group/idea its voice. From an original germinal joke (before Butler's spell in the more avant-garde Tin Huey) and appearance on a local compilation LP, the Waitresses grew into a well-known New York-based sextet (including ex-Television drummer Billy Ficca) churning out danceably funky pop tunes spiked with a few twists (not the least of which is Mars Williams' searing and satirical sax). Furthermore, Donahue's persona—she doesn't sing so much as carry a simultaneous conversation and tune—has been developed into the archetypal young, white, middle-class woman trying to sort out her identity while beset with standard societal conditioning on one hand and specious, voguish "alternatives" (the Sexual Revolution, the Me Generation) on the other. The Waitresses' combination of musical aplomb and lyrical acuity makes the first LP at once funny, sad and universally true.

The American EP contains a TV sitcom theme ("Square Pegs"), the wonderful Yuletide rap track ("Christmas Wrapping"), a live-for-TV take of an old Hueys-era Butler tune and more. The related English release is somewhat different, most notably lacking "Christmas Wrapping."

Bruiseology was recorded amidst serious personnel tension. (Donahue subsequently quit, was briefly replaced by Holly Vincent, but later rejoined.) Although Butler penned another batch of witty and wise songs about the exigencies of modern womanhood—perhaps less pointed but not far removed from those on the first LP—and the playing and production are fine, the formula doesn't wear all that well. The Waitresses have since broken up but the name continues to surface sporadically in concert listings. [jg]

WALL

Personal Troubles & Public Issues (Fresh/nr) 1981
Dirges & Anthems (Polydor/nr) 1982

The Wall hail from the northernmost reaches of England, which may explain the faint Scottish influence audible on their first album. Essentially a revisionist hardcore band, the Wall play a brand of punk that refuses to toe the genre line, employing different tempos (none of them too fast) and occasionally novel ideas to countermand the restrictions that make so many lesser groups sound alike. **Personal Troubles & Public Issues** (one side per subject) is a pretty decent record, with blazing guitars, clear vocals and relatively thoughtful lyrics. Like a heavy metal album, the sound is crisp and well-balanced, but the songs have much more interesting subjects than bats or hell. **Dirges & Anthems**, which comes with a three-song bonus single, refines and improves the approach somewhat, toning the guitars down a little and adding a bit of saxophone, acoustic guitar and even a reggae rhythm. The Wall seem to be pursuing an individual direction that only coincided with the thrash brigade for a short while.
[iar]

WALL OF VOODOO

Wall of Voodoo EP (Index-IRS) 1980
Dark Continent (IRS) 1981
Call of the West (Illegal/IRS) 1982
Granma's House (IRS/nr) 1984
Seven Days in Sammystown (IRS) 1985

Los Angeles' Wall of Voodoo makes junk music that can be extremely entertaining as long as you don't expect too much from it. Working in the same general cinematic groove as Devo, only taking their cues from westerns and noirs rather than science fiction, Voodoo generate a stiff (though human) sound that furnishes a vivid backdrop to Stanard Ridgway's semi-catatonic vocals. Wall of Voodoo is poised uneasily between machine music and rock'n'roll, a fine illustration of the conflict between the old and the new for the serious-minded. A more honest interpretation would describe Voodoo as classy Halloween music, scary but pleasantly so.

The EP includes among its four songs a wacked-out version of Johnny Cash's "Ring of Fire." On **Dark Continent** the band displays more polish, with tunes like "Back in Flesh" and "Full of Tension" benefitting from colorfully morose guitar and keyboards. **Call of the West**'s execution is livelier and more articulate, but just as spooky. The album contains the now-classic "Mexican Radio."

Ridgway left Wall of Voodoo in 1983 for a solo career; the band decided to replace him and continue. In 1984, British IRS released a compilation album, **Granma's House**, with all of Voodoo's best tracks, from "Ring of Fire" to "Mexican Radio."

Unveiling two new members (drummer Joe Nanini having departed as well), Wall of Voodoo returned to action with **Seven Days in Sammystown**, their first new album in three years. Ridgway's absence forced a major rethink of the band's sound and purpose; the record is adequate, but somewhat short of character and uncompelling. "Far Side of Crazy" and a dirgey cover of the mining oldie, "Dark as the Dungeon," are quite good, but the rest falls short; an attempt to mimic Ridgway ("Big City") fails.
[jy/iar]

See also *Stan Ridgway*.

WANDERERS

Only Lovers Left Alive (Polydor/nr) 1981

The brief liaison between members of Sham 69 and ex-Dead Boy Stiv Bators set the stage for the subsequent Lords of the New Church, and resulted in one album. Although begun as a Sham 69 record (with Bators replacing singer Jimmy Pursey), contracts prevented its release as such; under the Wanderers name, it attracted almost no attention. It deserved a better fate. Presenting legible rock with a strong political bent, **Only Lovers Left Alive** brings together loads of influences that had never been present in either faction's background, and synthesizes a varied, well-produced angry assault that's more radical in stance than music. In any case, the album is noteworthy for including a courageous rockified version of "The Times They Are A-Changin'."
[iar]

WANG CHUNG

Points on the Curve (Geffen) 1984
To Live and Die in L.A. (Geffen) 1985

HUANG CHUNG

Huang Chung (Arista) 1982

Despite their exotic name, this overdressed British band plays familiar post-Ultravox pop—with saxophone instead of keyboards and less of a heavy dance beat—on **Huang Chung**. A talented and proficient quartet, they lack only an identity and the first-rate songs that might have made it memorable.

Points on the Curve unveils several major changes, including a revised name, a slimmed-down trio lineup (no more sax) focused on singer Jack Hues and a different label. "Dance Hall Days" has dumb lyrics but a good, rhythmic sound and a strong hook; "Wait" has dumb, awkward lyrics ("evidently/there's a difficulty") but a clever

arrangement with synthesized strings and chimes adding punctuation. Elsewhere, they essay dance-funk and Foreigner-like pomposity. Having banished its facelessness, Wang Chung is revealed in all its mediocrity.

By the time they wrote and recorded the soundtrack for the movie *To Live and Die in L.A.* (a good title tune plus lots of expendable instrumentals), W.C. was merely a duo. At this rate, two more LPs should finish them off.
[iar]

WARSAW PAKT

Needle Time! (Island/nr) 1977

Out of London's exploding early punk scene came this novelty—an album that reached local shops *within 24 hours of the start of its recording!* The band wasn't anything extraordinary—just amateur working class thrash'n'bash—but the speedy creation of the record made quite a stir for a few moments. The record came packed in a mailing envelope covered with stickers and rubber stamps; the insert sheet includes a complete log of the 21 hours it took to finish. Bizarre. [iar]

WAS (NOT WAS)

Was (Not Was) (ZE-Island) 1981
Born to Laugh at Tornadoes (ZE-Geffen) 1983

Shattering all illusions of a division between "black music" and "white music," Detroiters David (Weiss) Was and Don (Fagenson) Was use undated soul and funk as a backdrop for making overt and implicit political statements, opening new doors for artists of all colors. The material on their eponymous first album leans on familiar elements from sources like Grace Jones and Stevie Wonder but blends in much humor and cleverness, making virtually every song an original gem, including the disco hits "Out Come the Freaks" and "Tell Me That I'm Dreaming," which includes mutilated found vocals from Ronald Reagan.

Born to Laugh at Tornadoes is a conceptual tour de force, a wacked-out collection of incongruous guest vocalists. Among the stars on parade: Ozzy Osbourne, Mel Torme, Mitch Ryder and Doug Fieger. Also in attendance: Wayne Kramer, Marshall Crenshaw, Kiss' Vinnie Vincent and many others. The songs—Was Bros. originals—typically mix wiseacre/devolution lyrics with muscular soul-funk-rock, making the album enjoyable on at least three levels—powerful dance music, cleverly worded smart-aleckdom, and super-session bizarreness.

The historical problem with a lot of dance music has been its rabid dissociation from intellect; more than almost any other group, Was (Not Was) obliterates that gap.
[sg/iar]

WATERBOYS

The Waterboys EP (nr/Island) 1983
The Waterboys (Ensign/nr) 1983
A Pagan Place (nr/Island) 1984
This Is the Sea (Ensign/Island) 1985

Mike Scott leads this bombastic Scottish band through hideously pompous over-produced epics that sound vaguely like Bruce Springsteen (horns and backing vocals)

crossed with the Alarm (overwrought drama and acoustic guitars) and topped off with a misbegotten impression of Bob Dylan (voice and lyrics). Scott seems to fancy himself the purveyor of some Important Message, but there's precious little worth receiving from these records. **This Is the Sea**, while hardly down-to-earth, shows Scott developing a bit of non-melodic songwriting skill, even as his production approaches are getting more and more absurd. Some of the tracks are so bizarrely realized that they're memorable if not enjoyable. If Scott ever decides to cover "MacArthur Park" I suggest we all head for the hills!
[iar]

BEN WATT

See *Everything but the Girl*.

WAVES

See *Katrina and the Waves, Kimberley Rew*.

WC3

WC3 EP (Fr. CBS) 1981

This French quartet has the '80s version of swinging '60s go-go beat down pat. They season it with atonalities and spooky effects (courtesy of keyboardist and sometime *chanteur* Francoise; there's no guitarist) as well as occasional shifts into unlikely rhythms. Emerging through all of this is the gruff Gallic growl of main vocalist Renaud Isaac, painting verbal pictures (in French) of themes like dancing, violence and boredom. The lyrics are actually quite clever in spots, and the music is catchy in its offbeat way.
[jg]

WEAPON OF PEACE

Weapon of Peace (Safari/nr) 1981
Rainbow Rhythm (Safari/nr) 1983

This seven-man ensemble's first album was produced by Bob Lamb (who's worked with UB40) and contains jazzy, upbeat, souled-out reggae with a positive message. A little too mellow and mainstream to be credible, but nice enough. **Rainbow Rhythm** finds the band getting a bit heavier and more topical, with "Society" and "Destiny" among their concerns. The horn charts add an incongruous Philly soul sound and the vocal stylings are likewise more American than Jamaican, making it not reggae but a smooth commercial derivative thereof.
[iar]

WEIRDOS

Who? What? When? Where? Why? EP (nr/Bomp) 1980
Action Design EP (nr/Rhino) 1980

LA's Weirdos were one of that town's earliest and most popular new wave bands; their first singles (including a 1977 Bomp EP) were routine genre fare. But by '79 they had evolved an intriguing blend of punk, psychobilly and gonzo rock with unsettling lyrics. The six songs on **Who? What? When? Where? Why?** present a wide variety of styles, all reasonably successful in conception and execution.

Action Design has only four numbers, and one of them is a needless soundalike version of the Doors' "Break on Through." The others are well-played, loud and fast, with less weirdness and more simple rock'n'roll directness. An interesting but inconsistent outfit. [iar]

STEFAN WEISER

See *Z'ev*.

HOWARD WERTH

Six of One and Half a Dozen of the Other (Metabop/nr) 1982

Werth's checkered career has included singing in lovable folk-pop deviants Audience, almost joining the Doors as Jim Morrison's replacement and putting out a single on California indie punk label Dangerhouse, backed by local LA talent (including a Wall of Voodoo member-to-be).

Funnily enough, this solo album (Werth had a prior LP out in 1975) is no cash-in job; here's a man who's finally found the musical climate he's been waiting for. There's one side of goofy-but-smart originals, his mellifluous, elastic voice a joy to hear telling of an encounter with an astrology nut, the virtues of "Meek Power" and other items of like value. The other side offers oldies of variable obscurity chosen wisely from rock's roots stockpile. The backing—by the likes of Billy Bremner, Carlene Carter and members of the Attractions—is impeccable, as is the shrewd production by Will Birch of the Records. Enough to turn the heads of fans of Dave Edmunds, Nick Lowe, et al. [jg]

WE'VE GOT A FUZZBOX AND WE'RE GONNA USE IT

164

We've Got a Fuzzbox and We're Gonna Use It EP (Vindaloo/nr) 1986

These four charming young lasses took over-the-top hairdos and a devil-may-care attitude straight into the Top 30 with this five-song EP. Proud of their lack of instrumental prowess (rightly so—it's a main part of their appeal), the Fuzzboxes simultaneously exploit and satirize the Page 3 mentality on great cuts like "X X Sex" and "She." Musically, the songs are built around rudimentary drums and guitar (yes, they do use their fuzzbox), occasional bass and unbridled enthusiasm. A real breath of fresh air. [dgs]

WHAM!

Fantastic (Innervision/Columbia) 1983
Make It Big (CBS/Columbia) 1984
The Edge of Heaven (nr/Columbia) 1986

Even if you despise this pair, you must admit they've had a fascinating story—from a legal row that almost scuttled their career to worldwide teenybop stardom and a groundbreaking engagement in China. Singer/producer/songwriter George Michael proved to be Wham!'s senior partner; guitarist Andrew Ridgeley receded further into the background. While the two albums cover a wide range of styles, the most consistent factor is their obnoxious phoniness.

Fantastic essays smug rap-funk ("Bad Boys" and "Wham Rap") and smooth Philly soul ("Love Machine," "Nothing Looks the Same in the Light") with equal lack of conviction. They may have cribbed the

idea, but never got any of the feeling. Vile.

Deciding that they didn't want to be black after all, Wham! decided to try being ultra-white. **Make It Big** locates a mindless pure pop format far better suited to the vacuous impersonality they project. "Wake Me Up Before You Go-Go" and "Freedom" may be giddily moronic, but at least have the ring of true commercial craftsmanship free of stylistic artifice. Otherwise, the LP consists largely of pop-soul that is so mild as to be soporific. If you thought Culture Club was too bland and easygoing, you haven't heard these boys. **Make It Big** is not just a record your parents could like, but your grandparents may find it their speed as well.

The duo dissolved in 1986 amidst legal tussles. **The Edge of Heaven** is a farewell cash-in compilation. [iar]

WHAT IS THIS

Squeezed EP (nr/San Andreas) 1984
What Is This (nr/MCA) 1985
3 out of 5 Live EP (nr/MCA) 1985

Wild, muscular rock-funk with a demented outlook, LA's What Is This bears more than a passing resemblance to the Red Hot Chili Peppers, but that's not surprising—guitarist Hillel Slovak formed What Is This after leaving the Peppers, whom he rejoined after making **Squeezed**. Chris Hutchinson and Jack Irons ride a fearsome rhythm behemoth, and Alain Johannes and Slovak both provide offbeat songs ("Mind My Have Still I" isn't even the weirdest), unnerving mental vocals and psycho guitar licks, making **Squeezed** a gut'n'butt-shaking experience you won't soon forget.

Cut as a trio, **What Is This** (produced by Todd Rundgren) is a less invigorating move towards the rhythmic rock mainstream. Some of the excitement remains, but not enough. The subsequent EP adds live versions of three numbers to a pair of album cuts. [iar]
See also *Red Hot Chili Peppers*.

WHERE'S LISSE?

Where's Lisse? EP (Glass/nr) 1982

Don't be put off by the stupid name. They're a bit scratchy, just barely keeping in step, but when the inchoate instrumental expression of this foursome threatens to unravel, they're pulled along by the steadfast, determined (double-tracked) vocals of John Novak. The playing's scruffy, but cut through the rough edging to the heart of it, and you'll find lean but proud melodies fighting to escape. [jg]

WHIRLWIND

Blowin' Up a Storm (Chiswick/nr) 1977
Midnight Blue (Chiswick/nr) 1980

This London quartet (named after a Charlie Rich Sun recording) was one of the first English rockabilly bands to emerge at a time when the music press was looking for the "next big thing" after punk. On its debut, **Blowin' Up a Storm**, Whirlwind—whether by design or simply limited competence—offers up a bare-bones style of rockabilly, with little or no concession to the advancement in recording quality

since the originals. The instrumentation is semi-traditional (one lead guitar, one muted-bass-strings rhythm guitar, electric bass and snare drum) and was recorded with no overdubbing, resulting in a sound that can charitably be called "thin." While painstakingly trying to recapture the simplicity of early rockabilly recordings, Whirlwind never manages to re-create the frenzied, fiery abandon that is really what it was all about. **Midnight Blue**, recorded over two years later, shows the group past its hang-ups about purity: the sound is filled out, the drummer plays an entire kit (albeit with amazing clumsiness at times) and pedal-steel guitar even finds its way onto one track. While an improvement over **Blowin' Up a Storm**, **Midnight Blue** still fails to present any clear reason why anybody would want to listen to it, when both the originals and far more imaginative updates like the Stray Cats are available. [ds]

WHIRLYWIRLD

Whirlywhirld EP (Aus. Missing Link) 1980

Guitar, bass, drums and electronics (not synthesizers, though) combine to make lots of staccato noise over which Ian Olsen can dispense his own brand of doom and gloom. This sort of amelodic anger has to be compelling to succeed, but Whirlywirld aren't and don't. Surprisingly, when the Sydney quartet gets relatively conventional on the final track, the savagery of their ska styling does indeed make you sit up and take note. [jg]

JAMES WHITE

See *James Chance*.

WHITE DOOR

Windows (Clay/Passport) 1983

White Door consists of two synthesists and a singer; with some guests, their album offers lovely pop-with-a-beat. Although the UK band's material and arrangements are not extraordinary for synth-pop, the way in which the fragile, ethereal vocals and durable dance music are blended on the best tracks ("Love Breakdown" is the standout) makes **Windows** more affecting than affected. [iar]

WHITE RUSSIA

East Side Story (Ger. Aladin) 1981

This quartet (evidently half-German, half-English) probably would have gone down quite well in the UK as late as 1979, but their brand of abrasive punk with the occasional pop-tune hook is too regressive for today's tastemakers and not blindly hardcore enough for skinheads to embrace. These guys can be lunkheads themselves, but usually quite acceptably so, and can rock with a vengeance. No earth-shaking songs but, out of sixteen tracks, there are only perhaps three or four clinkers. With a bit more guitar power (there's only one) these guys could really score with US punkoids, if they don't set their sights too high. [jg]

WHODINI

Whodini (Jive) 1983
Escape (Jive) 1984
Back in Black (Jive) 1986

Like Run—D.M.C., this two-man team from Brooklyn does something very original and exciting within the context of rap, blending in wit and variety to make entertaining records. On their debut, Jalil Hutchins and Ecstasy worked with three different producers—Thomas Dolby, Conny Plank and the Willesden Dodgers—to come up with an '80s version of "Monster Mash" ("The Haunted House of Rock"), two bouncy history-of-rap/rap-is-good numbers ("Magic's Wand" and "Rap Machine") plus a couple of alternate versions and three more cuts. Although the moderate tempo big-beat gets a bit numbing, the pair's sharp lyrics and straightforward delivery, plus countless bits of electronic flotsam and jetsam prevent serious tedium.

Escape brought Whodini under the talented studio wing of Run—D.M.C. co-producer Larry Smith, who created a smooth, semi-spare sound and did a lot of the writing as well. With fewer quirky synthesizer accents, the action centers on raps about the urban nightmare ("Escape (I Need a Break)"), failed romance ("Friends") and New York's all-night lifestyle ("Freaks Come Out at Night"), as well as other more egocentric topics. Airy without being simple, **Escape** is an appealing and innovative rap record.

With Grandmaster Dee (celebrated on an **Escape** song) officially expanding Whodini to a trio, **Back in Black** is more straightforward, with less reliance on fancy production and more concentration on varied, organic arrangements. However, while Whodini's music is getting stronger, their lyrical ideas aren't: all eight cuts cover familiar rap ground with no special outlook and only intermittent cleverness. [iar]

WIDE BOY AWAKE

Wide Boy Awake EP (nr/RCA) 1983

Ex-Ant bassist Kevin Mooney formed and leads Wide Boy Awake, an exciting interracial quartet which has so far released only some singles, the first two of which are collected on this American 12-inch. Hard to classify, the Wide Boys offer clever wordplay and a preponderant funk beat on "Slang Teacher," while square-dancing into wonderful country-tinged pop for "Bona Venture." Elsewhere, they try scratch cajun and dance-rock. [iar]

JANE WIEDLIN

Jane Wiedlin (IRS) 1985

Free of the Go-Go's, guitarist/songwriter Wiedlin's record is stylistically eclectic to a fault, and stresses goody-goody lyrical concerns too bluntly, but is also substantial, attractive and joyously reflects her newfound artistic freedom. "Blue Kiss" is an adorable love lament; "Somebody's Going to Get into This House" is sturdy dance-rock. "Where We Can Go" could have been done by her former band, while the moody "Modern Romance" would better suit the Motels. Wiedlin's not the world's strongest vocalist, but her enthusiasm and sincerity largely compensate. [iar]

KIM WILDE

Kim Wilde (RAK/EMI America) 1981

Select (RAK/nr) 1982 (Fame/nr) 1985
Catch as Catch Can (RAK/EMI America) 1983
Teases & Dares (MCA) 1984
The Very Best of Kim Wilde (EMI/nr) 1984

Scion of pre-Beatles teen idol Marty and sister of player/writer/producer Ricky, pouty, adorable Kim Wilde turned out to be a fairly talented pop singer herself. With sympathetic family support, she records catchy rock tunes that have HIT written all over their memorable choruses and hook-filled arrangements. The songs on **Kim Wilde**, penned by the two male Wildes, focus thematically on youth, which underscores Kim's own tender age but veers her a bit uncomfortably close (careerwise) to featherweight bubblegum. "Kids in America," "Chequered Love" and "Water on Glass" are wonderful confections though, and serve as an enjoyable update of the teenybop sounds popular a decade earlier.

Three years and several albums later, **Teases & Dares** makes it perfectly clear that this fresh-faced girl has grown into a woman, from the glamorous cover photo to the lyrics that challenge a man in a "cheap motel" to "stop giving up—you know you can't refuse me" and "go for the second time." Whew! The musical emphasis is also on maturity, abandoning simpleminded charm for intricate, modernized synthesizer rock. Ricki (little spelling change there) and his pop co-produced and are the LP's main tunesmiths, although Kim gets in a couple of her own this time; Ricki is the featured musician. Given less engaging songs and increased competition from the backing, Kim doesn't hit as many bullseyes on this LP. "Fit In" sounds like Laura Nyro; elsewhere she essays other styles that, more than anything else, point up her limitations as a singer. This woman should have stayed a teenager. [iar]

SCOTT WILK AND THE WALLS

Scott Wilk and the Walls (Warner Bros.) 1980

Encountering the line between artistic influence and stylistic plagiarism, Scott Wilk grabbed a copy of Elvis Costello's **Armed Forces** and blithely pushed ahead. Parts of this record are uncannily accurate impressions; the cover design and group photo do nothing to reduce the Costello/Attractions allusion. Funny thing, though—this album is tremendous! If you can ignore its derivative *raison d'etre*, you'll find powerful, well-crafted songs, impressive playing and production and an overriding sense of cohesion. An unexpected but disconcerting thrill. [iar]

ROBERT WILLIAMS

Buy My Record EP (A&M) 1981
Late One Night (A&M) 1982

Drummer/singer/composer Williams has played with some real heavyweights in his low-profile career: several years as a member of Captain Beefheart's Magic Band, tours with Bo Donaldson and the Heywoods, an LP with Hugh Cornwell. So it's hardly surprising that the credits on Williams' solo records read like a who's who of modern music. Appearing on these two discs are the likes of Mark and

Bob Mothersbaugh of Devo, a couple of Go-Go's, Cornwell, Danny Elfman, ex-Door Robby Krieger, ex-Wing Laurence Juber and a veritable orchestra-full of Beefheart and Zappa sidemen. So much for the illustrious company.

Musically, Williams has absorbed a lot of different styles and spews them back with alarming variety and an overriding sense of fun. From mock-raga (on a neat remake of "Within You Without You" from the LP) to straight pop-rock, heavy dance rhythms, reggae and jazz-funk-art-fusion, Williams tries everything and gets away with most of it. The four-song EP is a bit closer to Beefheart with Zappaesque lyrics; the album expands the musical scope and succeeds more in terms of accessible smart-aleck rock. [iar]

See also *Stranglers*.

JAMES WILLIAMSON

See *Iggy Pop*.

MARI WILSON

Showpeople (Compact Organization/London) 1983
Born Lucky [tape] (Compact Organization/nr) 1983
The Mari Wilson Chat Show [tape] (Compact Organization/nr) 1983

Joined by the Wilsations, crowned with an awesome beehive hairdo and dressed in formal evening wear, England's Mari Wilson attempts to singlehandedly effect a return to the days when singers were known as song stylists and the loudest instruments on a record were trombone and violin. As a pose, I can't fathom the appeal—this is so far removed from rock as to lose any satirical value and hardly aimed at people desirous of the real article. If the world was in need of a new Peggy Lee, wouldn't the call go out for a real middle-aged schmaltz-spooner?

Anyway, if you don't have a conceptual problem with it, **Showpeople** is a likable, grandly-produced and bountifully tuneful record. Wilson is an almost-very-good singer with a fair amount of versatility, judging by the mock-rock mixed in with the MOR crooning. The centerpiece and virtual statement of purpose is Wilson's smoky cover of "Cry Me a River," a hit for Julie London in 1957. The American release deducts two songs and shifts the running order.

Born Lucky is a live cassette recorded in 1982. Given the problems of recording an orchestra and vocalist in one take, the sound is a bit cluttered, but Wilson sounds swell, her big voice taking charge of the six numbers, most of them not from the studio album. The **Chat Show** tape is an hour of Mari talking and playing assorted recordings, including outtakes, demos and live cuts. [iar]

WINDBREAKERS

Any Monkey with a Typewriter EP (nr/Big Monkey) 1983
Disciples of Agriculture (Fr. Closer) 1985
Terminal (Homestead) 1985
Run (nr/DB) 1986

Mississippi singer/guitarists Tim Lee and Bobby Sutliff gave their band a terrible name (one hopes the reference is to jackets, not flatulence) but do bring something distinctly unique to the power pop

genre, reflecting more of an American than English influence with strange melodic turns and a ragged Southern vocal style. Following the release of a 1982 debut 7-inch, Mitch Easter produced **Any Monkey**, assisting the trio instrumentally as well. (Richard Barone of the Bongos also appears on the record.) The self-released six-song 12-inch is amateurish but well worth hearing. (**Disciples** is a French compilation.)

Recorded as a duo with Easter and other helping out, **Terminal** is a brilliant, raw pop-rock-folk record with insidious melodies, fuzzed-out guitars, bristly lyrics and unselfconscious sincerity. An appropriately atmospheric version of Television's "Glory"—produced by and played with the Rain Parade—subsequently led Lee to work separately in side ventures with Paraders Steven Roback (as Gone Fishing) and Matthew Piucci (as Distant Cousins).

Run is another collaboration with Easter, who at this point is virtually a (non-writing) member of the band. A bit less quirky (but just as engaging) than past releases, the electrically energized pop could have been mixed more evenly, but that's not a major distraction. Coolest song concept: the anxiety-ridden "Braver on the Telephone." [iar]

WINKIES

The Winkies (Chrysalis/nr) 1975

Best known for their role as Eno's just-post-Roxy Music tour band, the Winkies included Philip Rambow as well as future sidemen for Phil Manzanera, John Cale and Sean Tyla. Less under-endowed than immature, the sub-Stones pub-rock on this album sounds too presumptuously casual, too unfocused—like demos in a pricey studio, despite Guy Stevens' production—to support Rambow's lyrical pretensions and nasal Canadian twang. The sole standout is "Trust in Dick," written by Guy Humphreys, the only Winkie to become more obscure after the group dissolved. [jg]

See also *Philip Rambow*.

WIRE

Pink Flag (Harvest) 1977
Chairs Missing (Harvest/nr) 1978
154 (Harvest/Warner Bros.) 1979
Document and Eyewitness (Rough Trade/nr) 1981
And Here It Is . . . Again . . . Wire (Sneaky Pete/nr) 1985
Wire Play Pop (Pink/nr) 1986

In the beginning, this self-taught South London quartet were as much atavistic thrashers as many other bands of the time, yet **Pink Flag** demonstrated that they were honing a genuinely expressive minimalist style—abrupt, angry and often willfully odd. Even so, in the midst of the album's 21 (count'em) tracks were a pair of excellent, more conventional rockers, and perhaps the prettiest song ever by a punk band, "Fragile."

Chairs Missing is more mature, moving decisively beyond any simple punk pigeonhole with much greater scope. As on its predecessor, amid the anger of "Being Sucked in Again," the bile of "I Am the Fly," the neurotic anxiety of "Too Late," even the ironic detachment of "French Film Blurred," sat the pretty if abstruse "Outdoor Miner."

On **154**, producer Mike Thorne became more integral than on the first two LPs, acting almost as a fifth member, using keyboards and studio technique to stylize the sound. That was Wire's development—stylized and smoothed out—although still dissonant; more abstract and detached, with the venom and sardonicism more subtly conveyed. Thus refined, this brilliant groundbreaking band adjudged their experiment complete and broke up, with Bruce Gilbert and Graham Lewis creating Dome and Colin Newman pursuing a solo career.

Document and Eyewitness, an album plus a 12-inch EP recorded live, owes its raunchy sound as much to Wire's disdain of musical niceties as to dodgy recording. Audience sounds and other incidental noise are left in; for aficionados only. **And Here It Is . . . Again . . . Wire** is a career retrospective containing singles, album tracks and live cuts. **Wire Play Pop** likewise compiles seven old tracks, but limits its scope to Wire's extraordinary, trailblazing A-sides, including "Dot Dash," "I Am the Fly," "Mannequin" and "1-2-X-U." [jg/iar]

See also *Dome, Colin Newman*.

WIRE TRAIN

In a Chamber (CBS/415-Columbia) 1983
Between Two Words (CBS/415-Columbia) 1985

Like 415 labelmates Translator, San Francisco's Wire Train plays exceptional, character-filled modern folk-pop, using strong songwriting as a basis. (The two groups additionally shared a producer—David Kahne—whose brilliant efforts have undoubtedly contributed to the quality of both bands' records.) Wire Train achieves its style with a full-blooded guitar attack, echoey vocals and strong, rushed drumming. **In a Chamber** has wonderful, memorable tracks like "Chamber of Hellos" and "I'll Do You"; lesser creations at least *sound* just as good. A great debut album.

Between Two Words, despite Kahne's absence and an inadvisable version of Dylan's "God on Our Side" that unintentionally trivializes the song's earnest concerns, is an equally memorable album. Not all of the songs work, but those that do—"Last Perfect Thing," "Skills of Summer," "Love, Love"—have folk-derived melodic beauty and an uneasy emotional perspective that is not easily ignored. The writing/singing/guitar-playing duo of Kevin Hunter and Kurt Herr don't display a lot of range or depth, but they do give the group an unmistakable, invariably pleasing style. [iar]

WITCH TRIALS

The Witch Trials EP (nr/Alternative Tentacles-Subterannean) 1981

Jello Biafra of the Dead Kennedys was the brains and voice of this mysterious one-off studio project, recorded in England and released originally in France. With unidentified musicians providing guitar and synthesizer backing—an atmospheric drone on one side, jarring unpleasantness on the other—Biafra recites two dramatic tales of mayhem and chants two more

165

pieces of madness that exhibit his characteristic venom and wit. Witch Trials is an interesting detour from Biafra's work with the DK's, and he proves to be just as capable and clever in this vein.

[iar]

JAH WOBBLE

The Legend Lives On . . . Jah Wobble in "Betrayal" (Virgin/nr) 1980
V.I.E.P. EP (Virgin/nr) 1980
Jah Wobble's Bedroom Album (Lago/nr) 1983

STRATETIME KEITH/JAH WOBBLE

Steel Leg v the Electric Dread EP (Virgin/nr) 1978

JAH WOBBLE, JAKI LIEBEZEIT AND HOLGER CZUKAY

How Much Are They EP (Island/nr) 1981

JAH WOBBLE & ANIMAL

A Long, Long Way EP (JAH/nr) 1982

JAH WOBBLE—THE EDGE—HOLGER CZUKAY

Snake Charmer EP (Island) 1983

JAH WOBBLE & OLLIE MORLAND

Neon Moon (Island/nr) 1985

After falling out with John Lydon and Keith Levene, bassist Wobble left Public Image Ltd. and launched an on-again-off-again solo/collaborative career. He also played in a group called the Human Condition, and did a brief stint as a cab driver.

Wobble's anti-musical playfulness on **The Legend Lives On** is matched only by his horrid vocals. But then again, that's the appeal: the return to the d.i.y., no-rules punk tradition. Wobble accentuates his reggae pretensions, fiddles with electronics and overdubbing and plays shadowy, threatening bass. If nothing else, Wobble has (anti)style. Not to be taken seriously, as Wobble would probably be the first to admit.

V.I.E.P., which sounds like outtakes from the album sessions, reprises the LP's "Blueberry Hill." Twice. "Sea Side Special" is notable for its professionalism and use of brass. But it's for completists only.

Far more indicative of Wobble's real talent is the four-song 12-inch made with erstwhile Can members Jaki Liebezeit and Holger Czukay in 1981. Manifesting a dour modern landscape, Wobble's bass buttresses the dark tunes with style and precision that balance his earlier solipsistic sloppiness. Freed from ego, Wobble teeters at last towards art.

Unlike previous Wobble projects, **A Long, Long Way** is sweetly pop-like, treading on Joy Division territory (with assistance from guitarist Dave "Animal" Maltby). Especially interesting is "Romany Trail," which mixes "Peter Gunn" jazz with modern sensibilities. Top notch.

The Bedroom Album was recorded alone—you guessed it—in the master's chamber, with Animal

providing the only outside contact. A cross between a legit solo studio job and the kind of one-man-band who plays on street corners, the LP finds Wobble building unstable and polyrhythmic atmospheric instrumentals over which he intones ponderous lyrics with only the barest glimpses of melody or meter. The lengthy record requires a lot of patience, but is not without charm or appeal.

In collaboration with producer Francois Kevorkian, Czukay, Liebezeit, Animal and U2's guitarist (among others—Wobble certainly appears to make friends easily), he pounds out far slicker dance-rock on **Snake Charmer**, but it's all for nought, as the record is overstaffed and overstuffed, mixing repetitive rhythms with extraneous sounds to achieve audible boredom.

Wobble's 1978 pre-PiL 12-inch with Keith Levene, filmmaker (and future Big Audio Dynamite member) Don Letts and someone called Steel Leg is a bizarre assemblage of dub reggae and noisome doom-funk that has Levene playing drums and guitar while Wobble adds bass, synth and vocals. Whew!

[sg/iar]

WOLFGANG PRESS

The Burden of Mules (4AD/nr) 1983
Scarecrow EP (4AD/nr) 1984
Water EP (4AD/nr) 1985
Sweatbox EP (4AD/nr) 1986
The Legendary Wolfgang Press & Other Tall Stories (4AD/nr) 1986

Ever-changing and always challenging, London's Wolfgang Press is one of the more enigmatic groups on an already enigmatic label. Known better for their stylish Alberto Ricci record covers than their music, the trio comprises Michael Allen (vocals/bass), Mark Cox (keyboards) and Andrew Gray (drums).

The Burden of Mules is dark and cacophonous, an angry, intense slab of post-punk gloom that is best left to its own (de)vices. **Scarecrow**, however, makes the most of the band's better attributes with spotless production by Cocteau Twin Robin Guthrie. Allen's almost-spoken, heavily accented vocals sputter through a mix of up-front bass, rhythm guitar, synthesizers and creative percussion. Some dreary moments remain, but a send-up of Otis Redding's "Respect" reflects the lightened mood.

Water continues the band's evolution, but in a totally different direction. Over minimalist backing, Allen's vocals turn baladeerish: Frank Sinatra sifted through Joy Division. There's even a track called "My Way" that is curiously reminiscent of Burt Bacharach.

Continuing to work with Guthrie, the Wolfgang Press sounds fully mature and more musically adept than ever on **Sweatbox**. The EP strengthens and confirms their fundamental approach: the deconstruction and reconstruction of pop conventions in their own image. Put through the Wolfgang Press breakdown process, Neil Young's "Heart of Gold" becomes "Heart of Stone," in effect creating an original. **Sweatbox** also establishes the group's mastery of moving instrumentals.

The Legendary Wolfgang Press compiles the three EPs onto one disc, with some songs remixed and/or edited from their original form.

[ag]

WOODENTOPS

Straight Eight Bushwaker EP (Hol. Megadisc) 1986
Well Well Well . . .
(nr/Upside) 1986

In this era of retro-rock, revivals and ripoffs, it's not easy to find truly innovative pop music. That's what makes this quintet from Peckham so special—they literally defy categorization. Led by the exuberant Rolo McGinty, the Woodentops employ only the barest of essentials—keyboards, acoustic guitars, bass and rudimentary drums.

These two records chronicle a string of five brilliant singles. The first, released in Holland, collects six tracks. "Move Me," like many of their songs, builds to a manic crescendo before collapsing into a wall of sound; "Well Well Well" is held together with skittering drums and pulsating keyboard chords; "It Will Come" rushes along in a flurry of guitar, piano and good-natured mayhem. The Woodentops tend to throw caution to the wind on their B-sides, and the three here explore all sorts of new territory. The American release adds two more B-sides (from 12-inch singles) and substitutes a longer version of "Well Well Well" that has incredible keyboard and drum breaks.

[ag]

BRUCE WOOLLEY AND THE CAMERA CLUB

English Garden (CBS/nr) 1979
Bruce Woolley and the Camera Club (nr/Columbia) 1979

FIRMAMENT AND THE ELEMENTS

The Essential EP (nr/Press) 1983

Bruce Woolley came out of the Buggles camp, having co-written several of their songs, including "Video Killed the Radio Star." That song, as well as "Clean Clean," is reprised on **English Garden** (which was retitled for the US market), an LP of light power pop strongly reminiscent of the Move. Woolley's musical attitudes were doomed to commercial failure, as this music was too lodged in the '60s to make a dent in the futurist '70s, and the record vanished in the flood. The Camera Club, however, can claim fame of a sort in that Thomas Dolby was a member.

Woolley abandoned the past and discovered the future in the '80s. Along with his brother Guy, he formed a weird, somewhat experimental group, Firmament and the Elements. Their intriguing EP contains nice tunes as well as bizarre effects and tape sounds.

[sg/iar]

WRECKLESS ERIC

Wreckless Eric (Stiff/nr) 1978
The Wonderful World of Wreckless Eric (Stiff/nr) 1978
The Whole Wide World (nr/Stiff) 1979
Big Smash (Stiff/Stiff-Epic) 1980

ERIC GOULDEN

A Roomful of Monkeys (Go! Discs/nr) 1985

On the front of his first LP, the grinning Eric Goulden wears a badge proclaiming "I'm a mess," and a drop of the needle on the disc confirms it. Led by producer Larry Wallis (himself an ex-Pink Fairy), a motley crew whose previous

employers include Ronnie Lane, Marc Bolan and Ian Dury slosh together some mangy guitars, slurpy sax and cheesy organ to surround the strangled, semi-sodden vocals of this lovable scruffy runt from Brighton. All too often, though, catching the bits of perception and knowing desperation requires clearing the sonic mud, not to mention deciphering Eric's drawl.

All, that is, except on the brilliant "Whole Wide World," produced and mostly played by Nick Lowe. As if noticing that Lowe's well-defined pop sense seemed to bring out Eric's best, a series of producers then tried to clean up and dress up his sound. The next album's roster was only slightly less ragtag (Hollywood Brats holdovers and ex-Man man Malcolm Morley), helmed by Pete Solley. This time, though, a balance was obtained between Wreckless' innate, er, looseness and the clarity and sheer musicality needed to adequately present his tunes. As a result, **The Wonderful World** is a rollicking good time propelled by Eric's by-then trademark guitar chug.

No hits were forthcoming, though, and Stiff apparently decided to clean Eric's act up further, as is evident from the new-material first half of the double set, **Big Smash**. Fresh faces in the band (who also collaborated with him on songwriting) and decidedly more commercial-minded production unfortunately seemed to have sanded off all of Eric's edges. (The standout tune, "Good Conversation," is one he wrote alone; it's also the nastiest.)

Clearly establishing his merits once and for all, the other half of **Big Smash** is an irreproachable distillation of the first two LPs and a batch of singles. That disc had previously been issued separately in the US as **The Whole Wide World**, indicating—even to those who might have otherwise dismissed him—Eric's surprising resonance, not to mention his squandered and/or squelched potential.

For collectors of odd discs, the first LP was also issued as a brown-vinyl 10-incher, with two songs fewer.

Returning in 1985 under his own name and fronting a band containing such stalwarts as Norman Watt-Roy and Mickey Gallagher from the Blockheads, Goulden recorded and released his first LP in five years, **A Roomful of Monkeys**.

[jg]

WURM

See *Black Flag*.

X

Los Angeles (nr/Slash) 1980
Wild Gift (Slash) 1981
Under the Big Black Sun (Elektra) 1982
More Fun in the New World (Elektra) 1983
Ain't Love Grand (Elektra) 1985

KNITTERS

Poor Little Critter on the Road (Slash) 1985

EXENE CERVENKA & WANDA COLEMAN

Twin Sisters (nr/Freeway) 1985

Named after the band's hometown, X's debut album is identifiable as a forerunner of hardcore; simple unrestrained energy oftens threatens to crush the "realistic" tunes ("Sex and Dying in High Society," "Nausea," etc.), but never does. Certainly, the elements that give X their majesty on later LPs are already present: Billy Zoom's vibrant rockabilly/Chuck Berry guitar licks, D.J. Bonebrake's thundering drums, arresting vocal harmonies by Exene Cervenka and bassist John Doe, strongly reminiscent of early Jefferson Airplane. Doors organist Ray Manzarek produced the first four albums; on **Los Angeles**, the band saluted him by covering "Soul Kitchen."

Wild Gift constitutes a quantum leap forward, bringing **Los Angeles**' action blur into sharp focus. Zoom's ingeniously simple guitar transcends its influences, and the Doe/Exene harmonies attain a knifelike sharpness. Also, their songs are frequently as incisive as their voices: "We're Desperate," "In This House That I Call Home" and "White Girl," a spooky ballad, ambitiously peer into unglamorous realities without either diminishing or inflating their subjects. **Wild Gift** was such a success as an independent label release that the band's jump to a big company (where greater success has eluded them) was practically inevitable.

Though **Under the Big Black Sun** primarily refines the techniques of **Wild Gift**, it's no disappointment. Bonebrake's drums just get harder and harder, while Doe and Cervenka continue to expand their prowess as singers and songwriters. "Motel Room in My Bed" revives the sleaze motif of earlier LPs, and "The Have Nots," their finest composition to date, skillfully separates compassion from mawkishness.

The problematic **More Fun in the New World** is the work of a band filled with energy and ideas, but unsure how to apply them. As a result, this thoroughly respectable LP is too much like **Big Black Sun** to be fully satisfying. Sizzling tracks such as "Make the Music Go Bang!" and "I Must Not Think Bad Thoughts" would have worked fine on that previous disc, which is a bad sign for a band accustomed to growing by leaps and bounds. In "True Love Pt. £2," X wonders about its own relationship to American mainstream music without arriving at a clear answer. After the LP, they attempted to make contact with Top 40 by covering "Wild Thing" and fell flat.

An album by the Knitters—a part-time mostly-acoustic band consisting of X (minus Billy Zoom), Blaster Dave Alvin and a stand-up bassist—proved to be a glimpse into the future when, in early '86, Zoom left X to form his own band and Alvin gave up the Blasters (at least temporarily) to replace him. **Critter on the Road** records a sincere but futile attempt to imitate several varieties of folk and country music, from traditional to swing. The material mixes cleverly-cliché-laden originals (and an acoustified version of "The New World" for anyone who didn't realize what a weak song it is) with Merle Haggard and Leadbelly covers; Doe/Exene's wistful "Love Shack" is the record's standout.

Ain't Love Grand, the original lineup's final album together, is a hot (if styleless) rock'n'roll record that cuts the crap to bang out unprepossessing rave-ups like "Burning House of Love." On most songs, lead vocals are taken by Exene or Doe alone; the partial elimination of their harmonies is a distinct improvement, as is Michael Wagener's loud, gimmick-free production style. The biggest boner here, a misbegotten, amateurish cover of the Small Faces' timeless "All or Nothing," indicates that X—or at least some portion thereof—has never had a clue about rock music's heritage.

Twin Sisters is a spoken-word album of original poetry. [jy/iar]

XDREAMYSTS

Xdreamysts (Hol. Polydor) 1981

This Northern Irish combo moves in the general direction of Elvis Costello (**My Aim Is True** strain), but lightly, gingerly—like Any Trouble or the Keys—and make even those bands sound fully individualated and almost original by comparison. Oddly enough, it's on the slower numbers that songwriting singer/guitarist Uel Walls shows signs of the kind of maturity it would take to emerge from behind's E.C.'s shadow. [jg]

XMAL DEUTSCHLAND

Incubus Succubus EP (Ger. Zick-Zack) 1982
Fetisch (4AD/nr) 1983
Tocsin (4AD/nr) 1984

The dense, throbbing rock of this German quintet may be too strong for some; on the title track of the three-song EP, semi-tonic vocalist Anja Huwe bellows and shrieks with dark drama while the band drones and pounds out an unbelievably heavy track behind her, a horror movie cross between Siouxsie and the Banshees and Hawkwind.

The lineup for **Fetisch**, recorded in England, includes Huwe and three other women (guitar, keyboards, drums), plus a male bassist. With a slightly toned-down attack, Xmal Deutschland's drone loses some of its allure, and a full album's worth of onrushing chaos and numbing noise is more tedious than gripping.

Also recorded in London, but this time with mainstream producer Mick Glossop, **Tocsin** tempers the band's ugly side with economy, variety and restraint. They're still loud as hell and sound in spots like Hawkwind, but at this point, they're also at a nexus with Joy Division, using bleak noise to convey a variety of moods. With the subtlety and dynamics that were lacking, **Tocsin** clearly displays Xmal Deutschland to be cogent and invigorating. [iar]
See also *This Mortal Coil*.

X-RAY SPEX

Germ Free Adolescents (EMI International/nr) 1978

POLY STYRENE

Translucence (UA/nr) 1980

One of the most exciting groups of its time, X-Ray Spex was at once an ideal and atypical punk band. While boasting as much raw aggression as any of its peers, X-Ray Spex used distinctively different means of delivery, augmenting Jak Airport's obligatory buzzsaw guitar with Rudi Thompson's (Lora Logic's replacement) even-more-abrasive sax and giving center stage to Poly Styrene, a talented teenager who yowled witty lyrics with all the delicacy of a cat in heat.

X-Ray Spex's one LP collects some of the ace singles that made them such an early punk standout. (It doesn't contain their first outing, the wildly polemic "Oh Bondage, Up Yours!") Styrene's songs focus on the artificiality of modern life; hence such titles as "The Day the World Turned Day-Glo" and "Warrior in Woolworths." Whether the tune is a ballad or a crazed rocker, the band surges as if there were no tomorrow. And for them, there wasn't. A masterpiece!

Singer/leader Styrene (Marion Elliot) always seemed one of punk's most dispossessed souls, so perhaps her solo album following the band's dissolution should be viewed as a last stab at finding some sense of place in musical terms. A feeling of alienation still prevails, though; **Translucence** is so smooth and coolly delivered that one could easily miss the dark side in the lyrics. Jazzy cocktail-hour backing combines with Styrene's childlike visions to make the music's effect most elusive. Poly Styrene subsequently left music to join a Hare Krishna sect, but resurfaced commercially in early 1986. [jy/wk]
See also *Essential Logic*.

XTC

3D EP (Virgin/nr) 1977
White Music (Virgin/Virgin International) 1978 (nr/Virgin-Epic) 1982 (nr/Geffen) 1984
Go 2 (Virgin/Virgin International) 1978 (nr/Virgin-Epic) 1982 (nr/Geffen) 1984
Drums and Wires (Virgin) 1979 (nr/Virgin-Epic) 1982 (nr/Geffen) 1984
Black Sea (Virgin/Virgin-RSO) 1980 (nr/Virgin-Epic) 1982 (nr/Geffen) 1984
5 Senses EP (Can. Virgin) 1981
English Settlement (Virgin/Virgin-Epic) 1982 (nr/Geffen) 1984
Waxworks/Beeswax (Virgin/nr) 1982 (nr/Geffen) 1984
Mummer (Virgin/Geffen) 1983 (Virgin/nr) 1985
The Big Express (Virgin/Geffen) 1984

MR. PARTRIDGE

Take Away (Virgin/nr) 1980

DUKES OF STRATOSPHEAR

25 O'Clock EP (Virgin/nr) 1984

XTC has never been easy to categorize. At first they seemed like one more high-spirited new wave band, gleefully trampling on rock conventions set the day before. On **White Music**, XTC delights in dissonance, unresolved melodic lines and playful lyrics; guitarist Andy Partridge's hiccoughing vocals are matched by equally nervous music. Amid hyperactive material like "Radios in Motion" and "Spinning Top," only a version of Bob Dylan's "All Along the Watchtower" shows respect for the past.

The follow-up, **Go 2**, is even further out. The songs, mostly by Partridge, excoriate conformism and other hang-ups in kaleidoscopic imagery; music is alternately herky-jerky and menacing. (If that sounds too coherent, a bonus EP called **Go+** pulverizes five of the album's tracks with dub remixes.)

The band settled down on **Drums and Wires**, proving they can make commercial-sounding music without sacrificing their considerable intelligence. The departure of organist Barry Andrews, replaced by guitarist Dave Gregory, seemed to take some helium out of the arrangements. XTC's funhouse world on **Drums and Wires** is more accessible, but still booby-trapped: "Making Plans for Nigel," "Real by Reel," "Scissor Man," "Complicated Game." (As Mr. Partridge, a separately released "solo" album, **Take Away**, finds Andy playing more dub games with tracks from **Drums and Wires**.)

Black Sea refines this approach. Heedless of fashion, XTC here build up the music with multiple strains, undanceable rhythms, intricate interplay and gloriously literate lyrics. The dazzling result is probably the band's finest achievement: an album that, like its songs ("Respectable Street," "Towers of London"), unsentimentally employs the past to make new statements.

English Settlement continues in the same vein but succumbs to rococo excess. (Five songs were pruned from the British two-record set to fit it onto one US disc.) Partridge evidently feels compelled to match musical sophistication with like words; he unfortunately outdoes himself. His prolix lyrics on offbeat but straightforward topics (war, paranoia, even love) read better than they sing and, as recorded, must be read to be understood. **English Settlement** tilts like an over-frosted wedding cake. That it doesn't quite topple is a tribute to the band.

XTC's most winning material, much of it written by bassist Colin Moulding, invariably turns up on their EPs and 45s. **5 Senses** gathers a few non-LP sides from 1980 and '81. That EP has since been superseded by **Waxworks—Some Singles 1977-1982**, which cleverly assembles the band's singles, almost all drawn from albums, on one superb LP. The accompanying second disc, **Beeswax—Some B-Sides 1977-1982**, collects their non-LP B-sides—not deathless music, but inventive as always and decidedly unpretentious.

Following drummer Terry Chambers' departure, XTC next found themselves in a precarious position with their British record label, who were reportedly hesitant to release another brilliant but uncommercial album, a hitch that delayed the appearance of **Mummer** for quite some time. As far removed as it may be from the quirky pop that originally characterized XTC's music, it's a lovely record, resplendent in a quiet, rural sound and ethos. Co-existing with the invigorating whomp of "Great Fire" and the loud rock and disgusted lyrics of "Funk Pop a Roll," there's Partridge's rustic "Love on a Farmboy's Wages" and Moulding's lazy "Wonderland," offering a perfect summery escape from the pressures and excitement of rock. **Mummer** is Music for Picnics.

Continuing on as a trio, **The Big Express** finds XTC back in the world of urban reality, singing disgruntled songs about life in the big city, celebrating the alternative ("The Everyday Story of Smalltown"), but, more surprisingly, again playing full-blast rock rather than bucolic lyricism. Nonetheless, "All You Pretty Girls," incorporating a British folk idiom, is as catchy a number as they've ever done, and the record's overall sense of recharged enthusiasm is quite infectious.

XTC went pseudonymously psychedelic on the carefully-appointed satirical **25 O'Clock** mini-album. The day-glo watches and peace symbols of the cover match the six Rutlesque rewrites of '60s classics like "I Had Too Much to Dream Last Night." Unfortunately, the put-on is so clever and careful that it's not funny, merely notable for its accomplishment.   [si/iar]

See also *Robert Fripp, Shriekback.*

XYMOX

The Clan of Xymox (4AD/Relativity) 1985

Despite competent musicianship and complexity, this Dutch quartet's gothic dance gloom is more imitative than distinctive. On their Anglo-American debut, the right components are present but the record is disappointingly lacking in personality. Despite three alternating vocalists (deeply anguished to breathlessly fragile), jutting electric and acoustic guitars, sinewy bass and a wealth of synths, Xymox can't seem to make anything out of the ordinary happen, and only three songs approach memorability. What would have made a commendable EP flounders as an album.   [ag]

YACHTS

Yachts (Radar/Radar-Polydor) 1979
Without Radar (Radar/Radar-Polydor) 1980

Liverpool's Yachts were capable of alternating a scaled-down version of pomp-rock (faster, more cheaply tricked out, no instrumental exhibitionism) and '60s-influenced rock with that cheesy organ sound, not unlike an Anglicized Joe "King" Carrasco. And that in the service of humorously melodramatic caricatures of the usual boy/girl lyric fodder: love by letter ("Box 202"), unfair romantic competition ("Yachting Types," "Semaphore Love," etc.) Despite sympathetic production by Richard Gottehrer, **Yachts** sounds a bit tinny, and the group was unable to equal their mini-classic Stiff debut single ("Suffice to Say"), though the potential to do so is evident. Not being taken seriously because of funny lyrics may have taken its toll; on **Without Radar**, the jokes and even the previously solid songwriting sound as thin as Martin Rushent's uncharacteristically poor production.   [jg]

YANKEES

High 'n' Inside (London/Big Sound) 1978

This odd album by rock writer/musician Jon Tiven's band has some really good songs (mostly originals written or co-written by Tiven), guest appearances by Voidoid Ivan Julian, Alex Chilton and Hilly Michaels, and a musical range that covers MOR, power pop, Leon Russellish pseudo-gospel, devolved R&B, off-the-wall Spectorized production and more. **High 'n' Inside** is unpredictable and uneven, but well worth a listen or three.   [iar]

YAZOO

Upstairs at Eric's (Mute/Mute-Sire) 1982
You and Me Both (Mute/Mute-Sire) 1983

Yazoo (known as Yaz in the States) was one of England's most interesting synth-pop duets, mostly because of the sharp contrast provided by vocalist Alison Moyet's incredibly rich and soulful voice, a more powerful and emotive sound than you expect to hear paired with high-tech instrumentation. Along with ex-Depeche Mode synthesist/songwriter Vince Clarke, Yazoo represented a stylistic breakthrough that has proven influential in the development of electronic-based dance music.

Unfortunately, while **Upstairs at Eric's** is admirable for its experimentalism, it contains just one really striking song (the beautiful ballad, "Only You"), some moderately interesting quirky pop ("Too Pieces," "Bad Connection"), two solid dance numbers ("Don't Go" and "Situation") made tolerable by the band's talent and strengths and one truly awful piece of tape-looping ("I Before E Except After C").

You and Me Both, on the other hand, offers a better selection, from Moyet's defiant and atmospheric "Nobody's Diary" and funky "Sweet Thing" to Clarke's bouncy "Walk Away from Love." There are some serious low-points to be sure, but in general it's a more even and exciting album, further exploring the blend's possibilities.

Given the dynamic tension of the

partnership, it was hardly surprising when Moyet and Clarke decided, after two albums, to go separate ways: he to form the Assembly (later, Erasure) and she to a successful solo career. [ks/iar]

See also *Erasure, Alison Moyet*.

YEAH YEAH NOH

Cottage Industry EP (In Tape/nr) 1984
Weakling Lines EP (In Tape/nr) 1984
Prick Up Your Ears EP (In Tape/nr) 1984
When I Am a Big Girl (In Tape/nr) 1985
Cutting the Heavenly Lawn of Greatness . . . Last Rites for the God of Love (In Tape/nr) 1985
Temple of Convenience EP (In Tape/nr) 1986

Like In Tape labelmates the Creepers, this Leicester quartet (later quintet) displays some Fall influence (albeit less harsh) and makes things easy for record buyers by combining several releases onto a single disc. **When I Am a Big Girl** contains the entirety of the first three EPs, highlighted by "Cottage Industry," "Prick Up Your Ears" and "Starling Pillowcase and Why," which, like the rest of the record's songs, are unpolished, raw pop gems with smartass lyrics. Cymbal-less drums and chunky bass lines form a foundation for modest guitar work and Derek Hammond's deadpan baritone. Great fun.

Heavenly Lawn adds some well-placed psychedelic embellishments and a little (but just a wee bit) more production to the homespun sound. Lyrics are sharp as ever: "Home-Ownersexual" is the clever tale of a bored, dissatisfied housewife; "Stealing in the Name of the Lord" decries religious hypocrisy. Some earlier tracks pop up again in new versions, and the LP also contains the title track from the **Temple of Convenience** EP. Sadly, Yeah Yeah Noh disbanded upon that release but left behind a catalogue of great records, permeated with real d.i.y. spirit, warmth and humor. Don't miss out. [dgs]

YELLO

Solid Pleasure (Do It/Ralph) 1980
Claro Que Si (Do It/Ralph) 1981
Bostich EP (Do It/Stiff) 1982
You Gotta Say Yes to Another Excess (Stiff/Elektra) 1983
Yello EP (nr/Elektra) 1983
Stella (Elektra) 1985

Switzerland's Yello (Boris Blank, Dieter Meier and Carlos Peron—all non-musicians in the finest Brian Eno tradition) has harnessed the synthesizer to become one of the most important and creative bands working in the medium.

Solid Pleasure is a record of their exploration of the studio and instruments, surging with discovery and innovation. On this LP, Yello are dark experimenters of the highest order, treading fearlessly through a perilous forest of electronics. The music is a confident cross-pollination of lighthearted pop and avant-garde. Inspired.

Claro Que Si continues Yello's adventurous innovation, but applies it to dance music with stunning results. Meier's vocals, though limited in range, slide blissfully against Blank's synthesizer and backing vocals and Peron's tape effects to create a pop/disco album full of

evocative, warm tunes, evincing a dynamism rare in this sort of music. And they stay far away from pretensions, too.

Bostich presents new versions of songs from the albums, with an otherwise unavailable track, "She's Got a Gun," added to the US edition. Remakes aren't normally essential listening, but Yello proves they're one of the few bands capable of transfiguring old material rather than rehashing it, and with exquisite intelligence at that.

Signing to Elektra (will wonders never cease?), Yello made **You Gotta Say Yes to Another Excess**, which contains some of their most accessible dance music, although it would be far from accurate to call Yello commercial or mainstream. "I Love You" pushes a pulsing electro-beat and whispered vocals vaguely about driving, throwing in screeching tires to underscore the point. "No More Words" recites the title over herky-jerky rhythms and little else; "Great Mission" is a suave dramatic travelogue. The 23-minute EP that followed contains remixed, extended versions of three LP tracks plus "Bostich."

Stella adopts more of a Euro-disco sound, dropping most of the weirdness to play as straight as Yello ever could. Meier's vocals have gone from wondrously strange to cloying; several guest musicians provide vocals, piano, drums and guitar, making this Yello's most routine and least intriguing release. [sg/iar]

YELLOW MAGIC ORCHESTRA

Yellow Magic Orchestra (A&M) 1979
Solid State Survivor (Jap. Alfa) 1979 (Alfa/nr) 1981
Public Pressure (Jap. Alfa) 1980
X∞ Multiplies (A&M) 1980

BGM (A&M) 1981

Technodelic (Alfa) 1981
Service (Jap. Alfa) 1983
After Service (Jap. Alfa) 1983
Naughty Boys (Jap. Alfa) 1983
Naughty Boys Instrumental (Hol. Pickup) 1985
Sealed (Jap. Alfa) 1985

For the technology-minded Japanese (who, after all, do have their own musical logic and traditions), the rock medium most suited to adaptation, rather than bland mimicry, has been electronic-oriented pop. By their third LP, YMO represented to Japanese kids a heterodoxy almost equivalent to the Sex Pistols and, in Japan at least, many times as commercially successful.

None of the three members of YMO were musical neophytes at the outset: while recording his first solo LP, session keyboardist Riuichi Sakamoto met drummer Yukihiro Takahashi, who'd not only cut his own album but had been a member of the Sadistic Mika Band (Japan's well-known art-rock export who made three LPs for UK Harvest) and its offshoot, the Sadistics. The pair met bassist/producer Haruomi Hosono, a veteran of two historically important Japanese bands, while he was cutting his *fourth* solo LP. (He's done more since, but unlike his two bandmates, none of his solo records has been released in England or America. His most recent, **Video Game Music**, employs the electronic sounds of arcade games.)

Despite the pedigree, YMO's first LP is merely inane electro-disco distinguished only by efforts at diddling video-game blips and squonks into songs. **Solid State Survivor** (actually their second Japanese LP, later issued intact in the UK) is a quantum leap forward: clever instrumentals and excellent electro-rock tunes with terse, sharp English lyrics by Chris Mosdell. Takahashi's flat, inflexible vocals are a mixed blessing—no silly histrionics, but an air of cool detachment that's, at least initially, off-putting. **X∞ Multiplies** has two more fine tracks in this vein, but the rest of this Japanese half-hour 10-incher is given over to mostly unfunny comedy skits (and two humorous tries at Archie Bell and the Drells' "Tighten Up"). In the UK, the LP of the same name adds on the aural vid-bits from the first LP, but the US release retains only the title and the two good cuts, the rest being the best part of **Solid State Survivor**. **Public Pressure** is a live album.

BGM and **Technodelic** are both mixed bags. On the plus side, they explore new (for YMO) stylistic areas—"Strawberry Fields" gone synth, Germanic bleep strutting, bleak Anglo synth-rap—but little on either is as distinctive or just plain entertaining as Takahashi's or Sakamoto's solo work. Hosono's production (the first six YMO LPs, as well as discs by Sandii and the Sunsetz, Sheena and the Rokkets and others) has clarity but lacks the snap and depth that would make these two records come alive.

Service is a frustrating record for us non-Nipponese, since it alternates YMO tracks with cuts just as long as the songs by the comedic (?) theatre group S.E.T. It might be annoying to those who **do** speak Japanese, since no matter how good those bits may be, if you want to hear music, you won't appreciate the interruptions. It's doubly irksome because the songs are excellent. **Naughty Boys** has equally good songs without the comedy. The melodies on both discs are much more accessible and consistently pleasing than any of the previous YMO LPs with no noticeable shift in songwriting balance. (Beginning with **Service**, Peter Barakan, who's written lyrics for Takahashi's LPs, supplies them to YMO in place of Mosdell. Also, YMO produced these two albums as a group.)

After Service is a double live set, but the name has more to do with the order of its release than its content, drawing on previous records. **Sealed** is a four-disc boxed set. [jg]

See also *Riuichi Sakamoto, Yukihiro Takahashi*.

YELLOWMAN

Mister Yellowman (Greensleeves/Shanachie) 1982
Bad Boy Skanking (Greensleeves/Shanachie) 1982
Zungguzungguguzungguzeng (Greensleeves/Shanachie) 1983
King Yellowman (CBS) 1984
Nobody Move Nobody Get Hurt (Greensleeves/Shanachie) 1984
Galong Galong Galong (Greensleeves/Shanachie) 1985

Albino reggae toaster Yellowman (Winston Foster) parlayed his unusual looks and talent into overnight success. His music is versatile, engagingly comic in a dancehall style. Like his counterparts in

American rap, he's often swaggering, boasting about his toasting and his luck with the ladies. Because his strut is good-natured and backed up by fierce turntable work (his improv and raps are extraordinary), he's extremely convincing, and has become quite a sex symbol. Due to his sudden notoriety, however, more than two dozen Yellowman albums flooded the market in the early '80s. Many are so-so live sets, collections of singles and outtakes, Jamaican-only releases, or team-ups with other djs. The listing above contains only his most widely available studio LPs.

Mister Yellowman, the album that helped launch his international fame, remains among his best. Nearly every cut is strong, including "Mister Chin," "Two to Six Supermix" and the *My Fair Lady*-inspired "Yellowman Getting Married" (in the morning). While they often come close, none of his other records equal this consistency and easy versatility.

Zungguzungguguzungguzeng, for instance, isn't even in the same league. For one thing, it's misleading. Seven of ten cuts are actually duets with another dj (Fathead); they make an okay team, but their rapport is mostly in a rub-a-dub style, and the record bogs down as a result. Best is the title tune, a solo toast to the music of Michigan and Smiley's "Diseases"; worst is "Who Can Make the Dance Ram," a reworking of Sammy Davis Jr.'s "Candy Man."

Admirably, CBS tried to encourage Yellowman's versatility when he signed with the label, but the result, **King Yellowman**, is another mixed success. Most of Side One is fine ("What Dat," for instance), but the flip is a mess. Yellowman meets Material for "Disco Reggae," tries to "Reggae Calypso" and finally covers Frankie Ford's pop hit "Sea Cruise." All of these fusion attempts go wildly astray.

Less contrived versatility is evident on his later Greensleeves albums. **Nobody Move** is a bit spotty, but the strong cuts are really great. The title track, as well as "Strictly Mi Belly" and "Why You Bad So" are all cookers, guaranteed to make you rock and groove. **Galong** is also worth investigating, for it features an anti-Michael Jackson number called "Beat It"; "Reggae Win a Grammy," Yellowman's report on his trip to the awards ceremony; and "Skank Quadrille," a toast to Bunny Wailer's "Walk the Proud Land." [bk]

YOBS

See *Boys*.

PAUL YOUNG

No Parlez (CBS/Columbia) 1983
The Secret of Association (CBS/Columbia) 1985

From the failed ashes of the neo-soul Q-Tips emerged Paul Young, whose smoky voice quickly put him in the British, and later, American charts, singing a mixture of classics and originals. The cover material on Young's first solo album ranges from the likely ("Love of the Common People," "Wherever I Lay My Hat (That's My Home)," both of which are magnificent) to the surreal (Joy Division's "Love Will Tear Us Apart," which he slowly mangles beyond recognition). A few of the new songs are swell as well. The

169

Royal Family and the Fabulous Wealthy Tarts supply sympathetic backing; Laurie Latham's wide-screen production is appropriately lush without ever abandoning the rock basis that anchored classic Motown records of the '60s. **No Parlez** is a really solid pop album by an especially good singer. However, since Young is so reliant on material and accompaniment, he's equally (and randomly) capable of rubbish and excellence.

The Secret of Association, Young's follow-up as a big star, chooses its material far more judiciously, resulting in an exquisite collection that mixes appropriate covers with originals co-written by Young. Items like "Everytime You Go Away," "Bite the Hand That Feeds" and "I'm Gonna Tear Your Playhouse Down" show off both Young's carefully controlled vocals and Laurie Latham's exceptionally subtle production. Every clearly-articulated sound functions perfectly in the arrangements, resulting in seamless, emotionally resonant pop-soul creations that bear repeated listenings with ease. [iar]

YOUNG MARBLE GIANTS

Colossal Youth (Rough Trade) 1980
Testcard EP (Rough Trade/nr) 1981

Singer Alison Statton and the Moxham brothers, Philip (bass) and Stuart (guitar, organ) from Cardiff managed to stay together long enough to produce one oddball album before apathy got the upper hand. Using few overdubs, **Colossal Youth** re-creates the mythical ambience of a beatnik coffeehouse. Statton's gentleness and the soft accompaniment contribute to a hushed mood that's either soporific or enchanting, depending on your point of view (or blood pressure). Minimalism never had such polite advocates before. Statton subsequently formed Weekend, who have released several albums; Philip Moxham became the Gist.   [jy]

See also *Gist.*

YOUTH & BEN WATKINS

The Empty Quarter
(Illuminated/nr) 1984

Several years after opting out of Killing Joke, dreadlocked bassist Youth teamed up with former Hitmen vocalist Watkins (now also versed in keyboards, drums and guitar) to record **The Empty Quarter,** a legitimate play soundtrack. Forceful and musically intelligent, with layers of disembodied sound lunging and pulsing in and out, it's a striking collection of dramatic, largely electronic instrumentals that bear some Youth's former band's fury, mixed with subtlety and artsiness. Surprising.   [iar]

YOU'VE GOT FOETUS ON YOUR BREATH

See *Scraping Foetus off the Wheel.*

Y PANTS

Beat It Down (nr/Neutral) 1982

The women who comprised this eccentric New York trio play drums, keyboards (nothing fancy or high-tech), bass and ukulele. They also sing—such numbers as "The Shah Song," lyrics like "Don't be afraid to be boring" and adaptations of "Bert" Brecht. Mostly, though, the record consists of skimpy, dada music that is baldly amateurish but charming. The Y Pants offer no stylistic pretensions, merely highly idiosyncratic music for aficionados of the arcane, intelligent and delightful.   [iar]

THIERRY ZABOITZEFF

See *Art Zoyd.*

ZANTEES

Out for Kicks (Charly/Bomp) 1980
Rhythm Bound (nr/Midnight) 1983
The Zantees EP (nr/Midnight) 1984

The Zantees, a New York-based rockabilly combo, aren't too serious about their music, which makes **Out for Kicks** delightfully irreverent. Singing and playing with a spirit money can't buy and synthesizers can't replicate, they easily make the oldies ("I Thought It Over," "Cruisin'," three others) their own, and the originals ("Gas Up," "Blonde Bombshell," six others) sound like oldies. A futile gesture, perhaps, but a grand one. Poor recording quality adds atmosphere. (Bassist Rob Norris graduated to the Bongos.)

With a one-take-looseness sound on **Rhythm Bound**, method singer Billy Miller (co-publisher with drummer Miriam Linna of the excellent fanzine, *Kicks*) barks out such ethnic 'billy originals as "Tic Tac Toe" and "Money to Burn." Linna also vocalizes on a couple: "I Need a Man" and "I'm Ready." The guitar-picking Statile brothers' proficient chromatic single-string playing provide a dual carburetor rhythm thrust.

The subsequent 12-inch combines two tracks from the second album with a pair of blazing live oldies (one sung each by Miller and Linna).   [si/iar]

ZEITGEIST

Translate Slowly (Stiff/DB) 1985

Out of Austin, Texas—the rowdy college town that Stevie Ray Vaughan and the Butthole Surfers call home—comes an impressive debut from two guys and two girls making moody, melodic and occasionally stunning folk-rock with a deep debt to the '60s, although there's plenty of modern angst and a rootsy feel that's more western than country. John Croslin and Kim Longacre work up a Byrdsy guitar drone and evocative vocal interplay that either lulls with a tepid sonic wash ("Cowboys") or explodes with brooding fury ("Things Don't Change") and hot-breath passion ("Araby"). Croslin's dry-as-dust vocals mix equal measures of desire and distance, but harmonies soar on a remake of Willie Nelson's "Blue Eyes Crying in the Rain."   [kh]

ZERRA I

Zerra I (Mercury/nr) 1985

Todd Rundgren has said that, as a producer, he can make bands sound like anything they choose. Little doubt as to what this client asked for: they emulate a certain (far more talented) quartet of fellow Dubliners. (It's a wonder the guitarist doesn't call himself the Border or something.) Zerra I go for a big, bombastic sound (cf., Rundgren's Meat Loaf work), with lyrics full of grandiose imagery. On "Tumbling Down," singer Paul Bell majestically proclaims, "We see it, we hear it, we know, we say." Problem: they don't.   [dgs]

Z'EV

Elemental Music (nr/Subterranean) 1982
My Favorite Things (nr/

Subterranean) 1984
Berlin Atonal Vol. 1 (Ger. Atonal)
1984

STEFAN WEISER

Contexts & Poextensions EP
(nr/Subterranean) 1981

Elemental Music, recorded live in San Francisco, finds bald percussionist Z'ev (Stefan Weiser) creating an amorphous and utterly atonal wall of pulsating sound on instruments that are neither identified nor aurally identifiable. Although different from what one usually thinks of in terms of ambient music—this shit gets *loud!*—as a soundscape for the post-industrial wasteland, it's fine in a numbing sort of way.

The Weiser EP is a 7-inch that can be played at any speed (although it only makes sense at 78, where it sounds like something a cheap cassette recorder might have picked up inside a factory.) Z'ev/Weiser has also performed live as a featured musician in Glenn Branca's "Symphony £2," in which he did a lot of Neubautenish smashing together of large metal objects.

My Favorite Things collects nine live performances dating between 1979 and 1983. Z'ev's half of **Berlin Atonal**, an LP he shares with Psychic TV, is a typically exhausting side-long piece ("Titan Night") recorded live in Berlin (3 December 1983). [iar]

ZONES

Under Influence (Arista/nr) 1979

This offshoot of Midge Ure's pre-Rich Kids Scottish pop outfit, Slik, had strong players, two of whom—guitarist Willy Gardner and keyboardist Billy McIsaac—wrote good songs and one of whom (Gardner) had an attractive if limited vocal style, like a young hybrid of Mick Ronson and Dave Edmunds. But what to do with it all? Pop? Hard stuff? Commercial new wave? Reggae-pop? The Zones tried a little of everything without any forceful, unifying personality, despite passing nods to Mott and the Skids (which two Zones later joined). No bad cuts, but only one rises from enjoyable to exciting. [jg]

ZOUNDS

The Curse of Zounds (Rough Trade/nr) 1982

Someone must have slipped one of those post-anarcho-syndicalist pamphlets in with these guys' *Beano* comics! This is sturdy, above-average pop-punk with some surprisingly infectious hooks. But the foursome ain't just disaffected youngsters lookin' for a kiss (or any ol' white riot)—they're searching out the meaning of life in the post-industrial capitalist system. As long as you've got the tunes, guys—go for it! [jg]

TAPPER ZUKIE

Man Ah Warrior (Klik/nr) 1974
    (nr/Mer) 1977
MPLA (Jam. Klik) 1976 (Front
    Line/nr) 1978
Tapper Roots (Front Line/nr) 1979
Peace in the Ghetto (Front Line/nr)
    1979
In Dub (Front Line/nr) 1979
Black Man (Mobiliser/nr) 1979
Raggy Joey Boy (Mobiliser/nr) 1982
Earth Running (Mobiliser/nr) 1983

Though Tapper (or Tappa) Zukie isn't active in the reggae mainstream, his toasting, which combines staunchly Rasta lyrics with heavy roots accompaniment, has always enjoyed an audience. His rock notoriety was boosted in the late '70s via an association with the Patti Smith Group; **Man Ah Warrior** was reissued by Lenny Kaye on the Mer label. Cuts like "Simpleton Badness," "Viego" (the Jamaican sound system where he got his start) and "A Message to the Pork Eaters" fill the LP with dread, seasoned with irony and humor. Not to be missed.

MPLA is likewise classic and **Tapper Roots** is almost as good. **Peace in the Ghetto**, on the other hand, is lackluster and uninspired; despite the inclusion of the single "Phensic" (retitled "Dangerous Woman"), the rhythms are flabby, the toasting less interesting. Parting company with Virgin/Front Line, Zukie returned to Jamaica.

His work in recent years, released via his own Stars label, is decent if inconsistent. **Black Man** is sturdy, as is the first side of **Earth Running**, which features "The General," a tribute to the late General Echo. (Side Two, however, has two unconvincing disco cuts.) Zukie's latest release, **Raggy Joey Boy** has more singing than toasting. [bk]

Omnibus Press
No.1 for Rock & Pop books

A-Ha On Tour
An up-to-the minute photo book on the Norwegian pop sensation, featuring live pix from their Australian tour. Includes fold-out poster.
36pp, OP 44171

Back In The USSR:
The Untold Story Of Rock In The Soviet Union
by Artemij Troitsky
Russia's best known rock writer traces the history and development of pop and rock music in the Soviet Union from the fifties to the present day – a publishing first.
160pp, OP 44395

The Beatles Apart
by Bob Woffinden
A 'warts and all' investigation into the careers of John, Paul, George and Ringo after The Beatles.
144pp, PRP 10083

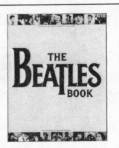

The Beatles Book
The most thorough and multifaceted critical examination of the Beatles music available, published to coincide with the release of the Beatles' music catalogue on compact disc.
176pp, OP 43439

Chuck Berry: Mr Rock 'N' Roll
by Krista Reese
The story of the most influential rock 'n' roll guitar player of all time.
128pp, PR 10029

Big Country:
A Certain Chemistry
By John May
The only official book about Big Country, the Anglo-Scottish quartet whose stirring music has won them a vast international following.
64pp, OP 43280

David Bowie Archive
by Chris Charlesworth
The first serious study of Bowie's life and career made available once again.
96pp, BOB 10021

David Bowie: In Other Words
by Kerry Juby
David Bowie's friends, relations and musical associates past and present talk in detail about his life and career; transcribed from the radio series of the same name.
128pp, OP 44114

Bowie: The Pitt Report
by Kenneth Pitt
The inside story of David Bowie's early career written by his manager from 1965-70. Highly acclaimed by Bowie fans.
230pp, OP 43256

David Bowie:
The Starzone Interviews
by David Currie
A collection of interviews and rare pix that have appeared in 'Starzone', the Bowie fanzine.
128pp, OP 43355

The Boy George Fact File
Masses of colour pictures of Boy George, the flamboyant leader of Culture Club. Includes full colour pull out poster.
36pp, OP 43207

From A Spark To A Flame:
The Chris de Burgh Story
by David Thompson
The official biography of Ireland's top singer/songwriter, written and produced with the full co-operation of de Burgh himself.
96pp, OP 43892

The Secret History of Kate Bush (and the strange art of pop)
by Fred Vermorel
This unique book traces the family history of this leading songstress, to reveal its influence on her life and spectacular career.
96pp, OP 42035

Eric Clapton:
A Visual Documentary
by Marc Roberty
A lavishly illustrated chronological survey of the career of Eric Clapton, rock's most illustrious blues guitarist. Illustrated, colour.
96pp, OP 43579

The Clash (Revised edition)
by Miles & John Tobler
The Clash, sole survivors of the summer of '77 were the only band to see beyond the posing and the safety pins and manage to come out of it alive.
Illustrated.
96pp, OP42613

Omnibus and Bobcat titles on all the above are available from good book, record and music shops.
In case of difficulty, contact Book Sales Limited, Newmarket Road, Bury St. Edmunds, Suffolk IP33 3YB.

Omnibus Press
No.1 for Rock & Pop books

The Complete Rock Family Trees
by Pete Frame
The work of the world's foremost rock archivist condensed into one volume.
64 fold out charts, OP 42811

The Elvis Costello Story
by Mick St Michael
The first major biography of Elvis Costello, the most important and critically acclaimed songwriter to have emerged in the UK in the past ten years.
128pp, OP 43561

Crosby, Stills & Nash: The Authorized Biography
by Dave Zimmer & Henry Diltz
A candid and detailed account of the career of CS&N written with the co-operation of the group and their associates.
272pp, OP 43066

Culture Club: Boy George In His Own Words Photobook
Masses of photographs, quotes from Boy George and the other members of the band plus a giant fold out full colour photo poster make this an ideal gift for fans.
32pp, OP 40872

The Cure
by Jo-Ann Greene
Records the progress of the enigmatic Robert Smith and his band from obscurity to success.
48pp, OP 43686

The Story Of The Damned
by Carol Clerk
The outrageous and hilarious story of the UK's longest surviving punk band; written with the group's total co-operation.
96pp, OP 44361

Deep Purple: The Illustrated Biography
by Chris Charlesworth
The definitive account of Deep Purple's stormy career, written with the band's co-operation. Illustrated, colour.
96pp, OP 42209

Depeche Mode
by Dave Thomas
The full story of one of the eighties' most successful electronic bands.
48pp, OP 43678

The Doors
by John Tobler & Andrew Doe
An illustrated account of the legendary LA rock band led by the late Jim Morrison – rock's most notorious singer.
128pp, BOB 10070

Duran Duran: Book Of Words
This official book of Duran Duran themselves puts into words the character and colour of their songs and their shows. Foreward by Simon le Bon. Illustrated.
96pp, OP 43116

Never Stop: The Echo and The Bunnymen Story
by Tony Fletcher
The absorbing story of Merseyside's top cult band, written and produced with their full co-operation.
128pp, OP 44353

Elvis: The Final Years
by Jerry Hopkins
Hopkins brings together all the elements of a sensational life. He talked to over seventy individuals to find the true story of the final years. Illustrated.
260pp, OP 41110

Peter Gabriel
by Armando Gallo
The first major study of the former Genesis singer turned solo star; compiled with the full co-operation of Gabriel himself and containing many rare photographs.
96pp, OP 43603

Genesis: From One Fan to Another
by Armando Gallo
A superb collection of Genesis photographs from their acclaimed biographer and archivist. A chronological history of the band is also included.
144pp, OP 42951

Genesis: I Know What I Like
by Armando Gallo
The acclaimed definitive Genesis biography republished due to popular demand. More than 300 photographs.
160pp, OP 44403

Omnibus and Bobcat titles on all the above are available from good book, record and music shops.
In case of difficulty, contact Book Sales Limited, Newmarket Road, Bury St. Edmunds, Suffolk IP33 3YB.

Omnibus Press
No.1 for Rock & Pop books

Heavy Metal A-Z (Revised)
by Paul Suter
The updated edition of the definitive encyclopaedia of Heavy Metal.
96pp, OP 43272

HM LPs
A full colour catalogue of Heavy Metal's outrageous album covers over the years.
Illustrated, colour.
96pp, OP 43983

Heavy Metal Thunder
by Philip Bashe
The music . . . its history . . . its heroes . . . the strongest and hottest musical style in the history of rock, here is the full story. Illustrated and with 32 pages of colour.
224pp, OP 43496

Hendrix
by Chris Welch
The reissue of Chris Welch's legendary biography of the great guitar man.
104pp, OP 41987

On Tour With INXS
by Donald Robertson
An on-the-spot account of the top Australian band's 'Listen Like Thieves' tour of their home country.
32pp, OP 44205

The Jam: A Beat Concerto
by Paolo Hewitt
The authorised biography, filled with rare photographs. As Paul Weller himself says, 'There is no more to be said on The Jam's formation and rise than is contained in this book.'
Illustrated, colour.
128pp, OP 42043

Elton John
by Chris Charlesworth
A concise illustrated biography of Birtain's most colourful and consistent rock performer.
48pp, OP 44080

Joy Division/New Order: Pleasure and Wayward Distraction
by Brian Edge
A critical and biographical analysis of the work of two of the most important and influential groups to have emerged in the UK since The Sex Pistols.
96pp, OP 43009

Kerrang! Heavy Metal Yearbook Volume II
Edited by Dante Bonutto
This year in Heavy Metal as seen by the staff of Kerrang! Britain's top-selling HM cult magazine.
128pp, SD 10017

Kerrang! Kalendar 1988
The calendar for heavy metal fans with poster-sized pictures of top HM acts.
585 × 435mm, 13 leaves, SD 10025

The Knebworth Festival Book
by Christina Lytton Cobbold
A year by year, blow by blow, account of the legendary rock festivals held in Knebworth Park.
96pp, OP 43587

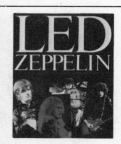

Led Zeppelin: A Visual Documentary
by Paul Kendall
Lavishly illustrated in colour and black & white, with rare photographs, posters, back stage passes, badges and memorabilia.
Illustrated, colour.
96pp, OP 41896.

Led Zeppelin In Their Own Words
Compiled by Paul Kendall
Here, in their own words, taken from interviews spanning their entire career, Led Zeppelin speak for themselves.
Illustrated.
128pp, OP 41284

London's Rock Landmarks
by Marcus Gray
First ever guide to London's Rock Landmarks: where the stars work, rest and play.
96pp, OP 43363

Madonna
A full colour photo-book of Madonna featuring live shots from her 'Virgin' tour.
32pp, OP 43462

Omnibus and Bobcat titles on all the above are available from good book, record and music shops.
In case of difficulty, contact Book Sales Limited, Newmarket Road, Bury St. Edmunds, Suffolk IP33 3YB.

Omnibus Press
No.1 for Rock & Pop books

Madonna: Her Story
by Michael McKenzie
The fullest account of Madonna's life to be published, now revised, updated and reissued by popular demand.
96pp, BOB 10088

Marillion
by Carol Clark
A concise illustrated story of Fish and his friends.
48pp, OP 43512

Marillion: The Script
by Clive Gifford
The first major biography of the immensely popular progressive rock band led by vocalist Fish.
96pp, OP 44304

1988: The New Wave Punk Rock Explosion
by Caroline Coon
'First published in the late seventies, Coon's articles from the Melody Maker remain an excellent guide to the first flush of punk in 1976.' RECORD MIRROR.
128pp, OP 41581

Jimmy Page: Tangents Within A Framework
by Howard Mylett
Jimmy Page is probably the most famous rock guitarist working today. This book is really a musical biography rather than a biography in the normal sense.
Illustrated, colour.
96pp, OP 42514

Pink Floyd: A Visual Documentary
by Miles
The standard reference work on The Floyd, now updated to include their world tour and performances of 'The Wall' at Earl's Court.
Illustrated, colour.
140pp, OP 40583

Queen: A Visual Documentary
by Ken Johnson
A comprehensive and lavishly illustrated guide to the music and career of one of the UK's most established superstar groups.
Illustrated, colour.
96pp, OP 43819

Rebel Rock: A Photographic Record Of The Sex Pistols
by Dennis Morris
A unique photo essay of the most influential punk band of all time.
Illustrated.
80pp, OP 43645

Regeneration: Chelsea, Generation X & Sigue Sigue Sputnik
by Ray Stevenson
Dramatic photo record of three influential bands featuring Tony James, leader of Sigue Sigue Sputnik. Text and live shots never published before.
52pp, OP 43934

Rolling Stones A-Z
by Sue Weiner & Lisa Howard
The ultimate Rolling Stones encyclopedia that collects everything there is to know about the Greatest Rock 'n' Roll Band In The World.
154pp, OP 43132

Sex & Drugs & Rock 'n' Roll
A candid look at the steamier side of rock 'n' roll, featuring scores of pictures the stars wish had never been taken. Includes free copy of Rockspeak – the rock dictionary.
96pp, OP 41953

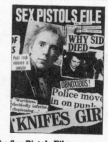

The Sex Pistols File
Compiled and photographed by Ray Stevenson
Well worth anyone's money.'
SOUNDS.
Illustrated.
72pp, OP 40302

Sex Pistols: The Inside Story
by Fred & Judy Vermorel
The incredible, true story of the Kings Road punks and their svengali manager Malcolm McLaren, whose influence continues to be felt – stronger than ever – ten years on.
240pp, OP 44312

Simple Minds
by Dave Thomas
The story of Glasgow's finest new wave band, generously illustrated and including a complete discography.
Illustrated, colour.
96pp, OP 43231

The Smiths
by Mick Middles
A detailed biography and appreciation of the Manchester quartet led by the eccentric Steven Morrissey.
Illustrated.
96pp, OP 43389

Omnibus and Bobcat titles on all the above are available from good book, record and music shops.
In case of difficulty, contact Book Sales Limited, Newmarket Road, Bury St. Edmunds, Suffolk IP33 3YB.

Omnibus Press
No.1 for Rock & Pop books

Born To Run:
The Bruce Springsteen Story
by Dave March
'Possibly the only essential rock biography so far written.'
NICK KENT, NME.
Illustrated.
192pp, OP 41011

The Supertramp Book
by Martin Melhuish
The definitive Supertramp biography, written with the full co-operation of the band.
Illustrated, colour.
192pp, OP 43637

Talking Heads
by Jerome Davis
The story of the most important and successful band to emerge from the New York art-rock scene of the mid-1970's.
144pp, OP 44338

Talking Heads: The Band And Their Music
by David Gans
The first full-scale biography and artistic analysis of a group which has changed the face of rock.
Illustrated.
160pp, OP 43942

Johnny Thunders: In Cold Blood
by Nina Guidio
In Cold Blood is a harrowing account of life in the fast lane of rock 'n' roll where the breaks have not been easy for this uncompromising rock outlaw.
128pp, JB 10004

The U2 File: Hot Press U2 History
Edited by Niall Stokes
A collection of articles, reviews and interviews from Ireland's top arts magazine which tell the story of U2 from their first Dublin concert in 1977 to their status as one of the world's most popular groups. Masses of colour and black & white pictures.
144pp, OP 43470

U2 - Stories For Boys
by Dave Thomas
A concise biography of Ireland's greatest ever rock band.
64pp, PRP 20421

U2 Visual Documentary
by Geoff Parkyn
The ultimate reference book on U2, the Dublin band led by charismatic singer Bono, who have conquered the world during 1987. From their earliest shows in Dublin to The Joshua Tree.
96pp, OP 44437

Uptight! The Velvet Underground Story
by Victor Bockris & Gerard Malanga
The Velvet Underground, formed in 1967 and disbanded in 1970, sell more records now than when they were together.
Illustrated.
128pp, OP 42142

Wham In Their Own Words
A full colour photo book of George Michael and Andrew Ridgeley with a giant fold out poster.
36pp, OP 43173

Wham Confidential: The Rise And Fall Of A Supergroup
by Johnny Rogan
The behind the scenes story of George Michael and Andrew Ridgeley: an astonishing indictment on the politics of power pop.
160pp, OP 44346

The Who: The Illustrated Biography
by Chris Charlesworth
A blow by blow account of The Who's tumultuous career that leaves few stones unturned.
Illustrated, colour.
96pp, OP 41607

Where Did Our Love Go? The Rise and Fall of the Motown Sound
by Nelson George
A compelling and definitive account of the most successful independent record label in the history of the record business.
Illustrated.
252pp, OP 43975

Viva Zappa!
by Dominique Chevalier
A comprehensive guide to the music and career of Frank Zappa, one of rock's most enigmatic figures.
Illustrated, colour.
128pp, OP 43900

The ZZ Top Story: Elimination
An illustrated and revealing biography of the most popular boogie band in the world.
96pp, OP 43447

Omnibus and Bobcat titles on all the above are available from good book, record and music shops.
In case of difficulty, contact Book Sales Limited, Newmarket Road, Bury St. Edmunds, Suffolk IP33 3YB.